WORLD WAR II AND SOUTHEAST ASIA

From December 1941, Japan, as part of its plan to build an East Asian empire and secure oil supplies essential for war in the Pacific, swiftly took control of Southeast Asia. Japanese occupation had a devastating economic impact on the region. Japan imposed country and later regional autarky on Southeast Asia, dictated that the region finance its own occupation and sent almost no consumer goods. GDP fell by half everywhere in Southeast Asia except Thailand. Famine and forced labour accounted for most of the 4.4 million Southeast Asian civilian deaths under Japanese occupation. In this ground-breaking new study, Gregg Huff provides the first comprehensive account of the economies and societies of Southeast Asia during the 1941–1945 Japanese occupation. Drawing on materials from 25 archives over three continents, his economic, social and historical analysis presents a new understanding of Southeast Asian history and development before, during and after the Pacific War.

GREGG HUFF is Senior Research Fellow at Pembroke College, University of Oxford. He is the author of *The Economic Growth of Singapore: Trade and Development in the Twentieth Century* and co-editor of and contributor to *World War II Singapore: The Chōsabu Reports on Syonan-to.* Gregg Huff has written numerous journal articles, including publications in the *Journal of Economic History, Economic History Review, Explorations in Economic History, Modern Asian Studies, Journal of Southeast Asian Studies, Economic Development and Cultural Change, Oxford Economic Papers, Cambridge Journal of Economics* and *World Development.*

WORLD WAR II AND SOUTHEAST ASIA

Economy and Society under Japanese Occupation

GREGG HUFF

Pembroke College,
University of Oxford

CAMBRIDGE
UNIVERSITY PRESS

CAMBRIDGE
UNIVERSITY PRESS

University Printing House, Cambridge CB2 8BS, United Kingdom

One Liberty Plaza, 20th Floor, New York, NY 10006, USA

477 Williamstown Road, Port Melbourne, VIC 3207, Australia

314–321, 3rd Floor, Plot 3, Splendor Forum, Jasola District Centre,
New Delhi – 110025, India

79 Anson Road, #06–04/06, Singapore 079906

Cambridge University Press is part of the University of Cambridge.

It furthers the University's mission by disseminating knowledge in the pursuit of education, learning, and research at the highest international levels of excellence.

www.cambridge.org
Information on this title: www.cambridge.org/9781107099333
DOI: 10.1017/9781316162934

First published 2020

Printed in the United Kingdom by TJ Books Limited, Padstow Cornwall

A catalogue record for this publication is available from the British Library.

Library of Congress Cataloging-in-Publication Data
Names: Huff, W. G. author.
Title: World War II and Southeast Asia : economy and society under Japanese occupation /
Gregg Huff, University of Oxford.
Other titles: Economy and society under Japanese occupation
Description: Cambridge, United Kingdom ; New York, NY : Cambridge University Press,
2020. | Includes bibliographical references and index.
Identifiers: LCCN 2020022973 | ISBN 9781107099333 (hardback) | ISBN 9781316162934
(ebook)
Subjects: LCSH: Southeast Asia – Economic conditions – 20th century | World War, 1939–
1945–Southeast Asia. | World War, 1939–1945 – Occupied territories. | Southeast Asia –
Social conditions – 20th century.
Classification: LCC HC441 .H84 2020 | DDC 940.53/59–dc23
LC record available at https://lccn.loc.gov/2020022973

ISBN 978-1-107-09933-3 Hardback

CONTENTS

FIGURES

TABLES

ILLUSTRATIONS

ACKNOWLEDGEMENTS

The idea of trying to write about World War II as it affected Southeast Asia originated many years ago as the result of a late-night conversation with Avner Offer. Throughout he has continued to offer advice and help for which I shall always be grateful. Reading and commenting on a manuscript of 180,000 words is a daunting task. I have been fortunate that both Andrew Bain and Dick DuBoff did just that, suggesting, re-shaping and greatly improving along the way. My debt to them is great. Mike Montesano undertook to read and correct the parts of the manuscript dealing with Thailand but in fact used his encyclopaedic knowledge of all things Southeast Asian carefully to go through the entire manuscript, some of it more than once, and make valuable corrections and suggestions. His many pages of detailed comments have saved me from numerous errors and have expanded my knowledge of Southeast Asia. Pierre van der Eng deployed his unrivalled insight into Indonesian economic history to correct and change much of my original attempt to deal with that country. Paul Kratoska warned me of various bibliographic errors in the citation of sources. So, too, did Panarat Anamwathana. I am indebted to both of them for conversations about Southeast Asia and for sharing some research material. Three anonymous Cambridge University Press referees made helpful and insightful comments on an early, partial manuscript. I owe a debt to them and to a fourth anonymous referee of the completed version of the manuscript for his/her careful reading and thoughtful remarks. Anne Booth, Michael Charney, Kevin Fogg, Trung Hoang, Gerry Sicat, Geoffrey Jones, Nick Snowden and Anthony Reid all read parts of the manuscript and provided constructive guidance. Shinobu Majima collaborated on various earlier parts of the manuscript in articles that we have published and has tried to help me avoid mistakes in Japanese names and citations. Mike Shand, University of Glasgow, drew the maps and designed the book illustration layout with consummate skill and unfailing good humour. Kathleen McCully copy-edited the book with understanding, skill and sensitivity. While no doubt errors remain in the book, all of the above have done much to reduce their number. Tjitske Wijngaard and Sarah Womack provided excellent and greatly appreciated research assistance. Pham Hyuen efficiently collected and processed data on the Vietnam famine.

23 December 1941 General Douglas MacArthur withdraws from Manila and declares it an open city. The Dutch military commander in Indonesia surrenders to Japanese forces.

24 December 1941 Japanese forces capture Wake Island. General MacArthur, Manuel L. Quezon and others evacuate to Corregidor.

25 December 1941 British surrender Hong Kong after a battle beginning on 8 December. Japanese bomb Rangoon for a second time.

26 December 1941 Manila is declared an open city.

2 January 1942 Japanese forces occupy Manila.

3 January 1942 Chiang Kai-shek named Supreme Allied Commander of the China Theatre, which includes Indochina and Thailand.

11 January 1942 Japan invades Indonesia, including Dutch Borneo.

13 January 1942 Japanese forces capture Kuala Lumpur.

16 January 1942 Japanese forces begin the invasion of Burma.

25 January 1942 Thailand declares war on the United States and Britain.

26 January 1942 Japanese forces begin their offensive towards Singapore from the north of Malaya. Allied forces, including British Indian Army units, are already deployed in the Middle East and North Africa, and without air or naval cover, the defence of Fortress Singapore is doomed to fail.

27 January 1942 Japanese Total War Research Institute (established December 1940 in Tokyo) draws up a draft plan for the establishment of the Greater East Asia Co-Prosperity Sphere. The plan envisages a Greater, a Smaller and an Inner Sphere. India is to be included within the Greater Sphere, or sphere of influence.

February 1942 Seni Pramoj, Thailand's minister in Washington, regards Thailand's declaration of war against the US as illegal and begins to organize the Free Thai (Seri Thai) movement in co-operation with the American Office of Strategic Services.

2 February 1942 Japanese forces invade Java.

7 February 1942 Britain accepts the assistance in Burma of the Chinese Expeditionary Force of China's National Revolutionary Army.

9 February 1942 Japanese Fifteenth Army is ordered to seize strategic places in Burma and soon occupies Moulmein.

15 February 1942 British surrender Singapore to Japanese forces.

18 February 1942 First Japanese air raid on Mandalay.

22 February 1942 General Douglas MacArthur leaves the Philippines.

27 February 1942–1 March 1942 Combined British, Dutch and American fleet is destroyed, opening the way for Japan to control the Indonesian archipelago. The Japanese navy is victorious in the Battle of the Java Sea.

28 February 1942 Japanese forces land on Java.

5 March 1942 Jakarta (Batavia) falls to the Japanese.

7 March 1942 Fall of Bandung, Java.

8 March 1942 Japanese troops occupy Rangoon; Japanese land in New Guinea.

12 March 1942 Japanese Southern Regions General Army prepares a plan to build one million tons of wooden ships in occupied territories.

15 March 1942 Chinese Expeditionary Force under General Wei Lihuang enters Burma.

23 March 1942 Japan occupies the Andaman Islands, about 250 miles southwest of Rangoon and a similar distance from the entrance to the Straits of Malacca.

24 March 1942 General MacArthur arrives in Australia.

5 April 1942 Japanese attack Colombo.

9 April 1942 Japanese attack Trincomalee in Ceylon (Sri Lanka).

10 April 1942 Beginning of the Bataan Death March in Philippines. After surrendering to the Japanese, some 11,000 Allied soldiers die during a 65-mile forced march.

18 April 1942 United States Doolittle bombing raid on Tokyo has an important psychological impact on Japan.

29 April 1942–1 May 1942 Lashio and Mandalay in Burma fall to Japanese forces.

5–8 May 1942 Battle of the Coral Sea. For the Japanese navy, the battle is a reversal but not a disaster.

6–8 May 1942 Allied forces surrender at fortresses of Bataan Peninsula and Corregidor in the Philippines.

20 May 1942 Allied forces complete withdrawal from Burma.

26 May 1942 Japanese begin planting of castor beans in Java to use as aviation fuel.

4–6 June 1942 Naval Battle of Midway during which Japan loses four carriers and the United States one. Midway is a decisive battle of the Pacific War because it ends Japanese supremacy on the high seas. The battles of the Coral Sea (May 1942) and Midway (June 1942) can be regarded as 'turning points' in the Pacific War. After these battles, Japan might have been ready to compromise for peace, but this was frustrated by Japanese Prime Minister Tōjō packing the Diet.

9 June 1942 Japan abandons its attempt to occupy Midway.

9 July 1942 Sukarno arrives back in Java from Sumatra, where he had been in exile since 1938.

21 July 1942 Burma Independence Army disbanded by the Japanese.

1 August 1942 Burma Executive Administration (Ba Maw government) installed.

7 August 1942–9 February 1943 Solomons and New Guinea campaigns. US Marines land on the island of Guadalcanal on 7 August 1942. Five months of bitter fighting between US and Australian forces and Japanese troops follow.

26 August 1942 Japan inaugurates the Burma Defence Army, the remnants of the disbanded Burma Independence Army.

November 1942 The Japanese government creates the Greater East Asia Ministry. Its purposes are: (1) to unify economic policies regarding labour, capital, transport, trade and natural resources; and (2) to protect and supervise Japanese interests. The Ministry's headquarters are in Tokyo and its chief Kazuo Aoki.

12–15 November 1942 Japanese are badly defeated in the naval Battle of Guadalcanal.

8 December 1942 Batavia officially renamed Jakarta.

30 December 1942 Mitani–Laval agreement signed in Vichy, France between Japanese ambassador Mitani and Premier Laval, binding Indochina to Japan's economic sphere.

31 December 1942 Five-year plan for cotton cultivation in Java announced.

January 1943 Japan withdraws from Guadalcanal, marking an end to the threat of a Japanese invasion of Australia. After Japan's retreat from Guadalcanal, its military position in Asia crumbles rapidly.

1 January 1943 Japanese diplomatic mission in Indochina is put under Japan's East Asia Ministry.

11 January 1943 Chinese nationalists form an official alliance with the United Kingdom.

22 January 1943 Prime Minister Tōjō announces in the Diet independence for Burma within a year and that the Philippines will also be granted independence.

28 January 1943 Prime Minister Tōjō announces the intention to re-organize Burma as an independent state.

31 January 1943 Japanese and Thai forces attack Yunnan in China, occupying several border towns.

7 February 1943 The last Japanese forces withdraw from Guadalcanal.

22 February 1943 Japan occupies Guangzhou Bay in China, having persuaded France to withdraw.

March 1943 Founding of the Southern Regions Development Bank, which will operate in Southeast Asia.

1 April 1943 Forced delivery of rice to the Japanese authorities begins in Java.

18 April 1943 Admiral Yamamoto, Japan's most brilliant military strategist and the architect of Pearl Harbor, is killed when his plane is shot down by American P-38 fighter planes.

20 April 1943 Japan's military administration of Sumatra separated from Malaya and placed under the 25th Army.

May 1943 Subhas Chandra Bose reaches Tokyo, and then, by June 1943, Sumatra from exile in Germany.

8 May 1943 Japan organizes an Independence Preparatory Committee to consider independence for Burma.

13 May 1943 The Allies begin to plan for the re-conquest of Burma.

11–30 May 1943 Japan defeated in the Battle of Attu, an island off the coast of Alaska in the Aleutians. The strategic location of Attu and the nearby island of Kiska give control of the sea lanes across the northern Pacific and are regarded by Japan as important because their occupation will prevent possible United States attacks from Alaska. The loss of Attu and Kiska, after fierce fighting in Arctic conditions, signals to Tokyo the need to begin massive build-ups in the occupied areas and to try to secure strong co-operation from local populations.

29 May 1943 The Japanese government accepts main principles for economic measures in the Southern Areas which stress that local manufacturing and food production should be increased to attain local self-sufficiency.

31 May 1943 Imperial Conference resolves to conclude a revised treaty of alliance with China; to grant Thailand border regions it had claimed in return for economic privileges; to implement a previous decision to grant Burma independence; to move towards independence for the Philippines; and to permit greater participation in political affairs for the peoples of Malaya, Sumatra, Borneo and Java.

1 June 1943 The United States begins submarine warfare against Japanese shipping.

17 June 1943 Prime Minister Tōjō refers to prospective independence for Burma and the Philippines in a speech to the Diet.

4 July 1943 Prime Minister Tōjō announces that the Shan states of Kengtung and Möng Pang in Burma are to be given to Thailand.

5 July 1943 Japan announces decision to transfer the Malayan states of Kedah, Perlis, Kelantan and Trengganu to Thailand.

1 August 1943 Burma Declaration of Independence, written by the Japanese, is issued. Prime Minister Ba Maw declares war on Britain and the United States.

16 September 1943 Burma Defence Army renamed (under Japanese direction) the Burma National Army.

23 September 1943 proclaimed 'National Service Day' in Burma in preparation for the first week of formal celebration of Burma's independence.

3 October 1943 Japanese establish Peta (*Pembela Tanah Air*, Defenders of the Homeland) as a volunteer army in Indonesia comprised of Indonesians.

9 October 1943 First cotton harvesting ceremony held in Surakarta, Indonesia. The Japanese are anxious to increase cotton production for the manufacture of textiles.

14 October 1943 Declaration of Philippine independence and the beginning of the government of José P. Laurel. Pact of Alliance signed between the Philippine Republic and Japan.

17 October 1943 Thailand–Burma railway completed. Preparations for construction had begun in June 1942 and actual construction started in November 1942.

18 October 1943 Japan transfers the Malayan states of Kedah, Perlis, Kelantan and Trengganu to Thailand.

25 October 1943 Thailand–Burma railway opening ceremony.

5 November 1943 Assembly of Greater East Asian Nations takes place in Tokyo. The Assembly is attended by President José P. Laurel from the Philippines and Prime Minister Ba Maw from Burma, but not Thailand's Prime Minister Phibun.

15 November 1943 General Louis Mountbatten takes charge of the South-East Asia Command.

December 1943 General Gōtarō Ogawa, formerly professor of economics at Tokyo's Imperial University and prominent member of the Diet, is sent to Burma as 'supreme economic advisor' with the brief that individual provinces in Burma should become self-sufficient. Ogawa remains in Burma until March 1944.

1–3 December 1943 Second Cairo Conference, at which Churchill and Roosevelt agree on scaling down operations in Southeast Asia and reducing naval and air assistance. Roosevelt and Churchill decide that landings in Europe prevent deployment of amphibious forces in Southeast Asia; Roosevelt informs Chiang Kai-shek, who was not present at the conference.

8 December 1943 Formation of Malay Defence Army and Corps after Japan announces its decision to form an army comprised of residents of Malaya.

27 December 1943 The Japanese formulate a plan to make Indonesia self-sufficient in paper.

1 January 1944 The Supreme Allied Commander issues a proclamation assuming responsibility for all of Burma.

11 January 1944 Burma State Bank opens, though the Japanese delay the issue of currency by the bank.

4 February 1944 Beginning of Japanese Arakan offensive, *Ha-Go*, in Burma.

Mid-February 1944 The United States mounts the largest carrier-launched air armada in history and blasts Japan's strategic Caroline Islands base at Truk, sinking from 19 to 26 ships and destroying an estimated 201 aeroplanes.

21 February 1944 Prime Minister Tōjō becomes army chief of staff.

March–April 1944 Allied counter-offensive triggers an all-out Japanese effort to fortify defences in Malaya.

March–July 1944 The Imphal–Kohima battle costs 30,000 Japanese dead and 20,000 wounded.

15 March 1944 Beginning of Japanese Imphal offensive, *U-Go*, in Burma. Imphal is the main Burma offensive.

1 April 1944 Bayah railway opens to transport coal from a mine in eastern Java.

24 May 1944 Japan begins construction in Indonesia of the central Sumatra (Pekanbara) railway, using 2,000 prisoners of war and 6,000 *romusha*.

June 1944 Report on 'The Present State of Material Power' is submitted to Japan's Supreme War Council, showing that Japan cannot carry on the war beyond the autumn.

June 1944 Setbacks for Japan beginning June 1944 include defeats in battles of the Marianas and the failure of the Imphal campaign in Burma.

15 June–10 July 1944 Battles of the Philippine Sea and Saipan greatly reduce Japanese air and sea power.

15 June 1944 Americans invade Saipan, one of the largest islands in the Marianas. American strategic air offensive against Japan begins from China. United States B-25 bombers use China bases to attack Japan.

July 1944 The Phibun government in Thailand is toppled by the National Assembly.

3 July 1944 Japanese forces, after suffering heavy loses, abandon any attempt to win the Battle of Imphal in India, marking a turning point in the Burma campaign.

8 July 1944 Saipan falls to United States forces and US operations against Guam begin. Japanese Prime Minister Tōjō had boasted that Saipan was 'impregnable'. Its loss causes the collapse of Tōjō's government. Saipan was at the very centre of the maritime defence ring around Japan. Its capture makes sea traffic between Japan and Southeast Asia almost impossible and allows US bombers easy access to Japan.

18 July 1944 General Tōjō falls from power as Japanese Prime Minister.

21 July 1944 United States forces invade Guam.

26 July 1944 Thailand's Prime Minister Phibun is ousted, partly because he would be unacceptable to the Allies and because it becomes obvious that Japan is losing the war. Phibun is replaced by Khuang Aphaiwong, who holds office until the defeat of Japan.

7 September 1944 Japan gives a public promise of eventual independence for Indonesia.

21 September 1944 President José P. Laurel invokes martial law in the Philippines.

23 September 1944 The Philippine Republic declares war on the United States and United Kingdom.

24 September 1944 The Allies bomb Jakarta.

October 1944 United States task force sweeps against the Ryukyus, a chain of Japanese islands, bringing Japanese economic lifelines under naval air attack for the first time.

18 October 1944 The United States' Philippine Campaign starts. The campaign makes the invasion of Indochina seem likely.

20 October 1944 United States forces land on Leyte in the Philippines.

23–26 October 1944 Battle of Leyte Gulf. After this battle Japan can no longer maintain open communications with Indonesia. The Battle of Leyte Gulf is, overall, the largest naval engagement in history. Japanese kamikaze attacks begin.

November 1944 United States B-29 bombers begin air raids on Singapore.

24 November 1944 United States air raids on Japan's home islands from the Mariana Islands begin. By August 1945, 27,059 planes have dropped 155,253 tons of bombs on Japan.

December 1944 In Burma the final Arakan offensive and Operation *Extended Capital* begins.

December 1944 Communications between Japan and Southeast Asia are virtually severed.

7 December 1944 Japanese Prime Minister Koiso Kuniaki declares that in the foreseeable future Indonesia will be granted independence.

January 1945 Japan makes a policy decision to take control of Indochina. By now, a United States invasion of Indochina is anticipated.

4 January 1945 British forces occupy Akyab, Burma.

9 January 1945 United States forces land on Luzon.

11–12 January 1945 Large-scale United States bombing of Indochina takes place.

17 January–August 1945 United States Air Force fire-bombing of Japanese cities causes mass destruction and high death tolls.

February 1945 Oil imports to Japan cease entirely by the end of February.

3 February 1945 United States forces launch an attack on Manila.

19 February 1945 30,000 US Marines storm the Japanese-held island of Iwo Jima, beginning one of World War II's bloodiest battles.

4 March 1945 Resistance of Japanese forces in Manila ends after street by street fighting. Between 3 February and the re-taking of Manila, 100,000 Filipino civilians die during the 'Massacre of Manila'. Close to 200,000 Japanese die during the battle for the Philippines.

7 March 1945 The Chinese Expeditionary Force takes Lashio, Burma. Chinese forces retake Liucheng, Guangxi Province.

9 March 1945 Japanese coup against French colonial administration in Indochina. The coup is followed by the setting up of the Japanese-sponsored Bao Dai (Emperor of Annam) government, which consists of Vietnamese nationalists.

9 March 1945 The United States starts incendiary bomb attacks on Japanese cities. Tokyo is devastated by incendiaries during the night. A massive Allied bombing campaign begins which causes the wholesale destruction of Japanese cities.

10 March 1945 American forces land on Mindanao in the Philippines.

20 March 1945 The British Indian Army takes Mandalay.

24 March 1945 Provisional government of General Charles de Gaulle announces it intends to form an 'Indochina Federation' within a 'French Union' with metropolitan hegemony over foreign affairs and defence. The

French Constituent Assembly is to determine participation in the Union, and the Governor-General to arbitrate between different parts of the Federation.

26 March 1945 Iwo Jima is declared secure by the United States after battle with Japanese forces beginning 19 February.

27 March 1945 Burma National Army rises against Japanese occupying forces. This day becomes Burma's 'Armed Forces Day'.

28 March 1945 Burmese rebellion against their former Japanese allies starts.

1 April 1945 Massive assault by United States forces on Okinawa begins.

17 April 1945 New Vietnamese nationalist government formed under Tran Trong Kim.

23 April 1945 Japanese withdraw from Rangoon.

3 May 1945 British troops capture Rangoon.

8 May 1945 Victory in Europe after the German surrender, allowing the transfer of Allied troops to the Pacific theatre.

28 June 1945 General MacArthur announces victory in the Philippines.

26 July 1945 At the Potsdam Conference, the Allies decide to divide Vietnam at the 16th parallel and allow Chiang Kai-shek to receive the Japanese surrender in the north, opening the way for the post-war stationing there of 200,000 Chinese Nationalist troops.

30 July 1945 Japanese government instructs its civilian population to collect acorns to stave off starvation.

6 August 1945 A five-ton uranium bomb, 'Little Boy', is dropped on Hiroshima.

8 August 1945 The Soviet Union declares war on Japan. Massive Soviet attack against Japan is launched across the frontier into Manchuria.

9 August 1945 The United States drops a plutonium bomb, 'Fat Boy', on Nagasaki.

13–14 August 1945 The United States Air Force fire-bombs Tokyo.

15 August 1945 Japan accepts the Potsdam Declaration. Emperor Hirohito announces the Japanese forces' unconditional surrender. The central Sumatra railway, begun in 1944 and which crosses central Sumatra, is completed.

15 August 1945 Responsibility for Indonesia is transferred from General MacArthur's HQ to General Mountbatten. He can do no more than order the Japanese 16th and 25th Armies to maintain law and order for the time being.

16 August 1945 Thailand's National Assembly declares null and void the declaration of war on Britain and the United States.

17 August 1945 Sukarno and Hatta proclaim Indonesian independence. José P. Laurel, now in Japan, issues a proclamation declaring the dissolution of his government.

18 August 1945 Subhas Chandra Bose killed in a plane crash in Taiwan.

18–19 August 1945 During the night, the Viet Minh take control of Hanoi.

23 August 1945 Hue taken by the Viet Minh.

25 August 1945 Saigon taken by the Viet Minh.

30 August 1945 Emperor Bao Dai, last monarch of the Nguyen Dynasty in Vietnam, formally abdicates in response to Viet Minh takeovers of major cities.

1 September 1945 Lieutenant Governor-General of the Netherlands Indies requests Lord Mountbatten of South East Asia Command to order Japanese troops to suppress the Indonesian Republican government.

2 September 1945 Formal Japanese surrender takes place on the USS *Missouri* in Tokyo Bay.

2 September 1945 Ho Chi Minh declares Vietnam a free and independent country and presents the Vietnamese 'Declaration of Independence'. The events of August 1945 are subsumed under the title, 'The August Revolution'.

5 September 1945 British Marines land in Singapore.

6 September 1945 Japanese army in East Java, except in Surabaya, disarm themselves and start 'self-internment'; first Allied troops arrive in Saigon.

9 September 1945 British Fifth Indian Division lands in Surabaya.

10 September 1945 Indonesians begin to counter-attack the British in Surabaya. The attack lasts for six weeks. Some 600 Indian troops defect from the British to join the Indonesians.

c. mid-September 1945 Chinese Expeditionary Force troops begin to arrive in north Vietnam.

23 September 1945 British and French forces mount a coup in Saigon; the Vietnamese war for independence starts.

29–30 September 1945 British troops land in Jakarta.

9 October 1945 The British hand over power to the French south of Vietnam's 16th parallel.

29 November 1945 British forces leave Indonesia.

10 February 1946 The Netherlands government announces its federal concept for Indonesia at the Conference of Malino.

2 March 1946 Ho Chi Minh elected president of Vietnam.

6 March 1946 The French government gives Ho Chi Minh and his party de facto if not formal recognition.

1 April 1946 Malayan Union formally proclaimed as part of a British plan to merge nine Malay states with Penang, Province Wellesley and Malacca. Singapore to become a separate Crown Colony.

23 April 1946 Manuel A. Roxas wins the Philippine presidential election.

30 April 1946 The US passes the Bell Trade Act which extends free trade arrangements between the US and Philippines for eight more years.

4 July 1946 The American flag is lowered and the Philippine flag raised in ceremonies to mark Philippine independence.

September 1946 Last units of the Chinese Nationalist army of Chiang Kai-shek leave northern Indochina.

November 1946 French forces seize Haiphong.

17 November 1946 Treaty of Tokyo (9 May 1941) annulled and Thailand returns Indochina provinces ceded to it under that Treaty.

23 November 1946 French forces bomb Haiphong.

19 December 1946 The Democratic Republic of Vietnam mounts attacks in Hanoi and elsewhere; fighting explodes in Hanoi. The First Indochina War begins.

27 January 1947 Aung San–Attlee agreement signed, setting out the methods by which Burma may achieve independence.

20 July 1947 Dutch troops invade Indonesian Republican territory in an officially described police action.

4 January 1948 Burma, as the Union of Burma, becomes independent from Britain with U Nu as the first Prime Minister.

1 February 1948 The Federation of Malaya comes into being after British abandonment of the Malayan Union.

9 March 1948 The Dutch establish a provisional federal government in Indonesia.

19 December 1948 Dutch airborne troops occupy Jakarta and within two weeks a number of other cities in Java and Sumatra.

1 August 1949 The Dutch and Indonesian Republicans sign an armistice.

27 December 1949 Indonesia achieves independence with the signing of a transfer of sovereignty in Amsterdam.

7 February 1950 The United States recognizes Vietnam as an independent state within the French Union.

19 March 1950 First American ships containing military equipment arrive in Saigon.

8 September 1951 San Francisco Treaty signed, after which Japan is restored to full sovereignty.

28 April 1952 The United States occupation of Japan formally ends.

22 October 1953 Laos recognized as a fully independent and sovereign state within the French Union.

9 November 1953 King Norodom Sihanouk declares Cambodian independence from France.

7 May 1954 Vietnamese army victorious in the Battle of Dien Bien Phu.

4 June 1954 Treaty ratified recognizing the independence of the state of Vietnam.

20 July 1954 First Indochina War ends. Delegates to the Geneva Conference partition Vietnam into two states divided at the 17th parallel with elections for reunification to be held in July 1956.

24 July 1954 Vietnam armistice signed in Geneva.

31 August 1957 Malaya becomes independent, leaving as colonies in Southeast Asia only Singapore and the territories of Borneo.

ABBREVIATIONS

ANM	Arkib Negara Malaysia (National Archives of Malaysia)
AOM	Centre des Archives d'Outre-Mer, Aix-en-Provence
AFFECO	Affaires économiques
GF	Fonds du gouvernement de fait
HCI	Haut commissariat pour l'Indochine
INF	Indochine nouveau fonds
RSTNF	Résidence supérieure du Tonkin nouveau fonds
AWM	Australian War Memorial
BE	Bank of England Records, London
	OV25 (Thailand)
	OV65 (Malaya, Singapore and Borneo)
	OV66 (Far East General)
	OV79 (Burma)
	OV85 (Dutch East Indies/Indonesia)
	OV85 (Indochina)
	OV149 (Philippines)
BT	Bank of Thailand Archives
IC	Indische Collectie, Instituut voor Oorlogs-, Holocaust- en Genocidestudies, (Collection Netherlands East Indies, Institute for War, Holocaust and Genocide Studies), Amsterdam
IER	Hitotsubashi University, Institute of Economic Research Library
IOR	India Office Records, British Library, London
IWM	Imperial War Museum
JISPB	Joint Intelligence Study Publishing Board
JM	Japanese Monographs
KITLV	Koninklijk Instituut voor Taal-, Land- en Volkenkunde (Royal Netherlands Institute of Southeast Asian and Caribbean Studies), Leiden
KKC	Kishi Kōichi Collection, Institute of Developing Economies, Japan External Trade Organization (IDE-JETRO)
LHC	Liddell Hart Centre for Military Archives, King's College, London Gracey Papers

MAGIC	Wartime Japanese diplomatic messages intercepted and decoded by the Allies
MFA	Ministry of Foreign Affairs, Japan, Diplomatic Archives, Navy Southeast Asia
MNA	National Archives of Myanmar, Yangon
NA	National Archives, Kew
NAC	National Archives of Cambodia, Phnom Penh
NAH	Nationaal Archief (National Archives), The Hague
NARA	National Archives and Records Administration, College Park, MD
NAS	National Archives of Singapore
NC	Nishijima Collection, Waseda University, Tokyo
NIDS	National Institute for Defense Studies, Tokyo Military History Research Centre
NIMH	Nederlands Instituut voor Militaire Historie (Netherlands Institute for Military History), The Hague
OSS	Office of Strategic Services
UP	University of the Philippines, Diliman, Main Library
USSBS	United States Strategic Bombing Surveys and Reports
WL	Weston Library, University of Oxford
VNA	National Archives Center I, Hanoi
FF	Fonds de la direction des finances
MH	Fonds de la mairie de Hanoi
RS	Fonds de la résidence supérieure au Tonkin

Preliminary Note

In the book, unless otherwise indicated, the description 'Chinese' refers to ethnic Chinese normally resident in Southeast Asia.

Blank spaces in tables indicate that data are not available.

Introduction

The 7 December 1941 attack on the United States at Pearl Harbor by Japan was a gamble. Japan was already entangled in a long-standing, probably unwinnable war in China, which since its outbreak in mid-1937 had cost 185,000 Japanese dead and billions of yen. Pearl Harbor opened a second military front and dangerously committed Japan, with a relatively small population and limited economic capacity, to a full-scale Pacific war. For Southeast Asia, the war brought three and a half years of Japanese occupation from the end of 1941 until Japan surrendered unconditionally on 15 August 1945. During this period, GDP in most Southeast Asian countries fell by half; 4.4 million civilians died prematurely; severe shortages of food and goods affected almost all Southeast Asians; and many lived in fear of draconian military rule. The present book explores why and how this happened.

Japan followed the operationally successful attack on Pearl Harbor with a clinically executed, swift occupation of all of Southeast Asia. Known as the Southern Regions in Japan, Southeast Asia covered 1.7 million square miles and had a population of some 145 million, double that of Japan (Figure I.1 and Table I.1). By May 1942, the Japanese military had control of a vast area of the Pacific and virtually all of Southeast Asia's six main countries of Burma, Thailand (Siam), Malaya (including the Straits Settlements of Singapore, Penang and Malacca), Indonesia (Netherlands India), Indochina (the five French administrative districts of Tonkin in the north, Annam in the centre and Cochinchina in the south, along with Laos and Cambodia) and the Philippines (Figure I.2). Japanese occupation swept aside colonial rule by Britain (Burma and Malaya), the Netherlands (Indonesia) and the United States (the Philippines). Thailand, part of Britain's informal empire, had its own government which remained in place as the Kingdom's nominal authority during the Japanese occupation.[1] A pro-Vichy French colonial regime in Indochina accepted Japanese occupation and was left in administration until a Japanese coup on 9 March 1945. In both Thailand and Indochina, however, Japan and its military held determining power.

[1] Aldrich, *Key to the south*, pp. 1, 4–7, 15, 25–30. On the strong position of the British Empire in Thailand's economy and 'stranglehold' on the supply of gunny bags, essential for the export of rice, see NA, FO 371/24756, Sir J. Crosby to Foreign Office, 21 October 1940.

Table I.1 *Southeast Asia pre-World War II population (000 persons)*

	1931	1938
Burma		
Lower Burma	7,964	9,066
Total Burma	14,667	16,824
Indochina		
Cochinchina	4,484	4,620
Total Indochina	21,450	23,030
Thailand	11,506	14,464
Malaya	4,348	5,004
Indonesia		
Outer Islands	19,009	
Java and Madura	41,718	
Philippines	13,405	16,000

Notes and sources: Burma: Figures for Lower Burma refer to the 1872 census area. The figures for 1938 refer to 1941. Hlaing, *Study*, p. 13. *Indochina:* The figure for 1938 refers to 1936. Brocheux and Hémery, *Indochine*, p. 254; Indochina, *Annuaire statistique 1943–1946*, p. 271. Population figures for Cochinchina refer to 1936 to 1938. Figures for 1931 and 1938 are from *Annuaire statistique 1931–32*, p. 53, *1943–1946*, p. 271. *Thailand:* Figures are from Kingdom of Thailand, *Statistical yearbook, 1937–38 and 1939–40*, p. 46 and refer to the census returns for 1929 and 1937. *Malaya:* The 1938 population figure is an estimate and assumes proportional population growth between 1931 and the 1947 census figure of 5,848,910 persons. Malaya, *Report on the 1947 census*, p. 39. *Indonesia:* Figures for 1931 refer to 1930 and are from Netherlands Indies, *Volkstelling, 1930*, vol. 8, p. 2. *Philippines:* The figure for 1931 is an estimate and from Philippines, *Yearbook of Philippine statistics 1940*, p. 24. For 1931 the figure refers to 1930. The figure for 1938 is for the census taken on 1 January 1939 and is from Philippines, Commission of the Census, *Special bulletin no. 1*, p. 3.

Occupation of Southeast Asia presented Japan with three problems which arose from the region's geography and demography and continually appear in various forms throughout this book. One was Southeast Asia's sheer geographic extent and a second its physical terrain, which channelled pre-war communications networks into north–south configurations. The insular nature of much of Southeast Asia and virtual absence of east–west transport across the region's mainland areas ran counter to Japanese military requirements and necessitated a heavy reliance on shipping and lengthy journeys to move men and materiel. Mountain ranges and jungles formed near-impenetrable barriers

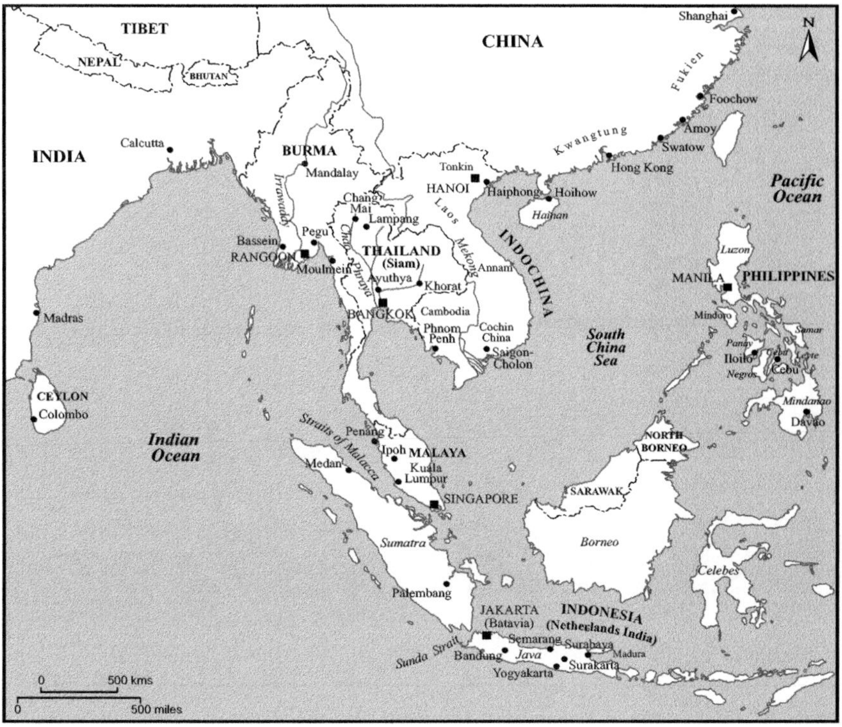

Figure I.1 Southeast Asia 1940

across Indochina and into Thailand, between Thailand and Burma, from one coast of Malaya to the other and across Sumatra. Japanese railway construction, notably the Thailand–Burma railway completed in October 1943, attempted to forge needed east–west transport links but these did not become available until at least the middle stages of the war and were no more than partially successful.

Southeast Asia's geographical size and population distribution created a third set of problems (Figure I.3). Because most of Southeast Asia was rural and sparsely populated, large numbers of Japanese military personnel and administrators would have been required to cover the region effectively. Japan countered this difficulty partly by administering through local elites. Puppet regimes were set up in Burma and the Philippines to try to gain popular support and bolster Japan's position in strategic areas: the Ba Maw government on 1 August 1943 and the José P. Laurel government on 14 October. The Tonkin delta in north Vietnam and Java had an administrative challenge of being exceptionally densely populated. In both areas, historic pressure on food and reliance on imported food at times of crisis put a premium on transport to avoid shortages.

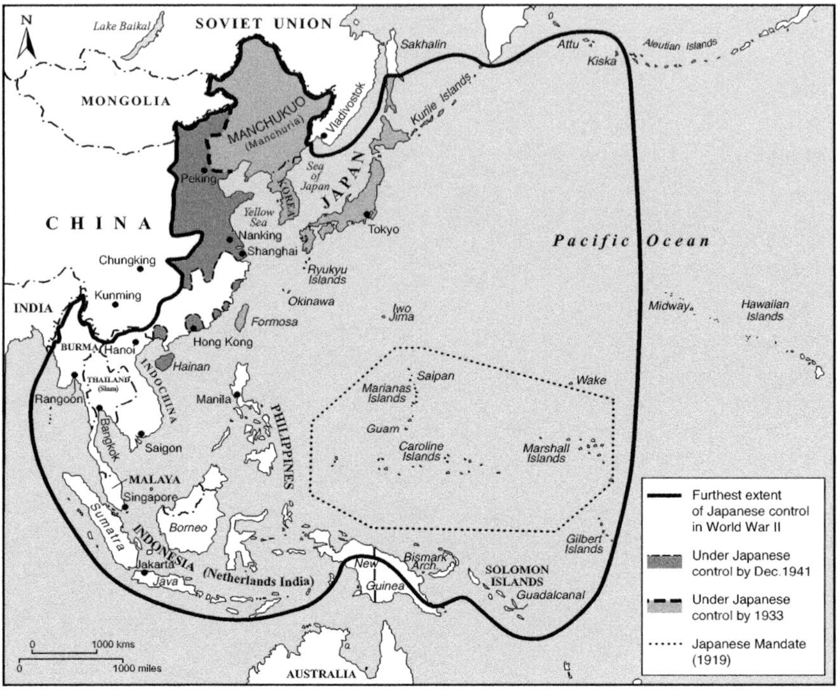

Figure I.2 Japanese Empire in East Asia May 1942
Source: Dower, *Embracing defeat*, p. 20.

Japanese military success was short-lived. Turning points in the war came as early as the first week of June 1942 with the Battle of Midway, a distant part of the Hawaiian group of islands, and, beginning in August 1942, the Battle of Guadalcanal in the Solomon Islands. By 1943, World War II began to cause great suffering for Japanese civilians. But even worse, often terrible, suffering was imposed on many Southeast Asians from the onset of occupation. By 1944, Thailand was the only country where national income was clearly above half of pre-war levels.

By the latter part of the war most Southeast Asians were malnourished, many seriously. Famine during 1944–45 claimed 3.4 million lives in Vietnam and Java; forced labour caused the deaths of hundreds of thousands more Southeast Asians. The number of Southeast Asian civilians who died due to occupation, about 3.1 per cent of the region's population, far exceeded all Japanese deaths, civilian and military, which resulted from World War II. Few moving monuments exist for the Southeast Asian civilian dead. There are no burial grounds comparable to the Piskaryov Memorial Cemetery for the famine victims of the 1941–44 Leningrad siege or the Kanchanaburi Cemetery in Thailand for Allied

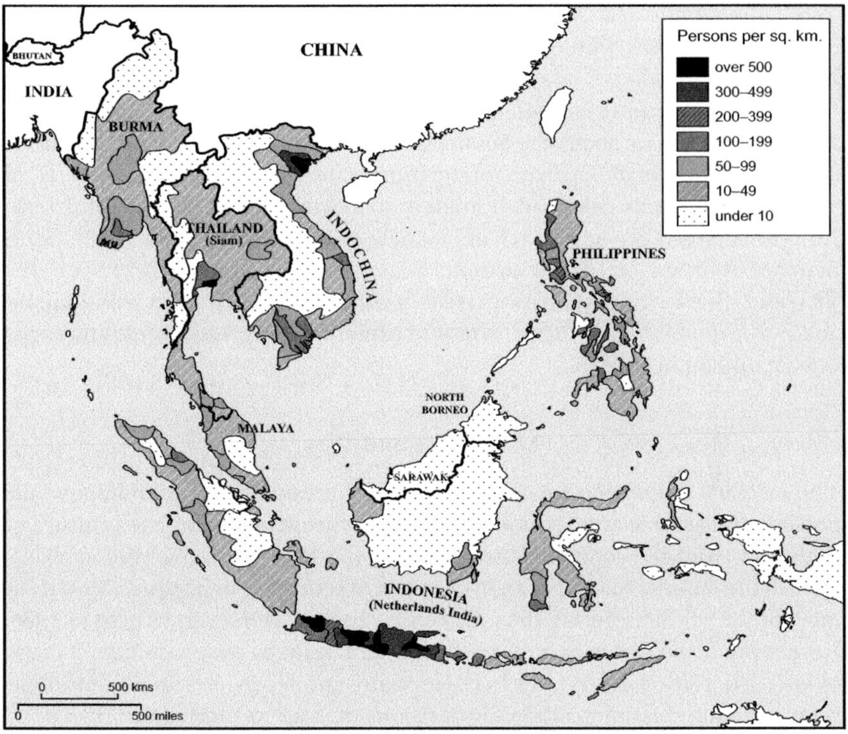

Figure I.3 Southeast Asia population distribution 1940
Source: Broek, 'Diversity and unity', p. 180.

war dead from labour on the Thailand–Burma railway (also known as the Siam–Burma railway and the Death railway). Japanese wartime infrastructure projects like railways, which might, to some extent, stand proxy for memorials, are now, if still traceable at all, little more than rusting relics partly overgrown with jungle.

Some commemoration attempts have been made, however. In 1962, after the unearthing in Singapore of the bones of thousands of Chinese massacred by the Japanese, the Singapore Chinese Chamber of Commerce gathered the bones and created the Civilian War Memorial, commonly known as the 'four chopsticks'. A three-metre high concrete memorial built in 1951 in Hanoi's Hop Thien charity cemetery where the remains of thousands of Vietnamese famine victims were interred had fallen into disrepair by 1954. The cemetery itself became buried beneath urban sprawl, making the 1951 monument virtually undiscoverable. In 2001, restoration work on the original memorial began as part of a modestly sized 'zone of recollection'. Its few visitors are mostly government officials and Japanese dignitaries who come periodically to 'recall' the famine dead.[2] In most histories of World War II, the great number of Southeast Asians who died as a result of Japanese occupation goes almost entirely unnoticed.

Comparatively little is written about how World War II affected Southeast Asia's economies or about the Southeast Asian civilians who died prematurely as a consequence of Japanese occupation. Literature on World War II in Southeast Asia deals chiefly with military manoeuvres, with the fate of British, American, Australian and Dutch in Japanese prisoner of war camps, with death marches inflicted on Allied prisoners and with European workers on the Thailand–Burma railway. The present book moves away from this military and European bias. Its principal aim is to explore the war's economic and social impact on Southeast Asia.

Economics and War

The primary motivation for war is frequently economic. Over and above the possibly pleasurable anticipation of war for some dictators are 'the pressure of population and the competitive struggle for markets'. These, Keynes explains, furnish the impulse for war as an instrument of economic policy and account for most of the conflicts during the nineteenth century. Moreover, writing in 1936, Keynes predicted that economic motives might again be the predominant cause of war.[3] He proved correct: for both Germany and Japan, economic considerations were the chief motivation for decisions that led to World War II.[4]

From the late nineteenth century onwards, Japan began to industrialize and in this depended heavily on selling manufactured goods in world markets in exchange for raw materials. As markets closed against Japanese goods in the 1930s and the world divided into economic blocs, Japan sought to escape the pressures of an acute lack of natural resources, a shortage of foreign exchange to buy the raw material inputs for industrialization, exclusion from external markets and the burden of a rapidly growing population. 'There is', contended General Hachiro Arita, Japanese army ideologist and Minister for Foreign Affairs from 1936 to 1940, 'scarcely any difference between economic and military pressure. If, indeed, there is a difference at all, it is nothing more than that between a gradual process of starvation and instant death'. For Japan, the formation of an economic bloc was a necessary 'measure of economic self-defence'.[5] In November 1941, just before Pearl Harbor, the reasoning behind

[2] MacLean, 'History reformatted', pp. 188–89, 213–14.

[3] Keynes, *General theory*, pp. 381–82.

[4] For Germany, see, for example, Barkai, *Nazi economics*, p. 157; Tooze, *Wages*, pp. 166–99, 219–22, 239–41.

[5] Arita, 'Greater East Asian sphere', p. 12. The economic causes of the war are well known; see, for example, Feis, *Road*, pp. 3–4; Butow, *Tojo*, pp. 328, 340–41; Matsuoka, 'New order in East Asia', pp. 1–5.

the decision for war, as later explained by wartime Prime Minister General Tōjō, was that 'rather than await extinction it were better to face death by breaking through the encircling ring [of the ABCD powers of America, Britain, China and the Dutch] to find a way for existence'.[6]

In Japan, the concept of an East Asian empire – a co-operative regional structure of subordinate nations that would form a self-sufficient economic bloc and, as a counterweight to western liberal capitalism, re-shape the global order – had a lengthy history. In 1918, Konoe Fumimaro (who as Prime Minister announced in 1938 Japan's New Order in East Asia) contrasted Japan as a 'have-not' nation with the 'haves' of Britain and the United States. The 'haves', Konoe went on to explain, denied the 'have-nots' equal access to the natural resources and markets of colonized areas. Unless this changed, Japan would be forced 'to destroy the status quo, just like Germany'.[7]

By the end of the 1930s, the idea, or perhaps more accurately the vision, of an East Asian economic bloc directed from Tokyo was rapidly gaining momentum as a national goal.[8] The Japanese desire for a New Order in Asia evolved into the concept of the Greater East Asia Co-Prosperity Sphere. This description became official on 1 August 1940. A sphere of control in Asia seemed to offer a solution to the acute natural resource poverty of the home islands, to encirclement by European powers and imminent economic strangulation, and to the perceived Japanese economic predicament of 'have-not' status. During the 1930s Japan had relentlessly sought access to Southeast Asian markets, and had been successful in penetrating them until halted by the rising protectionism of the colonial powers. A Co-Prosperity Sphere centred on Japan, it was argued, would enable the Japanese nation to assume its rightful place among the world's great powers.

The concept of a Greater East Asia Co-Prosperity Sphere had as its basis the economics of large areas. In this, Japan's sphere resembled Albert Speer's vision of the role of Germany in Europe as the central manufacturing core of a large free trade area, a single customs union to match those of the US, Russia and the British Empire.[9] An East Asia of Japan, Korea, Taiwan, Manchuria (Manchukuo), Southeast Asia and China would form an economic unit big enough to become, with appropriate modifications, essentially self-sufficient and effectively insulate Japan from the international economy. The envisaged Co-Prosperity Sphere would provide raw materials for Japanese industry and an assured market for Japanese manufactured goods.

Japan would have preferred to pursue its economic goals by peaceful means. But if that strategy failed, war was always considered to be the legitimate next

[6] Tōjō, *International Military Tribunal for the Far East*, Exh. 3655, cited in Feis, *Road*, p. 293.
[7] Oka, *Konoe Fumimaro*, pp. 10–13; see also Hata, 'Continental expansion', p. 313.
[8] Duus, 'Imperialism', p. 58.
[9] Milward, *New order*, pp. 146, 148.

economic policy step.[10] When the war in Europe and early German victories isolated European colonies in Southeast Asia, Japanese leaders identified an unrepeatable opportunity to take control of the region: Southeast Asian 'natural resources waited for Japanese picking like "fresh rice cakes off a shelf"'.[11] Southeast Asia would become a fundamental constituent of a Greater East Asia Co-Prosperity Sphere.

The Economics of War and Southeast Asia

Objectively, Japan had little chance of winning World War II, and almost none of outright victory. Fundamental determinants of the ability to win conventional wars are the means to finance them, access to resources and productive capacity. In all three respects, Japan was far behind the United States. The new economics of war builds on these points. Its central argument is that among major country combatants in conventional twentieth-century warfare, relative economic strength – measured as national output, an economy's transformation capacity to shift towards war-related production and degree of geographical vulnerability – is close to decisive in determining the outcome of war.[12]

For Southeast Asia, analysis of World War II, although relevant to the economics of war literature, must take a different tack. Events there relate to the literature because the economic weakness that prejudiced Japan's chances in World War II directly impacted Southeast Asia's economies and peoples. This study differs from the war economics literature, however, in that Southeast Asians themselves did not have economic motives for the war and were peripheral to its outcome. Rather, Japan's economic and military vulnerability shaped its policy approach to, and management of, Southeast Asia in ways that led to catastrophic economic and social collapse in what were essentially neutral countries.

Much of the book focuses on the economic aspects of military occupation. A substantial part of the study considers areas such as production, trade, currency, taxation, population movements, price controls, rationing, food availability, living standards and the provision of labour. Economics is fundamental to all of these and is either heavily influenced by an occupying administration

10 Butow, *Tojo*, p. 203.

11 Drea, *Japanese imperial army*, p. 209 and see Ike, *Japan's decision*, pp. xix, 134, 202, 238; KKC, file B1-209, Japan, Imperial Headquarters, *Gozen kaigi shidai: Tai Ei-Bei-Ran Sensō ni tomonau zaisei kin'yū no jikyū-ryoku handan ni kansuru setsumei yōshi (Ōkura Daijin)* [Minutes of Imperial Conference: Summary of explanation (by Finance Minister) on the financial durability of monetary and fiscal systems in relation to the war against Britain, America and the Netherlands], 5 November 1941.

12 Goldsmith, 'Power of victory'; Milward, *German economy* and *War, economy and society*; Ránki, *Economics*; Offer, *First World War* and 'War economy'; Harrison, *Accounting* and *Economics*; Broadberry and Harrison, *Economics*; Tooze, *Wages*; Rockoff, *America's economic way*.

or under its direction. Yet consideration of economic issues, particularly in wartime occupation, cannot have a wholly economic focus. After occupying Southeast Asia, military and civilian Japanese administrators immediately confronted major problems. Difficulties arose from the distance between Southeast Asia and Japan, from an exceptionally challenging Southeast Asian geography, from a continuously shifting military balance, from the cultural distance between Japan and all Southeast Asian countries, and from the need to exert social control over the local population. While all these problems were intertwined with economics, none had entirely, or even necessarily primarily, economic solutions.

Geography and War

The vastness of the Pacific and Japan's remoteness from Southeast Asia (2,888 nautical miles from Tokyo or Yokohama to Singapore, a minimum of about eight days' travel by sea) put a premium on shipping and air transport. So too did the large land area of Southeast Asia, its island configuration and north–south infrastructure bias. The extreme transport and supply difficulties that confronted Japan were further compounded by the rapidity and ease with which it occupied Southeast Asia along with much of the Pacific, and by the United States April 1942 Doolittle bomber raid on Tokyo, the latter causing the army to move further into China to destroy threatening Chinese air bases. In the Pacific, Japanese strategists decided in the spring of 1942 to extend military advance beyond the huge area already under Japanese control to include the Solomon Islands and Port Moresby, followed, if possible, by New Caledonia, Samoa and Fiji, the capture of Midway and temporary occupation of the Aleutians (Figure I.2). Japan's forces were, however, already stretched beyond Japanese economic and military capabilities and '[N]o amount of bravery could compensate for logistical impotence'.[13]

After the Pacific War's turning points in the summer of 1942, the military balance continuously shifted against Japan and its defensive perimeter began to contract. During late 1943 and 1944, Japanese losses of merchant and oil tanker tonnage soared. Over the course of 1944, American submarine and air attacks reduced Japan's merchant fleet to under a third, and by the end of the war to less than a fifth, of its 1941 tonnage.[14] In 1944, the inability to move refined products home or to war zones caused Japan to limit oil refinery operations in Southeast Asia; the last Japanese tanker convoy for Japan left Singapore on 19 March 1945 but probably never arrived.[15] With small and

13 Coox, 'Pacific war', p. 357, and see Drea, *Japan's imperial army*, pp. 226–27.

14 Andō, *Kindai nihon keizai shi yōran*, p. 139; see also USSBS, *Effects of strategic bombing*, pp. 41–44.

15 USSBS, *Oil*, pp. 6, 49; Parillo, *Japanese merchant marine*, pp. 143–44.

declining stocks of oil, aeroplanes were of little use except for kamikaze missions, which required fuel for only an outward flight. The sole military option still available to Japan was a last-ditch defence of the home islands where, moreover, if war had continued into the winter of 1945, there would probably have been famine.

A lack of shipping to carry goods from Southeast Asia to Japan and troops to the region was paralleled by acute intra-Southeast Asian transport shortages. Although Japan commandeered most Southeast Asian transport, this was insufficient for Japanese military needs. Shortages of fuel, lubricants and spare parts along with increasingly effective Allied bombing in Burma and Indochina further disrupted transport. By the war's late stages, transport systems in much of Southeast Asia functioned badly, if at all.

In large parts of Southeast Asia, the Japanese military instituted country autarky. The reasons for autarkic policies were to limit transport use and, for an army living off the land, to avoid the domino effect of a military loss in one region causing the loss of another due to food and materiel shortages. Deterioration in Japan's military situation led to country autarky becoming regional, or even sub-regional, autarky.

By mid-1943, a lack of regional shipping and land transport further contributed to pushing Southeast Asian countries towards autarky. Pre-war Southeast Asian countries and regions were so economically integrated and so interdependent, especially in regard to food, that the collapse of intra-regional and inter-country trade associated with the shortage of transport exacerbated the already steep economic decline caused by Southeast Asia's severance from the global economy.

Food supplies in Southeast Asia, especially outside rice-growing areas, were drastically reduced by ever more narrowly circumscribed autarky, mounting transport deficiencies, increased Allied bombing and greater control over food distribution which included delivery quotas for farmers and confiscation. The Burma delta, Cochinchina in the south of Vietnam and Central Thailand produced great surpluses of rice that were essential in feeding much of the rest of Southeast Asia but which during the war became largely or entirely unavailable to many food-deficit areas. In the food-deficit (net food-importing) countries of Malaya, Indonesia and the Philippines, the Japanese had to ration rice virtually from the start of occupation and then progressively rationed other foods. As the war continued, ration sizes were continuously cut. They fell to well below minimum calorie requirements in the largest cities, typically to even less in smaller cities, and to nothing in rural areas. Numerous Japanese campaigns encouraged Southeast Asians to grow their own food. These and Japanese dissemination of information on the preparation of substitutes for foods no longer available, especially rice, at best only partially countered scarcities.

Japanese War Finance, Shortages and Black Markets

The first financial principle of occupation is that the occupied country should bear the cost of its occupation. In Southeast Asia, since opportunities for finance through taxation or selling bonds were limited, this largely meant printing money. Japan paid for both its military and civilian expenditures in Southeast Asia and also for its imports from the region chiefly by issuing increasing quantities of currency. High inflation and finally hyperinflation inevitably followed.

Japan supplied few consumer goods to Southeast Asia and hardly any of the basic necessities such as cloth, thread, shoes and sandals, soap, matches, paper, batteries, light bulbs and essential medicines. Nowhere in pre-war Southeast Asia had industrialization been sufficiently advanced for the region to be self-sufficient in such goods. Southeast Asian countries had typically relied on imports for three-quarters or more of their annual consumption of textiles.

Clothing became almost universally hard to obtain, especially outside urban areas where few pre-war stocks existed. In Burma, thieves did a thriving business in stolen articles of clothing.[16] Graves in Manila were robbed to obtain clothes from the corpses, as well as for gold teeth.[17] By late 1943, gunny bags normally used to transport rice and sugar began to be worn as clothing. In Indonesia, some people even clothed themselves in sheets of crude rubber or, as a last resort, banana leaves.[18]

Nearly every Southeast Asian had to turn to substitutes for many basic manufactured goods and medicines, or go without. Middle-class Southeast Asians sold pre-war assets in order to buy consumer goods and food. In Manila and Singapore, specialized city-centre markets acquired institutional status as centres for the sale of gold, jewellery and other valuables. These items, after passing through networks of agents, brokers and dealers, often ended up in the hands of Japanese military personnel, Japanese civilians or Southeast Asians to give as presents to military officers who handed out contracts or other favours.[19]

Acute shortages of goods, high inflation and attempts at price controls led to the proliferation throughout Southeast Asia of black markets for food and all manner of goods. The Japanese themselves often resorted to black markets to secure otherwise unobtainable items like building materials, machinery, medicines and sometimes food. Intricate supply networks and a burgeoning informal economy emerged in the new environment of shortage, uncertain information and the advantage of contacts, especially with the Japanese military.

16 OSS, R&A 2015, *Japanese administration of Burma*, p. 43.

17 UP, Manuel A. Roxas Papers for the ms. Osmeña, 'Dear dad', p. 310; Agoncillo, *Fateful years*, pp. 583–84.

18 Stoler, *Capitalism*, p. 99.

19 Lee, *Singapore story*, p. 66.

Southeast Asian Labour and War

By mid-1943 in most of Southeast Asia, labour shortages replaced early labour gluts due to the Japanese need for workers to build airfields and defence installations against probable Allied invasion. The Japanese military required large amounts of labour because it had only limited manpower of its own in Southeast Asia and because Japan's approach was, wherever possible, to substitute labour for capital. Forced labour became a frequent solution to greater Japanese defence needs. Deception might be needed to recruit this labour, but Southeast Asian authorities frequently had a large role in obtaining workers. Indonesians in positions of leadership, including Sukarno, the Republic's first president, actively helped to recruit, often as conscripts, large numbers of *romusha*, a term that in Japanese meant unskilled manual labourers but who, in the context of the war, often amounted to forced labour.[20]

The Japanese war effort used Southeast Asians mainly in auxiliary, supporting and characteristically menial duties. Although in Burma and Indonesia the Japanese-trained substantial local armies, they never envisaged that these soldiers would fill a combat role in the defence of Southeast Asia, nor did they trust them to do so. Nevertheless, Japanese-trained armies in the two countries were of great significance because, as an organized military, they hastened independence and subsequently exerted a dominating influence on politics and economics.

Japanese Misperceptions and Mistakes

Main themes that run through this book include shortages, economic contraction, hunger, famine, dislocation, brutality and premature death. Three sets of Japanese misperceptions which can be identified are fundamental to many of these themes. Misperceptions were intertwined and led to mistakes which multiplied and became more disastrous for Japan and for Southeast Asia too as war and occupation continued. The cumulative effect was that any hope of realizing a Greater East Asia Co-Prosperity Sphere soon became unrealistic. Instead, by mid-1943 the Japanese military struggled against mounting odds to avert disaster, while for Southeast Asians suffering from occupation escalated.

Economic Weakness

One set of misperceptions relates to the weakness of Japan's home economy and, in light of this, the limits of Japan's ability to prosecute war. Second, the Japanese imperfectly grasped the nature of pre-war Southeast Asian economic development. It was not adequately understood what commodities and goods

[20] Sukarno, *Autobiography*, p. 192; Hill, *Journalism and politics*, pp. 25, 44.

Southeast Asia could supply to Japan and, moreover, how to use the market to obtain those goods that Southeast Asia was capable of producing. A third set of misperceptions comprised Japanese cultural misunderstandings of both the Allies and Southeast Asians.

A sharp disconnect existed between Japan's economic strength and its political ambitions. Japan started the war from an economically weak and geographically vulnerable position. These economic shortcomings were increasingly, and by 1944 ruthlessly, exposed. Initial Japanese military conquest caused Japan to misjudge Allied strength, depart from a strategy of a short war, and re-define the Greater East Asia Co-Prosperity Sphere far beyond the originally intended area bounded by Thailand, Indonesia and the Philippines in the south and the Pacific islands near Japan. Japanese leaders might have succeeded in their objective of strengthening the economy through annexing some part of Southeast Asia if they had acknowledged that Japan was economically equipped only for a short war and adhered to their original military strategy as planned by Admiral Yamamoto, or if they had tried to negotiate a peace settlement after early war defeats. Once war spread over most of the Pacific and lengthened beyond two years, Japan had no realistic chance of emerging victorious. As the conflict continued, Southeast Asia contributed less and less to Japan's economy. Instead of doing much to further the war effort, the occupation of all of Southeast Asia spread Japanese forces over a vast geographical area that was too large to defend and drew Japan into a disastrous military campaign in Burma.

A successful war economy must increase GDP and move decisively to the production of war-related goods. Japan failed to achieve the former and accomplished the latter only through drastic cuts in home consumption. Japanese GDP declined somewhat after 1939 and then stagnated from 1940 to 1944. The shift to a war economy was at the expense of a fall in consumer expenditure from about two-thirds of GDP in 1940 to two-fifths by 1944.[21] Japanese average daily food intake shrank from an estimated 2,250 calories in 1941 to 1,800 calories by 1944, followed by a large decline in 1945.[22] Japan's economic failings and inability fully to mobilize a war economy were magnified in Southeast Asia. Occupation left Southeast Asians heavily dependent on Japan for supplies of food and basic consumer goods but Japanese economic weakness soon made shipping goods to the region out of the question, even if Japan had wanted to do so.

Japan embarked on war with probably inadequate shipping to meet both the needs of its home economy and to transport men to and from as well as within Southeast Asia. The military mistakes of a failure to recognize the value of the convoy system to minimize the loss of merchant vessels or to foresee the

[21] Ohkawa and Shinohara, *Patterns*, pp. 259–60; see also USSBS, *Effects of strategic bombing*, p. 15, which gives somewhat different figures but makes the same point.

[22] USSBS, *Effects of strategic bombing*, pp. 32–33.

deadliness of Allied submarine warfare led to the growing loss of merchant vessels and oil tankers. A lack of steel, together with insufficiently innovative technologies in shipbuilding, made it impossible to replace damaged and sunk ships. By the spring of 1944, Japan had lost one of Southeast Asia's principal early contributions to the war effort: shipping losses and Allied interdiction of sea lanes meant that Indonesian oil could no longer reach Japan. Nor could Japan continue to obtain coking coal and iron ore from China to counter a serious steel constraint.

Southeast Asian Economy Misperceptions

The second set of misperceptions derived from an insufficient understanding of the Southeast Asian economy by Japanese planners and their inability realistically to assess how the region might contribute to the war effort and substitute for pre-war imports no longer available. During the war, the abundance of useful resources that Japan had expected Southeast Asia to yield never materialized. Nor could Southeast Asian industry provide many manufactured goods to Japanese forces in Southeast Asia.

In 1941, Southeast Asia was a collection of monoeconomies, specialized in just four main primary commodity staples – rice, rubber, tin and sugar. Pre-war development depended substantially, although not entirely, on small-scale or peasant producers. The basis for development was comparative advantage created by quite specific geographical characteristics. Southeast Asia's geography favoured the production of tropical crops, not temperate ones. The great rice-producing deltas of southern Burma and Indochina, low-lying and before late nineteenth-century export booms often swampy, were ill-suited to agriculture other than rice. In the Burma delta, fully a third of rice land was at most a foot above the high tide level and almost nothing grew, or could economically be grown, except rice.[23]

Apart from oil, bauxite and rice, Japan's economy was too small to use more than a fraction of the commodities in which pre-war Southeast Asia specialized. Nor did Southeast Asia offer Japan the easy access to resources anticipated before the war, the rice cakes available just for the taking. Rather, successful resource extraction posed difficult, and often intractable, problems of how to re-configure Southeast Asian output to the economic needs of Japan and an East Asia Co-Prosperity Sphere.

Substitution formed a key part of Japan's economic planning for war. Before the war, Japan relied on imports for nearly every strategic raw material. The United States supplied most of the oil Japan needed and much of the raw cotton for textile manufacture. Korea was the largest source of imported rice. The Japanese hoped to substitute conquest followed by production in the occupied areas for pre-war trade. Conquest in Southeast Asia would replace

[23] Dobby, *Monsoon Asia*, p. 182.

American oil with Indonesian. Control of Southeast Asia would provide an effectively unlimited supply of rice. That would be required since half of the Japanese labour force was in agriculture and many of these workers would have to become soldiers; because Korean rice output would fall as its economy moved from agriculture to the manufacture of war goods for Japan; and due to a need to feed conquered areas of China. However, Southeast Asia produced greater quantities of rice than Japan could use. A planned shift in Southeast Asia from some rice cultivation to fibre crops would help to make up for the cessation of cotton supplies from the United States and India and replace Indian jute, the raw material for gunny sacks. The Philippines was to grow cotton and only enough sugar for domestic consumption, since production in Formosa (Taiwan) already made East Asia essentially self-sufficient in the commodity and since the Philippines was an inefficient sugar producer.[24]

During its occupation of Southeast Asia, Japan's strategy of substitution was largely unsuccessful. None of the complexities of effective exploitation of the region was overcome. Geography and a tropical climate ill-suited to cotton and other fibre crops, compounded by Japanese insistence on techniques successful in Japan and Taiwan, often stood in the way.

For an occupier, agrarian economies of small cultivators like Southeast Asia's are more difficult to manage and exploit than developed industrial economies. Because in Southeast Asia producers were numerous and decentralized over large areas, compulsion only imperfectly substituted for incentives. Before the war, textiles and simple manufactures from the West, known as inducement goods, furnished the motivation for Southeast Asians to produce primary commodities and were fundamental to its economic development. Nevertheless, the Japanese made almost no attempt to use incentives as a means of stimulating and altering Southeast Asian output. One reason was, of course, that the Japanese economy could not supply Southeast Asia with consumer goods. Equally, however, the Japanese did not regard these as essential and chose instead to regulate prices and rely on a command structure. Even when crops like the cotton and jute specified in directives from Japanese planners might have been viable, farmers were disinclined to switch production or to tend new crops without either the reward of higher prices or consumer goods in exchange, especially if non-food crops threatened food security. In Vietnam, some farmers responded to compulsion to replace rice with jute by boiling the seeds before planting them or pulling up the young jute plants at night.[25] Even when jute was grown it was of variable quality.[26]

24 NARA, RG226, entry 16, box 144, 'Conditions in the Philippine Islands', 23 August 1942, p. 36.

25 Bui, 'Japan's role', p. 590; Le, *Impact*, pp. 181–82, 205–6, 217, 231, 242, 257 n. 14; Jose, 'Labor usage', p. 276.

26 AOM, GF/47, Letter Trac to Lemarque, Commissaire du Gouvernement aux Matières Textiles, 4 November 1944.

As the occupation continued, production incentives were continuously undermined by the way Japan financed occupation and by inflexible administered prices for Southeast Asian primary commodities. While Japan's technique of financing occupation chiefly through printing money successfully shifted a large part of the cost of occupation onto the occupied, it also led to high and increasing inflation. Rising prices for consumer goods combined with relatively inflexible primary commodity prices eroded incentives.

Japan intended that as part of the Co-Prosperity Sphere Southeast Asia would, like south-eastern Europe for Nazi Germany, remain essentially a producer of food and primary commodities. Even so, in conformity with Japan's policy of a military living off the land, it was anticipated that as part of the war effort Southeast Asia would produce much of what Japanese forces needed. By 1943, due to shipping losses, the army had entirely to support itself.[27] In response, the Japanese made greater efforts to adapt pre-war Southeast Asian plant and machinery and to manufacture locally what they needed. However, pre-war Southeast Asia had been so little industrialized, so dependent on imported components for manufactures, and so short of both skilled labour and capital that it could produce few manufactured goods for Japan's war effort.

Problems of weak pre-war industrialization also constrained Japan's extraction of Southeast Asia's minerals. Japan would have needed to invest capital, bring machinery, manufacture spare parts, invest capital and transfer large numbers of skilled workers to Southeast Asia to restore and develop mineral output in the region. However, all these inputs to industrialization were already in short supply in the Japanese home economy and at best could be directed to Southeast Asia only in small amounts. To some extent and notably in Indonesia, Japan made up for shortages of trained personnel by continuing for some time to employ pre-war European engineers and technicians.

As Southeast Asia's pre-war stock of lorries, buses, cars, trains and ships was commandeered by the Japanese military and deteriorated beyond repair, transport became an economic bottleneck. Increasingly, and by the end of the war almost wholly, Southeast Asians in Burma, Indonesia and the Philippines had to rely on pre-modern transport like bicycles, ox carts and country boats.[28] Due to a lack of transport, wide price variations, even between nearby areas, became a feature of wartime Southeast Asia.

By its nature, occupation is not a permanent state, and often a short-run phenomenon. However, Japan meant to dominate most of East and Southeast Asia for the foreseeable future and, as observed in 1943, meant to mould the 'vast area under its control into one homogeneous sphere which is more or less independent of the outside world'.[29] That, however, would never, even in the

27 JM 103, *Outline of administration*, pp. 4, 15.

28 OSS, R&A 1713, *Structure of the government of Burma*, p. 49.

29 '"Co-prosperity" takes shape', *The Economist*, 18 December 1943, p. 814.

absence of war, have been easily or swiftly accomplished. It implied a departure for Southeast Asia from decades of development as specialized components of the global economy and required fundamental economic and structural transformation. Japan had not prepared for this and during the war was unable to begin to transform Southeast Asia's economies. Instead, it destroyed Southeast Asia's pre-war economies.

Cultural Misperceptions

The third set of misperceptions was Japan's failure to understand the cultures of either Southeast Asia or the United States. Japanese cultural misperceptions of Southeast Asians included the belief that large numbers of them would adopt Japanese views and attitudes, or at least could be educated to do so; that long-established ways of thinking could easily be altered; that this could be accomplished through exhortation and force; and that progress could be expected despite an absence of the kinds of material incentives long a cornerstone of Southeast Asian economic development. Southeast Asian societies were viewed as so simplistic and backward that they could be managed effectively despite a lack of material goods. In November 1941, Japanese Finance Minister Kaya considered that compared to China it would be easy to maintain the livelihood of Southeast Asians 'because the culture of the inhabitants is low, and because the area is rich in natural products'.[30]

Japanese policy to re-orient Southeast Asian culture and exert social control over occupied countries was twofold. One strand, directed especially against the Chinese, was to disregard the deprivations of occupation for Southeast Asians and brutally to suppress any potential opposition. Japan's official November 1941 outline of administration in Southeast Asia made this clear: 'During the war, the great burdens which will fall on natives on account of the acquisition of natural resources and the process of making the army self-supporting must be borne with the utmost patience. Any requests regarding welfare, which are contrary to this object, will be refused.'[31]

Economic dominance by the Chinese in Southeast Asia gave Japan no option but to rely on them. The Chinese co-operated outwardly with Japan because, in the words of a former Japanese army officer writing after the war, 'they valued their lives and wanted to gain profits'.[32] Japan's arrival in Singapore was quickly followed by the systematic killing of some 20,000 Chinese, a war crime and an occupation strategy reminiscent of the Rape of Nanking (Nanjing). All groups of

[30] KKC, file B1-209, Japan, Imperial Headquarters, *Gozen kaigi shidai* [Minutes of Imperial Conference], 5 November 1941, 'Summary of explanation on financial durability of monetary and fiscal systems', p. 4 and translated in Ike, Japan's decision, p. 224.

[31] NA, WO203/6310, 'SEATIC Special intelligence bulletin', 1946, p. 2.

[32] JM 103, *Outline of administration*, p. 17.

Southeast Asians, even if, unlike the Chinese, considered potential allies of Japan, suffered verbal abuse and the ubiquitous Japanese practice of slapping a person's face for a misdemeanour, which might be failure to bow to a Japanese soldier or official. Minor infringements attracted severe treatment; a suspicion of anything more serious resulted in torture and often execution.[33]

The second strand of Japanese strategy was to change attitudes and convert Southeast Asians to a corporatist social behaviour like that in Japan, where individuals worked for the good of the state and accepted its benevolent rule. Towards this end, schools and classes for adults taught *Nihon-go* (the Japanese language). In all countries except Thailand and Indochina, the Japanese set up a plethora of organizations to try to link individuals to the state and inculcate a spirit of work and sacrifice. The names of Japanese-sponsored associations changed often, partly because if one was unsuccessful it was re-introduced in a new form.

At the outset of occupation, many of those in Southeast Asia, notably in Burma, Indonesia and Thailand, were either well disposed towards the Japanese or at least neutral. As Southeast Asia's economies were forced towards self-sufficiency and societies disintegrated, it became increasingly difficult to convince such Southeast Asians of the 'prosperity' element of Japan's Greater East Asia Sphere and its cultural mission. In an environment of acute shortages, social decay and draconian social repression, the Japanese promise of Asia for Asians lacked credibility. Japanese ideals never carried much weight in the Philippines. Filipinos doubted the idea of Asian brotherhood and considered their Christian morality superior to the Japanese, undercutting Japan's call for Asian solidarity. The mix of Spanish and American cultural heritage in the Philippines probably ensured complete Japanese failure in altering Filipino culture, as should have been obvious from the start.[34]

Throughout Southeast Asia, disillusion towards the Japanese took hold even where it had not at first been present. However, most Southeast Asians had a safety-first approach and tried to make themselves inconspicuous. Except possibly in Thailand, '[I]f someone suddenly set up a small wooden board, with something written in Japanese on it, at the gate of your house, you realized immediately [that it was needed by the army] and you quit promptly, bag and baggage'. Likewise the same person, an Indian journalist, recalled that: 'If you happened to be taking a stroll and saw some Japanese soldiers unloading cases of ammunition from a fleet of lorries, you just rolled up your sleeves and helped the war effort. If you tried to walk away, you would not get far; you would be lying on the road with a bleeding bayonet wound in your back.'[35] Even in Bangkok, despite Thailand's alliance with Japan, the 'Thais looked on

33 NARA, RG226, entry 16, box 144, 'Conditions in the Philippine Islands', 23 August 1942, p. 9; Hartendorp, *History of industry*, p. 67.

34 Friend, *Between two empires*, p. 232; Rōyāma and Takéuchi, *Philippine polity*, p. 260.

35 Sivaram, *Road to Delhi*, pp. 63–64.

helplessly, as Japanese officers and civilians occupied every available building in the city'.[36]

Cultural misperceptions on both the Japanese and Allied sides pre-dated the war. Before Pearl Harbor, influential opinion in the United States and Britain considered it obvious that Japan, a midget economy, would rationally assess its limitations and behave accordingly. Japan would act sensibly and not wage war, while if it did Japanese soldiers would be far inferior to Allied troops. Neither Churchill nor Roosevelt believed that Japan, already deeply enmeshed in China, would make war on the British Empire as well.[37] Government officials in the United States, including US Secretary of State Cordell Hull, misunderstood Japan culturally: they thought that, given Japanese economic weakness, American strategy in the run-up to war would deter Japan, not that it would be seen as a threat to Japan's very existence.[38]

In Japan, it was felt that America was too decadent and too materialistic a society wholeheartedly to pursue war. Social unrest would take hold in the United States as wartime sacrifices began to bite. Moreover, unlike the superior Japanese Yamato race, Americans lacked fighting spirit.[39] A short war and favourable peace would be possible after early Japanese gains: the United States would settle and cede Japan control of some part of Southeast Asia. Another incorrect perception was that decisive Japanese victories at the war's outset, and long supply lines for America, would discourage the United States from persisting in an Asian war and cause it to agree a peace and abandon support for China.[40]

Cultural misunderstanding persisted on both sides even as the war lengthened. By mid-1944, economic disaster for Japan was almost inevitable and could be foreseen with reasonable clarity by anyone possessing basic information.[41] In June 1944, a report to Japan's Supreme War Council titled 'The present state of material power' concluded that Japan could not continue the war beyond the autumn.[42] Although from a Western perspective Japanese surrender was the obvious choice, it was anathema to Japan's military culture and its leaders. Honour alone, as Offer has pointed out, can fuel conflict well beyond rationality and Japan's generals were determined to preserve this at any cost, including widespread starvation in the home islands during the winter of

36 Ibid., p. 62. On the Japanese takeover of any business or residential property that they wanted, regardless of whether it belonged to enemy nationals, Thai or Chinese, see NARA, RG59, entry 205, box 5834, file 892.00 233, J. Holbrook Chapman, 'General report on conditions in Thailand December 1941 to June 1942', 18 August 1942, p. 24; Reynolds, 'Anomaly', p. 253.

37 Allen, *Singapore 1941–1942*, p. 136; Jones, *Japan's new order*, p. 461.

38 Paine, *Japanese empire*, p. 156.

39 Earhart, *Certain victory*, pp. 256, 258, 301; Drea, *Japan's imperial army*, p. 226.

40 Paine, *Japanese empire*, p. 154.

41 USSBS, *Summary report*, pp. 15, 34.

42 Jones, *Japan's new order*, p. 435; USSBS, *Japan's struggle*, p. 2.

1945–46.[43] Furthermore, even in mid-1945, army leaders believed that, as well as maintaining honour, Japan could inflict such painful losses on invading American forces that it could get a peace settlement on Japanese terms and so still salvage material gain from the war.[44] Japanese leaders never expected the United States to require unconditional surrender.[45] In this, they misunderstood America's way of war. The American tradition, Rockoff explains, had long been to demand and accept nothing less than unconditional surrender.[46] There was little chance of departure from that tradition, as humiliating early defeats at the hands of the Japanese aroused American public opinion 'against [Japan] to such a degree that nothing short of her complete downfall would have satisfied it'.[47]

Continuing the war after mid-1944 resulted in millions of dead, most of whom were Southeast Asians, and acute suffering for nearly all civilians in Southeast Asia. In June 1944, when Japan was already beaten, the famines in Vietnam and Java could still have been avoided. At that point, too, a negotiated peace would have prevented the February 1945 Rape of Manila and the torture and death of tens of thousands of its inhabitants along with the city's total ruin.

Japan's surrender would also have averted wholesale physical destruction in Japan. The capture of Iwo Jima in March 1945 afforded a perfect natural aeroplane runway within easy striking distance of Japan, handing the United States an open bombing target. Relentless Allied bombing of Japanese cities was almost unopposed, since Japan, short of oil to fuel fighter planes, lacked effective air cover for its home islands. Bombing levelled all major Japanese cities except Kyoto. The 9 March 1945 firebombing of Tokyo was possibly the most destructive attack of all time.[48] Finally, two atomic bombs brought the war to a close. For Southeast Asia, the darkest period of its history had ended but a long, troubled aftermath of war and occupation lay ahead.

Conquest and Material Gains

Prior to World War II, the dominant liberal belief was that occupied territories yielded few resources to their conquerors.[49] Recent work has suggested that the experience of World War II, in both Europe and Asia, demonstrates the contrary: that war and occupation can go hand in hand with effective

43 Offer, 'Going to war', pp. 213–41.
44 Drea, *Japan's imperial army*, p. 250.
45 Paine, *Japanese empire*, p. 156.
46 Rockoff, *America's economic way*, pp. 46–47, 141, 158, 214, 220.
47 Jones, *Japan's new order*, p. 465.
48 Werrell, *Blankets*, p. 226.
49 Milward, *New order*, pp. 1–22.

economic exploitation.[50] This book challenges that possibility. It will be shown that Japan gained little from Southeast Asia and that the costs of the Pacific War for the Japanese home islands and people were enormous in terms of lost GDP, Japanese dead and obliteration of much of Japan's infrastructure. Nearly 3 million Japanese military personnel and civilians died as a result of the Pacific War. Of the about 2.3 million Japanese military deaths during the eight years of war starting in 1937, a half to two-thirds were from starvation or starvation-related causes together with the wounded and enfeebled who were induced, or forced, to commit suicide after leaving the front line.[51] In Southeast Asia, failures of Japanese military strategy and planning cut short initial exploitation and combined to stop the shipments of even militarily strategic goods. Yet high as Japanese war losses were, the costs for Southeast Asia of occupation were almost certainly greater.

For the Pacific War to have succeeded as an instrument of economic policy and been 'profitable' for Japan, it would have had to win the war, or end it in a position to negotiate a favourable peace. Although outright victory was always unlikely, it is conceivable that had Japan engineered a short war, a post-war settlement might have been achieved which acknowledged Japanese hegemony over some part of Southeast Asia. In the end, however, Japan's only choice was unconditional surrender. Japan's embarkation on the Pacific War could have been a great move in history to challenge outmoded Anglo-American dominance.[52] Instead, it resulted in American supremacy in the Pacific for the next three-quarters of a century.

[50] Liberman, *Does conquest pay?*

[51] Fujiwara, *Uejini shita eiyūtachi*, pp. 3, 128, puts the number of total war-related deaths at 3.1 million for 1937 to 1945. Dower gives a figure for Pacific War deaths of nearly 3 million in *Embracing defeat*, p. 22 and 2.7 million in *War*, p. 299. He suggests (*War*, p. 298) that only a third of military deaths were in actual combat; Fujiwara indicates that combat caused 45 per cent of military deaths.

[52] Duus, 'Imperialism', p. 66.

1

Southeast Asia in the Pacific War

This chapter has two main aims. One is to assess the reasons for the outbreak of war in the Pacific. Japanese economic motivations for war are given particular weight. Second, the chapter analyses Japan's economic plans for Southeast Asia at the outset of occupation, how these changed as the war turned against Japan, and the implications for Southeast Asia of Japanese military reversals and heavy merchant shipping losses.

By 1940, Japan's sense of injustice as a 'have-not' nation had festered for much of the previous decade. Moreover, the Japanese were, after two and a half years, bogged down in an unwinnable war in China. The December 1941 attack on Pearl Harbor was intended to solve both problems. This chapter begins with an analysis of Japan's 'have-not' status and the intention to reverse this by incorporating Southeast Asia into a Greater East Asia Co-Prosperity Sphere, thereby acquiring a 'fairer' share of the world's natural resources. Control over Southeast Asia was also expected to help solve Japan's 'China problem' by ensuring the severance of southern supply routes through Southeast Asia to Chiang Kai-shek's Nationalist Chinese troops.

The chapter goes on to examine Japan's strengths and weaknesses in embarking on a Pacific war where the United States would be its principal adversary. Again, resource deficiency and geography are major themes in the narrative. As a resource-poor island fundamentally dependent on shipping to bring food and most of the main requirements for war, Japan's geography made it highly vulnerable to wartime economic strangulation. Japanese strategists anticipated that occupation of Southeast Asia would substantially help to overcome this vulnerability.

During the war, however, Southeast Asia created a large net defence liability for Japan because the region was so extensive, so distant from the Japanese home islands and turned out to be of limited economic value for Japan's war effort. By mid-1943, after over a year of Japanese military setbacks, the Southeast Asian liability was starkly apparent. Continuous and escalating shipping losses exposed fundamental Japanese weakness. In response, at least for the duration of the war, Japan abandoned the effort to re-configure Southeast Asia as an integral part of the Greater East Asia Co-Prosperity Sphere. Instead, pressured by military imperatives, planners divided some

Southeast Asian countries into autarkic regions and attempted, for the first time, to realize a significant Southeast Asian manufacturing contribution from the region alongside its role as a raw materials supplier. During the approximately two years between this change of tack and Japan's surrender in August 1945, Southeast Asia was devastated economically.

Japanese 'Have-Not' Status and the East Asia Co-Prosperity Sphere

World War II was a confrontation between the 'have-not' nations of Germany, Japan and Italy and the 'haves', principally the United States and the United Kingdom with its vast resource-rich empire. Among the 'have-nots', none was more resource-poor than the Japanese Empire. Figure 1.1 compares the control of World War II combatants over 34 key raw materials: 15 metals, 8 non-metallic minerals, and 11 agricultural products. Japan wholly lacked 19 of the 34 materials and was self-sufficient or surplus in just five. Coal, oil, iron and cotton were fundamental to industrialization: of these Japan had self-sufficiency only in coal, and even here had to import coking coal to manufacture steel.[1] Germany and Italy resembled Japan in resource deficiency. By contrast, the United States and United Kingdom were between them self-sufficient or surplus in all but 5 of the 34 raw materials. Furthermore, both the United States and Britain could restrict access to strategic raw materials through effectively controlling resources in informal empires in Latin America and the Middle East. In July 1941, the American and British governments demonstrated their hold on Latin America: they blocked the export from the region to Japan of nearly all important war materials and by then had acquired the exclusive right to purchase almost all Latin American production of strategic materials.[2]

A somewhat different accounting of the 'have' and 'have-nots' than shown in Figure 1.1 analyses control of 40 significant industrial raw materials in 1939. Countries that would form the Axis were the leading producers of just 5 of the 40 materials (potash, mercury, rayon, staple fibre and natural silk). The Allies controlled 75 per cent or more of the output of most of the remaining 35.[3] Oil, the raw material essential for industrialization and war, had a quite uneven distribution. In 1941, the United States produced 62.5 per cent of world oil and Latin America a further 16.8 per cent; Japanese oil production accounted for 0.1 per cent of world output (Table 1.1).

For the Japan of the 1930s, resource poverty, population pressure, industrialization and the international payments system merged into an

[1] USSBS, *Summary report*, pp. 13–14; Cohen, *Japan's economy*, p. 114.
[2] Feis, *Road*, p. 243.
[3] Jones, 'Industrial capacity', pp. 197–98.

	Japanese Empire	Germany	Italy and colonies	United States	British Empire	France and colonies	USSR
Metals							
Iron	PD	PD	WD	SS	SS	ES	SS
Copper	SS	WD	WD	ES	SS	WD	PD
Lead	PD	WD	SS	SS	ES	WD	WD
Zinc	PD	PD	SS	SS	SS	WD	PD
Tin	WD	WD	WD	WD	ES	WD	WD
Bauxite	WD	WD	SS	PD	SS	ES	WD
Manganese	PD	WD	WD	WD	ES	WD	ES
Nickel	WD	WD	WD	WD	ES	SS	WD
Tungsten	PD	WD	WD	WD	SS	WD	WD
Chromium	PD	WD	WD	WD	ES	SS	PD
Vandaium	WD	WD	WD	WD	ES	WD	WD
Molybdenum	PD	WD	WD	ES	WD	SS	WD
Antimony	WD	WD	PD	WD	WD	PD	WD
Magnesite	WD	PD	PD	PD	SS	WD	SS
Mercury	WD	WD	ES	PD	WD	WD	SS
Non-metallic minerals							
Coal	SS	ES	WD	ES	ES	PD	SS
Petroleum	WD	WD	WD	ES	WD	WD	ES
Asbestos	PD	WD	PD	WD	ES	WD	ES
Graphite	SS	PD	PD	WD	ES	ES	PD
Sulphur or pyrites	ES	PD	ES	ES	PD	WD	PD
Phosphates	WD	WD	WD	ES	SS	SS	SS
Potash	WD	ES	WD	PD	WD	ES	SS
Platinum	WD	WD	WD	WD	ES	WD	ES
Agricultural products							
Rubber	WD	WD	WD	WD	ES	WD	WD
Cotton	WD	WD	WD	ES	PD	WD	SS
Wool	WD	WD	WD	PD	ES	WD	PD
Silk	ES	WD	ES	WD	WD	WD	SS
Flax	WD	WD	WD	WD	WD	SS	ES
Jute	WD	WD	WD	WD	ES	WD	WD
Hemp	WD	WD	ES	WD	WD	WD	SS
Manila (abaca)	WD	WD	WD	WD	WD	WD	WD
Sisal	PD	WD	WD	WD	SS	WD	WD
Vegetable oils	WD	WD	SS	ES	ES	SS	SS
Timber	PD	PD	WD	SS	SS	PD	ES

Key: ES exportable surplus; SS approximately self-sufficient; PD partly dependent on outside sources; WD largely or entirely dependent on outside sources.
Note: United States is US and dependencies but excludes the Philippines.
Source: Royal Institute of International Affairs, *Raw materials and colonies*, p. 29.

Figure 1.1 Japan and comparative raw material dependence 1936
Source: Royal Institute of International Affairs, *Raw materials*, p. 29.

argument for expansionism. This narrative, built largely on economic considerations, gained wide acceptance and formed the basis for Japan's decision to go to war. Investment in war could, if successful, add

Table 1.1 *World oil production 1938–1941 (million metric tons and %)*

	1938/40		1941	
	Tons	%	Tons	%
North America	173.7	61.3	191.0	62.5
Latin America	45.9	16.2	51.4	16.8
Soviet Union	29.4	10.4	33.2	10.9
Middle East	16.1	5.7	13.4	4.4
Indonesia, Borneo and Burma	9.7	3.4	8.8	2.9
Japan and Formosa	0.4	0.1	0.4	0.1
Continental Europe	7.9	2.8	7.5	2.5
World	283.1	100.0	305.7	100.0

Source: League of Nations, *World economic survey, 1941/42*, p. 75.

considerably to economic strength through widening the Asian zone of Japanese domination.[4]

Japan, the narrative began, needed further industrialization to accommodate a rapidly growing population and raise still relatively low living standards. Just 16 per cent of land in the home islands, densely populated and no bigger than California, was cultivable. Half of the population worked in agriculture, farming 3 per cent of the agricultural land of the United States but trying to feed a population half as large.[5] The industrialization essential for Japan, the argument continued, required great quantities of raw and manufactured materials. Almost all of these had to be imported. Imports had to be paid for with United States dollars or sterling as convertible currencies, and foreign exchange could be earned only through exporting. In the 1930s, however, Japanese exports were increasingly impeded by economic nationalism. Influential Japanese opinion interpreted 1930s measures against Japanese goods as a drama of 'hectic struggles between the "haves" and "have nots"', featuring every conceivable economic weapon from import tariffs and quotas to complete exclusion. In this economic war Japan was certain to suffer.[6] Trade restriction enacted in the 1930s against Japanese exports considerably strengthened arguments for an expanded Japanese Empire.

Limited war had already proved a profitable Japanese investment strategy. For Japan, the Sino-Japanese War of 1894–95 and the Russo-Japanese War of 1904–05 were, in cost-benefit terms, among modern history's 'most effective political and economical military operations'.[7] Conquest had enabled Japan to

[4] Milward, *War, economy*, p. 15.
[5] USSBS, *Summary report*, p. 26.
[6] Inouyé, 'Necessity', p. 240.
[7] Goldsmith, *Financial development of Japan*, p. 35.

acquire an East Asian empire of which Korea, Taiwan and Manchuria were the main constituents. A 1930s Japanese programme to increase the production of armaments quickly and the 1937 decision to take total control of Manchuria enhanced Japanese military power. Moreover, it made more compelling a Japanese return to the historically successful option of investing in war to build economic strength. War investment required more armaments and so greater imports of raw materials and capital goods. However, a surge in imports in conjunction with Japan's 1930s military build-up had already exerted pressure on the balance of payments, strengthening yet further the case for a larger empire.

A Greater East Asia Co-Prosperity Sphere, although variously defined geographically and never fully thought out, offered an apparent solution to Japan's 1930s economic problems. In a Co-Prosperity Sphere substantially self-sufficient in raw materials, external purchasing power would no longer be a constraint; Japan's balance of payments problem would evaporate. Bilateral trading arrangements mediated through Tokyo and the establishment of a yen bloc throughout the Co-Prosperity Sphere would enable Japan to pay in yen rather than in foreign exchange for raw materials needed for industrialization and military goods. Yen could always be printed if required, but that would probably be unnecessary: the food- and raw-material-producing constituents of a Japanese empire would need yen to pay for manufactured imports from Japan as the empire's industrial centre.[8] Any mechanism that forced Japan to reduce its debts in East Asia would be eliminated. Tokyo would be established, as a Thai government minister observed after Thailand's 1942 acceptance of the yen as a reserve currency, 'as the monetary centre of the Greater East Asia Co-Prosperity Sphere'.[9] 'It is the yen', Finance Minister Kaya told Parliament as Japan began to exert control over Southeast Asia, 'which is destined to become the standard of value in East Asia and Tokyo the centre of payments'.[10]

Japanese Rationale for War in the Pacific

Early World War II German military victories isolated European colonies in Southeast Asia. As late as June 1941, Japan's leaders remained unsure of how best to take advantage of this probably never-to-be-repeated opportunity to enlarge the Japanese Empire. The chance for swift action to expand into Southeast Asia was embodied in the popular phrase: 'Don't

[8] Matsuoka, 'New order in East Asia', pp. 1–5; Arita, 'Greater East Asian sphere', pp. 10–15; Yamada, 'Economic bias', pp. 876–81; Yasuba, 'Did Japan ever suffer', pp. 544, 555–57.

[9] BE, OV25/9, 'Monetary axis', speech by Nai Vanich Pananananda, Minister without Portfolio, Chief of Thailand Economic Mission, Tokyo, 19 June 1942.

[10] AOM, 1AP/883/20, 'L'effort moral et matériel du Japon dans la guerre du Pacifique', *c.* early 1942, p. 12.

miss the bus'.[11] Japanese leaders seriously considered the northern possibility of invading the Soviet Union instead of the southern strategy of the conquest of Southeast Asia. In opting for the latter, Japan took the more realistic and economically attractive route.

Apart from the obvious attraction of the Southeast Asia option – the effective separation of Southeast Asian colonies from their European mother countries due to war in Europe – Southeast Asia had three further advantages. One was that by August 1941, Japan was already in a strong position in Indochina after accommodation from Vichy France: Japanese diplomatic and military pressure had made the French colony effectively a Japanese economic colony and military protectorate. Indochina on its own could supply many of the commodities that Japan needed. In 1940, Colonel Kenryo Sato, then handling negotiations with the French colonial government in Hanoi, stressed Indochina's value for Japan: 'Our food question, to say the least, would be settled, and we would get plenty of timber, rubber, tin and all kinds of minerals . . . From the point of view of obtaining supplies alone, the advisability of seizing Indochina is incontestable.'[12] In October 1941, a Japanese mission of 151 arrived in Indochina to assess how its economy could contribute to Japan.[13]

Second, in late 1941 Japan was in a quagmire of war in China, where its forces were fighting a ground war over an area the size of the United States east of the Mississippi.[14] Nationalist Chinese forces could be supplied via Southeast Asia by two routes northwards: by the Burma Road and by rail from Haiphong (Figure 1.2). The Burma Road, because of its many bends, required 717 miles of track through mountainous and extremely difficult terrain to cover 360 miles from Lashio in Burma to Kunming in China. The other, less tortuous southern route to Kunming was by rail from Haiphong. In September 1941, Japan had cut this line by destroying the bridge at Lao Kay on the Vietnam–China border.[15] Once in control of Southeast Asia, Japan could both permanently end the rail link to Kunming and shut down the Burma Road. The latter, after being briefly closed by Britain in response to Japanese diplomatic pressure, had been re-opened in October 1940.

[11] Hata, 'Continental expansion', p. 310; Drea, *Japan's imperial army*, pp. 209–21; Coox, 'Pacific War', p. 324.

[12] LHC, MAGIC, 'Economic value of Indo-China to Japan', 5 July 1944, pp. 14–15, quoting a November 1940 message from Sato to Tokyo. In 1944, Sato was Chief of the Military Affairs Bureau of the War Ministry, Tokyo. MAGIC are wartime Japanese diplomatic messages intercepted and decoded by the Allies.

[13] See NAC, 14087, box 1160, 'Séjour à Phnom Penh du ministre du Japon Uchiyama Chef de la mission Japonaise au sud-Indochine', 29 November 1941, for Japanese interest in Cambodia. Uchiyama was accompanied by Japanese military personnel.

[14] Drea, *Japan's imperial army*, p. 194.

[15] Robequain, *Economic development*, pp. 362, 365; Allen, *Burma*, pp. 7–8.

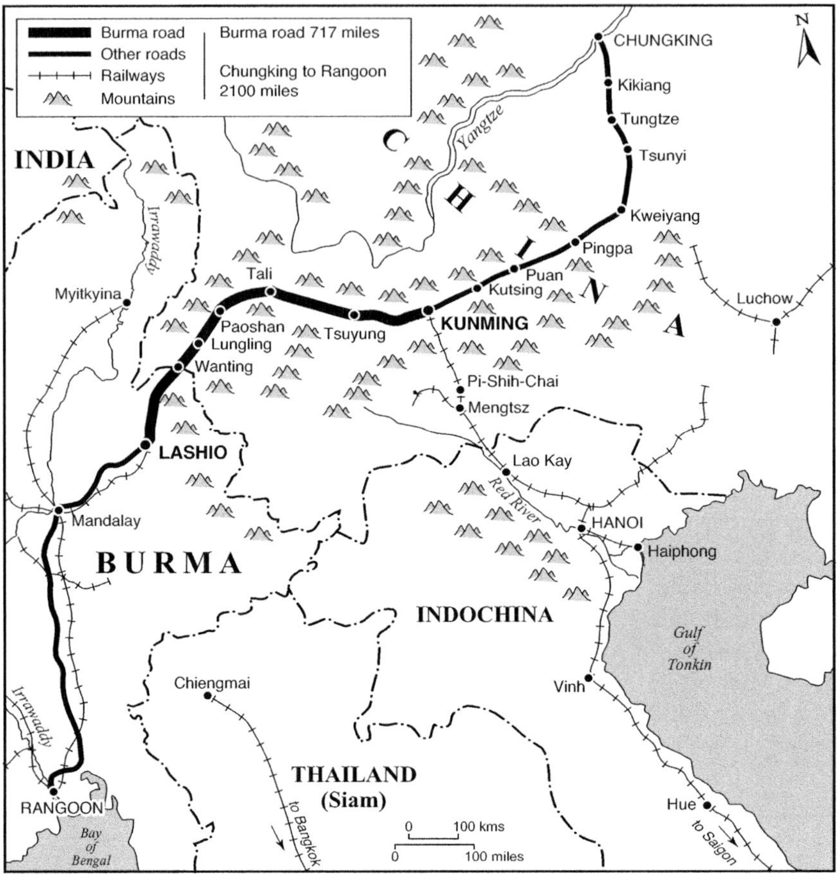

Figure 1.2 The Burma Road
Source: Paul French, *China Rhyming*, www.chinarhyming.com/2011/05/08/the-wartime-burma-road-map/

Third, as well as oil, Southeast Asia afforded a variety of useful, though less significant, resources. These included iron, nickel, rubber, tin, copper, lead and cobalt.[16] Indonesia, as well as a range of agricultural products, could supply mineral resources sufficient to go a considerable way towards giving Japan its 'fair' world share and remedying its 'have-not' status (Figure 1.3). Although in the long term Southeast Asia could substantially increase the resources available to a Japanese-directed Co-Prosperity Sphere, apart from oil, bauxite and

[16] For a list of resources that Japan planned to obtain from each area of Southeast Asia, see NA, WO203/6310, 'SEATIC Special intelligence bulletin', 1946, pp. 4–5. See also USSBS, *Japan's struggle*, p. 13.

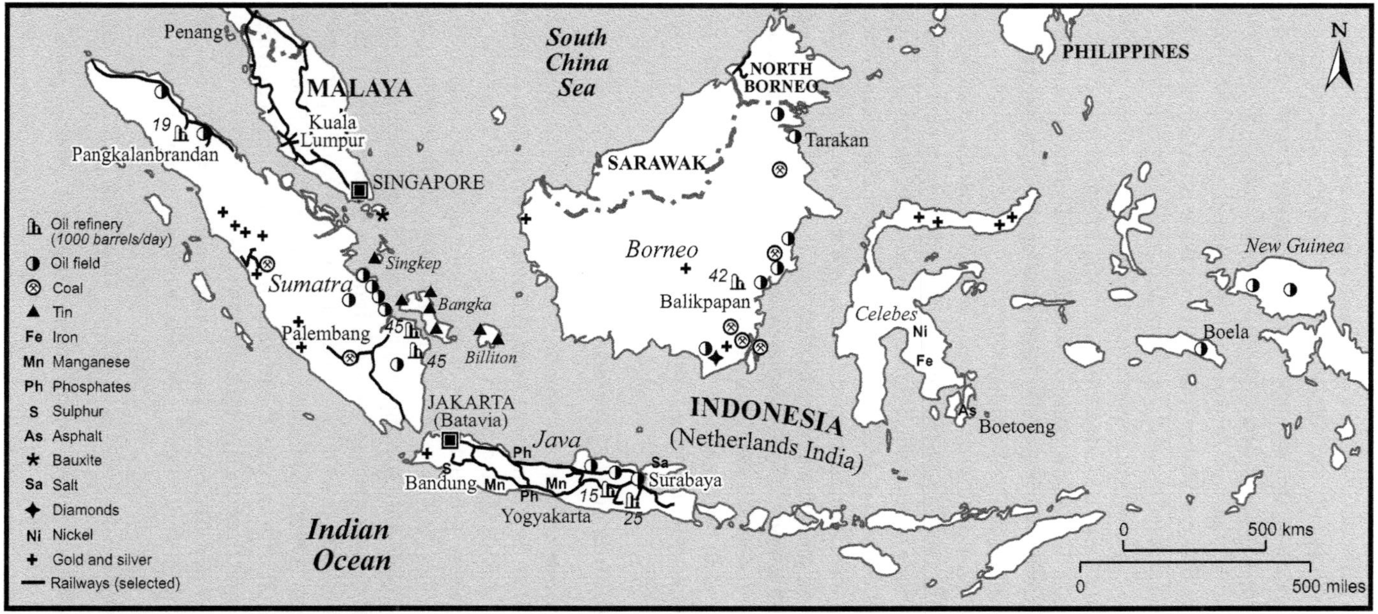

Figure 1.3 Southeast Asia natural resources
Source: Naval Intelligence Division, *Netherlands East Indies*, vol. 2, pp. 249, 253.

rice, the region's immediate contribution to fighting the war was slight. Above all for warfare, Indonesia had oil, the 'blood of battles which win victory'.[17] Japanese war leaders, a 1946 US Strategic Bombing Survey found, did not anticipate increasing Japan's miniscule home oil production: 'their eyes and calculations were fixed on the rich oil fields of the Netherlands East Indies [Indonesia]'.[18] Without this oil, Japan would have to draw on existing stocks, which would be exhausted after at most two years and possibly well before.[19]

The Greater East Asia Co-Prosperity Sphere could be justified, as many in Japan including the Prime Minister did, as a matter of survival. A semi-official explanation in July 1941 was that 'Japan in seeking its southward advance [to Southeast Asia] has no intention to attempt Imperialist aggression on the South Sea region, but it means to safeguard its economic independence.'[20] During 1940 and 1941, abortive negotiations with the United States and the Netherlands, from which Japan tried unsuccessfully to gain secure access to oil, made it seem likely that an East Asia Sphere to include some part of Southeast Asia could be realized only militarily. Japan viewed Southeast Asia as held in the grip of America, Britain, China and the Netherlands. The alternative to war, in the analysis of the small number of men, mostly in the military, who decided Japanese policy, was encirclement and economic suffocation.[21] However, there were formidable economic and geographical barriers to ending Western domination. For war to prove a profitable investment, it would need to be strategically well conceived, and short enough to avoid the full mobilization of American economic and military might.

Constraints on the Japanese War Options

Japanese economic power was far inferior to that of the United States. By developed country standards, Japan's was a tiny economy with limited capacity for war production. In 1940, United States GDP was nearly five times that of Japan (Table 1.2). Japanese productivity per man hour in all manufacturing industries was a quarter of American.[22] The United States accounted for two-fifths of world capital goods output compared to a mere 3.5 per cent for Japan. Low productivity and such a small capital goods industry severely constrained Japan's scope to produce armaments. So too did Japan's 1940 GDP per capita of GK (Geary-Khamis) 1990$2,874 compared to America's GK$7,010 per capita, since the lower GDP per capita, the smaller the leeway to reduce civilian consumption and re-direct productive capacity towards war.

Furthermore, the United States was Japan's principal source of vital raw materials, chiefly oil, iron and cotton, and also its main export market. In

17 Jones, 'Industrial capacity', p. 162.
18 USSBS, *Oil*, p. 45.
19 Jones, 'Industrial capacity', pp. 162–63, 171–78; USSBS, *Oil*, pp. 1–11, 40.
20 Yamada, 'Economic bias', p. 880.
21 Coox, 'Pacific War', p. 329.
22 Productivity figures are from Goldsmith, 'Power of victory', p. 79.

Table 1.2 *Japan and United States comparative economic strength 1940*

	Japan	United States
Population (000)	72,967	132,637
GDP 1990 (GK$000)	209,728	929,737
Per capita (GDP GK$)	2,874	7,010
% labour force in agriculture	49.5	18.1
% world capital goods output	3.5	41.7

Notes and sources: Maddison, *Historical statistics of the world economy*; Japan Statistical Association, *Historical statistics of Japan*, vol. 3, p. 389 and also www.stat.go.jp/english/data/chouki/19.htm, table 19–9; Carter et al., *Historical statistics of the United States*, vol. 2, p. 101; Milward, *War, economy*, p. 34. World capital goods output from Milward is for 1937. Agriculture includes forestry and fishing.

1936/37, the United States provided just under a third of Japanese imports and took a fifth of Japanese exports. In comparison, Asia as a whole supplied an only slightly bigger proportion than the United States of Japan's imports (Figures 1.4 and 1.5). These came mainly from India, which was an important supplier of cotton and provided 12.5 per cent of all Japanese imports, and from China and Manchuria, which accounted for 12.8 per cent of imports. Japan relied on North China for its major supply of good coking coal while Manchuria was a large source of pig iron.[23] Southeast Asia had relatively little importance for Japan, furnishing 9.9 per cent of Japanese imports and taking 11.5 per cent of exports.

Japan's geography compounded economic weakness to put it doubly at risk. As a small island cluster largely devoid of raw materials and unable to feed itself, Japan was fundamentally dependent on shipping for survival. In the event of war, Japanese naval vessels would have to secure Asian sea lanes and protect Japan's coastline. 'No country', observed the US Strategic Bombing Survey, 'could have been further from self-sufficiency with respect to raw materials than was Japan'; this made it 'desperately vulnerable to blockade operations'.[24]

A Pacific war would require Japan successfully to develop Southeast Asia as a substitute for raw materials previously imported from countries with which it was now at war. The great distance of any part of Southeast Asia from Japan would add to already heavy pressure on Japanese shipping (Figure 1.6). Although the conflict in China was primarily a land war, it nevertheless required substantial amounts of shipping. War in the Pacific would be principally a naval and air war, and place further large demands on shipping. Manila, the Southeast Asian capital closest to Japan, was 1,756 nautical miles (2,021 land miles) from Yokohama.

23 USSBS, *Effects of strategic bombing*, p. 13.

24 Ibid., and see p. 41; *Summary report*, pp. 18–20; and *Oil*, p. 31; see also Coox, 'Pacific War', pp. 377–80.

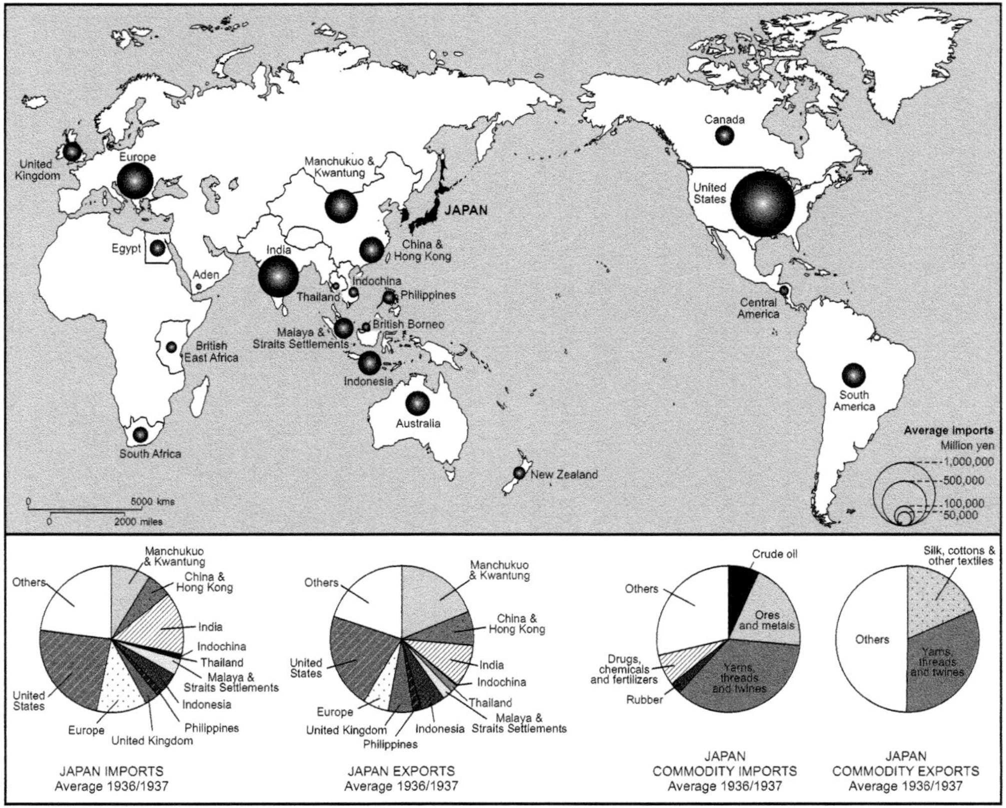

Figure 1.4 Japan geographical distribution of imports 1936/1937
Source: Japan, Ministry of Finance, *Bōeki nenpyō* [*Return of foreign trade*], 1937–1944–48.

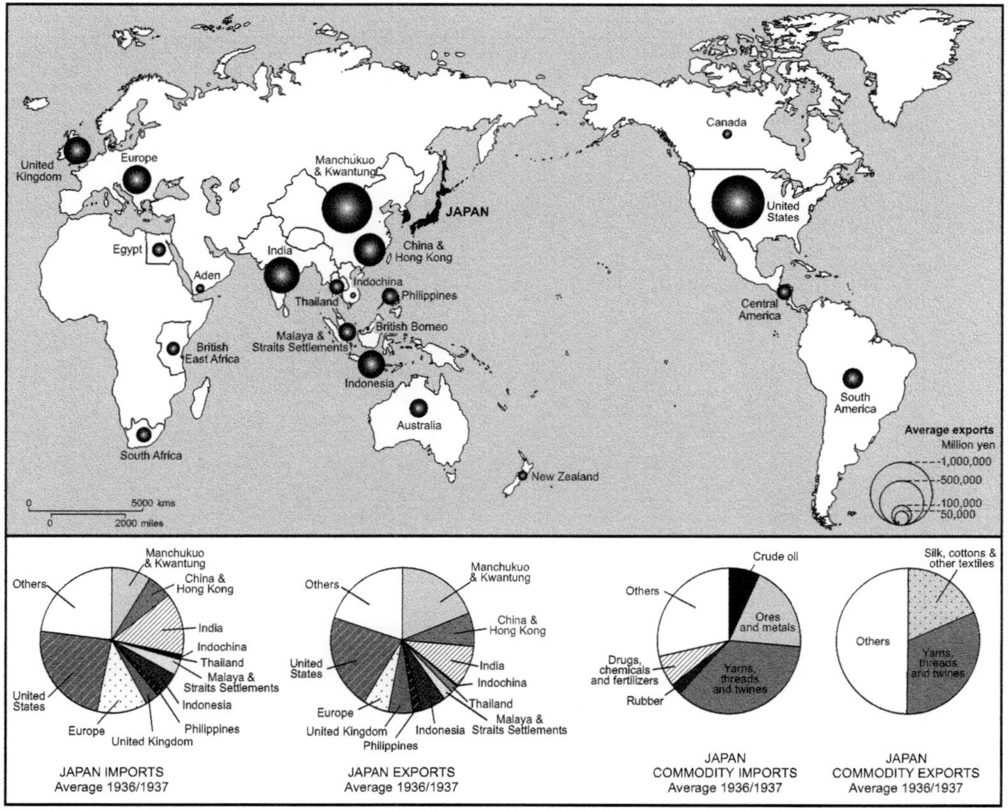

Figure 1.5 Japan export markets 1936/1937
Source: Japan, Ministry of Finance, *Bōeki nenpyō* [*Return of foreign trade*], 1937–1944–48.

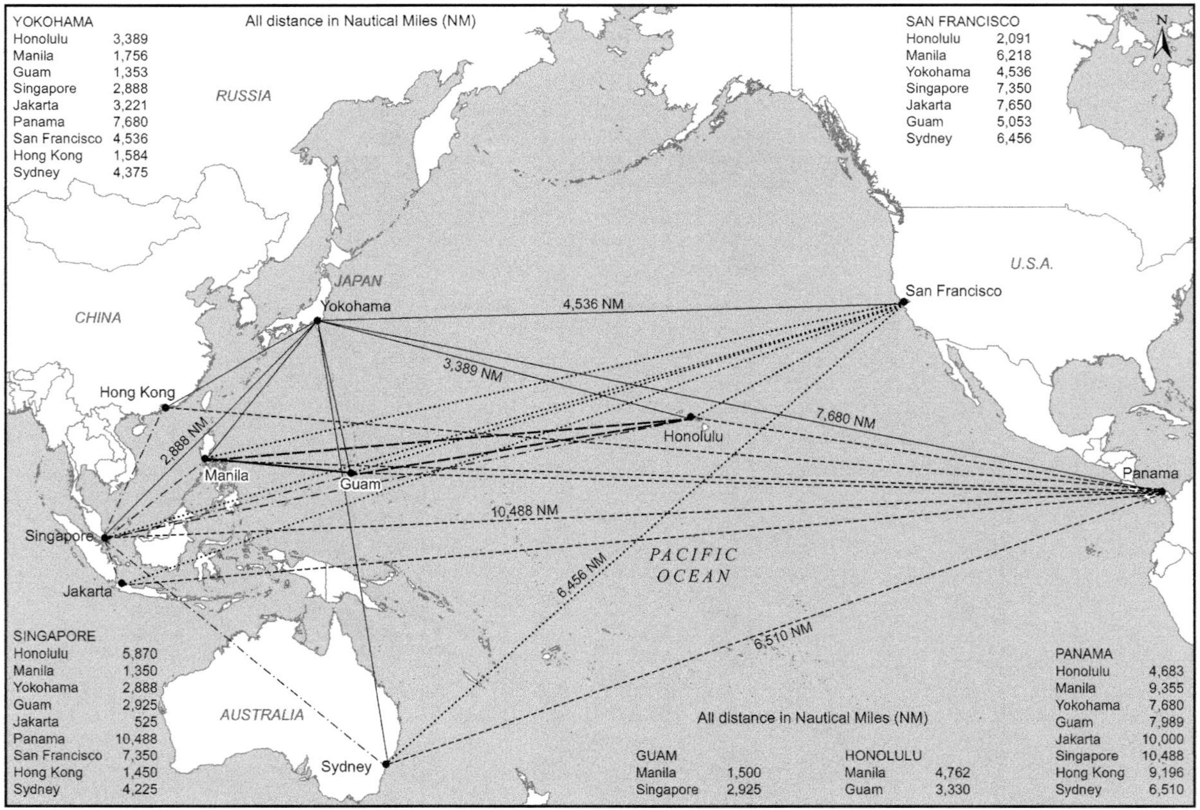

Figure 1.6 Pacific Ocean distances
Source: Cole, *Imperial military geography*, pp. 154–55.

Table 1.3 *World merchant fleet 1939 and 1946 (000 gross tons and %)*

	1939		1946	
	000 tons	%	000 tons	%
United States	9,000	15.4	27,000	47.7
British Empire	21,000	35.9	17,500	30.9
Japan	5,600	9.6	1,100	1.9
Norway	4,800	8.2	3,400	6.0
Germany	4,500	7.7	700	1.2
Italy	3,400	5.8	700	1.2
Netherlands	3,000	5.1	1,900	3.4
France	2,900	5.0	1,700	3.0
Greece	1,800	3.1	700	1.2
USSR	1,300	2.2	1,200	2.1
Denmark	1,200	2.1	700	1.2
Total	58,500	100.0	56,600	100.0

Note: Figures for the United States exclude the Great Lakes fleet. In 1946 the United States had, additionally, 11,000 tons in reserve.
Sources: United Nations, *Salient features*, p. 224; Milward, *War, economy*, p. 346.

Singapore was 2,888 nautical miles from the Japanese port and Rangoon further still. Ships would not travel much faster than 15 nautical miles an hour, placing Singapore at least eight days' sailing from Yokohama.[25]

In 1939, Japan's merchant fleet of 5.6 million tons ranked behind only those of the British Empire (21 million) and the United States (9 million tons) as the world's largest (Table 1.3). Nevertheless, for success in war Japan would have to build ships and use captured tonnage to meet essential requirements because of its lack of resources and consequent reliance on shipping, and because in a war merchant vessels would inevitably be damaged or sunk.

Political Context of War and Japanese Assessments

Japanese Foreign Minister Matsuoka, speaking at the 10 July 1941 Liaison Conference, summarized negotiations with America's Secretary of State Cordell Hull as: 'the United States is trying to destroy Japanese leadership in

[25] In 1940, nearly 300 Japanese cargo ships were rated at 12 knots and over and 37 per cent of Japanese cargo-passenger vessels were capable of speeds of 15 knots per hour or better. That compared with a speed of 10 knots for the average pre-war American freighter of the Hog Island type (Cohen, *Japan's economy*, p. 251).

East Asia'.[26] Japan, Hull stated on 24 July, must not be allowed to remain in Indochina because the South Sea area encompassed trading routes vital to American interests.[27] Two days later, the United States embargoed oil and scrap metal sales to Japan. This soon became an American–British–Dutch trade embargo which effectively denied Japan access to world raw material supplies. While Washington officials considered that the embargo would result in a Japanese climb-down, the military staff in Japan's American embassy asserted that it would drive Japan towards Malaya and Indonesia.[28] In Tokyo, Japanese leaders had to choose between war or backing down in the face of American pressure. They interpreted this pressure as an attempt 'to cheat Japan out of its deserved place on the earth' and forfeiture, at least for the foreseeable future, of Japanese imperial aspirations. The United States argued that Japan's war in China and control of Indochina menaced an 'open door' in Asia (the inviolability of the territorial integrity of countries and non-discrimination in commercial relations) and construed American policy as a justified warning to Japan.

By later 1941, Japan had been backed into a corner, characterized by Feis as a 'choice between dismal retreat and war'.[29] Tōjō, not long elevated to the prime ministership, famously summed up the 5 November 1941 Liaison Conference:

> [H]ow can we let the United States continue to do as she pleases even though there is some uneasiness? Two years from now we will have no petroleum for military use. Ships will stop moving. When I think about the strengthening of American defences in the Southwest Pacific, the expansion of the American fleet, the unfinished China incident, and so on, I see no end to difficulties. We can talk about austerity and suffering, but can our people endure such a life for a long time? . . . I fear that we would become a third-class nation after two or three years if we just sat tight.[30]

A combination of this predicament, years of intense Japanese militaristic nationalism and a government dominated by a military which operated outside civilian control may have made almost inevitable the final decision for war at the 27 and 29 November 1941 Liaison Conferences.

26 Ike, *Japan's decision*, p. 98; Liaison Conferences, which took place from late 1937 to 1944, were meetings between the government and military to discuss various issues and formulate policy. Major policy decisions agreed at the conferences were ratified by Imperial Conferences.

27 US Congress, House Committee on Armed Services, *United States-Vietnam Relations 1945–1967: Study Prepared by the Department of Defense* (Washington, 1971), bk. 7, B4. Cited in La Feber, 'Roosevelt, Churchill', p. 1278.

28 Aldrich, *Key to the south*, p. 331.

29 Feis, *Road*, p. 212 and for the quotation in the previous paragraph p. 341; see also Milward, *War, economy*, pp. 296–97.

30 KKC, file B1-209, Japan, Imperial Headquarters, *Gozen kaigi shidai* [Minutes of Imperial Conference], 5 November 1941; Tōjō's remarks are translated in Ike, *Japan's decision*, p. 238 and see p. 272.

As well as evoking a fight for national survival, supporters of war pointed to a lack of American fighting spirit and the vast distances across the Pacific from the United States west coast to Southeast Asia (Figure 1.6). For American forces to reach Singapore from San Francisco would require a voyage of 7,350 nautical miles (or 8,450 miles, a voyage of about 20 days for a ship averaging 15 knots an hour). If supplies from the US east coast passed through the Panama Canal, vessels had first to reach it, and then cover a further 10,488 nautical miles before arriving in Singapore. Even the distance of over 6,000 nautical miles from either San Francisco or Panama to Manila, the capital of the only United States colony in Southeast Asia, posed a formidable logistical challenge.

Nor in 1941 was America militarily prepared for war. Japanese views on American degeneracy and moral decay apart, Japan had reason to doubt any American commitment to a distant conflict. Although aware of American power, it would, Japan's General Staff reasoned, be several years before this could be brought to bear. By then Japan, in a short war marked by early crushing victories, could have control of a substantial part of Southeast Asia and its resources.[31] Those in Japan who did not doubt American imperial ambitions and willingness to underwrite these with military power could invoke a philosophy coloured strongly by fatalism. Ideological justification for a Greater East Asia Co-Prosperity Sphere was summoned from the rightness of a 'Holy War for Asian Liberation' which, at least among some, generated intense feelings.[32]

Pre-war Japanese Preparation and Plans for Southeast Asia's Occupation

Prior to war, Japanese civilian economists and political scientists provided no more than limited advice on how to manage and control Southeast Asia after occupation. Both government ministers and the armed forces preferred their own assessments and an emphasis on military matters. Civilians were not asked to formulate any plan for occupation. A large part of pre-war civilian input came from Japanese living in Southeast Asia who provided intelligence on economic and social conditions or military installations, but, like similar reports from a number of Japanese residents in various parts of the region working as spies, this information was not systematic nor frequently that useful. A lack of planning and preparation probably arose partly from Japan's assumption that the war would be short, making any management problem relatively insignificant. Possibly more important were that Southeast Asian societies were regarded as simple with few needs, and that the military and government ministers dominated pre-war thinking but were uncertain

[31] Drea, *Japan's imperial army*, pp. 218–21.
[32] Friend, *Blue-eyed enemy*, p. 55.

until the summer of 1941 whether the Soviet Union or Southeast Asia would be the preferable invasion target.

Insofar as academically trained civilians made a pre-war contribution, one of the main assessments related to Japan's chances of winning a Pacific war rather than how occupied Southeast Asian societies and economies were to be run. A notable (and prophetic) pre-war civilian evaluation was made in 1940. Under the orders of Iwakuro Takeo, Akimaru Jirō of Section 8 (Propaganda and Intelligence) of the army's General Staff Office organized a group of economists to assess Japan's capacity for war. They focused on Japanese industrial power and shipping tonnage, comparing its economy to the economies of the United States, the United Kingdom, Germany and the Soviet Union. On the basis of analyses of each of these countries, the *Akimaru Kikan* (the surname of the group leader and *Kikan* or *Tokumu* special military unit) prepared a report which measured Japanese economic war power as one-twentieth of Allied. Although this finding was reported to the Imperial Headquarters Liaison Conference in late August 1941, an Imperial Conference soon afterwards favoured war. Moreover, in the summer of 1941, even before official tabling of the *Akimaru Kikan*'s reports, they were said to have been burned. The basic research was, however, available to the Institute of Total War, inaugurated in April 1941. Its desktop simulation of a Pacific war concluded that Japan would not win.[33]

Formal planning for Southeast Asia's occupation by the military and the military-dominated government came remarkably late and took the form of broad policy guidelines, not detailed prescriptions. About nine months before the outbreak of the war and from early February to the end of March 1941, first-stage planning for the Southern Military Administration began, based on the research conducted by three officers, Colonel Obatake Nobuyoshi, Lieutenant Colonel Nishimura Otsuji and Lieutenant Colonel Budget Examiner Tōfuku Seijirō, within the General Staff HQ. The 15 reports of these officers influenced the outline of the plan submitted to the Imperial General HQ.[34] At the beginning of November 1941, the Implementation Plan of the Military Administration of the Southern Army appeared with policies for finance, trade development, resource acquisition and transport as well as administration. On 20 November, with war a near certainty, the Liaison Conference, as part of the 'Essentials of policy regarding the administration of occupied areas in the southern regions', adopted the three *gunsei* (military organization) principles of strategic materials acquisition in Southeast Asia, occupying army self-sufficiency and restoration of

[33] Majima, 'Chōsabu members', pp. 51–52, and 'The Chōsabu: its members', pp. 7–9, which discusses the research of those who did not join the Chōsabu; Ike, *Japan's decision*, pp. 124–63. The key decision of the 3 September 1941 Liaison Conference, and following this the 6 September Imperial Conference, was to continue negotiations with the United States and simultaneously prepare for war. If negotiations were not successful by the last ten days of October, Japan would go to war.

[34] Iwatake, *Gunsei ronshū*, pp. 22–27, and *Nanpō keizai shisaku*, vol. 1, pp. 24–27.

law and order in occupied areas. The 20 November 1941 document was the first definitive policy statement for military administration in Southeast Asia.[35] Finally on 12 December 1941, when war was already underway, the 'Outline of economic policies for the southern areas' became available.[36]

The rapidity with which the Japanese military took control of Southeast Asia, the lack of detailed instructions and the extent of the conquered region offered little choice other than what Japan did in Southeast Asia: to set up administrations based on pre-war structures and local personnel (Chapter 2). Rather than a product of careful planning, Japan's wartime empire emerged as ad hoc and haphazard.[37] Although before the war the Japanese had studied Southeast Asia's societies and cultures, most of those sent to occupied Southeast Asia lacked local knowledge and language skills.[38] Few people in Japan with knowledge of the Chinese in Southeast Asia were sent to the region and the Southeast Asian Command had just one person charged with Nanyang (Southeast Asian) Chinese affairs.[39]

Symptomatic of Japan's lack of an overall non-military determined pre-war economic strategy for Asia was that the Japanese government created the Greater East Asia Ministry only in November 1942. The Ministry, until mid-1944 under Kazuo Aoki, was a merger of existing government diplomatic missions and overseas agencies of the Asia Development Board. There were two stated aims. One was to unify economic policies regarding labour, capital, transport, trade and natural resources for the entire area controlled by Japan; the other to protect and supervise Japanese interests. In Southeast Asia, Malaya and Sumatra did not fall under the Ministry's remit because Japan's intention to retain them as permanent parts of the empire meant they were designated an 'integral territory' of Japan.[40] Elsewhere in the region the Ministry's responsibilities remained 'more prospective than actual, in so far as military government continued in some form throughout the war'.[41] Disseminating cultural propaganda became the main activity of the Ministry. It organized the November 1943 Greater East Asia Conference in Tokyo attended by Burma (Ba Maw), the Philippines (José P. Laurel) and Thailand (a government representative), but to which other Southeast Asian countries were not invited.[42]

35 Goto, *Tensions*, pp. 52–53, 78.
36 Ike, *Japan's decision*, pp. 249–53; Benda, Irikura and Kishi, *Japanese military administration*, pp. 1–3, 17–24; Yoshimura, 'Japan's economic policy', pp. 113–14.
37 Goto, *Tensions*, p. 77.
38 Kratoska and Goto, 'Japanese occupation', p. 539.
39 Akashi, 'Japanese policy', p. 62.
40 OSS, R&A 2072, *Japanese administration in Malaya*, p. 6; JM 103, *Outline of administration*, p. 44.
41 Beasley, *Japanese imperialism*, p. 238.
42 Jones, *Japan's new order*, p. 337.

Starting early in 1943, academics, organized as Chōsabu (research bureaus) were sent to most of Southeast Asia. Many of the members of these bureaus came from leading Japanese universities, notably the Institute of East Asian Economies at the Tokyo University of Commerce (the forerunner of the Institute of Economic Research at Hitotsubashi University). The reports of these Chōsabu did not begin to appear until late 1943. By the time Chōsabu policy prescriptions became available, insofar as they existed and the military acted on them, Japan was already playing a losing game of catch-up in the war and little could be done to ameliorate rapid economic and social deterioration in Southeast Asia.[43]

Course of the War and Japanese Shipping

In December 1941, the Western countries that had ruled Southeast Asia were remarkably ill prepared for Japan's invasion; its rapidity and effectiveness surprised no-one more than the region's colonial powers. On 8 December, Japan, able to use Indochina as a staging post, launched its attack in Southeast Asia. After brief resistance at landing points and about 100 Thai dead, Thailand allowed entry to Japanese troops.[44] Japan simultaneously invaded Malaya from the north at Kota Bahru. Because of the Peninsula's jungle terrain, the Allies considered unrealistic Japanese plans to move down the Peninsula to take Singapore. British capitulation in Singapore occurred just over two months later on 15 February 1942. Rangoon fell on 7 March and all of Indonesia on the ninth. Japan had already entered Manila, declared an open city by United States General Douglas MacArthur, on 2 January, and set up a Japanese military administration. By May 1942, Japan, having defeated Allied forces which outnumbered its troops by two or three to one, controlled all of Southeast Asia apart from small enemy holdings in the Philippines, Malaya and Burma areas and in Merauke on the south-east coast of what is now the Papua province of Indonesia.[45]

Japanese War Reversals

Japan held too large an area in the Pacific to be militarily defensible even before the spring 1942 decision to advance yet further. The May 1942 Japanese defensive perimeter extended far beyond Southeast Asia to include New Guinea in the south and part of the Aleutians in the north. Eastwards it reached almost to Hawaii (Figure 1.7). As the US Strategic Bombing Survey explained: 'By stretching and overextending her line of advance, Japan was committed to an expensive and exacting supply problem, she delayed the fortification of the perimeter originally decided upon, jeopardized her economic program for

[43] Huff and Majima, *World War II Chōsabu reports*, passim.
[44] Reynolds, 'Aftermath of alliance', p. 67.
[45] JM 103, *Outline of administration*, p. 2.

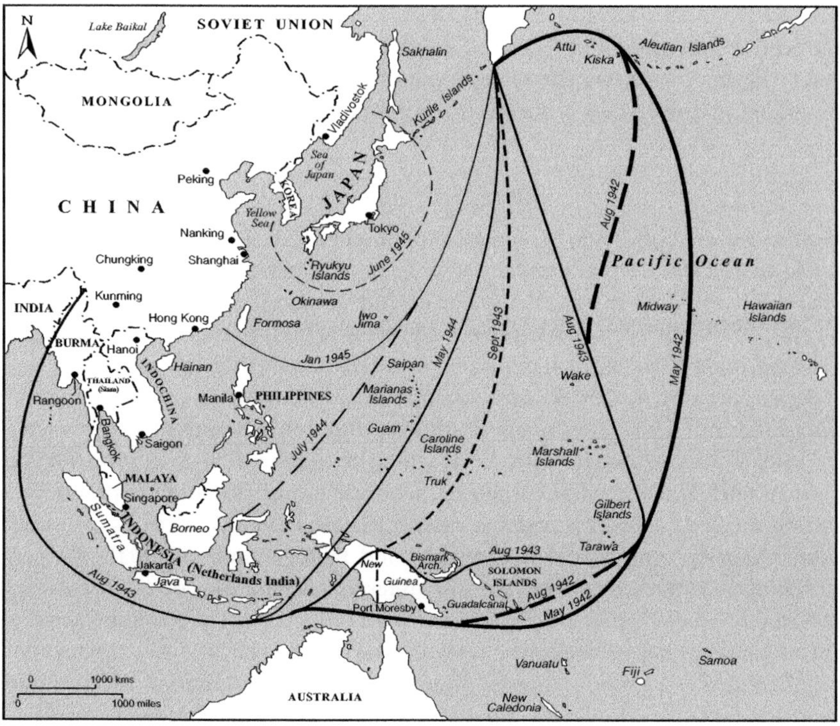

Figure 1.7 Japan defensive perimeters May 1942–June 1945
Source: Drea, *Japan's imperial army*, p. 233.

exploiting the resources of the area already captured, and laid herself open to early counter-attack in far advanced and, as yet, weak positions.'[46]

The Battle of Midway in June 1942 ended Japanese supremacy on the high seas and the naval Battle of Guadalcanal in November 1942 inflicted a further crushing defeat. Japan's defensive perimeter did not, however, begin to collapse until the summer of 1943, but then quickly contracted. Operational guidelines at the end of September 1943 to implement a new 'absolute national defence sphere' were outdated by May 1944 (Figure 1.7).[47] From late 1943, Allied attacks had damaged so much Japanese shipping that it became difficult to allocate vessels to Southeast Asia.[48] By the end of 1943, transport shortages also made it hard to move troops and left Japan fighting two separate wars: the Sino-Japanese War and the war against the United States in the Pacific. Japanese divisions still deployed in China at the end of the war were not there because of the force of Chinese armies but

[46] USSBS, *Summary report*, p. 4, and see pp. 3–5, 7, 27; Coox, 'Pacific War', pp. 354–59.
[47] Coox, 'Pacific War', pp. 352–53, 359; Wood, *Japanese military strategy*, p. 28.
[48] Iwatake, *Nanpō keizai shisaku*, vol. 1, pp. 117–18.

because Japanese merchant shipping was too compromised to transport them to the central and south-west Pacific where they were desperately needed.[49] By mid-1944, Japan was defeated economically.[50] Nevertheless, and tragically for Southeast Asians, the war continued for another year.

Japanese Shipping

On the eve of World War II, Japanese planners and military strategists utterly failed to realize the precariousness of Japan's merchant shipping capability. The army and navy always had priority in the scramble for resources and, as a result, at the start of the war Japan had no more, and probably less, merchant tonnage than it needed.[51] Early naval success and advance through Southeast Asia obscured the reality of insufficient merchant shipping as well as encouraging overconfidence and Japanese expansion into much of the Pacific.

Japan made a strategic mistake in going to war without planning for the vulnerability of its merchant shipping to attack, a miscalculation compounded during much of the war by three further mistakes. One was not building escort vessels to protect merchant shipping; a second, failing to understand the dangers of submarine attack; and the third, not quickly adopting the convoy system for merchant vessels. Japan began the war with approximately 6 million tons of merchant shipping including oil tankers. During the war, it built, captured or requisitioned 4.1 million tons of ships. However, construction, capture and requisitioning did not make up for losses at sea: between December 1941 and December 1943, serviceable merchant tonnage fell by more than a quarter and by December 1944 was less than a third of its pre-war figure (Table 1.4). When Japan surrendered in August 1945, out of the total of 10.1 million tons of shipping available to Japan during the war, 8.9 million tons had been sunk or damaged beyond use, leaving just 1.2 million operable tons.[52] Before the war, Japanese officials believed that the United States had an aversion to the use of submarines; US submarines accounted for 54.7 per cent of the 8.9 million tons of Japanese ships that were destroyed.[53] Japan entered the war with 9.6 per cent of world shipping; by 1946, it had only 1.9 per cent of the world total (Table 1.3).

During 1944 and 1945, the huge contraction of the Japanese defensive perimeter amplified the impact of the precipitate contraction in Japan's merchant

[49] Tohmatsu, 'Strategic correlation', pp. 422, 434, 439–40.

[50] USSBS, *Summary report*, pp. 14–15, 20, and *Japan's struggle*, pp. 2–4, 16; NA, WO203/1498, Japanese translation series no. 10, 2 August 1945 from the Nippon Hyoron, December 1944, pp. 2–3; Cohen, *Japan's economy*, pp. 197, 263, 266, 268; Coox, 'Pacific War', pp. 363, 377; Drea, *Japan's imperial army*, pp. 239–40.

[51] USSBS, *War against Japanese transportation*, p. 48, and *Effects of strategic bombing*, p. 41; Cohen, *Japan's economy*, pp. 251–55, 266.

[52] USSBS, *Summary report*, p. 11.

[53] Cohen, *Japan's economy*, pp. 50, 254; USSBS, *Summary report*, p. 11.

Table 1.4 *Japan merchant shipping 1941–1945 (000 tons, excludes tankers)*

	Tonnage afloat	Serviceable ships	Ships built	Ships sunk	Serviceable ships as % Dec. 1941
7 Dec. 1941	5,421	5,220	5		100.0
1 Dec. 1942	5,252	4,893	245	1,019	93.7
1 Dec. 1943	4,171	3,777	484	1,491	72.4
1 Dec. 1944	1,979	1,563	1,075	2,664	29.9
1 Aug. 1945	1,587	1,000	474	1,176	19.2
15 Aug. 1945	1,547				

Notes: 1. Serviceable ships are army ships, navy ships and serviceable civilian ships. The figure for serviceable civilian ships is an estimate which the USSBS based on Japanese sources.

2. Tonnage afloat does not correspond to ships built minus ships sunk because Japan added to total tonnage, mostly during 1942, through the addition of captured and salvaged ships and lost merchant ships due to their conversion to tankers.

3. December and August 1945 figures are for the shipping situation at the first of the month.

4. Some sources, for example Cohen, *Japan's economy*, p. 267 and Ránki, *Economics*, p. 159, show Japanese operable merchant shipping on 15 August 1945 as 557,000 tons. This figure is arrived at by excluding from operable tonnage ships cut off in the southern areas. That is not done in this table because cut-off shipping would still have been available for use in Southeast Asia.

Source: USSBS, *War against Japanese transportation*, p. 116.

shipping capacity (Figure 1.7). By August 1944, Japanese vessels were restricted to staying close to the shore and even these routes were dangerous (Figure 1.8). Because of this, between the start of the war and 1944, shipping time from Japan to Singapore increased two and a half times.[54]

Oil tankers, fundamental to Japan's ability to remain in the war, traced a different course than non-tanker tonnage (Table 1.5). During 1944, Japan greatly expanded tanker construction and, as a result, ended the year with substantially more capacity to transport oil than in 1941. Building tankers was in vain. After Japan's loss of Saipan in July 1944, the United States controlled tanker routes between Indonesia and Japan and, chiefly through submarine attack, started to destroy Japanese oil tankers at will. Finally, Japan made a last, desperate attempt to transport oil from Southeast Asia by submarine.[55]

54 USSBS, *War against Japanese transportation*, p. 49; Parillo, Japanese merchant marine, pp. 125–45 traces the shrinkage of shipping routes available to Japan.

55 USSBS, *Oil*, pp. 56–57, 88.

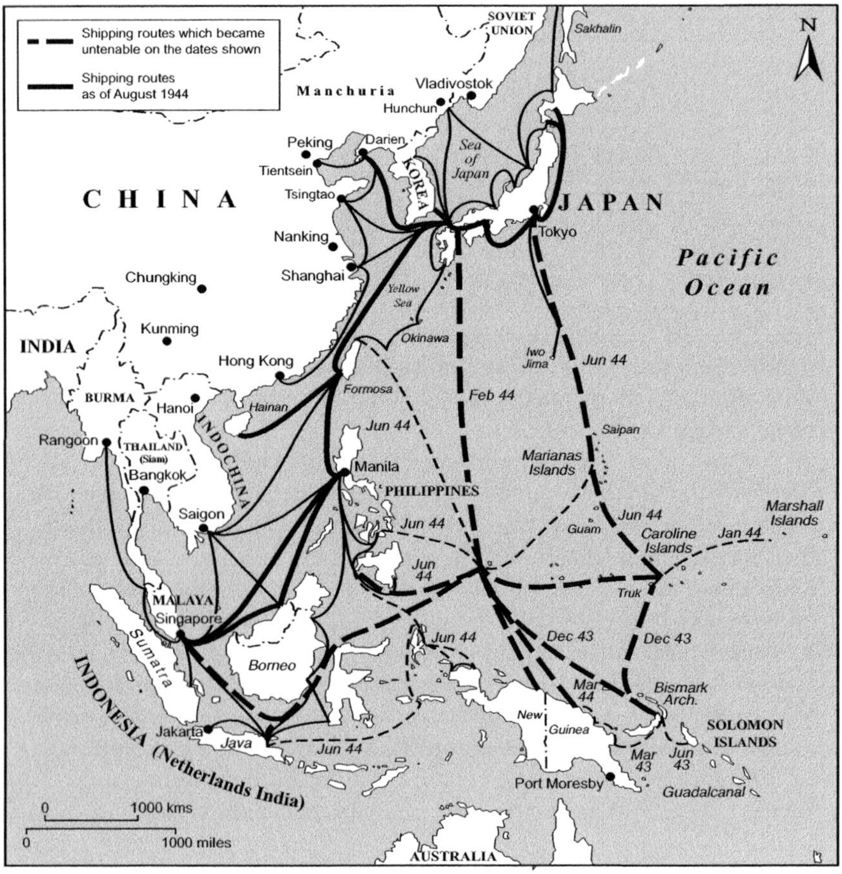

Figure 1.8 Changes in Japanese shipping routes 1943–1944
Source: United States, *Reports of General MacArthur*, vol. 2, part 2, plate 75.

Effect on Southeast Asia of Japanese War Reversals and Shipping Losses

Japanese naval defeats and merchant shipping losses, along with increasing Allied destruction of railways, affected Southeast Asia in four main ways. One was to contribute to drops in Southeast Asian output. Japan had little reason to encourage the production of goods in Southeast Asia if these could not be sent home or shipped elsewhere. After mid-1943, Japan imported few resources from Southeast Asia (Chapter 4).[56] By 1944, Japan could no longer transport much to its home economy even from the nearest Southeast Asian countries, and nothing from Burma. Merchant tonnage had to be prioritized for a few

[56] Cohen, *Japan's economy*, p. 110; Johnson, *Japanese food management*, pp. 135–39.

Table 1.5 *Japan merchant tankers 1941–1945 (000 tons)*

	Serviceable tonnage	Tankers importing oil to Japan	Tankers built	Tankers sunk	Serviceable tankers as % Dec. 1941
7 Dec. 1941	510		1		100.0
1 Dec. 1942	622	429	20	10	122.0
1 Dec. 1943	811	606	255	184	159.0
1 Dec. 1944	803	716	624	824	157.5
1 Aug. 1945	101	35	86	362	19.8
15 Aug. 1945	86	25			16.9

Note: In 1945, the collapse of tankers importing oil to Japan was mainly because Japan was cut off from supplies in Southeast Asia. The termination of convoys from Singapore occurred in March 1945. Tanker tonnage importing oil to Japan fell from 700,000 tons in January 1945 to 100,000 tons in April and thereafter declined continuously until the end of the war.
Source: USSBS, *War against Japanese transportation*, p. 118.

strategic exports from Southeast Asia, such as bauxite. From about mid-1943 there was also a fall in Japanese consumer goods arriving in Southeast Asia, although flows of these had never been more than tiny (Chapter 4).

Second, immediate military needs in Southeast Asia, not its potential role in a Co-Prosperity Sphere, became the overriding Japanese concern and grew increasingly pressing as the war continued to turn against Japan. War reversals forced Japan to abandon the concept of a Greater East Asia Co-Prosperity Sphere and to change fundamentally its approach to Southeast Asia. After the beginning of 1943, when the Allies instigated active air and sea operations in the south-east zone and Japanese shipping losses mounted, '[E]very army in the southern area was compelled to support itself independently and be self-sufficient against any emergency'.[57] Japanese strategists now looked to produce consumer and capital goods in Southeast Asia. By the spring of 1943 in Malaya, Japan began to announce a series of industrial and production plans, typically for implementation over a five-year period, to create military self-sufficiency and limit the need to supply the military from the home islands. Each country in Southeast Asia was to produce manufactured goods to support the Southern Army garrisoned there and perhaps also to supply Southeast Asian civilians to some extent. For civilians, Japan issued practical instructions, complete with numerous diagrams, on how to produce and mend goods like shirts and shoes.[58] Success in producing

[57] JM 103, *Outline of administration*, p. 4.

[58] Noda, *Nanpō jikatsu kyōhon*; ANM, 1957/0575122 Intelligence 506/10, 'Appreciation of Malaya, part I Pre-Japanese occupation', 20 July 1943, pp. 10–13; Kratoska, *Japanese occupation*, pp. 161–63.

manufactures in Southeast Asia was, however, at best partial, and throughout the region civilians and military alike had to rely heavily on a combination of imperfect substitutes and what could be obtained from a black market that marshalled pre-war materials and machines for sale to the highest bidder.

A May 1943 five-year production plan for essential materials such as iron ore, cement, soda, paper and fibre soon proved impractical because inputs of materials were scattered all over Southeast Asia and transport shortages effectively prevented shipments of critical materials from Japan itself. Some machinery did arrive in Southeast Asia. Textile machinery, made surplus by the attempt of Japanese planners to re-configure the home economy in favour of war production, was sent to Southeast Asian countries including Burma, Indonesia, the Philippines and Vietnam. Adaptation of the equipment proved difficult, however, and raw cotton remained in short supply. Only relatively small quantities of cloth were produced (Chapter 4).[59]

The third way that Japanese war reversals affected Southeast Asia was to increase the demand for Southeast Asian labour (Chapter 8). By the 1930s, there was chronic underemployment in the region and labour availability further increased during the early stages of the war because economic collapse threw large numbers of people out of work. After mid-1943, when it became likely that the Allies would invade Southeast Asia, labour shortages developed, mainly because the Japanese required large numbers of workers to build defence installations and the Thailand–Burma railway and to serve as military auxiliaries. Two further reasons for a scarcity of labour were the refusal of some Southeast Asians to work for the Japanese and, in the later stages of the war, the physical breakdown of large numbers of workers from sickness and lack of food.[60]

A fourth consequence of military defeats and shipping losses was to push Japan towards an increasingly Balkanized approach to Southeast Asia. Japanese strategists imposed regional, not just country, economic autarky in Indonesia, Burma and Malaya to try to create self-sufficient areas and prevent Allied conquest in one part of a country leading to the loss of other parts because of insufficient food and essential materials.[61] Even from the start in Java and Madura (which then had an identity separate from Java), Japanese administrative policies encouraged districts to evolve into separate economic blocks. Separation became even more pronounced after April 1943 with the introduction of a forced rice delivery system based on quotas for each residency.[62] Yet further fragmentation occurred after 1 October 1943 when it was decided to divide Java and Madura into 17 self-sufficient areas and ban trade between them.[63] A 1944 plan decreed that Burma

59 Nagano, 'Cotton production', pp. 188–92; Le, *Impact*, pp. 206, 211–12.
60 JM 103, *Outline of administration*, pp. 15–16.
61 Scott, 'Approach', p. 276.
62 Sato, *War, nationalism*, pp. 32–35.
63 De Jong, *Collapse*, pp. 231, 258.

should be self-sufficient, no longer within national boundaries alone but in four administrative regions as well.[64] Similarly, Japan's goal became not just 'autarky in Malaya as a whole but for each State and Settlement in it'.[65] Economic autarky seriously reduced living standards in Burma and contributed to famine in Java, as discussed in subsequent chapters.

For Southeast Asians, the bleakest years of the war began in mid-1943 and can be traced to the isolation of the region from the outside world; the exhaustion of pre-war stocks of basic consumer items and lack of goods from Japan; an inability to produce simple manufactures locally; a growing disruption of intra-country Southeast Asian communications; and the imposition of intra-country autarky. Much of the rest of the book deals with the impact of these changes. In the course of this discussion, it will become apparent that the 26 months beginning in mid-1943 rank as among World War II's darkest chapters for civilians anywhere.

Plan of the Book

Nine chapters and an Epilogue comprise the remainder of this book. Chapter 2 is concerned with how Japan administered Southeast Asia's six main countries and effected social control. Chapter 3 addresses how Japan financed the war in Southeast Asia. Wartime economic collapse in Southeast Asia is quantified, as far as possible, in Chapters 4 and 5. The contraction of the region's economies and unavailability of new clothing, soap and many basic manufactures led to the appearance of whole ranges of substitute goods. An examination of some of these substitutes and a discussion of rationing are the subjects of Chapter 6.

Food, living standards and population movements in rural areas and outside the main cities are the focus of Chapter 7, while Chapter 8 deals with a like range of issues for Southeast Asia's principal urban areas. The use of Southeast Asian labour by the Japanese is appraised in Chapter 9. Topics discussed include forced labour, Japan's policy of enslaving comfort women and the recruitment of workers for Japanese armed forces.

An accounting for both Southeast Asia and Japan of the war's costs and benefits is set out in Chapter 10. I arrive at an approximate total of Southeast Asian civilian loss of life due to the occupation and indicate the extent of wartime physical damage to the region's cities and infrastructure. Similar data for Japan afford a comparative yardstick. For large parts of Southeast Asia, occupation opened the way for post-war social and political transformations and weighed against an early recovery of GDP per capita to pre-war levels. These constituted the main legacies for the region of wartime occupation, assessed in the Epilogue.

64 OSS, R&A 2015, *Japanese administration of Burma*, p. 61. See also OSS, R&A 2077, *Economic reorganization of Burma*, pp. 3–4.

65 Malaya, *Report on the 1947 census*, p. 34.

2

Administration and Social Control in Southeast Asia

Japan had three main goals in Southeast Asia: resource extraction, maintenance of social stability and army self-sufficiency.[1] In administering Southeast Asia and controlling its peoples so as to meet these goals, Japan faced stark geographic, demographic and economic realities. The region was large, divided into several countries, overwhelmingly rural, and racially and ethnically varied. Against this, Japan had available only a relatively few administrators and limited manpower for military occupation, especially with so many administrators and soldiers required for the war in China. Japan's weak, badly overstretched economy further restricted resources that could be expended in Southeast Asia.

The main argument of this chapter is that in administering Southeast Asia, Japan had always to find ways to economize on scarce resources and make up for a lack of knowledge of the region and its variety of pre-war administrative systems, customs and languages. Where possible, as to a large extent it was, use was made of existing administrative structures. Japanese practice was to work through elite groups, and sometimes create them, which reduced the need for contact with the mass of the population and made less important the acquisition of local knowledge and language skills. Economically, the Japanese operated through monopolistic bodies. Monopoly was seen as efficient and rational and it limited the number of organizations with which administrators had to deal. A goal of social organization was, as in Japan, to make control self-enforcing through a neighbourhood system, which was built on a base of units of about 10 to 20 houses collectively responsible for the behaviour of each of their members and for allegiance to Greater Japan.

Of course, there were serious limitations to self-enforcement in societies which had their own cultural norms and which were diverse. Parts of Southeast Asia had a high proportion of recent immigrants or migrants and included large numbers of Chinese. Many of the latter looked to China and naturally supported it in the ongoing Sino-Japanese War. Japan implemented a twofold solution to its 'Chinese problem' and to populations increasingly disillusioned

[1] NA, WO203/6310, 'SEATIC Special intelligence bulletin', 1946, p. 2; JM 103, *Outline of administration*, pp. 1, 42.

by severe food scarcities and by Japanese denial of almost any consumer goods to Southeast Asians.

One aspect of the solution, viable in Thailand and Indochina, was to let an existing, pre-occupation administration try to deflect dissent and bear a share of the responsibility for worsening conditions. To some extent, a similar strategy was tried, but much less successfully, in Burma and the Philippines, with the creation during the latter part of 1943 of nominally independent governments. The other Japanese answer to the maintenance of social control and suppression of anything deemed 'anti-Japanese' was a draconian use of the military police. Units had relatively few men but made use of the former employees of colonial security services and large numbers of local informers, both ways of economizing on scarce Japanese resources.

Political and Administrative Arrangements

For the most part, Japanese administration maintained colonial Southeast Asian boundaries. Division of Southeast Asia into Areas A and B reflected the particular uses Japan had for different countries. Usage depended on their geographical and resource advantages, the scope for alliances within the region and the possibilities for different administrative modes (Figure 2.1). Thailand and Indochina, more or less allied with Japan, comprised Area B as distinct from those parts of Southeast Asia under formal military administration. There were immediate plans for the complete integration of Thailand and Indochina into the Greater East Asia Co-Prosperity Sphere.[2] Japan had little reason to be displeased with either the Thai or Indochinese French administrations, although this changed towards the end of the war. By 1942, both countries had accepted a status of Japanese military protectorates and economic colonies. As Chapter 3 shows, these two Southeast Asian countries, rather than those in Area A under direct military control, were the most economically exploited by Japan, if measured as a percentage of GDP transferred to the Japanese home islands.

Thailand and Indochina

Japan would have occupied Thailand and Indochina militarily if their armies had put up meaningful resistance.[3] They did not, and Thai and French co-operation had significant benefits. Co-operation avoided the need for large numbers of Japanese administrators and troops in the two countries and so

[2] On Japan's intentions for Thailand, see the 29 September 1942 Japanese document 'Outline of economic policy toward Thailand' in Swan, *Japan's economic relations*, pp. 249–53 and the discussion on pp. 209–16, 227.

[3] NA, WO203/6310, 'SEATIC Special intelligence bulletin', 1946, p. 1.

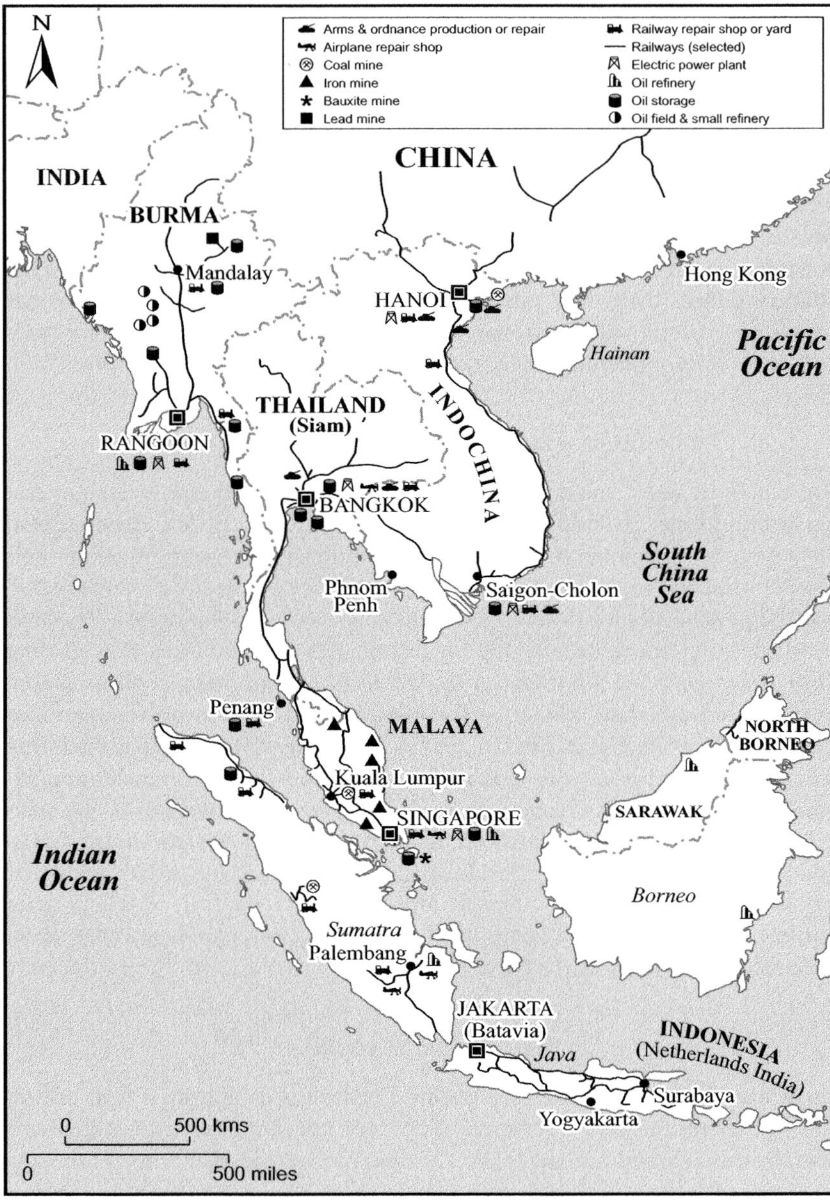

Figure 2.1 Southeast Asia strategic and mineral resources
Source: OSS, R&A 1286.1, *Additional strategic objective.*

saved on administrative resources and military manpower. What amounted to a form of indirect rule was possible.

In acquiescing to Japanese domination, neither Indochina nor Thailand had much choice. 'The fall of France in 1940', a United States intelligence report observed, 'left Indochina in a precarious and virtually helpless position.'[4] Throughout 1940 and 1941, Japanese demands for concessions from Indochina, including the stationing of troops in the country and favourable trade and currency arrangements, continuously increased.[5] The French administration of Governor-General Jean Decoux, appointed on 21 July 1940, managed 'to preserve its own authority, the presence of an army, French police and French business interests, but only at the grace of Japan, a political, economic and military collaboration with the Empire of the Rising Sun'.[6] Decoux's government remained in place in Indochina until a 9 March 1945 Japanese coup. By then, the Japanese could no longer leave Indochina under even nominal French rule because of doubts over the allegiance of many French administrators to Japan; because of the likelihood of Allied invasion of Vietnam; and because of Indochina's strategic location in the South China Sea and importance as a military and supply base.

Wartime Thai leaders drew on Thailand's long history of successfully avoiding colonization. They practised what has been described as a 'flexible "bamboo" diplomacy ... based on a realistic view of the world'.[7] During Japanese occupation, Thai leaders tried to retain as much independence as possible and, where feasible, moderate Japanese demands. Japan, as an Allied intelligence report observed in 1944, 'obtained nominal Thai collaboration at the price of nominal recognition of Thai sovereignty'.[8] Thailand had to yield to Japan on foreign affairs but internally retained freedom of action to a substantially greater extent than any other Southeast Asian country.[9]

Both the French and Thai administrations could point to benefits from bending to Japanese domination but not being broken by it. Until Japan's 1945 coup, Decoux's administration was able to work continuously to protect the economic interests of French nationals, secure rights and freedoms for

4 JISPB, *Joint Army-Navy intelligence study of Indochina*, chapter 10, 'People and government', p. 5.

5 See, for example, NA, WO106/4479, Agreement between Admiral Decoux, Governor-General Indochina and General Semitian, Head of Japanese Mission, 6 September 1941. The agreement gave the Japanese the right to station 40,000 troops in southern Vietnam and Cambodia, obliged the French to provide billets for them, limited the French to minimum troops necessary for national security and sharply restricted the movements of French forces.

6 Gorce, *L'empire écartelé*, p. 287.

7 Reynolds, *Thailand*, p. 236 and see preface.

8 OSS, R&A 2368, *Japanese domination*, p. 2.

9 OSS, R&A 552, *Thai cooperation*, pp. 1–2 and R&A 2368, *Japanese domination*, pp. 2, 18, 47–48.

French citizens and maintain an army. In Thailand, the government hoped for economic and territorial gains from being allied with Japan as the new, dominant power in Southeast Asia. Unlike in much of Southeast Asia, Japanese soldiers behaved well in Thailand, and the establishment by the Garrison Army of a separate army brothel helped to avoid a source of friction which had initially marked Japan's occupation.[10]

Although alliance with Japan enabled Thailand to prevent extensive Japanese interference with the rights and daily life of the Thai, the same was not true of Chinese living in the Kingdom. A number of 'patriotic' Chinese leaders were arrested; Chinese had to make substantial monetary contributions to the war effort; and Chinese in Thailand were required to fly the Japanese flag above the main entrance to their houses.[11] Japan pressured the Thai government to arrange the recruitment of Chinese workers for the Thailand–Burma railway and forced the expulsion of Chinese from the north of Thailand. When Chinese businesses were lost, as in both the north and Bangkok, it was the Japanese, not the Thai, who gained most.[12]

In 1932, military officers, conservative civil servants and young radical civilians had eliminated royal absolutism by staging a coup against Thailand's monarchy, after which they took control of the country, leaving a king as only the titular head of the Kingdom of Siam (Thailand from 1939). The coup was important for subsequent Thai economic development because it made a ruling circle of bureaucrats, not the throne, the centre of Thailand's emergent bureaucratic polity, facilitating joint wartime industrial ventures with the Japanese.[13] Beginning in December 1938, Plaek Phibunsongkhram (Phibun), formerly defence minister and an admirer of fascism and the nationalism of Hitler and Mussolini, became Prime Minister, succeeding another military officer as Thailand's premier. Phibun, who led Thailand's government for most of the war, embarked on a programme of nationalism and modernization which included specifying a change to 'appropriate', non-traditional, more western dress and emphasis on the Buddhist religion.[14] During the early 1940s there were, however, other important centres of power in Thailand, notably Pridi Phanomyong and the Regency.[15]

Although expediency dictated a treaty of alliance with Japan, Thailand's declaration of war against the United States and United Kingdom on

[10] Reynolds, *Thailand*, pp. 228, 151 and see pp. 136–39.

[11] OSS, R&A 2695, *Status of the Chinese*, pp. 37–38; OSS, R&A 2368, *Japanese domination*, p. 22.

[12] Skinner, *Chinese society*, p. 275; OSS, R&A 2368, *Japanese domination*, p. 26.

[13] Riggs, *Thailand*, p. 379.

[14] OSS, R&A 92, *Increased Japanese influence*, pp. 19–20; Numnonda, 'Pibulsongkram's Thai nation-building programme', pp. 235–41.

[15] Pluvier, *South-East Asia*, pp. 90–91; Ferrara, *Political development*, pp. 109–10; Smitabhindu, 'Domestic developments', pp. 39–42.

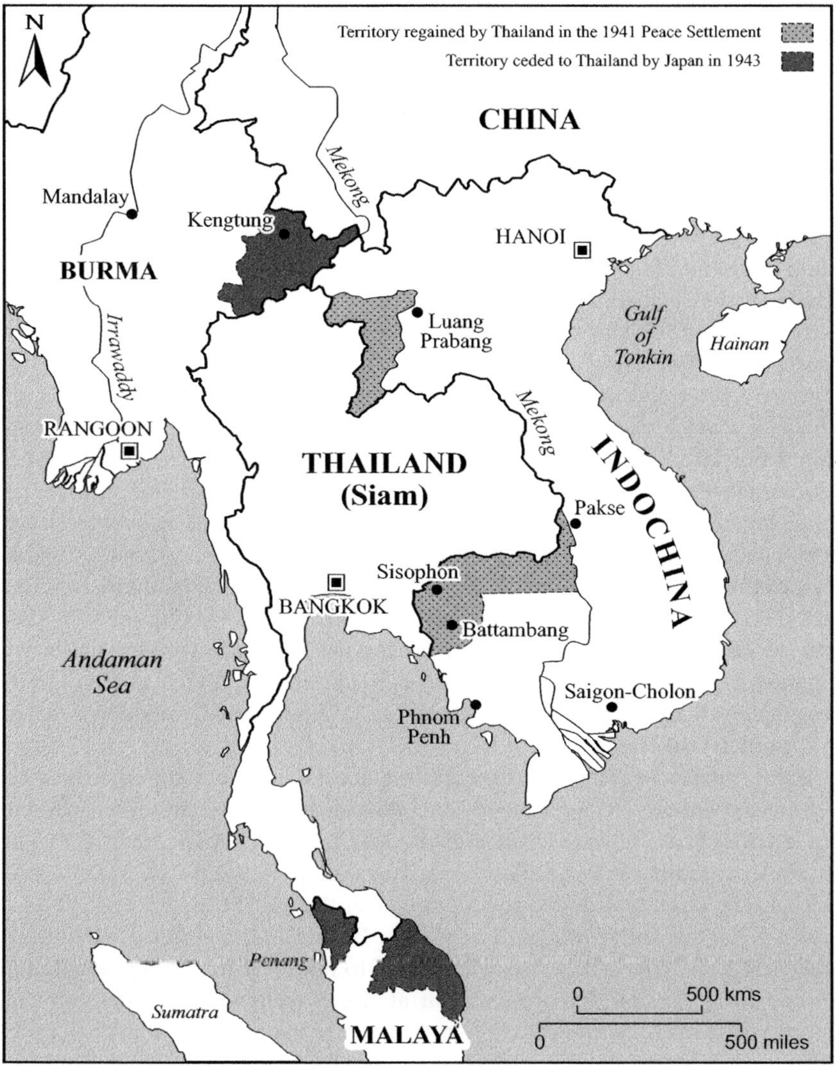

Figure 2.2 Thailand territory acquisition 1941–1943
Sources: Naval Intelligence Division, *Indo-China*, p. 486; Reynolds, *Thailand and Japan's southern advance*, pp. 154–55; Kratoska, *Japanese occupation*, p. 88.

25 January 1942 and abrogation of a June 1940 non-aggression treaty with Britain was not forced on it by the Japanese.[16] Rather, Phibun, even apart from

[16] OSS, R&A 2114, *Political aspects of Allied occupation*, pp. 3, 6–7; *Thailand no. 1 (1940) Treaty of non-aggression*, Cmd.6211.

his admiration for fascism and a Japanese military government, saw an opportunity for modernization and expansionism. Modernization, as indicated below and further discussed in Chapter 4, could be promoted through a mutually beneficial patron–client economic relationship with Japan. Japan had the technology, capital and machinery to support Thai efforts to industrialize and develop economically.

The advantage of expansion anticipated by Phibun was that association with Japan would further the creation of a Thailand mini-empire. Phibun aimed to build 'a greater Thai nation centred on Thailand that would encompass the whole of the region inhabited by the Thai race', including nearby areas in Burma, Indochina and China.[17] The Thai military had a 'blank cheque' to prosecute a war being fought against the French in Indochina and by January 1941 this had so swollen the budget that, according to the British financial advisor, the financial situation had become desperate: 'we are practically a busted community'.[18] However, Japanese intervention resolved border hostilities between France and Thailand. A settlement under the auspices of Japan favoured Thailand and recognized Thai irredentist feeling over territory which had been lost to the French in 1907. Thailand was given all of Cambodia west of the Mekong and north of Angkor Wat. In Laos, it gained Pak Lay, the area west of the Mekong in Luang Prabang, north-west Laos (Figure 2.2).[19] As part of Phibun's grandiose plan for an expanded Thailand, the Thai army invaded Burma's Shan states in May 1942. The territory Thailand acquired, recognized by Japan in an August 1943 treaty, became the United Shan States or Original Thai States.[20]

Japan, anxious to cement Thailand's place as a puppet state in the Co-Prosperity Sphere, sought to bolster Phibun's position and gain favour among the Thai. Towards this end, in August 1943 Japan made 'gifts' of substantial additions to Thailand's territory, at the expense of Malaya and Burma. Thailand was handed sovereignty over the four Malay states of Kedah, Perlis, Kelantan and Trengganu as well as Burma's Shan states of Kengtung and Mongpan (Figure 2.2). Japan also tried to reinforce the Thai government by according Thailand representation at the November 1943 Assembly of Greater East Asian Nations in Tokyo. The territorial transfers and Thailand's

[17] Murashima, 'Commemorative character', p. 1093 and 'Thai-Japanese wartime alliance', pp. 202–3.

[18] BE, OV25/8, W.A.M. Doll telegram to the Bank of England's Governor, Sir Otto Niemeyer and Sir David Waley, 23 January 1941 and see NARA, RG59, entry 205, box 5834, file 892.00/217, W.A.M. Doll to Frederic Dolbeare, American Foreign Affairs Advisor in Thailand, 19 November 1940.

[19] Robequain, *Economic development*, p. 366; NA, HS1/71, F.C. Jones, 'Thailand part A political', 7 October 1941, p. 7.

[20] Murashima, 'Commemorative character', pp. 1059, 1087, 1092–95; Aldrich, *Key to the south*, pp. 115–16, 370. In 1945, the Shan states were ceded back to the British.

participation at the Assembly may have marked the high point of Phibun's relations with Japan.[21]

Even by the time of the 1943 territory transfers, however, strains between the Japanese and the Phibun administration were apparent. The transfers seem to have been achieved more by assignment than mutual agreement and were reluctantly received by the Thai government. Diplomatic messages from Japan's ambassador revealed that by transferring the territories the Japanese aimed to counter unhappiness in Thailand over the war and take 'positive steps' to strengthen Phibun's political position. Phibun himself apparently did not encourage the transfers.[22] They increased Thailand's administrative burdens, including the need to supply rice to northern Malaya, and did not offer full sovereignty because Japan retained important rights in the Malay states. Moreover, territorial gains would prove lasting only if Japan won the war.[23] The Japanese reportedly used the 30-day period between the signing of the transfer treaty and its implementation to plunder the four Malay states.[24] After the war, the states in Burma and Malaya given to Thailand again became part of their pre-war countries. Retrocession to Indochina of territories which had been gained by Thailand between 1941 and 1943 was negotiated as part of the 1946 Washington Conference.[25]

The July 1944 Japanese loss of Saipan and resulting fall of the Tōjō cabinet encouraged a Thailand National Assembly vote against Phibun on a domestic issue. By then, too, the public blamed Phibun for war shortages and distress.[26] Phibun and his cabinet were forced to resign on 22 July 1944. Despite the overthrow of Phibun by elements opposed to his Japan policy and, additionally, the existence of a Free Thai (Seri Thai) faction and guerrilla resistance to occupation, the Japanese did not move formally to govern Thailand. Some evidence suggests, however, that this was contemplated late in the war.[27]

The Japanese decision to leave in place a Thai government may have been partly because the new, post-July 1944 Thai administration, in which Pridi Phanomyong was the power behind the cabinet, was not antagonistic to Japan. It was also unclear what benefit formal control would have yielded: the

[21] OSS, R&A 2368, *Japanese domination*, pp. 47–48. According to Reynolds, however, by later 1942 Phibun and his colleagues had become thoroughly disillusioned with the Japanese. Reynolds, *Thailand*, p. 113.

[22] LHC, MAGIC, 'Japanese-Thai negotiations concerning the cession to Thailand of territory in the Shan states and Malaya', 14 October 1943, pp. B2–B3 and see Goto, *Tensions*, p. 62.

[23] Naval Intelligence Division, *Indo-China*, pp. 485–86; OSS, R&A 552, *Thai cooperation*, pp. 19–20; LHC, MAGIC, 'Japanese-Thai negotiations', 14 October 1943, pp. B4–B5; Reynolds, *Thailand*, pp. 154–59.

[24] LHC, MAGIC, 'Summary 546', 23 September 1943, p. 5.

[25] Chandler, *History*, p. 215; Stuart-Fox, *History*, p. 66.

[26] OSS, R&A 1931, *Problems confronting the Free Thai movement*, p. 4.

[27] Wyatt, *Thailand*, p. 249.

Japanese still dominated Thailand militarily and the Thai had to observe existing treaties lest Japan take over the administration of their civil affairs. A further reason to avoid a formal assumption of power was that Japan was already short of administrators and hard pressed elsewhere in Asia.[28]

A possible advantage for the Japanese of having a stable Thai administration in place was that if at the end of the war Japan failed to hold Burma, as by 1944 seemed likely, Thailand could appear independent and yet serve as a pro-Japanese buffer state between Indochina and Burma.[29] A buffer was desirable because of Indochina's great strategic advantages. These included its location in the South China Sea, the role of Saigon along with Singapore as a nerve centre for Japanese military operations, and the availability of rice, timber and minerals in Indochina in quantities sufficient for many of the needs of a Greater East Asia Co-Prosperity Sphere (Figure 2.1). Following Japan's surrender and before the arrival of the Allies, Thai and Japanese dignitaries took turns in staging numerous farewell social events for one another.[30]

Burma, Philippines, Malaya and Indonesia

A 26 November 1941 agreement between Japan's army and navy divided between the two services the administration of Southeast Asia that would be occupied, apart from Thailand and Indochina (Area B). In military-administered Southeast Asia, the army would be in charge of Java, Malaya, British Borneo, Burma and the Philippines and these constituents of the region were, other than Burma, planned for as Area A. The navy would have only subsidiary authority in the designated army areas but principal control in Dutch Borneo, Celebes (Sulawesi), Moluccas (Maluku) and the Lesser Sunda Islands. The administrative division of Southeast Asia was partly intended to avoid conflict between the army and navy, a marked feature of Japan's World War II experience. Division also had as a rationale that the army would oversee more densely populated areas while the navy was in charge of areas with sparse populations, mainly the many islands of the Indonesian archipelago.[31] In pre-war planning, the Japanese had identified Indochina and Thailand as areas for Japanese manufacturing and industrial enterprise but envisaged Area A only as a source of raw materials. The 12 December 1941 Outline of Economic Policies

28 OSS, R&A 2368, *Japanese domination*, pp. 2, 12, 17, 48–49 and R&A 2114, *Political aspects of Allied occupation*, pp. 1, 6–10.

29 On Thailand's strategically central location, see NARA, RG59, entry 205, box 5835, file 892.00/9-3044, Dwight Bulbly, 'The importance of Thailand's political future', September 1944, p. 1.

30 Reynolds, *Thailand*, pp. 227, 236.

31 Benda, Irikura and Kishi, *Japanese military administration*, pp. 5, 7, 17. Burma was not mentioned as in Area A in an 8 December outline of economic policies but for purposes of discussion here it is useful to include it in Area A.

for the Southern Areas made this clear: 'As a basic principle, no manufacturing industries shall be promoted [in Area A] with the exception of certain industries (such as shipbuilding, and maintenance industries required for the upkeep of equipment needed in the development of resources).'[32] However, beginning in mid-1943, Japan had to depart from this policy because army self-sufficiency required the production of basic goods by local industries and, to a lesser extent, because shortages of essential goods for Southeast Asians were escalating (Chapter 4).

Within Area A, Malaya and Sumatra, discussed below, were particularly important as sources of raw materials, while the Philippines and Burma had considerable significance for Japan due to their strategic locations (Figures I.1 and 2.1). Burma, on the western perimeter of the Co-Prosperity Sphere, was seen as a gateway to both China and India and at the time of the designation of areas also as a buffer between the Japanese East Asian and the British Empires.[33] The Philippines had great strategic importance because it sat astride the sea routes between Japan and Southeast Asia.

At the outset of the war, Japan was still undecided whether Burma and the Philippines would be granted independence.[34] A greater strategic than economic role for both countries in the Co-Prosperity Sphere helps to explain why Japan set up puppet governments in them and invited their leaders to the 1943 Assembly of Greater East Asian Nations.[35] Japan needed to mobilize popular support in Burma and the Philippines to solidify its position in them and considered that the best way to achieve this was through indigenous leadership, with the proviso that Japan itself retained considerable, and ultimately determining, power. Effective Japanese control was, however, always elusive and moved further and further out of reach as the war continued.

Burma was already in a deplorable state in May 1942, when Japan first began to try to manage the country. Looting and violence were rife and transport was at a standstill.[36] By the end of 1942, a deteriorating situation was becoming a political liability.[37] An announcement in the Diet at the beginning of 1943 that Burma would be given independence did not bring stability. Neither, in August, did a declaration of independence for Burma, written by the Japanese, nor the appointment of Ba Maw as head of state (*Adipadi*) of a Burmese government. Ba Maw had already succeeded in May 1943 in enlisting support from 'responsible' members of the Burmese elite for a 22-person Burma Independence Preparatory Committee. Many of the 22 were Burmans (the majority ethnic group, now sometimes referred to as Bama) and nine were

32 Benda, Irikura and Kishi, *Japanese military administration*, pp. 20–21, 38.
33 Goto, *Tensions*, p. 93.
34 NA, WO203/6310, 'SEATIC Special intelligence bulletin', 1946, pp. 22–23.
35 Ohta, 'Japanese military occupation', p. 35.
36 OSS, R&A 2015, *Japanese administration of Burma*, 10 July 1944, p. 9.
37 OSS, R&A 1253, *Problem of law and order in occupied Burma*, p. 10.

Thakins ('masters', a designation assumed by members of the League of Burmans, literally the We Burmans Association [DoBama Asi-ayon], and including a highly influential group of 30 young Burmese nationalists formed in the 1930s). The Japanese had hoped that Ba Maw's mobilization of support from prominent Burmans, as well as a Karen on the Committee to represent that minority ethnic group, would stabilize Burma, but it did not.[38] Disorder was already entrenched, and Burman nationalism had taken on a dynamic which left no role for the Japanese. Ba Maw found himself in the impossible position of not only being fully committed to collaboration with Japan but also of being expected by the Japanese to personify Burma's political and social aspirations as the leader of an independent government.[39]

In January 1944, in an attempt to rescue Burma from chaos and shore up Japan's military position, Tokyo despatched General Gōtarō Ogawa to Rangoon as 'Supreme Advisor to the Burmese Government'. Ogawa, formerly professor of economics at Tokyo Imperial University and Minister of Commerce and Industry in 1936–37, was a prominent member of the Diet and in the latter 1930s had served as Vice Minister of Finance.[40] During his three-month stay in Burma, Ogawa drew up a plan to re-organize Burma and its economy. The plan outlined a complete re-organization of provincial administration, decreed a drastic policy of forced utilization of land and labour resources in support of war needs, made a central bank operational, and established a new model War Collaboration Committee to supervise the entire programme.[41] As an economist and planner, Ogawa favoured command, not market, solutions, an approach in keeping with Japanese military thinking and policy elsewhere in Southeast Asia.

By early 1944, however, when Ogawa's plan began to be implemented, the Japanese were living on borrowed time in Burma. The economy had collapsed to such an extent that it is unlikely that any plan could have succeeded, even a more realistic one that recognized Burma's high degree of economic integration and gave scope to the market. Ogawa left Burma a legacy of state direction and the beginnings of a central bank. After independence from Britain in 1948, Burma adopted much of Ogawa's programme of land and labour utilization, and Burmese politicians drew on the Central Bank as a ready, but ultimately inflationary, source of finance.

38 OSS, R&A 2015, *Japanese administration of Burma*, p. 20, R&A 1278, *Personnel of 'independent' Burma*, pp. 1–4 and R&A 1526, *Psychological warfare problem*, p. 3.

39 OSS, R&A 2015, *Japanese administration of Burma*, p. 28.

40 Burma Intelligence Bureau, *Burma*, vol. 2, pp. 18, 180; OSS, R&A 2077, *Economic reorganization of Burma*, 1944, p. 2. Both sources specify Tokyo Imperial University as Ogawa's affiliation but some other sources indicate Kyoto Imperial University.

41 OSS, R&A 2077, *Economic reorganization of Burma*, pp. 1–2 and R&A 2015, *Japanese administration of Burma*, pp. 62–64.

After occupying the Philippines, the Japanese recruited a Filipino elite and obtained, if to varying degrees, its co-operation. Most Filipinos, however, had always rejected Japanese nationalism and rejection quickly turned to hostility and hatred towards Japan. The distinguished Philippine politician, Manuel Roxas, was, for example, a 'reluctant collaborator'.[42] Elite recruitment did not mobilize support for the Japanese from the masses. They were unconvinced by the idea of a Japanese-granted independence and promises of 'the Philippines for the Filipinos' and 'the door of freedom unlocked'. Scepticism arose partly because before the war the Philippines already had been granted considerable political autonomy by the United States and given a promise of independence, and partly because of widespread distaste for the Japanese and their culture.[43] The October 1943 Declaration of Philippine independence and new government of Laurel left the Filipino public unimpressed.

For Japan, involvement in the Philippines was an essay in frustration and disappointment. It proved impossible to win Filipino friendship or convince Filipinos to act in a more Japanese fashion, including the acceptance of the corporatist ideals of society in Japan rather than American individualism. The Japanese considered the Filipinos spoiled and aimed to simplify their lives, abolish luxuries and eradicate all American ideas.[44] Filipinos were regarded as having an exaggerated sense of rights at the expense of social duties and welfare and in need of spiritual re-education.[45] Associations formed by Japanese to try to organize Filipinos and gain support included Makapili (Patriotic Association of Filipinos), United Nippon and the Kalibapi (Association for Service to the New Philippines).[46] The Kalibapi meant, according to an official pamphlet, 'action, service and union for the NEW PHILIPPINES' and societal linkage 'in toil, in hardship, and in happiness'.[47] Benigno S. Aquino, elected speaker of the wartime Second Philippine Republic, acted as the driving force behind the Kalibapi. Like other Japanese-inspired organizations, the Kalibapi attracted little support and insofar as it did, a significant part of this was in Aquino's home province of Tarlac.[48] A Filipino song, referring to the

[42] OSS, R&A 1752.2, *Status of the Philippine puppet government*, p. 4 and R&A 3208 *Philippines: finale of the puppet government*, p. 2; see also Roxas, 'Brief summary', pp. 244–50.

[43] Philippines, Japanese Military Administration, *Our independence*, pp. 3, 10.

[44] NARA, RG226, entry 16, box 144, 'Conditions in the Philippine Islands', 23 August 1942, pp. 2, 36–37; JM 103, *Outline of administration*, pp. 31, 34; NA, WO203/6310, 'SEATIC Special intelligence bulletin', 1946, p. 23.

[45] Rōyama and Takéuchi, *Philippine polity*, p. xiii.

[46] Hartendorp, *History of industry*, pp. 138–39.

[47] Philippines, Japanese Military Administration, *Ano ang Kalibapi?* [*What is the Kalibapi?*], pp. 14–15.

[48] OSS, R&A 1752.2, *Status of the Philippine puppet government*, pp. 12–17; Rōyama and Takéuchi, *Philippine polity*, p. 275.

ubiquitous Japanese practice of slapping faces (which could mean bleeding and a black eye), ran: 'I'm a slap-happy Jappy, Since I joined the Kalibapi'.[49]

The black market in rice, dealt with in Chapter 8, revealed how little control either Laurel's administration or any other official body, including the Japanese military, exercised. Provincial mayors and gangs ran whole areas of the Philippines to their personal advantage. Over large parts of the Philippines between the end of 1943 and 1945 the authority of Laurel's government 'existed largely on paper, and not in fact'.[50]

Throughout the Philippines, numerous Filipino guerrilla units operated independently, often little co-ordinated with each other, and became firmly entrenched. About half of the units were led by American officers who remained after the surrender of US forces in May 1942. Guerrillas, with the advantages of island terrains of mountains and jungle and of knowing the local people and trails, forced the Japanese to abandon their attempted 'extermination' of insurgents in favour of a campaign of 'pacification'. If anything, however, Filipino guerrillas grew in numbers.

For much of the war, extensive guerrilla resistance restricted the safe movement of the Japanese to the so-called lines and points – the corridors along railways or main roads and the towns. In Leyte, for example, guerrillas were already established by the time Japan occupied the island. It was impossible for Japanese forces, spread as thinly as one soldier per 3.67 km^2, to neutralize the guerrillas; they frequently attacked Japanese garrisons in the lowlands.[51] Adding to overall disorder in the Philippines, bands of guerrillas might fight not only the Japanese but sometimes each other, as the Huks (Hukbalahap or *Hukbo ng Bayan Laban sa Hapon* [People's Army against the Japanese]) did with non-Huk organizations in central Luzon in 1944.[52]

Even towards the end of the war, Japan had no plans for the independence of Java or Malaya and Sumatra.[53] The last two areas, administered together by the 25th Army until April 1943, were regarded as permanent Japanese colonies. They comprised 'the geographical centre of communication' in Southeast Asia, the nuclear zone of the Empire, 'the core of JAPAN's Southern strategy'. All aspects of these areas were to be stringently controlled.[54] Sumatra's oil made it

49 Hartendorp, *Japanese occupation*, p. 451 and *History of industry*, p. 72; On the physical effect of a slap, see NAS, Oral History, Abdeali K. Motiwalla, p. 34.

50 OSS, R&A 1752.2, *Status of the Philippine puppet government*, p. 10.

51 Ara, 'Food supply problem', pp. 64–65.

52 OSS, R&A 2357S, *Guerrilla resistance*, pp. 1–2; Pluvier, *South-East Asia*, p. 310; Ikehata, 'Japanese occupation period', pp. 5–7.

53 IC, 400–1443, Statement of Yamamoto Moichirō, 'Indonesian independence movement during Japan's occupation', 1946?, p. 2; Benda, 'Beginnings', p. 73; OSS, R&A 2072, *Japanese administration in Malaya*, pp. 5–6.

54 NA, WO203/6310, 'SEATIC Special intelligence bulletin', 1946, p. 23 and see p. 31; Benda, Irikura and Kishi, *Japanese military administration*, p. 169.

too valuable for the Japanese ever to surrender control. For Malaya, colonial status ensuring tightly monitored operation within the orbit of the Co-Prosperity Sphere was desirable because of the country's location at the centre of Southeast Asia and because its peninsular coastline stretched the length of the Straits of Malacca. Moreover, Singapore was Southeast Asia's most important port and the geographical centre of communications in the region (Figure 2.1).

Hasty British withdrawal from Malaya led to an almost complete breakdown of order, which forced the Japanese army, when it took over, to use its personnel to staff many of the government offices. While trying, as elsewhere in Southeast Asia, to make use of the Chinese for their business acumen, the Japanese identified the country's Malays as a favoured group. The Japanese occupiers contributed to bitter post-war racial conflict in Malaya by working through a Malay elite, promoting Malays in the civil service, and using Malays as informers.[55] By contrast, ethnic Chinese comprised most of the guerrilla bands that emerged in Malaya. In early 1945, according to a former captain in the Indian army: 'In small towns and in the interior of the Malay peninsula, the guerrillas can be called the real masters. It is only in the towns where the Japanese military is stationed that the guerrillas do not exercise complete control.'[56] Such a strong guerrilla foothold made highly likely the near anarchy that reigned in Malaya after the sudden Japanese surrender (Epilogue).

Muted Malayan nationalism suited the Japanese preference to retain Malaya as a colony. Insofar as nationalism was a force in Malaya, it largely focused on China in the case of the Chinese and India for the Indians. A group of radical Malay nationalists hoped for the formation of a Malay-dominated state formed in union with Indonesia. While this received a degree of sponsorship from the Japanese, the idea of a pan-Indonesia did not become an important nationalist force.[57]

Java presented Japan with a much more intractable problem than Malaya. As elsewhere in Southeast Asia, the Japanese approached the mobilization of collaboration in Java by co-opting local elites: 'Plans must be made to use local potentates, according to their present dignity and ability as an organ of the military administration.' A similar tactic existed in North Borneo for the use of 'native princes'.[58] For a time after occupying Indonesia, a lack of personnel forced the Japanese to rely on Dutch administrators and technicians.[59] That, however, was a minor difficulty which, in any case, the Japanese partly solved by promoting Indonesians to higher government positions.

55 Abu Talib Ahmad, *Malay Muslims*, pp. 102–6, 120.
56 NARA, RG226, entry 19, box 147, R&A XL10747, *Interrogation on Malaya*, 1 June 1945, p. 3.
57 Cheah, *Red star*, pp. 50–53; Taufik Abdullah, 'Nationalist activities', p. 126.
58 NA, WO203/6310, 'SEATIC Special intelligence bulletin', 1946, p. 24.
59 Sato, 'Administrative changes', pp. 92–93 and see p. 102; Sutter, *Indonesianisasi*, p. 146.

A main Japanese goal in Indonesia was to construct a Javanese nationalism directed against the West and favouring *Dai Nippon* (Great Japan). Japanese strategists saw Islam as a potential ally in gaining the support of Indonesians. Between 1942 and 1945, the Japanese gave representation of Islam a privileged position and assiduously cultivated Islamic leaders. Rural religious leaders were accorded special attention and brought into the mainstream.[60] During the 40 months of occupation, Islam became a strong political force in Indonesia and the pre-war nationalism of a small urban intelligentsia was joined by a new, broadly based rural nationalism.[61] By giving leading nationalists social prestige and prominence, the Japanese forged them into a true elite group.[62] Japanese occupation shook the foundations of rural society in Java. The outstanding developments during the Japanese occupation were a greater Islamization and the tremendous increase in national consciousness.[63]

In contrast to Dutch colonialism, Japan sponsored political organization on a large scale. While a major purpose of these organizations, semi-military in character, was to create Indonesian nationalism in support of the Japanese war effort, they had the important effect of 'spread[ing] a militant anti-Westernism through the entire population'.[64] Japanese sponsorship extended to numerous movements, including many youth groups, with a bewildering array of names, to build Javanese co-operation and enthusiasm for Japanese goals. Mass organizations in Java aimed at persuading people to make sacrifices for the Greater East Asia Co-Prosperity Sphere included the Pergerakan Tiga A (Triple A movement, March 1942), PUTERA (Centre of the People's Power or Concentration of the People's Energy, March 1943) and Jawa Hokokai (Java Public Service Association, March 1944).[65] Youth movements were the most radical Japanese departure.[66] They often featured physical training and sought to instil in young Indonesians a Japanese-like spirit and appreciation of Japan. While inspiring Indonesian nationalism, Japanese efforts failed to achieve the desired orientation towards Japan and support for it.[67]

As part of an effort to encourage an Indonesian nationalism hostile to the West, the Japanese identified Sukarno, who had established the Nationalist Party (*Partai Nasional Indonesia*) in 1927, and Mohammad Hatta, and enlisted

60 Taufik Abdullah, 'Nationalist activities', pp. 117–18.
61 Benda, 'Beginnings', pp. 81–82, 'Indonesian Islam', pp. 361–62 and 'Structure', pp. 136–37.
62 Benda, *Crescent*, p. 169.
63 Kahin, *Nationalism*, p. 128; Benda, *Crescent*, p. 150.
64 Feith, *Decline*, p. 7.
65 Benda, *Crescent*, p. 192; Cribb, 'Institutions', pp. 102–13; Taufik Abdullah, 'Nationalist activities', pp. 114–19.
66 Benda, 'Japanese interregnum', pp. 77–78.
67 Kahin, *Nationalism*, pp. 109–10.

their help as likely organizers. Both had long been prominent anti-colonial leaders and agitators. Sukarno had been arrested on various occasions and in 1933 banished to Flores, while Hatta had been detained in 1934 and sent to Boven Digul in New Guinea. In promoting nationalism, the Japanese made extensive use of Sukarno and enhanced his standing, as he later recalled: 'Imamura [General and commander of the army of occupation] was pleased with my oratory ... he placed newspapers and planes at my disposal. He allowed me mass rallies. I addressed 50,000 at one meeting, 100,000 at another. Sukarno's face, not just his name, penetrated the archipelago.'[68] Although Sukarno and Hatta had their own nationalist agenda different from Japan's, they apparently regarded compliance with the Japanese as the best hope for Indonesian independence. Indonesian nationalists were, however, disappointed by Indonesia's exclusion from the 1943 Assembly of Greater East Asian Nations.[69] That implied that Japan did not envisage an independent Indonesia.

During the occupation, efforts to mobilize Javanese support were increasingly undermined by Japanese resistance to Java's (and so also all of Indonesia's) independence. Finally in September 1944, Japan, badly needing to mobilize support from Indonesians against likely Allied invasion, announced that Indonesia would be granted independence. Whether it was intended to deliver on this promise is doubtful. On 17 August 1945, just after the Japanese surrender, Sukarno and Hatta, pushed by younger, more radical nationalists, declared Indonesian independence. The declaration became one of many ingredients in a progression towards revolution which included large numbers of Indonesians given military training by the Japanese, stocks of weapons made available by them and, after the war, a power vacuum in Indonesia until the British army began to arrive at the end of September 1945.

Economic Administration

This section investigates how the Japanese sought to organize and control the distribution of food and goods to Southeast Asians and production of the region's primary commodities. In both instances, the Japanese philosophy can be summarized as an ideal of a government-regulated system, army supervision, co-operative enterprise and monopoly, monopsony or oligopoly. Economic concentration was deemed the most efficient organizational form because it eliminated duplication and waste and because co-operation maximized societal good. Although monopolistic organization had the advantage

[68] Sukarno, *Autobiography*, p. 179.

[69] NIMH, 011/3, International Prosecution Section, Netherlands Division, November 1946, Statement of K. A. de Weerd, 'The Japanese occupation of the Netherlands Indies', pp. 57–58. Taufik Abdullah, 'Nationalist activities', p. 121.

of saving on Japanese administrative resources by limiting the number of people with whom administrators had to deal, it did not prove successful either in the production of primary commodities or in the distribution of goods to Southeast Asians. Production was generally inefficient and corruption became widespread. Qualified managerial personnel were in short supply and not all Japanese put in charge of estates and mines had sufficient local and technical knowledge. Problems of management were compounded by the collapse of markets for nearly every commodity. That made it difficult, if not impossible, for private enterprise, whether directed by large Japanese conglomerates or individual Japanese-appointed managers, to operate profitably. Nor was the army allowed to make a profit. Finally, and importantly, the Japanese choice of economic organization assumed that Southeast Asians, as Asians, would recognize and respond to monopoly's efficiency attributes and that, in any case, traders could be effectively organized and managed. During the war, however, among most Southeast Asian traders, and many Japanese too, black market opportunities to profit from scarcities of food and goods prevailed over economic goodwill and the implementation of official economic directives.

Distributive Organization

For the distribution of food and consumer goods, the Japanese had no option but to work through pre-war distributors. That meant reliance on Chinese and, to a lesser extent, Indian traders. Japanese planners acknowledged this but hoped somewhat to reduce dependence on the Chinese by bringing Japanese merchants on 'a gradual and planned basis' into the acquisition and distribution of commodities at an intermediate level.[70] To some extent this happened naturally: in Thailand, for example, the arrival of the military was soon followed by 'an influx of Japanese merchants and tradesmen'.[71] Possibly because Burma had far fewer Chinese traders than other Southeast Asian countries, the Nippon Trading Company took over much of the country's wholesale distributing business.[72] Organization of Southeast Asia's vast body of small, often family, firms took the form of grouping them into 'associations' or 'unions'. These extended to practically every activity and typically, as in the Philippines, reached down to the smallest retailers.[73]

Wholesale and retail distributive organizations for the allocation of food and consumer goods were known as *kumiai* and analogous to Japan's non-

[70] Benda, Irikura and Kishi, *Japanese military administration*, p. 39 and see p. 169; Trager, *Burma*, p. 48.

[71] BT, Bank of Thailand, *Bank of Thailand economic and financial report, 1945*, p. 30.

[72] OSS, R&A 2015, *Japanese administration of Burma*, p. 58.

[73] Hartendorp, *History of industry*, pp. 91, 92–93 and *Japanese occupation*, pp. 501, 503–4, 596.

voluntary co-operatives, or *nōkyō*. *Kumiai* in Malaya, for example, included associations regulating trade in fish, meat, eggs, vegetables, rice and piece goods. Singapore had previously had only one monopoly, for opium, but '[N]ow everything was a monopoly. There was even a *kumiai* for charcoal and firewood, and a *kumiai* for nightsoil. We were hedged in by *kumiais*. We could not move an elbow without coming into contact with some *kumiai*.'[74] These aspects of retailing in Malaya were paralleled in Java by the Japanese preference for monopoly and organization of Chinese merchants into a single association.[75]

In wartime Southeast Asia's distributive trades, the replacement by monopoly of pre-war competition between numerous small traders bred corruption and hoarding. Traders in Malaya used exclusive purchase and distribution rights to withhold supplies from regulated markets and sell instead at higher black market prices.[76] According to a contemporary observer, *kumiai* 'became government-protected compartments of the Black Market ... Every *Kumiai* was nothing but a monopoly to fleece the public. As soon as a *Kumiai* for any particular commodity was formed, that commodity soon disappeared from the markets and became difficult to get. As a result, prices soared.'[77] Several heads of *kumiai* were said to have become multi-millionaires.[78]

Traders in Burma countered official price regulation by withholding their goods from the market. Wealthier Burmese consumers had to buy clandestinely and poorer ones to do without. Only officials could buy at controlled prices. Two Japanese attempts to set up effective price controls failed.[79]

Japanese regulation of the purchase and distribution of rice in Southeast Asia largely copied Japan's Rice Distribution and Control Law of 1939. Controls were, however, neither uniform between areas nor constant over time.[80] As rice availability contracted in response to low and, in real terms, decreasing administered prices, Japanese controls became more comprehensive and extended to delivery and allocation quotas. For rice, as was observed more generally for Indonesia, almost invariably the Japanese solution to problems of distribution was to set up a control board or organization.[81] However, Japanese attempts at a greater regulation of rice in Southeast Asia were typically outpaced by a local response of increased evasion and decreased production.

[74] Low, *When Singapore*, p. 64.
[75] Sutter, *Indonesianisasi*, p. 172.
[76] Chin, *Malaya upside down*, pp. 88–90; Low and Cheng, *This Singapore*, pp. 128–29; Kratoska, *Japanese occupation*, pp. 172–73.
[77] Chin, *Malaya upside down*, p. 88.
[78] ANM, 1957/0572010, Lau Siew Foo and J. C. Barry, 'A brief review of Chinese affairs during the period of Japanese occupation', *c.* September 1945, p. 2.
[79] OSS, R&A 2015, *Japanese administration of Burma*, pp. 48–54.
[80] Kurasawa, 'Transportation and rice distribution', p. 33; Johnson, *Japanese food management*, pp. 187–93.
[81] Sutter, *Indonesianisasi*, p. 199.

There were, however, some exceptions to Japanese reluctance to look for market solutions. For example, in May 1944 the threat of serious food shortages led to a relaxation of export–import regulations to allow barter trade between Malaya on the one hand and Thailand and Indochina on the other. Singapore's rice trade was liberalized at about the same time.[82] By the spring of 1944, after repeated regulatory attempts had failed to secure sufficient rice to maintain Singapore's population even at a low nutritional level, the Japanese partially freed the import of rice and allowed private Chinese traders to obtain rice in Thailand for sale on the Singapore open market (Chapter 8).

Organization of Production

The Liaison Conference of 12 December 1941 had set out the principle which became the primary Japanese objective for guiding the organization of production in Southeast Asia: 'to fulfil the demand for resources vital to the prosecution of the present war'.[83] The March 1942 Outline on the Conduct of Military Administration in Occupied Areas divided the management of production between the military and qualified individuals selected as subcontractors or as commissioned enterprises and working under military supervision. Coal and oil, strategically vital raw materials, were under direct military management. Early in 1942 in Indonesia and Malaya, the importance of quinine to the war effort caused this anti-malarial medicine, too, to be placed under direct control by the Japanese army.[84] In the March 1942 Outline, phosphates were at first to be mined by subcontractors but were later to come under some form of direct military management. Major pre-war exports such as rubber and copra, which had been confiscated but did not require active development, would be allocated to private enterprise under military supervision.

For the most part, private Japanese business was put in charge of managing Southeast Asia's agricultural and industrial enterprises. The reliance on existing Japanese companies, it has been observed, was symptomatic of the lack of any policy to develop the economies in Southeast Asia in a systematic way.[85] It may also have been partly due to Japan's need quickly to establish administrative and enterprise structures. Japanese companies, typically with a lead firm specified for each Southeast Asian enterprise, were selected and designated by the Sixth Committee under the Cabinet. Nominated firms included medium-sized enterprises, but more often were large industrial and financial conglomerates, the

[82] OSS, assemblage 43, R&A 2280.1, *Handbook of Japanese industry*, pp. 411–12.
[83] Benda, Irikura and Kishi, *Japanese military administration*, p. 17.
[84] JM 103, *Outline of administration*, p. 14. Sutter, *Indonesianisasi*, pp. 152–53; Kratoska, *Japanese occupation*, p.165.
[85] Okazaki, 'Strategies', p. 34.

zaibatsu.[86] In army-occupied Southeast Asia, close to 1,300 Japanese companies set up operations, including 525 industrial firms, 224 in commerce and trade, 190 in agriculture, 133 in mining and 49 in forestry. The Mitsui group had 240 firms and the Mitsubishi group a further 125.[87]

Initially, a policy of dividing up resource exploitation among two or more companies was meant to avoid the semblance of monopoly. Later, however, monopoly was not necessarily seen as a problem as, for example, in Indonesia where army authorities ultimately found it more expedient to deal with just one organization.[88] Over the course of the war, the administration and management of a number of the pre-war export industries varied as Japanese administrators tried to find more effective regulation arrangements. Sometimes resource exploitation was re-allocated to private enterprise from military management, but in other instances the military took over from failing Japanese businesses.

From the beginning, Thailand and Indochina were exceptions to the plan for extensive military involvement in, and management of, resource development because both retained their pre-war governments and because both were seen as offering investment opportunities for Japanese companies. In Thailand, Japanese investment accorded with plans to re-organize the economy and incorporate the Kingdom as a full member of the Greater East Asia Co-Prosperity Sphere.[89] A blueprint policy adopted by the Liaison Conference of 29 September 1942 determined that Japan would take control of all aspects of the Thai economy fundamental to the prosecution of the Greater East Asia War and the economy of East Asia.[90] Subsequent policy decisions, notably 'Matters concerning Thailand' in September 1942, confirmed this.[91] By 1944, Japanese had joint control of many Thai state and private industries, including the Thai Rice Company and the Thai Tin and Rubber Company. There were also a number of joint industrial ventures (Chapter 4). Although Phibun's Thai government saw advantages in Japanese involvement in the economy, it was unable to resist economic domination by Japan. Japan not only exercised military control but could back this up with an economy far stronger than Thailand's.

Japan strengthened its economic position in Thailand through close ties with Thai officials, of whom Wanit Pananonda was said to be notorious, but which included a number of leading cabinet members and government

[86] Benda, Irikura and Kishi, *Japanese military administration*, pp. 36–39; Hara, 'Daitōa', p. 9; Okazaki, 'Strategies', p. 34.
[87] Hikita, 'Japanese companies' inroads', pp. 174–76; Kobayashi, '"Kyōei ken" to Nihon kigyō', p. 117.
[88] Sutter, *Indonesianisasi*, p. 156.
[89] Swan, 'Japan's intentions', pp. 141–43.
[90] Reynolds, *Thailand*, pp. 134–35.
[91] Swan, *Japan's economic relations*, pp. 209–16, 249–53.

officials. Wanit had been in Japan's pay before the war and was, until his suicide in May 1944 following arrest on charges of illegal transactions in gold bullion, influential in wartime negotiations with Japan. As well as being head of the Foreign Trade Bureau and Chairman of an Economic Mission to Japan, Wanit held influential positions in Phibun's wartime cabinet, including that of Deputy Minister of Finance. Because of his important official positions and perhaps also through being Chairman of the Board of Directors of the newly established Bank of Thailand, Wanit was able to secure offices such as manager or director of the Thai Rice and Thai Rubber companies.[92]

In Indochina, a May 1941 economic co-operation agreement with Japan led to an influx of Japanese firms which increased after a further December 1942 agreement to modify and extend the earlier accord. It allowed Japanese to engage in business and own land in Indochina on the same basis as Indochinese nationals. Mitsui Bussan Kaisha, the biggest Japanese company in Indochina, was given a monopoly to export rice to Japan. Dainan Koosi, the longest-established Japanese company in Indochina, expanded its Indochinese operations through affiliates which acted as purchasing agents for the army and navy. Most Japanese companies in Indochina invested in agricultural production, the timber industry and mining and minerals. The Japanese company Compagnie Indochinoise de Commerce et d'Industrie formed three joint ventures with French companies to mine chromium, manganese, iron ore and phosphates for export to Japan.[93] French business realized some benefits from co-operation with the Japanese, and the Decoux administration was reasonably successful in resisting a Japanese takeover of the economy and protecting its lucrative areas for French interests.

To exploit already developed, less strategic resources like rubber, sugar and timber in military-occupied Southeast Asia, Japan set up umbrella control organizations, agreed in consultation with the Tokyo government and dominated by the *zaibatsu*.[94] For resource mobilization in Burma, a network of Japanese control organizations, or unions, was established. These included the Nippon Burma Rice Union and the Nippon Burma Timber Union. The latter, apparently dating from 1942, was a commercial combine in which Mitsui Bussan Kaisha, Mitsubishi, Ataka Shōkai and Toyo Menka Kaisha participated.[95] The Philippines economy fell under the domination of a series of complementary

[92] OSS, R&A 2368, *Japanese domination*, pp. 32–33; OSS, R&A 2114, *Political aspects of Allied occupation*, pp. 6–7. See also R&A 2368, *Japanese domination*, pp. 54 and 56 for lists of principal pre-war Japanese companies in Thailand and Japanese firms mentioned since the invasion of Thailand.

[93] Le, *Impact*, pp. 184–88.

[94] Bisson, *Japan's war economy*, pp. 87–89; Cohen, *Japan's economy*, pp. 68–69.

[95] Burma Intelligence Bureau, *Burma*, vol. 2, p. 56; Pe, *Narrative*, p. 55. For a full listing of Japanese companies, see NARA, RG226, entry 154, box 79, file 1306, 'Japanese companies operating in Burma', 27 September 1944.

monopolies. These included six Mitsui-affiliated companies including the Mitsui Bussan Company, Mitsui Mining Company and Mitsui Agricultural Commerce and Forestry. The Japanese created a Philippine Cocoa Purchasing Union with headquarters at the offices of the Japanese firm Daidō Bōeki Kaisha.[96] In July 1944, in recognition of Philippine independence, Japan handed 20 government corporations to the Laurel administration, although probably more in name than reality. Among these were the National Coconut Corporation, Philippine Sugar Association and Manila Tobacco Association as well as railway, gas and shipping corporations or associations.[97]

In Malaya, rice imports from Thailand became the monopsony of a large trading firm, Mitsubishi Shoji Kaisha.[98] For rubber, a syndicate of 18 Japanese firms operated through a contract with the army as the Syonan [Singapore] Rubber Association (Syonan Gomu Kumiai). But this latter, even with the benefit of administered prices, could not counter the collapse of demand for rubber and failed to make a profit. In response, a 1943 re-organization allocated three-fifths of enemy rubber estates to the military administration.[99] Six Japanese companies took over the operation of Indonesia's foreign-owned, mostly Dutch, sugar holdings. These had not been estates in that they did not have their own estate land but rather factories that had grown sugar cane on leased farm land. Apportionment of sugar mills was on the basis of the size of the companies' sugar holdings in Taiwan and so favoured enterprises which were already large there. Control of all European estates in Sumatra passed to Japanese companies.[100] As it became clear that many estates in Java, Sumatra and Borneo were economically non-viable, they were effectively closed and turned over to workers for subsistence cultivation.

Cultural Policies

As part of an overall strategy to dominate Southeast Asians and integrate them into a Japanese Empire, Japan made determined efforts to disseminate its language and culture.[101] A November 1941 directive from Tokyo determined that 'Native inhabitants shall be so guided as to induce a sense of trust in the Imperial forces'. Another directive, formulated just before the attack on Pearl

96 Hartendorp, *Japanese occupation*, pp. 207–10; Steinberg, *Philippine collaboration*, pp. 86–88.
97 OSS, R&A 1752.2, *Status of the Philippine puppet government*, pp. 8–9.
98 Kurasawa, 'Transportation and rice distribution', p. 55.
99 OSS, R&A 2072, *Japanese administration in Malaya*, pp. 32–33; NARA, RG226, entry 16, box 1472, no. 128585, OSS, R&A Branch, Regular Intelligence Reports, 'Malaya under the Japanese, March 1945', p. 17; Sutter, *Indonesianisasi*, p. 153; Kratoska, *Japanese occupation*, pp. 233–34.
100 Sutter, *Indonesianisasi*, pp. 153, 155.
101 Benda, Irikura and Kishi, *Japanese military administration*, p. 33.

Harbor, advised that 'winning the hearts of the peoples under our rule is extremely vital to the prosecution of the war'.[102] But the Japanese did not win hearts and minds and their initiatives to re-shape Southeast Asian culture to fit into a Japanese-dominated Greater East Asia Co-Prosperity Sphere almost entirely failed.

Failure had multiple explanations. One was that few Southeast Asians could manage the Japanese language, *Nihon-go*, and another that Japan lacked the resources to deploy large numbers of teachers and educational materials to Southeast Asia. Third, the Japanese made themselves so unattractive and hated as a people and culture that not many Southeast Asians aspired to emulate them (even though initially Southeast Asians had often been well disposed). Finally, shortages of food and goods erased any lingering incentive to believe in the Japanese vision or in its superiority. For Southeast Asians there was no escaping the heavy-handed methods and racial disdain practised by the occupying Japanese. Convinced that they were a superior race, the Japanese, Thein Pe Myint observed, 'treated Burmese arrogantly and thought nothing of slapping them about the face'.[103] The Japanese slogans used throughout Southeast Asia, 'Same race, same culture' and 'One colour, one race', had a hollow ring.[104]

Education and Language

The thrust of Japanese educational policy was to control education, not develop it. Instruction in Japanese and insistence on the everyday use of *Nihon-go* had direction and domination as objectives. Thailand, as in many other respects, was an exception, as also was Indochina. In Thailand's schools, classes in English, French and Chinese were abolished in favour of Japanese, which became a compulsory subject, but Thai remained the main medium of instruction as well as the Kingdom's administrative language.[105] Similarly, in Vietnam French and Vietnamese were the administrative languages and the ones in which children were taught.

Japan sought to exert cultural influence in Thailand in more subtle ways than by dictating educational policy. In the 1930s, the Japanese were already vigorously pursuing a cultural programme in the Kingdom. This was formalized in July 1942 by a cultural treaty with Thailand.[106] Cultural efforts directed at the Thai received considerable indirect support from Japanese merchants,

[102] Ibid., pp. 2, 47.
[103] Taylor, *Thein Pe Myint's 'Wartime traveler'*, p. 107.
[104] Low, *When Singapore*, p. 121; Benda, 'Beginnings', p. 67 and see p. 70.
[105] OSS, R&A 552, *Thai cooperation*, p. 2 and R&A 301, *Social conditions, attitudes and propaganda in Thailand*, p. 13.
[106] OSS, R&A 92, *Increased Japanese influence*, pp. 12–14; OSS, R&A 2368, *Japanese domination*, pp. 35–45.

officials and professionals resident in Thailand. During the war, the Japanese published two daily newspapers in Bangkok, one in Chinese and the other in Japanese, and exercised control over one or more Thai-language newspapers.[107] However, Phibun's nationalist-oriented cultural policies effectively countered Japanese hopes for a Japanization of Thai culture.[108]

In Malaya, Burma and the Philippines, the Japanese, although attempting to eradicate English, were forced to recognize that it was the only possible *lingua franca*.[109] After the Japanese banned Dutch in Indonesia, Indonesian afforded the most effective means of communication. Although Japanese was taught in all schools, *Bahasa Indonesia* (Indonesian language) became the sole official language for administration and for all education above the third year of primary school.[110] Although the vernacular *Bahasa Malajoe* had been widely used in colonial Indonesia and included a lively newspaper and book press and radio broadcasts, it has been argued that a greater use of Indonesian as a language contributed to a common bond that encouraged nationalism.[111] Manila's principal streets were given Japanese names, but Singapore's were not.[112] In Indochina, French rule precluded an alteration of street names but soon after the March 1945 Japanese coup, officials in many of Vietnam's provinces submitted detailed lists of changes to Vietnamese names.[113]

Japanese officials persisted in a determination that all Southeast Asians learn Japanese and think and act like Japanese.[114] Schools in Malaya, Burma and the Philippines that re-opened during the occupation all taught Japanese. In Malaya, Japanese language teaching and cultural studies took up most of the day. The fall of Singapore was described as the beginning of three and a half years of 'educational twilight' throughout Malaya.[115] In the Philippines in September 1943, just 45 secondary schools, two-fifths of the pre-war number, were open, including only two in Manila.[116] Japanese policy in Burma was

[107] OSS, R&A 2368, *Japanese domination*, pp. 35–44.
[108] Reynolds, *Thailand*, pp. 135–36; OSS, R&A 2368, *Japanese domination*, p. 50.
[109] Burma Intelligence Bureau, *Burma*, vol. 2, p. 33; OSS, R&A 2072, *Japanese administration in Malaya*, p. 44; Low, *When Singapore*, p. 84; JM 103, *Outline of administration*, p. 34.
[110] Kahin, *Nationalism*, p. 132; Benda, *Crescent*, p. 276.
[111] Jones, *Japan's new order*, p. 373; Anderson, 'Languages', pp. 105–6; Takir Alisjahbana, 'Indonesian language', pp. 389–90; Thomas, 'Educational remnants', p. 632.
[112] NARA, RG226, entry 16, box 144, 'Conditions in the Philippine Islands', 23 August 1942, p. 9.
[113] AOM, GF/24 contains numerous files dated April and May 1945 with details of proposed changes.
[114] Burma Intelligence Bureau, *Burma*, vol. 2, pp. 46–49.
[115] Malayan Union, *Annual report on education . . . 1946*, p. 2.
[116] Hartendorp, *Japanese occupation*, p. 603; OSS, R&A 2380, *Education in the Philippines*, p. 14.

to eradicate the English language; Rangoon University re-opened in February 1944 but with less than 10 per cent of its pre-war enrolment.[117]

Older Southeast Asians were encouraged to speak Japanese with slogans like one in Singapore: 'Do you wish to always be a rickshaw puller? If not, learn your *Nippon* [*Nihon*]-*go*.'[118] Even a smattering of Japanese could facilitate rapid promotion.[119] Lee Kuan Yew, just 19 years old when Japan invaded but later Singapore's Prime Minister, was among those who saw the advantages of learning Japanese and by doing so got a job at Domei, the military-controlled Japanese news agency.[120]

In Malaya, as elsewhere in Southeast Asia, clocks were moved to Tokyo time and a concerted effort was made to instil Japanese habits, customs, discipline and outlook.[121] Employees at the Kuala Lumpur Town Board fell in at 8 a.m. sharp, faced the Imperial Palace in Tokyo and bowed, then did physical training for half an hour, followed by a compulsory course in *Nihon-go* for an hour on alternate days.[122] One morning, Malayan Hospital staff, perceived as bowing incorrectly, stood to attention in the sun for an address in Japanese on how to bow before undergoing two hours of strict supervision to learn the correct technique.[123] In Indonesia, men and women who passed a sentry and did not bow would be slapped.[124] Filipinos were made to celebrate Foundation Day, marking the over 2,500 years during which Japan had never been invaded; on the Emperor's birthday public buildings and homes were 'asked' to display the Japanese flag. Singapore residents were told when to put out a Japanese flag and any household without a flag had to purchase one.[125] Although such requirements were relatively minor, they were indicative of an unrelenting Japanization effort. The Japanese, observed a Filipino who lived through the occupation, 'might much better have gone slower, used a policy of "attraction" instead of almost naked coercion'.[126]

Outwardly, Southeast Asians prudently adopted the trappings of Japanese manners. In Malaya, everyone bowed to Japanese personnel. They also bowed to passing cars since it was unlikely that anyone except Japanese would be

[117] Burma Intelligence Bureau, *Burma*, vol. 2, p. 126; Christian, *Burma and the Japanese invader*, p. 357.
[118] NA, HS1/114, 'Interrogation of British soldiers formerly prisoners of the Japanese' in 'Far East: Malaya, general intelligence policy: progress reports', p. 11.
[119] Sivaram, *Road to Delhi*, p. 64.
[120] Lee, *Singapore story*, pp. 62–64.
[121] Chin, *Malaya upside down*, pp. 148–55; NAS, Oral History, Chew Cheok Hai, p. 52; Sivaram, *Road to Delhi*, p. 64.
[122] ANM, 1957/0292046, R.C. Selangor 269/1947, *Report of the Kuala Lumpur Town Board 1946*, p. 3.
[123] Malayan Union, *Report of the medical department 1946*, p. 4.
[124] Sukarno, *Autobiography*, p. 181.
[125] NAS, Oral History, George Edwin Bogaars, p. 38.
[126] Hartendorp, *Japanese occupation*, p. 215 and see pp. 211–21.

riding in them.[127] That was a reasonable supposition: petrol was scarce and only cars operating for the Japanese had a legal right to this fuel.[128]

An unyielding insistence that Southeast Asians adhere to Japanese culture alienated most of them from their occupiers. Even in Thailand, the most lightly occupied Southeast Asian country, by the second half of 1942 'arrogant Japanese behavior and war-induced economic problems had created widespread resentment among the general population'.[129] Not all Indonesians could accept the Japanese belief in themselves as a Chosen Race, superior to all others. The concept of a divine Emperor clashed head on with the Islamic faith.[130] In Indochina, a French official reported from the northern Indochinese province of Lao Kay (Lào Cai) that '[o]n the whole, people hate the Japanese'.[131] Ba Maw later described the Japanese in Burma as 'domineering and blinded by delusions of their own racial grandeur and Asian destiny'.[132] They were disliked in Burma for instituting forced labour, requisitioning carts and animals, and face slapping.[133] This last was considered by Burmese as a particularly great humiliation and intensely resented.[134]

Social Organization and Control

This section first briefly considers Vietnam and Thailand and then explores three aspects of social organization and control used in military-administered Southeast Asia by the Japanese. One was *tonari-gumi*, which copied Japanese practice, under which groups of people were expected to monitor the conduct of one another and enforce correct behaviour; a second, jurisdiction over supplies of food and its distribution; and the third, the Japanese military police. The last were the backbone of an approach to social control which relied heavily on fear to subdue local populations.

In Thailand and Indochina, the continuance of pre-war governments enabled Japan substantially to devolve to these administrations problems of social control, although the Japanese always had occupying troops at their

127 NARA, RG226, entry 19, box 0158, 'Journey of the Burma special research commission', 10 May to 2 August 1942, p. 2.
128 ANM, 1957/0575131 Intelligence 506/30, 'Appreciation of the economic position of Malaya under the Japanese', 30 June 1944, p. 6.
129 Reynolds, *Thailand*, p. 113.
130 Benda, *Crescent*, p. 127.
131 AOM, INDO/NF/11021, Bulletin de Renseignements du Centre Orientation et Liaisons Indochine, 10 September 1945, p. 6.
132 Ba Maw, *Breakthrough*, p. 274; for a similar evaluation, see Taylor, *Thein Pe Myint's 'Wartime traveler'*, p. 234.
133 IOR, Clague Papers, Mss Eur E252/44, 'Situation in Burma during the period shortly before the British evacuation and the withdrawal of the Japanese from Burma', *c.* March 1945, p. 1.
134 Khin Myo Chit, *Three years*, p. 4.

disposal if needed. As already indicated, in Thailand Japanese policy focused on supporting Phibun, working through the military and seeking influence with the Thai elite. In Indochina, the Decoux administration had strong fascist traits and supported Vichy France and the Axis. Decoux himself swore enthusiastic allegiance to Marshal Pétain and worked to instill in Vietnam youth a culture, including physical education and sports, which could be described as tropical fascism.[135] The Vichy slogan, 'Work – Family – Fatherland', was prominently displayed in wartime Indochina, and for Decoux evoked the true and traditional aspirations of the Indochinese masses.[136] In the southernmost Vietnamese administrative district of Cochinchina, the Japanese, anxious for a local power base, operated through two religious-cum-political organizations, Hòa Hảo and the Cao Đài, each of which maintained their own militias.[137]

Social control in military-administered Southeast Asia presented Japanese officials and Japan's military with more of a challenge than in Indochina and Thailand, where there were still pre-war administrations. The four military-administered countries and British Borneo formed a collection of societies alien to the Japanese and furthermore different from one another. By early 1938 in the home islands, Japan had some 96,900 economic police, one for about every 750 persons.[138] Manpower on this scale could not be deployed in Southeast Asia. Shortages of food and goods created a potential for social unrest. It was desirable to avoid serious hunger because this could become a cause of widespread protest and because Southeast Asian workers were needed to contribute to the war effort. If social unrest took hold it might assume its own momentum and spiral beyond easy remedy.

Neighbourhood Associations

Tonari-gumi was a pyramid structure with a base of neighbourhood units of about 10 to 30 houses. Above these, the pyramid narrowed sharply towards its apex. Section heads were responsible for a number of neighbourhood units and overseeing the section heads was a small number of headmen or supervisors. Collective responsibility, and tied to this the threat of collective punishment, was key to the system. Members of neighbourhood units were told to patrol their own small area and report any disturbance, diseases or activities in opposition to occupation administrations. Neighbourhood associations,

135 Shipway, *Decolonization*, p. 69.
136 Marr, *Vietnam 1945*, pp. 72–73.
137 OSS, R&A 1249, *Japanese penetration in French Indo-China*, pp. 1–3; Tràn, 'Japan and Vietnam's Caodaists', pp. 185–88; NAC, 23220, box 2743, 'Activités Caodaistes', 29 March 1943; Brocheux, 'Economy of war', pp. 322–33.
138 Scherer, 'Drawbacks', p. 117.

Philippines radio announced in February 1943, 'should be regarded as an effort of every peaceful community to do away with undesirable elements'.[139]

The speed and comprehensiveness with which neighbourhood associations were successfully introduced in occupied Southeast Asia varied considerably. Over the whole of Java, *tonari-gumi* of 10 to 20 houses, depending on local circumstances, were established in just three months, although apparently not until late 1943. Explicit Islamic approval of the associations probably made villagers more willing to accept them. Rationing in urban Java was entrusted to neighbourhood chiefs. In Jakarta's (formerly Batavia) informal (non-modern) economy, the *rukun tetangga* or *tonari-gumi* drew the city's so-called *kampong* (traditional village) dwellers into a network of administrations more closely than ever before.[140] As well as the collection and distribution of goods, the *rukun tetangga* were responsible for fire-fighting, funerals and education and served as a local source of information for the government.[141]

The Japanese instituted the neighbourhood system less quickly in Malaya than Java but ultimately fairly comprehensively. In Singapore, *tonari-gumi*, founded in September 1943 and called the Peace Preservation Corps, comprised 5,500 neighbourhood units of 30 households, 55 sections and 550 subsections, each with a leader. Corps also existed in Penang, Malacca, Selangor, Perak and probably elsewhere in Malaya. The corps registered all families in a neighbourhood and so, as well as monitoring local behaviour, served as a form of census and a basis for the distribution of rations.[142]

In the Philippines, the system of neighbourhood associations, created by executive order in August 1942, met considerable early resistance but by April 1943 was said by the Japanese to be functioning in 600 towns and in Manila, where it had 900,000 members in 1,789 districts and 13,192 associations, implying an average of 68 persons per association. Heads of families were required to patrol at night and report suspicious persons or wrongdoers, on pain of fines or other punishments for failure to do so. The rationing of some items, including soap, lard, matches and sugar, was through associations.[143]

The slow and incomplete introduction of *tonari-gumi* in Burma was symptomatic of the country's endemic social disorder. In rural areas, villages were traditionally divided into 10-house *gaungs* but by the 1940s this had often

[139] Hartendorp, *Japanese occupation*, p. 452.

[140] IC, 400–1443, Yamamoto Moichirō, 'Indonesian independence movement', 1946?, pp. 12–13; De Jong, *Collapse*, p. 258; Benda, *Crescent*, p. 157; Abeyasekere, *Jakarta*, p. 142.

[141] Cribb, *Gangsters*, pp. 40–41.

[142] OSS, R&A 2072, *Japanese administration in Malaya*, pp. 20–21; OSS, R&A 2423, *Singapore under Japanese domination*, pp. 2–3; NARA, RG226, entry 16, box 1472, no. 128585, OSS, R&A Branch, Regular Intelligence Reports, 'Malaya under the Japanese, March 1945', p. 6 and RG226, entry 19, box 297, R&A XL20728, *Notes on group attitudes in southern Malaya*, 2 October 1945, p. 6.

[143] Hartendorp, *Japanese occupation*, pp. 452–53.

given way to management by a village headman and his assistants. Although the Japanese tried to revive a modified version of the 10-house system for purposes both of census and counter-espionage, how far they succeeded is unclear. An initiative in General Ogawa's 1944 plan for Burma was to organize neighbourhood associations in Rangoon. The system was also extended to Insein, Pyapon and Maubin Districts, but this was not announced until February 1944 and so could have had little effect on the maintenance of order. Nor is it likely that the neighbourhood associations were able to enforce a commodity control programme, a designated part of their role from the end of 1943.[144]

Food and Control

The control Japanese administrators had over food and its distribution as rations, also examined in subsequent chapters, provided a lever which could be used to forestall possible social unrest. Although during the war rations fell continuously and to well below minimal nutritional requirements, rationing helped to diffuse possible protest by distributing some food widely within larger concentrations of population and by providing a nutritional floor for urban residents. Rationing was critical to the survival of many Southeast Asians. Because rationing was increasingly confined to cities, especially the larger ones, and Southeast Asia's population was overwhelmingly rural, the need to supply food was comparatively limited and distribution could concentrate in areas where the danger of disturbances was greatest. The collapse in exports led to widespread rural unemployment and many of those thrown out of work drifted to cities. Once there, these rural arrivals often found themselves outside the rationing system because they were not registered with the Japanese authorities. Although this created serious problems of hunger and famine, notably in Java, major problems were not reported, perhaps owing to censorship. The potential for protest was, however, low because dispossessed rural arrivals appear to have been unorganized and often were in a debilitated state on arrival in cities.

Large numbers of Southeast Asians worked for the Japanese, a common advantage of which was being paid in food. Amounts of food distributed in this way varied but even small quantities created a dependence on Japanese regimes and allowed them a degree of leverage through an ability to withhold food, a power which encouraged, among recipients at least, a tacit acceptance of the status quo. Working for the Japanese might be the only way for Singaporeans to obtain sufficient food. As one Singapore resident later recalled, the Japanese in effect said: 'If you don't work for us, you don't get

[144] OSS, R&A 2015, *Japanese administration of Burma*, pp. 32–33, 54, 61; Burma Intelligence Bureau, *Burma*, vol. 2, pp. 132–33.

any rice.'[145] Wages in food were particularly important in food-deficit areas including Java, Malaya and the Philippines. Large numbers of Javanese worked voluntarily as *romusha* to get food. Including these workers and other, forced-labour *romusha*, by November 1944 the Japanese provided rice for 2.6 million Javanese.[146]

In Singapore in March 1944, some 70,000 people were employed by Japanese companies or the military and most, if not all, had food priority. That also applied to another 60,000 Singaporeans, making the total for priority rationing around 130,000 or 38 per cent of the entire workforce. A small minority working for the army were especially favoured and had a monthly rice ration of 30.4 lbs (459.6 grams a day for a 30-day month). While the general ration provided far less than the bare minimum for survival, those with priority status received an officially listed daily ration of 420 grams (1,428 calories) of white rice and 1,922 calories overall, although they probably often sold some of their rations on the black market.[147]

Military Police and Security Organizations

Japanese military police operating in Southeast Asia were the *kempeitai* for the army and their navy equivalent, the *tokkeitai*. Each was charged with monitoring political loyalty, ensuring acquiescence to Japanese rule and countering dissent or anything construed as anti-Japanese. The two groups of military police had absolute authority and could act with near-total freedom from legal checks.[148] They were, together, instrumental in the maintenance of order in Southeast Asia and central to an explanation of why there was so little trouble during the occupation years. Fear of the military police was reinforced by the constant threat that any Japanese could exact punishment for the most trivial offence or perhaps just on a whim.

145 NAS, Oral History, Heng Chiang Ki, p. 75.

146 Kurasawa, 'Mobilization', p. 156; van der Eng, *Food supply*, p. 37; Sato, *War, nationalism*, p. 33.

147 Huff and Majima, *World War II Singapore*, pp. 39, 275–77, 335–52 and see table 7.9 for nutritional values of priority rations; NIDS, Sōchōshi dai 35 gō, *Shōnan tokubetsu shi wo chūshin to seru bukka taisaku* [Counter-measures for prices in Syonan Municipality], Nanpō Gunsei Sōkanbu Chōsabu (Kirita Naosaku), Shōwa 19. 03 (March 1944), passim; Nansei Gunsei –16 Japan, Southern Military Administration Chōsabu, Report no. 12: *Syonan ni okeru minzoku betsu saitei seikatsu jittai chōsa: Minzoku betsu jūyō seikatsu hitsujuhin ni kansuru kakaku sūryō oyobi hitsuju no teido no chōsa wo chūshin ni shite* [A study of the real state of the lowest living standard of ethnic groups in Syonan Municipality: a study focused on prices, quantity and degree of the need of daily necessities according to various ethnic groups], by Yamada Isamu, Kawai Mikio (Singapore: Southern Military Administration Chōsabu, October 1943), p. 9.

148 OSS, R&A 3186S, *Kempei*, p. 1.

There are three main reasons why Japan's military police could oversee Southeast Asian societies with relatively few personnel and sparing use of resources. One was that Southeast Asia's population was largely rural: low urbanization limited the scope for organized resistance. A second, more important, reason was the use of large numbers of Southeast Asians who received training from the *kempeitai*, had local knowledge and were in touch with day-to-day events. While some 3,000 *kempeitai* operated in Burma, Java had just 697.[149] They, however, employed 958 Indonesians who had worked for the colonial Dutch intelligence.[150]

The Japanese demanded complete control of the Indochinese police system in the autumn of 1941 and again in November 1942.[151] Each time, the French successfully resisted. Indochina retained its pre-war security service, the Sûreté générale, dreaded in its own right. Already in 1940, with the defeat of France and Japan's forcible entry to Indochina, the colonial authorities had moved to implement policies to neutralize any threat from the Vietnamese population, reinforcing the Sûreté générale and giving it wider powers.[152] With the arrival of Japanese soldiers, civilians had the *kempeitai* to fear as well.

In Malaya, the Japanese formed a Special Secret Police Corps made up of young, healthy recruits from the pre-war police force willing to swear loyalty to the Emperor. The Corps, directly under the authority of the Japanese army, were reported to be 'the most dreaded of all [the police] and notorious for their cruelty'.[153] In Malaya, a civil servant recalled that:

> One could not live in Negri Sembilan in the last months of 1945 without being reminded frequently of the legacy of reported atrocity which some Japanese had left behind them. At this street corner it was said a man had been chained to a tree to die by inches; in that building there had been torture and beating up. The *kempeitai*, in particular had left the FMSVF [Federated Malay States Volunteer Force] building for their 'interrogations' and the odour of sadism clung to it.[154]

Throughout Southeast Asia, the Japanese military police made extensive use of local informers. They had, it was reported to Dutch intelligence, 'native spies everywhere'.[155] Among Indochina's most effective Sûreté agents were *métis*

149 OSS, R&A 3186S, *Kempei*, pp. 2, 4.
150 Post, 'Policing society', p. 153.
151 AOM, NF/1102, 'Contrôle Japonais sur l'administration Française en Indochine', 14 September 1944, p. 3.
152 Marr, *Vietnam 1945*, p. 72.
153 OSS, R&A 2072, *Japanese administration in Malaya*, p. 13.
154 WL, Heussler Papers, MSS. Brit. Emp. s 480, J. M. Gullick, 'My time in Malaya', June 1970, pp. 32–33.
155 NIMH, 010A/10, Netherlands Forces Intelligence Service, 'Interrogation of three Boeginese survivors of a ship-wrecked crew of 10', 24 July 1944, p. 1; Sukarno makes a similar point: Sukarno, *Autobiography*, p. 181.

(people of mixed Euro-Vietnamese heritage), abandoned by their French fathers but offered education and employment by the colonial government.[156] The military police in Malaya particularly used women working in restaurants, bars, brothels and offices as informers.[157] In Burma, as well as a system of informers distributed two to a square mile, marketplaces had white wooden boxes in which people could leave names.[158]

The third, and most important, explanation for the effectiveness of the *kempeitai* and *tokkeitai* in maintaining order was that these security services routinely employed extreme methods of interrogation and torture. These were so brutal that few dared oppose or openly question Japanese rule. In Singapore, although agitation might have been anticipated because of the city's overwhelmingly Chinese makeup, acceptance of Japanese rule was total.[159] Burma's civilian population was described as 'thoroughly cowed' by the police.[160] In both Singapore and Burma, the civilian reaction is unsurprising: under *kempeitai* control, even Shanghai, notorious for an extensive underworld, relapsed into comparative law and order.[161] While it was wise to avoid the military police at all cost, as one moved about Singapore, any Japanese were to be given a wide berth. Military sentries might brutally slap a person and then require hours of standing in the sun for not bowing or not having bowed to satisfaction.[162] As a Singaporean recalled, '[I]t was just the law of the sword, they used to chop off heads and all that kind of thing . . . a kind of strict military discipline control over the city'.[163] As stories of *kempeitai* torture and beheadings spread, people in Indochina wondered if even the oppressive French might have been better.[164]

Because the security services stood behind the system of *tonari-gumi*, its effectiveness as an instrument of social control cannot be fully evaluated. For the policing of neighbourhood associations, the *kempeitai* were the ultimate enforcers of group responsibility.[165] In Burma's system of ten-house *gaungs*, it was the duty of village headmen to arrest those who were unco-operative and send them not to the police but to the Japanese.[166]

156 Marr, *Vietnam 1945*, p. 72.
157 NARA, RG226, entry 19, box 147, R&A XL10747, *Interrogation on Malaya*, 1 June 1945, p. 5.
158 Khin Myo Chit, *Three years*, p. 18; OSS, R&A 1713, *Structure of the government of Burma*, pp. 49–50.
159 OSS, R&A 2423, *Singapore under Japanese domination*, p. 1.
160 OSS, R&A 1713, *Structure of the government of Burma*, p. 50.
161 OSS, R&A 3186S, *Kempei*, p. 3.
162 NAS, Oral History, Wong Kee Hung, p. 36; see also Baey Liam Peck, p. 34.
163 NAS, Oral History, George Edwin Bogaars, pp. 26, 39.
164 Marr, *Vietnam 1945*, pp. 91–92.
165 OSS, R&A 3186S, *Kempei*, p. 2.
166 OSS, R&A 2015, *Japanese administration of Burma*, 10 July 1944, pp. 32–33.

The response of the military police and army to protest by Southeast Asians was truckloads of troops and arrests.[167] Anyone arrested by the Japanese was in danger of being brutally tortured and then killed. In Singapore, someone in Bukit Timah raised a Chinese flag: two days later the Japanese came and 'took over and then they slaughtered all the Chinese in Bukit Timah'.[168] When informed (incorrectly) that a Singapore man and his brother were communists, the *kempeitai*, after arresting the suspects, burned alive several women and children in their house.[169] After the March 1945 coup in Indochina, the *kempeitai* turned the Saigon Chamber of Commerce into a prison, rounded up Frenchmen suspected of working for the resistance and brutally tortured them.[170]

Torture, perhaps followed by decapitation as a favoured form of execution, was systematically and routinely used by the military police and also practised by the Japanese military. Terror tactics were a deliberate policy to intimidate Singapore's population in order to secure social and economic control, as Lee Kuan Yew notes.[171] In Malaya, where the Japanese were wary of the Chinese and less concerned to win over the local population than in some other countries, torture was widely known to be an acknowledged procedure and was encouraged.[172] The Japanese military could, and often did, torture and execute Southeast Asians, but the *kempeitai* was the institution particularly associated with these practices. During the war, an escalation of extreme measures in large areas of Southeast Asia was partly because the *kempeitai* – as Friend observes for the Philippines and Indonesia and was also true of the German SS – 'tended to develop independent power and a distinct outlook, composed of fascist spirituality, nationalist fanaticism, free-floating sadism, and power-grabbing separatism'.[173] An alternative, but incomplete and unconvincing, explanation for Japanese behaviour is that security organizations were manned by partially literate, almost entirely unaccountable, Japanese peasants.[174]

Numerous independent contemporary accounts of *kempeitai* torture, graphic and harrowing, suggest that it would have been better to die immediately than be tortured, even if one might have survived.[175] In fact, execution

167 Lucas, *One soul*, p. 49.
168 NAS, Oral History, Baey Lian Peck, pp. 20–21.
169 Low and Cheng, *This Singapore*, pp. 48–49.
170 Allen, *End of the war*, p. 106.
171 Lee, *Singapore story*, p. 71. See also Hartendorp, *Japanese occupation*, p. 454; Burma Intelligence Bureau, *Burma*, vol. 2, pp. 41–51.
172 ANM, 1957/0572010, 'Brief review of Chinese affairs', *c*. September 1945, pp. 2–3.
173 Friend, *Blue-eyed enemy*, p. 68; Milward, *German economy*, pp. 155–56. On torture in Japan of foreigners, see Grew, *Ten years*, pp. 459–60.
174 Ooi, *Japanese occupation*, p. 54.
175 Hartendorp, *Japanese occupation*, pp. 606, 642.

frequently followed torture, and Burma's prison population fell because of this.[176] It was standard practice to inflict brutal torture on anyone suspected of transgression before interrogating them. In Burma, a culture of suspicion was fed by the country's networks of informers and a Japanese 'spymania'.[177] To be suspected of any crime – for example, dealing in British or American currency, listening to the BBC or smuggling – was almost certain to lead to torture.[178] If one person in a house was wanted the Japanese might torture everyone.[179] The pulling out of a victim's fingernails was frequent and vicious beatings usual. Water torture, followed by jumping on the stomach until water came out of the victim's orifices, was said to be the most dreaded of the Japanese methods.[180] In Burma, a witness of any crime or alleged crime stayed in the hands of the *kempeitai* for an average of three months during which he underwent all conceivable forms of torture.[181] Japanese police in Celebes were known as '*toekang poekoel*' (craftsmen in beating).[182]

Contemporary accounts document Japanese torture. These are so numerous, and the further corroboration by testimony to the Tokyo War Crimes Trial (International Military Tribunal for the Far East) so compelling, that it is clear that torture was institutionalized.[183] Men were typically the victims of torture but women were not exempt, as shown by the account of weeks of appalling interrogation of Sybil Kathigasu, a nurse suspected of treating injured Malayan guerrillas.[184] In Indochina, torture and murder were commonly inflicted on civilians in the name of quashing espionage, and rape, mainly of French women, was also frequent.[185] Of the many accounts of torture, the following helps to elucidate why many Southeast Asians so feared and hated the Japanese:

> Pinching the back of your hands with pliers was only the beginning. Gashing all over the body with a knife and sprinkling salt over the gaping wounds, cutting the limbs gradually beginning from the fingers and toes, singeing the body, pouring boiling water on the body, putting the person in the scorching sun to be thrashed non-stop the whole day, suspending

176 Burma Intelligence Bureau, *Burma*, vol. 2, pp. 41–51.
177 Ooi, *Japanese occupation*, pp. 49, 53, 58, 82; Pe, *Narrative*, pp. 22–23; Nu, *Saturday's son*, p. 106.
178 Chin, *Malaya upside down*, p. 124; Malayan Union, *Annual report on education . . . 1946*, p. 3; NARA, RG226, entry 16, box 144, 'Conditions in the Philippine Islands', 23 August 1942, p. 9.
179 Khin Myo Chit, *Three years*, pp. 40–43.
180 He, *Syonan interlude*, p. 184.
181 Pe, *Narrative*, pp. 22–23.
182 NIMH, 010A/18, Netherlands Forces Intelligence Service, Nofis interrogation report no. 184, part 3, 18 October 1944, p. 5.
183 Totani, *Tokyo War Crimes Trial*, pp. 168–69, 181.
184 Kathigasu, *No dram of mercy*, pp. 141–49; see also Khin Myo Chit, *Three years*, p. 44.
185 Totani, *Tokyo War Crimes Trial*, pp. 181.

> a person with feet up and beating him with an iron rod, and severing the joints of the limbs, tying a man down to a ladder and keeping him in the water with his face downwards were some of their methods ... And to think that in every town and village through-out Burma there would be a good number of people who had gone through all this ... In Rangoon there was a spacious ground with bamboo fencing at the junction of the Kokine Road and Goodliffe Road which was a miniature Hell on earth. People living around and those who had to pass that way heard the piercing shrieks of agonised victims.[186]

The *kempeitai* had, however, what for them were lighter moments. N. I. Low remembered a man pointed out as a mechanic who had once worked for the Singapore rubber magnate, Tan Kah Kee:

> This man's hands were tied together by a rope; the free end of the rope was fastened to the seat of a motor-cycle ... As [the motor cycle] gathered speed, the mechanic had to run faster and faster, finally to stumble and fall and be dragged along. The sight of a man frantically running a losing race with a motor-cycle was a welcome change for the Kempeitai, relieving the tedium of their severer duties.[187]

Conclusion

There always was a chasm between the philosophies and conduct, economic and cultural, of the peoples of the Southeast Asian countries occupied by Japan and those of the Japanese. During the war, the gulf was all the greater because the military dominated Japanese thinking in the administration of Southeast Asia. Ba Maw, although an apologist for Japan, understood this:

> As for the Japanese militarists, few people were so mentally race-bound, so one-dimensional in their thinking ... The militarists saw everything only in a Japanese perspective ... For them there was only one way to do a thing, the Japanese way; only one goal and interest, the Japanese interest; only one destiny for the East Asian countries, to become so many Manchukuos [Manchurians] or Koreas tied forever to Japan.[188]

Southeast Asians needed, in Japan's view, to think and act like Japanese, to implement new modes of economic organization, to adopt a new outlook and language, and to internalize a new set of values.

Japan's economic and cultural objectives in Southeast Asia were impossible to achieve quickly, or perhaps at all, and certainly not under conditions of scarcity, repression, shortages of trained administrators and the backlash from

[186] Khin Myo Chit, *Three years*, pp. 42–43; see also Nu, *Burma*, pp. 22–23; Ba Maw, *Breakthrough*, pp. 278–79.

[187] Low, *When Singapore*, p. 15.

[188] Ba Maw, *Breakthrough*, p. 185.

Japanese military defeats. It has been suggested that even if General MacArthur had not returned to the Philippines, Filipino resistance, active and passive, might have toppled the Japanese regime.[189] In Taiwan, Lee Kuan Yew pointed out, Japan had managed to gain an acceptance of its administration and culture but it never succeeded in doing so in Korea. He went on to suggest that Malaya was a sufficiently young, diverse and culturally malleable society that acceptance of Japanese rule and thinking would have come within 50 years.[190] Whether the same would have been true of other Southeast Asian societies is problematic. Because of their well-established cultural traditions, it might have taken a very long time, if ever, for Japan to transform them sufficiently to effect genuine social and cultural incorporation into a Greater East Asia Co-Prosperity Sphere.

[189] Rōyama and Takéuchi, *Philippine polity*, pp. x–xviii.
[190] Lee, *Singapore story*, p. 78.

3

Finance for Japan's Occupation

Even before the outbreak of war, Japanese financial policy was clear: Southeast Asians would themselves provide much of the finance for war in the region. This chapter explores Japanese financial policies and their implications in three main respects. One is to identify wartime, 'market-purchased', resource transfers from Southeast Asians to the Japanese. Excluded from these transfers are resources that the Japanese directly confiscated and labour extraction. Although Japanese exploitation through transfers quantified in this chapter fell short of Nazi levels, it was still substantial. In Indochina, during one year transfers reached as much as over a third of GDP.

Second, the chapter analyses how Japan financed resource extraction. Its financial techniques of occupation costs (the costs of occupation being paid by the occupied country), military scrip (unbacked military notes) and bilateral clearing arrangements were similar to those of Nazi Germany. Money creation was, however, considerably less important in Europe than in occupied Southeast Asia.

Third, this chapter quantifies the monetary and inflationary consequences of Japanese financial policies for Southeast Asia. Even though transfers to Japan were chiefly financed by printing money, Southeast Asian inflation was checked to some degree because of the usefulness of Japanese-sanctioned money as a medium of exchange and because of Japanese legal restrictions on use of alternative currencies. Legal restrictions were the essence of Keynes' plan for how Britain should pay for World War II.[1] Unlike Keynes' forced saving programme, however, in Southeast Asia, Japan looked predominantly to seigniorage – the ability of government, with a monetary monopoly, to finance expenditure by issuing money – as a way to pay for war. Adequate revenue from seigniorage depends on avoiding too much inflation and this, in turn, relies on the public being willing to hold, or being forced to hold, currency issued by the government. Japanese restrictions to ensure that Southeast Asians used, and so held at least for a period, government-issued money also featured in the Sino-Japanese War and echoed coercive powers

[1] Keynes, 'How to pay'.

employed historically, for example during the Terror in revolutionary France.[2] In Southeast Asia, legal restrictions on the use of money help to explain why hyperinflation appeared only late in the war.

Legal restrictions backed by strict enforcement were not, however, the whole Southeast Asian story. In the rice-producing areas of Thailand, Indochina and Burma, peasant rice growers held Japanese notes as a store of value. This peasant holding of money helped to keep inflation multiples close to those of money supply increase.

Occupation Patterns, Banking, Exchange Rates and Scrip

Patterns of occupation finance followed other Japanese administrative arrangements. The pre-war governments which remained in place in Thailand and Indochina were left to determine how to pay for resource transfers specified by Japan. By contrast, in Malaya, Burma, Indonesia and the Philippines, Japanese military administrations directly controlled finance and the issue of currency.

Among Japan's first occupation acts was to revalue the yen and in each Southeast Asian country set a unit of the prevailing currency equal to one yen. Compared to 1937 exchange rates, in different countries the yen gained from 35 per cent to 101 per cent in value, making goods in Southeast Asia cheap for Japan. The amount of overvaluation, if not overvaluation itself, was, however, partly by chance, since a reason for currency parity was to facilitate eventual monetary union in East Asia. Exchange rates were, in any event, secondary for Japan, because of its intention to supply few goods to Southeast Asia. Even so, had Japan, at some future date, paid its wartime debts to countries in the region, the amounts would have been substantially reduced by the enforced devaluation of Southeast Asian currencies. Writing in 1950, the British financial advisor to Thailand cited that country's wartime status as a creditor to Japan and observed that Japan's devaluation of the baht was 'co-prosperity with a vengeance, Japan getting the prosperity and leaving Siam with only the co-'.[3]

In occupied Western Europe, Germany took over the banks and used local stock markets as tools to effect financial repression through forcing citizens of occupied countries to hold government bonds at negative real interest rates.[4] Japan, however, lacked these options in Southeast Asia and, partly because of this, made little use of local financial institutions. Southeast Asia's principal

[2] Sargent and Velde, 'Macroeconomic features', pp. 503–7.

[3] Kingdom of Thailand, *Report of the financial adviser 1941–1950*, p. 53; Kingdom of Thailand, Department of Commerce and Statistics, *Statistical yearbook 1939–40 to 1944*, pp. 168–69.

[4] Bloc and Hoselitz, *Economics*, p. 61; Oosterlinck, 'French stock exchanges' and 'Sovereign debts'.

banks were European and assuming control of them would not have helped the Japanese much. The European banks were merely branches with head offices in the metropolitan countries and, as so-called exchange banks, their chief function was to finance foreign trade. They did limited deposit banking, made few long-term loans, and served chiefly European customers (now either outside Southeast Asia or interned) along with, through a comprador system, a few Chinese. After occupation, European banks, cut off from their head offices and without European personnel, lacked both institutional structure and assets. Although in Indonesia the cultivation banks had assets in the form of crops still to be produced, there was no market for these after occupation and the banks went out of business. Stock markets in Southeast Asia were poorly developed or non-existent and so, like the banks, offered at most restricted scope to help in financing the war.

Throughout Southeast Asia, pre-war banks associated in any way with Allied countries were shut down.[5] This meant the closure, and eventual liquidation, of almost all European banks. These included the three great British banks – the Hongkong and Shanghai, the Chartered Bank of India, Australia and China, and the Mercantile Bank of India – as well as the Java Bank, the Netherlands Trading Society and the National City Bank of New York. Since pre-war Southeast Asian banking had revolved around European banks, their closure largely eliminated banking in Southeast Asia.[6] The Yokohama Specie Bank and the Bank of Taiwan were made the vehicles through which the military and Ministry of Finance in Tokyo organized banking in Southeast Asia.[7]

The Japanese allowed local Asian banks to re-open during 1942 and 1943 but recognized that they were of slight value. Asian banks were tiny compared to the European banks and served a restricted, ethnically specific, clientele. Furthermore, the Asian banks had relied on their European counterparts, and so the London head offices of these banks, as 'central banks'. After re-opening, local Asian banks did relatively little business, except in Thailand, where, helped by inflation, the number of incorporated commercial banks increased from three in 1939 to nine by 1945.[8]

5 Huff, 'Monetization' and 'Financial transition' discusses pre-war Southeast Asian financial structure in detail.

6 OSS, assemblage 44, R&A 2629, *Financial programs of Japan*, pp. 227–28, R&A 2072, *Japanese administration in Malaya*, p. 28 and R&A 1433, *Political and economic changes effected by the Japanese in Malaya*, pp. 30–31.

7 Anon., 'Monetary situation in the south', p. 561; OSS, assemblage 44, R&A 2629, *Financial programs of Japan*, pp. 227–28, R&A 2072, *Japanese administration in Malaya*, p. 28 and *Political and economic changes in Malaya*, pp. 30–31.

8 BT, Bank of Thailand, *Economic report, 1945*, p. 29 and *1947*, pp. 10–11; Kingdom of Thailand, *Report of the financial adviser 1941–1950*, p. 56; Emery, *Financial institutions*, pp. 567–68.

Money in Thailand and Indochina continued to be issued by their own monetary authorities. In 1942, Thailand established the Bank of Thailand as a central bank to supply currency but probably also to avoid the establishment of a Japanese-controlled bank and as a symbol of nationalism.[9] During the war, however, and for a time thereafter, the Bank did not fully function as a central bank. It undertook no business pertaining to commercial banks and could do almost nothing to combat wartime inflation. The Bank's early post-war functions were the issue and management of notes and government loans, the keeping of government balances and reserves, and the control of foreign exchange transactions. In the judgement of the British Financial Advisor, writing in 1947: 'we have no one in the country with even an inkling of what is really meant by Central Banking, with the one exception of Price Viwat' [first governor of the Bank of Thailand].[10] In time, however, the Bank's role expanded. Viwat was frightened by Thailand's high wartime inflation and anxious to restore financial stability as quickly as possible after 1945. During the post-war years, the Bank, under Viwat's leadership and that of Dr Puey Ungphakorn, stood as an important institutional legacy of Japanese occupation and assumed an important role in controlling the money supply and inflation.[11]

For Southeast Asia other than Thailand and Indochina, Japan printed military scrip, possibly beginning as early as January 1941.[12] Scrip, literally campaign money given to Japan's invading forces, was legal tender only in the occupied territory for which it was issued. As before the war, currencies were denominated in rupees, dollars, guilders and pesos for Burma, Malaya, Indonesia and the Philippines respectively. With 'appropriate' pictures – banana plants for Malaya and Indonesia, pagodas for Burma – scrip looked markedly different from pre-war notes. It incorporated 'none of the refinements of the Japanese-sponsored currencies in North and Central Occupied China'.[13] Print quality was, the Japanese acknowledged, 'appalling' and it deteriorated as the war continued.[14] Before then, however, Japan's occupation currencies attracted derisive names: 'banana money' in Malaya and Indonesia, 'Mickey Mouse money' in the Philippines.

9 Muscat, *Fifth tiger*, pp. 67–68.

10 BE, OV25/21, W.A.M. Doll letters to the Bank of England Governor, Sir Otto Niemeyer, 28 April 1947, 25 March 1946 and 'Note on the establishment of the Central Bank of Thailand, 25 September 1942; and see Yang, *Multiple exchange rate system*, pp. 17, 24.

11 Warr and Nidhiprabha, *Thailand's macroeconomic miracle*, p. 27.

12 Shibata, *Senryōchi kin'yū seisaku*, p. 532; Shimazaki, *En no shinryaku shi*, pp. 364–94; Longmuir, *Money trail*, p. 32.

13 King, *Money*, p. 23.

14 NIDS, Nansei Gunsei –17 Japan, Southern Military Administration Chōsabu, Report no. 23: *Zairai tsūka kaishu mondai ni tsute* [Withdrawal of local money] by Higuchi Gorō (Singapore, December 1943), p. 7.

Before long, the Yokohama Specie Bank, and in the Philippines the Bank of Taiwan, replaced the military for the issue of scrip. A specialist bank, the Southern Regions Development Bank, was set up to finance Japanese business, industry and long-term resource development in Southeast Asia. However, Southeast Asian economic development did not materialize on the scale envisaged and probably partly because of this the Bank took over the issue of scrip. A further reason may have been that because Bank loans in Southeast Asia were in scrip a separate issuing authority was unnecessary.

The Southern Regions Development Bank started issuing scrip in April 1942, although in some areas not until 1943. Notes remained identical to those used by the military and the Yokohama Specie Bank and were still printed in Tokyo.[15] Like the Yokohama Specie Bank, the Southern Regions Development Bank functioned as no more than a conduit through which currency passed on its way to the military and into circulation.[16]

Over the first year or so of the war, in the military-occupied countries pre-war colonial currencies were allowed to circulate at par alongside Japanese military scrip. Some foreign currencies also circulated, for example the US dollar in the Philippines.[17] Subsequently, however, scrip drove colonial monies from open circulation through a combination of the operation of Gresham's Law that bad money drives out good and, as later discussed, because of strong Japanese coercion beginning around late 1942.

Payments and Transfer of Goods to Japan

In Malaya, Indonesia, the Philippines and Burma, the Japanese transferred resources to themselves simply by printing the required amount of currency (scrip). Acquiring currency to spend in Thailand and Indochina was slightly more complicated. However, as this section shows, the effect was like issuing scrip, since Japan gave no money or credits convertible into tangible goods in exchange for local Thai or Indochinese currency. This section goes on to identify large Southeast Asian payments to the Japanese and the need to finance these by money creation.

[15] Shibata, 'Monetary policy', p. 712.

[16] Swan, 'Thai-Japan relations', pp. 320–21; Cohen, *Japan's economy*, pp. 95–96; Ránki, *Economics*, p. 303; OSS, R&A 2451, *Control of inflation in Japan*, pp. A41–A42 and assemblage 44, R&A 2629, *Financial programs of Japan*, p. 238.

[17] OSS, assemblage 44, R&A 2629, *Financial programs of Japan*, pp. 215–16, 237; Cribb, 'Political dimensions', p. 114; Longmuir, *Money trail*, p. 125; Romualdez, 'Financial problems', p. 460.

Occupation Costs, Bilateral Clearing Arrangements and Yen Credits

Japan used baht in Thailand and piastres in Indochina to buy goods it exported and to meet local military and administrative (occupation) costs. When Japanese officials, after some negotiation with the Thai or Indochinese governments, specified currency requirements, the Yokohama Specie Bank credited at the Bank of Japan in Tokyo the accounts of the Bank of Thailand or Banque de l'Indochine with the yen equivalent of baht or piastres to be given to Japan. These Southeast Asian 'central banks' then credited the Yokohama Specie Bank in Bangkok or Saigon with local currency for military use.[18]

Yen credited to Thailand and Indochina were 'special' but, in reality, merely paper credits without practical use. They could neither be spent in Japan nor used to purchase imports from Japan.

Although occupation costs typically exceeded actual military and administrative costs, bilateral clearing agreements negotiated with Thailand and Indochina were potentially an even more powerful means of extraction. They gave Japan purchasing power in these two countries that was limited only by three factors: the physical capacity to provide goods and services to Japan; how much of these goods Japan could use; and the availability of shipping to carry goods.[19] As such, bilateral agreements suited not just wartime finance but Japan's long-term goals of integrating Southeast Asia into the yen bloc and creating an empire in East Asia.

Payments to Japan

Thailand, Indochina and Indonesia provided the greatest volume of resources to the Japanese. Wartime national income estimates can be used to evaluate transfers as a share of GDP (Table 3.1). For all three countries, exploitation was substantial at arbitrary, wartime exchange rates, and even larger at pre-war (market) exchange rates. Between 1942 and 1945, Thailand's payments to the Japanese averaged 6 per cent of GDP at wartime rates and a little over 9 per cent at 1937 rates. Payments made by Indochina at Japanese wartime rates rose from 9.1 per cent of GDP in 1942 to 25.4 per cent by 1945. At 1937 market exchange rates, 1945 payments were over a third of GDP. Indochina made such large payments, probably the biggest in Southeast Asia, because it was a principal Japanese military and logistical base in Southeast Asia; because until

[18] BE, OV25/9, Extract from *Bangkok Times*, 'Japan-Thailand economic co-operation. New agreement now signed. The system of settlement', 4 May 1942; Kingdom of Thailand, *Report of the financial adviser 1941–1950*, p. 55; AOM, 1 AFFECO/289, Franco-Japanese accords: 'Modalities d'application de l'exchange de lettres, 1942' and 'Note: Négociation d'un nouvel accord financier entre l'Indochine et le Japon', Vichy, 23 December 1942.

[19] Viwat, *Wiwatthanachaiyanuson*, pp. 399–402; OSS, R&A 4409, *Financial relations between Siam and Japan*, p. 6.

Table 3.1 *Southeast Asia payments to Japan 1941–1945*

a) 000 Thailand baht

	GDP current prices	Yen credits	Yen credits as a % of GDP at wartime exchange rates	Yen credits as a % of GDP at 1937 exchange rates
1942	2,531,956	61,000	2.4	3.8
1943	4,218,629	176,050	4.2	6.5
1944	7,119,363	520,840	7.3	11.4
1945	12,505,066	800,910	6.4	10.0

b) 000 Indochina piastres

	GDP current prices	Occupation costs and trade surplus	Occupation costs and trade surplus as a % of GDP at wartime exchange rates	Occupation costs and trade surplus as a % of GDP at 1937 exchange rates
1941	1,919,810	183,503	9.6	13.1
1942	2,267,014	205,213	9.1	12.4
1943	2,829,739	191,014	6.8	9.2
1944	3,423,568	405,377	11.8	16.2
1945	3,710,565	943,948	25.4	34.8

c) 000 Indonesia guilders

	GDP current prices	Change in money supply	Change in money supply as a % of GDP at wartime exchange rates	Change in money supply as a % of GDP at 1937 exchange rates
1942	4,330,250			
1943	8,849,400	990,097	11.2	21.4
1944	23,517,900	1,302,015	5.5	10.6
1945	145,778,780	1,176,991	0.8	1.5

Source: Chapter appendix.

1944 it was Japan's largest single wartime source of rice; and because the pro-Vichy colonial government was in no position to resist demands from Tokyo.[20]

[20] Robequain, *Economic development*, pp. 367–73. By 1942, Japan almost completely controlled Indochina's surpluses (Chapter 4). See also Decoux, *A la barre de l'Indochine*, pp. 440–50.

Table 3.2 *Thailand and Indochina composition of payments to Japan 1941–1945*

	Payments to Japan	Occupation costs %	Trade surplus %
a) 000 Thailand baht			
1942	61,000	14.8	85.2
1943	176,050	93.0	7.0
1944	520,840	87.2	12.8
1945	800,910	96.8	3.2
b) 000 Indochina piastres			
1941	183,503	31.2	68.8
1942	205,213	41.7	58.3
1943	191,014	61.4	38.6
1944	405,377	88.8	11.2
1945	943,948	99.1	0.9

Source: Chapter appendix.

During the war, the composition of Thai and Indochinese payments to Japan altered radically as Japan lost control of Pacific shipping lanes and increased military expenditure and troop numbers in Southeast Asia in response to the apparent near certainty of Allied invasion. Initially, available merchant shipping and Japan's war needs at home, mainly for rice, made trade surpluses the chief component of payments (Table 3.2). By the last two years of the war, however, occupation costs comprised over 90 per cent of payments because Japan no longer had shipping to transport goods from Southeast Asia and because Japan's emphasis shifted towards the defence of Southeast Asia. After reaching 11.2 per cent of GDP in 1943, or nearly twice that at pre-war rates, payments from Indonesia fell sharply. Japan's chief demand on Indonesia was for oil, but during 1944 systematic American submarine and air attacks decimated the Japanese tanker fleet, cutting Japan off from Indonesian oil (Chapter 1).[21]

A number of resource transfers from Southeast Asia to Japan cannot be reliably quantified; the payments shown in Table 3.1 are a lower bound of total transfers. Although the plunder of commodities was not especially great – it included, for example, four months' supply of crude oil from Indonesia and between 60,000 and 150,000 tons of rubber from Malaya – it was considerable

[21] Nenryō Konwa Kai, *Kaigun nenryō shi*, Part one, p. 664; USSBS, *Effects of strategic bombing*, pp. 41–44.

in regard to all types of transport.[22] Rolling stock and rails were taken from around Southeast Asia for Japanese railway construction projects in the region. The Japanese military took most motorized transport and ships. Additionally, a high proportion of Southeast Asians did at least some 'voluntary' work for the Japanese war effort and large numbers were co-opted as forced labour (Chapter 9). That amounted, at the least, to a tax on Southeast Asians, as did forced deliveries of food at below market prices.

Why Weren't Payments from Southeast Asia Larger?

Total resource transfers to Japan seem unlikely anywhere in Southeast Asia to have approached the 1943 high point of the over 50 per cent of GDP that Nazi Germany extracted from France through occupation costs set far above the actual cost of occupation.[23] Even in Indochina, Japan was unable to achieve exploitation on such a scale.[24] There were four main reasons for the comparatively smaller payments from Southeast Asia to Japan than France to Germany, all of them economic rather than financial. One was that in Southeast Asia a low standard of living limited available surpluses that could be appropriated. Second, Southeast Asia's highly specialized monoeconomies, which before the war exported mainly rice, rubber, tin and sugar, produced all these commodities in far greater quantities than the Japanese economy could use. Third, by 1944 Japan found it difficult to carry home even those commodities it needed because of severe shortages of merchant shipping. Fourth, rapid initial conquests boxed Japan into diverting resources to try to maintain its vast Pacific defensive perimeter.

Financing Payments

War can be financed by selling bonds at home or internationally, through taxation, and by printing money. In Southeast Asia, the Japanese relied heavily, and increasingly, on money creation and its associated seigniorage. Table 3.3 details this for Thailand and Indochina, the two countries for which data exist. In 1940 in Thailand, the budget had already increased dramatically due to spending on defence. During the war, in both Thailand and Indochina government revenue lagged well behind expenditure. Conventional government expenditure alone gave rise to modest budget deficits. These combined with occupation costs and trade surpluses with Japan to create large budget deficits. Currency issues, measured in Table 3.3 by the annual change in money supply,

22 Milward, *War, economy*, p. 165.

23 Occhino, Oosterlinck and White, 'How much', p. 7.

24 For discussion of this, see LHC, MAGIC, 'Economic value of Indochina to Japan', 5 July 1944, pp. 13–16.

Table 3.3 *Thailand and Indochina methods of financing government expenditure and payments to Japan 1941–1945*

a) million Thailand baht

	Conventional government expenditure	Yen credits	Total government expenditure	Government revenue % of expenditure	Money % of expenditure	Gold from Japan % of expenditure
1941	198.9		198.9	80.9	31.5	
1942	200.0	61.0	261.0	56.5	36.5	5.7
1943	261.1	176.1	437.1	48.4	60.6	6.6
1944	390.7	520.8	911.6	31.4	56.7	6.6
1945	425.2	800.9	1,226.1	25.7	75.7	2.0

b) million Indochina piastres

	Conventional government expenditure	Occupation costs and trade surplus	Total government expenditure	Government revenue % of expenditure	Money % of expenditure
1941	151	183.5	334.5	45.1	19.8
1942	181	205.2	386.2	46.1	65.7
1943	171.6	91.0	362.7	42.9	78.6
1944	219.1	405.4	624.5	31.1	51.5
1945	299.7	943.9	1,243.7	19.3	75.8

Note: Money is the change in money supply and from official statistics. Columns 4 (government revenue as a percentage of total government expenditure) and 5 (money as a percentage of total government expenditure) do not add to 100% in any calendar year. But they average 101% over the five years for Thailand and 95% for Indochina. Some increases in money supplies must have leaked out into the hands of merchants, shopkeepers, black market operators and the like, but the numbers strongly indicate that money creation was used to finance government operations. There were also small sales of bonds in the two countries but data for these sales are not available.

Source: Chapter appendix.

largely filled the gap. From 1943 onwards, in Thailand and Indochina money creation financed half to three-quarters of total government spending.[25] The proportion of government finance obtained from printing money was almost certainly as large, and probably larger, in the four military-administered Southeast Asian countries, since there Japan had merely to issue scrip as required.

Even if Japan had not favoured the 'direct means' of selling special yen and issuing scrip, alternatives to this financing of expenditure through money creation were limited. Neither the Thai and Indochinese governments nor Japanese military administrations had any possibility of borrowing internationally. Although in Japan war finance depended on financial institutions' purchases of government bonds, nowhere in occupied Asia was their sale attempted on any scale.[26] Given the elimination of most of the pre-war banks in Southeast Asia, this is hardly a surprise.

Japanese lack of interest in bond finance was not, however, entirely shared by Southeast Asian governments which, beginning in 1943, looked to soak up excess purchasing power and restrict inflation. Doubts over the viability of bond sales in Indochina, and the advisability of their limited use, were confirmed by experience in Burma.[27] In August 1943, bonds issued by the Ba Maw government went on sale in Rangoon and rural areas. While the local press hailed the issue as a great success, the absence of further issues suggests otherwise.[28] Thailand's government issued 30 million baht of 3 per cent saving bonds in 1944. It also gave bonds at 1 per cent interest to compensate for the February 1945 demonetization of 1,000-baht notes.[29] The main example of bond finance was in the Philippines. Japan did not liquidate the pre-war state-owned Philippine National Bank, which was made to purchase most of a substantial amount of bonds issued by the Laurel government.[30] However, with the partial exception of Philippine bonds, none of the wartime Southeast Asian saving, taxation or bond schemes went far towards reducing the need to finance through money creation.

Governments and Japanese administrators did, however, try to use taxation and savings campaigns to raise resources. Taxation was difficult because the wartime collapse in exports and per capita income largely destroyed pre-war

[25] Cf. BT, Bank of Thailand, *Economic report, 1945*, p. 24: '[T]he Government resorted to printing paper money to meet their revenue deficits'.

[26] Cohen, *Japan's economy*, pp. 88–90; OSS, R&A 2451, *Control of inflation in Japan*, p. A42; USSBS, *Effects of strategic bombing*, p. 91.

[27] Le, *Impact*, p. 244.

[28] Burma Intelligence Bureau, *Burma*, vol. 2, pp. 108–9.

[29] BT, Bank of Thailand, *Economic report, 1945*, p. 28; Viwat, *Wiwatthanachaiyanuson*, p. 91; Kingdom of Thailand, *Report of the financial adviser 1941–1950*, p. 53.

[30] Romualdez, 'Financial problems', p. 459; OSS, assemblage 44, R&A 2629, *Financial programs of Japan*, pp. 245–46.

Southeast Asian tax structures.[31] In response, the Japanese made considerable efforts to substitute for these in order to limit money creation. Both the Asian news media and Allied intelligence describe numerous saving schemes, for example in March 1944 a 'gigantic saving campaign' in Malaya.[32] Taxes included 'voluntary' gifts levied mainly on Chinese businessmen, but also Singapore's Chettiar Association, as well as the extensive use of lotteries. Gambling was taxed, as were amusement parks, cockpits, bicycles, hand carts, taxi dancers (women at public dances with whom men purchased a ticket to dance), restaurants and coffee shops, the last three associated with Singapore's striking wartime increase in prostitution.[33]

Dynamics of Japanese Finance for Occupation and War

Governments and military administrations, Keynes remarked, rely on seigniorage to finance themselves when no other methods exist.[34] That was not, as indicated above, strictly true in Southeast Asia. However, for much of the war the issue of currency and resultant seigniorage was an effective, as well as near costless, way for Japan to tax the mass of the population and finance occupation.[35]

Links between Money Demand, Inflation and Seigniorage

The links between money demand, inflation and seigniorage clarify how Japan financed military expenditure in Southeast Asia and why it faced increasing difficulty in obtaining this finance. Real money balances, or money's actual purchasing power, are defined as the face or nominal value of money divided by the price level. The term real balances is used to denote the proportion of their income that people wish to hold as cash. Typically, real balances fall in response to inflation: people are less willing to hold cash when its real value (what it will buy) declines. A desire to offload money in response to its falling real value implies an increase in money's velocity of circulation, that is to say the speed at which money changes hands within the economy, and this makes

31 NIDS, Nansei Gunsei –15 Japan, Southern Military Administration Chōsabu, Report no. 6: *Sumatra Higashi Kaigan Shū wo chūshin to seru inflation mondai ni tsuite* [Problems of inflation in the east coast residency, Sumatra] by Higuchi Gorō (Singapore: Southern Military Administration Chōsabu, June 1943), p. 39.

32 OSS, assemblage 44, R&A 2629, *Financial programs of Japan*, p. 211.

33 On 'voluntary' gifts, see Tan, *Extortion* and on a Chettiar donation of $100,000 to wounded Japanese soldiers NARA, RG226, entry 16, box 431, no. 38483, OSS, R&A Branch, Regular Intelligence Reports, 'Fortnightly intelligence report, 8 May 1943', p. 7.

34 Keynes, *Tract*, p. 37.

35 Cf. Palairet, *Four ends*, pp. 142–47 on German finance for its World War II occupation of Greece.

a rise in prices likely. The mechanics of this process can be examined by using the quantity theory of money:

$$M/P = kY$$

where M is the nominal money supply, P the price level at which goods and services are traded and Y is real national income. In the Cambridge formulation of the quantity theory, the community holds real money balances (M/P) in some proportion, k, of real income. This k (and its reciprocal 1/k, the velocity of circulation of money) are regarded as fairly constant. If so, kY on the right-hand side of the equation also remains approximately constant, and the relationship between money supply, M, and prices, P, will be more or less proportional. A 10 per cent increase in money supply leads to a 10 per cent rise in prices if the equation is to hold.

The variable k, and so circulation velocity, are considerably less constant when inflation is high and never constant in conditions of hyperinflation. When prices are rising rapidly and people expect this rise, the anticipated cost of holding money is also high. The customary response to a higher cost of something, in this case money, is to demand less of it. People seek to rid themselves of money before its real value falls further and it will command fewer physical goods. In the terminology of economics, liquidity (money) preference is low because money is losing value so rapidly that people want to hold it for as short a time as possible. Eventually, printing more currency with no corresponding increase in goods available will cause people to lose confidence in the value of money; velocity of circulation then takes off. Hyperinflations are always a monetary phenomenon and in these velocity multiplies far more rapidly than money supply.

Money fulfils two important functions in an economy. One is to provide a medium of exchange: people find money convenient to make everyday purchases and payments. As well as this so-called transactions demand for money, it may serve as a store of value. In this role, money is held to buy goods or to invest at a later date.

Seigniorage – the revenue government receives from money creation at any point in time – is the difference between the cost of printing money and its face value. However, government printing of money to use for its own purchases will tend to bid up prices and reduce money's real value. Insofar as the public still finds uses for money and so attempts to replenish real balances, the resulting increase in money holdings generates seigniorage. It does so through implicit taxation. Known as the inflation tax, the tax on holding money balances is measured as the rate of inflation (the tax rate) times real money balances (the tax base). The relationship of what governments can receive as seigniorage is quadratic: an increase in money supply increases seigniorage revenue (with which the government can buy goods and services) but increasing money supply leads to inflation which reduces the real money supply and so diminishes the tax base. As this latter increasingly dominates and people become ever more unwilling to hold money because of its falling real value, seigniorage is progressively destroyed as a source of government revenue. For seigniorage to be an effective tool of government finance the public must somehow be persuaded (or forced) to hold money.

Wartime Southeast Asian GDP and Japanese Needs for Finance

In analysing high inflation and hyperinflation, it is customarily assumed that real incomes remain stable (an unchanged quantity of goods and services). If so, the demand for money is not reduced by less need for money due to lower incomes.[36] As indicated in the Introduction and further explored in Chapter 4, Southeast Asia experienced not stable real incomes but large income falls. These falls (a lower Y in the Cambridge version of the quantity theory) almost certainly reduced the transactions demand for money to make daily purchases and payments. Furthermore, reports of Japanese war reversals probably decreased willingness to hold scrip (money) by reducing its attractiveness as a store of value.

At the same time as economic forces were causing the demand for money to fall, Japan needed to raise more finance in Southeast Asia: a worsening war outlook made it necessary to hire large numbers of Southeast Asians to erect coastal defences, build airfields and so forth. As early as October 1943, the construction of facilities like ports and airbases was said to account for Malaya receiving more military money than other occupied countries in the region and causing a price spiral.[37] In Indochina, the biggest single item in a large budgetary increase for the first six months of 1944 was the construction and equipping of airfields. Expenditure escalated during 1944 and even more in 1945.[38] Since Japanese finance for war and occupation expenditure relied chiefly on seigniorage from printing money, this led to greater monetary expansion. But consequent upwards inflationary pressure threatened the ability to finance occupation and war through seigniorage and made hyperinflation much more likely.

[36] Cagan, 'Monetary dynamics', pp. 31–33.

[37] NIDS, Nansei Gunsei -16 Japan, Southern Military Administration Chōsabu, Report no. 15: *Malaya ni okeru tsūka kin'yū mondai* [Problems of currency and money in Malaya] by Hayawaka Yasumasa (Singapore: Southern Military Administration Chōsabu, October 1943), p. 9.

[38] LHA, MAGIC, 'Budget for Japanese military expenses in French Indo-China for January-June 1944', 23 December 1943; MAGIC, 'Excerpts from 7 June report by Ambassador Yamamoto on situation in Thailand', 19 June 1945, p. A4; NA, FO371/53959, 'Second report on Japanese financial manipulations in French Indo China' by Lt. Colonel T. H. Sweeny, 19 January 1946.

Money Supply and Inflation in Southeast Asia

Money creation and inflation time series for Thailand and Indochina contrast markedly with those for the four military-administered Southeast Asian countries (Table 3.4). Divergence, described in this section, is evident both in the magnitude of inflation (lines 1, 4, 7 and 9) and the quantity of currency issued (lines 2 and 5). Numerous attempts at price controls were ineffective (Chapter 6).

Between 1942 and 1945, inflation and money supply relationships in Thailand and southern Indochina (Cochinchina and the lower part of Annam, together represented by Saigon) appear to satisfy even the naïve quantity theory (an identity in which prices rise proportionately to money supply and velocity of circulation is not taken into account). The price level in Thailand at the end of occupation compares, at 7.1 times December 1941 prices, to a 6.9-fold increase in money, although inflation data may somewhat understate actual price rises.[39] However, in both countries measures to decrease money supply helped to limit inflation. In February 1945, Thailand reduced the money supply by some 30 per cent after demonetizing the 1,000-baht note, while in March 1945 Indochina limited withdrawals from banks for individual depositors to 2,000 piastres per month.[40]

A separate price index exists for Hanoi (northern Indochina) but not separate money supply figures. The Hanoi index (and other data) indicates a 15-fold increase in wartime prices.[41] The remainder of this chapter refers to southern Indochina around Saigon rather than Indochina (or even Vietnam) as a whole. One reason for this is the lack of money supply data for northern Indochina around Hanoi. More important, the north was a rice-deficit area, and being a rice-surplus region like southern Indochina was a key consideration in explaining the holding of real balances.

Burma was the only military-administered country comparable to Thailand and Indochina in its production patterns. Data for Burma are for Rangoon, and so, like Thailand and southern Indochina, indicative of the demand for money in a rice-surplus area. Unlike Thailand and Indochina, however, Burma was subject to instability associated with political uncertainty and some of the most intense fighting in the Southeast Asian theatre. Although a lack of data for 1942 and 1943 hampers analysis, from Japan's initial bombing of Rangoon on 22 December 1941 to the city's occupation by the Japanese on 8 March 1942, and

39 Ungphakorn and Suvarnsit, 'Fiscal and other measures', p. 70.

40 Kingdom of Thailand, *Report of the financial adviser 1941–1950*, p. 53; AOM, HCI 2/226, 'Mémoires Yokoyama', section 7. These memoirs, written soon after the end of the war in response to a request from the French, represent a first-hand account of events surrounding the famine. The letter accompanying the transmission of these memoirs is dated 25 August 1946. Yokoyama was perhaps the most important Japanese economic and political advisor in Indochina.

41 NA, T236/108, telegram from SACSEA to War Office, 1 September 1945.

Table 3.4 *Southeast Asia characteristics of money and inflation during the Japanese occupation 1942–1945*

	Burma	Malaya	Thailand	Indonesia	Indochina Saigon	Philippines
1. Ratio of prices at the end of occupation to prices at its beginning	1,856.5	11,226.5	6.9	32.0	3.6	889.3
2. Ratio of quantity of currency at the end	16.4	25.1	7.1	11.0	5.7	28.0
3. Ratio of (1) to (2)	11.3	447.3	1.0	2.9	0.6	31.8
4. Average rate of rise in prices (% per month)	16.9	16.3	4.0	7.9	2.7	18.4
5. Average rate of rise in quantity of currency (% per month)	6.3	7.4	4.1	5.6	4.1	9.0
6. Ratio of (4) to (5)	2.7	2.2	1.0	1.4	0.7	2.0
7. Average rate of rise in prices during last year of occupation (% per month)	27.1	30.5	5.4	7.6	2.8	32.3
8. Ratio of (7) to (4)	1.6	1.9	1.4	1.0	1.0	1.8
9. Average rate of rise in prices during last two months of occupation (% per month)	72.1	86.8		14.0		37.2
10. Ratio of (9) to (4)	4.3	5.3		1.8		2.0
11. Real balances at end of occupation as a % of real balances at its beginning	9.0	2.0	102.7	34.3	171.8	3.2

Source: Chapter appendix.

possibly until March 1943, prices appear to have risen much faster than money supply. However, during the next 21 months, until December 1944, when money supply increased by about a factor of 10, prices rose only slightly faster. This changed between January and August 1945, which encompassed Rangoon's fall in May: Burma's money supply less than doubled but prices rose 21.4 times so that by the war's end Burmese prices had increased by a factor of 1,857.

In Malaya, the Philippines and Indonesia, price rises also outdistanced monetary expansion. Malaya appears the extreme example: by the end of the war money supply had multiplied 25.1 times while prices were 11,000 times higher. However, the Philippines and Indonesia might well show similar money supply and price histories if data were available for the final weeks of the war when the Japanese issued particularly large quantities of currency.

Earlier work on Southeast Asia almost universally refers to wartime hyperinflation. But by either the Cagan (prices rising 50 per cent a month) or Reinhart–Rogoff (40 per cent) criteria, hyperinflation was not typical until late in the war.[42] Only the Philippines had a 40 per cent monthly price rise or more before 1945. Even there, inflation did not reach 40 per cent until August 1943. Between November 1943 and January 1945, monthly Philippine inflation exceeded 50 per cent on three occasions, but fell back to a lower level the next month. Malaya never approached 40 per cent monthly inflation until the final days of the war in August 1945. Burma became hyperinflationary only in the last two months of the war as retreating Japanese troops desperately drew on their monetary stocks to obtain food and supplies.

Real Balances

This section explores contrasting trends in real balances. In Thailand, Indochina (Figures 3.1 and 3.2) and, before 1945, Burma, despite high inflation real balances were well maintained (Figure 3.3). By contrast, in Malaya and the Philippines real balances fell sharply over time (Figures 3.4 and 3.5). More importantly, in all five countries Japan could finance occupation by printing money because real balances held up sufficiently well that hyperinflation was largely avoided. Why, then, did Southeast Asians continue to hold money to the extent they did when its value was being comprehensively debauched?

Malaya, the Philippines and Indonesia

The path of real balances during high inflation or hyperinflation is complicated. Surely, as suggested above, as prices skyrocket, people demand less

[42] Cagan, 'Monetary dynamics', p. 25; Reinhart and Rogoff, *This time*, p. 5. European hyperinflations, as described by Sargent ('Ends'), far outstripped price rises in wartime Southeast Asia.

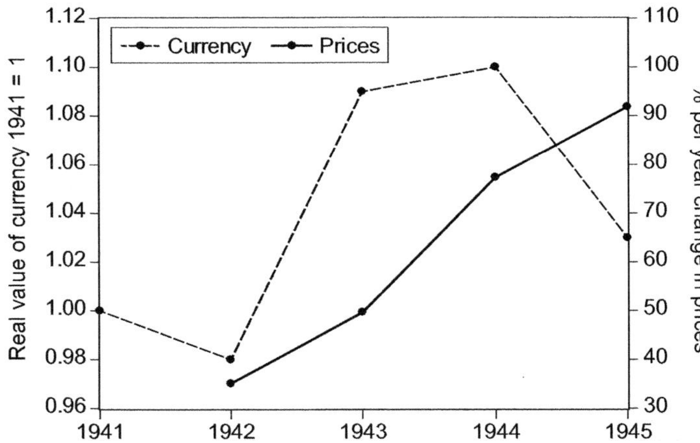

Figure 3.1 Thailand end-of-year index of real value of currency and rate of change in prices 1941–1945
Source: Chapter appendix.

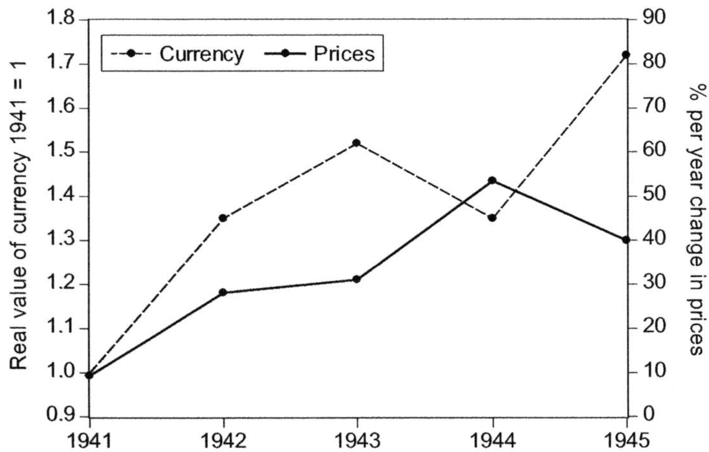

Figure 3.2 Indochina end-of-year index of real value of currency and rate of change in prices 1941–1945
Source: Chapter appendix.

money because its real value falls and the cost of holding currency rises (Figures 3.4 and 3.5). Initially, however, real balances may rise because, as Keynes observed, people are so accustomed to considering money the ultimate standard that they hoard it and postpone purchases.[43] Moreover, even after

[43] Keynes, *Tract*, p. 40.

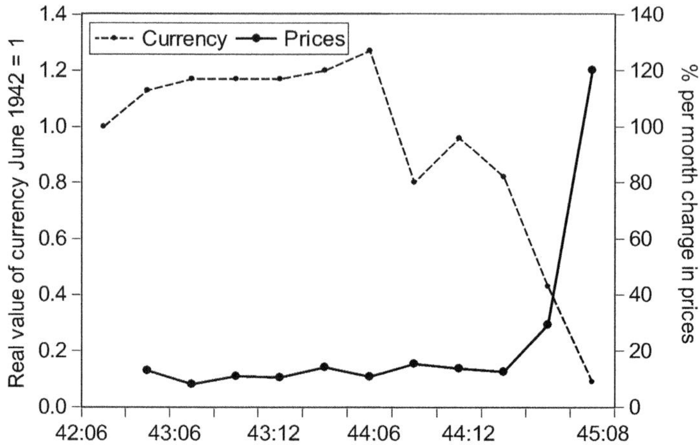

Figure 3.3 Burma end-of-month index of real value of currency and rate of change in prices June 1942–August 1945
Source: Chapter appendix.

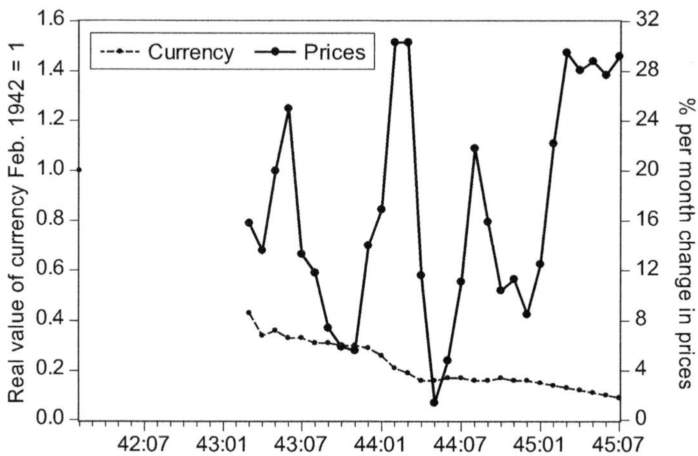

Figure 3.4 Malaya end-of-month index of real value of currency and rate of change in prices February 1942–July 1945
Source: Chapter appendix.

real balances start to fall, the decline is often erratic and marked by reversals.[44] In Malaya and the Philippines, there was insufficient willingness to hold scrip – the

[44] Cagan, 'Monetary dynamics', p. 27. See also the example of initial increases in money stock in the Soviet hyperinflation in Bernholz, 'Currency substitution', p. 301.

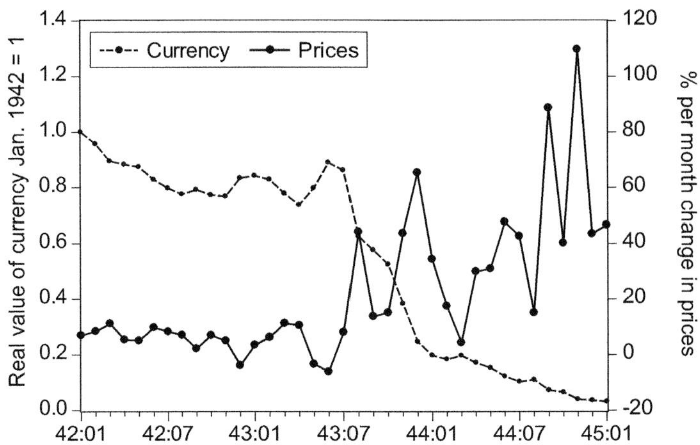

Figure 3.5 Philippines end-of-month index of real value of currency and rate of change in prices January 1942–January 1945
Source: Chapter appendix.

banana and Mickey Mouse money – to support more than brief rises in real balances. Balances fell irregularly but inexorably. By August 1945, real balances in Malaya stood at 2.0 per cent of their level at the onset of occupation, while in January 1945 the Philippine figure was 3.2 per cent. In July 1945, Indonesian real balances were a third of their initial level.

Four principal reasons explain why scrip was held in military-administered Southeast Asia. To begin with, military decrees and coercion provided strong incentives to hold currency. After the first year of occupation, Japanese administrations outlawed the use of pre-war currencies. Their mere possession was deemed criminal and led to draconian punishment.[45] A second reason is that good money substitutes for scrip were not available. Japanese-enforced autarky supported Japanese monetary monopoly by largely cutting off access to substitute currencies. Indonesia was an exception. The circulation of pre-war Dutch colonial currency was permitted, possibly because of a lack of sufficient Japanese currency and possibly because some Japanese officials had obtained large quantities of the pre-war money and found it a profitable speculation as the guilder continuously appreciated against Japanese-issued

[45] NIDS, Nansei Gunsei -17 Japan, Southern Military Administration Chōsabu, *Zairai tsūka kaishu mondai ni tsute* [Withdrawal of local money] (December 1943), p. 17; NA, CO852/510/24, C. D. Adhearne, 'The Malayan currency problem', 22 June 1943, p. 1 and WO203/390, BMA to SACSEA, 12 January 1945 referring to document 24 November 1945 from Troopers concerning transactions in Japanese currency; NARA, RG226, entry 16, box 208, 'Economic conditions in the Philippines', 15 October 1942, p. 7; NIMH, 010A/1, Netherlands Forces Intelligence Service, 'Report on interrogation of De Has', 23 January 1943, p. 21; Chin, *Malaya upside down*, pp. 123–24.

notes.[46] In the Philippines, the only monetary substitutes left were the clandestine use of pre-war monies and various guerrilla currencies. Many of the latter had been printed in America for distribution to anti-Japanese groups throughout the Islands.[47]

A third reason to hold scrip was its considerable transactional benefits. The many monopoly buying and distributing organizations begun by the Japanese all dealt in scrip and so ensured its widespread use.[48] With the disappearance of pre-war export markets, Japanese buying organizations were the principal, or even the only, outlet for export staples like rubber and tin in Malaya and sugar and abaca (Manila hemp) in the Philippines. Malayan and Philippine staple producers could only obtain income to buy basic necessities by selling their output to Japanese buyers. Local (barter) demand for the staples was slight or non-existent since they were of little local use. In areas specialized in producing rice, its surfeit undermined barter demand. Money payments to the large numbers of labourers and other workers employed by the Japanese were all in scrip. Furthermore, nearly everyone in the military-administered countries needed scrip for the many taxes levied by the Japanese, to obtain rationed goods including food and clothing, and for any other market transaction.

Fourth, although confidence in scrip fell because the Allies announced that it would become worthless after Japan surrendered, not all Southeast Asians believed this propaganda.[49] Almost certainly, a number of people continued to hold scrip in the likelihood that, even if Japan lost the war, it would still have some value. A rational basis for this belief is confirmed by actual Bank of England strategy. It was elliptically set out in a telegram: '[we] have to redeem Japanese occupation currency most important that the impression should be created that we do not (repeat not) contemplate such redemption'.[50] In stressing that for Burma scrip must be accorded post-war value, the Bank of England's Governor, Sir Otto Niemeyer, found, for the commercial banks and for himself, it 'inconceivable that the reoccupying Power would create a

46 BE, OV85/2, 'Monetary, banking and credit system during the Japanese occupation period 1942/1945', Enclosure with Batavia despatch to Foreign Office, 1 April 1946, p. 2.

47 BE, OV149/1, United Kingdom, Overseas & Foreign Office, 'The Philippines', 5 July 1945, p. 1.

48 There were, of course, exceptions to a continued substantial transactions demand. By the second half of fiscal 1944 in North Borneo, each local district had become self-supporting. Under these conditions, 'the natives sold food only in exchange for some other goods which eventually led to a complete barter system'. JM 103, *Outline of administration*, p. 67.

49 NIDS, Nansei Gunsei –17 Japan, Southern Military Administration Chōsabu, *Zairai tsūka kaishu mondai ni tsute* [Withdrawal of local money] (December 1943), p. 4.

50 BE, OV79/16, Draft telegram in reply to telegram of 20 February 1943 from Commander-in-Chief in India; see also NA, T247/4, 'Post-war currency in Malaya', 2 December 1942 in which J. M. Keynes states that Japanese notes need not necessarily be redeemed at the same rate as pre-occupation notes.

position in which the Burmese could not use the money in their pockets'.[51] Similarly, informed observers of the Philippines anticipated that the Japanese peso would not be entirely repudiated.[52]

As the war went on, scrip was, however, increasingly shunned as a store of value. By the war's latter stages in Malaya, 'only the most stupid were lulled into a sense of wealth' by holding large quantities of Japanese notes. Others 'who had amassed "fortunes" quickly changed the paper money into commodities, and substantial investments'.[53] Apparently, given the opportunity even the clerks in Japanese banks changed their pocket money into British currency.[54] Axis reversals especially eroded scrip as a store of value. In Malaya: 'Every time there was an Axis defeat, particularly Japanese defeats, prices of goods jumped up. Every Allied victory ... and every visit of B-29s over Malaya, caused spurts of prices in foodstuffs. Saipan, Iwojima, Manila, Rangoon, and Okinawa were inflation spring-boards.'[55], Prices in the Philippines rose each time air-raid precautions and defence drills were held in Manila.[56] Insofar as money, as distinct from jewels or durable goods, remained a store of value, it largely constituted pre-war currencies exchanged among those considered trustworthy.

One example of this appears in the wartime memoirs of a young girl in Malaya. She recounts the sale of the family car to a Japanese who, to the family's surprise, responded to a request to pay in British money (Malayan dollars which replaced the Straits dollar in 1938) and returned the next day, smiling and with the cash. The money, she remembers, 'was to see us through most of the war ... mother would take out one note at a time and sell it on the black market ... By the end of the war, we had no car and no more British notes, but we had managed to stay alive, and that was saying something'.[57]

Thailand, Indochina and Burma

In Thailand and Indochina, real money balances were impressively persistent (Figures 3.1 and 3.2). The same appears to be true of Burma during the periods of direct military rule and of the Ba Maw government, but not after the country's 1945 descent into military chaos (Figure 3.3). Burma suggests that balances were maintained for more important reasons than the identity or near

[51] BE, OV79/16, Niemeyer to Sir David Waley, 8 March 1944.

[52] BE, OV149/1, A. G. Kellogg, Hong Kong and Shanghai Bank to A. Morse, Hong Kong and Shanghai Bank, 14 June 1944.

[53] Chin, *Malaya upside down*, p. 45.

[54] NIDS, Nansei Gunsei –17 Japan, Southern Military Administration Chōsabu, *Zairai tsūka kaishu mondai ni tsute* [Withdrawal of local money] (December 1943), p. 6.

[55] Chin, *Malaya upside down*, p. 45.

[56] Jose, 'Rice shortage', p. 211.

[57] Aisha Akbar, *Aishabee at war*, p. 134.

identity of pre-war and wartime notes and a continuity of governments (true of Indochina and Thailand). Those reasons were that peasants produced for the market and tended to hoard money. The maintenance of real balances in Thailand, Indochina and Burma is especially striking, because of the expected negative relationship between money demand and inflation and because of the quantity theory of money's implicit assumption of constant real income. In fact, the large falls in Southeast Asian real incomes would lower the transactions demand for money through decreasing the quantity of goods to buy. Less transactions demand would reduce the demand for real balances and so increase the likelihood of hyperinflation. By contrast, a continued holding of large real balances despite high inflation and a declining nominal value of money would facilitate Japanese finance for the war through seigniorage.

Real balances in Thailand stayed approximately constant and in Indochina appear to have risen. In Burma, after an apparently sharp fall, real balances stabilized and remained near or above their March 1943 level until December 1944. During 1945, however, balances collapsed after the British launched two major offensives followed by the capture of Mandalay on 20 March and the fall of Rangoon on 3 May. In August 1945, real balances in Burma were 9 per cent of their June 1942 level.

Thailand, Indochina and Burma had transactional motives for holding money similar to Malaya and the Philippines. Burmese transactions were 'largely (if not entirely) based on Japanese-issued rupees'.[58] These were, a wartime Burmese government official recalled, the only legal currency and an unwillingness to accept them 'meant imprisonment, torture or death'.[59] The Thai and Indochinese governments helped to sustain a demand for money through policies to support producers by buying their output.[60]

The unchanged physical appearance of the Indochinese piastre, and nearly identical appearance of the Thai baht, may seem to bolster a store of value motive for high real balances. But the principal explanation lies elsewhere. High real balances in Thailand, Indochina and, for part of the war, Burma are explained mainly by the fact that all three economies were dominated by numerous small peasant rice growers. Unlike producers in the rice-deficit areas, they could easily achieve food self-sufficiency (if not necessarily adequate nutrition), since rice and some other basic foodstuffs could be obtained through household production or barter for this output. Such small rural cultivators tend to hoard money, even in the face of inflation. Under inflationary conditions, Keynes observed, as 'more money flows into the pockets

58 BE, OV79/16, 'Burma – reoccupation, 27 April 1944'. And see 'A false step in Burma', *The Times*, 22 May 1945, which made the same point.

59 Pe, *Narrative*, p. 93.

60 OSS, R&A 1715, *Indochina's war-time government*, pp. 33–34, R&A 2695, *Status of the Chinese*, p. 26 and R&A 2589, *Rubber industry*, p. 7.

of the peasants, it tends to stick there'.[61] For Thailand, it was observed that only 20 or 25 per cent of notes in circulation were in Bangkok: 'The rest are in the provinces, where they largely disappear into farmers' hoards: and the demand of the provinces for fresh supplies of notes is a never ceasing one.'[62] In Burma, villagers in rice-producing districts insisted on payment in Japanese currency: 'They thought it was better than British and enjoyed the feeling of wealth which they got by carrying away large wads of brand new Jap notes.'[63] Even when brought to the cities, rural dwellers like Indochina's Cao Đài religious sect apparently had consumption patterns little affected by inflation. In Saigon, the Japanese relied heavily for their workforce on the Cao Đài who, being vegetarians, 'ate simple food with lots of vegetables, rice, and seeds. Any extra money they earned was channeled back to their families or to their temples'.[64]

Peasant money illusion (mistaking nominal for real values of money) may not, however, fully account for the holding of money in rice-surplus areas. Producers in these areas had limited spending opportunities because local production generally provided no more than small quantities of inferior substitutes for pre-war imported manufactures and because Japan sent few goods to Southeast Asia.[65] Given this absence of manufactured goods, and so long as a post-war redemption of wartime notes could be anticipated, as seemed especially likely in Indochina, Thailand and Burma, it was rational to hold money. Peasants probably realized that manufactured goods would become more abundant after the war and prices would decline dramatically.

Seigniorage and the Inflation Tax

Seigniorage is made up of two elements: revenue from changes in real money balances and the inflation tax. Normally, the change in real money balances from one period to the next accounts for about half of seigniorage and can be its main component in an economy experiencing high real growth. However, Japanese finance in wartime Southeast Asia relied chiefly and increasingly on taxation through inflation (Table 3.5).

[61] Keynes, *Tract*, p. 66.

[62] Kingdom of Thailand, *Report of the financial adviser 1941–1950*, p. 55. The same hoarding behaviour was repeated in Thailand's 1949–51 inflation. Despite a large increase in money supply, prices did not rise to any comparable extent. Apparently, 'a large volume of notes were simply hoarded, mainly by up-country producers'. Viwat, *Wiwatthanachaiyanuson*, p. 268.

[63] IOR, M4/306, A. K. Potter, 'Currency policy, Burma', 31 May 1945 and see 'Two currencies in Burma: introducing new notes', *The Times*, 9 June 1945.

[64] Tràn, 'Working', p. 291.

[65] Robequain, *Economic development*, pp. 381, 383; Ingram, *Economic change*, p. 164; Numnonda, *Thailand*, pp. 88–92; Le, *Impact*, p. 188; Jose, 'Labor usage', p. 270; Pe, *Narrative*, p. 55.

Table 3.5 *Southeast Asia composition of seigniorage 1942–1945*

	Seigniorage	Change in real base % seigniorage	Inflation tax % seigniorage
a) Thailand million baht			
1942	70.6	−9.5	109.5
1943	130.9	26.3	73.7
1944	144.1	1.6	98.4
1945	134.8	−16.3	116.3
b) Indochina Saigon million piastres			
1942	198.0	61.6	38.4
1943	169.7	34.5	65.5
1944	124.8	−47.2	147.2
1945	261.3	48.8	51.2
c) Burma million rupees			
1944	44.4	10.3	89.7
1945	12.4	−308.3	408.3
d) Malaya million Straits dollars			
1942	23.2	−585.9	685.9
1943	14.9	−309.6	409.6
1944	9.6	−273.1	373.1
1945	4.8	−123.5	223.5
e) Philippines million pesos			
1942	72.1	−55.0	155.0
1943	25.5	−551.0	651.0
1944	7.4	−678.1	778.1
f) Indonesia million guilders			
1942	263.7	69.6	30.4
1943	141.3	−44.8	144.8
1944	83.3	−347.5	447.5
1945	36.8	−103.6	203.6

Note: For 1945, Burma seigniorage data are until the end of June 1945 and for Malaya and Indonesia seigniorage data are until the end of July 1945.
Source: Chapter appendix.

Nevertheless, important differences are apparent between rice-surplus Thailand, Indochina and Burma, where real balances were generally maintained, and Malaya, the Philippines, Indonesia and Burma after 1944, where they were not. In Thailand and Indochina, high real balances, despite high inflation and falling GDP, allowed increasing amounts of seigniorage to be realized at relatively low tax rates. Between 1942 and 1944, seigniorage in Thailand doubled while the inflation tax (although still near 100 per cent) fell somewhat. In 1945, however, the contribution of real balances became negative as Thais sought to avoid the tax of inflation.

To try to preserve seigniorage elsewhere than in Thailand and Indochina, Japanese military administrators had to rely on high inflation taxes (for example, 778.1 per cent in the Philippines in 1944) to try to offset strongly negative changes in real balances. That did not, however, prevent a sharp fall in seigniorage as populations sought to avoid taxation. As this happened, inflation instability in Southeast Asia tended to rise at the same time that real seigniorage was tending to decline (Table 3.5).

Monetary Overhang

Monetary expansion to finance war creates a potentially serious post-war problem of strong inflationary forces generated by a large stock of money. After World War II, Southeast Asian countries faced this problem of 'monetary overhang' due to wartime money supply expansion.[66] A seemingly obvious way to avoid monetary overhang is to repudiate a wartime currency. That, however, is somewhat unusual because it abruptly leaves the public without means of payment. Just as Niemeyer made that point for Burma, it was anticipated that in the Philippines Japanese currency would not be entirely repudiated as this would impose 'too much of a hardship on the small rank and file' in taking much, perhaps all, of their wealth away from them.[67]

Some, but not all, of post-war Southeast Asia avoided monetary overhang. Exceptions were Indochina, which inherited a large stock of money, Thailand and Indonesia. The cost of living index for Saigon workers, 100 in 1941 and 360.1 in 1945, reached 3,226.6 in 1949.[68] However, it is unclear how much of this post-war inflation was due to an overlarge money supply and how much to the First Indochina War (1946–54). Thailand inherited a greatly increased stock of baht

[66] Barendregt, *Dutch money purge*.

[67] BE, OV149/1, A. G. Kellogg to A. Morse reporting a conversation with representatives of the Philippine National Bank in New York, 9 June 1944.

[68] Indochina, *Annuaire statistique, 1943–46*, p. 301, *1947–48*, p. 285; Vietnam, *Annuaire statistique du Viêtnam, 1949–1950*, p. 283.

printed for the Japanese. The Kingdom effectively wrote off its yen credits although a relatively small amount of gold on deposit with the Bank of Japan was recovered in 1949.[69]

When the Dutch returned to Java and Sumatra, they controlled only some large cities and had to co-exist with Indonesian Republican forces. In Borneo and eastern Indonesia, the Dutch were able to establish their own NICA (Netherlands Indies Civil Administration) money. It could not, however, successfully be introduced in Java and Sumatra because the Dutch occupied such a small part of these islands and could offer few goods in exchange for NICA currency. Little option existed but to accept a continued use of Japanese scrip, which was used by Indonesian Republicans and widely recognized and accepted in the countryside. Moreover, as the only way to finance their urban administrations, the Dutch put into circulation a large amount of Japanese scrip captured from the banks, the Kolff printing works in Jakarta and elsewhere. They further authorized the Japanese to print yet more scrip to pay for supplies requisitioned from them. When on 6 March 1946 the Dutch, and on 31 October 1946 Indonesian Republicans, finally issued their own currencies, these further added to Indonesia's grossly overlarge stock of money and helped to stoke already high inflation.[70]

Elsewhere in Southeast Asia, post-war administrations sidestepped monetary overhang. The Philippines and Malaya both demonetized Japanese currency.[71] Nor, contrary to expectations, was it accorded post-war value in Burma.

Demonetization exchanged the challenge of monetary overhang for that of how to re-start a monetary economy. In Singapore, although new currency was put in circulation after Japanese scrip was declared worthless, this could not be done instantaneously and for some time many people had no money. Japanese 'banana money' could be picked up freely from the gutters. Barter was a partial substitute and cigarettes served as a form of money and 'could buy almost anything'. However, few people except the British military had any cigarettes.[72]

The Philippines underwent a 'monetary crisis'. In September 1944 in Manila, discarded Japanese pesos littered the streets.[73] Monetary transactions were limited 'only to the most elemental needs', since Japanese notes were outlawed and the banks closed after Manila was almost entirely destroyed by

69 Kingdom of Thailand, *Report of the financial adviser 1941–1950*, pp. 54–55; Ingram, *Economic change*, pp. 165, 168.
70 Cribb, 'Political dimensions', pp. 113–36; Wing and Nasution, 'Indonesian economic policies', pp. 41–42.
71 'P.I. currency is stabilized on 2–1 base', *Shanghai Evening Post*, 5 January 1945.
72 Gilmour, *With freedom*, pp. 103–4.
73 BE, OV149/1, A. F. Handcock, Hong Kong and Shanghai Bank to A. Morse, Hong Kong and Shanghai Bank, 19 June 1945.

the Japanese and by American bombing.[74] Nor would US army authorities recognize as legal tender pre-war notes issued by the Philippine National Bank or money which had been printed by the guerrillas with US army permission.[75]

Burma's sudden lack of money created considerable disruption. By August 1945, Japanese notes were no longer used in Rangoon but they were in some rural areas, including in the delta.[76] Because peasants in the rice-growing districts had relied on Japanese notes they had no British Burma currency. The British solution was to extend interest-free loans to peasant cultivators in small coins likely to be spent – 24 rupees (US$7.23) for those working one yoke of oxen and 36 rupees for more than a yoke.[77]

Conclusion

Japanese expectations for the gains from war in Southeast Asia – the realization of a Greater East Asia Co-Prosperity Sphere – went well beyond the use of financial arrangements to exploit Southeast Asia. Finance was but one component of Japan's strategy to achieve the economic advantages of a large, Japanese-controlled empire in East Asia. Nevertheless, Japanese financial policy in Southeast Asia revealed, perhaps as much as anything, the reality of Japan's vision of shared prosperity in a new Asian economic order.

After deciding on war to pursue empire and the creation of a Co-Prosperity Sphere, Japan had to rely on inflation as the main way to finance occupation in Southeast Asia. Japanese war planners probably saw that inflation had other advantages. Although in the longer term high inflation might well re-order Southeast Asian societies, this was not inconsistent with the aim of replacing the pre-war order with Japanese Empire. At the same time, inflation offered an efficient means of wartime finance. It avoided the enforcement problems of overt taxation in a large geographical area with a predominantly rural population and over which Japanese officials, forced to take charge of administration in four countries, were thinly spread. Tax collection was further complicated by the erosion of a tax base in Southeast Asian countries after the wartime collapse of the region's export economies.

74 UP, Roxas Papers, Toribio Teodoro, 'Philippine manufacturing industries', 12 July 1945, p. 5.

75 NARA, RG319, entry 85A, box 1366, file 208481, 'Intelligence report: economic situation', 5 October 1945, p. 2.

76 OSS, R&A/SEAC no. 23-R in NARA, RG226, entry 154, box 81, file 1427, 'Burma economic review July–August', 21 August 1945, p. 1; OSS, R&A/SEAC no. 8-R in NARA, RG226, entry 154, box 81, file 1406, *Economic conditions in the Rangoon area May–June 1945*, 29 June 1945, p. 3.

77 IOR, M4/306, 'Currency in Burma', 17 September 1945; 'Currency problems in Burma', *The Times*, 24 May 1945; Longmuir, *Money trail*, pp. 96–101.

To fund the war effort, Japan imposed administratively set exchange rates, required Southeast Asian governments to issue massive amounts of currency, and in Thailand and Indochina enacted a yen bloc of bilateral trading arrangements. The combined effect was to create large international debts in Southeast Asia for which at the time, and probably in the future had Japan won the war, it intended to give nothing in exchange. It is striking that even military-administered Southeast Asia had comparatively moderate, Latin American-like inflation for much of the war and hyperinflation only near its end when Japan had clearly lost. Southeast Asia's wartime inflation experience is testament to a combination of strict Japanese controls and the transactions benefits of holding money despite its rapidly depreciating real value. Stanley Fischer advocates legal requirements to use domestic rather than a foreign currency as one way for governments to capture seigniorage.[78] Revolutionary France, some 150 years before Japan's occupation of Southeast Asia, successfully backed up monetary monopoly and legal requirements to use government currency with the guillotine for offenders. Likewise, Japan implemented its own effective, if drastic, enforcement mechanisms, which also included death. Both for France and Japan, rigorously enforced legal restrictions ensured that seigniorage could largely finance war.

In Southeast Asia, a continuing demand for real balances enabled Japan to avoid issuing as much new money as would have been required if the demand for real balances had been less and therefore the rise in prices greater. Scrip, occupation costs, clearing arrangements and seigniorage afforded Japan a low-cost way to finance occupation and gain control of Southeast Asian resources. In the end, however, major Japanese failures in naval strategy and in the protection of oil tankerage and other merchant shipping told heavily. These failures prevented Japan from realizing the full exploitative potential of the financial measures analysed in this chapter.

[78] Fischer, 'Seigniorage', p. 306.

Illustration 1 Japanese bicycle troops enter Saigon July 1941 (Popperfoto #79657005). Japanese occupation of Indochina before World War II was a principal factor in the US decision to embargo oil shipments to Japan (Chapter 1).

Illustration 2 Japanese troops mop up in Kuala Lumpur January 1942 (IWM HU2776). Japanese forces moved swiftly down the Malay peninsula to capture Singapore on 15 February 1942 (Chapter 1).

Illustration 3 The Burma Road (NARA box 349 228183).
The road, notable for its difficult terrain, was a lifeline for Allied supplies to Nationalist China (Chapter 1).

Illustration 4 Japanese occupy the Nicobar Islands October 1942 (Getty Images #92425276).
By May 1942, Japan had planted its flag over 1.7 m square miles of Southeast Asia (Chapter 1).

Illustration 5 US Navy Helldiver flies over a stricken Japanese oil tanker January 1945 (NARA_US Navy).
The Allies decimated Japanese shipping, which as early as 1943 became basic to the increasingly perilous Japanese military and economic position (Chapter 1).

Illustration 6 Allied propaganda leaflet: Japanese soldier leading a weeping Thai elephant (NARA RG226 entry 144 box 133 file 1312).
The wartime status of Thailand, allied with Japan, was somewhat ambivalent, and the Allies launched concerted propaganda campaigns to try to win popular Thai support (Chapter 2).

Illustration 7 Japanese occupation currency (Author's collection).
The Japanese made Southeast Asians pay the cost of their occupation, and did this mainly by printing military currency of the kind pictured here (Chapter 3).

Illustration 8 Philippine guerrilla notes (author's collection).
The United States printed and distributed currency to Philippine guerrilla groups as a way for them to finance themselves (Chapter 3).

Illustration 9 Lottery ticket issued by the Japanese in Singapore (NAS, 19980005535–0110).
Lotteries were extensively used by the Japanese to tax Southeast Asians (Chapter 3).

4

National Product and Trade

Within a year of its 1942 occupation, Japan began to inflict on Southeast Asia one of the great macroeconomic crises in modern economic history.[1] Over the next 32 months the crisis continued to deepen and by 1945 ranked among the largest economic contractions anywhere during the last two centuries. In this chapter, I attempt, with the data available, to analyse and compare across countries the wartime collapse in Southeast Asian income, output and trade.

The aim of this chapter and Chapter 5, taken together, is to substantiate estimates, set out below, that between 1938 and 1945 real GDP per capita in all Southeast Asian countries except Thailand plummeted by about half, and perhaps even by two-thirds in Malaya and the Philippines. I use a combination of quantitative and qualitative evidence and build analysis around a modified version of the six sectors identified by John Kendrick as the main components of the economy: farming (agriculture), mining, transport, manufacturing, public utilities and services.[2] Chapters 4 and 5 evaluate all of these sectors except services and show declines in each consistent with GDP per capita contractions of 50 per cent or more by the early months of 1945. Japan's GDP per capita also fell sharply, dropping by 53 per cent between 1940 and 1945. In 1946, it remained 50 per cent less than before the war and by 1950 had recovered to just two-thirds of its pre-war level (Table 4.1). During the 1950s, however, Japan grew rapidly, while GDP per capita of several Southeast Asian countries languished below pre-World War II levels.

Southeast Asian agriculture and mining are considered in the present chapter which, departing from Kendrick typology, also examines trade because of its critical importance for Southeast Asia, with its high degree of economic specialization in export-oriented primary commodity production. Trade provided the outlet for the bulk of the region's most important agricultural and mining commodities and, in return, the means for obtaining nearly all consumer items essential to the everyday life of Southeast Asians. Chapter 5 focuses on transport, public utilities and manufacturing.

[1] For comparative macroeconomic crises in modern history, see Barro and Ursúa, *Macroeconomic crises*.

[2] Kendrick, *Productivity trends*, pp. 133–88; see also Gallman, 'Gross national product'.

Table 4.1 *Southeast Asia and Japan GDP per capita 1870–1950*

a) 1990 (Geary-Khamis $)

	Burma	Malaya	Thailand	Indonesia	Indochina	Philippines	Japan
1870	504	683	608	517	505	624	737
1900	699		784	734		673	1,180
1913	685	954	841	869	727	988	1,387
1929	814	1,766	793	1,017		1,413	2,026
1938	740	1,452	826	1,057	831	1,440	2,449
1939		1,708	826	1,038	886	1,508	2,816
1940			841	1,104	803	1,507	2,874
1941			846	1,158	763		2,873
1942			743	925	698		2,818
1943			812	738	659		2,822
1944			759	579	515		2,659
1945			682	512	407		1,346
1946			716	527	473	646	1,444
1947			775	602	498	875	1,541
1948			838	694	512	993	1,725
1949			826	758	562	1,025	1,800
1950	396	1,665	836	784	658	1,070	1,921

b) 1938 = 100

	Burma	Malaya	Thailand	Indonesia	Vietnam	Philippines	Japan
1870	68.1	47.0	73.6	48.9	60.7	43.3	30.1
1900	94.5		94.9	69.5	0.0	46.7	48.2
1913	92.6	65.7	101.8	82.3	87.4	68.6	56.6
1929	110.0		96.0	96.3		98.1	82.7
1938	100.0	100.0	100.0	100.0	100.0	100.0	100.0
1939		117.6	100.0	98.3	106.6	104.7	115.0
1940		0.0	101.8	104.5	96.6	104.6	117.4
1941			102.4	109.6	91.8		117.3
1942			90.0	87.6	83.9		115.1
1943			98.3	69.9	79.3		115.2
1944			91.9	54.8	62.0		108.6
1945			82.6	48.5	48.9		55.0
1946			86.7	49.9	57.0	44.9	59.0
1947			93.8	57.0	59.9	60.8	62.9
1948			101.5	65.7	61.6	68.9	70.4

Table 4.1 (*cont.*)

b) 1938 = 100

	Burma	Malaya	Thailand	Indonesia	Vietnam	Philippines	Japan
1949		0.0	100.0	71.8	67.6	71.1	73.5
1950	53.5	114.7	101.2	74.2	79.1	74.3	78.4

Notes: 1. For details of the GDP sources and estimates, see Appendix to Chapter 3, pp. 425–26.
2. Comparable 1990 GK$ figures for United States per capita income are: 1938: $6,126; 1945: $11,709; and 1950: $9,561.

Sources: Maddison Project Database, version 2013, pp. 627–51; van der Eng, *Long-term growth in Malaysia, 1910–2010*; van der Eng, *Thailand estimates of GDP based on Sompop's work*; van der Eng, 'Real domestic product of Indonesia', pp. 368–69; Jean-Pascal Bassino, personal communication, Vietnam national income, 6 Feb. 2011; Malaya, *Report on the 1947 census*, p. 39.

Services, the last of Kendrick's six sectors, are not treated separately but considered throughout the book. As earlier analysis suggested, and subsequent chapters will make increasingly apparent, services are unlikely to have added to GDP during the war. A large share of financial services disappeared with the closure of most banks and the replacement of pre-war currencies by military scrip (Chapter 3). Employment in the services sector increased considerably but this largely reflected the need for people, thrown out of work by the collapse of export industries and domestic commerce, to find alternative employment in activities like hawking or standing in queues. Rather than augmenting GDP, such improvised activities did little more than divide up existing work among more people. They were a way to supplement available rations and own food cultivation with some additional income. An obvious expansion of services also occurred in the spread of black markets to most parts of Southeast Asian life, in prostitution, and in the collection for sale and recycling of discarded items such as rags, cardboard, newspapers, bottles, old bits of metal and even cigarette butts. Goods were in such short supply that everything, even if previously considered 'useless and trashy', now became difficult to get and had value: 'There was literally nothing which was not worth something.'[3]

Pre-war Economy and Wartime Collapse

In 1940, Southeast Asian economies ranked among the world's most open and most specialized. Throughout the region, growth had been strongly export-led,

[3] Chin, *Malaya upside down*, p. 193.

and exports were almost wholly some combination of agricultural and mineral products. Specialization was heavily weighted in favour of just four commodities: rice, rubber, tin and sugar. Together primary production and trade accounted for three-fifths to two-thirds of GDP in most Southeast Asian countries and as much as three-quarters of GDP in Malaya due to its exceptional openness. Because of such extreme specialization, agriculture and mining were central to the pre-war growth of Southeast Asian GDP as well as to its wartime collapse (Tables 4.1 and 4.2).

For the determination of national income, exports, investment and government spending are autonomous expenditures or injections to the circular flow of income. In pre-war Southeast Asia, exports were the dominant form of autonomous expenditure and so also the main determinant of national income. Investment was small, as was government spending. Little foreign capital flowed to Southeast Asia. The region's primary producers self-financed much of capital formation through their own effort of clearing and improving land. Governments generally tried to restrict spending, operate with a limited administrative apparatus and balance the budget. In this last, they almost invariably succeeded over a short period if not always every year.[4]

Net exports fluctuated in response to world demand but were typically large. The economy adjusted to swings in the external balance. When net exports fell so too did money income. A consequent reduction in consumption through the income effect was reinforced by a decrease in the money supply. It contracted under the classic or colonial currency board system which dominated throughout Southeast Asia for most of the pre-war period and in which money supply depended chiefly on an export surplus.[5]

An analysis of the post-1900 Philippines applies equally to the whole of Southeast Asia: 'In the absence of national income data, the best indicators of economic growth may be the foreign trade statistics.'[6] Before the war, in Southeast Asia not only did the growth in primary commodity exports typically outpace expansion in total agricultural and mining output but, furthermore, because exports usually exceeded combined imports of goods and services they yielded the necessary surplus on current account for export-led growth and money supply increases.[7]

Because during the Japanese occupation nothing fundamentally changed these pre-war macroeconomic relationships and because there was little new investment or much government spending, the collapse in exports led directly to large falls in national income. The Southern Regions Development Bank was set up to finance

4 Huff, 'Globalization, natural resources', pp. 127–55.
5 Huff, 'Monetization', pp. 311–19.
6 Sicat, 'Philippine economy' (1964), pp. 6–7 and re-stated in Sicat, 'Measurement', p. 25.
7 The net effect of such an injection to the economy would, however, have been offset to the extent that profits were remitted abroad although, like the current account surplus indicated above, magnitudes are unclear.

Table 4.2 *Southeast Asia composition of GDP by sector 1939–1945*

		%						
	GDP	Agric., fishing, mining	Trade	Manufacturing	Transport	Utilities	Services	Total
***Burma* (million current Rs.)**								
1938–39	1,275	55.1		5.6	2.8	8.1	28.4	100.0
***Thailand* (million 1950 baht)**								
1939	18,828	43.8	18.6	13.5	5.1	0.1	18.9	100.0
1940	19,387	43.8	18.8	13.6	5.1	0.1	18.6	100.0
1941	19,850	44.0	18.8	13.6	5.1	0.1	18.4	100.0
1942	17,738	42.3	18.3	13.3	5.0	0.1	21.0	100.0
1943	19,740	43.1	18.9	13.6	5.1	0.1	19.2	100.0
1944	18,783	42.3	18.6	13.4	5.0	0.1	20.6	100.0
1945	17,191	41.0	18.0	13.1	4.9	0.1	22.9	100.0
***Malaya* (million 1960 Straits $)**								
1939	2,635	53.7	18.3	6.7	4.5	0.9	15.9	100.0
1940	3,532	56.3	19.1	6.0	4.5	0.9	13.2	100.0
***Indonesia* (billion 1983 rupiahs)**								
1939	19,517	49.3	9.9	12.5	8.9	0.1	19.3	100.0
1940	20,917	49.1	9.9	11.9	8.1	0.1	20.9	100.0
1941	21,971	49.5	9.6	11.6	8.4	0.1	20.8	100.0
1942	17,321	45.0	9.1	14.2	7.9	0.1	23.7	100.0
1943	14,749	54.2	8.6	13.3	5.1	0.1	18.7	100.0
1944	11,199	52.0	9.1	14.0	3.8	0.1	21.0	100.0
1945	9,553	49.9	9.1	14.3	4.0	0.1	22.6	100.0
***Indochina* (million 2000 piastres)**								
1939	1,474	64.6		22.0			13.4	100.0

Table 4.2 (*cont.*)

		%						
	GDP	Agric., fishing, mining	Trade	Manufacturing	Transport	Utilities	Services	Total
1940	1,347							
1941	1,290							
1942	1,189							
1943	1,132							
1944	893							
1945	691							
***Philippines* (million 1985 pesos)**								
1939	1,23,695	39.0		18.0		1.3	41.7	100.0

Notes: Burma: Manufacturing is the entry in the source for processing. Utilities include public utilities and public authorities. *Thailand:* Manufacturing includes construction which accounts for about 18% of the total. *Malaya:* Refers to Malaya including Penang and Malacca but excludes Singapore. Manufacturing includes construction which accounts for 38.9% of the total. *Indonesia:* Manufacturing includes construction. It declined from 11.3% of the total in 1941 to 5.7% in 1945. *Indochina:* Data are for 1938 and refer to Vietnam only. Manufacturing includes the category handicraft which accounts for 21.7% of manufacturing in the table. Data for the deflator are for working-class cost of living. For Saigon for 1945 data are an average for the first two quarters. Because of high inflation near the end of the war, which is not reflected in a deflator for only the first two quarters, GDP for 1945 is probably overstated. Moreover, the Hanoi consumer price index rose much more than Saigon's and use of the Hanoi index would give lower wartime GDP than shown in the table. GDP estimates can therefore be regarded as an upper bound. *Philippines:* Manufacturing includes construction which accounted for 7.5% of the total. Utilities include gas only.

Sources: Burma: Burma, *National income*, pp. 1–2, 5, 10. *Thailand:* van der Eng, *Thailand estimates. Malaya:* van der Eng, *Historical estimates. Indonesia:* van der Eng, 'Real domestic product of Indonesia', pp. 367–69. *Indochina:* Thien, 'Economic development', p. 72; J.- P. Bassino, personal communication. *Deflator:* Vietnam, *Annuaire statistique du Vietnam, 1949–1950*, pp. 283, 289. *Philippines:* Hooley, 'American economic policy', p. 481.

Japanese business, industry and long-term resource development but sustained investment never materialized and the Bank took over the issue of scrip (Chapter 3). Japanese industrial efforts concentrated on trying to adapt and use pre-war manufacturing capacity; this was only partially accomplished, even after mid-1943 when it was decided to try to supply the military with goods manufactured in Southeast Asia. Such Japanese investment as occurred was mainly aimed at patching up infrastructure, the provision of redundant textile machinery and a concerted but futile attempt to build usable wooden boats, as well as greater efforts to turn pre-war Southeast Asian manufacturing capacity to war production. If anything, conventional government expenditure fell because, Thailand and Indochina apart, the Japanese relied on adapting existing administrative structures and cut pre-war programmes including education, health services and hospitals, welfare provision and malaria eradication. However, military spending did replace, though partially, pre-war government expenditure.

Throughout the occupation, regional activity contracted as markets shrank due to the direct effects of dwindling exports and near disappearance of intra-regional commerce. Falls in the contributions of trade and commodity production to GDP were intensified by the collapse of transport, attenuation of public utility provision and shortages of manufactured goods. Japanese price controls added to the economic squeeze by reducing incentives for farmers to produce for local markets. Transport shortages and, by 1943, Japan's policy of enforced autarky within areas of the same country, worked in tandem to split national economies into localized enclaves. Market segmentation probably widened income inequalities in most, perhaps even all, of the region. For Southeast Asia, enforced enrolment in the Greater East Asia Co-Prosperity Sphere disrupted trade, both external and internal, deterred specialization within agriculture and mining, and wiped out dynamic gains that had flowed from all trade.

Once Southeast Asia was occupied and no longer had access to global markets, pre-war development went quickly into reverse. The other economic sectors, considered in this chapter and in Chapter 5, contracted along with the steep decline in the primary commodity and trade sectors and at about the same rate (Table 4.2). Export specialization, a loss of global markets and wartime Japanese economic policy substantially explain drops in commodity output and trade. In turn, these falls adversely impacted transport, utilities and manufacturing.

Pre-war commodity exports had been exchanged to meet most of Southeast Asia's need for basic consumer items, manufactured materials and capital equipment. Japan's failure to step in as an alternative source of supply left large gaps in the availability of manufactures and inputs needed for production. Utilities and transport contracted as trade disappeared. Each sector depended on items such as spare parts, tyres, fuel and lubricants previously obtained from abroad but which, after late 1941, became almost entirely unavailable.

In Southeast Asian countries, manufacturing accounted for at most a fifth of GDP, and typically much less. A large share of this contribution consisted of primary commodity processing which, except for rice milling and some rubber milling in Thailand and Indochina, soon became largely redundant owing to a lack of demand for Southeast Asia's main export commodities. During the war, manufacturing activity across the region probably fell somewhat less than other economic sectors due to Japanese production for the military. However, the manufacture of many basic consumer goods became impossible because the collapse of trade forced Southeast Asian economies towards near-total autarky and necessary inputs were locally unobtainable.

After occupation halted imports of nearly all essential finished goods, Southeast Asians became heavily, often exclusively, reliant on a supply of manufactures that consisted of goods already in Southeast Asia in December 1941 – the so-called 'stock economy'. Since Southeast Asia had always depended on a steady flow of imported consumer goods, pre-war stocks, as was observed of Burma, were meant to supply populations for a relatively short period.[8] By 1944, if not before, pre-war supplies were effectively exhausted. Japanese occupation left Southeast Asia economically stranded. Because of the lack of basic goods and often food, living standards for ordinary Southeast Asians probably declined even further than the roughly halving of GDP per capita which, I argue in the next section, occurred during the war.

GDP Per Capita

During World War II in Southeast Asia, 'economic life receded from modernity' and countries retreated 'toward an isolation and autarchy that harked back to precolonial times'.[9] Data for real GDP per capita, although incomplete and partly reliant on informed estimates, strongly support this judgement. Except in Thailand, the data show plunges in real per capita Southeast Asian GDP of around 50 per cent during the Japanese occupation and indicate the intensification of a macroeconomic crisis that had, as early as 1944, driven incomes in the region back to late nineteenth-century levels (Tables 4.1 and 4.2). Incomes bottomed in 1945 and in some countries took decades to regain pre-war levels. In all of Southeast Asia except Thailand, widespread malnutrition, severe economic dislocation, forced labour and, in Vietnam and Indonesia, mass famines checked or often temporarily reversed, population growth. Since the Japanese occupation ended inwards migration to Southeast Asia, no movement of young, able-bodied workers to the region was available to help maintain wartime GDP by offsetting per capita income falls through higher average labour inputs.

Quantification of GDP and its components is difficult but imperative. It can, however, be at best approximate, chiefly because the margin for error associated with so deep an economic collapse, especially in the region's exports, is substantial.

[8] Burma, *Burma's new order plan*, p. 38.
[9] Bastin and Benda, *History*, p. 127.

For Southeast Asia, yearly estimates of wartime GDP exist for three countries, the work, cited in Table 4.1, of van der Eng for Indonesia and Thailand and Bassino for Vietnam (which accounted for some 83 per cent of Indochina's population). Matters are further complicated by the need to account for domestic production of substitute goods in several areas, as well as the shift to home production, neither of which can be tracked with any reliability. The difficulty in reaching figures for national income itself is magnified by the different impacts on each of the Southeast Asian countries, and on regions within them, of the massive macroeconomic contraction that gripped Southeast Asia during the entire course of the war.

Thailand was the Southeast Asian outlier: between 1938 and 1944, GDP per capita fell by a modest 8.1 per cent, and even in 1945 remained at 82.6 per cent of its 1938 level. Thailand's economy benefited from its military alliance with Japan through avoiding extensive physical destruction from war; through its role as a supply base, especially for rice, for Japan's war effort; through government support efforts, notably for rice production; and through manufacturing ventures as part of the attempt by Phibun's government to initiate greater industrialization. The southern areas of Thailand, which produced rubber and tin for export, lost income due to the collapse in demand for those commodities, although this was partly offset by government buying of tin at around half of pre-war prices and purchases of rubber to stockpile. Furthermore, Thailand was able to sell rice, often by smuggling, to food-deficit Malaya and Indonesia. While the extent of these sales is unclear, during 1944 and 1945, when Japan liberalized Singapore's rice trade, Singapore replaced Japan as Thailand's largest export market.

During the two years prior to the outbreak of war, Indonesian GDP per capita rose partly because of increased exports of oil, rubber and tin arising from demand created by Western and Japanese stockpiling in anticipation of war (Tables 4.1 and 4.2). The last relatively normal pre-war year was 1939. Between then and 1945, van der Eng estimates, GDP per capita in Indonesia plunged by more than 50 per cent and became roughly equivalent to what it had been in 1870 (Table 4.1). De Jong concurs with the magnitude of this contraction and Booth assesses it as 'plausible'.[10] However, perhaps even more than for most of Southeast Asia, Indonesian data mask large regional variations. These arose from Indonesia's geography of numerous islands, the lack of wartime transport within and between different Indonesian areas, and Japanese-imposed regional autarky in Java. Japanese policies to restrict trade and stimulate handicrafts pushed Javanese villages 'toward the extremes of self-sufficiency' and 'an almost pre-modern state of autarky'.[11] While occupation stimulated small home industries and this helped to arrest falling GDP, it is unlikely that village production went far towards offsetting aggregate declines.

In Indochina, economic decline started earlier than in Indonesia partly due to growing Japanese controls over the economy, including over rice exports.

[10] De Jong, *Collapse*, p. 237; Booth, *Indonesian economy*, p. 50.
[11] Geertz, *Social history*, pp. 60–61.

Controls began at the end of the 1930s, and by July 1940 included the rationing of some foods.[12] During the early years of the war, however, an expansion of local industries helped to support the Indochinese economy and in 1943 GDP per capita remained at over four-fifths of the 1940 level, despite the near absence of imports apart from a few goods arising from Japanese government initiatives, including a public works programme (Tables 4.1 and 4.2). The maintenance of GDP at a level not entirely adrift of 1940 is partly explained by import-substituting industrialization which was promoted by the French administration.[13] A 38 per cent drop in GDP per capita between 1943 and 1945 reflected severe transport disruption, US air attacks, mass famine in Tonkin and North Annam and extreme instability resulting from the March 1945 Japanese coup, followed by the Indochinese Communist Party/ Viet Minh revolution in August. By early 1945, industrial activity had ceased except in sectors important to the Japanese war effort. Faced with economic breakdown, 'the main problem was to ensure the survival of the population'.[14]

Because income declines in Indochina started from an already low level, wartime decreases were particularly serious, especially for those in the poorer, northern half of Vietnam. The post-1943 fall in incomes reduced Indochina's GDP per capita to possibly the region's lowest. In 1945, average per capita income, at 1990 GK$407, was half the 1938 level and on a par with today's poorest African countries.

Three main considerations in evaluating wartime Southeast Asian GDP are the degree to which exports fell, the extent to which wartime physical destruction prevented production, and the indirect effects of a lack of transport and loss of infrastructure. In all three respects the Philippines and Burma suffered greatly. Damage to capital stock in the two countries increases the likelihood that in both declines in GDP per capita may have exceeded half. Sicat extrapolates backwards for the Philippines to calculate a drop in 1940 GDP of 50 per cent by 1943 and 70 per cent in 1945. He considers, moreover, that even a fall of 70 per cent may be an understatement due to the decimation of capital stock.[15] That included the near-total destruction of Manila and devastation in many other cities and larger towns which in the latter 'left little but the names and the sites'.[16] Between 1938 and 1946, a fall of over three-fifths in the combined index of Philippines physical production supports Sicat's estimate of a 70 per cent wartime contraction of Filipino national income and indicates that the fall of half, suggested above, may be a conservative figure.[17]

12 Verney, *L'Indochine*, p. 209.

13 OSS, R&A 1715, *Indochina's war-time government*, pp. 9–10, 33–34; 'L. A.', 'L'Indochine depuis la guerre', pp. 1–8.

14 Le, *Impact*, p. 270 and see pp. 270–72.

15 Sicat, 'Philippine economy' (2015), pp. 197, 201, 202.

16 Hartendorp, *History of industry*, p. 153.

17 Spencer, *Land*, p. 223; Steinberg, 'Ambiguous legacy', p. 180.

In Burma, the 1946/47 volume of output was 60 per cent of that in 1938/39.[18] This may understate national income decline between the end of the 1930s and 1945 due to wartime falls in transport, services, utilities and trade. Omitting strictly military traffic, the Japanese occupation soon reduced Burma's foreign trade to probably less than 5 per cent of its normal pre-war level.[19] In 1950, GDP per capita in Burma was just slightly above half that in 1938 and apparently well below what it had been in 1870 (Tables 4.1 and 4.2).

It is unclear whether Burma's 1950 GDP figure should be attributed to further post-war decline or if it reflects some recovery after 1945, but the latter seems more likely. The observations of informed contemporaries, although from outside the country, are revealing. British intelligence reported a 'drastic decline in living standards'; Burma had to adjust to a 'lower, handicraft stage of existence'. Even this was seriously hampered by a shortage of raw cotton which left a proportion of the population wearing gunny bags for clothing.[20] The country, concluded one scholar, returned to a standard of living last seen in the 1880s and 1890s.[21] 'Both in internal transport and external trade', according to another observer of the Japanese occupation, 'Burma was thrown back a century, without warning or prior preparation.'[22] During the war, as well as crisscrossing armies, endemic civil war and plagues of roaming bandits and dacoits, Burma had to cope with a breakdown in transport and, after 1943, its division into four administrative districts, each meant by the Japanese to become economically self-sufficient.[23] Burma's northern rice-deficit areas and rice-surplus south became effectively separated.

Malaya underwent a severe contraction in GDP, probably by a half to three-fifths, but which might have been ten percentage points more or less (Tables 4.1 and 4.2). The pre-war Malayan economy had the world's highest per capita exports and depended heavily on selling rubber and tin to the West. Output of both commodities dropped precipitately and they became largely unsaleable except for some Japanese buying. After the war, however, Malaya's extreme export specialization worked in reverse. A rubber tapping holiday necessitated by the war rested rubber trees, and a consequent later increase in productivity helped Malaya to benefit from the Korean war boom when, as just before the Pacific War, raw materials were in high demand for the war and for stockpiling.

Commodity Output

In this section I discuss wartime production in each of the region's main countries and how changes in production relate to the above GDP per capita

18 Burma, *National income*, p. 2.
19 Burma Intelligence Bureau, *Burma*, vol. 2, p. 173.
20 Ibid., vol. 2, pp. 175–76, 193–94, 198.
21 Christian, *Burma and the Japanese invader*, p. 355 and *Burma*, p. 124.
22 Andrus, *Burmese economic life*, p. 335.
23 OSS, R&A 2077, *Economic reorganization of Burma*, pp. 3–4.

estimates. Commodity analysis facilitates comparison across countries. It is fundamental to an assessment of falls in national income in Burma, Thailand and Indochina, since all three were so heavily specialized in producing rice for export. Due to a similar reliance on rubber and tin, Malaya and Indonesia's Outer Islands, but not Java, can also be considered chiefly through a discussion of these two staples.

The Philippines and, because of Java, Indonesia had more varied economies than those of Malaya and the three mainland rice-growing countries. Accounting for declines in commodity outputs and GDP in Indonesia poses Southeast Asia's most difficult challenge because of its size; because of economic differences between Java, with over two-thirds of all Indonesians, and the Outer Islands; and because of Java's high population density and economic diversity. As well as sugar, Java had large estate rubber, tea and coffee industries, while Javanese smallholders grew substantial amounts of rubber, copra, tobacco, coffee and tea. Furthermore, in both Java and the Philippines rice comprised a high share of total output. In 1941, Java attained rice self-sufficiency for its some 50 million people while the Philippines relied relatively little on imported rice to feed its population of over 16 million. Food output, particularly rice, is discussed in Chapter 7 in conjunction with a consideration of living standards and famine. It is worth observing here, however, that in Java by 1945 the area cultivated with food crops had fallen by 30 per cent.

All Southeast Asian countries had considerable non-export or traditional sectors, but because of large subsistence components these sectors were not central to an explanation of changing commodity output and GDP, the focus of this chapter. For this reason a discussion of traditional sectors is postponed until Chapters 7 and 8 on standards of living and levels of urbanization. Nevertheless, it should be noted here that declines in welfare among a number of traditional sector populations, including those in the north of Vietnam, northern Burma and some Philippine islands, were among the most damaging outcomes of Southeast Asia's wartime occupation.

Rice-Surplus Countries: Burma, Thailand and Indochina

Before the war, Asia, including Southeast Asia, both grew and consumed most of the world's rice. Burma, Thailand and Indochina produced the great bulk of exportable surpluses. Each of these three Southeast Asian countries had large expanses of land around river deltas specialized in growing rice to the near exclusion of other crops (Figures 4.1, 4.2 and 4.3). Rice accounted for 71 per cent of the total acreage under crops in Burma, over 90 per cent of the cultivated area in Thailand, and in Indochina, in Vietnam's southern region of Cochinchina, occupied three-quarters of land under cultivation.[24] While outside the mono-

[24] Robertson, 'Rice export', pp. 244–45; Ingram, *Economic change*, pp. 50–51.

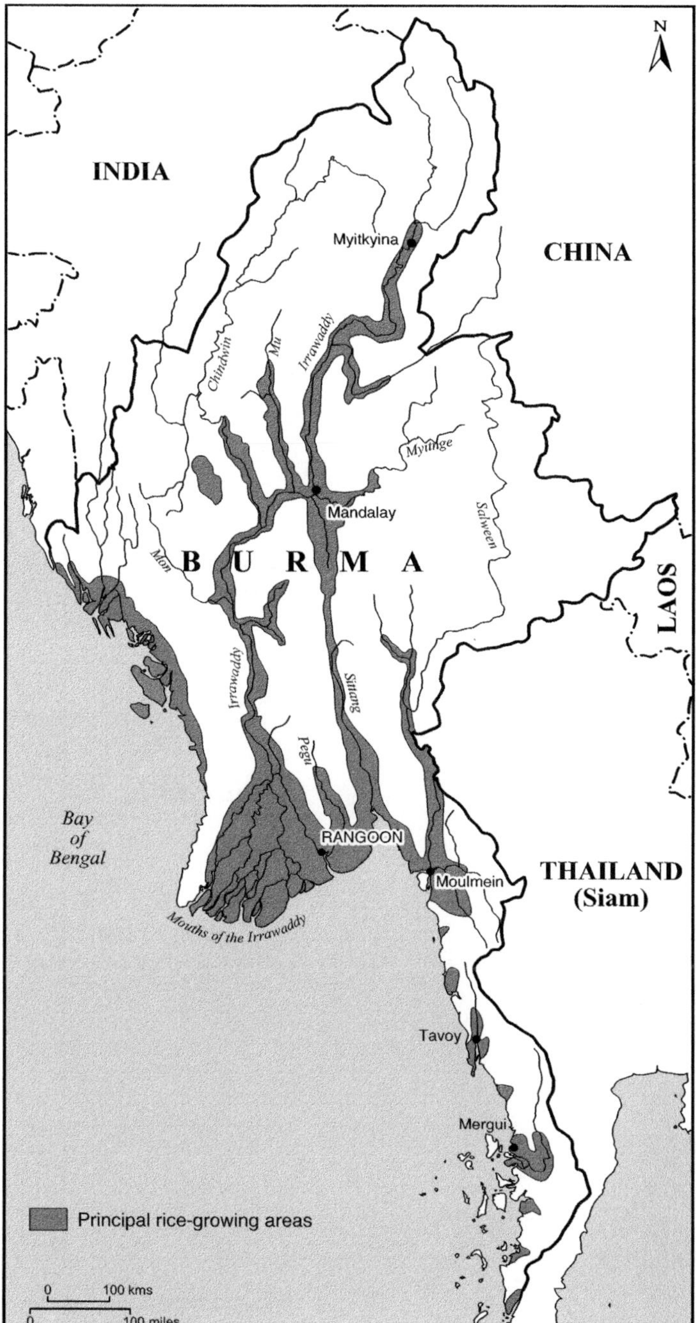

Figure 4.1 Burma rice-growing areas
Source: Fisher, *South-east Asia*, p. 453.

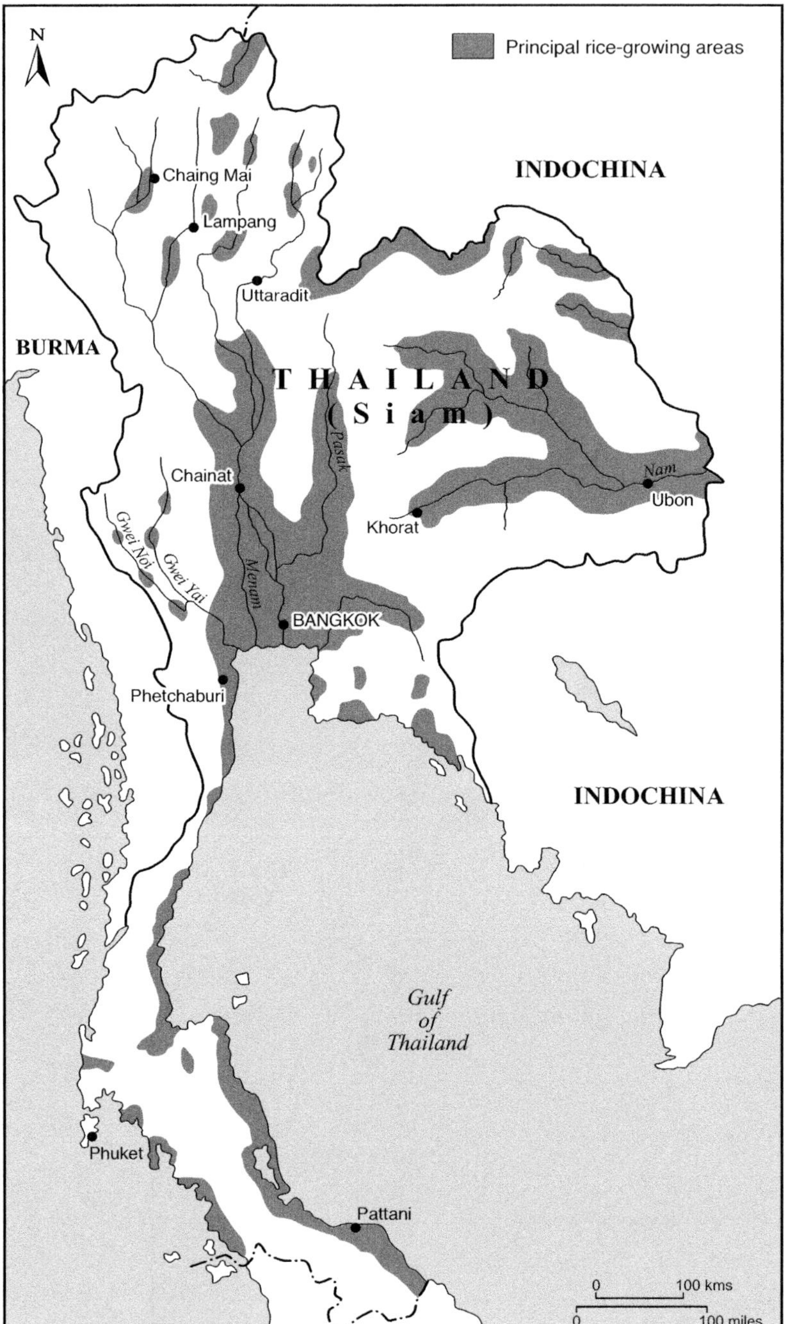

Figure 4.2 Thailand rice-growing areas
Source: Fisher, *South-east Asia*, p. 498.

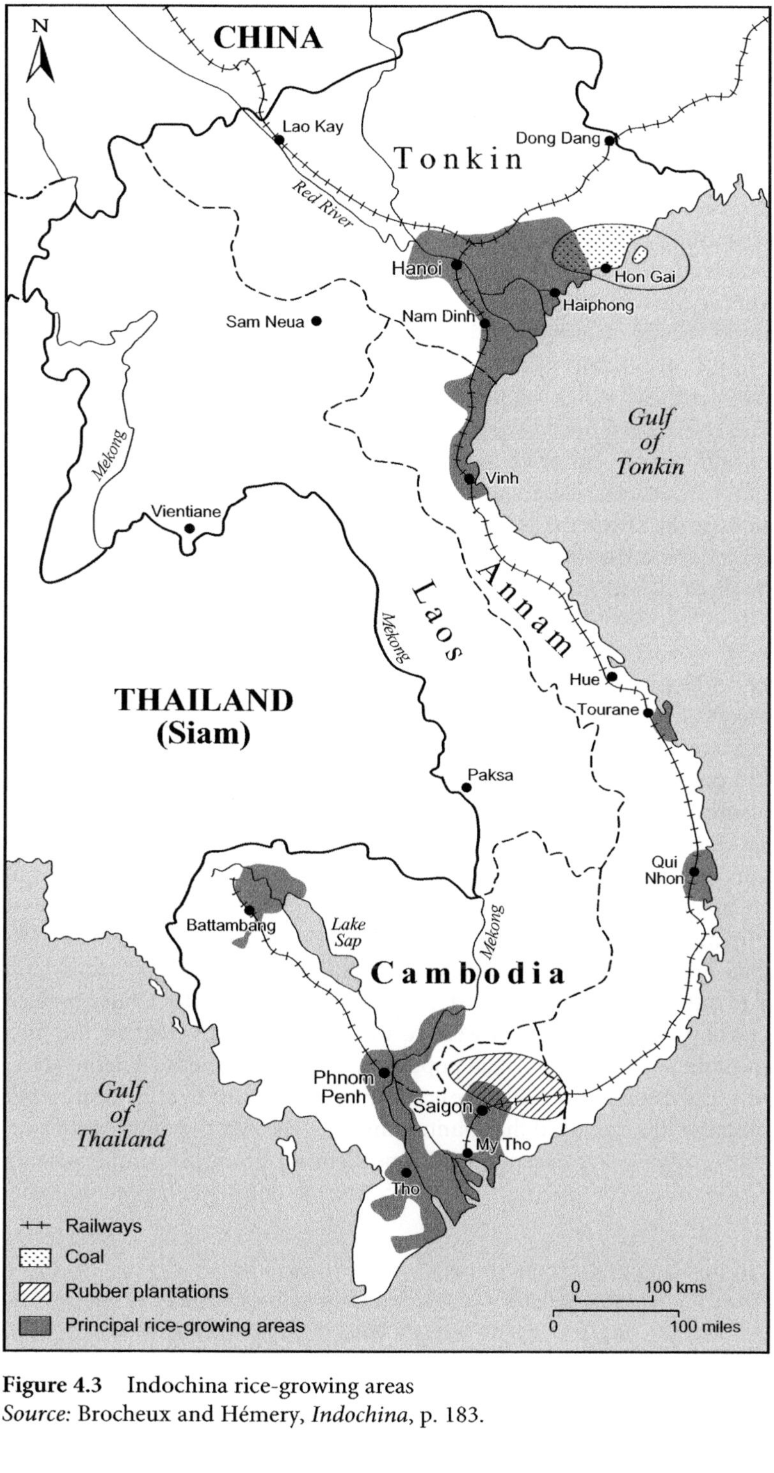

Figure 4.3 Indochina rice-growing areas
Source: Brocheux and Hémery, *Indochina*, p. 183.

crop areas of Burma, Thailand and Indochina much of Southeast Asia also grew rice, this was chiefly for local consumption or traded with nearby areas.

In the three rice-specialized Southeast Asian countries, rice normally accounted for three-fifths or more of exports. Rice from the three countries was essential in feeding large parts of the rest of Asia. Burma sent most of its rice to India, notably Bengal, although some went to Europe; Indochina supplied China and to a lesser extent Southeast Asia; and Thailand, often via Singapore, had a predominantly Southeast Asian market (Figure 4.4). The dependence of non-rice-specialized Southeast Asia on the region's main rice producers became crucial during the war, when rice shipments were impaired or ceased altogether.

Although reliant on large rice imports to feed a population in which rice accounted for 60 per cent of calorie consumption, Japan stood aloof from the three large Southeast Asian suppliers (Table 4.3). During the 1920s, Korea and Taiwan had been developed by Japan as cheap sources of rice to ensure Empire food self-sufficiency and at the same time allow the low urban wage levels needed for competitive Japanese industrialization.[25] Reflective of this cheap rice policy, in the latter 1930s Japan imported almost no rice from Southeast Asia, looking instead to its Korean and Taiwanese colonies.

The prelude to war and then the incorporation of Southeast Asia into the Greater East Asia Co-Prosperity Sphere radically altered pre-war trade patterns (Table 4.3). As early as 1940, Japan began to import large quantities of rice from all of the three main Southeast Asian suppliers. Between the later 1930s and 1941, imports from Korea and Taiwan more than halved as labour was moved out of rice cultivation and into war-related industrial production.

Beginning in 1942, however, strategic dictates, in which shipping capacity soon became key, forced Japan to reverse its policy of obtaining rice mainly from Southeast Asia. Burma was abandoned in 1942 as a rice source because of its distance from Japan and consequent demands on shipping. Thailand followed in 1943 and Indochina in 1944. Japanese imports from nearby Korea and Taiwan only partly made up for the loss of Southeast Asian rice. Moreover, although in 1944 Japan purchased 494,000 tons of rice from Indochina, 300,000 tons were shipped to other parts of Southeast Asia and 18,000 tons to China to feed Japanese troops; just 37,000 tons went to the home islands.[26] During the final two years of the war, Japan's civilian population suffered severe food deprivation.

Burma was the Southeast Asian rice economy most affected by a falling demand for rice because this impacted the country immediately after the outbreak of war; because its economy was exceptionally dependent on producing and exporting rice; and because rice milling was the country's only significant industrial

[25] Hayami, 'Rice policy', pp. 24, 29; Shu, *Growth*, pp. 71–80.

[26] LHC, MAGIC, 'Japanese purchases and shipments of Indo-China rice', 30 March 1945, pp. 1, 10–11. Table 7.1 gives a slightly different figure for Japanese purchases and does not give exports by direction.

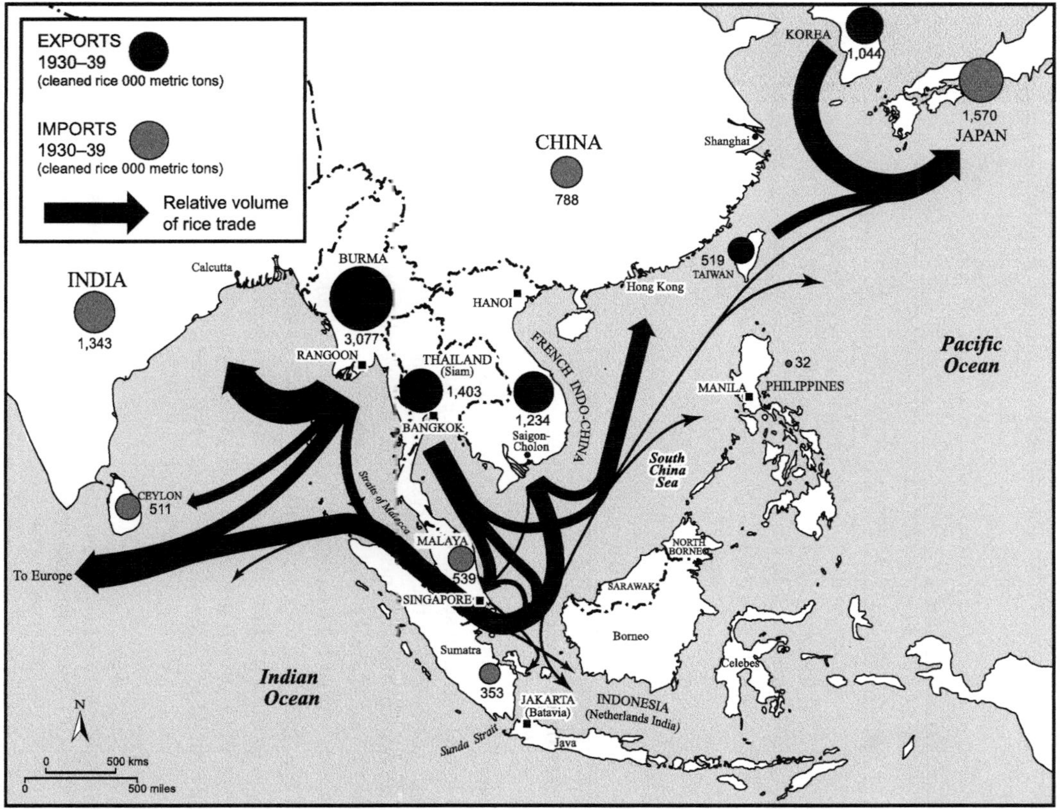

Figure 4.4 Geographical distribution of Southeast Asian rice trade 1930–1939
Source: Wickizer and Bennett, *Rice economy*, p. 87.

Table 4.3 *Japan rice imports 1936/38–1945*

a) 000 metric tons

	Burma	Indochina	Thailand	Korea	Taiwan	Total
1936/38	0	0	47	1,437	814	2,297
1939	0	0	26	948	660	1,634
1940	556	461	313	66	464	1,860
1941	500	677	461	551	328	2,517
1942	55	741	628	873	284	2,581
1943	29	688	164	0	302	1,183
1944	0	39	35	583	217	874
1945	0	0	0	227	41	268

b) % of 000 metric tons

	Burma	Indochina	Thailand	Korea	Taiwan	Total
1936/38	0.0	0.0	2.0	62.6	35.4	100.0
1939	0.0	0.0	1.6	58.0	40.4	100.0
1940	29.9	24.8	16.8	3.5	24.9	100.0
1941	19.9	26.9	18.3	21.9	13.0	100.0
1942	2.1	28.7	24.3	33.8	11.0	100.0
1943	2.5	58.2	13.9	0.0	25.5	100.0
1944	0.0	4.5	4.0	66.7	24.8	100.0
1945	0.0	0.0	0.0	84.7	15.3	100.0

Source: Cohen, *Japan's economy*, p. 369.

activity.[27] By 1943, Burma's rice exports were a tenth of their 1937/39 average (Table 4.4). An almost total disappearance of export demand, coupled with often chaotic conditions in the countryside, caused a fall in rice production of approximately two-thirds and a near halving of acreage planted with rice. The collapse of Burma's rice industry and forced retreat towards subsistence production are consistent with a fall in national income of about half, suggested earlier.

A number of factors in Burma contributed to the increase in fallow area, but central to most of these was a sharp drop in rice prices.[28] The lack of a market for rice drove down prices and cultivators began to sow only enough rice for family needs.[29] Low prices made the cultivation of paddy unattractive

[27] Spate, 'Beginnings', pp. 75, 88.

[28] MNA, Intelligence Bureau, Government of Burma, Simla, report 25, 16 September 1943, p. 6; Burma, *Season and crop report 1944*, pp. 2–13.

[29] MNA, 1/590 Intelligence Bureau, Government of Burma, Simla, report 25, 16 September 1943, p. 6.

Table 4.4 *Burma, Indochina and Thailand rice acreage, production and exports 1937/39–1950*

	Burma			Indochina			Thailand		
	Area 000 acres	Production 000 metric tons	Exports 000 metric tons	Area 000 acres	Production 000 metric tons	Exports 000 metric tons	Area 000 acres	Production 000 metric tons	Exports 000 metric tons
1937–39	12,433	7,193	3,350	12,685	6,957	1,419	8,617	4,547	1,382
1940	12,518	6,894	3,123	11,816	6,846	1,586	9,518	4,923	1,326
1941	12,325	7,738		12,207	6,944	944	9,923	5,120	1,599
1942	10,697	5,752		12,133	7,222	974	10,948	3,854	991
1943	7,635	3,053	336	12,792	7,071	1,024	10,370	5,536	739
1944	6,501	2,545		12,419	5,971	499	10,155	4,928	477
1945	6,496	2,677		12,419	4,871	45	9,406	3,572	305
1946	7,910	3,844		12,419	5,966		9,955	4,442	684
1947	8,597	5,440		12,419	6,340		12,062	5,506	513
1948	9,798	5,164		12,419	6,016		13,029	6,835	1,019
1949	9,017	4,581		12,419	6,579		13,170	6,684	1,319
1950	9,150	5,403	1,378	12,419	7,151		13,850	6,782	1,843

Table 4.4 *(cont.)*

	Burma			Indochina			Thailand		
	Area 000 acres	Production 000 metric tons	Exports 000 metric tons	Area 000 acres	Production 000 metric tons	Exports 000 metric tons	Area 000 acres	Production 000 metric tons	Exports 000 metric tons
1937–39 = 100									
	Area	Production	Exports	Area	Production	Exports	Area	Production	Exports
1937/39	100.0	100.0	100.0	100.0	100.0	100.0	100.0	100.0	100.0
1940	100.7	95.8	93.2	93.1	98.4	111.8	110.4	108.3	95.9
1941	99.1	107.6	–	96.2	99.8	66.5	115.2	112.6	115.7
1942	86.0	80.0	–	95.6	103.8	68.7	127.0	84.8	71.7
1943	61.4	42.4	10.0	100.8	101.6	72.2	120.3	121.8	53.5
1944	52.3	35.4	–	97.9	85.8	35.2	117.8	108.4	34.5
1945	52.2	37.2	–	97.9	70.0	3.2	109.1	78.6	22.1
1946	63.6	53.4	–	97.9	85.8	–	115.5	97.7	49.5
1947	69.1	75.6	–	97.9	91.1	–	140.0	121.1	37.1
1948	78.8	71.8	–	97.9	86.5	–	151.2	150.3	73.7
1949	72.5	63.7	–	97.9	94.6	–	152.8	147.0	95.4
1950	73.6	75.1	41.1	97.9	102.8	–	160.7	149.2	133.4

Sources: Burma: Saito and Lee, *Statistics*, pp. 81, 94; Andrus, *Burmese economic life*, pp. 164, 338. *Indochina:* Indochina, *Annuaire statistique, 1943–1946*, pp. 90–91, 277. Figures for production and area are for Vietnam and from Bassino and Blaise, 'Linking pre-1945 and post-1954 series', p. 423. *Thailand:* Wilson, *Handbook*, pp. 118–19; Manarungsan, *Economic development*, pp. 210–11.

compared to 'easier and quicker ways of obtaining money' including trade, war-related occupations and other manual labour. As prices fell, it became hard, and by 1944 almost impossible, to obtain cultivation loans from big landlords, and even when rice was planted its value might turn out to be less than the cost of reaping so that the crop was left to be scorched by the sun. Fields in more remote areas were abandoned because the risk of being attacked by dacoits and 'bad characters' outweighed the likely return on rice.[30]

Cultivators were also hampered by shortages of plough cattle, or during the ploughing season found their services and those of their cattle and carts commandeered for Japan's war effort. Large numbers of plough cattle were lost to slaughter to feed the Japanese army or died from 'sunstroke' when taken for long journeys to transport military stores and equipment. Others died as disease spread from one area to another due to a lack of veterinary services. Yet another reason for output declines was the occupation by the Japanese military of rice land for the construction of aerodromes or other installations.[31]

Thailand's rice exports were by 1944 only about two-fifths of pre-war levels but production changed little and the area under rice increased (Table 4.4). These last two considerations were significant in preventing a wartime fall of Thailand's national income on a scale equivalent to elsewhere in Southeast Asia. Part of the explanation for the wartime maintenance of rice production and acreage is that, compared to Burma, exports were a relatively small share of total output. A more important reason is probably that Thailand's exports fell less than official figures indicate. Unlike Burma, situated on the Southeast Asian periphery and with pre-war rice exports largely controlled by European merchants, Thailand was centrally located in Southeast Asia and rice was purchased by both the Thai Rice Company, set up as a state enterprise in November 1938, and ethnic Chinese dealers and millers, historically dominant in the rice trade. The Thai Rice Company aimed to compete with Chinese traders and by 1941 had a semi-monopoly position as an exporter.[32] During the war, the Company bought paddy and milled rice from farmers for re-sale at a slight discount to small Thai vendors for distribution throughout Thailand.[33] Chinese dealers and millers could, whether through sanctioned trade or smuggling, draw on trading links with other Chinese in Thailand's traditional markets of Singapore, Malaya and Indonesia. For much of the war there was a 'considerable trade' by Chinese-organized coastal junks travelling from Thailand and along both the east and west coasts of Malaya. The junks carried mainly rice and dried fish. Allied

30 The quotations in this paragraph are from Burma, *Season and crop report 1944*, pp. 4, 2.

31 Burma, *Season and crop report 1944*, pp. 2–13; MNA, 1/5 86 British Military Administration report, November 1945, p. 10.

32 NA, CO852/568, A. G. Baker, 'The Siamese rice trade with Malaya', 27 August 1945, p. 2; NA, HS1/71, F.C. Jones, 'Thailand part B economic', 15 October 1941, p. 4.

33 Anamwathana, 'Economic policy', pp. 33, 102; Suehiro, *Capital accumulation*, pp. 123–26.

submarine commanders could apparently distinguish between Japanese and Chinese vessels and usually let the Chinese pass.[34]

Acreage data for Indochina appear suspiciously similar from 1944 onwards, but until 1944 output figures suggest that rice production held up well (Table 4.4). Indochina's rice industry, and therefore also GDP, was bolstered by Japanese demand and, as also for rubber, by government support for the industry. The 1944 fall in output was partly owing to Japan's lack of shipping to carry rice to the home islands even from relatively nearby southern Vietnam and partly to the poor 1944/45 harvest in northern Vietnam. For want of transport either to Japan or the north of Vietnam, where there was famine, rotting rice piled up in Saigon-Cholon (Chapter 7).

Rubber: Southeast Asia

During the war, control of Southeast Asian rubber production brought little benefit to the Japanese war economy due to tiny Japanese demand but massive Southeast Asian supply. Japan had a small automotive industry (the chief user of rubber) and so required no more than an insignificant fraction of world production. Nor did the denial of rubber to the Allies have the great benefits anticipated by Japan because of American stockpiles of rubber and because of the development of synthetic rubber.[35]

The acute disparity between Southeast Asia rubber production and Japanese needs led the bulk of the export sectors of the Malayan and Outer Islands Indonesian economies to shut down, causing GDP to fall sharply in both Malaya and Indonesia. Short-term solutions to arrest decline may not have existed or, if they did, were not found. For Japan, a longer-term consideration, discussed below, was that wartime maintenance of productive capacity in the rubber (and also the tin) industry and Southeast Asia's position as a monopoly world supplier would enable a post-war Greater East Asia Co-Prosperity Sphere that incorporated Southeast Asia to extract monopoly commodity rents from western countries.

In 1940, Southeast Asia provided 85 per cent of world rubber exports, while Japan absorbed no more than about 5 per cent of world rubber production.[36] Most of world output of natural rubber, both in 1940 and in the medium term as immature rubber acreage came into bearing, depended on Malaya, where production concentrated along the west coast, and on Indonesia (Figure 4.5; Table 4.5). Each country had, in 1940, just under two-fifths of world rubber acreage; Southeast Asia as a whole accounted for 91.3 per cent of world acres planted in rubber. Even apart from a pre-war build-up of rubber stocks, the plunder of some 60,000 to 150,000 tons of rubber from Malaya, and the about

34 OSS, R&A 2695, *Status of the Chinese*, p. 43.

35 ANM, 1957/0575122 Intelligence 506/10, 'Appreciation of Malaya, part I Pre-Japanese occupation', 20 July 1943, p. 2.

36 Bauer, *Rubber industry*, p. 391; Knorr, *World rubber*, p. 249.

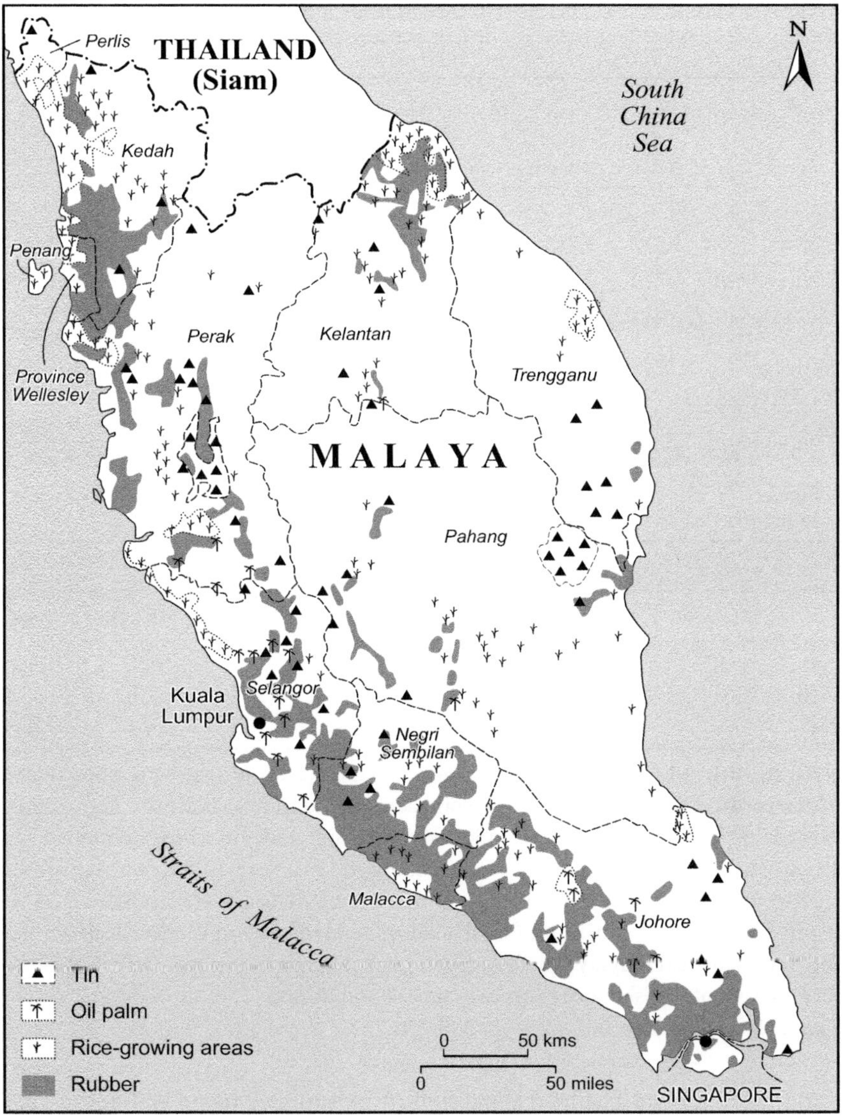

Figure 4.5 Malaya distribution of primary commodity production
Source: International Bank for Reconstruction and Development, *Economic development of Malaya*, p. 125.

39,000 tons produced in Indonesia before the occupation but exported during it, already went a long way towards supplying Japan's war needs.[37] During the

[37] Department of Economic Affairs, Batavia, 'Produce shipped', p. 56; Milward, *War, economy*, p. 165; OSS, R&A 2589, *Rubber industry*, p. 35.

Table 4.5 *Southeast Asia rubber production and exports 1939–1941*

a) Area planted in rubber end of 1940 (000 acres)

	Malaya	Indonesia	Thailand	Indochina	Other Southeast Asia	Others	Total
Mature area							
Estates	1,817	1,286	0	273	150	398	3,924
Smallholdings	1,295	1,706	299	19	308	306	3,933
Total	3,112	2,992	299	292	458	704	7,857
Immature area							
Estates	290	281	0	38	10	44	663
Smallholdings	79	100	120	1	16	28	344
Total	369	381	120	39	26	72	1,007
Total mature and immature	3,481	3,373	419	331	484	776	8,864

b) % of world exports

	Malaya	Indonesia	Thailand	Indochina	Others	Total
1939	36.6	37.4	4.2	6.6	15.2	100.0
1940	38.8	38.5	3.1	4.6	15.0	100.0
1941	37.8	41.8	3.0	3.3	14.1	100.0

Note: In 1940, Southeast Asia had 91.3% of the total of world mature and immature rubber acreage; Malaya had 39.3% of world acreage and Indonesia 38.1%. The region's four main producers of Malaya, Indonesia, Thailand and Indochina accounted for 85.0% of world rubber exports in 1940 and 85.9% in 1941. Several of the acreage figures are approximate, notably the ones for Indonesian and Thailand smallholdings. Almost all acreage in Sarawak consisted of smallholdings, while acreage in British North Borneo and Burma divided roughly equally between smallholdings and estates. Other Southeast Asia consists of British North Borneo, Sarawak and Burma.
Source: Bauer, *Rubber industry*, pp. 380, 391.

war, Indochina and Thailand alone could have supplied Japan with more than enough rubber, and the same was true of tin.[38]

After occupying Southeast Asia, one of Japan's principal economic policy problems was how to manage the region's non-food staple industries. Bound up with the decisions taken by Japan was the fate of workers employed in rubber production. On the one hand, there was little point in producing rubber on the

[38] ANM, 1957/0575122 Intelligence 506/10, 'Appreciation of Malaya, part I Pre-Japanese occupation', 20 July 1943, p. 2.

same pre-war scale that served global markets but only marginally Japan and East Asia. But any large fall in production would create unemployment. That would threaten social stability and undermine the Japanese claim to a prosperous, self-sufficient Co-Prosperity Sphere. Furthermore, post-war control over a raw material as strategic as rubber (or tin) would transfer to the Co-Prosperity Sphere economic power which before the war had been seen as unfairly favouring the United States and Britain. Despite an early preference to replace substantial *hevea* acreage with other crops, the eventual Japanese choice was to look to long-term control over natural rubber and the possibility of post-war monopoly rents. Japanese planners assessed rubber as 'a key asset for their post-war trading position'; only small amounts of *hevea*, often near towns and old rubber trees, were cut down to clear land for food crops.[39] Similarly, in Indonesia, Japanese authorities wanted 'to keep up the productivity of rubber plantations for future needs'.[40] Just 12 per cent of East Sumatra's 640,000 acres of rubber was commandeered and felled in favour of food production.[41]

Immediately after occupation, rubber production plummeted throughout Southeast Asia. During 1943 and 1944, Malayan rubber exports hovered at around a quarter of their 1937/39 level. By 1944, exports of rubber from Indonesia were a fifth of those in 1937/39 and in 1945 a twentieth (Table 4.6). Although Japanese technicians and scientists devised numerous ways to use rubber, including in the manufacture of petrol and lubricants, this still left large, unusable quantities in Singapore. The fall in Malayan rubber output goes a considerable way towards explaining that country's wartime contraction in GDP, because of rubber's extreme importance to the economy and linkages with substantial income multiplier effects. The 1931 census showed that rubber cultivation engaged some 661,000 persons, a third of Malaya's working population. It was the sole occupation of over three-quarters of these workers and was the principal activity of a large proportion of the remaining quarter returned in the census as in 'other and multifarious' agriculture.[42]

In Thailand, rubber production fell sharply although the government, anxious to have the industry in a strong post-war position, purchased rubber equivalent to half of 1940 production and stockpiled it.[43] The impact of falling output was largely confined to southern Thailand, where rubber growing concentrated as a smallholder industry. Smallholders, about 70,000 in number and mostly ethnic Chinese, had typically used previously uncultivated land to begin growing rubber as a subsidiary source of income. Since, as discussed below, Thai smallholders could be largely self-sufficient in the absence of an

[39] OSS, R&A 2589, *Rubber industry*, p. 13 and see pp. 27, 29; White, *Business, government*, pp. 79–80.

[40] OSS, R&A 3170 and second edition of assemblage 22, *Programs of Japan in Java*, p. 172.

[41] Pelzer, *Planter*, pp. 124–25.

[42] Malaya, *British Malaya: a report on the 1931 census*, p. 99.

[43] OSS, R&A 2589, *Rubber industry*, pp. 7, 41, 47.

Table 4.6 *Southeast Asia rubber and tin exports 1937/39–1950*

a) Metric tons

	Rubber				Tin			
	Malaya	Indonesia	Thailand	Indochina	Malaya	Indonesia	Thailand	Indochina
1937/39	414,981	386,123	40,271	57,333	54,494	32,090	15,595	2,226
1940	558,144	548,945	45,266	64,600	81,995	45,536	13,186	2,132
1941	584,229	660,000	47,010	50,300	61,268	53,372	16,077	70
1942	98,883	203,000	11,901	37,800	15,952	9,898	7,823	314
1943	88,814	102,000	4,976	36,100	26,417	19,085	6,028	356
1944	123,831	73,830	3,048	200	9,551	7,008	3,402	195
1945		20,000	2,032	100	3,150	1,050	1,319	14
1946	403,067	197,751	20,321	136,979	8,535	6,423	784	451
1947	656,775	283,131	45,722	51,707	27,433	15,936	4,976	107
1948	709,406	439,683	96,422	42,066	45,519	30,613	11,523	39
1949	682,278	450,358	97,606		55,781	29,033	9,329	
1950	705,240	741,343	110,896		58,423	32,102	10,833	

b) 1937/39 = 100

	Rubber				Tin			
	Malaya	Indonesia	Thailand	Indochina	Malaya	Indonesia	Thailand	Indochina
1937/39	100.0	100.0	100.0	100.0	100.0	100.0	100.0	100.0
1940	134.5	142.2	112.4	112.7	150.5	141.9	84.6	95.8
1941	140.8	170.9	116.7	87.7	112.4	166.3	103.1	3.1
1942	23.8	52.6	29.6	65.9	29.3	30.8	50.2	14.1
1943	21.4	26.4	12.4	63.0	48.5	59.5	38.7	16.0
1944	29.8	19.1	7.6	0.3	17.5	21.8	21.8	8.8
1945		5.2	5.0	0.2	5.8	3.3	8.5	0.6
1946	97.1	51.2	50.5	238.9	15.7	20.0	5	20.3
1947	158.3	73.3	113.5	90.2	50.3	49.7	31.9	4.8
1948	170.9	113.9	239.4	73.4	83.5	95.4	73.9	1.8
1949	164.4	116.6	242.4		102.4	90.5	59.8	
1950	169.9	192.0	275.4		107.2	100.0	69.5	

Note: During the war, falls in rubber exports considerably exceeded falls in production. After the war, accumulated stocks began to be exported. The figures for production were: rubber: 1940: 72,200; 1941: 76,100; 1942: 75,200; 1943: 74,800; 1944: 61,400; 1945: 12,000; 1946: 20,300; 1947: 38,560; 1948: 43,875.

Sources: Malaya: Drabble, *Malayan rubber*, p. 309; Lim, *Economic development*, p. 328; OSS, R&A 2589, *Rubber industry*, p. 4; Yip, *Tin mining industry*, p. 399.

Indonesia: Rubber: Data are for production not exports and are from a personal communication from Pierre van der Eng based on his *Growth and productivity change*. For somewhat different data, which are available for some years, see Indonesia, Department of Economic Affairs, Central Bureau of Statistics, *Statistical pocket book of Indonesia 1941*, pp. 80, 86, and also Indonesia, Department of Economic Affairs, 'Economic data on Indonesia', pp. 9, 11. *Tin:* Data are for exports. Tin ore is converted to tin concentrate. Data are from a personal communication from van der Eng. *Thailand:* Manarungsan, *Economic development*, pp. 217–19. For tin, the source does not specifically state that these are exports. *Indochina:* Indochina, *Annuaire statistique, 1943–1946*, pp. 277, 280; *1947–1948*, pp. 216–17.

income from rubber, they were not seriously affected by falling wartime demand.[44] Although many rubber estates in Thailand ceased production, labourers on them tended to migrate to other, more remunerative occupations, creating a shortage of estate labour after the war.[45]

During the war, Indochina alone exceeded pre-war rubber output due to systematic French government buying for a National Rubber Stock and purchases by private French firms. No rubber was exported in 1944 but all Indochinese production was bought for incorporation into a national reserve for French industry. By the end of 1944, Indochinese rubber stocks of about 161,000 tons, including 133,000 tons for the national reserve, were the largest in Southeast Asia and rubber acreage was slightly greater than before the war.[46] New warehouses built in Saigon-Cholon to store rubber were, by 1944, stuffed with it.[47] In 1945, however, output fell by more than four-fifths due to the ending of government support, the Japanese coup in March and political instability. After the war, the French sold most of the surplus rubber, although some was destroyed by the Viet Minh.[48]

Across Southeast Asia, the economic and social effects of the sharp drop in rubber production differed greatly. Divergences arose mainly from the contrasting production structures of estates and smallholdings. In Malaya, estate rubber comprised just under three-fifths of rubber acreage (Table 4.5). Estates were holdings of at least 100 acres but usually much larger and managed by expatriate Europeans in charge of an Asian labour force. Indians, especially Tamils recruited from Madras, formed the bulk of Malayan estate workers. By contrast, Malayan smallholdings, although technically under 100 acres, were often around 5 to 15 acres and tended by family labour with possibly one or two hired workers. Smallholder land was mainly on the more economically developed west coast of Malaya and worked by Chinese or Malays.

The division of land ownership obtaining in Malaya was reversed in Indonesia where smallholders, after rapid interwar increases in planting, cultivated nearly three-fifths of rubber land. Smallholdings accounted for only about half of rubber output in 1940 due to large immature acreage and were principally in the Outer Islands of Sumatra and Borneo; the latter had almost no estate rubber. Indonesian estates concentrated in Java and Sumatra and relied heavily on Javanese labour. Estates were almost entirely foreign owned, mainly by Dutch and Britons.

In Malaya and Indonesia, the main economic impact of the wartime drop in rubber production fell on Asian estate workers. From 1943 onwards,

44 Ingram, *Economic change*, pp. 101–4; Manarungsan, *Economic development*, pp. 107–17.

45 NA, WO203/2647, 'Summary of economic intelligence (Far East) no. 130', 15 October 1945, p. 3.

46 AOM, INF/1267, 'Rapport sur les problèmes économique depuis l'armistice', 3 February 1945, pp. 34–5; OSS, R&A 2589, *Rubber industry*, pp. v, 7, 11, 48, 49, 58.

47 OSS, R&A 2589, *Rubber industry*, p. 58.

48 Wormser, *Quelques facteurs*, p. 17; Aso, *Rubber*, p. 171.

worsening food shortages made it increasingly difficult to maintain rubber estates and their labour forces. Although in a number of instances Malayan and Indonesian estate workers were told to grow their own food on land cleared of rubber, this and other attempts to provide adequate food for estate populations were generally no more than partially successful. During the war, Malaya's estate population halved to 190,000; just 70,000 were an active estate workforce and about two-fifths of these individuals only grew food (Chapter 7). In Malaya, displaced estate workers provided some of the most extreme examples of malnutrition, starvation and, especially among migrants to large urban areas, destitution (Chapters 7 and 8). The difficult wartime circumstances faced by many Indonesian rubber estate workers during the war are discussed below, in conjunction with the similar plight of labourers on Indonesian estates growing other crops.

Among Malayan rubber smallholders, family access to nearby uncultivated land had often allowed the planting of *hevea* alongside a continuation of subsistence production. Crop diversification gave these smallholders an economic flexibility that put them in a far stronger position than estate workers to weather the wartime collapse in the demand for rubber. In the depressions at the beginning of the 1920s and 1930s, Malayan smallholders had turned to a greater, or even complete, reliance on cultivation of non-*hevea* land while they awaited better times.[49] A similar strategy could be used during the war. When it was over, Malayan smallholders quickly resumed rubber production, and by the end of 1946, 80 to 85 per cent were again tapping.[50]

The wartime collapse in the rubber industry had a more varied impact on Indonesian rubber smallholders than Malayan. Although smallholder expansion, as in Malaya, had relied heavily on abundant land, different approaches to land utilization divided Outer Islands smallholders into two types.[51] One group of smallholders, almost certainly the less numerous of the two, consisted of migrant Javanese planters who, because they lacked agricultural experience and familiarity with the Outer Islands, tended to specialize solely in rubber. The other group comprised previously established farm households which, as in Malaya and Thailand, planted rubber on nearby unused land but retained earlier subsistence crops or inter-planted *hevea* between existing subsistence crops. During the war, the option of falling back on subsistence crops allowed these smallholders, unlike their migrant Javanese counterparts, to sidestep the worst effects of the closure of a market for rubber. Although neglecting their

[49] Grist, *Outline*, pp. 163–68. On similar peasant behaviour in the 1950s, see Swift, 'Accumulation', p. 326. Bauer, 'Some aspects', p. 197 notes the ability of Malay rubber cultivators to return to paddy production.

[50] Malayan Union, *Report on agriculture in Malaya 1946*, p. 9.

[51] van der Eng, *Agricultural growth*, pp. 234, 236; see also, Pelzer, *Pioneer settlement*, pp. 24–25.

rubber trees after rubber became unsalable, Indonesian smallholders stubbed (cut down) plantings and trees on only a limited scale.[52]

Tin: Malaya, Indonesia and Thailand

Tin, like rubber, was in far greater supply in Southeast Asia than Japan required. In 1937, Malaya produced 78,787 tons and Indonesia 40,417 tons of total world tin output of 211,033 metric tons. Taking into account the smaller Southeast Asian producers of Thailand and Burma, the region accounted for 65.1 per cent of all tin production. Japan produced 2,293 tons of the metal and, together with imports, consumed 8,321 tons of tin, equal to 3.9 per cent of world output.[53]

Malayan tin production, which had reached an all-time peak in 1940 as several countries, especially the United States, scrambled to build stockpiles, fell sharply after the Japanese occupation (Table 4.6). In 1942, output of 16,000 tons was less than a third of 1937/39 average production and reflected the need to repair deliberate pre-occupation Allied damage to mining equipment, including the sinking of dredges, and the need to re-organize mining under Japanese management. Although during 1942 most tin came from Chinese gravel pump and hydraulic mines, Japanese technicians showed considerable ingenuity in bringing dredges back into production. By the end of the year 70 dredges, about two-thirds of the pre-war total, were again working. During 1943, this helped output to recover to a wartime peak of 26,400 tons, just under half its 1937/39 average. Also important in the 1943 recovery was the transfer early that year of the management of mines from Japanese administrators to about ten Japanese mining companies. They took over and operated foundries, previously owned by Chinese, to repair and maintain dredges and make mining tools for Chinese mines.[54]

After 1943, the Japanese were anxious to continue restoring Malayan production to pre-war levels, perhaps partly because tin is easily stored, and because of shipments to Germany, which in 1943/44 took 7,000 tons of tin. Output could not, however, be maintained even at its 1943 level and dwindled to 9,600 tons in 1944 and 3,200 tons during 1945. A lack of lubricating oils, and the use of poor, generally plant-based, substitutes, took a heavy toll on machinery and further added to a need for spare parts, already in short supply or entirely lacking. Production also dropped due to the widespread sabotage of mines, especially those distant from the larger towns, by anti-Japanese guerrillas. Furthermore, mining labour became increasingly unavailable because

[52] Department of Economic Affairs, Batavia, 'Native agriculture and its recovery', p. 167.

[53] International Tin Research and Development Council, *Statistical year book 1938*, pp. 12–13; Commodity Research Bureau, *Commodity year book 1939*, pp. 574, 578.

[54] Yip, *Tin mining industry*, p. 290.

workers had been taken forcibly to work on the Thailand–Burma railway, had fled to the jungle fearing shipment to the railway, or could not be induced to work for Japanese companies even with the incentive of rice rations. After the war, little mining machinery remained operative. Wholesale looting of essential components of dredges like electric gears and brass bearings supplied a black market in which Chinese miners and small business owners were eager buyers.[55]

Despite tin being a principal Malayan export and mining an important industry in much of western Malaya, the economic impact of the collapse in tin production was far less than for rubber. That was because Malayan tin mining employed a comparatively small labour force and was chiefly a European industry, due to the need for dredges to reach many deposits and other capital requirements. In 1931, the tin industry employed only 79,400 people, about 4 per cent of Malaya's working population.[56]

Some of the same Japanese companies that assumed management of Malayan mining also took control of Malaya's great pre-war European smelting works. These had been operated by the Straits Trading Company (STC) at Butterworth in Province Wellesley, Penang and on the island of Pulau Brani off Singapore, and by the Eastern Smelting Company in Penang. Hasty European evacuation as Japanese troops advanced left the Butterworth works and the plant of the Eastern Smelting Company virtually intact. During the war, Japanese tin smelting concentrated at these two sites; no tin was smelted at Pulau Brani. Its works had been disabled by STC employees and then subjected to wanton destruction by an apparently almost hysterical British military squad.[57]

Pre-war tin production in Indonesia, the other main Southeast Asian source of the metal, centred on two small islands, Banka and Billiton, near Singapore and was controlled by Dutch enterprise. Output fell dramatically during the occupation, dropping to just over a fifth of its 1937/39 average by 1944 and 3.3 per cent in 1945 (Table 4.6). However, the economic consequences of this reduction were limited because Indonesian tin mining employed comparatively few workers and existed as an enclave with few linkages to other parts of the economy. In 1920, the introduction of bucket dredgers on Billiton had allowed 150 men working three eight-hour shifts to move as much earth and tin ore as formerly required 4,000 or 5,000 workers. Probably, the main linkage created by the Indonesian mines was to a smelter in Arnhem in the Netherlands where most of the tin ore had been sent for smelting.[58]

55 Malayan Union, *Annual report on the mines department 1946*, pp. 22–30; Yip, *Tin mining industry*, pp. 289–96; NARA, RG226, entry 136, box 53, file 136, SEATIC no. 147, 17 May 1945.

56 Malaya, *British Malaya: a report on the 1931 census*, p. 99.

57 Tregonning, *Straits tin*, pp. 56, 62–63; Yip, *Tin mining industry*, pp. 289–96.

58 Naval Intelligence Division, *Netherlands East Indies*, vol. 2, pp. 262–64; Dick et al., *Emergence*, pp. 104, 139.

In Thailand, tin production concentrated on both sides of the peninsula in the south and on the island of Phuket. As in Malaya, by World War II mining depended largely on bucket dredging and European companies, including the Singapore-based Straits Trading Company. In 1937/39, European companies accounted for two-thirds of Thai production of 15,349 tons, although they engaged only about a third of a mining labour force of around 17,000. During the war, almost all miners, whether working in dredging or for one of Thailand's numerous small mines owned and mainly manned by ethnic Chinese, lost their jobs as tin production halved from its 1937/39 level to 7,694 tons in 1942 and just 1,298 tons by 1945. Chinese mining largely ceased and many European companies permanently gave up business. In 1940, western capital investment in Thai mining was estimated as 110 million baht (UK£10 million) but at the end of the war stood at £5.9 million.[59] Little is known about the wartime economic collapse of mining in Thailand but, combined with the sharp contraction of rubber production in the south and localized shortages of rice, it must have spread depression through that region which, furthermore, was poorly suited for rice cultivation. The wartime revival of local Chinese tin smelting would not have compensated for the loss of mining work and this smelting industry died out once the war ended.[60]

Bauxite: Indonesia and Malaya

Southeast Asia was Japan's only Co-Prosperity Sphere source of bauxite, essential for the manufacture of aircraft and so more valuable than tin for the war effort. Japanese imports from Southeast Asia rose from 275,000 tons in 1940 to 909,000 tons by 1943 before dropping to 376,000 tons the next year. In 1945, imports fell to almost nothing due to the severance of shipping links between Southeast Asia and Japan.

Indonesia was Japan's main Southeast Asian supplier of bauxite. Production centred on the island of Bintan and its neighbouring islands in the Riouw archipelago where during the war 6,000 prisoners of war were brought to work in the mines.[61] Between 1941 and 1943, Japan succeeded in more than doubling Indonesian bauxite production to 650,000 tons. However, output fell sharply during the last two years of the war (Table 4.7).

In Malaya, Japanese tin mining companies assumed responsibility for extracting bauxite, iron ore and coal along with a whole range of less significant

[59] Kingdom of Thailand, *Statistical yearbook 1939–40 to 1944*, pp. 535–41; Manarungsan, *Economic development*, pp. 151–53.

[60] Ingram, *Economic change*, p. 101.

[61] ANM, 1957/0575122 Intelligence 506/10, 'Appreciation of Malaya, part I Pre-Japanese occupation', p. 4; LHC, MAGIC, 'The Japanese aluminium program', 14 April 1944, pp. A36–A40.

Table 4.7 *Indonesia bauxite, coal and copper production 1936/38–1950 (000 metric tons)*

	Bauxite	Coal	Copper ore
1936/38	193.0	1322.1	6.7
1939	230.7	1796.6	23.5
1940	275.2	2009.4	55.5
1941	274.3	2029.0	55.6
1942	297.7	1533.5	27.8
1943	649.8	1038.0	43.1
1944	275.0	753.0	58.5
1945	164.0	337.0	0.0
1946	0.0	207.7	0.0
1947	24.6	222.9	0.0
1948	450.2	539.8	0.0
1949	678.0	662.0	0.0
1950	531.0	804.0	0.0

Source: Pierre van der Eng, private communication.

minerals.[62] A pre-war Japanese bauxite mine in Johore was re-started in 1942 and a new deposit in Malacca began to be worked in 1943. Between 1942 and 1944, Malaya exported 253,450 tons of bauxite to Japan. On an annualized basis, exports for the three years therefore compared almost identically to the 85,000 tons of bauxite mined in 1939. Despite this maintenance of pre-war levels of bauxite production, Malaya accounted for only about 16 per cent of all Southeast Asian bauxite sent to Japan. Although Malaya exported some 120,000 tons of iron ore to Japan, that was a tiny share of Japanese imports, which came almost entirely from outside Southeast Asia.[63]

Oil: Indonesia's Outer Islands and Burma

Oil is fundamental to war, and since Japan itself produced almost no oil, Southeast Asian wells and refining capacity were central to Japanese war planning and strategy. Although Southeast Asia, mainly the Indonesian islands of Sumatra and Borneo and to a lesser extent British Borneo and Burma, accounted for just 2.9 per cent of world oil production in 1941, output on this scale would have been sufficient for Japanese requirements (Figure 4.6).[64]

[62] Malayan Union, *Annual report on the mines department 1946*, pp. 22–30; Yip, *Tin mining industry*, pp. 289–96.

[63] Malayan Union, *Annual report on the mines department 1946*, pp. 23–25; USSBS, *Effects of strategic bombing*, pp. 189–96; OSS, R&A 2137, *Industrial facilities in Malaya*, p. 35.

[64] League of Nations, *World economic survey 1941/42*, p. 75.

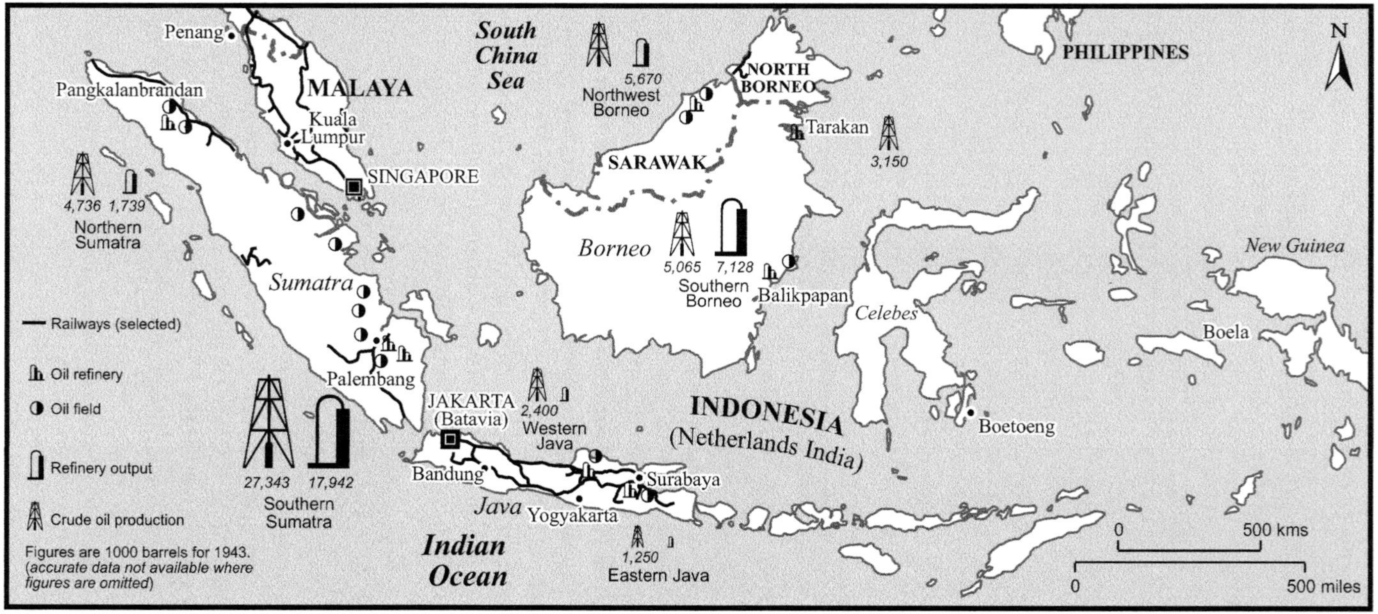

Figure 4.6 Indonesia oil production and refining
Source: USSBS, *Oil*, pp. 78–79.

Table 4.8 *Japan planned and actual Indonesian oil supplies 1940–1945 (fiscal years, million barrels)*

	Planned Japan oil consumption	Actual production Indonesia	Planned Indonesia shipments to Japan	Shipments from Indonesia received in Japan	Consumed in Southeast Asia or lost at sea
1940		65.1			
1942	35.9	25.9	1.9	10.5	15.4
1943	34.6	49.6	12.6	14.5	35.1
1944	35.9	36.9	28.5	5.0	32.0
1945		6.5		0.0	6.5

Notes: 1. The first two columns refer to all oil and the last three to crude oil and so are not strictly comparable.
2. Planned Japan oil consumption included army, navy and civilian.
3. Planned oil consumption and planned imports are from the Cabinet Planning Board, which before the war estimated Japan's oil requirements for war from 1942 to 1944. In 1944, Japan, which had started with an inventory of 51 million barrels in 1942, ended with an inventory of zero. These data indicate Japan's planned heavy reliance on Indonesian oil. It was anticipated that by 1944 Indonesia would supply four-fifths of Japan's oil requirements.
4. For 1945 data are for April to August or September.
Source: USSBS, *Oil*, pp. 38–40, 49–50, 77.

The close fit between Japanese demand for oil and Southeast Asian supply prevented a large wartime contraction in oil production. A drop in oil output does relatively little to account for falls in Southeast Asia's GDP. Japan, not Southeast Asia, was mainly affected by output changes.

By December 1941, Japan had stockpiled a projected two years supply of oil. Japanese planners anticipated that in a Pacific war of over two years Indonesia would supply four-fifths of ongoing oil requirements.[65] The oil industry in Burma had little wartime importance for Japan. Burma accounted for a tiny share of world oil output and, furthermore, wells were located principally in the somewhat remote Magway district in central Burma west of the Irrawaddy River, and heavily bombed by the Allies.[66]

After the outbreak of war, the Allies attempted to destroy Southeast Asia's oil installations, but with varying success. Japanese engineers, helped by some pre-war oil company staff and workers, soon largely restored pre-war

[65] USSBS, *Oil*, pp. 38–40, 49–50, 77. In 1944, planned consumption was estimated to be 35,900 barrels and imports from Indonesia 28,500 barrels.

[66] Andrus, *Burmese economic life*, pp. 116–22; OSS, R&A 2753, *Japanese use of Burmese industry*, pp. 20, 22.

Indonesian oil production. It peaked in 1943 at over three-quarters of 1940 output (Table 4.8). In November of that year, the refinery at Palembang was fundamental to Japan's military capacity and because of this ranked as the most important Allied target in Southeast Asia for air attack.[67] Most crude oil and all refinery output came from the Indonesian islands of Sumatra and Borneo; British Borneo and Java produced small amounts of crude (Figure 4.6). A high proportion of refined oil went to Singapore for onwards shipment to Japan and war theatres in Southeast Asia and China.

Although until 1944 Indonesian oil production and shipments exceeded pre-war Japanese targets, Japan's oil stocks fell continuously (Table 4.8). During the final two years of the war, shortages of spare parts and lubricants compromised Indonesian production. But Japan's overriding problem, as explained in the first chapter, was the destruction of its tanker capacity by Allied submarines and aircraft. During 1944, crews on tankers departing Southeast Asia embarked on what became near-suicidal voyages; the home islands received less than a fifth of the oil shipped from Indonesia. Japan could no longer effectively continue the Pacific War and was forced into desperate measures such as kamikaze flights and the transport of oil by submarine.

Agriculture: Indonesia

While rubber in Indonesia has already been considered, it is discussed here as part of the country's diversified export agricultural sector, which also included sugar, tobacco, coffee, tea and copra. Assessment of Indonesian export agriculture is complicated because production spread over a number of islands, involved a variety of crops, and often concentrated in relatively small areas; because output divided between estates and smallholders, with the latter incompletely recorded; and because some of the crops important as export commodities (for example, tobacco and sugar) were also consumed domestically (Figure 4.7). Nevertheless, the devastating impact of war and occupation on agricultural output is not in doubt. Export crops typically declined by much more than the estimated halving of GDP.

For Indonesia, the term cash (as distinct from food) crops denotes agricultural exports which may sometimes also be referred to as non-food crops such as rubber, tea and coffee. Cash crops were grown both on estates and by smallholders. Unlike in Malaya, the Indonesian cut-off point differentiating estates from smallholdings was not clearly specified according to acreage. Rather, the distinction was based on definitions of land tenure: for previously uncultivated land, foreign-owned estates operated leaseholds for a maximum term of 75 years, or in the case of leased farm land had leaseholds of 2.5 years. Smallholders cultivated what were in effect freeholdings. Despite some

[67] OSS, R&A 1286, *Selection of s. o. objectives in the Southeast Asia theatre*, pp. A1–A2.

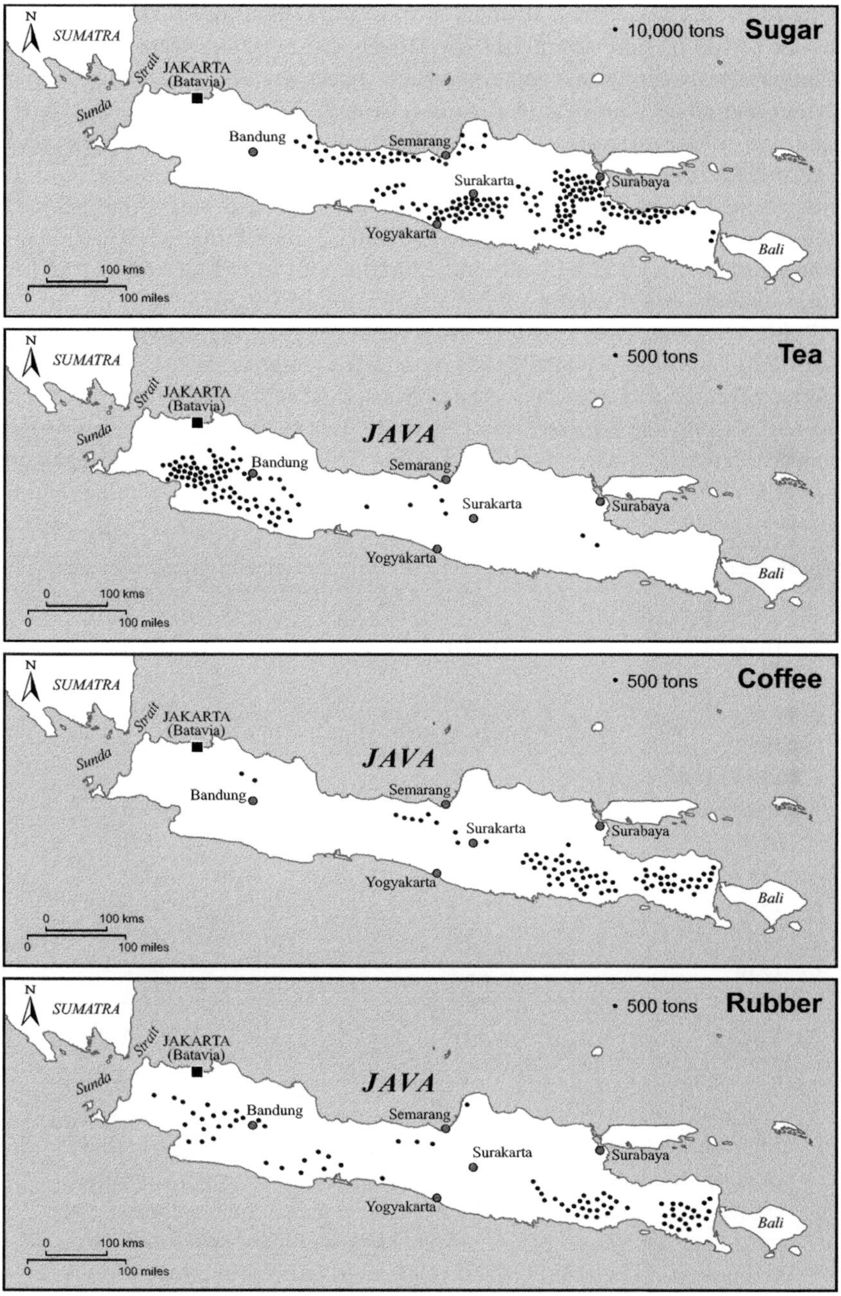

Figure 4.7 Java geographical distribution of principal export crops
Source: Stamp, *Asia*, p. 443.

definitional ambiguity, for practical purposes the difference between the two modes of Indonesian agriculture is relatively clear. Estates were holdings of usually at least hundreds, and often thousands, of acres. They were almost always owned by European companies, generally Dutch but also British or other non-Indonesian enterprises, and managed by expatriate Europeans who directed a large native labour force that might include a high proportion of migrant, usually Javanese, workers. Smallholders, although sometimes referred to as peasant cultivators, were, more accurately, small farmers who relied on household labour and frequently some hired labour to produce cash crops for domestic sales or for export.

Table 4.9 summarizes as index numbers for 1936/38 to 1950 total Indonesian estate and cash crop production in Java and the Outer Islands. Until 1942, the output of cash, and especially estate, crops rose substantially as production recovered from still depressed markets in the late 1930s and responded to the buoyant demand of stock building for war. During the Japanese occupation,

Table 4.9 *Indonesia estate and cash crop production 1936/38–1950*

	Estate crops	Cash crops
1936/38	100.0	100.0
1939	115.1	101.0
1940	120.8	103.8
1941	126.1	110.5
1942	68.1	67.3
1943	40.1	49.6
1944	27.7	35.2
1945	10.1	21.3
1946	3.7	51.5
1947	3.2	71.3
1948	22.1	88.2
1949	43.6	85.0
1950	46.3	142.8

Note: The key estate and cash crops were sugar, rubber, tea, coffee, tobacco, copra and palm oil. Smallholders in Java grew all the key estate and cash crops except palm oil, although relatively little coffee and rubber. In Java, rubber and sugar were chiefly estate crops but copra was almost entirely a smallholder crop. Rubber was the principal smallholder crop in the Outer Islands, although smallholders there also produced large amounts of coffee and copra and a significant quantity of tobacco. In the Outer Islands, smallholders grew more rubber than estates, although there were small and unreported amounts of palm fruits or tea.
Source: van der Eng, 'Real domestic product of Indonesia', p. 367.

output drops were continuous and extreme because Japan's home islands had little, if any, use for most of Indonesia's main export crops. A collapse in real prices undermined a main incentive to produce; and great disorganization reigned as the Japanese authorities struggled to find the best way to manage and re-shape estate production. In trying to accomplish this, the authorities faced enormous transport difficulties due to the loss of ships, railway disrepair and the disruption or unavailability of what regular shipping services still existed. Furthermore, key agricultural inputs such as imported fertilizer were no longer available.

At first, Japanese administrators, mainly through the *Saibai Kigyō Kanri Kōdan*, (Agricultural Estate Management Corporation) financed and oversaw estates. Then, under the shortened name *Saibai Kigyō Kanri*, this organization also attempted to manage estates, while from 1 June 1944, control over estates was ceded to Japanese companies or private individuals.[68] By 1944, estate crop output was a quarter, and cash crop production a third, of 1936/38 levels. Decline persisted in 1945, when the production of estate crops bottomed at 10.1 per cent of that in 1936/38 and cash crops fell to 21.3 per cent. Even in 1950, the estate sector produced less than half as much as in the late 1930s. Many estates were still not operating, because owners or managers had not been able to return due to continued lawlessness in rural areas; because estates were occupied by workers or local Indonesians whose occupation was condoned by the authorities; and because of the destruction of processing facilities. By contrast, aggregate cash crop output, lifted by smallholder rubber production in response to Korean war-driven demand, rose far above its pre-war level.

Tables 4.10 and 4.11 show for Java and the Outer Islands respectively output of principal estate and non-food smallholder crops. The tables omit less important crops, for example oil palm grown on estates. Nevertheless, disaggregation of the main components which comprise the index numbers in Table 4.9 provides a picture of trends in the output of Java and Outer Islands export crops.

In Java, along with rubber, sugar, tea and coffee were chiefly estate crops; smallholders produced mainly copra and tobacco. Estate production of sugar and tea declined sharply from the outset of occupation, and by 1945 had substantially ceased. Southeast Asia produced large surpluses of sugar, whether measured against world demand or the needs of a post-war Co-Prosperity Sphere in which Taiwan was already a large, highly efficient sugar producer. In response, the Japanese decided to limit Indonesian sugar output to about 650,000 tons a year, approximately two-fifths of pre-war production and deemed sufficient for local consumption. Of a pre-war total of 120 active and reserve Indonesian sugar mills, only 51 were left intact. Others were used to make butanol or alcohol or adapted to a variety of industrial purposes (Chapter 5). However, well before 1944, when sugar output had contracted sharply to under a third of its 1940 level and below the amount targeted for local consumption, there was said to be such

[68] Prillwitz, 'Estate agriculture', pp. 13–14; Keppy, *Politics*, pp. 146–53.

Table 4.10 *Java main estate and non-food smallholder crops 1940–1950*

a) 000 metric tons

	Sugar		Tea		Coffee		Rubber		Copra		Tobacco	
	Estate	Smallholder	Estate	Smallholder	Estate	Smallholder	Estate	Smallholder	Estate	Smallholder	Estate	Smallholder
1940	1,606.6	84.6	49.7	20.1	33.0	8.4	99.1	1.8	6.3	234.3	10.5	83.2
1941	1,677.0	85.6	49.5	17.8	37.1	8.3	116.8	2.2	6.0	225.3	9.0	81.5
1942	1,340.0	66.3	19.4	14.5	38.7	8.1	32.0	0.9	4.0	222.6	6.8	65.2
1943	682.9	52.0	2.0	14.7	43.2	7.9	25.4	0.4	0.0	226.2	4.5	45.0
1944	496.8	37.5	1.5	14.7	12.7	7.8	24.3	0.2	0.0	226.2	2.5	12.2
1945	282.3	22.3	0.5	14.7	10.0	7.6	5.0	0.0	0.0	224.0	0.0	4.5
1946	20.0	18.5	1.0	14.8	1.5	6.6	8.7	3.6	0.0	228.7	0.0	2.0
1947	25.0	18.8	1.5	15.0	3.3	5.0	5.9	6.9	0.1	236.2	0.0	2.0
1948	42.4	21.6	11.8	17.2	9.3	3.3	39.9	10.7	0.5	243.6	3.5	3.4
1949	223.8	45.4	22.9	19.4	10.6	4.0	63.3	11.0	1.4	250.5	3.7	13.0
1950	277.1	54.4	31.0	19.8	10.6	4.0	73.3	27.9	0.9	253.6	2.8	22.5

b) 1940 = 100

	Sugar		Tea		Coffee		Rubber		Copra		Tobacco	
	Estate	Smallholder	Estate	Smallholder	Estate	Smallholder	Estate	Smallholder	Estate	Smallholder	Estate	Smallholder
1940	100.0	100.0	100.0	100.0	100.0	100.0	100.0	100.0	100.0	100.0	100.0	100.0
1941	104.4	101.2	99.6	88.6	112.4	98.8	117.9	122.2	95.2	96.2	85.7	98.0
1942	83.4	78.4	39.0	72.1	117.3	96.4	32.3	50.0	63.5	95.0	64.8	78.4
1943	42.5	61.5	4.0	73.1	130.9	94.0	25.6	22.2	0.0	96.5	42.9	54.1
1944	30.9	44.3	3.0	73.1	38.5	92.9	24.5	11.1	0.0	96.5	23.8	14.7
1945	17.6	26.4	1.0	73.1	30.3	90.5	5.0	0.0	0.0	95.6	0.0	5.4
1946	1.2	21.9	2.0	73.6	4.5	78.6	8.8	200.0	0.0	97.6	0.0	2.4
1947	1.6	22.2	3.0	74.6	10.0	59.5	6.0	383.3	1.6	100.8	0.0	2.4
1948	2.6	25.5	23.7	85.6	28.2	39.3	40.3	594.4	7.9	104.0	33.3	4.1
1949	13.9	53.7	46.1	96.5	32.1	47.6	63.9	611.1	22.2	106.9	35.2	15.6
1950	17.2	64.3	62.4	98.5	32.1	47.6	74.0	1550.0	14.3	108.2	26.7	27.0

Source: van der Eng, *Growth and productivity change.*

Table 4.11 *Indonesia Outer Islands main estate and non-food smallholder crops 1940–1950*

a) 000 metric tons

	Tea		Coffee		Rubber		Copra		Tobacco	
	Estate	Smallholder	Estate	Smallholder	Estate	Smallholder	Estate	Smallholder	Estate	Smallholder
1940	19.3	0.0	6.3	38.4	183.6	264.5	29.9	709.2	12.6	18.8
1941	20.1	0.0	3.9	36.1	219.0	322.0	31.0	648.2	11.0	18.5
1942	7.9	0.0	4.3	33.6	60.1	110.0	26.0	522.1	8.3	14.8
1943	5.8	0.0	4.0	30.2	36.5	39.7	10.0	481.0	5.5	10.0
1944	2.8	0.0	2.0	25.0	24.5	24.8	0.0	393.4	2.5	2.8
1945	1.2	0.0	0.5	16.5	10.0	5.0	0.0	295.8	0.0	0.5
1946	0.0	0.0	0.1	8.4	11.3	174.2	0.0	351.3	0.0	0.1
1947	0.0	0.0	0.2	5.1	7.7	262.6	1.2	498.3	0.0	0.2
1948	1.1	0.0	0.5	12.5	63.8	325.2	11.2	628.2	1.2	0.5
1949	4.4	0.0	0.3	16.5	108.7	267.3	14.5	749.6	5.6	1.7
1950	4.4	0.0	0.5	35.0	104.8	535.4	13.0	758.2	4.3	2.9

b) 1940 = 100

	Tea		Coffee		Rubber		Copra		Tobacco	
	Estate	Smallholder	Estate	Smallholder	Estate	Smallholder	Estate	Smallholder	Estate	Smallholder
1940	100.0		100.0	100.0	100.0	100.0	100.0	100.0	100.0	100.0
1941	104.1		61.9	94.0	119.3	121.7	103.7	91.4	87.3	98.4
1942	40.9		68.3	87.5	32.7	41.6	87.0	73.6	65.9	78.7
1943	30.1		63.5	78.6	19.9	15.0	33.4	67.8	43.7	53.2
1944	14.5		31.7	65.1	13.3	9.4	0.0	55.5	19.8	14.9
1945	6.2		7.9	43.0	5.4	1.9	0.0	41.7	0.0	2.7
1946	0.0		1.6	21.9	6.2	65.9	0.0	49.5	0.0	0.5
1947	0.0		3.2	13.3	4.2	99.3	4.0	70.3	0.0	1.1
1948	5.7		7.9	32.6	34.7	122.9	37.5	88.6	9.5	2.7
1949	22.8		4.8	43.0	59.2	101.1	48.5	105.7	44.4	9.0
1950	22.8		7.9	91.1	57.1	202.4	43.5	106.9	34.1	15.4

Source: van der Eng, *Growth and productivity change.*

widespread and constant complaint of sugar shortages as to make this a feature of Indonesian life (Table 4.10). During the war, sugar exports from Indonesia were negligible, and while sugar channelled to the Japanese for local consumption was over half of available supplies and Indonesians consumed more sugar in the absence of other foods, these uses together do not appear to account for shortages.

A 1946 Dutch analysis by the Acting Chief Officer of Sugar Affairs explained sugar shortages as the outcome of the maintenance until June 1945 of official sugar prices at their pre-war level, high and increasing inflation, and hoarding by numerous Chinese dealers who could buy sugar at the official price but did not then re-sell it to retailers. While not an ideal commodity to store, sugar became a principal inflation hedge for Chinese dealers. Sugar acquired this role for several reasons. One was a universal demand due partly to its usefulness and partly to a lack of other food substitutes. Another was sugar's divisibility and expectations of acute post-war shortages. It was estimated that by the end of the war Chinese dealers held some 832,000 tons of sugar, equivalent to more than a quarter of the total of wartime Javanese sugar output shown by Table 4.10.[69]

During the occupation, large areas of tea were destroyed, either to free land for food crops or to plant rami for fibre, castor as a source of vegetable oil to serve as a lubricant, and pyrethrum to use as an insecticide. Only 50 of about 220 pre-war estate tea factories were left in operation and these processed only small amounts of tea. As discussed in the Chapter 5, factories on some 20 estates were converted into manufacturing centres. On most estates, however, factory parts were removed, while in a number of instances the buildings themselves were demolished. The closure of most tea estates removed an important source of income for a large number of Javanese workers: before the war in Java, sugar employed approximately 529,000 regular estate workers and other estates a further 435,000 workers. Tea estates accounted for a sizeable share of this non-sugar employment.[70]

Coffee was an exception to an immediate downwards wartime trend; estate output rose markedly through 1943. Although coffee, unlike tea, factories remained largely intact, by the end of the war output had slumped to a fifth of its 1936/38 level. By then, approximately 30 per cent of coffee bushes had been stubbed with the intention of planting rami, castor beans, derris or food crops.[71] Among Javanese smallholders, only copra output remained much the same as before the war, because coconut palms are not easily cleared to grow food crops, because they were owned by smallholders, and because copra provides an edible fat. Tobacco production, however, subsided to almost nothing as the plants were

[69] Rodenburg, 'Java's sugar supply', pp. 25–29; Centraal Bureau voor de Statistiek, 'De economische toestand van Nederlandsch-Indie', p. 119.

[70] Netherlands Indies, *Volkstelling 1930*, vol. 8, p.122; Nishijima and Kishi, *Japanese military administration in Indonesia*, p. 268 give a figure of 2 million tea estate workers but this seems unlikely to be correct and if it is must have included both the workers and their families.

[71] Prillwitz, 'Estate agriculture', pp. 15–16.

uprooted, mainly because the local market for tobacco and tobacco products collapsed and the land was used to plant food crops.

Estate agriculture was much less prominent in the Outer Islands than in Java (Table 4.11). Together with rubber, tobacco and tea were the main Outer Islands estate crops. Outer Islands smallholders produced substantial amounts of tea, coffee, copra and tobacco. Although by 1945 coffee and copra production stood at under a third of 1936/38 levels, local consumption probably helped to avoid even sharper output falls. However, tea and tobacco output dropped to near zero.

In East Sumatra, estate workers, if no longer in waged employment, often lacked a fall-back like that for non-specialized smallholders. During the occupation, a third of tea acreage, along with 12 per cent of rubber and 16 per cent of oil palm land, was cleared, parcelled into lots of 0.6 hectares, and issued to landless cultivators to grow their own food. So long as that proved feasible, or if displaced workers could find other land and start to grow food, this would have mitigated the worst effects of a loss of employment and of the food rations that had formed a part of their wages. However, for many former workers subsistence cultivation proved unsuccessful or was not tried. In East Sumatra, and also in Java (Chapter 8), a drift of people to the towns evidenced the straitened circumstances of displaced estate workers.[72]

Agriculture: Philippines

Japanese occupation destroyed Philippine export agriculture probably to an even greater extent than Indonesian, although a near-total lack of wartime production data, partly due to Japan's failure to control the countryside, restricts quantification to pre- and post-war comparisons. In the index of Philippine physical production, a fall in agriculture from 98.0 in 1940 to 58.2 in 1946 – far less than declines in manufacturing and mining and so also the combined index – fails to reflect adequately the drop in agricultural exports (Table 4.12). These comprised only about half of agricultural production, since before the war 50 to 55 per cent of cultivated land was devoted to subsistence crops, mainly rice, *palay* (unmilled or rough rice) and *canotes* (sweet potatoes).[73]

Half of all Filipino agricultural workers grew rice. So large a food sector helps to explain why the pre-war Philippines, where three-quarters of the population were rice-eaters, was 96 per cent self-sufficient in rice.[74] Domestic production supplied the rice-eating population with an average of 341 grams (1,220 calories) per day.[75] However, large parts of the country, particularly those specialized in export production as well as Manila and larger towns, were heavily deficit in rice and starchy foods. This geographical imbalance of production, along with an acute lack

[72] Pelzer, *Planter*, pp. 124–25.

[73] Hainsworth and Moyer, *Agricultural geography*, p. 14.

[74] Sacay, 'Food supply', p. 204; Hainsworth and Moyer, *Agricultural geography*, p. 31.

[75] Sacay, 'Food supply', p. 204.

Table 4.12 *Philippines index of physical production 1937–1950*

	Combined index	Agricultural	Manufacturing	Mining
1937	100.0	100.0	100.0	100.0
1938	98.2	85.3	109.1	129.4
1939	93.4	82.8	98.8	152.3
1940	109.9	98.0	117.1	165.0
1946	38.7	58.2	21.0	2.0
1947	75.6	79.5	77.5	16.8
1948	85.3	86.4	89.4	36.0
1949	91.3	92.2	94.7	49.1
1950	98.2	97.6	103.1	58.6

Sources: United States, Department of State, *Economic survey mission to the Philippines*, p. 6; Philippines, 'Central Bank statistical bulletin', p. 109; Spencer, *Land*, p. 224.

of transport, contributed to severe food shortages in the Philippines by 1943, and to subsequent localized famine (Chapters 7 and 8). Shortages affected workers in export-specialized agriculture differently according to contrasting agricultural production structures although, as throughout the Philippines, the impact of scarcities also varied with proximity to a food-surplus region and the willingness of regional politicians to ship food to deficit areas. During the war in Bicol (Kabikulan), for example, an area in the far south of Luzon highly specialized in growing abaca, inhabitants were nearly 'forced to revert completely to material life'.[76] Smallholders predominated in three of the four main agricultural export industries – copra, abaca and tobacco – and access to land gave them an opportunity to turn to growing subsistence crops. Tobacco, for example, was produced both on estates, totalling 15, and by smallholders, some 75,000 in number.[77]

Agrarian organization in the production of sugar, by far the most important export crop, was complex and included a large contingent of landless workers. The structure of production was pyramidal: it had a broad base of transient labourers and tenant farmers, above which were a smaller number of peasant proprietors and then, many fewer still, large landowners. Luzon had about equal contingents of peasant proprietors (working an average of two to five hectares) and tenant farmers. In the Visayas, transient labourers, known as *sacadas*, predominated but there were also many peasant proprietors.[78]

Although the sugar industry, localized in southern and central Luzon, Panay and Negros, occupied a relatively small part of the Philippine Islands, in 1939 it

[76] Owen, *Prosperity*, p. 157.

[77] Hainsworth and Moyer, *Agricultural geography*, p. 29.

[78] Friend, 'Philippine sugar industry', p. 181.

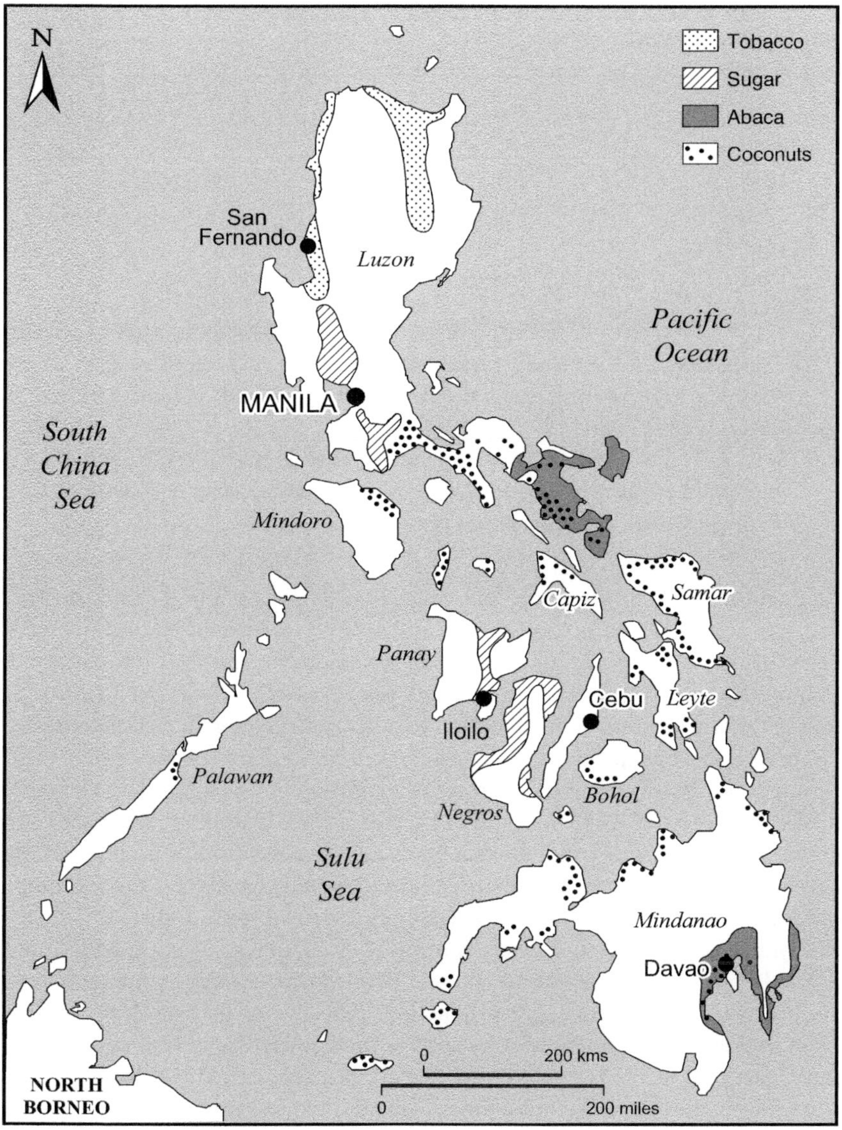

Figure 4.8 Philippines geographical distribution of principal export crops
Source: Robequain, *Malaya, Indonesia*, p. 280.

directly supported over 2 million people and indirectly a further 4 million, in total almost two-fifths of the entire population (Figure 4.8).[79] Annual average sugar exports of just over 800,000 tons in 1935/39 represented most Philippine

[79] Ibid.

Table 4.13 *Philippines main agricultural crops chiefly for export 1935/39–1950*

	Sugar	Copra	Abaca	Tobacco (cigars) pieces 000
1935/39	806	305	168	201,980
1946	12	185	30	
1947	77	905	82	
1948	355	801	99.5	
1949	661	633	75	
1950	621	708	93	

Note: For 1946 onwards, sugar data are for crop years 1945–46 (entry for 1946), 1946–47 (entry for 1947) and so forth.
Sources: Hainsworth and Moyer, *Agricultural geography*, p. 64; Honrado, 'Philippine sugar', pp. 195–96; Rodrigo, 'Coconut industry', p. 200; Cruz, 'Philippine fiber industry', p. 124.

production; local consumption took only about a fifth of output (Table 4.13).[80] Because of this export predominance and a large number of landless workers engaged in sugar-growing, Japan's determination drastically to contract Philippines sugar production to no more than enough for domestic consumption left many formerly employed in the industry struggling to feed themselves.

Three main considerations explain Japan's decision to cut sugar output.[81] First, although the world's second-largest sugar exporter, the Philippines was a highly inefficient producer: yields were the lowest per acre of all the main sugar cane growing countries.[82] Second, uneconomic sugar production had no place in the Co-Prosperity Sphere because its needs could be adequately met by Taiwanese output. Third, a chronic world oversupply of sugar meant that, unlike for Malayan and Indonesian rubber, control of Philippines sugar exports would not yield post-war commodity rents for a post-war Co-Prosperity Sphere.

For Japan, Philippines sugar production, reflective of its historical development, represented high opportunity costs of foregone land and labour. Although sugar occupied just 6.0 per cent of the total cultivated area, this had soils which were among the best in the Philippines.[83] In addition, sugar entailed a substantial labour cost. Production had expanded onto abundant frontier land and also relied heavily on the use of cheap, plentiful labour. Dependence on exports to

[80] Sacay, 'Food supply', p. 204.
[81] NARA, RG226, entry 16, box 208, 'Economic conditions in the Philippines', 15 October 1942, pp. 26–27, 29; Agoncillo, *Fateful years*, pp. 524–26.
[82] Honrado, 'Philippine sugar', p. 191; Larkin, *Sugar*, p. 55.
[83] Hainsworth and Moyer, *Agricultural geography*, p. 24.

a protected market in the United States had supported a bloated and inefficient industry. The plan for an autarkic Co-Prosperity Sphere was to re-deploy land and labour devoted to sugar to plant cotton and other fibre crops or for subsistence cultivation. Cotton was especially favoured but attempts to grow it failed (Chapter 5).

After mid-1943, much of the sugar cane harvested in the Philippines was only crudely refined for local markets or made into fuel alcohol. Automobiles and trucks in Manila at first ran on 92 per cent alcohol and 8 per cent gasoline but subsequently only on alcohol.[84] By 1943 in Manila and other parts of the Philippines, sugar began to be rationed.[85] At the end of the war, the Philippines sugar industry was in ruins. Just five mills (compared to 45 sugar centrals and a number of small mills in 1940) functioned to process the 1945/46 crop and produced just 12,000 tons of sugar (Table 4.13). A lack of spare parts and destruction left most mills inoperable. Wartime disruption had dispersed sugar farmers, workers and administrators. No sugar was exported in 1946 but exports re-started on a limited scale in 1947.[86]

Together, coconut products, abaca and tobacco accounted for about two-fifths of pre-war Philippine exports.[87] Only copra, which before the war averaged around 25 per cent of exports and accounted for a third of world production, survived the war relatively unscathed. The trees are perennials and, although with lower wartime yields due to neglect and abandonment, went on bearing nuts. Between 1935/39 and 1946, copra output, normally about half of all coconut products with coconut oil comprising most of the rest, fell by roughly 40 per cent. Beginning in 1946, a world shortage of vegetable fat drove up prices for copra and other coconut products and copra exports more than doubled from pre-war levels (Table 4.13).[88]

Abaca, responsible for some 10 per cent of pre-war exports, was the only one of the main pre-war Philippines agricultural exports in which Japan had a strong strategic interest, even allowing for the manufacture from sugar of alcohol as a fuel. Unique soil conditions in the Bicol region of southern Luzon and Davao in Mindanao, where most abaca was grown, gave the Philippines a virtual world monopoly in the production of abaca (Figure 4.8). The plants afforded unrivalled qualities in the manufacture of cordage because their fibres were the only natural fibres that would not swell in salt water. However, armies used even more abaca than navies because of haulage needs and the use of an abaca core in steel cables to provide flexibility.[89]

84 Hartendorp, *Japanese occupation*, p. 349; Kerkvliet, 'Withdrawal', p. 179.
85 Hartendorp, *History of industry*, p. 88.
86 Larkin, *Sugar*, p. 237; Hainsworth and Moyer, *Agricultural geography*, pp. 20, 24.
87 Hainsworth and Moyer, *Agricultural geography*, pp. 38–40.
88 Rodrigo, 'Coconut industry', pp. 199–200.
89 Hainsworth and Moyer, *Agricultural geography*, p. 29; Hartendorp, *Japanese occupation*, p. 357.

Before the war, Japanese firms in Davao controlled about half of Philippines abaca production. This, and abaca's place among the world's strategic raw materials, made Japan anxious to maintain pre-war output. It fell, however, due to shortages of fuel for machine stripping of the fibre and also of labour.[90] In 1946, abaca output was less than a fifth of that in 1935/39, although in 1947 it reached half of its pre-war level (Table 4.13).

Tobacco, some 5 per cent of pre-war exports, was grown all over the Philippines but especially in the Cagayan Valley in Luzon.[91] Before the war, large quantities of both leaf and cigars were exported, mainly to the United States. After occupying the Philippines, the Japanese took control of the Manila Tobacco Association, a pre-war organization of manufacturers, but the manufacture of cigars does not appear to have been pursued. The Philippines, like the other Southeast Asian countries, relied heavily on imported cigarettes. After occupation, the sale of cigarettes at controlled prices increasingly drove pre-war supplies onto the black market until stocks were exhausted. Homemade cigarettes began to be offered on the streets of Manila by pedlars but these sales were outlawed and the pedlars jailed.[92]

Southeast Asian–Japanese Trade

Japanese planners envisaged Southeast Asia during the war and in a post-war Co-Prosperity Sphere as a 'colonial-like' periphery specialized in primary commodity production. The region might, in time, have become a major source of primary commodities for the Co-Prosperity Sphere and, in turn, looked to Japan, and possibly also Korea, as industrial centres supplying manufactured goods. During the war, however, that reciprocity was conspicuously absent. Little was exported to Southeast Asians, partly because Japan could not adequately feed and clothe its home population; partly because shipping was lacking; but mainly because, as already described, Japan determined even before the war to allocate Southeast Asia a bare minimum of goods. This section documents how few goods Japan sent to Southeast Asia and the collapse in the region's exports to Japan.

Japanese import and export data record the great bulk of wartime Southeast Asian commerce, since countries in the region had little opportunity to trade except with Japan. In addition to Japanese statistics, national trade data exist only for Thailand and Indochina. Indochinese, Thai and Japanese data are used to analyse trade flows between Southeast Asia and Japan. Because of high Japanese inflation, the trade statistics by value shown in Table 4.14 greatly distort physical trade levels. In the absence of a deflator for Japan's trade with

[90] Hartendorp, *Japanese occupation*, pp. 357–58.
[91] Hainsworth and Moyer, *Agricultural geography*, p. 29.
[92] Hartendorp, *Japanese occupation*, pp. 351–53.

Southeast Asia, the table includes an index of Japanese wholesale prices. The following discussion uses this index to approximate real trade.

Prior to World War II, Japan's main trading partner was the United States (Chapter 1). Southeast Asia was relatively unimportant, accounting for about 10 per cent of both Japanese imports and exports. Nor for Southeast Asia was Japan that important, since the latter obtained rice almost entirely from Korea and Taiwan and imported small amounts of most Southeast Asian raw materials. While Southeast Asia's imports of Japanese manufactured goods increased markedly in the 1930s, the region still imported manufactures chiefly from Europe and the United States (Table 4.14).

During the war, although Southeast Asia's share in Japan's trade rose, trade values and volumes fell dramatically. Beginning in 1941, exports to the region spiralled downwards and by 1944, in real terms, were around 15 per cent of their level three years previously. Southeast Asia's share of Japan's imports continued to increase until 1942, mainly due to rice from Indochina and Thailand, and reached a quarter of total Japanese imports. The region did not, however, provide the

Table 4.14 *Japan trade with Southeast Asia 1936–1948*

	Million current yen			Million current yen			
	Imports from Southeast Asia	Total imports	Southeast Asia % of total imports	Exports to Southeast Asia	Total exports	Southeast Asia % of total exports	Japan price index 1936 = 1
1936	274.8	2,763.7	9.9	290.8	2,693.0	10.8	
1937	374.0	3,783.2	9.9	386.7	3,175.4	12.2	1.2
1938	272.1	2,663.4	10.2	219.2	2,689.7	8.1	1.3
1939	295.2	2,917.6	10.1	235.5	3,576.4	6.6	1.5
1940	554.4	3,452.7	16.1	301.1	3,655.8	8.2	1.7
1941	693.1	2,898.6	23.9	306.5	2,650.9	11.6	1.8
1942	433.4	1,751.6	24.7	234.6	1,792.5	13.1	2.4
1943	460.0	1,924.4	23.9	305.4	1,627.4	18.8	2.7
1944	219.0	1,947.2	11.2	186.1	1,298.2	14.3	3.3
1945	49.1	956.6	5.1	15.9	388.4	4.1	3.1
1946	0.0	4,068.7	0.0	14.2	2,260.4	0.6	18.9
1947	415.6	20,264.8	2.1	2,451.8	10,148.0	24.2	51.0
1948	3,063.2	60,287.2	5.1	11,264.1	52,022.1	21.7	149.6

Note: Price indexes are for wholesale prices in Japan and only approximate orders of magnitude. Prices are actual (as opposed to the official price index) wholesale prices from Cohen, *Japan's economy*, p. 97.

Sources: Japan, Ministry of Finance, *Nihon gaikoku bōeki nenpyō* (Return of foreign trade of Japan), 1937–1944–48; Cohen, *Japan's economy*, p. 97.

bonanza of raw materials anticipated by pre-war Japanese planners. By 1942, real trade was roughly a third of what it had been in 1940. In the final two years of the war, both Southeast Asia's share of Japanese imports and the region's goods imported by Japan dwindled to insignificance (Tables 4.14, 4.15 and 4.16).

As was the Japanese intention, membership of the Greater East Asia Co-Prosperity Sphere dramatically re-oriented Southeast Asian trade. It became largely limited to Japan. Between 1942 and 1944, well over 90 per cent of Indochina's exports went to Japan. It, in turn, was the source of from half to three-quarters of

Table 4.15 *Japan imports from Southeast Asia 1938/39–1945*

a) Total current yen and % of total

	1938/39	1940	1941	1942	1943	1944	1945
Total yen 000	283,678	554,401	693,101	433,428	459,963	219,040	49,095
Indochina	8.3	17.6	23.2	51.7	28.8	10.2	0.6
Thailand	1.8	9.6	26.4	38.5	10.7	4.7	0.2
Malaya	38.2	23.0	6.6	0.8	21.7	37.9	95.5
Burma	4.1	13.7	12.2	2.7	1.1	2.8	0.0
Philippines	14.9	11.0	8.0	1.7	12.0	7.7	2.3
British Borneo	4.4	2.5	1.3	1.7	4.1	5.5	0.0
Indonesia	28.2	22.6	22.2	2.9	21.7	31.3	1.4
Total %	100.0	100.0	100.0	100.0	100.0	100.0	100.0

b) Per capita current yen imports to Japan

	1938/39	1940	1941	1942	1943	1944	1945
Indochina	1.0	4.2	7.0	9.7	5.7	1.0	0.0
Thailand	0.3	3.5	12.2	11.2	3.3	0.7	0.0
Malaya	21.7	25.5	9.2	0.7	19.9	16.6	9.4
Burma	0.7	4.5	5.0	0.7	0.3	0.4	0.0
Philippines	2.7	3.8	3.5	0.5	3.5	1.1	0.1
British Borneo	15.1	16.4	11.1	8.7	22.8	14.4	0.0
Indonesia	1.2	1.8	2.2	0.2	1.4	1.0	0.0

Notes: 1. Imports include re-imports.
2. Malaya includes the Straits Settlements and the Malay peninsula.
3. Population data are for 1938 apart from British Borneo which are for 1939 and Burma and Indonesia which are for 1941. The British Borneo population (except Sarawak) for 1939 and the Indonesia population for 1941 are estimated by using census figures (1931 for British Borneo and 1930 for Indonesia) and assuming annual population growth of 1.2%. The Sarawak figure is a 1939 headcount.
Source: Japan, Ministry of Finance, *Nihon gaikoku bōeki nenpyō* (Return of foreign trade of Japan), 1937–1944–48.

Table 4.16 *Japan exports to Southeast Asia 1938/39–1945*

a) Total exports (000 current yen) and % of total

	1938/39	1940	1941	1942	1943	1944	1945
Total yen	227,360	301,149	306,547	234,550	305,403	186,148	15,919
Indochina	1.1	0.9	14.8	61.6	31.8	11.7	11.9
Thailand	14.4	16.4	21.4	28.3	28.8	5.9	20.0
Malaya	10.0	8.6	3.2	0.7	6.4	28.9	24.9
Burma	8.3	7.3	3.5	1.9	4.2	5.5	0.0
Philippines	12.6	8.9	4.4	0.6	9.8	19.7	7.6
British Borneo	0.4	0.4	0.2	0.2	0.9	2.7	0.0
Indonesia	53.2	57.6	52.5	6.7	18.2	25.6	35.6
Total %	100.0	100.0	100.0	100.0	100.0	100.0	100.0

b) Per capita current yen exports to Japan

	1938/39	1940	1941	1942	1943	1944	1945
Indochina	0.1	0.1	2.0	6.3	4.2	0.9	0.1
Thailand	2.2	3.3	4.4	4.4	5.9	0.7	0.2
Malaya	4.5	5.2	2.0	0.3	3.9	10.8	0.8
Burma	1.1	1.3	0.6	0.3	0.8	0.6	0.0
Philippines	1.8	1.7	0.8	0.1	1.9	2.3	0.1
British Borneo	1.1	1.4	0.6	0.6	3.2	6.1	0.0
Indonesia	1.7	2.5	2.3	0.2	0.8	0.7	0.1

Notes: 1. Exports include re-exports.
2. Malaya includes the Straits Settlements and the Malay peninsula.
3. Population data are for 1938 apart from British Borneo which are for 1939 and Burma and Indonesia which are for 1941. The British Borneo population (except Sarawak) for 1939 and the Indonesia population for 1941 are estimated by using census figures (1931 for British Borneo and 1930 for Indonesia) and assuming annual population growth of 1.2%. The Sarawak figure is a 1939 headcount.
Source: Japan, Ministry of Finance, *Nihon gaikoku bōeki nenpyō* (Return of foreign trade of Japan), 1937–1944–48.

Indochinese imports (Tables 4.17 and 4.18). Thailand was never as dependent on Japan as Indochina. But in 1942 Japan took almost three-quarters of Thai exports and provided over three-fifths of Thailand's imports (Tables 4.19 and 4.20).

Similar trade statistics are not available for other Southeast Asian countries, because they began Japanese occupation as conquered dependencies and were not considered sovereign like Thailand or a colony like Indochina. However, the trade reliance on Japan of the other Southeast Asian countries would have been as high as, and probably higher than, Thailand's and Indochina's. Just as

Table 4.17 *Indochina exports by direction 1939–1945*

a) Value of exports (million current francs)

	1939	1940	1941	1942	1943	1944	1945
France	1,130.1	675.9	161.6	0.0	0.0	0.0	0.0
French colonies	170.6	186.2	209.9	98.2	63.1	25.3	0.0
Japan	153.1	815.7	1,599.3	2,338.8	1,996.0	793.2	133.1
United States	418.7	644.3	159.8	0.0	0.0	0.0	0.0
China	169.2	441.8	307.6	11.0	16.5	7.2	8.6
Hong Kong	310.6	528.4	164.8	0.1	1.1	2.3	0.1
Macao	n.a.	n.a.	111.9	8.1	27.5	0.2	0.6
Thailand	14.2	11.8	2.8	9.0	6.6	22.3	9.6
Singapore	356.0	332.1	113.1	0.0	0.6	0.0	0.0
Indonesia	37.7	12.2	6.5	0.0	0.0	0.0	0.0
Philippines	75.9	11.5	9.0	0.0	0.3	0.3	0.1
Others	659.6	293.8	22.0	6.8	14.4	14.3	27.2
Total	3,495.7	3,953.7	2,868.3	2,472.0	2,126.1	865.1	179.3

b) % of exports

	1939	1940	1941	1942	1943	1944	1945
France	32.3	17.1	5.6	0.0	0.0	0.0	0.0
French colonies	4.9	4.7	7.3	4.0	3.0	2.9	0.0
Japan	4.4	20.6	55.8	94.6	93.9	91.7	74.2
United States	12.0	16.3	5.6	0.0	0.0	0.0	0.0
China	4.8	11.2	10.7	0.4	0.8	0.8	4.8
Hong Kong	8.9	13.4	5.7	0.0	0.1	0.3	0.1
Macao	n.a.	n.a.	3.9	0.3	1.3	0.0	0.3
Thailand	0.4	0.3	0.1	0.4	0.3	2.6	5.4
Singapore	10.2	8.4	3.9	0.0	0.0	0.0	0.0
Indonesia	1.1	0.3	0.2	0.0	0.0	0.0	0.0
Philippines	2.2	0.3	0.3	0.0	0.0	0.0	0.1
Others	18.9	7.4	0.8	0.3	0.7	1.7	15.2
Total	100.0	100.0	100.0	100.0	100.0	100.0	100.0

Note: For 1942–44, data for Kouang-Tcheou-Wan (Guangzhouwan) are included under the destination 'French colonies'. For earlier years, these data are listed separately as Kouang-Tcheou-Wan and it is unclear if the data are also included under French colonies. Kouang-Tcheou-Wan, a small enclave on the southern coast of China and a leased territory, appears to be the main destination within French colonies for Indochina exports.

Sources: Indochina, *Annuaire statistique, 1939–1940*, pp. 146–47, 164–74; *1941–1942*, pp. 154, 171–83; *1943–1946*, pp. 156–57, 179–86.

Table 4.18 *Indochina imports by direction 1939–1945*

a) Value of imports (million current francs)

	1939	1940	1941	1942	1943	1944	1945
France	1,332.80	769.2	285.2	9.2	0.1	0.3	0.0
French colonies	78.0	61.5	35.5	52.6	78.0	13.6	7.6
Japan	40.1	31.3	336.4	1,142.8	1,258.1	337.8	50.7
United States	99.3	238.2	191.2	8.6	0.0	0.0	0.0
China	115.9	140.7	441.3	165.1	141.3	71.1	77.1
Hong Kong	166.2	258.1	161.0	7.1	18.7	49.5	0.7
Macao	n.a.	n.a.	226.3	10.5	14.1	0.1	0.0
Thailand	41.3	31.0	13.6	41.5	167.0	151.7	30.1
Singapore	100.7	120.9	70.0	1.1	0.2	0.2	0.0
Indonesia	104.4	144.9	51.7	2.4	1.0	18.5	4.7
Philippines	2.5	9.3	116.7	2.3	0.0	0.0	0.0
Others	313.1	233.8	71.6	19.3	6.9	8.4	3.6
Total	2,394.30	2,038.90	2,000.5	1,462.5	1,685.4	651.2	174.5

b) % of imports

	1939	1940	1941	1942	1943	1944	1945
France	55.7	37.7	14.3	0.6	0.0	0.0	0.0
French colonies	3.3	3.0	1.8	3.6	4.6	2.1	4.4
Japan	1.7	1.5	16.8	78.1	74.6	51.9	29.1
United States	4.1	11.7	9.6	0.6	0.0	0.0	0.0
China	4.8	6.9	22.1	11.3	8.4	10.9	44.2
Hong Kong	6.9	12.7	8.0	0.5	1.1	7.6	0.4
Macao			11.3	0.7	0.8	0.0	0.0
Thailand	1.7	1.5	0.7	2.8	9.9	23.3	17.2
Singapore	4.2	5.9	3.5	0.1	0.0	0.0	0.0
Indonesia	4.4	7.1	2.6	0.2	0.1	2.8	2.7
Philippines	0.1	0.5	5.8	0.2	0.0	0.0	0.0
Others	13.1	11.5	3.6	1.3	0.4	1.3	2.0
Total	100.0	100.0	100.0	100.0	100.0	100.0	100.0

Note: For 1942–44, data for Kouang-Tcheou-Wan (Guangzhouwan) are included under the source 'French colonies'. For earlier years, these data are listed separately as Kouang-Tcheou-Wan and it is unclear if the data are also included under French colonies. Kouang-Tcheou-Wan, a small enclave on the southern coast of China and a leased territory, appears to be the most important source within French colonies for Indochina imports.

Sources: Indochina, *Annuaire statistique, 1939–1940*, pp. 146–47, 164–74; *1941–1942*, pp. 154, 171–83; *1943–1946*, pp. 156–57, 179–86.

Table 4.19 *Thailand exports by country and region 1941–1945 (current baht)*

	1941		1942		1943		1944		1945	
	000 baht	%	000 baht	%	000 baht	%	000 baht	%	000 baht	%
Southeast Asia	96,214	33.2	25,335	18.4	55,678	48.1	76,863	81.6	73,860	82.6
Singapore	39,829	13.7	4,959	3.6	25,565	22.1	32,801	34.8	47,134	52.7
Penang	44,689	15.4	4,351	3.2	7,358	6.4	15,709	16.7	8,233	9.2
Malay states	10,035	3.5	6,643	4.8	13,300	11.5	13,024	13.8	14,813	16.6
British Borneo	525	0.2	974	0.7	0	0.0	8,130	8.6	812	0.9
Burma	168	0.1	187	0.1	1,227	1.1	415	0.4	114	0.1
Indochina	143	0.0	4,564	3.3	7,676	6.6	4,695	5.0	2,399	2.7
Indonesia	759	0.3	1,130	0.8	552	0.5	2,089	2.2	355	0.4
Philippines	66	0.0	2,527	1.8	0	0.0	0	0.0	0	0.0
Japan and possessions	113,002	39.0	97,379	70.7	47,355	40.9	6,411	6.8	809	0.9
Japan	109,426	37.7	97,322	70.7	46,997	40.6	6,381	6.8	809	0.9
Formosa	22	0.0	5	0.0	0	0.0	0	0.0	0	0.0
Korea	1,109	0.4	0	0.0	0	0.0	0	0.0	0	0.0
Manchuria	2,445	0.8	52	0.0	358	0.3	30	0.0	0	0.0
Hong Kong	38,429	13.2	1,888	1.4	1,411	1.2	225	0.2	13,330	14.9
China	35,655	12.3	9,606	7.0	7,041	6.1	3,118	3.3	1,019	1.1
India	490	0.2	0	0.0	0	0.0	0	0.0	0	0.0
United Kingdom	553	0.2	0	0.0	0	0.0	0	0.0	0	0.0
United States	3,022	1.0		0.0		0.0		0.0		0.0
Others	2,719	0.9	3,499	2.5	4,244	3.7	7,620	8.1	440	0.5
Total	290,084	100.0	137,707	100.0	115,729	100.0	94,237	100.0	89,458	100.0

Source: Kingdom of Thailand, *Annual statements of foreign trade 1942–1945*, p. 92.

Table 4.20 *Thailand imports by country and region 1941–1945 (current baht)*

	1941		1942		1943		1944		1945	
	000 baht	%	000 baht	%	000 baht	%	000 baht	%	000 baht	%
Southeast Asia	39,527	23.4	23,624	23.4	71,819	35.4	112,256	71.6	106,115	97.1
Singapore	16,423	9.7	1,524	1.5	13,343	6.6	32,021	20.4	36,873	33.7
Penang	11,233	6.7	10,802	10.7	18,442	9.1	15,568	9.9	10,757	9.8
Malay states	1,498	0.9	6,319	6.3	15,903	7.8	32,600	20.8	25,409	23.2
British Borneo	0	0.0	0	0.0	0	0.0	0	0.0	0	0.0
Burma	115	0.1	477	0.5	10,996	5.4	1,008	0.6	871	0.8
Indochina	799	0.5	3,108	3.1	7,265	3.6	27,829	17.8	31,624	28.9
Indonesia	7,691	4.6	1,391	1.4	5,647	2.8	3,230	2.1	581	0.5
Philippines	1,768	1.0	3	0.0	223	0.1	0	0.0	0	0.0
Japan and possessions	53,769	31.8	62,322	61.8	107,179	52.9	37,253	23.8	1,397	1.3
Japan	53,477	31.7	60,396	59.9	102,798	50.7	36,310	23.2	1,397	1.3
Formosa	264	0.2	1,408	1.4	4,116	2.0	917	0.6	0	0.0
Korea	28	0.0	295	0.3	28	0.0	0	0.0	0	0.0
Manchuria	0	0.0	223	0.2	237	0.1	26	0.0	0	0.0
Hong Kong	17,079	10.1	799	0.8	689	0.3	544	0.3	1,715	1.6
China	13,837	8.2	9,106	9.0	21,256	10.5	4,293	2.7	24	0.0
India	6,429	3.8	11	0.0	0	0.0	0	0.0	3	0.0
United Kingdom	7,727	4.6	102	0.1	210	0.1	1	0.0	62	0.1
United States	23,713	14.0	2,488	2.5	15	0.0	0	0.0	19	0.0
Others	6,758	4.0	2,349	2.3	1,593	0.8	2,327	1.5	0	0.0
Total	168,839	100.0	100,801	100.0	202,761	100.0	156,674	100.0	109,335	100.0

Source: Kingdom of Thailand, *Annual statements of foreign trade, 1942–1945*, p. 91.

with incorporation of Southeast Asia into a yen area, the Japanese aim in regard to trade went beyond economic exploitation: it was that the economic ties of trade, like those of currency, would make it politically impossible for Southeast Asian countries to separate from Japan.

From 1941 to 1943, Japan began to shift any supply of goods to Southeast Asia strongly in favour of its allies of Thailand and Indochina (Table 4.16). Between 1938/39 and 1941, Indonesia, reflecting its large population and successful 1930s market penetration by Japanese exporters, took over half of the goods Japan sent to Southeast Asia. None of Southeast Asia's other countries accounted for as much as a fifth of Japanese exports to the region. After 1941, the physical quantity of Japanese exports to Southeast Asia fell dramatically. Insofar as Japan supplied Southeast Asia with any consumer and manufactured items, these went predominantly to Thailand and Indochina. The two countries accounted for almost 90 per cent of Japanese goods that reached Southeast Asia in 1942 and three-fifths in 1943.

Per capita exports to Southeast Asia measured in Japanese yen tell a similar story and emphasize the sparseness of supply from Japan (Table 4.16). In 1942, at the height of Japan's favouritism of Indochina, Japanese shipments to Indochina averaged on a per capita basis just 6.3 yen worth of goods. The peak for Thailand was 5.9 yen in 1943. Per capita exports to other Southeast Asian countries were generally negligible with the 1944 exception of Malaya due to shipments of machines and metal goods. These exports partly reflected the new, mid-1943 desire to make Singapore an industrial centre and partly Japanese defence needs. In 1944, machinery, sent mainly to the Straits Settlements, accounted for over half of Japanese exports to Malaya. If shipments to the military were taken into account and excluded from the figures in Table 4.16, this would reduce imports available to Southeast Asians

The balance of trade between Southeast Asian countries and Japan affords a measure of exploitation and shows that this was considerable (Table 4.21). In most years, Southeast Asia ran substantial trade surpluses with Japan. Surpluses in 1941, Indochina apart, pre-dated Japanese control. Trade deficits for Thailand in 1943 and 1944 are partly explained by sharp falls in rice sent to Japan but probably are also due to Japan's shipment of goods for the military, since import statistics show the receipt of few consumer or capital goods. Although data for Southeast Asia for 1942 to 1945 alone reduce the magnitude of surpluses, they do not alter the overall picture. There is, moreover, a large understatement of surpluses because of the enforced devaluations of Southeast Asian currencies (Chapter 3).

Thailand, Indochina and Malaya accounted for the bulk of the Southeast Asian trade surplus; Japan imported few goods from the Philippines and almost nothing from Burma. Obtaining goods from Burma was not a priority: its distance from Japan, pressure on Japanese shipping capacity and more than enough rice from Thailand and Indochina discouraged trade. The sharp declines in Japan's trade deficit with Southeast Asia after 1942 gave an appearance of less one-sided trade. This evening up of exchange did not represent more goods

Table 4.21 *Southeast Asia trade balance with Japan 1941–1945 (000 current yen)*

	Exports to Japan	Imports from Japan	Trade balance (X-M)	% of Southeast Asia trade surplus
Thailand				
1941	182,903	65,649	117,254	
1942	166,902	66,462	100,440	
1943	49,169	87,833	-38,664	
1944	10,250	10,910	-660	
1945	89	3,178	-3,089	
			175,281	24.5
Indochina				
1941	160,654	45,377	115,277	
1942	223,984	144,380	79,604	
1943	132,260	97,034	35,226	
1944	22,275	21,761	514	
1945	312	1,897	-1,585	
			229,036	32.0
Indonesia				
1941	153,704	161,007	-7,303	
1942	12,751	15,733	-2,982	
1943	99,818	55,520	44,298	
1944	68,452	47,563	20,889	
1945	692	5,675	-4,983	
			49,919	7.0
Burma				
1941	84,789	10,739	74,050	
1942	11,715	4,495	7,220	
1943	4,861	12,720	-7,859	
1944	6,159	10,301	-4,142	
1945	0		0	
			69,269	9.7
Malaya				
1941	45,991	9,893	36,098	
1942	3,337	1,637	1,700	
1943	49,329	19,600	29,729	
1944	83,019	53,830	29,189	
1945	46,867	3,960	42,907	
			139,623	19.5
Philippines				
1941	55,772	13,361	42,411	
1942	7,472	1,328	6,144	
1943	55,096	30,053	25,043	

Table 4.21 (*cont.*)

	Exports to Japan	Imports from Japan	Trade balance (X-M)	% of Southeast Asia trade surplus
1944	16,838	36,672	-19,834	
1945	1,135	1,210	-75	
			53,689	7.5
Total Southeast Asia trade surplus			716,817	100.0

Source: Japan, Ministry of Finance, *Nihon gaikoku bōeki nenpyō* (Return of foreign trade of Japan), 1940–41–1944–48.

going to Southeast Asia, however, but a precipitate decline in trade. As the war continued, Japan sent fewer and fewer goods to Southeast Asia, while at the same time the Japanese could not import much from Southeast Asia due to growing shortages of shipping and overall contraction of economic activity.

Trade: Thailand and Indochina

National trade data collected by the authorities in Thailand and Indochina reveal how starved the whole of wartime Southeast Asia was of consumer items and manufactured goods. The data show this for three reasons. One was that most Japanese exports went to Thailand and Indochina, and a second that Southeast Asia itself produced few of its own basic consumer and capital goods. Third, after 1941, if goods were to come from anywhere, it would have to have been from Japan. But even to Thailand and Indochina, Japan's favoured trading partners, the Japanese sent no more than trickles of goods. Thai and Indochinese trade statistics help to reveal sharp declines in living standards and the truth of the remark that to Burma, Japanese ships brought only 'arms and ammunition, *sake* and comfort women'.[93]

Tables 4.22 and 4.23 show the volume of Thai and Indochinese imports from Japan and classify them as consumer or capital goods. For Thailand, consumer items divide into two types. One, notably foodstuffs and fuels, was obtained from regional suppliers. Reflecting Japanese control of trade and transport, imports of these goods contracted sharply, and by 1944 stood at around a fifth of 1941 levels.

The second type of consumer goods, textiles and thread, comprises goods which were major pre-war imports and which wartime shipments from Japan

[93] Pe, *Narrative*, p. 55.

Table 4.22 *Thailand import volume of consumer and capital goods 1941–1945*

	Quantities	Volume in 1941	1941 = 100 1942	1943	1944	1945
Consumer goods						
Fish, dried and salted	000 kg	693.0	27.4	30.6	19.8	8.6
Sugar, manufactured	000 kg	32,458	21.0	33.7	13.8	14.0
Beer	000 litres	1,659	33.3	22.5	2.4	0.0
Kerosene	000 litres	20,044	58.0	40.2	10.4	3.6
Paraffin	000 kg	1,429	2.9	29.0	2.2	6.6
Matches	000 boxes	21	15,573.0	8,834.2	25,229.3	7,751.7
Quinine	000 kg	8.2	3.8	71.4	6.5	4.7
Toilet soap	000 kg	150	28.9	3.6	40.4	47.9
Cigarettes	000 kg	204	3.3	11.6	21.7	0.8
Cotton prints	000 pieces	334	13.6	8.7	2.0	0.8
Shirting	000 pieces	2,138	11.3	13.4	2.5	0.3
Artificial silk	000 kg	1,674	22.8	14.3	2.6	0.0
Sewing thread	000 kg	186	51.3	19.5	7.5	2.6
Capital goods						
Liquid fuel	000 litres	51,528	25.0	35.9	21.9	6.1
Benzine	000 litres	28,811	8.6	50.9	23.4	9.0
Cotton yarn, grey	000 kg	3,480	2.3	0.1	0.2	0.2
Raw cotton	kg	7	417.8	757.0	1,210.1	150.3
Paper	no. 000	433	5.8	2.2	0.2	0.1
Cordage and rope	000 kg	1,299	8.2	57.9	31.5	14.7
Gunny bags	000 bales	34	65.7	38.1	165.5	0.8
Machine belting	000 kg	78	24.9	24.8	72.7	6.7
Sewing machines	000 machines	6.5	4.6	10.8	12.3	3.1
Metal bars, sections	000 kg	5,328	6.5	18.9	7.0	0.4
Galvanized sheets	000 kg	3,879	0.5	0.1	2.6	0.2
Nails	000 kg	4,932	2.5	3.3	2.9	1.2
Iron and steel manufs.	000 kg	4,259	9.5	9.1	5.5	2.6
Chemical products	000 kg	9,352	25.3	37.5	5.3	3.0
Bicycles	no. 000	6.0	111.7	59.9	22.3	4.3
Automobiles	no.	1,392	23.6	5.5	7.7	5.7
Automobile parts	000 kg	363	11.5	81.3	17.8	3.4
Automobile tyres	000 tyres	24	50.3	22.2	21.6	22.9

Note: Cordage and rope includes coir and Manila hemp. Nails include wire nails and other nails. Shirting includes white, grey, dyed and Turkey red.
Source: Kingdom of Thailand, *Annual statements of foreign trade, 1942–1945*, pp. 1–53.

Table 4.23 *Indochina volume of imports 1937/39–1946*

	Wheat flour 000 tons	Cotton fabric 000 tons	Cotton thread 000 tons	Iron and steel bars 000 tons	Teak 000 tons	Raw cotton 000 tons	Gunnies 000 tons	Petrol and refined oils 000 tons	Automobiles number	Auto chassis number	Bicycles and spare parts tons	Inflatable tyres and tyre treads tons
1937/39	23	8.4	1.4	21.4	30.2	11.1	26.3	75	1892	497	959	1,326
1940	20	3.8	1.1	22.8	30.0	11.7	21.0	85	922	382	421	1,213
1941	15	4.6	2.3	5.7	17.5	13.3	17.0	23	252	756	65	833
1942	0	4.6	1.0	0.2	12.5	0.5	12.0	1	51	75	278	391
1943	0	2.0	0.1	0.9	6.3	0.0	9.4	0.2	28	11	318	214
1944	0	0.3	0.0	0.1	2.1	0.0	1.6	0.2	0	0	44	55
1945	0	0.0	0.0	0.0	0.0	0.0	0.0	0.0	0	0	2	0
1946	6	2.0	0.1	9.0	0.0	4.1	15.3	37	0	0	51	777

Source: Indochina, *Annuaire statistique, 1943–1946*, pp. 293–94.

might have replaced. By Southeast Asian standards, Thailand had an indigenous textile industry of some significance because weaving continued to exist, mainly in the north-east and to a lesser extent elsewhere in the north. Largely as a result, before the war, about a third of the quantity of textiles consumed in Thailand was woven domestically, either from imported yarn or domestically grown cotton.[94] Nevertheless, that left Thailand, especially Central Thailand, chiefly dependent on textile imports, and beginning in 1942, imports of both textiles and almost all other consumer items progressively fell. By 1944, imports of most consumer goods were less than 4 per cent of 1941 levels. Matches were an exception, but the index numbers for them are misleading in regard to living standards. Before the war, most matches were produced locally and imports were small. After the Japanese occupation, matches were in short supply because of a contraction of production by local Chinese-owned firms which could not secure necessary raw materials (Chapter 5).

Pre-war Thailand produced almost no capital goods. During the war, any such goods would have had to come as imports from Japan. For the most part, however, new and replacement capital goods were unavailable. The difficulty in initiating new industrialization, despite government promotion attempts, is apparent from the lack of imports of capital equipment and manufactured materials like machine belting, galvanized iron and metal manufactures. Chronic shortages of fuel and lubricants for machinery would further have hindered industrialization. The import of gunny bags fell less than most other imports because they were needed to ship rice. Sharp increases in raw cotton imports between 1942 and 1944, shown by Table 4.22, are discussed in Chapter 5 in conjunction with Japan's efforts to boost textile manufacturing in Southeast Asia.

The Japanese supply of manufactures to Indochina was as meagre as it was to Thailand (Table 4.18). Indochina had a relatively large domestic textile industry by Southeast Asian standards, but nevertheless relied heavily on imports of gunny sacks and cotton goods, the latter accounting for 14.1 per cent of all Indochinese imports in 1937.[95] Over the course of the war, imports of fabric and thread fell effectively to zero. So too did imports of raw cotton to supply a small Indochinese textile manufacturing sector. The near-disappearance of tyres and tyre treads and a drop to almost nothing of imported petrol and refined fuels (none of which Indochina produced locally) seriously restricted the use even of Indochina's continuously falling stock of working vehicles.

Shipping: Thailand and Indochina

Port traffic at Bangkok and Saigon tells a story similar to trade but from a different angle (Tables 4.24 and 4.25). At Bangkok, the explanation for the much higher

[94] Ingram, *Economic change*, pp. 118–19.

[95] AOM INF/1267, 'Rapport sur les problèmes économique depuis l'armistice', 3 February 1945, pp. 7–8; Indochina, *Annuaire statistique 1937–1938*, pp. 162–66.

Table 4.24 *Bangkok ships cleared with cargo 1941–1949*

a) Number and tonnage

	Inwards		Outwards	
	No.	000 tons	No.	000 tons
1941	419	521	547	791
1942	56	134	91	254
1943	86	133	113	188
1944	47	35	74	51
1945	18	7	14	3
1946	246	235	246	277
1947	418	513	461	599
1948	559	800	627	1,104
1949	651	1,068	742	1,459

b) 1941 = 100

	Inwards		Outwards	
	No.	000 tons	No.	000 tons
1941	100.0	100.0	100.0	100.0
1942	13.4	25.7	16.6	32.1
1943	20.5	25.5	20.7	23.8
1944	11.2	6.7	13.5	6.4
1945	4.3	1.3	2.6	0.4
1946	58.7	45.1	45.0	35.0
1947	99.8	98.5	84.3	75.7
1948	133.4	153.6	114.6	139.6
1949	155.4	205.0	135.6	184.5

c) Japanese ships as % of total

	Inwards		Outwards	
	No.	000 tons	No.	000 tons
1941	13.1	26.7	21.2	43.5
1942	91.1	95.5	94.5	98.4
1943	44.2	75.2	52.2	81.9
1944	19.1	48.6	36.5	62.7
1945	33.3	2.1	57.1	11.0

Notes: 1. The explanation for the higher number and tonnage of Japanese ships with cargo cleared outwards than inwards is that Japanese ships arrived in ballast and so without cargo but carried cargo away from Thailand.
2. During the war, apart from Japanese vessels, Thai ships were virtually the only ships clearing outwards from Bangkok.
Sources: Kingdom of Thailand, *Report of the financial adviser, 1941–1950*, p. 17; Kingdom of Thailand, *Annual statements of foreign trade, 1942–1945*, pp. 81, 83.

number and tonnage of ships with cargo cleared outwards than inwards is the dominance of rice and its bulkiness and seasonality. After the late autumn harvest, ships came to Bangkok in ballast to lift rice. While these ships arrived at Bangkok without cargo, they had rice cargoes outwards. A similar pattern apparently persisted during occupation. The Japanese used special rice boats and informed Thailand's government that these ships had no space for goods shipped to Thailand. These would have to come by regularly scheduled steamers.[96] Large vessels virtually disappeared from Bangkok harbour as trade fell, and as the Allies systematically destroyed Japan's merchant fleet. Furthermore, by February 1944, Bangkok's port was being subjected to air attack.[97] Between 1941 and 1944, the number of ships inwards to Bangkok fell from 419 to 47. In 1945, just 18 ships arrived.

Inwards shipping tonnage decreased even more dramatically than outwards, and by 1944 was less than 7 per cent of 1941 tonnage. At first, Japanese ships dominated at Bangkok. Beginning in 1943, however, their importance declined sharply, because Japan's military position worsened and because after 1942 Thailand was allowed to trade with other Japanese-controlled areas. Thai traders, mostly ethnic Chinese, took advantage of this and forged wartime links with other parts of Southeast Asia, notably Singapore.[98]

Shipping at Saigon remained at a higher absolute level than at Bangkok, but nevertheless between 1943 and 1945 the number of ships outwards dropped by over 85 per cent and tonnage by two-thirds. In 1943, the great imbalance between outwards merchandise (1,209,000 tons) and inwards (182,500 tons) reflects bulky rice cargoes and the paucity of Japanese exports to Indochina. Especially during 1944 and 1945, a further reason for falls in both shipping and merchandise handled at Saigon was that ships called further south at Cap Saint Jacques to avoid Allied bombers flying from bases in China.

Conclusion

The Japanese occupation of Southeast Asia became a 'natural experiment' of an abrupt shift from highly globalized to autarkic economies: occupation suddenly reversed the economic environment in a region which, for the seven previous decades, had been fundamentally shaped by free trade, comparative advantage and integration into the world economy as one of its most highly specialized components. The GDP measures set out at the beginning of this chapter are approximate. But the chapter's marshalling of evidence on the

[96] LHC, MAGIC, 'Economic', 17 September 1942, p. 7.

[97] On the danger for shipping in Bangkok harbour, see LHC, MAGIC, 'Economic', 2 February 1944, p. 9 and 'Digest of 8 December report from Ambassador Yamamato on the situation in Thailand', 3 January 1945, p. A1.

[98] Numnonda, *Thailand*, p. 87.

Table 4.25 *Saigon port traffic 1943–1946*

	1943		1944		1945		1946	
	No.	000 tons	No.	000 tons	No.	000 tons	No.	000 tons
(a) Ships inwards	576	1,533.9	267	785.7	134	705.1	475	1,586.9
(b) Ships outwards	575	1,540.20	277	774.9	104	549.3	475	1,616.9
(c) Merchandise inwards		182.5		50.8		105.1		460.2
(d) Merchandise outwards		1,209.9		370.2		13.1		402.3

Source: Indochina, *Annuaire statistique, 1943–1946*, p. 125.

consequences of Japanese occupation for commodity output and trade – the engines of Southeast Asia's economies – makes it difficult to accept that, Thailand apart, per capita incomes in Southeast Asia could have fallen by less than half during the war. In several instances, the facts point to even greater decline. Chapter 5, which takes up the sectors of transport, public utilities and manufactures, builds upon and supports this assessment of trends in GDP during the war years.

5

Transport, Public Utilities and Industrialization

In analysing agriculture and mining, Chapter 4 dealt with two of the six sectors that Kendrick identified as the main components of an economy in an industrial age. This chapter presents evidence for three more of Kendrick's sectors – transport, public utilities and manufacturing. The chapter divides into two parts: the first considers transport and public utilities, the second manufacturing. I argue that wartime trends in these sectors paint a picture that accords with the estimated losses in GDP of half or more presented in Chapter 4.

Neither transport and public utilities nor manufacturing directly accounted for a large share of GDP. Table 4.2 indicates that the direct contribution of transport and utilities was no more than 5 to 10 per cent. Manufacturing may have been about a fifth of Indochinese GDP, but elsewhere in Southeast Asia it was at most about 15 per cent and probably well below that in Burma and Malaya. Even taken together, transport, utilities and manufacturing could have exerted only a relatively small direct impact on GDP and not one sufficient to reverse trends described in Chapter 4. Moreover, reversal was unlikely as Japan was stretched at home. It had few resources to invest in Southeast Asian transport or utilities and, as indicated in the last chapter and discussed in the second part of this chapter, made little effort to develop Southeast Asian manufacturing until mid-1943.

The indirect effects of wartime declines in transport and utilities could, however, be large and both sectors impacted indirectly on GDP through extensive backward and forward linkages to other economic sectors. At the aggregate level, efficient transportation reduces costs in many industries (while inefficient transportation increases these costs), and confers mobility on labour and capital. Additionally, there are unintended or unforeseen impacts such as congestion and a diversion of resources from some firms and industries.

During the war, acute transport shortages developed throughout Southeast Asia. Modern transport, other than for military use, became virtually unavailable. The military's commandeering of almost all automobiles, lorries, railways and ships would not in itself have necessarily reduced GDP, but it did so because the armed services often lacked adequate fuel and parts to operate the transport they had. For Southeast Asians, if buses and trams functioned, it was with much reduced services. Coastal and inland shipping services on which most of Southeast Asia depended to move food and goods sharply declined or even disappeared. Local wartime construction of infrastructure and some ships along with a greater use of conveyances like bullock carts and rickshaws contributed to a limited extent to GDP but in no way made up for either direct or indirect losses. Japanese railway construction, chiefly in Thailand and Burma, added to transport capital in these two countries but mostly at the expense of its depletion in other parts of Southeast Asia. New railways relied heavily on rolling stock, locomotives and track from Southeast Asia's existing railways, not imports from Japan. The construction of state highways in Thailand virtually stopped during the war because available funds were transferred to build military roads. When the war ended, existing roads had fallen into such disrepair that their rehabilitation and improvement took all the efforts of the Highways Department for the next three years.[1] In October 1942, an American intelligence report on the Philippines observed that whether industry and commerce revived to some extent 'will depend largely on the ability of the Japanese and the Civil Administration to solve the transportation problem'.[2] No solution proved possible in the Philippines or anywhere else in Southeast Asia. By the late stages of the war, probably well under half of pre-war transport operated.

Large wartime contractions in the transport and utility sectors reinforced declines in GDP analysed in Chapter 4 when transport was unavailable to move goods and food, leaving the latter to rot; when industries which might have operated efficiently could no longer do so; when workers were fatigued from long journeys to work; and when power stations ceased to function so that factories lacked electricity or gas supplies to operate. In Burma, Malaya and the Philippines, Allied sabotage just before occupation considerably reduced available public utilities and these were often restored slowly, and frequently no more than partially. Furthermore, throughout Southeast Asia and even in main cities, equipment for utilities operative at the time of occupation was often not replaced after damage or loss. As the war continued, insofar as public utilities still functioned, their operation became patchy due to inadequate fuel stocks and a lack of spare parts.

Manufacturing had fewer indirect effects than transport and utilities. Southeast Asian countries relied so heavily on imports of manufactures that linkages from local manufacturing to other sectors of the economy were less than for transport and utilities. However, manufacturing linked backwards to a demand for labour and raw materials and forwards to furnishing some inputs for industry and, importantly, to providing final consumption goods crucial to giving an incentive for food production. Along with low food prices and forced deliveries, the lack of manufactured goods to exchange for food discouraged its production and added to the problem of feeding people.

1 Kingdom of Thailand, *Report of the financial adviser 1941–1950*, p. 46.

2 NARA, RG226, entry 16, box 208, 'Economic conditions in the Philippines', 15 October 1942, p. 2.

Estimates in Table 4.2 and evidence in this chapter suggest that by 1945 public utilities and transport had fallen by at least as much as other components of GDP, and possibly by more. Through indirect effects, declines of this magnitude in transport and utilities could not but drag down other economic sectors. Manufacturing, hindered by many of the same shortages that affected transport and utilities, fell roughly in line with contraction in the other four economic sectors discussed in this chapter and in Chapter 4. By mid-1943, as Southeast Asia's economies spiralled downwards, a collapse in manufacturing was already underway, seemingly unstoppably.

PART I: TRANSPORT AND PUBLIC UTILITIES

Pre-war Southeast Asian economic development and geography left Japan a poor transport legacy from which to construct its war effort. Japanese military operations, as well as Southeast Asians themselves, suffered from Japan's occupation strategy to have the armed forces rely as much as possible on whatever they found in Southeast Asia rather than on supplies from Japan. Although after occupation the Japanese monopolized modern transport, pre-war Southeast Asia had insufficient motorized vehicles, shipping and transport infrastructure for the needs of a modern military. Added to this, growing shortages of spare parts, lubricants and fuel together with Allied bombing reduced transport and infrastructure facilities, making them progressively more inadequate.

Southeast Asian Transport and Geography

Problems of insufficient transport encountered by Japan when occupying Southeast Asia were greatly compounded by Southeast Asian geography and the region's pattern of pre-war economic development. As mainland Asia's southernmost extensions, Burma, Thailand, Malaya and Indochina were predisposed to a predominately north–south geographical configuration, since international shipping ran near the tips of these countries. Furthermore, almost all the main rivers in these countries run north–south. From the 1870s onwards, geography was reinforced by the transformation of Burma, Thailand, Malaya and Indochina into export economies: railways and roads for the carriage of primary commodities to world markets focused on Rangoon, Bangkok, Singapore and Saigon-Cholon as the ports nearest to the world east–west shipping route which bisected Southeast Asia after the inauguration of the Suez Canal. Railway lines, although sometimes branching to form tree-like networks, generally paralleled major rivers or the coastlines, and ran north–south. In adhering to geography, infrastructure ensured that internal communications focused on a single port city in the south (Figure 5.1).

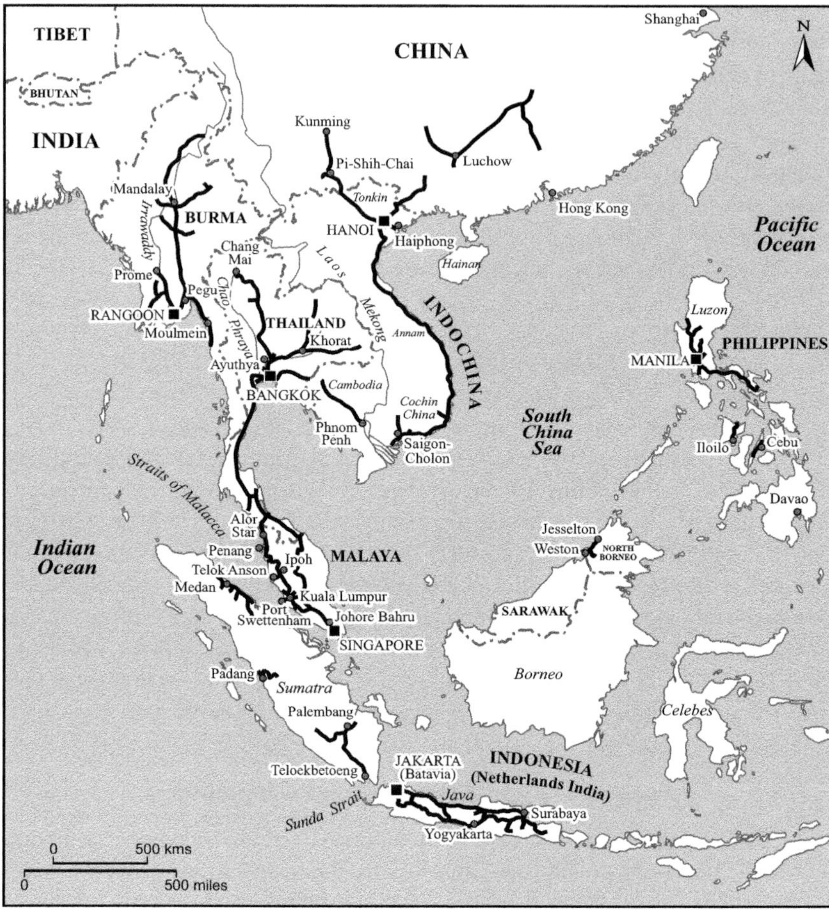

Figure 5.1 Southeast Asia railways 1939
Sources: Burma: OSS, R&A 1286.1, *Additional strategic objective*; R&A 1992A, *Burma (situation report no. 1)*, pp. 7–16; and R&A 1992, *Burma (New Delhi area report no. 1)*, pp. 1–11. *Malaya:* Federated Malay States Railways, *Fifty years*, p. 2. *North Borneo*: Naval Intelligence Division, *Netherlands East Indies*, vol. 2, p. 483. *Thailand*: Kakizaki, *Laying the tracks*, p. 36; Ingram, *Economic change*, pp. 85–86. *Indonesia*: Reitsma, *Gedenkboek der staatsspoor- en tramwegen in Nederlandsch-Indië*, pp. 72–73, 75–76; Naval Intelligence Division, *Netherlands East Indies*, vol. 2, maps between pp. 428–29. *Indochina*: Indochina, *Annuaire statistique*, 1937–38, fold-out map; JISPB, *Joint Army-Navy intelligence study of Indochina*, chapter 11, section 'Transport and telecommunications'; Naval Intelligence Division, *Indo-China*, p. 423. *Philippines*: Spencer, *Land and people*, p. 76; Worcester, *Philippines*, pp. 622–23, end map.

As opposed to Southeast Asia's north–south transport pattern, Japan's military needed links that connected Southeast Asia east–west by land. These would afford the shortest routes through Southeast Asia and would economize on scarce shipping. East–west road and rail communications across central Southeast Asia, starting from the key Japanese military logistics base of Haiphong, would circumvent the need to travel around the tip of Indochina to reach Bangkok and the need to sail from Bangkok around the tip of Malaya to reach that country's west coast and, further to the west, Burma. Bangkok served as a transshipment centre for military supplies for Thailand and Burma, although a sandbar at the mouth of the Chao Phraya (Menam) River forced ships of more than 15 feet draught to load and unload cargo by lighters at an anchorage outside the bar.[3]

In 1941, almost no east–west roads or railways crossed the borders of Southeast Asian countries. Neither Saigon-Cholon nor Hanoi was linked to Bangkok by more than secondary and dirt roads. Saigon-Cholon and Phnom Penh were not connected by railway, although the Saigon and Mekong Rivers, with their associated canal system, provided a water transport route. In the absence of a direct rail route from Saigon to Bangkok, the normal method of transporting freight overland from Saigon was by river boat up the Mekong to Phnom Penh and then by rail to Bangkok.[4] Railway construction envisaged by the Japanese would have crossed central Indochina to join Hanoi with the Thai railway system in north-east Thailand beyond Khorat, shortening the journey from Hanoi to Bangkok by hundreds of miles. But a railway across the Annamite Cordillera, a 1,100 km (680 mile) range of mountains through Vietnam, Laos and north-east Cambodia, was never undertaken. It would have been expensive in men, materials and time and would still have left the important port of Saigon-Cholon without direct rail access to Bangkok.[5] Age-old caravan trails to China traversed Burma's land frontier, but no modern means of communication crossed it until 1939, and even then did not involve Thailand.[6] Although the Thai and Burma railway systems were only about 250 miles apart, they were separated by a near-impenetrable barrier

3 OSS, R&A 2595, *Selected industrial installations in Thailand*, p. 51.

4 LHC, MAGIC, 'Economic: Tokyo', 2 February 1944, p. 9. For a map of two possible ways to close the gaps in rail lines to link Vietnam and Bangkok, see NA, WO208/516, 'Railway developments in S. E. Asia', 8 March 1944. Just before the outbreak of war, a missing section of the line between Phnom Penh and Bangkok was completed (Figure 5.2), allowing direct rail connection between Phnom Penh and Singapore via Bangkok if railways were open (NARA, RG59, entry 205, box 5834, file 892.00 233, Chapman, 'Conditions in Thailand December 1941 to June 1942', 18 August 1942, p. 28).

5 LHC, MAGIC, 'Bangkok to Tokyo', 4 June 1942, pp. 9–10; Robequain, *Economic development*, p. 385.

6 Burma Intelligence Bureau, *Burma*, vol. 2, p. 174.

of mountains and jungle. There was no continuous road across Lower Burma, between Rangoon and either Moulmein to the east or Bassein to the west.[7] No direct east–west route existed in Malaya: freight and troops from Bangkok or Saigon to Kuala Lumpur or Penang had to go several hundred miles south and then repeat this distance northwards.[8] The lack of railways or roads across central Sumatra meant that transport from one side of the island to the other required sailing around it.[9]

At the outset of the war, for Indochina, Thailand, Malaya and Burma there were, time and cost apart, two further reasons to minimize the use of shipping. One was that in December 1941 Japan's merchant fleet was probably already too small to meet the needs of the home economy and the logistical requirements of its forces in the Pacific.[10] Second, the insular geographies of Indonesia and the Philippines would necessitate large amounts of shipping. Although by the 1930s Java had a rail system comparable in density to European countries, the island nevertheless also relied on an extensive network of coastal shipping.[11] For the economies of other Indonesian islands, coastal shipping was essential. The same was true of the Philippines, a collection of 7,083 islands, because its economy divided among several large islands and because of a mountainous terrain often extending to near the sea and covered by dense forest. The Philippines had just 14,250 miles of road, of which only 7,500 miles were first-class roads. Two-thirds of first-class roads were in Luzon, mostly around Manila.[12]

The military importance of better east–west land transport in Southeast Asia was obvious to Japanese planners, who by early 1942 had studied various possibilities.[13] Construction of east–west transport links across Southeast Asia soon became imperative. Mounting shipping losses were one factor. Another was growing Allied control of Southeast Asian waters, which forced Japanese vessels to take circuitous routes within the region to try to avoid enemy ships and aircraft. As shipping became ever more difficult, Japan increasingly depended on Thailand's railways to move supplies and troops coming via Indochina to ports along the Indian Ocean, strengthening the case for a rail link from Thailand to Burma.

[7] Andrus, *Basic problems*, p. 22; Allen, *Burma*, p. 8.
[8] OSS, R&A 1007, *Japanese use of land transport*, p. 17.
[9] De Jong, *Collapse*, p. 243.
[10] USSBS, *Effects of strategic bombing*, p. 41.
[11] Naval Intelligence Division, *Netherlands East Indies*, vol. 2, p. 414, figure 7.
[12] NARA, RG226, entry 16, box 1004, 'Report on railroads of the Philippine Islands', October 1943, pp. 1–3.
[13] LHC, MAGIC, 'Economic', 20 April 1943, p. 6; 'Economic', 2 May 1942, p. 2; 'Economic', 11 May 1943, pp. 6–8; 'Bangkok to Tokyo', 4 June 1942, pp. 9–10; 'Economic', 21 September 1942, p. 6; and 'Military', 23 December 1943, p. 7.

The military need for east–west transport across Southeast Asia explains the decisions to construct two rail lines: one across the Kra Isthmus, agreed with Thailand on 6 June 1943, and the other to provide transport between Thailand and Burma (Figure 5.2).[14] The Thailand–Burma railway, which linked Bangkok to Moulmein in Burma via Ban Pong and Three Pagodas Pass, afforded Japan the quickest and most direct way to transport military supplies and soldiers to and from Burma. By avoiding shipment from Thailand or Indochina around the Malay peninsula and then up to Rangoon, the 320-mile railway link across Thailand and through the jungle of Burma saved a 2,000-mile sea voyage each way. Even so, the Thailand–Burma railway did not afford a continuous line to northern and central Burma: supplies still had to be transshipped at Moulmein and carried across the Salween River by ferry (Figure 5.2).[15] The Kra Isthmus and Thailand–Burma railway projects are discussed in Chapter 9 on labour because of the large number of Southeast Asians and Allied prisoners who worked on them.

Japanese planners also talked of a Tokyo to Singapore railway (with a ferry service from Japan to Korea) that would traverse south China, link to Thailand's railway system and then use its connection with Malaya to reach Singapore. But this east–west linkage, grandiose compared to any that might have been constructed in Southeast Asia, would have required, first, effective occupation of south China and then the construction of hundreds of miles of railways in China. The latter scheme would have consumed resources such as iron and steel far in excess of anything that Japan could mobilize during the war.[16]

A strand of contemporary analysis in Japan, and a view perhaps still with traction among some observers, regarded shipping as the constraint from which all of Japan's wartime problems flowed. An intelligence extract, reproducing an August 1943 argument in the Japanese newspaper *Mainichi Shimbum*, summarizes this:

> Whatever one may say, the greatest worry of all is the question of shipping. If only we had ships, the greater part of our difficulties could easily be overcome, and most of our problems solved. Owing to lack of ships, we are obliged to make unnatural self-sufficiency plans and superfluous efforts become necessary. Again, as we haven't got the ships, the smooth flow of goods between the various regions of the Co-prosperity sphere is impossible, and instead of the unified construction of the Co-prosperity

[14] LHC, MAGIC, 'Bangkok: Singora', 28 June 1943, p. 4 and 'Military', 5 December 1943, pp. 1–3; OSS, R&A 2368, *Japanese domination*, p. 46.

[15] OSS, R&A 1286.1, *Additional strategic objective*, p. 1–2.

[16] Robequain, *Economic development*, p. 386; USSBS, *Summary report*, p. 15.

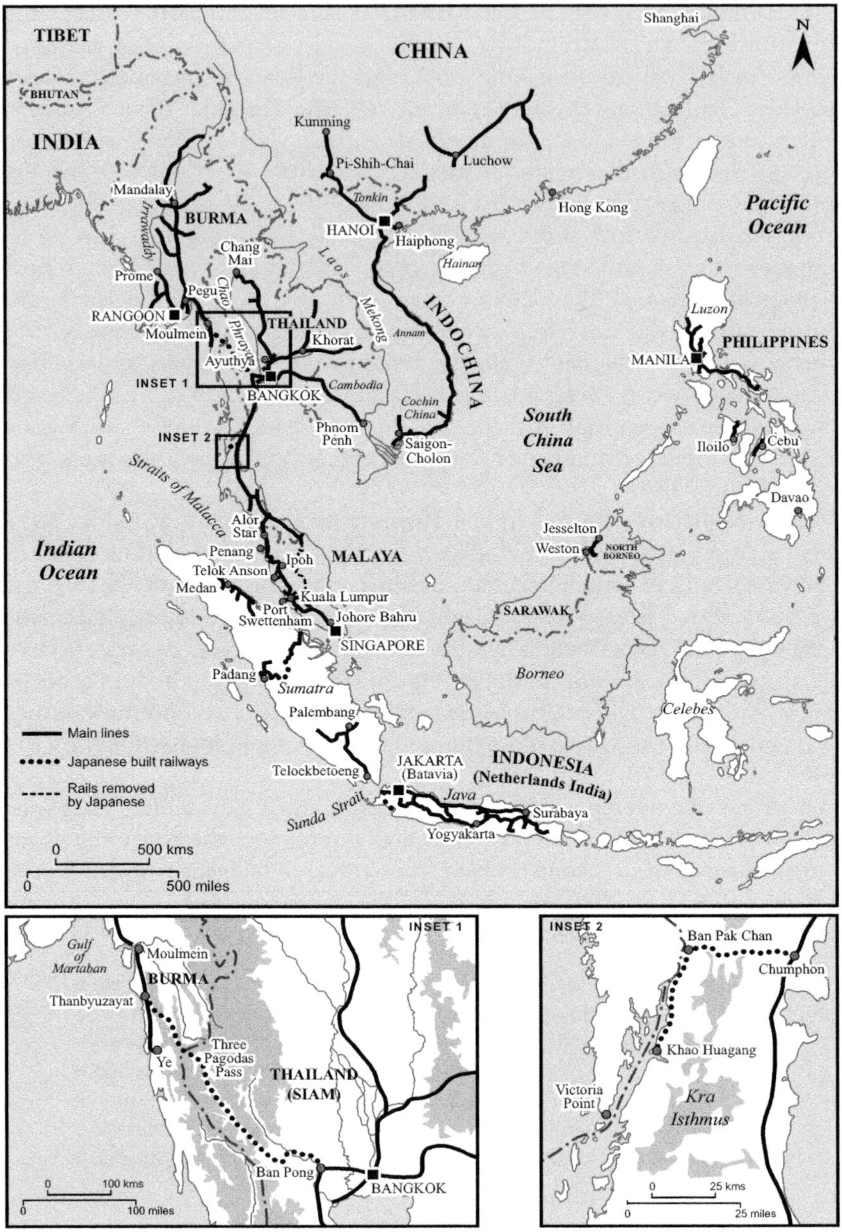

Figure 5.2 Thailand–Burma and Kra Isthmus railways
Sources: Rawson, 'Two new railways', pp. 85–88; Fisher, 'Thailand–Burma railway', pp. 85–97.

> sphere as a whole, the various regions are being developed separately and independently. If only we had the ships, these problems would all be solved and remedied at once.[17]

While a lack of shipping was a major Japanese wartime difficulty, this book makes it clear that Japan's failings in the Pacific War went far beyond that. They were systemic and rooted in fundamental misperceptions about Japan's economic strength and the nature of Southeast Asia's economies and societies, including pre-war regional transport facilities.

Thailand

Consistent with its slow pre-war economic growth and slight urbanization outside Bangkok, Thailand had less modern infrastructure than any other Southeast Asian country. The Kingdom had fewer roads than even the Philippines, although an area nearly twice as large. No trunk road connected Bangkok to the rest of the country; motor vehicles could comfortably travel at most 20 miles beyond central Bangkok. Goods, including about four-fifths of rice, were carried chiefly by punt-like boats along rivers and canals. Bullock caravans were the chief means of road transport outside Bangkok. Thailand's railway mainly catered for passengers, but before the war these numbered fewer than a million each year, about one-fifteenth of the population.[18] By early 1944, Thailand's rail transport suffered delays because the reserve supply of carbon brushes for diesel-electric locomotives was exhausted.[19]

Even apart from the Japanese–Thai alliance, Thailand's few, short roads and small stock of motor vehicles afforded the Japanese little scope for requisitioning transport other than the railway. The Southern Army took charge of it, setting up a Japanese military station at every place with a Thai station and controlling the traffic schedule.[20] Bangkok, as Thailand's sole large city and main port, was, together with the railways, an obvious Allied bombing target, but the capital's physical infrastructure remained relatively unscathed until the war's late stages. Before then, the theft of electric light cables, which thieves sometimes replaced with lighter wire, reduced the supply of electricity to Bangkok. Electricity continued to be generated, however, until 4 April 1945, when Allied bombs hit Bangkok's two power stations and ended electric power until after the war.[21] In the countryside, Allied air attacks damaged various

[17] ANM, 1957/0575122 Intelligence 506/10, 'Appreciation of Malaya, part II Post-Japanese occupation', 20 July 1943, pp. 2–3.

[18] Dobby, *Southeast Asia*, p. 285; Ouyyanont, 'Bangkok', p. 101; Stamp, 'Siam', p. 218.

[19] LHC, MAGIC, 'Bangkok', 30 March 1944, p. 11.

[20] OSS, R&A 2368, *Japanese domination*, p. 30; Sivaram, *Road to Delhi*, p. 100; Reynolds, *Thailand*, p. 143.

[21] OSS, R&A 2595, *Selected industrial installations in Thailand*, p. 1; Chaya, *Passing hours*, pp. 5–6, 79.

small but strategic railway lines and bridges at points including Nakhon Chaisi on the Ban Pong line in Central Thailand and Ban Dara and Mae Chang on the Chiang Mai line. Chiang Mai itself was temporarily cut off from the shipment of goods from Bangkok. Northern Thailand, heavily reliant on rail transport, suffered from a 1944–45 dry season bombing of the railways.[22]

Burma

Like Thailand, Burma had limited infrastructure, and during the war this declined more than in any other Southeast Asian country, partly because it was the country most fought over and the one most cut off from Japan. Considerable destruction, from Japanese bombing and an Allied denial policy, occurred even before occupation. Well before occupation ended no part of Burma's infrastructure remained intact. By 1943, coastal shipping was little more than numerous wooden ships of 100 to 300 tons capacity which were most active between Moulmein and Khao Huagang (Gao Fachi) in Thailand near Victoria Point on the Kra Isthmus (Figure 5.2).[23] Pre-war Burma had just 4,400 miles of main roads, almost all of which ran north–south, and in 1939 22,300 vehicles of all types. The Irrawaddy River, navigable for 900 miles, provided Burma's chief transport artery, and the early loss of much of river shipping crippled communications.[24] An Allied scorched earth policy was more effective in Burma than in most of Southeast Asia, and upon occupation the Japanese probably had available less than half of the Irrawaddy Flotilla Company's fleet of 600 ships.[25] During the war, hundreds of boats on the Irrawaddy disappeared as a result of concealment or deliberate scuttling for retrieval later, and storms during 1944 greatly worsened shortages by sweeping away 600 to 700 boats.[26] By 1945, river transport was mainly confined to country craft, power-driven vessels having suffered heavily from bombing attacks.[27]

Transport in Burma by land was probably even more impaired than by water. Although the Japanese military monopolized all but pre-modern land transport, including the railways, and also requisitioned some bullock carts, this still fell short of its needs.[28] The main rail line in Burma paralleled the Irrawaddy, and at first the railways were kept running partly through the use of

[22] LHC, MAGIC, 'Effects of Allied air attacks on Thai rail communications', 21 February 1945, pp. B1–B4; Reynolds, *Thailand*, p. 205.

[23] Andrus, *Burmese economic life*, p. 342.

[24] OSS, R&A 44, *Resources of Burma*, p. 9.

[25] Burma Intelligence Bureau, *Burma*, vol. 2, p. 224.

[26] Pe, *Narrative*, p. 58.

[27] NA, FO371/46363, Ministry of Economic Warfare, 'Six-monthly report: survey of economic developments in the Far East', 31 December 1944, p. 32.

[28] OSS, R&A 2015, *Japanese administration of Burma*, p. 54.

30 locomotives brought from Malaya.[29] Due to a lack of coal, locomotives were converted to burn wood. However, Allied bombing increasingly hampered railway operations and damaged a number of key railway bridges. The Japanese were, however, a contemporary Burmese observer remarked, 'about the fastest bridge builders I have seen, heard or read about'.[30] By 1944, trains often ran only at night, and engines were camouflaged or otherwise hidden during the day. Only some 126 of 350 locomotives remained in a useable condition.[31]

The occupying forces did, however, in Burma as elsewhere in Southeast Asia, attempt to repair and augment transport and communications infrastructure. The Japanese restored Burma's telegraph service, as well as re-opening telegraphic communications throughout much of Southeast Asia during 1943.[32] They also undertook, for military purposes, considerable road construction in Burma, including an all-weather road beside the Thailand–Burma railway, a highway between Prome and Taungup in Arakan (Rakhine), a road northwest from near Bassein to Arakan, and numerous strategic roads in the Chin Hills and Upper Chindwin district.[33] However, shortages of tar and nails made the maintenance of road bridges difficult. Moreover, a lack of vehicles, spare parts and petrol limited road transport; by March 1944, if not before, transport services for civilians were 'at a standstill, so that food is growing scarce in the north'.[34] The solution to 'paralyzed internal transport' and economic revitalization, decreed by Gōtarō Ogawa in 1943 as Supreme Advisor to the Burma government, was a large-scale mobilization of ox carts and use of country boats.[35]

In Rangoon, public electricity was reinstated only in July 1943. Until then, kerosene oil and candles were the only means of lighting for most residents. Without street lighting, few ventured far from their homes at night. Although the Rangoon Electric Tramways power station was restored, frequent power failures occurred. Electric trams ran intermittently, although apparently trolley buses did not operate for the duration of the occupation.[36] Oil and kerosene to run buses was hard to obtain; Rangoon's transport officer tried to alleviate the shortage by advertising for used motor oil. Passengers frequently had to push buses to get them started.[37]

29 Burma Intelligence Bureau, *Burma*, vol. 1, p. 75.

30 Pe, *Narrative*, p. 10; OSS, R&A 1992A, *Burma (situation report no. 1)*, pp. 8–9; OSS, R&A 2753, *Japanese use of Burmese industry*, pp. 28–29; Andrus, *Burmese economic life*, p. 342.

31 Burma Intelligence Bureau, *Burma*, vol. 2, pp. 225–26.

32 Ibid., vol. 2, p. 230.

33 Ibid., vol. 2, pp. 227–28.

34 OSS, R&A 1253, *Problem of law and order in occupied Burma*, p. 12 and see OSS, R&A 2015, *Japanese administration of Burma, p. 9;* Burma, *Burma's new order plan*, p. 68.

35 OSS, R&A 2077, *Economic reorganization of Burma*, p. 2 and see pp. 2–3.

36 OSS, R&A 2753, *Japanese use of Burmese industry*, p. 36.

37 Burma Intelligence Bureau, *Burma*, vol. 2, pp. 122–28.

Indochina

Indochina may at first have gained from Japanese investment in infrastructure. Japanese entrenchment in Indochina during 1940 and the country's strategic and economic importance to the Co-Prosperity Sphere gave strong motives for early infrastructure investment, from which Indochina's economy benefited. The Japanese constructed a number of roads, completed a highway from Saigon-Cholon to Luang Prabang far up the Mekong River in Laos, and in late 1941 closed a short gap between the Thai railways at Aranyaprathet and the Phnom Penh–Mongkolborey line. Extensive airfield construction, although for predominantly military purposes, also injected investment into the economy.[38]

Unlike in Malaya and Indonesia, the Japanese took relatively little equipment from Indochina's railway. This may have been partly because of the difficulty in moving it to rail construction projects elsewhere, although five locomotives and a number of freight wagons were sent from the Phnom Penh–Brattambang railway to Thailand.[39] Before 1944, American bombing did not seriously impair the Transindochinois, the main railway running from Saigon-Cholon to Hanoi, but during the last 18 months of the war largely crippled it. Since goods traditionally went mainly by coastal vessels, not rail, bombing and mining along much of the Vietnamese coast seriously impacted Vietnam's economy and hindered the shipment of food to the famine-affected north (Chapter 7).

With the interdiction of Indochina's rail and sea traffic, road transport might have seemed an option. It could not, however, effectively link Vietnam because of its long, narrow geography and wartime damage to bridges. Road transport was, furthermore, in increasingly short supply. Before the war, 3,500 to 4,000 heavy goods vehicles had operated in Indochina, divided about equally between public and private use, but by April 1944 transport utilization had fallen by between a third and a half due to a lack of tyres, spark plugs and spare parts. A similar shortage of tyres caused public transport to be cut by 40 per cent.[40]

Philippines

As in Burma and Vietnam, and consistent with large falls in GDP, three and a half years of war reduced transport and public utility infrastructure in the Philippines to a fraction of pre-war levels. As well as destroying the Philippine economy, World War II 'left the infrastructure devastated; rehabilitation took

[38] Robequain, *Economic development*, p. 385.

[39] OSS, R&A 1007, *Japanese use of land transport*, p. 5.

[40] VNA, FF 15154, 'Le problème économique et la question des transports', 18 April 1944, p. 26.

a decade'.[41] Throughout Southeast Asia, the lack of transport fragmented economies into ever smaller, local units and in the Philippines this was pronounced.

Philippine geography dictated a heavy reliance on transport by water, but this became difficult almost from the start of the war. In 1938, 3,337 vessels engaged in inter-island trade, of which 67, with an aggregate net tonnage of over 50,000 tons, were steamers. By the time of the Japanese occupation, the destruction of all inter-island ships of any size left only sailing *bancas* (boats of traditional Philippine design about 50 to 70 feet in length). These were able to carry just a fraction of the freight needed to supply Philippine industries.[42] Communication between the islands 'reverted to the most primitive state'.[43] The lack of boats and other materials caused a sharp decline in fishing.[44]

In August 1942, severe road transport problems almost immediately forced the Japanese to license trucks and supply them with petrol to bring food to Manila.[45] Except for official or semi-official vehicles, cars and trucks virtually disappeared from the roads while those which remained ran on alcohol or charcoal.[46] Non-official transport soon became a matter of private negotiation: individuals with small boats or trucks advertised in newspapers.[47] To make the most of transport by bullock carts, in 1942 the government prohibited the slaughter of *carabao* (domestic water buffalo) without a licence, which was granted only for an animal unfit for work.[48] Buses around Davao ceased operation at the end of January 1944 due to shortages of fuel and spare parts.[49]

Railways, which ran much of the length of Luzon, functioned no more than partially (Figure 5.3). In December 1941, American bombing destroyed or seriously damaged 70 per cent of the rolling stock of the Manila Railroad as well as shop machinery and numerous bridges, storage tanks and other installations. However, Japanese engineers managed to restore some railway services. These included connections to the Luzon countryside, which allowed Manila's main train station to become a black market centre for rice carried to the city by smugglers (Chapter 8).

41 Larkin, 'Philippine history', p. 624.
42 NARA, RG226, entry 16, box 208, 'Economic conditions in the Philippines', 15 October 1942, p. 8; see also Hartendorp, *Japanese occupation*, p. 198.
43 Hartendorp, *Japanese occupation*, p. 206.
44 Lear, *Japanese occupation*, pp. 139, 166.
45 NARA, RG226, entry 16, box 144, 'Conditions in the Philippine Islands', 23 August 1942, pp. 48–49.
46 Hartendorp, *Japanese occupation*, p. 494.
47 Hartendorp, *History of industry*, p. 93 and *Japanese occupation*, pp. 206–7.
48 NARA, RG226, entry 16, box 208, 'Economic conditions in the Philippines', 15 October 1942, p. 11.
49 LHC, MAGIC, 'Economic: Manila: Davao', 7 April 1944, p. 12.

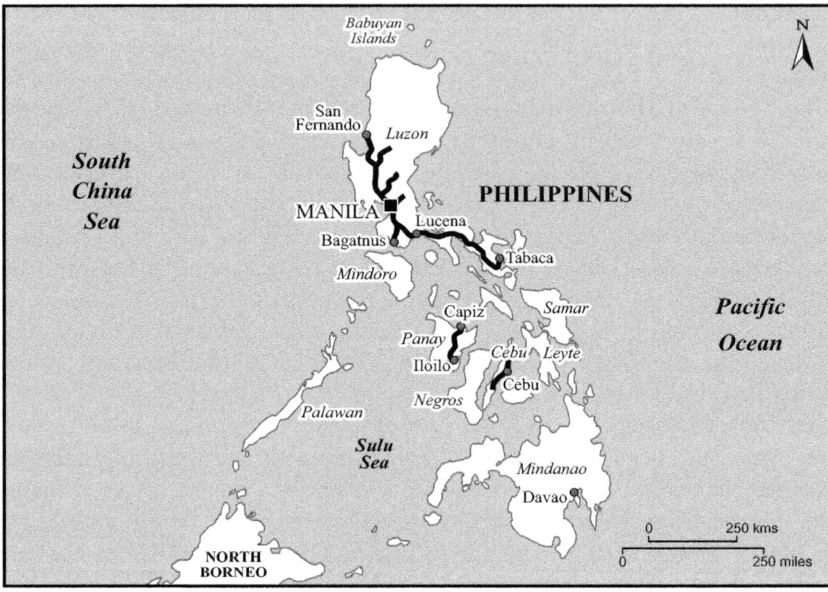

Figure 5.3 Philippines railways 1939
Sources: Spencer, *Land and people*, p. 76; Worcester, *Philippines*, pp. 622–23, end map.

As early as August 1942, transport in Manila was essentially limited to *carromatas* (horse-drawn carriages), bicycles and electric street cars.[50] Buses in Manila, hampered by poor fuel substitutes, often found difficulty in negotiating inclines and getting onto bridges and might require passenger help.[51] Fuel shortages soon forced electricity and gas companies to burn coconut oil and shells and restricted power supplies in Manila. In March 1942, people were urged not to waste electric power, and the use of electricity for advertising or display was prohibited.[52] The Manila Gas Company finally shut down in November 1944 when the coconut oil, coconut shells and firewood on which it had depended for fuel were re-allocated to the Japanese navy.[53] When Manila was re-taken in March 1945, no utility service remained even in partial operation: 'there was no light or power, no gas, no telephone service, no transportation, little shelter, no food, and, most serious of all, there was no

[50] NARA, RG226, entry 16, box 144, 'Conditions in the Philippine Islands', 23 August 1942, p. 50.
[51] Hartendorp, *Japanese occupation*, p. 206 and *History of industry*, p. 92.
[52] NARA, RG226, entry 16, box 208, 'Economic conditions in the Philippines', 15 October 1942, p. 25.
[53] Hartendorp, *History of industry*, p. 95.

water', this last because the defeated Japanese blew up a number of strategic points in the city's water supply.[54]

Malaya

A substantial part of the Malayan railway, mainly the east coast line, was taken elsewhere in Southeast Asia. Removals, principally to build the Thailand–Burma railway, included 276 miles (444 km) of running line and 57 miles (92 km) of second line and siding (in all, a quarter of total track mileage of 1,321 in 1935), about half of the system's 5,800 wagons and a third of locomotives (Figure 5.2).[55] Replacement wagons, locomotives and other railway equipment were brought from Java, but less than were taken. Although by August 1942 the Japanese re-opened the main, west coast, line of the Malayan railway as far as Kuala Lumpur, a more or less regular through service to Bangkok was not running until August 1943 and in 1945 took six days instead of the pre-war two.[56] In Malaya, shortages of rail and lorry transport meant that ordinary Singapore businessmen who lacked 'official pull' could do little trade.[57] By 1945 a third of locomotives in Malaya were out of service, a third needed repair and a third ran poorly.[58]

Electricity generating plants in Malaya were badly damaged by the Allies in 1942 before surrender. During the occupation, a lack of lubricants, oil and equipment further impaired operations.[59] Although the Singapore Gas Works, which supplied the city's gas lights, was re-started by the Japanese, lighting remained restricted. In March 1943, the Syonan Municipality Gas Factory generated daily half a million cubic feet of gas compared to 1.2 million before the war and just 840 of Singapore's 4,050 gas lamps functioned. Electricity generation for the city was similarly curtailed.[60]

Public transport in Singapore so deteriorated that by the latter half of 1944 only a third of trams and buses were in service. Singapore had numerous car dumps where hundreds of workmen prepared large numbers of damaged cars, lorries and armoured vehicles for shipment to Japan as scrap. With motorized

54 Ibid., pp. 180, 189.

55 Malayan Union, *Railways report 1946*, p. 1; Federated Malay States Railways, *Fifty years*, p. 1.

56 ANM, 0575122 Intelligence 506/10, 'Appreciation of Malaya, part I Pre-Japanese occupation', 20 July 1943, p. 13; NARA, RG226, entry 16, box 1472, no. 128585, OSS, R&A Branch, Regular Intelligence Reports, 'Malaya under the Japanese, March 1945', p. 12.

57 Chin, *Malaya upside down*, p. 36.

58 Malayan Union, *Railways report 1946*, p. 1.

59 Malayan Union, *Report of the electricity department 1946*, p. 1.

60 NIDS, Nansei Gunsei – 29 Japan, Southern Military Administration, Department of General Affairs, Research Office, *Syonan tokubetsu shi jūyō kōjō genjō gaikyō* [An overview of important industrial factories in Syonan Municipality] (Singapore: Southern Military Administration, Department of General Affairs, March 1943), p. 6.

vehicles hardly available and petrol scarce, Singaporeans increasingly turned to rickshaws, bullock carts and horse carriages for transport.[61] Japanese researchers recommended that the production of oxcarts and pushcarts be increased to supplement lorries, which were in short supply.[62] By 1944 and 1945, Perak's public works department had resorted almost entirely to bullock cart transport.[63]

Indonesia

Before the war, the Indonesian islands were linked to one another and to surrounding parts of Southeast Asia by a dense network of steamer services and small vessels. Steamers were mainly owned by two companies. One was the Singapore-based Straits Steamship Company (SSC), which operated 55 of 81 local steamers based on Singapore and provided services covering 78 ports in the region, including many in Indonesia; the other the Dutch-controlled Koninklijke Paketvaart Maatschappij (KPM) (Figure 5.4).[64] The KPM was central to intra- and inter-island communications. It had 134 ships and called at every major Indonesian port and most of the minor ones. There were, in addition, several small Chinese steamer companies. During the first nine months of the war, the sinking of 1,200 vessels in Malaya and Sumatra alone greatly reduced shipping. Moreover, the KPM and SSC fleets were decimated and scattered, severely limiting local cargo transport. The KPM lost 77 ships.[65] Prior to the fall of Singapore in February 1942, 21 SSC ships, about a quarter of its fleet, had avoided capture and left Southeast Asia for destinations across the Indian and Pacific oceans and even the Mediterranean. Overall, during the war 31 SSC vessels were lost.[66]

By late 1942, in the waters around Indonesia and Malaya, a 'regression of shipping to primitive forms', created a need for staging posts, since sailing vessels were unable to travel long distances or in rough seas. Singapore emerged as a hub for staging-post arrangements and also as a centre for the associated black market trade in rice (Chapter 8). Towards the end of the war, only small sailing vessels appeared in the seas around Indonesia.[67] During the last phase of the war, islands

61 NA, CO273/673/2, 'Conditions in Singapore in the late summer of 1944', 5 February 1944, p. 4; National Archives of Singapore, *Syonan years*, pp. 220–21.

62 IER, Azb: 5 Japan, Malayan Military Administration Chōsabu, Report no. 47: *Shōnan tokubetsu shi rōmu jijō chōsa: Hōjin keiei kōjō wo chūshin to shite* [A study of the labour situation in Syonan Municipality focused on factories managed by Japanese], by Izawa Kōzō, Ōmura Junzaburō (Taiping: Malayan Military Administration Chōsabu, October 1944), p. 7.

63 WL, MSS. Ind. Ocn. s. 172, T. G. Seshan, 'Resume of works done during the period January 1942–August 1945: roads and bridges', 8 December 1945, p. 6.

64 Straits Settlements, *Report of the commission to enquire into trade*, I, p. 96, IV, p. 250.

65 Twang, *Chinese business élite*, p. 92 and see Fruin, *Het economisch*, p. 42.

66 Tregonning, *Home port Singapore*, pp. 196, 228.

67 Twang, *Chinese business élite*, p. 96 and see p. 92.

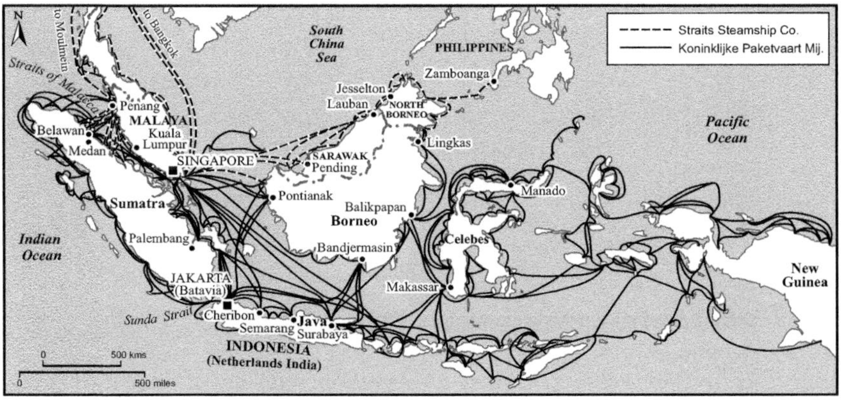

Figure 5.4 Indonesia local shipping 1939
Sources: De Boer and Westerman, *Een halave eeuw paketvaart*, p. 119; Tregonning, *Home port Singapore*, p. 162.

outside Java and Sumatra became isolated due to the sinking and destruction of much small shipping. For these islands, trade came 'practically to a standstill, so that the process of impoverishment and pauperization of the local population reached a most acute stage'.[68]

Java, crisscrossed 'by what may be fairly called a metropolitan network of railways', had more railway equipment removed than anywhere else in Southeast Asia (Figure 5.5).[69] In 1947, 3,200 tons of rails, 1,100 carriages and 25 locomotives from Java could be traced to Singapore and Malaya, six locomotives to Indochina, and undetermined quantities of rails and bridges to Burma.[70] Rolling stock was also taken to Manchuria and Thailand.[71] After the war, recovery of the rail system to its pre-war capacity would have required 300 passenger carriages, 2,000 goods wagons, 150 steam and diesel locomotives and 55,000 tons of steel rails.[72] A lack of shipping prevented the movement of coal from Sumatra for Java's railway, which burned teak instead. By 1944, large expanses of Indonesia's teak forests had been denuded, causing serious ecological damage, and the Japanese, having exhausted seasoned teak, began to fell green teak and increasingly to use other wood fuels including rubber trees. However, rubber wood yielded fewer calories than teak and rubber sap gummed locomotive engines.[73]

68 Department of Economic Affairs, Batavia, 'Economic prospects of Indonesian islands', p. 2.
69 Fisher, 'Economic myth', p. 184.
70 De Vries, 'Tracing', p. 36.
71 Anon., 'History of railways in Indonesia', p. 4.
72 Netherlands, Centraal Bureau voor de Statistiek, 'De economische toestand van Nederlandsch-Indie', p. 121.
73 Sato, *War, nationalism*, pp. 186–88; Kurasawa, 'Rice shortage', p. 640.

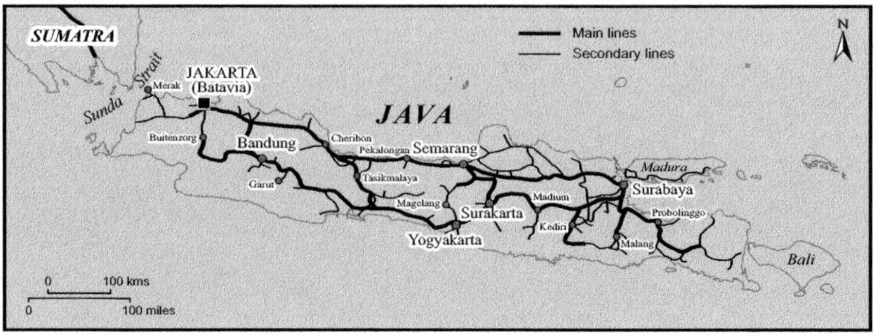

Figure 5.5 Java railways 1939
Sources: Reitsma, *Gedenkboek der staatsspoor- en tramwegen*, p. 73; Naval Intelligence Division, *Netherlands East Indies*, vol. 2, pp. 415–17.

In Jakarta, street lighting more or less disappeared because gas lamp posts were taken in a drive for scrap iron.[74] Nearly all of Indonesia's stock of motor vehicles was lost during the war.[75] With the curtailment of motorized passenger transport, in a number of cities the Japanese introduced the three-wheeled pedicab, known locally as the *becak* (*betjak*).[76] Its introduction and the shortage of petrol led to an increase in *becak* driving in Jakarta, although by 1944 owners of these vehicles had to use wooden tyres.[77] Also by then, ox carts and strips of rubberized roads had appeared in Jakarta. Plans were announced, but probably not implemented, to provide urban transport by constructing 20,000 horse- and ox-drawn carts and organizing their owners into regional associations.[78]

Summary and Comparisons

Although the direct contributions to GDP of transport and utilities eventually fell everywhere in Southeast Asia, differences in timing and extent were considerable. Declines were the greatest and most immediate in Burma and the Philippines. The eventual deterioration of transport services to perhaps a third and certainly not more than two-fifths of the pre-war level left large areas economically isolated and had considerable indirect impacts on GDP. North–south transport in Burma depended fundamentally on the artery of the

[74] OSS, R&A 3170 and second edition of assemblage 22, *Programs of Japan in Java*, p. 231.
[75] Department of Economic Affairs, Batavia, 'Economic condition of Indonesia', p.126.
[76] OSS, R&A 3170 and second edition of assemblage 22, *Programs of Japan in Java*, pp. 235–36; Sutter, *Indonesianisasi*, p. 164.
[77] Abeyasekere, *Jakarta*, p. 141; Sato, *War, nationalism*, p. 171.
[78] Sutter, *Indonesianisasi*, pp. 226–27.

Irrawaddy River, and communications were crippled by the loss of over half of Irrawaddy Flotilla Company ships and disappearance of a large share of small private craft. Road building and the transference of capital goods from elsewhere in Southeast Asia for the Thailand–Burma railway, both almost exclusively for military purposes, added to capital stock but fell far short of offsetting capital decline in other parts of the transport sector. In the Philippines almost nothing was done to make good the decimation of local shipping, basic to inter-island transport. Water and road transport in the islands reverted to late nineteenth-century levels. Railway services in Luzon were only partially re-established. Manila's gas company functioned at much reduced levels at the start of Japan's occupation and by November 1944 not at all.

Functioning transport and utilities in Indonesia and Malaya declined progressively and by late 1944 by about half. Unlike mainland Southeast Asia, the two countries were too distant from Allied airbases in China to suffer the same bombing destruction to infrastructure as in Burma, Indochina and Thailand. However, the loss of most local shipping, principally the vessels of the KPM and SSC, badly affected both countries, especially Indonesia. Java's once superb railway network lost significant capital stock. Locomotives in Java, with no coal to burn due to a lack of coastal shipping to transport it, had to adapt inefficient fuel substitutes. Gas and electricity supplies in Singapore were never more than partially re-established and by early 1943 began to encounter reductions due to shortages of lubricants and fuel. It is unclear how far substitutes, including horse- and ox-drawn carts, may have made good the increasing Indonesian and Malayan losses in motorized transport, but declines in efficiency must on their own have been considerable. In late 1944 in Singapore, when 30 lorries should have been available to bring food from collection points in Malaya, the actual fleet was only 11 and 3 of these had broken down. Some perishable foods were left to rot for lack of transport.[79]

The direct GDP contributions of transport and utilities remained strongest in Thailand and, until 1943, in Vietnam. Road construction in Thailand added to GDP, as did inflows of capital equipment for the Thailand–Burma railway, which was situated mainly in the Kingdom. The effective takeover by the Japanese of Thailand's rail system did not reduce its GDP contribution, although it must have had adverse indirect effects in hampering resource flows in the non-Japanese military part of the Thai economy. Unlike most other principal Southeast Asian cities, Bangkok lost power supplies only near the end of the war.

[79] IER, Azb: 3 Japan, Malayan Military Administration Chōsabu, Report no. 44: *Syonan tōnai shokuryō zōsan saku ni tsuite* [Policy for increasing food production on Syonan island] by Yamada Isamu (Taiping: Malayan Military Administration Chōsabu, October 1944), pp. 16–20.

At first, Indochina may have been a net gainer in the transport sector as a result of Japanese investment in railway and road projects. But petrol, like all oil products, had come as imports to Indochina, and as early as July 1941 the exhaustion of stocks began to impede the operation of automobiles and lorries. The lack of tyres and need to make do with locally produced tyre re-treads constrained lorry transport, which became increasingly problematic.[80] By the latter part of the war, both private motorized and public transport had decreased by around half. Moreover, beginning in mid-1943 and throughout the remainder of the war, Allied bombing cut the Transindochinois railway in numerous places and, along with the mining of coastal waters, effectively severed transport links between north and south Vietnam (Chapter 7). Whatever transport capacity remained was monopolized by the Japanese military. By mid-1944, Vietnam, although probably not Cambodia and Laos, had, like Indonesia and Malaya, lost half or more of its transport.

PART II: MANUFACTURING AND INDUSTRIALIZATION

On the eve of World War II, the base of Southeast Asian manufacturing remained quite narrow. A large share of manufacturing consisted of primary commodity processing, while a high proportion of manufactures required by Southeast Asia came as imports. No country approached self-sufficiency even in textiles. Additionally, throughout Southeast Asia the bulk of modern manufacturing in all sectors was in European, not Asian, hands. Beginning at the end of the 1930s, a number of colonial governments, aware of an extreme dependence on imports and in preparation for military defence, initiated some industrialization, but this had progressed relatively little when the Pacific War started.

After occupation, the Japanese inherited the two strands of Southeast Asian industry, a small modern manufacturing sector and the remnants of traditional nineteenth-century handicraft output. Large parts of modern manufacturing involved processing primary commodities for which, oil, rice and bauxite apart, Japan had limited immediate use. Often, Japanese technicians tried to adapt to alternative uses the machinery of pre-war primary-commodity-processing industries. These efforts, like all wartime manufacturing, were hampered by a lack of inputs, spare parts, transport and also technicians. Only a relatively small number of Southeast Asians were technically trained; Japan did not have enough technicians to send many to Southeast Asia; and practically all Europeans had left, had been killed or were interned.

Nor would it be easy to expand the second, traditional strand of Southeast Asian industry to supply Japanese troops and to make up for a lack of

[80] VNA, FF 15154, 'Le problème économique', 18 April 1944, pp. 23–24.

consumer goods available to Southeast Asians. In 1940, village home industry met about a seventh of Indonesia's textile requirements and a quarter of demand in Burma.[81] The about a third of Thailand's textile consumption produced domestically was high by Southeast Asian standards.[82] Although this textile output came almost entirely from traditional techniques, these were not readily disseminated to other Thai, despite necessity and Japanese efforts to do so. Even if techniques were successfully taught, traditional handicrafts usually depended on imported raw materials, notably yarn, now unavailable.

Japanese wartime policy towards Southeast Asian manufacturing and industrialization fell into two phases. Initially, the concept of a Greater East Asia Co-Prosperity Sphere shaped policy, in which Southeast Asian industrialization played little part. A March 1942 military administration directive for the navy, but also applicable to the army, explained that in occupied Burma, Malaya, Indonesia and the Philippines, 'In keeping with the policy of utilizing the Southern areas as a supplier of raw materials for our country and as a market for our products, the fostering of manufacturing industries in the occupied areas shall be discouraged'. The directive excepted only industries needed to develop resources or which utilized rubber and copra.[83] This approach made sense viewed in light of limited pre-war Southeast Asian industrialization. It would have been difficult, and probably impossible, quickly to develop manufacturing from its low starting point and under wartime conditions of shortage. As a March 1942 Allied intelligence report concluded in regard to a Southeast Asian country with more manufacturing than usual in the region: 'The industrial development of Indo-China is slight and could contribute very little to military enterprise.'[84] The Philippines exemplified Southeast Asia's lack of manufacturing. Although an overwhelmingly agrarian economy, there was just one firm in the country that made farm implements and it employed fewer than 100 people.[85] Japan could not expect to turn Southeast Asian ploughshares into swords on any very significant scale because the region manufactured so few of the former.

The second phase of Japanese policy towards Southeast Asian industry began in May 1943.[86] War reversals, the growing shortage of shipping and

81 Department of Economic Affairs, Batavia, 'Economic condition of Indonesia', p. 123; Hlaing, 'Trends', pp. 105–6.

82 Ingram, *Economic change*, pp. 119–21.

83 'Outline on the conduct of military administration in occupied areas' (14 March 1942), in Benda, Irkura and Kishi, *Japanese military administration*, p. 38. In the same volume, see also 'Outline of economic policies for the southern areas' (12 December 1941), pp. 20–21. Japanese policy did not regard Thailand and Indochina as occupied.

84 OSS, R&A 719, *Strategic survey of Indo-China*, p. 42.

85 Rōyama and Takeuchi, *Philippine polity*, p. 282.

86 For descriptions of this new industrialization policy, see Hayashi and Hikita, 'Japanese business', p. 236; Kratoska, *Japanese occupation*, pp. 161–63; ANM, 0575122 Intelligence 5O6/10, 'Appreciation of Malaya, part I Pre-Japanese occupation', 20 July 1943, p.10.

a military strategy of autarky forced a re-consideration of the industrial contribution that Southeast Asia's economies might make to the war effort. Furthermore, consumer goods had become so scarce that outputs from traditional industry were needed not just for military self-sufficiency but to help maintain social stability. Food apart, one of the most critical shortages affecting Southeast Asian consumers was clothing and textiles.

Textile production

After mid-1943, as Japan turned its attention towards supplies of clothing and textiles for Southeast Asia, two options were theoretically open. One was for home island factories to send goods to Southeast Asia. In 1941, however, Japanese policymakers had rejected the possibility of supplying consumer goods to Southeast Asia, and as early as 1943, even assuming a change of heart, exporting to the region would have been extremely difficult because of a lack of goods as well as shipping. By March 1943, 91 per cent of all Japanese textile plants had been switched to war production; no more than 5 per cent continued to produce textiles.[87] Between 1937 and 1944, in Japan the net supply of cotton cloth decreased from 2,184 million square yards to 51 million square yards; the availability of woollens declined similarly. Few, if any, additional supplies of silk or synthetic fibre compensated for the lack of cottons and wool.[88]

The other option, and the one Japan pursued, was to promote local Southeast Asian textile manufacture to make up for pre-war imported textiles. All countries were sent old Japanese textile machinery. Almost universally, the machinery was of little use because technicians and workers trained to operate and repair it were lacking, because lubricants and fuel were in short supply, and, crucially, because only small amounts of cotton or other fibre crops were locally available. With the partial exception of Thailand, Japanese attempts to increase the output of cotton and other fibre crops such as sisal were unsuccessful, mainly because of unfavourable climatic and soil conditions and because low prices gave farmers no incentive to shift production from existing crops.

Burma, with 550,000 acres under cotton, was the only important cotton producer in Southeast Asia, normally growing about half of the cotton equivalent of local textile consumption.[89] However, textile machinery which arrived in July 1943, followed in November by spinning machines with the aim of

[87] Ránki, *Economics*, p. 236.

[88] USSBS, *Effects of strategic bombing*, pp. 32–33.

[89] Burma, *Report on the progress of cotton work 1939–40*, pp. 1–2; Burma, *Season and crop report 1943*, p. 7 and *1944*, p. 7; Andrus, *Basic problems*, pp. 9, 44–45.

making Burma self-sufficient, had limited applicability.[90] No more than about an eighth of cotton grown in Burma was spun there: Burma's many weavers relied mainly on imported yarn or silk, which gave a much finer cloth than could be spun from local cotton. Most of Burma's pre-war raw cotton exports went to Japan.[91] Furthermore, although in 1939/40 Burma harvested 12,800 tons of raw cotton, yields varied greatly according to climatic conditions and fell sharply due to wartime disruption.

Pre-war raw cotton production in Thailand averaged 2,300 tons annually but, boosted by the absence of imported cotton goods, rose to 14,000 tons in 1943.[92] That, however, still fell far short of enough cotton for a self-sufficient Thai textile manufacturing industry. In 1944, the Thai government, perhaps encouraged by this jump in output and to provide the raw material for imported Japanese machinery, planned to ask farmers to convert a sixth of areas sown in rice and other grains to cotton.[93] That does not appear to have happened, however, since in 1948 and 1949 raw cotton production averaged a little over 5,000 tons. Although in the early post-war years cotton cultivation did not maintain wartime gains, agricultural diversification through the expansion of tobacco, oil seeds and maize had its origins during the war.[94]

Elsewhere in Southeast Asia, Japanese plans for cotton production and textile manufacture were less successful than in Burma and Thailand. Textile machinery reached Malaya during the second half of 1943 and in 1944 but, hampered by a shortage of cotton, used rags and other waste substitutes.[95] Cotton plants introduced in Malaya by the Japanese rapidly reached a considerable height only to be spoiled by the rain.[96]

Before the war, the Philippines imported over 80 per cent of its textile requirements. Nearly all cotton used for local manufacture was also imported, mainly from the United States. In January 1943, the Philippines had some 20,000 usable spinning machines, sufficient for the production of about 10 per cent of pre-war cotton cloth consumption.[97] To try to replace pre-war textile imports and supply an indigenous manufacturing industry with cotton, the Japanese, relying on a combination of exhortation and compulsion, launched a programme to grow the crop in the Philippines. It proved a 'colossal failure, not only because of the people's indifference but also because the cotton crops were planted either in unsuitable places or out of season. Pests

90 OSS, assemblage 43, R&A 2280, *Handbook of Japanese industry*, p. 105.
91 OSS, R&A 2753, *Japanese use of Burmese industry*, p. 46.
92 Ingram, *Economic change*, pp. 120–21.
93 OSS, assemblage 43, R&A 2280.1, *Handbook of Japanese industry*, p. 313.
94 Silcock, *Thai agriculture*, pp. 53–55.
95 NA, WO203/2647, 'Economic intelligence no. 132', 12 October 1945, pp. 7–8.
96 ANM, 1957/0575131 Intelligence 506/30, 'Appreciation of the economic position of Malaya', 30 June 1944, p. 5.
97 OSS, assemblage 43, R&A 2280, *Handbook of Japanese industry*, pp. 107–8.

like leafhoppers also caused havoc to the cotton crop.'[98] Japanese planners apparently did not know, or had forgotten, the history of Philippines agriculture. It was 'replete with experimental attempts to grow cotton . . . experiments not attended by conspicuous success'.[99] In the absence of raw cotton, plans to re-organize the textile industry were stillborn and a great number of imported Japanese spindles left redundant.[100] Although self-sufficiency in clothing materials was promised for the end of 1944, by then the Philippines produced practically no textiles.[101]

Pre-war Indochina's manufacture of cotton textiles accounted for only about half of the annual consumption of cotton goods, and less than a third of the cotton in this output was locally sourced.[102] In May 1943, Japan undertook to send Indochina 80,000 spindles and 3,000 looms for the stated purpose of making the army and the Indochinese people 50 per cent self-sufficient in clothing, but probably to clothe other parts of the Empire as well. However, the virtually insoluble problem of how to secure enough cotton for this undertaking was left to the French colonial government. In 1940, Indochinese textile producers had imported 53,500 bales of ginned cotton, mostly from India, as against 6,000 bales produced locally. Although maximum potential domestic production was 15,000 bales of ginned cotton, the new Japanese machinery had the capacity to process 40,000 bales for spinning and 54,000 bales for weaving.[103] In 1943, Indochinese cotton supplies were sufficient for only 10 per cent of the pre-war production of Indochina's traditional and modern textiles mills. Local raw material supplies did almost nothing to make good this shortfall, since between 1942 and 1944 the output of raw cotton increased less than 10 per cent (from 5,650 tons to 6,203). In light of so slight an increase, the realization of much textile output followingTokyo's establishment in late 1943 of a new spinning mill in Saigon and weaving mill in Tonkin seems doubtful.[104] Obstacles to manufacturing gunny sacks were similar to those for cotton textiles. Due to a lack of raw materials and equipment, in 1944 a factory built near Hanoi to manufacture a million gunnies a month made less than 15 per cent of that number.[105]

98 Merino, 'Introduction', p. xii.

99 Golay, *Philippines*, p. 41; NARA, RG226, entry 16, box 208, 'Economic conditions in the Philippines', 15 October 1942, p. 28.

100 Nagano, 'Cotton production', pp. 171–95.

101 OSS, R&A 2280, *Handbook of Japanese industry*, pp. 126–27.

102 OSS, R&A 2594, *Selected industrial installations in Indo-China*, p. 42.

103 LHC, MAGIC, 'Economic', 23 May 1943, pp. 14–17; 'L. A.', 'L'Indochine depuis la guerre', p. 4.

104 'I. G. M. I', 'L'effort d'industrialisation, p. 187; Indochina, *Annuaire statistique 1941–1942*, p. 89, *1943–1946*, p. 92.

105 Le, *Impact*, p. 206.

A second component of Japanese plans to increase Southeast Asian clothing and textile production was a return to nineteenth-century handicraft and cottage production. While traditional weaving and some spinning continued to exist in all Southeast Asian countries, an expansion of these activities was particularly emphasized in Burma and Thailand, perhaps because each grew significant amounts of cotton and had large handloom industries. The idea of a resurgence of tradition resonated with Burma's government: Ba Maw's 1944 'New Order Plan' envisaged vegetables being grown in every garden, a handloom in every home, and every woman spinning and weaving as well as working in the fields; the plan's slogan was 'Sow and Spin in Every Home'.[106] In Thailand by 1943, the Ministry of Industry had become interested in popularizing spinning and weaving in rural areas. During that year, in co-operation with the agriculture and interior ministries it organized 14 spinning classes with 8,917 trainees and 92 spinning and weaving classes with 4,496 trainees, as well as providing instruction in making gunnies and rope.[107]

While Thailand and Burma grew some cotton for local weaving, other Southeast Asian countries were less well placed in this regard. In the Philippines, hand weaving ceased during the war due to the lack of raw materials. That included a hand loom industry in the Ilocos provinces which prior to the war had produced some 5 million yards of cotton goods, such as piece goods, blankets and towels.[108]

In 1940–41, Indonesia imported some 80 to 85 per cent of the textiles it consumed.[109] Japanese planners saw traditional industry as a way to counter Indonesian dependence on foreign textiles. In Java, a million manual spindles, each requiring one operative, were to be constructed, and by April 1945 210,000 spindles had been built.[110] However, traditional textile machinery, like the disused machines sent from Japan for local textile production, was of limited worth due to the availability of no more than small amounts of cotton or yarn. In October 1943, a Japanese report observed of Java that 'the production of handmade cotton textiles, which were widely woven on the island, became impractical because the import of cotton and cotton thread ceased.

[106] Burma, *Burma's new order plan*, p. 39; OSS, R&A 2753, *Japanese use of Burmese industry*, p. 8; for not dissimilar sentiments of what Burmese objectives should be, see Than, *Burma my first five year plan*.

[107] OSS, assemblage 45, *Manpower in Japan and occupied areas*, vol. 2, p. 220; OSS, assemblage 43, R&A 2280.1, *Handbook of Japanese industry*, p. 314.

[108] NARA, RG226, entry 19, box 0412, J. Bartlett Richards, 'Textile manufacture in the Philippines', 24 January 1945; UP, Roxas Papers, Teodoro, 'Philippine manufacturing industries', 12 July 1945, p. 9.

[109] van der Eng, 'Why didn't colonial Indonesia', p. 1049.

[110] Sato, 'Relocation', p. 256; OSS, R&A 3170 and second edition of assemblage 22, *Programs of Japan in Java*, pp. 145, 191, 216; and see Noda, *Nanpō jikatsu kyōhon* for diagrams and techniques for self-help.

The cotton machines went unused and many workers lost their jobs'.[111] The fibre materials used with traditional hand looms, pre-war Indonesian textile machinery, and equipment brought from Japan derived from sources such as sisal, kapok, castor, banana and pineapple plants, and hemp.[112]

Industrialization Scope: Burma, Thailand and the Philippines

Three of Southeast Asia's six main countries offered few possibilities to establish wartime manufacturing even after the 1943 policy to favour it. Burma and Thailand were Southeast Asia's least industrialized countries; manufacturing would have had to start from a low base and, moreover, one eroded by the effects of occupation. Manufacturing in the Philippines consisted mainly of primary commodity processing, and a few first-stage import-substituting industries, and was not much greater than in Burma or Thailand. Departing Allied troops put a proportion of Philippine manufacturing beyond early repair, and subsequent instability, shortages of almost all inputs and a lack of transport combined to discourage its rehabilitation and, indeed, the utilization of other pre-war manufacturing.

Burma

In Burma, rice milling and saw milling, which together employed some three-fifths of all factory workers, were the mainstays of the manufacturing sector. Apart from these industries and the other extractive industry of oil refining, Burma's industrial development was 'negligible'.[113] An assessment of Burma at the start of the war emphasized that 'There are few industries in Burma ... Basic industries are almost entirely absent'.[114] During the war, the fall in exports of rice, timber and oil led to a sharp drop in primary commodity processing and so in most manufacturing in Burma.

It is remarkable in light of Burma's slight pre-war industrialization and heavy Allied bombing that 'for two years, the Japanese fed, clothed and transported their armies in Burma almost without help from Japan'.[115] That was partly because Japan's chief use of Burmese industry was to support the

[111] NIDS, Japan, Java Military Administration, *Gunseika ni okeru Java – Madura no shokuryō jijō to sono taisaku* [The food conditions and its measure in Java and Madura under the military administration] (Jakarta: Java Military Administration, October 1943), p. 28.

[112] OSS, R&A 3170 and second edition of assemblage 22, *Programs of Japan in Java*, pp. 216, 217, 219, 220.

[113] Spate, 'Beginnings', p. 88; Hlaing, 'Trends', p. 106.

[114] OSS, R&A 44, *Resources of Burma*, p. 6.

[115] OSS, R&A 2753, *Japanese use of Burmese industry*, p. 1.

occupying forces.[116] However, provision for them also necessitated Japanese manufacturing initiatives to supply military needs. Goods manufactured for the army included shoes, uniforms and aluminium hardware, substitute petrol and some arms and ammunition; cottage industries were organized to make paper, cigarettes, ironware, lacquer and varnish. Numerous tanneries, often producing leather of dubious quality, sprang up.[117] The outstanding feat of Japanese wartime ingenuity was to manufacture electric light bulbs and at least 15 diesel engines at the port of Syriam opposite Rangoon. Additionally, the Japanese used steel obtained by refining scrap iron to build two steel ships and adapted existing engineering facilities to repair, as well as railway rolling stock, military trucks and tanks.[118]

Nevertheless, Japanese wartime manufacturing in no way made up for the losses in Burma of pre-war industry. The wartime drop in primary-commodity-processing industry alone would have been sufficient to account for this shortfall, but, in addition, traditional industry contracted. Prior to occupation, about 230,000 people wove cotton on hand looms and produced annually some 30 million yards of cloth, mainly for cotton *longyis*, the standard dress in Burma. The looms were fed mainly by imported yarn, which became unavailable during the occupation. That left local cotton growing and spinning as the sole source of cloth. It did not, however, come close to compensating for the fall in cloth output after the loss of yarn imports, and provided only a rough quality *longyi*, since Burma grew short, not long, staple cotton.[119]

Wartime manufacturing in Burma declined along with other economic sectors. Decline was hastened by Allied bombing. By October 1944, the Japanese had to leave bombed industrial buildings unrepaired and work in various small scattered buildings on adjacent sites.[120]

Thailand

As late as 1919, manufacturing in Thailand was 'quite unimportant'.[121] Apart from primary commodity processing, the manufacturing sector probably consisted of fewer than ten factories. Manufacturing increased during the

116 NARA, RG226, entry 154, box 79, file 1309, 'Industrial objectives in Burma', July 1943, pp. 1–2.

117 MNA, 1/9 Village industries, L.U. G. Tripp, HMG, Ministry of Supply memo, 14 November 1945.

118 OSS, R&A 2753, *Japanese use of Burmese industry*, pp. i, 24–25, 31, 34.

119 MNA, 1/9 Village industries, letter from Lt. Gen. GOC in-c Twelfth Army to HQ ALFSEA, August 1945; NA, WO203/2647, 'Summary of economic intelligence (Far East) no. 137', 19 January 1946, p. 3.

120 NARA, RG226, entry 154, box 79, file 1308, OSS, Washington, DC, Patricia Barnett, 'Burma industrial file', 14 October 1944.

121 Ingram, *Economic change*, p. 133 and for discussion in the rest of this paragraph, see pp. 119–23, 132–48.

interwar years, but in 1937, including rice and lumber milling, employed just 1.6 per cent of the labour force. Most manufacturing was small scale. Rice mills and saw mills accounted for over a third of the some 107 firms employing 50 or more workers. Among the remaining firms, there were six shipbuilders and six rubber goods manufacturers, a brewery, a cement factory and a machine shop. Other Thai manufacturing was predominantly first-stage import-substitution industry such as the manufacture of aerated water, soap, cigarettes, matches and shellac and printing and binding.

During the war, there was a smaller drop in manufacturing activity in Thailand than elsewhere in Southeast Asia, even though, due to bombing in late 1944, the cement factory ceased to operate, as in April 1945 did Bangkok's two power stations.[122] Between 1941 and 1945, manufacturing fell relatively little as a share of GDP which, in turn, contracted considerably less than elsewhere in Southeast Asia (Table 4.2). The first and most obvious of the three main explanations for the maintenance of a relatively high level of Thai manufacturing was that Thailand, unlike Burma, sidestepped intense fighting. The manufacturing sector suffered relatively little wartime destruction. Nor, in contrast to the Philippines, was there destabilization associated with an extensive guerrilla movement. The alliance with Japan partly explained this relative tranquillity in Thailand. Co-operation with Japan and Thailand's willing incorporation as a puppet state within the Greater East Asia Co-Prosperity Sphere also contributed to the second and third explanations for a continued comparatively high level of wartime manufacturing activity.

The second explanation was that both rice milling and saw milling, the backbone of Thai industry, accorded with the Co-Prosperity role envisaged for Thailand as a source of primary commodities useful to Japan and others in the sphere. Rice exports from Thailand to Japan remained high until 1943. Subsequently, Thailand, accorded some freedom of action by virtue of its alliance with Japan, could send rice to other Southeast Asian countries. That probably helps to account for continued Thai rice output at about pre-war levels, although rice milling became impaired by a shortage of milling stores including lubricating oil and belting.[123]

Saw milling was central both to Japanese plans for a Co-Prosperity Sphere and to the war effort because of the need in Japan for wood and its use for construction and shipbuilding in Bangkok. In the autumn of 1943, Bangkok became a centre for building wooden ships, the wood for which kept some 30 local saw mills, including 4 large formerly European-operated mills, in

[122] OSS, R&A 2595, *Selected industrial installations in Thailand*, p. 44; NA, FO371/46363, Foreign Office, 'Six-monthly report: survey of economic developments in the Far East', 30 June 1944, p. 31 and Ministry of Economic Warfare, 'Six-monthly report', 31 December 1944, p. 35.

[123] NA, CO852/568, Baker, 'Siamese rice trade', 15 August 1945, p. 7.

constant operation and sometimes running at night. Teak was used for only some ships; most were built of *mai-deng*, a variety of hardwood that better suited quick construction. At the peak of shipbuilding in 1944, some 12 Bangkok yards, approximately double the pre-war number, operated on a 24-hour basis. Many of the Bangkok-built boats were between 100 and 250 tons and powered by sails and auxiliary motors, the latter dismantled from small vessels in Japan and shipped to Mitsubishi in Bangkok. After early 1945, shipbuilding tapered off, due partly to a shortage of engines and partly to the futility of boat-building in the face of Allied submarine warfare. Many Japanese who had overseen the Thailand shipbuilding programme were recalled to Tokyo.[124]

Third, the initiation between 1942 and 1944 of a number of new industrial ventures contributed to Thai manufacturing output. War and occupation brought together a pre-existing Thai government desire for greater industrialization and similar Japanese ambitions for Thailand as a member of the Co-Prosperity Sphere. Extensive state involvement in, and sponsorship of, Thai manufacturing began after the 1932 revolution. Manufacturing received a considerable boost as part of the nationalist, anti-Chinese, modernizing agenda of Prime Minister Phibun following his assumption of the premiership in 1938. An even larger push during the war came from alliance with Japan and a perceived need for import-substituting manufacturing arising from shortages of many basic goods. Local Thai manufacture of such goods would complement Thailand's principal Co-Prosperity role as a source of raw materials and expand the Thai market for more complex Japanese manufactures. Moreover, the spread of manufacturing in Thailand would strengthen Japan's economic presence in the country as a supplier of capital goods, technical knowledge and almost all equipment needed by the Thai army and navy.

Many new wartime undertakings consisted of first-stage import-substitution industry; most had some form of Thai government sponsorship; and most gave Japan a large role as a supplier of capital goods or as a participant in joint Thai-Japanese companies. New government-sponsored companies begun in 1942 with the intention of supplanting local Chinese enterprise included the Thai Minerals and Rubber Company, the Thai Wood Company and the Thai Industrial Development Company. Japanese business became not just a source of plant and machinery but also a government ally able to promote the desired industrialization and Thai-ification of the economy, even though the latter generally also depended on incorporating the business ability of Chinese Thai. The Thai Industrial Development Company purchased its soap-making machinery from Mitsui; the Thailand Spinning and Weaving Company, a state enterprise established in 1943, bought materials from Kanebo Spinning and Weaving Company; and the Dai Nippon Textile

[124] OSS R&A 2595, *Selected industrial installations in Thailand*, pp. 28, 35–36.

Company sold large numbers of spindles and looms to Thai mills. Japanese companies set up machinery for sugar, paper, shellac, alcohol, rubber and caustic soda factories. Companies which became joint Thai-Japanese ventures during the war included the semi-state Thai Rice Company, the Thai Tin and Rubber Company and the Japan-Thai Textile Company. In 1943, a joint Thai-Japanese paper manufacturing enterprise was formed, as were the Thai Steamship Company of Hongkong and two joint Thai-Japanese textile manufacturing companies, one of which was a partnership with Dai Nippon Textile Company to create the Japan-Thai Textile Company.[125]

Increased state scope for industrialization through joint Thai-Japanese projects fit well in a Thai social structure where government employment was one of the only outlets for educated young men. Previously foreign companies that were liquidated and reorganized with Thai managers or members of the board included the Thai-Fibre-Cement Company, the Thai Navigation Company, the Thai Electric Corporation and Thai Industries, Ltd. For Thais, nationalized enterprises as employers were 'most attractive – monopolies free of competition – mills, banks, purchasing and shipping industries all generously subsidised by government funds'.[126] In extending the opportunities for state industry and also in creating a greater role for local Chinese business expertise, the Japanese occupation expanded and enhanced a complementary relationship in Thailand between government and private-sector Chinese acumen, to which the Epilogue makes further reference.

While the installation of new industrial plant and equipment helped to support Thailand's GDP, this addition to investment does not appear to have resulted in any large addition to manufacturing output. Many of the new enterprises did not get underway until 1943 or even 1944. Moreover, these undertakings, like all Thai manufacturing, typically depended on imported raw materials, the wartime unavailability of which resulted in low and falling output or prevented production from starting at all. Although the Dai Nippon Thai Rubber Industrial Company was registered in 1941, factory construction was delayed by a lack of building materials, and in March 1944 was still not completed.[127] Textile machinery installed in Thailand required cotton well in excess of existing domestic production and neither raw cotton nor yarn could

125 OSS, R&A 2695, *Status of the Chinese*, pp. 26–28; OSS, R&A 2368, *Japanese domination*, pp. 31–32; OSS, assemblage 43, R&A 2280.1, *Handbook of Japanese industry*, p. 313; OSS, R&A 2589, *Rubber industry*, p. 43; Suehiro, *Capital accumulation*, pp. 122–33. The Thai Rubber Company was set up in May 1941 as a joint Thai-Japanese venture between Thailand's government and Mitsui Bussan and probably later became the Thai Tin and Rubber Company. See Swan, *Japan's economic relations*, p. 110.

126 OSS, R&A 1712, *Structure of the government in Thailand*, p. 66.

127 OSS, assemblage 43, R&A 2280.1, *Handbook of Japanese industry*, p. 282 and R&A 2589, *Rubber industry*, p. 43.

be imported.[128] Before the war the Thai Match Company had produced some 259 million matches a year, but beginning in 1942 output dropped sharply due to a lack of potassium, and during 1944 amounted to just 18 million matches, 7 per cent of the pre-war level. Similarly, Thailand manufactured 80 per cent of its own soap before the war but the wartime shortage of caustic soda considerably reduced production.[129] Although for most basic goods, including textiles, matches and soap, the wartime drive for industrialization was almost entirely unsuccessful in countering shortages and preventing rationing (Chapter 6), it extended state control over the economy and helped to set the pattern for Thailand's post-war industrialization.

Philippines

In the pre-war Philippines, processing industries comprised a major part of the manufacturing sector. Apart from sugar milling, which must be sited close to growing areas, most manufacturing centred in Manila. Modern industry other than primary commodity processing included the manufacture of shoes and shirts, and the San Miguel brewery, but was sufficiently slight to occasion the observation that industrial production 'has not yet outgrown the handicraft stage'.[130] The bulk of Manila manufacturing was low-productivity, low-wage handicraft production. Cigar making, embroidery and *chinelas* (slipper or wooden clog) manufacture employed tens of thousands of metropolitan Manila workers organized in establishments ranging from large factories to individual workers in a putting out system. A few textile factories operated, sometimes with obsolete machinery, but because of a large market for textiles and because most of these came from abroad, as a share of total imports they ranked second only to steel products and machinery, accounting for 20 per cent, and in some years for as much as 30 per cent, of all Philippine imports.[131]

During the war, manufacturing in the Philippines largely ceased to function and, if anything, probably fell more than the estimated drop in GDP of some three-fifths. New 'manufacturing' which sprang up in the provinces such as weaving, pot making, soap factories and the production of clogs and slippers represented a return to traditional and cottage industry and substitution for unavailable pre-war supplies.[132] Such industries did little to counter the collapse in pre-war manufacturing.

[128] OSS, assemblage 43, R&A 2280.1, *Handbook of Japanese industry*, p. 313.

[129] OSS, R&A 2595, *Selected industrial installations in Thailand*, pp. 60, 62.

[130] Kurihara, *Labor*, p. 9.

[131] Doeppers, *Manila*, pp. 17–35; UP, Roxas Papers, Teodoro, 'Philippine manufacturing industries', 12 July 1945, p. 9; United Nations, *Economic reconstruction: Philippine Republic*, p. 9.

[132] OSS, assemblage 33, *Programs of Japan in the Philippines*, pp. 384, 411–12.

Beginning in 1942, a large section of the Islands' manufacturing disappeared with the loss of primary commodity processing. According to a contemporary report, during three and a half years of occupation, output of 35 locally produced basic raw materials used by Philippine industries was 'negligible'.[133] As well as the near-total cessation of sugar milling (Chapter 4), the processing of tobacco, copra and rubber more or less ceased. Soon after occupation, the Japanese made efforts to re-start industry, and to supply the military took over Manila's main brewery and sugar refining, rope and tobacco factories. But in October 1942, manufacturing functioned on only a limited scale owing to the destruction by the departing Americans of transport and practically all stores of fuel, lubricants and raw materials. Manila rope factories were hindered by a shortage of abaca, and coconut oil factories by a lack of transport for copra. Civilian experts brought from Tokyo in 1942 to rehabilitate industry were described by Allied intelligence as having 'frankly admitted that the task seems hopeless'.[134]

An inauspicious first year did not discourage the Japanese from frequent announcements during 1943 and 1944 of plans to repair pre-war industries and start new ones, but little happened in either regard.[135] Many existing factories were stripped of machinery and equipment for installation in plants used for war repairs; other factories were diverted from their original use to war production.[136] In July 1944, the army transferred seven corporations and factories to the Philippines government but kept control of a further 17 deemed important for the war effort.[137] War output, of course, contributed to GDP, although probably not much to the availability of goods to Filipinos, for whom clothing was among the most acute of the shortages. Late in the war, the Japanese attempted to counter the lack of paper by bringing to the Islands a paper mill intended to become operative in 1947, which the National Development Company subsequently inherited.[138]

Malaya

Parallel wartime strands of manufacturing developed in Malaya. One, as in other parts of Southeast Asia, consisted of local enterprises, often no more than

133 UP, Roxas Papers, Teodoro, 'Philippine manufacturing industries', 12 July 1945, p. 3.

134 NARA, RG226, entry 16, box 208, 'Economic conditions in the Philippines', 15 October 1942, p. 20 and see pp. 9–12, 19–20.

135 OSS, assemblage 43, R&A 2280.1, *Handbook of Japanese industry*, p. 363 and assemblage 33, *Programs of Japan in the Philippines*, p. 384.

136 UP, Roxas Papers, Teodoro, 'Philippine manufacturing industries', 12 July 1945, p. 4.

137 NARA, RG226, entry 16, box 976, file 346188, 'Philippine Islands, transfer of industrial concerns', 27 July 1944.

138 NARA, RG319, entry 319, box 2271, J. Bartlett Richards, 'Philippine economic conditions – 1946', p. 17.

cottage or household industries, which grew up to produce substitutes for previously imported consumer goods such as textiles, matches, soap, glue, paper and toothpaste. These activities added to GDP and employment, but were remarkable principally for the adaptability and inventiveness of local entrepreneurs (Chapter 6). In Malaya, this strand of manufacturing, dominated by Chinese, showed a mushroom-like growth in quickly establishing itself after occupation.[139]

A second strand of manufacturing, more capital-intensive and larger in scale, almost entirely involved production for the Japanese military. Japan made little attempt in Malaya, or generally in Southeast Asia, to manufacture consumer goods. Manufacturing for Japan's military largely made use of prewar industrial facilities and machines and focused on Singapore. One reason for this locational choice was that Singapore's industrial facilities and manufacturing industry complemented its great military importance as a service, repair and storage centre (cf. Figure 2.1). Second, most Malayan industry was already in Singapore. It had Malaya's principal repair facilities, its main engineering firms and its only auto assembly plant, a Ford factory built in 1939.[140] Penang and Kuala Lumpur were both much smaller than Singapore, and manufacturing in each, other than tin smelting in Penang, chiefly consisted of producing consumer items for the local market.

Beginning in 1940, when the outbreak of war in Europe made it apparent that Malaya would be cut off from normal supplies, Malayan firms were organized to provide as many war goods and repair facilities as possible. New production lines included the manufacture of mines, shell cases and revolvers. Singapore began to build diesel engines and a local automobile firm converted trucks into armoured vehicles. When Singapore fell, the Japanese took over Singapore's engineering works, foundries and machine shops, for the most part largely intact. However, the industrial facilities of the British naval base on the north of the island were 'pretty well destroyed' by the departing British and had to be restored. So, too, did the facilities of the Singapore Harbour Board, which, together with its five dry docks, was placed under the control of Mitsubishi.[141]

After occupying Singapore, the Japanese moved to adapt industry there for military requirements. Some essential machinery was shipped from Japan to Singapore, and some came from Indonesia, but against these additions to capital stock a considerable amount of machinery was transferred from Singapore to Sumatra.[142] United Engineers, Malaya's sole large engineering firm, which had branches throughout the peninsula, was converted to a munitions factory. According to one intelligence report, work at the Singapore site continued 24

[139] Malayan Union, *Report on the British military administration*, p. 110.
[140] OSS, R&A 2137, *Industrial facilities in Malaya*, p. 3.
[141] Ibid., p. 13 and see pp. 1–13.
[142] Malayan Union, *Report on the British military administration*, p. 109.

hours a day on a shift system.[143] Cement was essential for the war, and since it was not manufactured in pre-war Singapore, the machinery and equipment for its production had to come from Japan for installation at Batu Caves in Malaya.[144] Two Japanese firms, the Yokohama Rubber Company and the Central Rubber Company, brought some machinery from Japan to manufacture rubber goods, mainly for the military. Production was, however, hampered by the low quality of locally produced chemicals and labour shortages due to an inability to supply workers with adequate rice rations.[145]

During 1942 and the first half of 1943, manufacturing almost certainly contributed much less to national income than before the war, and so became part of the wartime fall in GDP. Decline was probably caused partly by the difficulties of shifting towards war production – even though the departing British had already made a start in putting manufacturing on a war footing – and of establishing new management and control structures. Moreover, primary commodity processing, which fell sharply, had accounted for a large share of pre-war manufacturing. Singapore's some 25 pre-war rubber mills became largely redundant; pineapple canning, a major industry before the war, fell into complete decay, and machinery was removed from the factories. The Japanese dismantled the Straits Trading Company's damaged Singapore smelting plant and took one of its large generators to a sub-station on Penang island. Tin smelting, which had needed ten furnaces, was replaced by various units, including some for the manufacture of sulphuric acid, a printing works and, in one furnace, the melting of spent cartridge cases.[146]

By mid-1943, in keeping with self-sufficiency initiatives elsewhere in Southeast Asia, Japan planned to go well beyond existing manufacturing in Singapore. The Production Materials Control Act and the Key Industrial Goods Act aimed to develop heavy and chemical industries in Singapore and other parts of Malaya.[147] In Singapore, despite its better industrial base than most other large Southeast Asian cities, the establishment of such industries would have marked a major historical departure. Singapore had never been an industrial centre, nor was it located anywhere near one. The city would have been the likely location for the manufacture of basic consumer goods for the Malayan market but before the war even such import-substituting industry had hardly developed. For example, pre-war Malaya imported practically all its

[143] NA, CO273/673/2, 'Conditions in enemy-occupied Malaya', 5 February 1944, p. 5.

[144] NA, WO203/2647, 'Economic intelligence', 29 October 1945, pp. 7–8.

[145] NA, WO208/1532, 'Economic intelligence', 29 October 1945, pp. 1–2; see also WO203/2647 for this report.

[146] Malayan Union, *Report on the British military administration*, p. 113; Tregonning, *Straits tin*, pp. 59–62.

[147] NA, CO273/673/1, 'Conditions in enemy-occupied Malaya', 'Intelligence report no. 15', 9 October 1943, p. 78.

consumption of cotton piece goods and artificial silk piece goods.[148] Malaya, Singapore included, was 'dependent upon importation for all machines, plant, iron and steel, raw materials, etc.'.[149] It lacked a substantial base of capital goods and chemical industries. Wartime Japanese industry in Malaya was 'largely equipped by the cannibalization of machinery ex British firms' workshops'.[150] In Singapore, to extract automobile fuel from rubber, 'Machinery was cannibalized, engine fan belts were made from old airplane tires and smoked sheets, and straw mats were waterproofed as a substitute for unavailable paper or gunny sacks'.[151]

The transformation of Singapore envisaged by Japanese planners would at best have been difficult and was probably impossible. It would have required large quantities of imported goods and a trained labour force, neither of which was obtainable under wartime conditions or quickly achievable even in peacetime. Unsurprisingly, plans announced in September 1943 for heavy industrialization and in 1944 to make Malaya a self-sufficient industrial centre did not come to fruition. The intended Singapore production of large quantities of steel, automobile tyres and electric bulbs failed to materialize.[152]

After about mid-1943, manufacturing, along with Malayan GDP, continuously contracted. Like other economic sectors, manufacturing was increasingly hindered by a lack of fuel, lubricants, power supplies, spare parts and transport, which rendered machinery partially, or even wholly, inoperative. Labour became a major constraint. By later 1944, poor transport and food shortages compromised work effort and contributed to high factory absenteeism (Chapter 9).[153]

Despite many failures, Japanese efforts to develop Malayan industry did have some wartime success. New factories and industries were, however, dictated by necessity and not by any consideration of commercial viability.[154] Their sole

148 ANM, 1957/0575131 Intelligence 506/30, 'Appreciation of the economic position of Malaya', 30 June 1944, p. 4.

149 ANM, 1957/0572698, 'Technical estimates of requirements for rehabilitation of government and public utility undertakings for Malaya', 12 June 1944, p. 1; see also OSS, R&A 2137, *Industrial facilities in Malaya*, p. 3.

150 ANM, 1957/0571877, ALFSEA conference, item 9c, 'Sponsored industries', *c.* 15 December 1945, p. 1.

151 NARA, RG226, entry 19, box 317, R&A XL23209, *Malaya–Japanese penetration of the rubber manufacturing industry*, 12 October 1945, p. 3.

152 OSS, assemblage 43, R&A 2280.1, *Handbook of Japanese industry*, p. 234; NARA, RG226, entry 16, box 1472, no. 128585, OSS, R&A Branch, Regular Intelligence Reports, 'Malaya under the Japanese, March 1945', pp. 14, 18; ANM, 1957 /0572056, O. W. Gilmour, 4 May 1944, pp. 5–6.

153 IER, Azb: 5 Japan, Malayan Military Administration Chōsabu, *Shōnan tokubetsu shi rōmu jijō chōsa* [Study of the labour situation in Syonan Municipality] (October 1944), p. 20.

154 ANM, 1957/0571877, ALFSEA conference, item 9c, 'Sponsored industries', *c.* 15 December 1945, p. 1;

purpose was 'to meet the urgent needs of war production and their equipment was of poor quality and their design often inefficient. Few of them had any prospect of a permanent future'.[155]

Indonesia

During the war, Indonesia's manufacturing dropped both more slowly and markedly less than GDP (Table 4.2). In 1943, manufacturing still stood at 83.5 per cent of its 1941 level, but in 1944 plunged to below two-thirds of pre-war activity, and in 1945 fell yet further. Between 1941 and 1945, manufacturing contracted by 43.1 per cent compared to 54.3 per cent for the economy as a whole. As a result, the share of manufacturing in GDP increased from a little over 10 per cent in 1941 to more than 13 per cent by the end of the war.

Although hardly industrialized and with no more than a weak technological base, pre-war Indonesia, as indicated by the 1941 GDP manufacturing share of around 10 per cent, had some significant industry. Much of this, as elsewhere in Southeast Asia, involved commodity processing. Java was easily the most industrialized Indonesian island, but even it relied on imports for a large share of almost all basic consumer items and was far from self-sufficient in cotton goods.

In the 1930s, the Dutch colonial government had been planning for more industrialization and beginning in 1940 made further plans to establish substantial manufacturing in Java to avert the shortages that would result from an inability to import manufactured goods due to the outbreak of war in Europe. Industrialization was to be balanced, and combine light industry to cater for Indonesian consumers with heavy and metallurgical industries to provide manufactured materials and capital goods. A large industrial complex would be sited along Java's north-east coast between Rembang and Surabaya.[156]

Japanese occupation cut short these Dutch industrialization plans for Indonesia, leaving Japan with the problem of how to supply manufactured goods to its military on the islands, as well as to civilian populations.[157] The initial Japanese response was twofold. One part was to concentrate almost exclusively on manufacturing for the military and more or less ignore Indonesians; the other was to try to use or adapt machinery already in Indonesia, and so attempt only relatively limited manufacturing. Beginning in about mid-1943, Japanese industrialization policy, as in other parts of

155 Malayan Union, *Report on the British military administration*, p. 109 and see pp. 108–9; for much the same conclusions, see NARA, RG226, entry 19, box 317, R&A XL23209, *Malaya–Japanese penetration of the rubber manufacturing industry*, 12 October 1945, p. 3.

156 Department of Economic Affairs, Batavia, 'Economic condition of Indonesia', p. 123; van der Eng, 'Government promotion', pp. 176–200; Sato, 'Relocation', p. 253.

157 Kubo, 'Higashi Ajia', p. 65.

Southeast Asia administered by Japan, changed with the acceptance of the 'Main principles for economic measures in the southern kō areas'.[158] Although manufacturing remained chiefly for the military, Japanese war reversals necessitated greater industrialization than at first envisaged, both to meet the new goal of regional Indonesian autarky and to provide a greater output of war goods. As with the Dutch three and a half years previously, the Japanese aim became to offset Indonesian economic isolation through local manufacturing.

During the initial phase of Japan's policy towards manufacturing, some facilities could simply be taken over and run by Japanese. Ishihara Sangyō K.K. (Ishihara Industry Co.), in addition to mining and shipping enterprises, managed electric wire and sulphuric acid factories in Surakarta and a graphite electrode factory in Bandung.[159] Industries that would ease life for Japanese replaced similar Dutch endeavours. Kirin Brewery took over beer factories in Jakarta and Surabaya. Morinaga & Co. operated chocolate and confectionery factories in Surabaya and dried vegetable and milk-treatment factories in Malang.[160] By September 1942 in Surabaya, a paper box factory, a match factory and leading industrial mills manufacturing daily necessities were said to be operating.[161] Rehabilitation and a return to production for most industries had been accomplished by the end of 1942.[162]

Pre-war manufacturing could not, however, supply numerous military needs. Commodity-processing industries provided a large part of the existing plant and machinery that could be turned to war production. Oil refining, located almost entirely in Sumatra and Borneo, and the mining and processing of bauxite and rice milling were the only manufacturing activities associated with primary commodities that were of much use to the Japanese. Java's sugar and tobacco industries were dispensable and their cannibalization furnished a substantial part of the basis for Japanese wartime industrialization. The conversion of this machinery to wartime purposes and use of existing stocks of fuel and lubricants helped to prevent an early collapse in manufacturing. Some parts were taken from rubber estate machinery, but much less so than from tea and sugar factories. Over three quarters of Java's tea factories ceased to operate. Some 20 tea factories were converted to produce war goods, including explosives, chemical products, electric batteries, automobile spare parts, textiles and paper. Factory parts from the other 150 tea estates were removed for use elsewhere, and estate buildings were often demolished.[163] About three-fifths of pre-war sugar mills (some 69 of the total of 120 pre-war mills) were adapted to other uses. Many of these mills were turned into

[158] Hayashi and Hikita, 'Japanese business', p. 236; Sato, 'Relocation', pp. 249, 253.
[159] Hayashi and Hikita, 'Japanese business', p. 241.
[160] Ibid., p. 242.
[161] OSS, R&A 3170 and second edition of assemblage 22, *Programs of Japan in Java*, p. 224.
[162] Sutter, *Indonesianisasi*, p. 160.
[163] Prillwitz, 'Estate agriculture', pp. 14–15.

machine shops; others began to produce butanol and alcohol or paper, caustic soda, paints or medicines. Often the lime kilns of sugar mills were used to produce cement.[164]

During the occupation, manufacturing became widely dispersed across Java and was moved to the Outer Islands. The dismantling of pre-war machinery and a mix-and-match approach to its re-assembly facilitated dispersal. Transport shortages, a need for nearby machine and repair industries, and Japan's policy of military self-sufficiency explain the spread of manufacturing. In the Outer Islands, manufacturing catered for urgent requirements such as for soda, hand-made paper, matches and medicines.[165]

The closure of Dutch enterprises and opportunities to manufacture consumer goods imported before the war did not lead to a large new class of Indonesian entrepreneurs. Japanese filled almost all the top positions in former Dutch firms. During the first year of occupation, virtually no new Indonesian industrial enterprises were founded.[166] The emergence of locally produced substitutes for previously imported items like textiles, shoes and soap depended mainly on cottage and handicraft industries, and frequently also on using pre-modern production methods. Such methods were the principal Japanese strategy for meeting Indonesian consumption needs. Japanese training programmes and self-help manuals with numerous diagrams aimed to teach Indonesians to make shoes, clothing and simple machines and to increase the use of hand looms.

Japan's decision to extend and develop Indonesian industry faced probably insurmountable obstacles by mid-1943. Nevertheless, planning remained ambitious. A 'War Power Increase Period' from May to July 1944 set goals of increased production in 36 factories and the initiation of 83 new factories to include shipyards, spinning mills and plants to manufacture caustic soda, carbide, carbon black, sulphuric acid, zinc oxide, automobile parts, drugs, batteries, paper, glass and so forth. Wooden shipbuilding was regarded as an especially important industry, and the construction of new electric power plants at several locations was planned.[167] During the first year of occupation, Dutch nationals who had held key positions in the economy such as production engineers and laboratory scientists remained in their jobs. By April 1943, however, all the Dutch had been interned.[168] That left in Indonesia only a small number of technicians and engineers who could contribute to industrialization. All of Java had just 235 qualified Indonesian engineers, 1,297 skilled and semi-skilled labourers, and 22 electricians. There were only 29 repair factories

164 Rodenburg, 'Java's sugar supply', p. 29; Fruin, *Het economisch*, p. 45.

165 Department of Economic Affairs, Batavia, 'Industries', p. 21.

166 Sutter, *Indonesianisasi*, p. 173.

167 OSS, R&A 3170 and second edition of assemblage 22, *Programs of Japan in Java*, pp. 210, 227, 243.

168 Sutter, *Indonesianisasi*, p. 171.

and an additional 3 for electrical equipment.[169] Moreover, by 1943 even existing manufacturing, increasingly hampered by a lack of fuel, lubricants, spare parts and transport, had begun to collapse (Table 4.2). As well as facing the same difficulties, the establishment of new industry envisaged by Japanese planners would have taken place under conditions of autarky. Virtually all materials, parts and machinery had to be available in Indonesia or capable of manufacture there. Neither condition was realistic for an economy so little industrialized as Indonesia's.

Indochina

In Indochina, manufacturing activity remained high in 1941 and 1942. That may have continued through the first half of 1943, after which, in a second phase, manufacturing began sharply to contract.[170] In its buoyant phase, manufacturing was bolstered, and in major respects transformed, by both French colonial government and Japanese military industrial initiatives. During the latter half of the war, however, manufacturing decline was continuous and precipitate due to increasing shortages of almost all inputs, a lack of transport, Allied bombing damage and the March 1945 Japanese coup. Between 1941 and 1945, the percentage fall in manufacturing may have exceeded the estimated more than halving of overall GDP.

In the late 1930s, Indochina remained little industrialized. The largest industrial concentration was in Cholon, the twin city to Saigon, where some 30 rice mills, each several storeys of corrugated iron with high chimneys, were visible for miles. The mills operated with imported American or German machinery, as did six saw mills. Tonkin, chiefly Haiphong, had two modern spinning and weaving mills, several alcohol distilleries, a lumber mill, match factories, brick and lime kilns and cement plants. Vietnam's several vegetable oil extracting factories and soap works generally relied on crude presses. A number of breweries produced about 50,000 hectolitres of beer annually, mainly for Europeans and wealthy Asians. The Indochinese chemical industry consisted of two oxygen plants, some small paint and varnish establishments and four factories making explosives and fireworks, mostly the firecrackers traditional to Vietnamese and Chinese.[171]

French colonial government promotion of Indochinese industrialization began in 1938, after the reversal of long-standing metropolitan opposition to

[169] Reid and Akira, *Japanese experience*, p. 244. Alternative estimates were 2,551 skilled and semi-skilled labourers and 91 electricians. See also Sato, *War, nationalism*, p. 189.

[170] Le, *Impact*, p. 234 argues for a high level of manufacturing until mid-1943.

[171] OSS, R&A 719, *Strategic survey of Indo-China*, p. 42; JISPB, *Joint Army-Navy intelligence study of Indochina*, chapter 8, 'Cities and towns in French Indochina', pp. VIII-I-VIII-3; OSS, R&A 2594, *Selected industrial installations in Indo-China*, pp. 42–61; Robequain, *Economic development*, pp. 275–84.

colonial manufacturing. The government in France now saw colonial industry as important on the grounds of self-sufficiency and national defence, and began to direct the economy towards these goals.[172] Unlike the abrupt end to Indonesian and Malayan colonial industrialization initiatives after Japanese occupation, those of the French colonial government remained in place and evolved for most of the war, often in conflict with, and as a means of defence against, Japan's agenda for Indochina's manufacturing sector and greater Japanese economic dominance.

In 1940, partly in response to the joint pressures of constant Japanese attempts to assert greater economic control in Indochina and Indochinese economic isolation, the Vichy government increased the authority of Governor-General Decoux and his independence from the French Ministry of the Colonies. With Indochina cut off from metropolitan support and trade after the fall of France in June 1940, the Indochinese government, using its enhanced authority, initiated a programme of public works for the unemployed and sponsored a number of schemes to start new manufacturing and expand existing industries.[173] Typically, colonial government schemes had the dual purpose of attempting to make up for now unavailable imports needed to maintain local industry and supplying Japanese military requirements. In response to acute shortages of petrol, the government converted some alcohol distilleries to the production of an alcohol substitute. Other distilleries manufactured industrial alcohol or butanol for the Japanese military to use as aviation fuel.[174] French Indochinese industrial successes dated from 1941, and included the manufacture of black powder (a dynamite substitute) for mines, potassium chlorate for matches, carbonate of soda, phosphorous and various, mostly vegetable-based, substitutes for lubricants for automobiles and steam-driven machinery.[175] Several metal moulding plants and refineries were built in Tonkin.[176]

Small Vietnamese and Chinese industry and local handicraft production responded vigorously to opportunities created by the cessation of imports, and some entrepreneurial families became wealthy in the space of two or three years. To try to co-ordinate and channel the outburst of local entrepreneurship, the French organized artisan exhibitions and set up the Conseil de la Production industrielle and the Comités locaux de l'artisanat.[177] Small firms emerged to make machine tools, spare parts, pharmaceutical substitutes,

172 'I. G. M. I.', 'L'effort d'industrialisation', pp. 161, 163; 'L. A.', 'L'Indochine depuis la guerre', pp. 6, 16.

173 OSS, R&A 1715, *Indochina's war-time government*, pp. 9–10, 34.

174 OSS, R&A 2594, *Selected industrial installations in Indo-China*, pp. 1–41.

175 'D. S. E.', 'Mise au point sur la situation actuelle', p. 8.

176 Vu, 'Political and social change in Viet-Nam', p. 160.

177 NAC, 32640, 'Au sujet du concours artisanal de Hanoi', 3 November 1942; AOM, GF/10, 'Propositions de gradés de manvarimat formmulies à l'occasion du concours de l'artisant

carbonate of soda for soap, potassium chlorate, low-quality bicycle tyres and tyre re-treads.[178] Insofar as textiles were available during the war, a large share was supplied by handicraft producers. As well as handicraft textile production, the Indochinese authorities encouraged cottage industries like handmade paper manufacture.[179]

Despite a commitment to supply Japan with 700,000 tons of rice annually, the rice industry and its key manufacturing activity of milling remained under the control of the French colonial government. Beginning in February 1941, a committee, initially named the Comptoir des Riz et Maïs and subsequently the Comité des Céréales, was set up to regulate rice and corn. Japanese efforts to take over rice milling were resisted, first through the device of committees to which Mitsui Bussan Kaisha was denied admission, and then in late 1943 by requisitioning the use of rice mills.[180]

In Indochina, as throughout Southeast Asia, Japan's main objective for manufacturing was its re-orientation towards military requirements. Predominantly, this involved plant and equipment available in Indochina. Part of the French government strategy was to resist the Japanese through considerable collaboration with them. Able to take advantage of this, the Japanese managed substantially to direct manufacturing and for many of their needs relied on French supply. Lumber production, including saw milling, was, however, one of the few industries over which Japanese control was total. The industry was strategically important to Japan because of its great emphasis on plans to build wooden ships and the need for wood to construct barracks, warehouses, railway sleepers and barrels. A Japanese consortium acquired local saw mills and brought equipment from Japan to construct its own mills. Foundries and machine shops formerly linked to shipping and railways were also taken over for the programme of building wooden ships and the repair of military equipment.[181]

In mid-1943, Japan's government directed Japanese companies to begin new manufacturing to supply the military. By then, however, the time for significant expansion had passed, and little was done to offset the start of a decline in manufacturing. In 1943, Mitsui established a Saigon foundry to make parts for the navy, and in 1944, with French interests, started a factory to produce calcium chloride for welding. Plans in 1944 by three separate firms, Mitsui, Mitsubishi and Nomura, to manufacture tyres may not even have been

Indochinois de 1944' (documents 1944 and 1945); Marr, *Vietnam: state, war*, p. 318; 'D. S. E.', 'Mise au point sur la situation actuelle', pp. 7–8.

178 Marr, *Vietnam: state, war*, p. 318; Le, *Impact*, pp. 235–37.

179 OSS, assemblage 43, R&A 2280.1, *Handbook of Japanese industry*, pp. 275–76, 283.

180 AOM, GF/34, 'Rapport au conseil de l'Indochine', 3 February 1945, p. 14; OSS, R&A 1715, *Indochina's war-time government*, pp. 70–71.

181 OSS, R&A 2594, *Selected industrial installations in Indo-China*, pp. 72–74; Le, *Impact*, pp. 206–7.

implemented; if they were, any output was probably small.[182] The colonial government bureaucracy, resolute in a policy of passive resistance, frustrated repeated Japanese attempts to gain control of a Haiphong cement plant, and for about a year between 1943 and May 1944 obstructed the acquisition of two alcohol distilleries.[183]

Over the course of 1944, manufacturing in Indochina progressively shut down, and during 1945 effectively ceased. In May 1944, the shortage of shipping caused the Japanese to suspend the mining of coal, bauxite and iron, low-grade manganese and chrome ores, except for local needs.[184] Wooden shipbuilding was largely abandoned in mid-1944, after grandiose plans had resulted in a minimal output of ships.[185] Allied bombing destroyed a number of factories, including the Haiphong cement plant and the Nam Dinh cotton mill in Tonkin.[186] In 1943, the production of rubber tyres and tubes was considerable, but dropped sharply in 1944 due to shortages of canvas and steel wires, and for the first quarter of 1945 totalled just 60 tons.[187] By April, after the Japanese coup, most manufacturing plants had closed.[188]

Summary and Comparisons

The Japanese occupation did not transform Southeast Asian industry but functioned on an ad hoc basis and relied heavily on cannibalizing and adapting whatever machinery was at hand. Wartime experience, however, left a strong desire among many Southeast Asians for more industrialization in their own nations. Southeast Asia had too limited a pre-war industrial base for transformation to be possible during the short period of occupation and the interruption to trade and lack of access to critical imports largely precluded even the beginnings of an 'industrial revolution'. These realities faced Japan in mid-1943 when it hoped to develop manufacturing both to provide military goods and to help make up for shortages of consumer items and manufactured goods. As a British intelligence report explained for Malaya: 'Japanese claims to be successfully industrializing Malaya are not credible. There was little industrialization before the war and despite the attempts to establish sericulture and

182 Le, *Impact*, p. 212; LHC, MAGIC, 'Hanoi', 14 February 1944, p. 10; OSS, R&A 2589, *Rubber industry*, p. 53.

183 Le, *Impact*, pp. 212–14.

184 LHC, MAGIC, 'Economic value of Indo-China to Japan', 5 July 1944, p. 12; Le, *Impact*, p. 233.

185 LHC, MAGIC, 'The wooden shipbuilding program in Thailand and Indo-China', 23 May 1944, pp. A1–A19; Le, *Impact*, pp. 209–10.

186 OSS, R&A 2594, *Selected industrial installations in Indo-China*, p. 44; NA, FO371/46363, Foreign Office, 'Six-monthly report', 30 June 1944, p. 30; Le, *Impact*, pp. 235, 271.

187 OSS, R&A 2589, *Rubber industry*, pp. 51–53; OSS, R *Japanese industry in Japan*, p. 283; Le, *Impact*, p. 236.

188 Le, *Impact*, pp. 271, 238.

other new industries it is unlikely that much can be done owing to the shortage of tools and plant.'[189] Japanese-directed manufacturing had largely to be limited to attempts to patch up pre-war industry as far as a lack of essential lubricants and spare parts permitted and to convert pre-war agricultural processing and mining machinery to wartime uses.

Burma and the Philippines had, even by Southeast Asian standards, slight industrial bases before the war. In both countries, commodity processing was the most important pre-war industry. However, since Japan could not use sugar from the Philippines or rice from Burma, processing activity languished during the war. Japanese initiatives in Burma to manufacture for the military hardly made up for the decline in rice milling. In the Philippines, virtually all sugar mills ceased to function and restoring large parts of the rest of the manufacturing sector proved beyond the Japanese. Both countries depended on a revival of traditional industry and handicrafts to provide some consumer goods. Just as it had for Ba Maw in wartime Burma, in some other countries after the war the traditional sector struck a responsive chord of a return to the past. In Indonesia, a large section of the political elite, although wanting steel mills for their symbolic value, was not drawn to the image of an industrial society.[190]

Thailand paralleled Burma and the Philippines in exceptionally weak pre-war industrialization but it had a more positive World War II story. The Kingdom avoided the intense fighting that damaged industries in Burma and the Philippines and, unlike these countries, its chief manufacturing component of rice milling, although facing shortages of ancillary inputs by 1945, continued to operate at near pre-war levels. Saw milling in Bangkok expanded in response to Japanese demand for wood. Industrial planning and the acquisition of plant, equipment and technical expertise, all with Japanese help, moved forwards during occupation. Although Japan left Thailand these industrial legacies, they were not matched by wartime increases in output, principally owing to an inability to obtain essential inputs.

In both Malaya and Indonesia there were substantial Japanese efforts to establish manufacturing during the war. Because of Singapore, the Japanese designated Malaya as an industrial centre, while Java's large population and strategic location made it an obvious place to try to expand manufacturing when, beginning in mid-1943, Japanese policy favoured this approach. In both countries, most of the new wartime manufacturing enterprises, having been established in response to need and under hothouse conditions, did not survive long into the post-war period (Epilogue).

[189] ANM, 0575122 Intelligence 5O6/10, 'Appreciation of Malaya, part II Post-Japanese occupation', 20 July 1943, p. 3.

[190] Feith, *Decline*, pp. 36–37.

Vietnam, encouraged by Paris, had started to develop an import-substituting industry three years before the outbreak of war. After 1941, French administrators in Vietnam actively implemented this policy and included in it chemical and metal industries. Japanese firms also began substantial new industry in Vietnam, mainly to serve military needs. There was an upsurge in local artisan production. By 1944, however, manufacturing began to contract and within a year effectively closed down.

CONCLUSION

In this chapter and Chapter 4, I have examined in some detail five of the six sectors identified by Kendrick as the basis for any but a subsistence economy. Apart from a few exceptions, the picture has been one of precipitate declines, with falls in one sector impacting other sectors and reinforcing compression of the economy. Formal estimates of GDP per capita are limited to Thailand, Indonesia and Vietnam, together with a well-informed evaluation of income in the Philippines. On this basis and on the evidence presented here and in Chapter 4, one cannot avoid the conclusion that, Thailand apart, GDP per capita in Southeast Asia halved during the Japanese occupation.

Chapter 6 considers two wartime aspects of Southeast Asian economic contraction and lack of manufacturing. One is the numerous substitutes devised to try to replace previously imported goods. Substitution did not, however, make up for acute shortages, which made inevitable price controls and rationing, the chapter's other main subjects.

6

Shortages, Substitutes and Rationing

In wartime occupied areas, the supply of goods is often highly inelastic for two reasons. One is that existing stocks are not easily augmented in the absence of pre-war levels of imports. The other is that adequate local substitution for previously imported items may prove difficult.[1] World War II Southeast Asia was an extreme example of both of these causes of supply inelasticity and its consequences. Acute shortages arose from the region's highly specialized economic development, to the exclusion of even many essential goods; from Japan's policy of sending almost no goods to counter supply shortfalls; and from real difficulties in substituting local production for pre-war imports.

Dire shortages of most goods, a falling availability of rationed items and surging prices created strong incentives to manufacture local substitutes for previously imported goods. Japanese military policy to achieve self-sufficiency wherever possible provided yet more impetus to import-substitution industrialization, and beginning in 1943 Japanese war reversals gave this added urgency. Nevertheless, as Chapter 5 argued, new wartime industrialization was slight even when its instigators were Japanese and its chief purpose was to support the war effort. Intermediate inputs and capital goods needed to set up import-substitution industries were often lacking, because they had previously come as imports and were unobtainable under wartime conditions. If this was not a constraint, a major barrier to industrialization was still the region's minimal pre-war production of even simple manufactured goods, and consequent lack of appropriate machinery and an industrial heritage. A Southeast Asian industrial platform of engineers, technicians and skilled labour was woefully inadequate to launch any substantial new industry.

Limited import substitution and restricted imports of raw and manufactured materials left Japanese and Southeast Asians alike often reliant on imperfect, makeshift adaptations and substitutes. Some of these are considered in the first section of this chapter, which explores the extent of wartime scarcity in Southeast Asia and shows the ingenuity of both occupiers and occupied in trying to counter the limited availability of goods by adapting materials at hand.

[1] Bloc and Hoselitz, *Economics*, p. 81.

Severe shortages and wholesale currency expansion generated strong upwards price pressure. Price controls are typically needed to complement rationing but, as in many other poor, primary-producing countries during World War II, these proved ineffective everywhere in Southeast Asia despite widespread and persistent attempts at implementation.[2] That left rationing, discussed in the chapter's second section, as the principal tool to regulate the distribution of most basic consumer goods.

Substitutes

Southeast Asia's limited industrial base and the almost total absence of supplies shipped from Japan would clearly have made import-substituting industrialization in Southeast Asia difficult, and often unrealistic. According to a high-ranking Japanese official, no areas apart from Java and Malaya had the ability to produce basic necessities such as clothing to supply even the needs of the Southern Army in the southern part of its command. The same official, apparently describing Indonesia's Outer Islands, reflected that: 'I really only understood the nature of a colonial economy, and how different it is from an independent national economy [after I came to] Indonesia, where there was not even a single iron-works, chemical factory, or carbide factory, and even the necessary technology and attendant facilities such as electricity, radio communications and medicine production were lacking.'[3] Civilian populations, although in areas more industrialized than this, faced acute scarcities, or frequently the unavailability, of many basic manufactured goods. Under these circumstances, necessity and high and escalating prices for absent or hard-to-obtain goods led to continuing attempts to devise some manner of substitutes. This section describes a few of the many, often seemingly unlikely, substitutes that emerged in Southeast Asia.

Three features are apparent in much of this substitution. First, substitutes were frequently quite inferior replacements for unavailable goods. Second, the production of substitutes was often highly labour-intensive and, even for commodities in extreme surplus like rubber, could require unrealistically large amounts of locally available raw materials. While this partly reflected the low cost of labour and large oversupply of a few commodities, it was also the consequence of limited industrial machinery and technical knowledge in pre-war Southeast Asia. Third, Southeast Asians and Japanese alike, constrained by near-total autarkic economies, had to make do with on-the-spot materials. The range of these was remarkably narrow. That helps to explain why across Southeast Asia different inputs were used to produce substitutes for the same good.

Of the numerous items that were essential but difficult or impossible to obtain, textiles and oil products, including petrol, lubricants and kerosene,

[2] Wallace, 'Price control', pp. 60–62; Prest, *War economics*, p. 23.

[3] Reid and Akira, *Japanese experience*, p. 237.

were the most important. Oil shortages reduced GDP through constraining economic activity, plagued the Japanese military and affected almost all Southeast Asians by restricting the transport of goods for civilians. Textile shortages, chiefly reflected in a lack of clothing and thread to repair it, were less serious for the military than for civilians. The military could requisition whatever textiles were available; few civilians wove their own cloth and most had to look to the market or rely on rations. By the latter part of the war, the chance of obtaining textiles from either of these sources was, for the majority of Southeast Asians, almost nil. In Indonesia by 1944, all clothing, except old, worn clothes, had disappeared from markets, and even a black market for used clothing no longer existed.[4] Indonesians collected rugs and scrap cloth to make clothing.[5] The general Singapore ration in early 1944 for cotton textiles of one yard per person per year was, as a Japanese research report observed, 'so small that it is virtually useless'.[6] In Manila, a wholly inadequate textile ration led to a brisk business in old clothes. Clothing marts appeared at Bambang Street in Sta. Cruz and Dart Street in Pacò.[7]

Other basic items in acute shortage nearly everywhere included soap, matches, cigarettes, paper and medicines. In Malaya, a tobacco industry mushroomed overnight into a 'considerable undertaking' to replace pre-war cigarette imports.[8] Matches, however, were not easily made locally, because good substitutes for chlorate of potash and other chemicals previously imported did not exist.[9] In the Philippines, where chemicals had been imported from Sweden, splitting matches in half economized on their use. As this required some skill, others made a wicker lamp from a tin can filled with coconut oil or, in the provinces, went back to the flint-and-tinder of earlier times.[10]

The limited range of locally available materials with which to produce substitutes put a premium on improvisation with whatever could be found, as in Malaya where spoons and forks were fashioned out of sheet aluminium

4 NAH, 2.21.266, Ch. O. van der Plas, 'Third report on conditions in the Netherlands Indies', 23 September 1944, p. 2; Sato, 'Occupation: economy', p. 268.

5 OSS, R&A 3170 and second edition of assemblage 22, *Programs of Japan in Java*, p. 214.

6 NIDS, Nansei Gunsei –18 Japan, Southern Military Administration Chōsabu, Report no. 35: *Syonan tokubetsu shi wo chūshin to seru bukka* taisaku [Counter-measures for prices in Syonan Municipality] by Kirita Naosaku (Singapore: Southern Military Administration Chōsabu, March 1944), p. 26. A 1945 report gives a clothing allowance in Malaya of one garment per year per household: NARA, RG226, entry 16, box 1472, no. 128585, OSS, R&A Branch, Regular Intelligence Reports, 'Malaya under the Japanese, March 1945', p. 22.

7 Agoncillo, *Fateful years*, p. 583.

8 Malaya, *Report on the 1947 census*, p. 34.

9 ANM, 1957/0290034, Selangor, *Annual Report of the Customs and Excise Department 2602* (1942), p. 6.

10 Agoncillo, *Fateful years*, p. 582; Hartendorp, *Japanese occupation*, p. 353 and *History of industry*, p. 88.

salvaged from the wreckage of downed Zeros and Flying Fortresses.[11] Burmese villagers obtained parachute cloth, literally from the skies, and found it useful.[12] In response to a law that private individuals could not hold tin, Singapore traders and speculators had the metal turned into spoons. These were used in coffee shops and private homes.[13] Guerrilla forces, operative in much of the Philippines, found numerous ways to adapt and innovate. One unit in Leyte had to compensate for the lack of a printing press, printing papers and ink with which to print their own currency. They utilized wooden blocks made by local engravers and ink concocted by a resident chemist, and printed on wrapping paper, grade three notebook paper or whatever other paper could be scavenged.[14]

Substitution for metals, all in chronic shortage, was particularly difficult due to a lack of capital equipment. Scrap metal of any sort became valuable, and existing structures were cannibalized. By September 1943, large numbers of homeowners in Manila had begun to tear down their dwellings in response to high prices for galvanized iron, roofing nails, lumber and other building materials.[15] In Malaya, Japanese firms turned old barbed wire and wire-ropes into wire-nails of up to three inches long for trade-packing and light construction work.[16]

Materials which found the most varied use in making substitutes frequently corresponded to the main Southeast Asian exports. The inputs most commonly used to create substitutes were rubber, rice, sugar, copra, pineapples and some tropical plants. In Malaya and also Burma, oil extracted from rubber was a common petrol substitute, but had the disadvantages of yielding less power than petrol, emitting a foul smell when burned and soon clogging engines.[17] While rubber oil alone worked poorly as a fuel, mixing it with benzene gave somewhat better results.[18]

Nor was gasoline efficiently made from rubber. Before the war, Malaya consumed 83,000 tons of gasoline. Fully to replace this amount would have required 1.7 million tons of rubber, three times Malaya's normal yearly production, and the construction of many more liquefaction factories.[19] Singapore traders carried rubber oil, made locally in large quantities and readily available on the open market, to Thailand where it could be exchanged for rice. Several Japanese factories in Malaya made rubber oil.[20]

11 Malaya, *Report on the 1947 census*, p. 34.
12 Spate, 'Burmese village', p. 542.
13 Chin, *Malaya upside down*, p. 175.
14 Lear, *Japanese occupation*, p. 149.
15 Hartendorp, *History of industry*, p. 600.
16 Chin, *Malaya upside down*, p. 172.
17 NARA, RG226, entry 16, box 937, no. 79807, OSS, R&A Branch, Regular Intelligence Reports, 'Commercial and industrial items, 4 July 1944', p. 4; OSS, R&A 2753, *Japanese use of Burmese industry*, p. 56.
18 Chin, *Malaya upside down*, p. 169.
19 OSS, R&A 2589, *Rubber industry*, p. 31.
20 ANM, 1957/0575131 Intelligence 506/30, 'Appreciation of the economic position of Malaya', 30 June 1944, p. 5; OSS, R&A 2423, *Singapore under Japanese domination*, p. 4.

Rubber was, however, just one of many possible fuel substitutes. Taxis in Singapore ran on charcoal, as did some automobiles.[21] Cars in Indochina also used charcoal, possibly mixing it with anthracite to improve performance.[22] Charcoal, when made from mangrove as in Malaya, yielded a fuel hot enough to make pig iron assaying at 70 to 78 per cent.[23] In Burma, petrol was manufactured from the sap of kanyin trees and from rice, as well as from rubber.[24] The Philippines produced no oil and, beginning in August 1942, buses fuelled by coconut-charcoal were introduced in Manila.[25] Motorized transport in Indochina depended chiefly on fuel distilled from rice; cane sugar grown in the Philippines was used to try to mimic high-grade fuel and also to produce paper.[26] Chemists in Indochina concocted a rice, maize or sugar substitute for aviation fuel, although one with octane levels that only allowed aeroplanes to operate at relatively slow speeds.[27] By contrast, sugar was scarce in Malaya, and in response some people began profitable businesses in extracting sugar from toddy (the buds of coconut trees).[28] Toddy, or sometimes wood, was also distilled to extract acetic acid for coagulating rubber.[29] A kerosene replacement in Indochina was concocted from a mixture of oils derived from fish, copra and groundnuts.[30]

During the later stages of occupation, growing shortages of lubricants hindered raw material processing and industrial production by causing machines to seize up. Heated cotton seed oil substituted as a lubricant in the Philippines. In Indochina, lubricants were derived from local vegetable oils.[31] Crude red palm oil, mixed with foreign-made oils and greases to add strength, was used by Malayan mines, factories and transport workshops.[32] At the beginning of 1944, castor oil plants were grown along Indonesian roadsides and on all available idle land to increase the supply of lubricating oil for aeroplanes.[33]

[21] Shinozaki, *Syonan*, p. 60.

[22] NA, FO371/35915, 'Economic situation in Indochina', 1943, p. 8.

[23] NARA, RG226, entry 19, box 0033, R&A/SEAC, Memo K-21, *Intelligence bearing upon Japanese intentions in South-East Asia*, November 1944, p. 3.

[24] Pe, *Narrative*, p. 60.

[25] Hartendorp, *History of industry*, p. 2.

[26] OSS, R&A 2594, *Selected industrial installations in Indo-China*, p. 1; LHC, MAGIC, 'Economic', 4 September 1942, p. 8.

[27] OSS, R&A 2594, *Selected industrial installations in Indo-China*, p. 1.

[28] ANM, 1957/0290034, Selangor, *Report of the Customs and Excise Department 2602* (1942), p. 7.

[29] NARA, RG226, entry 16, box 1472, no. 128585, OSS, R&A Branch, Regular Intelligence Reports, 'Malaya under the Japanese, March 1945', p. 16; NARA, RG226, entry 19, box 297, R&A XL23209, *Malaya–Japanese penetration of the rubber manufacturing industry*, 12 October 1945, p. 10.

[30] AOM, GF/34, 'Rapport au conseil de l'Indochine', 3 February 1945, p. 5.

[31] Ibid., p. 5.

[32] Chin, *Malaya upside down*, p. 168.

[33] OSS, R&A 3170 and second edition of assemblage 22, *Programs of Japan in Java*, p. 194.

Rubber found a number of uses apart from providing a raw material for fuel oil, although none could absorb more than an insignificant amount of the surpluses piling up in Southeast Asia's rubber-growing regions. Boats, horse-shoes, canteens, rice cookers and asphalt substitutes, intended for airport runway and other surfaces, all incorporated rubber as a principal material. In Burma, Japanese technicians made rubber into a leather substitute for belts and for bayonet, cartridge and signal lantern cases. Because there was a severe shortage of gunnies, part-rubber bags were used to transport rice and all-rubber bags to carry mineral oils.[34] A lack of equipment to manufacture inner tubes led to the appearance of solid rubber tyres on cars and bicycles; wood tyres might otherwise have to make do.[35]

Gunny sacks, although in short supply for shipping rice or sugar, were the most usual Southeast Asian cloth substitute, despite the drawbacks of itching badly and harbouring lice. In Java, shorts made from gunny cloth were a prize for the delivery of 15 rat tails.[36] Some Burmese complemented clothing made from gunnies with jackets of mosquito netting.[37] Clothing substitutes in Indochina, clothing made from Malaya and Indonesia, generally more exotic than practical, included kapok and pineapple leaves, castor oil and banana plants, fan palms and sisal hemp fibres.[38] The bark of fibrous trees provided the material for clothing in parts of rural Indonesia and was used in that country's Bakken province to make rope.[39] Sheet rubber was adapted in Malang (East Java) to make sarongs, *kebayas* (blouses) and trousers.[40] In mountain Java, people clothed themselves in old tyre tubing.[41] Even so, it was not uncommon for people in rural areas to go naked for want of clothing. In Malaya, Japanese firms manufactured clothing and blankets for the military from rags and waste materials.[42]

Writing paper and other types of papers had only partial, rather imperfect, substitutes. Paper was variously produced from slang grass, rice husk or coconut husk (South Borneo), pineapple fibre or bamboo (Malaya) and

34 OSS, R&A 2753, *Japanese use of Burmese industry*, pp. 22, 34, 38–39, 55; OSS, R&A 3170 and second edition of assemblage 22, *Programs of Japan in Java*, pp. 211, 224.

35 NA, WO208/1532, 'Economic intelligence August 1942–October 1945', p. 35.

36 Lucas, *One soul*, p. 40.

37 Burma Intelligence Bureau, *Burma*, vol. 2, p. 198.

38 AOM, GF/34, 'Rapport au conseil de l'Indochine', 3 February 1945; OSS, assemblage 43, R&A 2280.1, *Handbook of Japanese industry*, p. 347; OSS, R&A 3170 and second edition of assemblage 22, *Programs of Japan in Java*, pp. 215–19.

39 OSS, R&A 3170 and second edition of assemblage 22, *Programs of Japan in Java*, p. 193; Aragon, 'Japanese time', p. 57. Bakken may be a mispelling of Banten.

40 NIMH, 010A/24, Netherlands Forces Intelligence Service, 'Compilation of NEFIS interrogation reports', 31 October 1944, p. 13; Lucas, *One soul*, p. 40; Sato, *War, nationalism*, p. 77.

41 Hefner, *Mountain Java*, p. 71.

42 NA, WO203/2647, 'Summary of Economic Intelligence (Far East) no. 132', 29 October 1945, p. 7.

straw or sometimes cotton and rice stalks (Indonesia).[43] Japanese in Malaya made recycled paper from locally collected waste paper.[44] Coconut husk waste yielded a form of cardboard in the Philippines.[45]

While garments had to be mended until they literally fell apart, cotton thread was hard to obtain. Plant fibres afforded one thread substitute, and also had several other uses. In Singapore, the fibres of pineapple plants were used to make fishing nets, belt conveyor hoses and tyres. The fibres were extracted in a process remarkable for high labour-intensity, by women scraping the pineapple leaves with small knives. A woman could glean just four to five ounces of fibre a day. It was estimated that Malaya could produce 2,000 tons of fibre a year by employing 36,000 female workers and using 250,000 pineapples daily.[46] In Pontianak, rope was made from pineapple fibres.[47]

Soap, in short supply everywhere, could be made with many alternative ingredients. Coconut oil was perhaps the most usual. It was mixed with mangrove ash in Borneo.[48] In the Philippines, where thousands of small Chinese soap manufacturers appeared, tobacco ash or various plant barks were used.[49]

Some substitutes were perhaps even more improbable than those already described. Discarded cigarette butts yielded the raw ingredient to produce a dye in Indonesia after the nicotine content had been extracted to manufacture insecticides.[50] The Public Works Department in Perak, lacking cement to repair cracks and crevices in pavements, experimented with a mixture of lime and powdered bricks but without much success.[51]

Substitutes for medicines were difficult to find. In Selangor and also in Indonesia, rubber oil mixed with some kerosene was sprayed on mosquito breeding areas in the hope of reducing the need for quinine as an anti-malarial agent.[52] Local substitutes for quinine, apparently made from dung beetles, were devised in

[43] OSS, assemblage 43, R&A 2280.1, *Handbook of Japanese industry*, p. 356; OSS, R&A 3170 and second edition of assemblage 22, *Programs of Japan in Java*, p. 225.

[44] OSS, assemblage 43, R&A 2280.1, *Handbook of Japanese industry*, p. 275; NA, WO203/2647, 'Economic intelligence, no. 134', 26 November 1945, p. 15.

[45] OSS, assemblage 43, R&A 2280.1, *Handbook of Japanese industry*, pp. 278, 347 and assemblage 33, *Programs of Japan in the Philippines*, p. 411.

[46] NIDS, Nansei Gunsei – 29 Japan, Southern Military Administration, *Syonan tokubetsu shi jūyō kōjō genjō gaikyō* [Overview of industrial factories in Syonan Municipality] (March 1943), p. 13.

[47] OSS, assemblage 43, R&A 2280, *Handbook of Japanese industry*, p. 106.

[48] NARA, RG226, entry 19, box 0158, 'Burma special research commission', 10 May to 2 August 1944, appx. F, p. 1; Ooi, *Japanese occupation*, p. 59.

[49] Hartendorp, *History of industry*, pp. 355–56.

[50] OSS, R&A 3170 and second edition of assemblage 22, *Programs of Japan in Java*, p. 220.

[51] WL, MSS. Ind. Ocn. s. 172, K. N. Sinnathamby and T. G. Seshan, 'Resume of works done during the period Jan. 1942–Aug. 1945: buildings', 3 December 1945, p. 2.

[52] ANM, 1957/0290027, Selangor Sanitary Board, *Annual report 2602*, p. 1 and 1957/0292046, *Report of the Kuala Lumpur Town Board 1946*, p. 4; OSS, R&A 3170 and second edition of assemblage 22, *Programs of Japan in Java*, p. 224.

the Philippines.[53] People in Singapore used shark oil as a dietary supplement and a sort of medicine.[54] Medical research in Malaya found that tinctures for medication could be extracted from a local shrub.[55] The basis for vitamin B and C pills came from rice bran and tangerines in Indonesia.[56] However, in the Philippines, fake aspirin tablets manufactured from starch were labelled by local sellers as *diyenwain* pronounced 'gen you wine' in Tagalog and adapted to its spelling as an inventive transliteration of American English 'genuine'.[57] In 1944, the Burma government, having concluded that the country must turn towards indigenous cures, set up a committee and engaged Japanese experts to study local medical roots and herbs.[58] The population of Borneo increasingly responded to a lack of medicines by appealing to medicine men and the spirits.[59]

In war economies, labour and raw materials often substitute for capital, as is evident from a number of the substitutes already described. In some instances, however, the labour intensity of substitution, encouraged by cheap labour and Japanese access to unlimited currency, was extreme. Although constrained by a shortage of production materials, the Japanese nevertheless pushed ahead with tyre manufacturing in Thailand. In June 1944, it took 14 days for four workers to produce one solid rubber tyre; the manufacture of four tyres a day required 14 tons of rubber a year.[60]

Rationing

Throughout Southeast Asia, quantities of consumer goods available for rations decreased during the war because pre-occupation stocks were depleted; because of a continuously widening gap between controlled and black market prices; and because of a lack of transport to secure and distribute goods. For the distribution of goods, the authorities in occupied Southeast Asia typically adopted a consumption policy analogous to that in Britain and the Soviet Union during World War II.[61] Basic consumer items were rationed and sold at frozen or only slowly adjusted prices, while the prices of other goods were left free to rise on the open market. The fundamental principle behind this rationing system was to guarantee a minimum standard of living.

53 NARA, RG226, entry 19, box 0158, 'Burma special research commission', 10 May to 2 August 1944, appx. F, p. 1.
54 Shinozaki, *Syonan*, p. 60.
55 Chin, *Malaya upside down*, p. 170.
56 OSS, R&A 3170 and second edition of assemblage 22, *Programs of Japan in Java*, p. 221.
57 Agoncillo, *Fateful years*, p. 583.
58 Burma, *Burma's new order plan*, pp. 40–41.
59 Ooi, *Japanese occupation*, p. 59.
60 OSS, R&A 2589, *Rubber industry*, pp. 43–44.
61 On a consumption policy of rationing, see Milward, *War, economy*, p. 239.

Initially, Japanese administrators in Singapore adopted a rationing system similar to the British colonial government's after the outbreak of war: registers were kept by retailers to control amounts given as rations. However, beginning in August 1942 rationing, like schemes usual in other parts of Southeast Asia, was through cards (or elsewhere variously tickets or coupons) issued to individuals.[62] Possession of a card entitled the bearer to purchase a specified amount of rationed goods at controlled prices. In the Philippines for clothing, a system of points deducted according to the choice of goods gave some scope for consumer preference, as did cloth coupons in Malaya.[63] Rationing generally lacked consistency between areas, as for example in Indonesia in late 1943, where, in the absence of a planned and unified rationing ticket system, rations were determined by certificates issued by the heads of administrative units.[64]

Rationing Characteristics

Patterns of rationing in Southeast Asia had three general features. One was that although rationing might at first extend to smaller towns and rural areas, and in Thailand included municipalities, as the war went on it increasingly concentrated in the largest cities. This localization of rationing helped to attract people in rice-deficit countries to the main urban centres and created problems of population inflows (Chapter 8).

Second, as in other poor, mainly primary-producing countries in the Middle East and in India, rationing in Southeast Asia was made difficult by a lack of adequate records of population and dealers.[65] The Japanese tried to gauge rationing requirements, reduce an inequitable distribution of key commodities and also assert social control by taking censuses in some areas, for example in 1943 in Singapore and in Rangoon, and using these as a basis for rationing. While a census similar to Rangoon's was ordered in Burma's districts, it was probably never taken.[66] Outside Rangoon a plan was devised to try to achieve a fairer distribution of salt and other essential commodities by channelling rations through village associations.[67] In cities, mainly in rice-deficit areas, large migrant inflows posed allocation and identification problems. Migrants tended, notably in Indonesia, often not to have been included in Japanese

62 NA, CO852/327/9, 'Food supplies Malaya', 1942, p. 2; Kratoska, *Japanese occupation*, p. 255.

63 Hartendorp, *Japanese occupation*, p. 504.

64 NIDS, Japan, Java Military Administration, Gunseika ni okeru Java – Madura no shokuryō jijō to sono taisaku [Food conditions in Java and Madura] (October 1943), ch. 2, section 7.

65 Prest, *War economics*, pp. 20, 204.

66 Burma Intelligence Bureau, *Burma*, vol. 2, p. 73 and vol. 1, p. 68.

67 OSS, R&A 2753, *Japanese use of Burmese industry*, p. 44; Burma Intelligence Bureau, *Burma*, vol. 2, p. 143.

population counts or censuses. Rationing cards in Hanoi were given to the family head but fair allocation was particularly a problem when this was a woman, due to uncertainties as to name changes and correct names.[68]

A third general characteristic of rationing, like much else in Southeast Asia's wartime economic history, was contrasts in the composition of rationed items between the region's rice-deficit and rice-surplus economies. Rice was easily the most important constituent of rationing throughout areas previously partly reliant on outside sources of supply. In Malaya (including Singapore), Indonesia and the Philippines, rationing began almost from the outset of occupation because of the need to supply rice as the staple food. Along with rice, principal among the many items rationed in Malaya were salt and sugar. These commodities were also rationed in the Philippines, together with soap, lard, cigarettes and matches.[69] In Indonesia, in addition to rice, kerosene, coconut oil and soap were strictly rationed.[70] As shortages worsened, rationing throughout Southeast Asia typically applied to a growing list of items. By October 1944, for example, foods rationed in Singapore included tapioca, sweet potatoes, bananas, green chillies, papaya, pineapples and spring onions, all sold at prices set by the Syonan Rationing Association's Department of Fruit and Vegetables.[71]

Chronic shortages and rationing made queue-standing a recognized 'profession' for many unemployed and older and less agile Southeast Asians. In urban Malaya, for those lacking other work, queuing and the sale of rationed goods at enhanced prices was 'always a possible source of livelihood'.[72] Queuing from soon after midnight became the norm in Singapore and Manila to try to obtain food rations, but with no guarantee of success. Large numbers of Singapore's pre-war household servants left domestic service because 'they could earn much more money by joining the "queues" for cigarettes, for fish, for meat'. When successful, 'the proceeds of a long wait could be disposed of at ten times the sum paid'.[73] In Manila, too, large time costs to try to obtain food made the re-sale of rationed goods a common practice. People waiting for rice rations might have 'to stand in line for the greater part of the day' or even all night.[74] Filipino humour, much given to word play, had it that the Philippines was no longer 'Pilipinas' but 'Pilapinas', 'pila' meaning queue.[75]

[68] AOM, RSTNF/1393, Delegation special Hanoi, 'Rapport d'inspection', 11 January 1945.
[69] Hartendorp, *Japanese occupation*, p. 498.
[70] NIMH, 010A/6, Netherlands Forces Intelligence Service, 'Report based on the interrogation of 32 Javanese', 3 July 1944, p. 3.
[71] IER, Azb: 3 Japan, Malayan Military Administration Chōsabu, *Syonan tōnai shokuryō zōsan saku ni tsuite* [Policy for food production on Syonan island] (October 1944), pp. 18–20.
[72] Malaya, *Report on the 1947 census*, p. 34.
[73] Low and Cheng, *This Singapore*, p. 127 and see Low, *When Singapore*, p. 63.
[74] Hartendorp, *History of industry*, p. 82.
[75] Jose, 'Rice shortage', p. 212; Agoncillo, *Fateful years*, pp. 551–52.

The rice-surplus countries of Burma, Thailand and Indochina faced a different rationing problem from their deficit counterparts, since rice shortages arose from distributive difficulties, not a lack of quantity. While acute rice shortages appeared in some parts of these countries, including northern Vietnam and Burma, surpluses built up in pre-war rice export areas. In the latter, rice was freely available, although the components of a nutritionally sufficient diet might be lacking, as they were in Lower Burma (Chapter 7). Prior to the war, much of Burma's salt had been imported from Germany. Labourers especially required salt and during the war it often became, as in Burma, a rationed commodity in Southeast Asia.[76] However, even in the war's early stages the authorities in these countries also found it necessary to ration a range of goods. Rationing in Indochina extended to sugar, matches, soap and all textiles and, in the north, rice as well.[77] Thailand had already started to ration gasoline, kerosene and fuel oil in May 1941 and by June 1942, after Japanese occupation, acute shortages of all kinds of imported products developed.[78] By then, ration coupons had been issued for use in Bangkok and Thonburi for rice, lard, soap, sugar, fuels and matches.[79] In Bangkok and other municipal areas, distribution, in exchange for coupons issued to heads of households, was through so-called rationing shops. These were either existing stores or set up specifically for rationing, and had to be owned by a Thai, a stipulation intended to push Thai into retailing and competition with shops run by ethnic Chinese who lacked Thai citizenship. The Thai Warehouse Company was established in March 1943 to buy and store basic goods like sugar and matches for rationing. Shares in the enterprise were offered only to Thai.[80] To try to deal with high clothing prices by 1944, Thailand, as well as starting spinning and weaving classes, put ginned and unginned cotton under government control in Bangkok and 23 provinces. Cotton goods, including material and made-up garments, were subject to price controls and rationed by a ticket system.[81]

Rationing Quantities

While the aim of governments in Southeast Asia remained to guarantee at least a subsistence level of essential foods and/or consumer goods, rationed amounts increasingly failed to reach this target. Shortfalls cut badly into consumption everywhere but had an especially detrimental effect on living standards in rice-

[76] OSS, R&A 2753, *Japanese use of Burmese industry*, pp. 43–44.
[77] AOM, GF/34, 'Rapport au conseil de l'Indochine', 3 February 1945, p. 8; Robequain, *Economic development*, p. 383.
[78] NARA, RG59, entry 205, box 5834, file 892.00 233, Chapman, 'Conditions in Thailand Dec. 1941 to June 1942', 18 August 1942, pp. 24, 25, 31.
[79] Numnonda, *Thailand*, p. 93.
[80] Anamwathana, 'Economic policy', pp. 64–70.
[81] OSS, assemblage 43, R&A 2280.1, *Handbook of Japanese industry*, pp. 313–15.

deficit areas, since throughout Southeast Asia rice was a staple food. Data on rationing levels are relatively abundant for Singapore, but scattered for elsewhere in Southeast Asia. Nevertheless, it is clear that by 1944 in Indonesia and the Philippines rations of rice and substitute food staples had fallen to a fraction of amounts at the beginning of occupation. In Manila, at the onset of occupation, rations of 300 grams of rice compared favourably with pre-war rice consumption of 300 to 350 grams (an average of 0.78 of a pound) a day. By May 1944, however, rations were 60 grams each of rice and sweet potatoes. During the latter part of 1944, food rationing became irregular and soon stopped altogether.[82]

In Singapore in a little over two years between September 1942 and November 1944, rice imports allocated to the city by the Japanese dropped by over half (Table 6.1). The fall in official rice imports led to a sharp contraction in rice rations and a disproportionate one for Singaporean civilians (Table 6.2). As late as November 1942, the ration for Japanese and Singaporeans alike was 20 catties a month (403.2 grams per day in a 30-day month, equivalent to 1,443 calories). By mid-February 1944, the monthly ration given to Japanese was 12 catties but just 8 for Singapore males (161.3 grams a day and 577 calories), 6 catties for females and 4 catties for children.

Male rice rations of 8 catties were far below minimum daily calorie requirements of at least 1,700 calories for productive work and 2,000 to 2,250 calories for an adequate food intake. Japanese rationing authorities had somehow to react to the drop in rations in order to maintain work effort at a functioning level among workers essential to the war effort. The Singaporean preference for white rice added to the difficulty of achieving this goal. Even in normal

Table 6.1 *Rice imports allocated to Municipal Singapore (bags of 100 kg monthly)*

Sep-42	110
Dec-42	105
Apr-43	90
Aug-43	76
Oct-43	55
Feb-44	44
Apr-44	50.5
Nov-44	52.5

Source: NA, WO 203/4499, Rice – SEAC territories, Oct. 1945.

[82] Jose, 'Food production', p. 80.

times white rice was favoured to an extent that it endangered well-being through deficiencies in niacin and vitamin B1, the causes of pellagra and beriberi respectively. During the war, along with inadequate quantities of rice, the problem of nutrition was compounded by insufficient overall food availability and by obtainable foods being grossly deficient in protein, oils, fats and vegetables. The Japanese responded in February 1944 by boosting rice rations for those in essential heavy work to 19 catties monthly (383 grams a day in a 30-day month) and allocating 15 catties a month to other essential workers. Apparently, however, additional rations to those regarded as doing essential jobs only partially achieved the intended aim since these priority workers were known to sell rations on the black market (Chapter 8).

Continuous falls in official Japanese rice imports to Singapore and therefore also rations left non-essential workers facing very considerable food deficits. Although some 'illicit' or 'illegal' smuggled rice had always reached Singapore for black market sale, amounts in no way made up for the large falls in Japanese-controlled official imports. Beginning in November 1942, in response to worsening rice rations for non-essential Singaporeans, Japanese rationing authorities began to rely on the distribution of rice substitutes, principally tapioca (calorific but seriously short of nutritional value). A further Japanese rationing strategy which started in April 1944 was rice brought to Singapore by so-called private importers (now legalized) and available for distribution through the Japanese rationing system at below market prices. However, these quantities of rice fell far short of furnishing adequate rations, even assuming that individuals could, in practice, secure stated rations.

In addition to rationed rice, the April 1944 Japanese strategy to deliver more rice to Singapore allowed private importers to sell some of their cargos on the open market. These importers did not, however, transport nearly enough rice to the city to remedy large food shortfalls by later 1944. Singaporeans, like their counterparts in rice-deficit Southeast Asia, had substantially to rely for a livelihood on what they could grow, catch and afford to purchase on the black market. For ordinary Singaporeans, consumption of staple foods probably continued to fall throughout the Japanese occupation, as well as being grossly inadequate in rationed basic goods. Cloth rations in Singapore amounted to about three yards of fabric and three ready-made pieces a year for a family of eight, approximately equivalent to the early 1944 ration, indicated above, of one yard per person per year.[83]

Because Tonkin in north Vietnam was, in sharp contrast to the south, a rice-deficit area and, moreover, during late 1944 and 1945 in the grip of severe famine (Chapter 7), rice rationing had many similarities to Singapore and other deficit areas such as the Philippines. As usual in Southeast Asia, rations

[83] ANM, 1957/0572010, 'Treatment of the people of Malaya during the Japanese military occupation', Memorandum, extraordinary general affairs section of the Koumintang, Selangor branch, p. 5.

Table 6.2 *Municipal Singapore rice and food rations March 1942–May 1945 (rice catties per month unless otherwise specified)*

	Rice per person per month	Rice per Japanese per month	Rice per male per month	Rice per female per month	Rice per child per month	Essential military factory workers	Essential workers heavy	Essential workers ordinary	Non-rice rations
10 Mar. 1942–15 Nov. 1942	20	20							
16 Nov. 1942–31 Jan. 1943	17								1 catty soybeans
1 Feb. 1943–31 Aug. 1943	14	17							
7 Mar. 1943									Sale of tapioca and soya bean bread From Feb. 1944, for rations of tapioca flour bread & noodles, rice flour & beans, see notes.
1 Sept. 1943–31 Oct. 1943	12	14							
1 Nov. 1943–10 Feb. 1944			12	9	6	5 extra per month			

11 Feb. 1944 onwards (except Japanese from July 1944, see n. 8)	12	8	6	4		11 extra per month	7 extra per month

Notes: 1 catty = 1.33 lbs.

1. 20 Mar. 1942 onwards: Official rice prices were (per catty): lime rice: 7 cents; whole rice 10 cents; broken rice 8 cents.
2. 16 Nov. 1942 to 31 Jan. 1943: 1 catty of soya beans per person per month.
3. 7 Mar. 1943: Sale of tapioca and soya bean bread.
4. 15 Feb. 1944: Tapioca noodles were sold to the public 1 catty per card at all markets.
5. 17 Apr. 1944: Tapioca flour bread rations were distributed through retailers at 6 cents a loaf at: 1–3 persons, one loaf; 4–6 persons two loaves; 7–9 persons three loaves and so on.
6. Apr. 1944: Because of confusion in the markets, the sale of tapioca noodles was entrusted to heads of wards. They in turn sold to heads of teams for onward sale to householders. Rations every three days were: 1 to 5 persons: 1 catty; 6 to 10 persons: 2 catties; and so on. Municipal and government employees were given 7 catties of rice extra per month.
7. May 1944: Essential workers received 5 catties of rice extra each from private importers' stock (one month only).
8. July 1944: Japanese rice ration increased to 19 catties of rice and 2 catties of pullet (or pulut, possibly meaning glutinous rice in Malay) or bee hoon (rice vermicelli) per person.
9. Sept. 1944: 3 catties of extra rice sold to the public from private importers stock at $2.80 per catty.
10. Nov. 1944: Availability of 1 catty of rice, 1.5 catties of rice flour and 0.5 catty of beans from private importers' stock, all at $2.80 per catty. It is unclear how much was available per person or over what time period.
11. Dec. 1944: Supply to the public (but not municipal and government servants) of bread and tapioca noodles stopped; 5 catties of rice and cereals sold to the public available from private importers' stock.
12. May 1945: Bread supply to municipal and government servants stopped.

Source: NA WO 203/4499 Rice—SEAC territories Oct. 1945. See also, WO 203/2647, 'Summary of economic intelligence no. 130, 15 Oct. 1945', p. 5.

were chiefly available in the large cities and their suburbs.[84] Rice rationing in Hanoi was by ticket obtained through registration, principally by the heads of families. In August 1943, 210,166 rations were distributed but this declined to 197,671 in February 1944 and then yet further to 183,419 in June and 181,237 in October, mainly because bombing in December 1943 and April 1944 caused people to leave the city.[85]

While rations in Hanoi were known to be inadequate, forcing recourse to the black market for additional rice, the number distributed nevertheless exceeded Hanoi's apparent December 1943 population (Chapter 8), perhaps because of difficulties in controlling fraud but also due to the inclusion of suburbs and population inflows encouraged by the onset of famine.[86] In his January 1945 report, the inspector for administrative affairs for Hanoi municipality cited the distribution of 130,000 rations to those in the urban periphery, and pointed out that this implied a much larger peripheral population, since infants under 2 years of age received no rations, those aged 2 to 5 a quarter ration and children between the ages of 5 and 10 a half ration. The report made several recommendations for controlling cityward migration, not only by those who had worked in agriculture but also by small traders, employees and servants and their families. It was suggested that newcomers without evidence of stable employment be refused ration cards so that 'Hanoi and its suburbs are not swollen by useless mouths and people without work'. A further idea was that migrants should contribute to public works projects.[87]

Rationing and Income Distribution

Rationing schemes can sometimes try to address, and may reduce, social inequalities, as for example in World War II Britain. That was not, however, a goal of rationing in Southeast Asia. Evidence discussed in Chapters 7 and 8 suggests that, if anything, inequalities in the region widened during the war, because as rations fell and black market prices rose, low earners, often with the disadvantage of relatively inflexible nominal wages, found it increasingly difficult to afford basic goods, particularly food in rice-deficit areas. The plight of many of those who migrated to large cities but remained outside the rationing system became desperate.

Where the Japanese offered priority rations, the policy attempted to maintain real food wages and altered income distribution. In Singapore, preferential rationing extended to the some 70,000 employed by the military or by Japanese

84 Marr, *Vietnam 1945*, p. 101.

85 AOM, RSTNF/1393, Municipalité de Hanoi, Rapport d'inspection, 29 January 1945, pp. 25–26.

86 Marr, *Vietnam 1945*, p. 102; AOM, RSTNF/1393, Municipalité de Hanoi, Rapport d'inspection, 29 January 1945, p. 29.

87 AOM, RSTNF/1393, Municipalité de Hanoi, Rapport d'inspection, 29 January 1945, p. 47 and see pp. 46–49.

firms.[88] The possibility of maintaining non-food real wages, probably partly with the proceeds from selling priority rations, was, of course, compromised by high prices and by a lack of goods to buy. Nevertheless, priority rationing left many on the island markedly better off than their counterparts employed in non-Japanese-run sectors of the economy, and placed a quantity of rice at their disposal that may not have been a great deal less than many had commanded before the war.

Price Controls and Black Markets

Successful rationing depends on a general acceptance by the public. Its willingness to comply with rationing, if combined with an availability of sufficient goods, avoids straining compliance beyond breaking point. In World War II Southeast Asia, neither of these constituents existed. While rationing helped to achieve social control (Chapter 2), growing scarcities left people no alternative but to go outside the rationing system and turn to the black market. Even had there been a greater supply of goods, the spectacle of the routing of Western colonial rulers and then the pressures of occupation might still have eroded the social order to an extent that rationing and price control could never be more than partially effective.

Price Controls

Japanese administrators and governments in Thailand and Indochina no doubt understood the complementarity between rationing and price controls but could do little to enforce the latter and prevent their near-total breakdown. It was, a French civil servant in Indochina concluded, simply impossible to cap prices of essential goods.[89] Attempts at price control were never much observed in the Philippines except as a joke. In Manila, the *Tribune* published official food prices. However, purchasers who cited these were rudely advised by market traders to go to the newspaper's office to buy; 'Tribune price' came into vogue in Manila as a derisive term. Scant notice was given to price controls by Manila street vendors, who remained undeterred by government-staged public humiliations such as a 'profiteers cage' in central Manila and various tortures and displays, including scores of offenders being roped together and paraded through the streets.[90]

In Rangoon, scarcities of some goods were so acute that bazaar-sellers held raffles for the right to buy available supplies.[91] Beginning in 1942, merchants in

88 IER, Azb: 5 Japan, Malayan Military Administration Chōsabu, *Shōnan tokubetsu shi rōmu jijō chōsa* [Study of the labour situation in Syonan Municipality] (October 1944).
89 AOM, INF/c141d1267, 'Rapport du Commissaire Martin', 3 February 1945, p. 18.
90 Agoncillo, *Fateful years*, p. 539 and see pp. 537–39, 572; Hartendorp, *History of industry*, p. 84.
91 Burma Intelligence Bureau, *Burma*, vol. 2, p. 212.

Thailand were liable to a fine or five years in prison for failure accurately to report the amount and value of their stocks. A lack of compliance continued, however, and led, in 1943, to the enactment of the stiffer sanctions of execution or life imprisonment.[92]

Indonesian authorities attempted, with at best partial success, to enforce price control for a number of commodities deemed important to the maintenance of some reasonable standard of living. Regulations issued in March 1942 specified ceiling prices set at 1 January 1942 levels. As inflation continued, a series of controls with upwardly revised prices followed. In April 1944 in Jakarta, controls widened to 24 items including rice. A year later, in April 1945, an official effort in the city to regulate prices and the distribution of necessities extended to rice, cereals, coconut oil, sugar, tea, fruit, vegetables, salt, dried fish and clothing.[93] Throughout Southeast Asia, the picture which resulted from rationing and an attempt to impose controls was generally, as in Burma, 'one of inefficiency and distress'.[94]

Black Markets

By mid-1943, a struggle for survival forced most Southeast Asians to rely on black markets, not just rationing and a measure of price controls for some goods. Black markets appear throughout this book and only noted here is their increasing importance as official rations dwindled, as stated entitlements became more difficult to obtain, as price controls failed, as prices for rationed goods progressively lost touch with demand, and as scarcities for non-rationed goods became more acute. Medicines and pharmaceuticals were notable for their escalating black market prices.[95] Indochina had a vibrant black market in pharmaceuticals; insulin, quinine, emetine (for dysentery) and renal medicines fetched particularly high prices.[96] In Hanoi at the beginning of 1945, the black market in rice was reported as 'flourishing'.[97]

Along with near-total supply inelasticity and high inflation, two further considerations contributed to driving up black market prices and encouraging hoarding. One was the award in Japanese-administered areas of distribution rights on an exclusive or cartelized basis, giving retailers monopoly power (Chapter 2). In Burma, the newspaper *New Light of Burma* reported in August 1943 that, 'As soon as prices were controlled everything disappeared.

92 Numnonda, *Thailand*, p. 93; NARA, RG59, entry 205, box 5835, file 892.00/11-2444, Bill Powell, 'Political conditions in Thailand', 22 September 1944, p. 9.

93 OSS, R&A 3170 and second edition of assemblage 22, *Programs of Japan in Java*, pp. 137–39, 142–43.

94 Burma Intelligence Bureau, *Burma*, vol. 2, p. 74.

95 Chaya, *Passing hours*, p. 57; Agoncillo, *Fateful years*, p. 572.

96 Marr, *Vietnam, state, war*, p. 544.

97 AOM, RSTNF/1393, Municipalité de Hanoi, Rapport d'inspection, 29 January 1945, p. 46.

As soon as the control is lifted the goods will reappear suddenly.'[98] Similar disappearance and re-appearance, often on the black market, was the norm in Malaya after the formation, under Japanese auspices, of official monopoly trading organizations. These *kumiai* were established for a whole range of basic commodities but once they were set up Malayans found that traders withdrew the commodity from the open market (Chapter 2).[99] In Bangkok, efforts to facilitate a flow of goods were ineffective, since under conditions of scarcity 'no one would sell their commodities without huge profits notwithstanding the price control orders'.[100] There were numerous arrests of Chinese for hoarding canned foodstuffs, beverages, soap, flour and thread, both in Bangkok and in the provinces, as, for example, in Phitsanulok in the Lower North of Thailand, where the Governor had 50 shopkeepers arrested.[101]

A second reason for escalating prices was that Japanese themselves often had to buy on the black market. Japanese civilians received few imported goods from Japan, while the military, expected to supply its own needs locally, could try to meet these by drawing on more or less unlimited supplies of currency. During the first half of 1943 in Indochina, a lengthy official report on the black market, commenting on the failure of numerous legislative measures to control prices and their escalation, concluded that it would be impossible to restrain prices unless the money supply could be controlled.[102] Filipinos had to bid for rice not just with Japanese civilians but with the Japanese military, who could pay high prices.[103] In Indochina, Japanese and local residents competed in the black market for vegetables, poultry and cloth.[104] Japanese in the Philippines paid 'astronomical sums' for iron, medicine, galvanized sheet metal and other necessary military materials.[105]

Black markets spawned a new class of Southeast Asians, commented on here and further discussed in Chapter 8 in regard to Manila and Singapore. In Burma, occupation produced several Rangoon Indian millionaires and multimillionaires. One was said to have 'started business with a couple of lorries and a dozen rowdies, looted some of the big stores and godowns in Rangoon after their owners had fled, stored away the stuff secretly and become prominent in the black market after the Japanese occupation'. Others went into the black market with goods of their own and made a fortune.[106] Along with their

[98] Burma Intelligence Bureau, *Burma*, vol. 2, p. 212.
[99] Chin, *Malaya upside down*, p. 88.
[100] Numnonda, *Thailand*, p. 94 and see pp. 94–95.
[101] OSS, R&A 2695, *Status of the Chinese*, pp. 44–45.
[102] VNA, FF 133394, 'Sur le contrôle des prix', 11 August 1944, p. 110.
[103] Garcia, *Documents*, p. 250; Jose, 'Rice shortage', p. 209.
[104] VNA, FF 133394, 'Sur le contrôle des prix and la lutte contre le marché noir', 11 August 1944, pp. 79–95.
[105] Agoncillo, *Fateful years*, p. 572.
[106] Sivaram, *Road to Delhi*, p. 150.

accomplices, an easily distinguishable group of 'speculators and middlemen' emerged, Burma's 'New Order Brokers'. Typically, these men bought up scarce commodities, sold them to the Japanese army at a huge profit and benefited from favours from the military.[107] Recognizable by the Shan bag or leather briefcase that they invariably carried, the New Order Brokers became 'the Nouveau Riche of New Order Burma'.[108] Thailand's social structure, if perhaps mainly in Bangkok, became more nuanced: 'A new class of citizens was born – the *nouveau riche* whose business morality could be summed up as "more smuggling . . . more money".'[109] After 1945, at least some of these individuals, aided by post-war controls and shortages, seem likely to have become part of a group of 'fabulously wealthy rice hoarders and smugglers'.[110] Elsewhere, too, in Southeast Asian the wartime *nouveau riche* established themselves as prominent members of post-war society.

During the war, the black market became a way of life throughout Southeast Asia. In Malaya, people came to think of it as normal: 'when the stage arrived at which the public was compelled to pay black-market prices for such things as bus-tickets, railway-tickets, cinema-tickets, cloth-coupons, and even newspapers, the situation was beyond redemption'.[111] Even in Thailand, the Southeast Asian country least economically affected by the Japanese occupation, black marketeering and profiteering took over as the norm: 'cheating became a widespread "sport" and cheating the Japanese, a national duty'.[112]

Conclusion

The acute shortage of consumer goods was one of the most prominent features of wartime Southeast Asia. This chapter has discussed two possible responses to shortages. Efforts to devise substitutes for scarce and unavailable goods were largely a market response, while rationing served as the government response and became a principal means of regulating the distribution of numerous basic consumer goods. Substitution, although markedly imperfect, was, to some extent, a palliative to wartime shortages. However, in the face of rampant black markets and spiralling prices, rationing was essential. For many it provided a floor from which Southeast Asians could work towards achieving at least a minimum standard of living. By doing so, rationing contributed towards the preservation of civil order, a main Japanese goal.

107 NARA, RG226, entry 154, box 81, file 1398, Japanese control of government finance in Burma, p. 10; IOR, Clague Papers, Mss Eur E252/44, 'Situation in Burma', p. 12.

108 Pe, *Narrative*, p. 67; see also Taylor, *Thein Pe Myint's 'Wartime traveler'*, p. 234.

109 Numnonda, *Thailand*, p. 95.

110 Yang, *Multiple exchange rate system*, p. 35.

111 Chin, *Malaya upside down*, p. 37.

112 Numnonda, *Thailand*, p. 95.

7

Food and Famine in Southeast Asia

For almost all Southeast Asians, whether rural or urban dwellers, food was the single most important determinant of health and living standards. Among the great majority of urban dwellers and those exchanging their income for food, it accounted for half to two-thirds of total expenditure. Proportions of implicit family income were similar for rural dwellers more or less totally reliant on producing their own food. This chapter, although commenting on various aspects of the standard of living, focuses largely on the changing wartime access to food in rural Southeast Asia. Food availability is also considered in Chapter 8 on Southeast Asia's main cities during the war. However, that chapter has urbanization as its principal focus, since all of the region's main cities experienced some combination of large population outflows and inflows, the latter typically driven by people from rural areas in search of food.

Pre-war Southeast Asia's high economic specialization and integration ensured that the entire region would suffer varying degrees of food scarcity once Japanese policies and limited transport restricted the operation of markets. Moreover, pre-war food availability was delicately balanced in Southeast Asia's two densely populated areas of Tonkin and North Annam in Vietnam and Java in Indonesia. In both, population had long pressed on food supplies, and any external shock threatened food security. To be certain of adequate food, Java and northern Vietnam needed to be able to call on outside sources of supply. During the war, with this safety valve blocked, falls in food output caused major famines.

Elsewhere in Southeast Asia, areas which before the war had relied on trade for many basic foodstuffs were now subject to serious and growing food shortages. That was true of virtually all of Malaya. People in Central and Upper Burma, the Philippines and Indonesia, too, found themselves cut off from essential food supplies due to a lack of transport and economic autarky. By the end of the war, malnutrition was general in Malaya. Famine deaths occurred in some areas of the Philippines, mainly in mountain provinces but also in Manila, and possibly in Burma as well.[1]

[1] United Nations, *Economic reconstruction: Philippine Republic*, pp. 12–13.

Even Southeast Asia's three great rice-exporting regions in Burma, Thailand and Indochina went short of some foodstuffs. Although this was no more than a moderate problem in Thailand, scarcities were serious in Lower Burma. Rice prices there fell below pre-war levels, but many people were unable to obtain other basic foods, many of which had previously come from Central Burma. By 1945, the majority of those in Rangoon and probably also in the surrounding rural areas of Lower Burma were malnourished.

Famine: Vietnam and Java

This section has two aims.[2] One, fundamentally empirical, is to address the issue of whether the famines in Vietnam and Java were distributional or food availability deficit (FAD).[3] In a distributional famine, even though the amount of available food may fall, enough still exists to feed everyone. People starve because their endowments such as land and labour skills and/or entitlements are insufficient to command adequate food. In this context, entitlements are defined as the set of alternative commodity bundles available to a person using the totality of his or her rights and opportunities. An entitlement to food would consist of some combination of its cultivation, purchase with income earned from work, or being given food by others, for example as rations or through relief efforts. Food availability deficit famines occur, not for distributional reasons, but because a fall in food supply is so large that, even supposing more or less equal distribution, there is insufficient food to go around. It is argued in this section that both Vietnam and Java had food availability deficit famines.

An analysis of famine inevitability and preventability is the section's other main aim. I argue that in a famine area in the context of war, while decisions for war and the existence of erratic weather are exogenous, human agency is not. Voluntary action may avert a potentially avoidable famine or may fail to do so, possibly due to misguided policies. The second of these two possibilities applied to both Java and Vietnam. In Java, the decisions of the occupying Japanese military led to mass famine. Famine in Vietnam, notwithstanding highly unfavourable weather and wartime bombing, might well have been sidestepped if one or more of three main groups had moved to supply food to the famine-affected Tonkin delta and North Annam. Those whose decisions could have made a difference included the French, who administered Vietnam until the 9 March 1945 Japanese coup, the Japanese military who occupied Vietnam, and the Americans who bombed the country.

[2] Discussion of the Vietnam and Java famines draws on Huff, 'Causes and consequences' and 'Great World War II Vietnam', where more detailed analysis can be found.

[3] Distributional or entitlements famines are discussed in Sen, *War*, 'Ingredients of famine analysis', pp. 433–64 and *Poverty*; and food availability deficit famines in Ó Gráda, *Black '47* and 'Ripple'; Campbell, 'Nature'; Garnaut, 'Quantitative description'.

Exploration of human agency draws on the work of Ellman and his distinction between FAD_1 and FAD_2 famines.[4] For the former, feasible human actions to avoid famine do not exist. Ellman shows this to be true of the 1941–44 starvation of Leningrad and Ó Gráda identifies the Great European famine of the 1310s as in the FAD_1 category.[5] By contrast, FAD_2 famines are differentiated by the existence of 'feasible policies that could have prevented the famine (or at any rate substantially reduced the number of victims)'.[6] I demonstrate that both Java's and Vietnam's were FAD_2 famines and indicate what could have been done to avert them. Even in an FAD_2 famine, endowments and entitlements matter. An account which utilizes these concepts shifts the focus from the Malthusian nature of FAD famines towards uncovering which population groups were most at risk. In Vietnam and Java, the landless and those dependent on wage labour were by far the most likely to die during the famine.

Famine Magnitude

For both Vietnam and Java total famine mortality is impossible to establish, as it is for most famines.[7] Estimates of Vietnam's famine-induced deaths vary considerably from a lower bound of about 700,000 to an upper one of 2 million, the latter enshrined in Vietnamese communist mythology.[8] Marr suggests a million deaths in Tonkin and the two North Annam provinces of Than Hoa and Nghe An over a five-month period.[9] The only number which resembles an official count is 1.3 million total deaths: a million in northern Vietnam and 300,000 in central Vietnam which would include North Annam. However, examination of archive records reveals this total to be little more than an estimate.[10] A million dead over a five-month period, as indicated by Marr, is probably nearest the truth.[11] That would amount to 8.3 per cent of the 1943 population of Tonkin and the North Annan provinces of Than Hoa and Nghe An and 7.9 per cent of the total Tonkin and North Annam (Than Hoa, Nghe An and Ha Tinh) populations of 12,708,700. Acceptance of 1.3 million deaths would raise mortality to 10.2 per cent of the 1943 population of all of Tonkin and North Annam, while for either 1.0 million or 1.3 million a tighter definition of Vietnam's famine-affected area which restricted it to the Tonkin

4 Ellman, '1947 Soviet famine', p. 621.
5 Ó Gráda, *Famine*, p. 232.
6 Ellman, '1947 Soviet famine', p. 621.
7 Ó Gráda, *Famine*, p. 92.
8 'Declaration of independence of the Democratic Republic of Vietnam', in Chen, *Vietnam*, appendix 2, p. 356.
9 Marr, *Vietnam 1945*, p. 104.
10 AOM, GF/12, 'Report to the Minister of the Interior (Le Nhiep)', November 1946.
11 Marr, *Vietnam, 1945*, p. 104.

delta and North Annam (Than Hoa and Nghe An) would substantially increase mortality percentages to 10.0 per cent for a million deaths and 13.0 per cent for 1.3 million.

In Java by 1944, as recent histories point out: 'a very high death rate was recorded', 'starvation was widespread' and people dying by the roads were a common sight.[12] At the time, however, there seems to have been remarkably little comment on famine or effort to quantify it, although possibly some quantification was attempted in destroyed Japanese records. Post-war estimates vary from De Jong's some 2 million, or close to 1 in 20 Javanese, to the around 3 million suggested by Friend, although this includes deaths caused by a lack of medical attention and executions as well as hunger and disease.[13] De Vries arrives at a total of 2.45 million 'lost souls', but this seems to encompass births that would have occurred in the absence of Japanese occupation.[14]

Reconstruction of demographic data affords the only reliable means of endeavouring to quantify Java's famine. Van der Eng provides a thorough analysis of available data and his figure of about 2.4 million deaths above what otherwise might have been expected is probably near the actual number.[15] While staggering, and some 5.7 per cent of Java's population of about 42 million, in terms of proportionate impact this was well below the Vietnamese famine.

Ecology and Population Pressure

Both Vietnam and Java had complex ecologies and fragile equilibria between population and food. For Vietnam, indigenous ingenuity and, from the late nineteenth century, French hydraulic engineering had allowed large increases in rice production in both the Red River delta in Tonkin in the north of Vietnam (Figure 7.1) and the Mekong River delta in Cochinchina in the south (Figure 7.2). The contrast between the two deltas, separated by some 1,700 kilometres, was, however, fundamental. In Cochinchina, an extensive system of French-constructed canals linked existing waterways and substantial inwards migration transformed frontier land into one of the world's three major rice-exporting areas. Despite migrant inflows, pre-World War II Cochinchina remained relatively thinly populated. French hydrology had a quite different impact on northern Vietnam. Dykes holding back the Red River (also called the *Song Hong* as in Figure 7.1) prevented most of the delta from being flooded and allowed rice production and therefore population

12 Kurasawa, 'Forced delivery', p. 70; Sato, *War, nationalism*, p. 203 and see pp. 33, 128 and 'Economic soldiers', p. 131.

13 De Jong, *Collapse*, pp. 235, 280–81; Friend, *Blue-eyed enemy*, p. 264 and *Indonesian destinies*, p. 34.

14 De Vries, 'Vital statistics', pp. 18–19.

15 van der Eng, *Food supply*, p. 38.

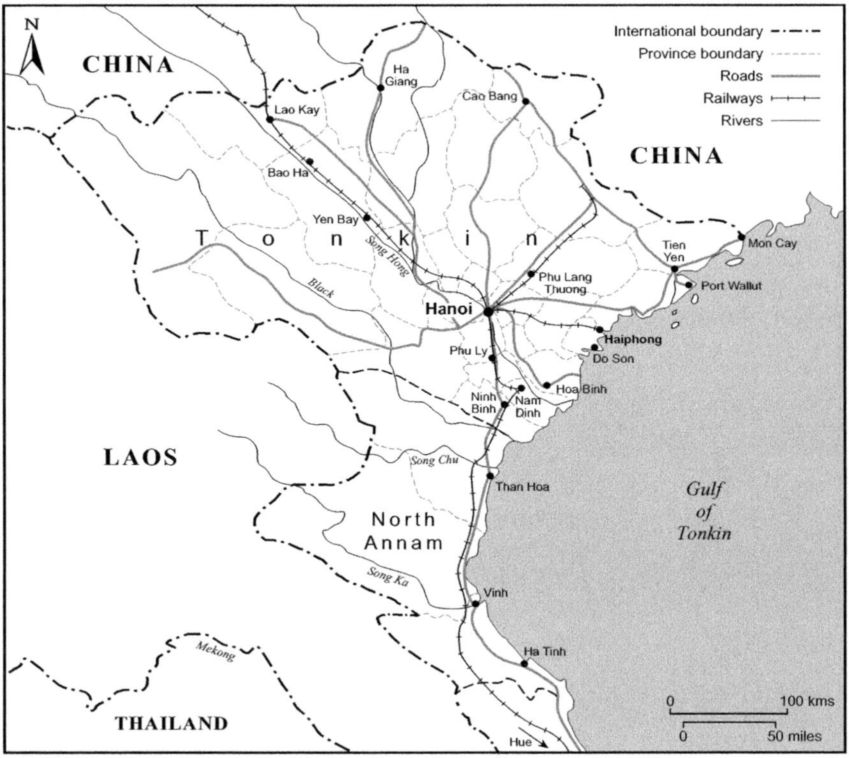

Figure 7.1 North Vietnam railways, roads and rivers
Source: Indochina, *Atlas de l'Indochine.*

continuously to expand. By the 1930s, the Red River delta, which stretched southwards from Haiphong along Tonkin's east coast for 150 kilometres to encompass the province of Ninh Binh and extended far inland, was among the world's most densely populated areas. Densities typically ranged between 250 and 500 persons per square kilometre, but in four provinces averaged over 700 persons per square kilometre (Figure 7.3). Population continuously threatened to outstrip food availability.

As early as the 1920s, Tonkin's population consumed as food some 80 per cent of the rice it produced.[16] In the delta, scarce land and abundant labour resulted in an intricacy of rice cultivation that, observed a French civil servant, made difficult an incorporation of yet more labour. It was already like gardening.[17]

[16] Office of Population Research, 'French Indo-China', p. 74.

[17] AOM, INF/2749, 'Principes généraux de la future économie Indochinoise', *c.* July 1941, p. 10. Cultivation had, in the minute and individual attention given rice plants, the character of horticulture. Gourou, *L'utilisation*, p. 240.

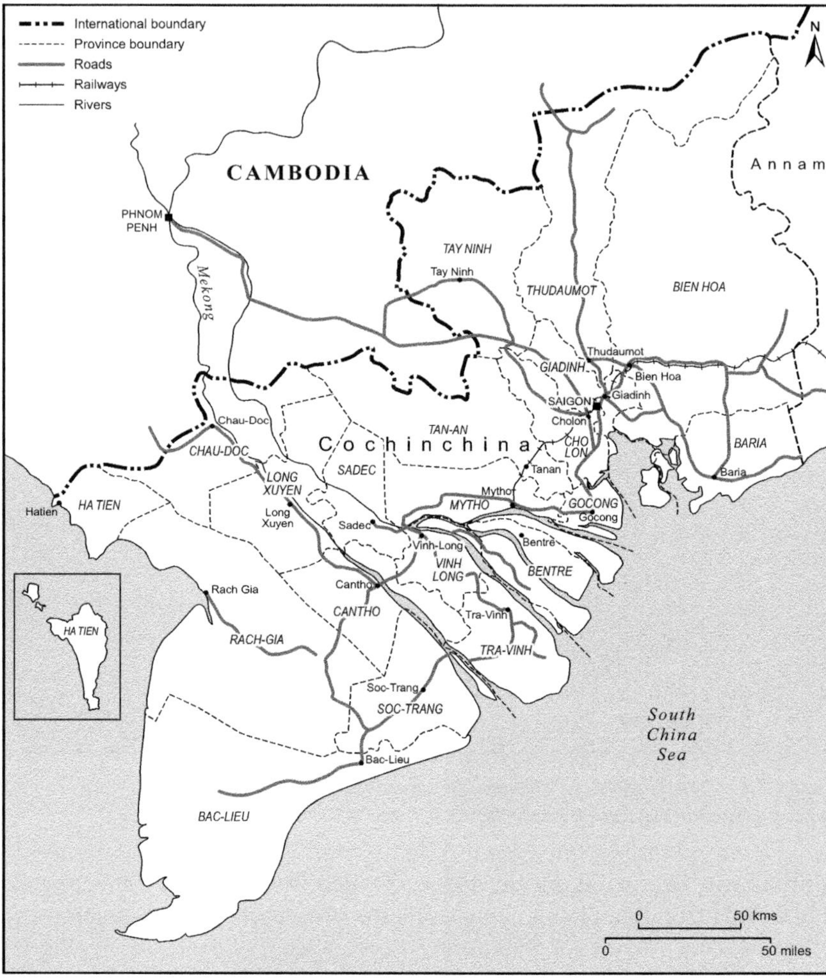

Figure 7.2 Cochinchina and Mekong River deltas
Source: Indochina, *Atlas de l'Indochine.*

Acute overpopulation, both in Tonkin and in North Annam, was accommodated only through an extremely unequal social structure that left most people vulnerable to shocks. In the late 1930s, the delta population of some 7 million included between 2 and 3 million day labourers and a further million unemployed or underemployed.[18] Between 50 and 60 per cent of families were virtually or wholly landless. Unpredictable, often violent, tropical weather

[18] Khérian, 'Les méfaits', pp. 478, 498–99; Brocheux and Hémery, *Indochina*, p. 265.

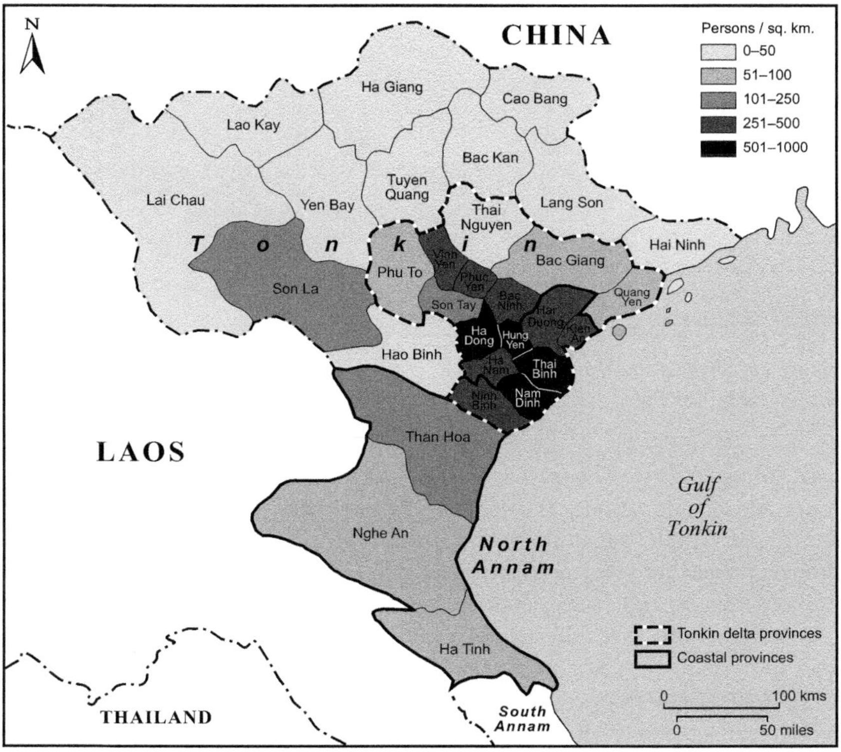

Figure 7.3 Tonkin and North Annam population density 1943
Sources: Indochina, *Atlas de l'Indochine;* Indochina, *Annuaire statistique 1943–1946*, p. 89.

placed these people at risk: 'in a normal year the poorest section of the population (50% to 60%) is barely sustained, but only slightly unfavourable circumstances suffice to make this population suffer from a dearth in the pre-harvest season'.[19] The poor typically ate only one meal a day and had enough to eat for no more than four months of the year, mainly after harvests, which were also the only time they could achieve a predominantly rice diet. Otherwise, they relied on somehow being able to buy or borrow rice and on greater consumption of potatoes, corn and taros.[20]

Java's ecology was no less remarkable than Vietnam's. Food crop cultivation, which extended over much of the available land, divided between irrigated and non-irrigated regions. The former, known as *sawah*, consisted of flooded fields in lowlands and on terraced hillsides, and in farm agriculture was

[19] Gourou, *Standard of living*, p. 14 and see p. 6.

[20] Office of Population Research, 'French Indo-China', p. 75; Nguyen, *Le problème*, pp. 9, 11, 18; Marr, *Vietnam 1945*, p. 97.

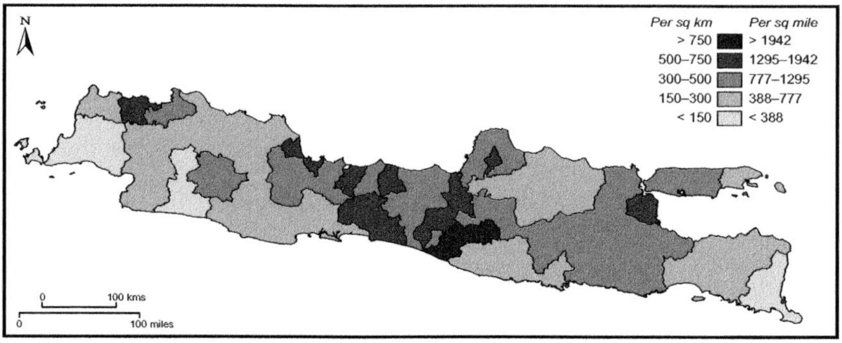

Figure 7.4 Java population density 1930
Source: Naval Intelligence Division, *Netherlands East Indies*, vol. 2, p. 134.

used almost exclusively to grow rice. Because mineral plant food was carried in water, *sawah* cultivation was capable of greater expansion than if rice had been dependent wholly on its immediate soil. Non-irrigated, rain-fed fields also produced rice, but were generally used to grow other crops including cassava (tapioca), maize and sweet potatoes.

Already in the 1890s, Java's population was seemingly at a natural ceiling and the island verged on overpopulation given the current technology. Nevertheless, numbers could continue to expand due to intricate irrigation, Java's rich volcanic soil, the reliance of *sawah* cultivation on water-borne nutrients, public investment in head works and channels for irrigation, the time and effort of individuals on irrigation at terminal levels (farmers' fields which received communal village investment), and the drainage of fields and migration to upland areas.[21] By the 1930s, population density in Java averaged 318 persons per square kilometre, but in parts of the centre densities were between 500 and over 750 per square kilometre, comparable to the Tonkin delta and the most thickly peopled regions of India and China (Figure 7.4).

Plantation agriculture, which covered some 1,378,000 acres, and to a much lesser extent factories, provided some outlet for Java's large pool of surplus labour. However, plantation and factory work, including Java's many sugar factories, was mostly seasonal and so unstable.[22] During the war, Javanese estate workers, landless and probably lacking the capital and skills to begin subsistence cultivation, found themselves at serious risk of being unable to obtain food. The problem became more pervasive throughout the war because Japanese occupation cut Indonesia off from the global economy. Without this market, estate cultivation continuously contracted. By 1944, it had largely ceased.

[21] Cf. Gourou, *Tropical world*, pp. 100–1; Geertz, *Agricultural involution*, pp. 29–34.
[22] Naval Intelligence Division, *Netherlands East Indies*, vol. 2, pp. 179, 284, 290–91.

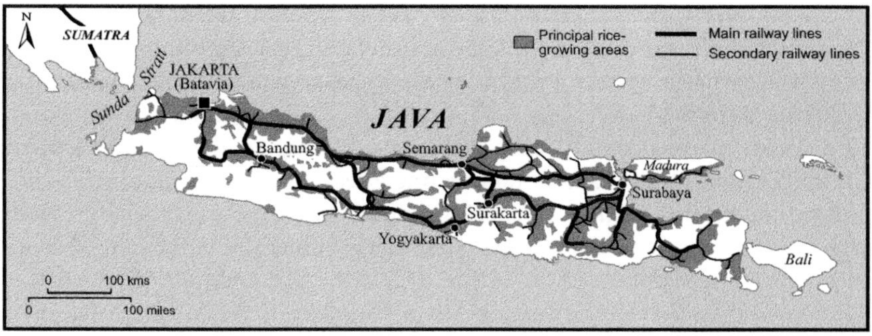

Figure 7.5 Java principal rice-growing areas and main railway lines 1940
Sources: Robequain, *Malaya, Indonesia*, p. 203, figure 5.1.

Rice was the Javanese staple and a favoured food, but by the 1930s per capita daily consumption averaged only about 230 grams, and comprised some two-fifths of the average Javanese diet.[23] To complement rice, pre-war Javanese depended on crops such as sweet potatoes, maize and cassava. Crucially, Java split into rice-surplus and rice-deficit regions, the latter principally in the east and south of the island (Figure 7.5). Beginning in 1933, although most rice continued to be traded and transported privately, the government initiated a programme of intervention in the rice market to ensure supplies for deficit areas. The flow of rice supplies and their equalization across provinces became fundamental to the island's food security. Java's extensive transport network allowed the achievement of a delicate balance of intra-province specialization and interdependence between surplus and deficit regions.[24] On the eve of World War II, Java had become self-sufficient in rice through carefully gauged production incentives and a complex delivery and storage system. In 1941, supplies between surplus and deficit areas were adjusted through the transport of 900,000 tons of rice by rail, 300,000 tons by truck and 150,000 tons by water, in all over 29 per cent of Java's rice harvest.[25]

Food Availability and Famine Causation

Although in Vietnam some famine was already evident in 1943 due to a typhoon in September 1943 and output falls at the end of the year, food shortages did not become severe until 1944 after the second rice harvest in

[23] Ibid., p. 170; Kurasawa, 'Mobilization', pp. 116, 16; van der Eng, *Food supply*, pp. 3, 8.

[24] On pre-war Java's highly integrated rice market, see van der Eng, 'Market responses', pp. 62–79.

[25] Anon., 'De rijstpositie van Nederlandsch-Indie' [The rice situation in the Dutch Indies], *Economisch Weekblad voor Nederlandsch-Indië*, vol. 12, no. 11, 25 May 1946, pp. 81–82; Department of Economic Affairs, Batavia, 'Rice production in Indonesia', p. 10; van der Eng, 'Regulation and control', p. 197.

November, normally the larger of the two. The typhoon season, which occurs along Vietnam's east coast in the later summer and early autumn, was extreme in 1944. Coastal provinces were hit by the weather shocks of three successive typhoons and a tidal wave. The 1944 August to October rainfall was more than 50 per cent above normal levels, and somewhat higher than in 1937, when famine loomed. While rainfall reflects one effect of the typhoons, it does not capture their consequences in causing rainfall intensity over a short period, high tides to which coastal areas are particularly vulnerable in the rainy season, and, above all, major ruptures in the dykes, the preservation of which was fundamental to preventing large parts of the delta from flooding. The Red River flowed six to seven metres above the surrounding land, serious breaches in dykes led to severe flooding, and in coastal provinces 230,000 hectares of rice were destroyed, equivalent to a loss of not far short of 200,000 tons of rice at 1942 yields.[26] According to a contemporary report from Nam Dinh province, which formed part of the delta's coastal complex, due to the earlier bad weather the November 'harvest was almost completely lost' and 558,383 people were left destitute: '[T]hese poor people have absolutely nothing to eat'.[27] Tonkinese lacking food in the countryside tried to eat anything: paddy husks, roots of banana trees, clover, tree bark.

Two main features of the wartime falls in rice output are evident from Table 7.1. One is that overall they were not large. Between 1942 and 1944, in Tonkin and North Annam output was 12.5 per cent down on the 1942 figure of 1,467,000 tons. The impact of the decline must, however, be assessed in light of the precarious margins of subsistence at which so many peasants in the two provinces lived. Further important considerations are the sudden and seemingly unanticipated nature of the falls; the apparent lack of rice stocks available to peasants and their practice of relying on the ability somehow to obtain rice during a large part of the year; and the exceptionally cold 1944–45 winter. Rice stocks were low partly because in the autumn of 1943 peasants had been ordered to sell rice surpluses to the French government, while the bad winter of 1944–45 ruined a large quantity of supplementary (non-rice) crops and prevented additional planting of some supplementary crops.[28] The effect of cold weather was intensified by the scant clothing available to many individuals. Japan sent almost no textiles to Vietnam to make up for pre-war imports and Vietnam produced only some of its textile requirements (Chapters 4 and 5). Tonkin peasants had depended almost entirely on buying their clothing.[29] By 1944, large numbers of people, as well as having little to eat, had few, if any, clothes to wear.

[26] Catling, *Rice*, p. 350.
[27] AOM, GF/6, Le Tông-dôc, 'Namdinh', 20 March 1945, p. 1.
[28] Nguyên, 'La famine', pp. 89–91; Vu, 'Other side', pp. 297–98.
[29] Gourou, *Les paysans*, p. 561.

Table 7.1 *Vietnam, Tonkin and North Annam rice output and exports 1941–1945 (000 metric tons)*

	Vietnam rice output	Tonkin and North Annam rice output	Eight coastal provinces rice output	Eight coastal provinces fall in rice output as % total fall in Tonkin and North Annam	Total Vietnam rice exports	Total Vietnam rice exports to Japan	Shipments of southern rice to Tonkin	Japanese rice stocks in Vietnam at end of war
1941	6,944.0				944.5	583.3		
1942	7,222.0	1,466.7	856.2		974.2	961.9	126.7	
1943	7,071.0	1,422.8	818.4	86.1	1,023.5	1,007.8	29.7	
1944	5,971.0	1,283.8	643.3	126.0	498.5	497.1	6.8	
1945	4,871.0				44.8	44.8		60.0

Notes: 1. For 1941, data on rice output by province were not published.
2. The eight coastal provinces are Kien An, Hai Duong, Thai Binh, Nam Dinh and Ninh Binh in Tonkin, and Than Hoa, Nghe An and Ha Tinh in Annam. Paddy output is converted to rice at a conversion rate of 0.6349, which is the conversion given in Gourou, *Standard of living*, p. 13. Data for 1944 are for 1943/44, for 1945 for 1944/45 and so forth.
3. Rice output and export figures are for Indochina as a whole but the contribution of its non-Vietnam constituents was negligible.
4. Rice exports shown as going to Japan include paddy and cargo rice but the great majority of exports were whole white rice. These last were (in tons): 1942: 581,099; 1943: 833 134; 1944: 418,267; 1945: 41,352. By 1944, most rice exports to Japan went, in fact, to other parts of Southeast Asia to feed Japanese troops and a small amount of rice went to China for the same purpose. Just 37,000 tons of rice was exported to Japan. See LHC, MAGIC, 'Japanese purchases and shipments of Indo-China rice', 30 March 1945, pp. 1, 10–11.

Sources: Rice output and exports: Indochina, *Annuaire statistique, 1941–1942*, pp. 87, 176, 188, 283; *1943–1946*, pp. 90–91, 188, 277. Data for rice exports to Japan in NA, WO203/2647, S.A.C., S.E.A., Economic Intelligence Division, 'The rice situation in Cochin China', are almost identical to export data for Japan in Indochina, *Annuaire statistique*, cited above. *Shipments of southern rice:* Gaudel, *L'Indochine Française*, p. 230. *Japanese rice stocks:* NA, FO371/53959, Lt. Col. T. H. Sweeny, 'Second report on Japanese financial manipulations in French Indo China', p. 3.

A second, crucial, feature of falls in the harvest between 1942 and 1943, and again between 1943 and 1944, was their high degree of localization. Output declines were concentrated in eight coastal provinces. Five were in Tonkin's delta (Hai Duong, Kien An, Nam Dinh, Ninh Binh and Thai Binh) and the other three in North Annam (Figure 7.3). Between 1942 and 1944, the drop in output of 24.9 per cent in these eight coastal provinces more than accounted for the overall decrease in output in all of Tonkin and North Annam; output in other, non-coastal provinces rose (Table 7.1). Declines in coastal rice output are almost entirely explained by sharp drops in yields rather than in area planted in rice. Yields probably fell mainly because flooding ruined rice which had been planted. It is important to note from the table that by 1945 almost no rice was being shipped to Japan. From 1944 onwards, large rice surpluses accumulated in Saigon in the south.

The eight coastal provinces were not necessarily those which were most densely populated (Figure 7.3). The imperfect association between population density and output falls, but strong correlation between output declines and coastal provinces, points to the importance of the weather shock of the typhoons, tidal wave and floods in triggering famine. If in 1944 output in the eight coastal provinces had been the same as in 1942, or probably even in 1943, it seems likely that famine would not have occurred or, if it had, would certainly have been less severe.

Data for Tonkin, although not Annam, allow the calculation of average daily per capita grams of rice available for consumption. Table 7.2 uses this data and shows for 1942 to 1944 available rice if it had been distributed equally in each province. Data in the table do not allow for the French requisition of rice, which began in 1943 to build up stocks in the north because a lack of transport from Cochinchina made it difficult to bring rice from there. Under normal transport conditions, rice shipments from south to north probably would have been instituted.

Although requisitions may have acted to decrease total available rice, availability appears to have depended chiefly on the harvest. However, requisitions would have affected distribution and among Vietnamese would probably disproportionately have favoured those in large cities. Requisitioned rice was distributed, largely to urban areas, as rations, confiscated by the Japanese military and stored against eventual need. Although in August 1945 the Japanese, after a build-up of forces, still had just 30,000 troops in northern Vietnam, they also stored rice. The main Japanese storage of rice was, however, in Cochinchina where there were 70,000 Japanese troops and rice stocks by the end of the war of some 60,000 tons (Table 7.1).[30]

[30] NA, WO106/4627, 'Brief summary of the position in Indochina', 12 March 1945 and FO371/53959, 'Second report on Japanese financial manipulations in French Indo-China', pp. 2–3.

Table 7.2 *Tonkin rice availability and famine deaths by province January to May 1945*

	1943 population thousands	Area 1,000 km²	1943 population density persons per km²	1942 rice output grams per capita per day	1943 rice output grams per capita per day	1944 rice output grams per capita per day	% fall in rice available in 1944 compared to 1942	Jan.–May 1945 401,271 famine deaths as % of province population
Coastal provinces								
Hai Duong	843.5	2.3	366.7	429.4	411.9	321.3	25.2	4.8
Kien An	428.7	0.9	476.3	300.1	262.1	245.6	18.2	7.8
Nam Dinh	1,233.4	1.5	822.3	256.5	224.2	176.3	31.3	10.4
Ninh Binh	406.2	1.6	253.9	455.0	327.6	258.8	43.1	10.1
Thai Binh	1,139.8	1.5	759.9	324.3	288.0	257.5	20.6	7.2
Total and averages	4,051.6	7.8	519.4	336.1	295.6	244.9	27.1	8.3
Other Tonkin delta								
Bac Giang	311.8	5.2	60.0	460.0	507.4	495.5	-7.7	
Bac Ninh	543.5	1.1	494.1	285.6	322.6	274.8	3.8	0.9
Ha Dong	961.4	1.7	565.5	238.4	258.4	264.1	-10.8	1.3
Ha Nam	596.2	1.2	496.8	220.7	186.0	173.8	21.2	2.7
Hung Yen	533.3	0.9	592.6	316.1	254.5	283.6	10.3	1.9
Phuc Yen	202.1	0.7	288.7	334.3	318.2	341.7	-2.2	1.1
Phu Tho	351.7	3.7	95.1	141.7	105.1	174.0	-22.8	1.5
Son Tay	210.6	1.0	210.6	491.4	502.0	487.9	0.7	2.7
Thai Nguyen	153.5	3.5	43.9	298.6	250.4	506.7	-69.7	1.8
Vinh Yen	296.2	1.1	269.3	398.3	391.8	390.3	2.0	1.2

Table 7.2 (*cont.*)

	1943 population thousands	Area 1,000 km^2	1943 population density persons per km^2	1942 rice output grams per capita per day	1943 rice output grams per capita per day	1944 rice output grams per capita per day	% fall in rice available in 1944 compared to 1942	Jan.–May 1945 401,271 famine deaths as % of province population
Other Tonkin delta	4,160.3	20.1	207.0	291.5	286.1	297.8	-2.2	1.5
Total Tonkin	8,211.9	27.9	294.3	313.5	290.8	271.7	13.3	4.8

Notes: 1. Available data are for 8,211,900 persons of a total Tonkin 1943 population of 9,851,200 which includes 119,700 in Hanoi and 65,100 in Haiphong. The delta province for which no data exist is Quang Yen.

2. Population data for 1942 are the population for 1943 and per capita output may therefore be somewhat understated. Similarly, population data for 1944 are the 1943 population and per capita output may be overstated or, possibly more likely, somewhat understated because famine deaths caused total population to fall between 1943 and 1944.

3. Paddy output is adjusted for rice on the basis that one ton of paddy equals 0.6349 ton of milled rice, as given in Gourou, *Standard of living*, p. 13.

4. Available grams per day assumes consumption of 85% of rice output as assumed in Marr, *Vietnam 1945*, p. 97. In comparison, in Tonkin from 1918 to 1930 average human consumption was 80% of total rice production (Office of Population Research, 'French Indo-China', p. 74).

5. Marr argues (*Vietnam 1945*, p. 97) that 297 grams per day would have been 'perhaps barely enough for everyone to survive until June 1945'.

6. For coastal provinces the percentage of deaths shown for total and averages includes Hanoi, where deaths were 2.7% of the population and Haiphong, where the percentage was 9.4%.

7. The source lists Phy-ly which was the county town of Ha Nam province. Data for Phy-ly have been included for Ha Nam.

Sources: Indochina, *Annuaire statistique, 1941–1942*, p. 87; *1943–1946*, pp. 27, 89; AOM, GF/3.

Table 7.2 shows the percentage changes in rice available for consumption in 15 Tonkin provinces (accounting for 84.4 per cent of Tonkin's population) and the distribution across 14 of the 15 provinces of 401,271 deaths from 1 January to 20 May 1945 attributed to famine. Between 1942 and 1944, in the 5 Tonkin coastal provinces, rice availability fell by between 18.2 per cent and 43.1 per cent. On a population weighted basis, the fall averaged 27.1 per cent. Declines in available rice in Tonkin's coastal provinces – with one exception not matched in any of Tonkin's other provinces – correlated closely with deaths as a percentage of population but not with population density. Tellingly, falls in available rice occurred between 1942 and 1944 and the 401,271 deaths between 1 January and 20 May 1945, a temporal ordering suggestive of causation. During the first five months of 1945, Tonkin's five delta coastal provinces accounted for over four-fifths of deaths ascribed to famine. Death rates were between 7.2 and 10.4 per cent of the population in all the provinces except Hai Duong, where the rate was 4.8 per cent. A death rate in Haiphong (Tonkin's second-largest city) of 9.4 per cent of the city's population is consistent with mortality data for surrounding coastal provinces, but mainly reflects famine victims from elsewhere.

Marr suggests that if available rice in Tonkin and North Annam had been shared absolutely equally, famine would have been avoided. He stipulates the 'barely enough' amount of rice for subsistence as 297 grams per day between November and the May–June harvest.[31] Consumption of 297 grams equates to 1,065 calories. That intake was below, or at best not much above, the basal metabolic rate (the level at which no surplus for physical activity exists) which, as a benchmark, is around 1,080 calories for women aged 18 to 30 and 1,450 for men aged 18 to 60.

Table 7.2 indicates that by 1944 per capita available rice exceeded Marr's subsistence threshold in only one Tonkin coastal province. Even with totally equal sharing, almost none of the coastal areas would have had available as much as a daily average of 297 grams of rice. To obtain subsistence quantities of rice, most coastal provinces would have had to trade with neighbouring provinces or obtain supplies from outside Tonkin and North Annam. Trade with neighbouring provinces was, however, not permitted by the French government, apparently partly so that the authorities could secure any surplus to supply urban centres.[32] In any case, precious little surplus for exchange existed elsewhere in Tonkin. Supposing that consumption for everyone of 297 grams a day had been possible, this would probably still have had to be supplemented by potatoes, maize or taros, which by the time famine struck could not be grown because of the exceptionally cold winter. In comparison to a subsistence level of 297 grams, Gourou identified 400, and Nguyen 500,

[31] Marr, *Vietnam 1945*, p. 97.
[32] AOM, HCI 2/226, 'Mémoires Yokoyama', p. 90.

grams as the average daily rice ration for a Tonkinese, but stressed that this was insufficient for a working man.[33]

Although famine reached its peak during the winter and spring of 1944–45 preceding the June harvest, it continued to claim lives through the summer and autumn of 1945 and into 1946. During the first half of 1946, some 20,000 people died, mainly in remote villages missed by communist relief cadres and volunteers. Finally, in June 1946, with the help of good weather and a good harvest, the spectre of mass famine was banished. In November 1946, the north had a good rice crop.[34]

Unusually good harvests in Java in 1942 and 1943 helped to mitigate declining food availability, although abnormally low rainfall in 1944 probably adversely affected rice output.[35] Rice, however, normally accounted for no more than 45 per cent of Javanese calorie consumption and, furthermore, rice

Table 7.3 *Java harvested area of main food crops 1940–1950*

	1940	1941	1942	1943	1944	1945	1946	1950
a) 000 hectares								
Irrigated paddy	3,724	3,743	3,687	3,789	3,310	2,877	3,016	3,352
Upland paddy	365	357	338	343	262	241	244	223
Maize	1,983	2,229	2,214	1,812	1,399	1,488	1,150	1,622
Cassava	1,041	1,003	976	950	829	551	626	711
Sweet potatoes	209	205	189	180	259	349	227	154
Peanuts	251	259	253	291	175	99	144	223
Soya beans	418	440	481	384	185	141	246	325
Total	7,993	8,237	8,139	7,749	6,419	5,833	5,729	6,610
b) 1941 = 100								
	1940	1941	1942	1943	1944	1945	1946	1950
Irrigated paddy	99.5	100.0	98.5	101.2	88.4	76.9	80.6	89.6
Upland paddy	102.2	100.0	94.7	96.1	73.4	67.5	68.3	62.5
Maize	89.0	100.0	99.3	81.3	62.8	66.8	51.6	72.8
Cassava	103.8	100.0	97.3	94.7	82.7	54.9	62.4	70.9
Sweet potatoes	102.0	100.0	92.2	87.8	126.3	170.2	110.7	75.1
Peanuts	96.9	100.0	97.7	112.4	67.6	38.2	55.6	86.1
Soya beans	95.0	100.0	109.3	87.3	42.0	32.0	55.9	73.9
Total	97.0	100.0	98.8	94.1	77.9	70.8	69.6	80.2

Source: van der Eng, 'Regulation and control', p. 195.

[33] Gourou, *Standard of living*, p. 13; Nguyen, *Le problème*, pp. 7, 11.
[34] Marr, *Vietnam: state, war*, pp. 321, 327, 329, 382.
[35] Brennan, Heathcote and Lucas, 'War and famine', pp. 25–30.

crop failures would typically have been offset by dry season production of non-rice food crops, particularly sweet potatoes and cassava. The revealing statistic, and one fundamental to explaining famine, is that in 1944 Java's harvested area was almost a quarter less than it had been in 1941 and by 1945 29.2 per cent less (Table 7.3). Taking 1937/41 as 100, paddy production was 81.2 in 1944 and 65.9 in 1945, while the corresponding index numbers for maize were 57.1 and 42.9.[36] Between 1941 and 1945, sweet potatoes, planted as a quick and easily obtained source of calories and as a crop not commandeered by the Japanese, were the only main food crop for which harvested hectarage rose. The expansion was, however, far too small to make up for sharp contractions in harvested areas of other food crops (Table 7.3).

The wartime fall in harvested area was accompanied by a catastrophic decrease in average per capita food availability. In this regard, however, official data probably overstate the actual drop in yields because of an under-reporting strategy at the end of the war and still in 1946 by local authorities to reduce the chance of farmers being compelled to hand over surplus production for token compensation and possibly also owing to an attempt to try to lower farmers' land tax liabilities by enabling them to claim dispensation due to crop failure. To estimate likely yields, van der Eng applies to the 1945–46 harvested area for five main food crops average yields at the beginning of the Japanese occupation and uses these to arrive at total output and average per capita calorie supply. During the Japanese occupation, both fell continuously and substantially.[37] However, average per capita daily calorie supply per residency, shown by Table 7.4 and Figure 7.6, does not take into account trade between residencies, calories possibly available for other than the five main food crops, or foreign trade, although the latter was seriously curtailed during the war.[38] As against this and not factored into Table 7.4 is that in 1944, yields of rice, but not dry season crops, were probably compromised by drought that year and so dropped in comparison to the harvest under normal rainfall conditions.[39]

Calorie counting by residency emphasizes Java's geographically unequal food production. In 1941, while calorie supply per head over the island as a whole averaged 2,068 calories, five residencies had over 2,600 calories and six under 1,700 calories. At that time, however, trade between residencies and colonial government policy worked to equalize calorie supply. Despite this, the Japanese banned inter-residency rice trade which, by greatly impeding an equalization of supplies, magnified the seriousness of wartime output falls.

36 Department of Economic Affairs, Batavia, 'Economic condition of Indonesia', p. 117.

37 van der Eng, *Food supply*, pp. 26–27, 70–71 and 'Regulation and control', pp. 193–95.

38 Calories from food crops other than the main crops may have averaged as much as 230 to 250 calories per person per day. See van der Eng, 'Regulation and control', p. 193.

39 van der Eng, *Food supply*, pp. 18, 25 and 'Regulation and control', p. 198; Department of Economic Affairs, Batavia, 'Export of pre-war agrarian produce', p. 167.

Table 7.4 *Java per capita daily calorie supply 1940–1946*

		1940	1941	1942	1943	1944	1945	1946	1944 as % of 1941	1945 as % of 1941
West Java	Bariten	1,647	1,642	1,505	1,538	1,363	1,139	1,217	83.0	69.4
	Jakarta	1,327	1,409	1,349	1,175	991	896	1,148	70.3	63.6
	Bogor	1,436	1,341	1,413	1,295	1,007	973	976	75.1	72.6
	Priangan	1,626	1,565	1,416	1,408	1,161	1,288	1,263	74.2	82.3
	Cirebon	1,917	1,804	1,700	1,526	1,205	1,377	1,216	66.8	76.3
Central Java	Pekalongan	1,758	1,920	1,824	1,498	1,049	1,024	1,132	54.6	53.3
	Semarang	2,373	2,624	2,344	2,015	1,997	1,869	1,592	76.1	71.2
	Pati	2,217	2,439	2,118	1,944	1,242	1,473	1,337	50.9	60.4
	Banyumas	2,440	2,688	2,295	2,059	1,478	1,577	1,449	55.0	58.7
	Kedu	2,375	2,705	2,468	2,017	1,568	1,690	1,511	58.0	62.5
	Principalities	1,944	2,036	2,093	1,720	1,298	1,621	1,450	63.8	79.6
East Java	Madium	1,839	1,980	1,868	1,560	835	975	1,295	42.2	49.2
	Bojonegoro	1,664	1,748	1,394	1,199	899	690	735	51.4	39.5
	Surabaya	1,493	1,561	1,430	1,465	1,231	1,053	1,027	78.9	67.5
	Kediri	2,093	2,370	2,172	1,748	1,167	1,224	1,399	49.2	51.6
	Malang	2,250	2,603	2,377	1,866	1,405	1,237	1,227	54.0	47.5
	Besuki	3,354	3,245	2,971	2,762	2,502	2,386	2,228	77.1	73.5
	Madura	2,049	2,105	2,033	1,893	1,892	1,508	1,359	89.9	71.6
	Java average	1,989	2,099	1,932	1,705	1,349	1,333	1,309	64.3	63.5
	Coefficient of variation	0.23	0.25	0.23	0.22	0.30	0.30	0.23		

Notes: 1. Data do not take into account trade across residency borders nor imports and exports of rice to or from Java.

2. Calories from rice varied considerably between areas of Java and between residencies. In West Java, rice provided about two-thirds of calories, in Central Java almost two-fifths, and in East Java between about a third and two-fifths.

Sources: van der Eng, *Food supply*; Leo Keukens, 'With nothing but our lives', http://leokeukens.com/wp-content/uploads/2013/04/java_new_map_medium_colordots.jpg.

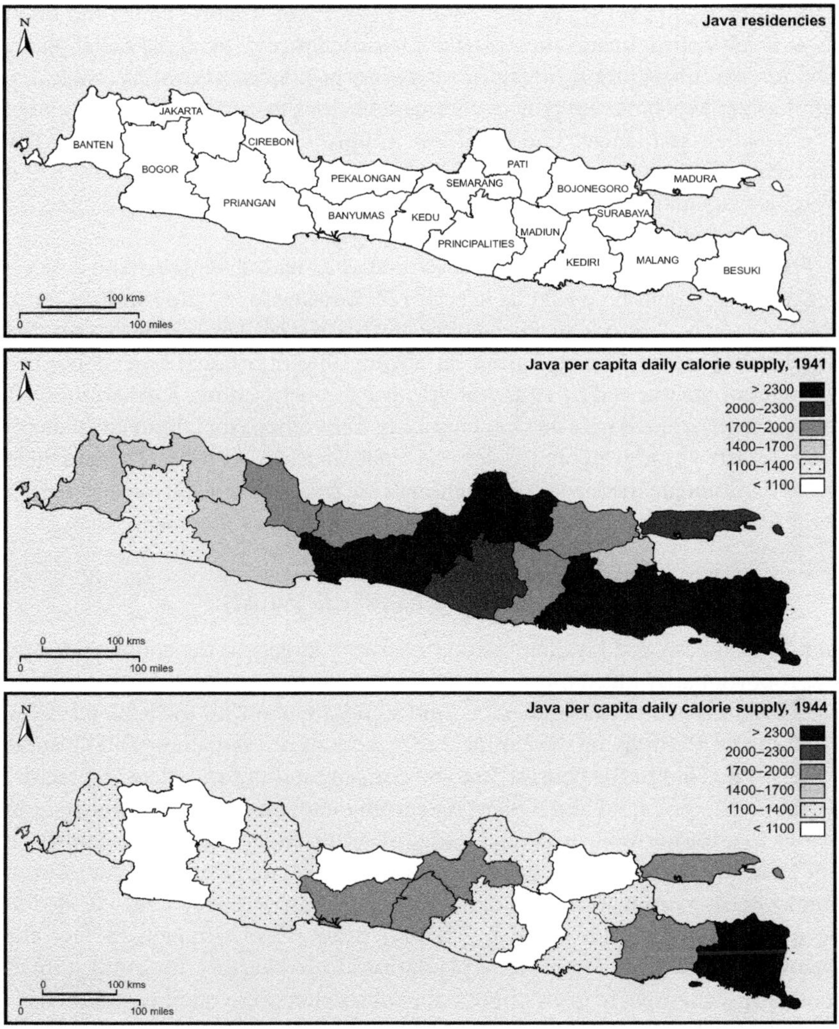

Figure 7.6 Java average per capita daily calorie supply 1941 and 1944
Source: van der Eng, *Food supply*, p. 79.

Between 1941 and 1944, net calorie supply per person per day from the main crops (calculated as total estimated production in Java divided by the island's total population) fell from the 2,068 indicated above to 1,316. Every residency experienced a drop in calorie consumption per capita. The average fall across all residencies was 35.7 per cent. During 1945, supplies remained at the same low level. Decline was markedly uneven among residencies, with large falls in many of the most deprived residencies. By 1944, 5 of Java's 17 residencies had average per capita calorie supplies of less than 1,100 calories and a further 6 had under 1,400 calories (Table 7.4 and Figure 7.6). Calorie consumption at these levels approximates no more than maintenance of the basal metabolism. The uneven distribution of calories between provinces, shown by Table 7.4, emphasizes why Japanese policies, discussed below, to outlaw the movement of rice between residencies and ruthlessly suppress black market trade in rice exacerbated Java's famine. Depending on how much and to whom rice was distributed, Japanese storage of 154,000 tons of rice in 1944 may have added to the famine but does not explain it.[40]

Falls in calorie availability were so great that, even had all food been more or less equally shared, famine would have occurred. Java's wartime drop in food availability would be dramatic in any country. In Java, the fall can only be described as disastrous, because it started from an already low nutritional base, continued throughout the war and by 1944 was already extremely serious. Furthermore, the fall was hard to ameliorate by switching away from other expenditure in favour of food, which already accounted for the bulk of almost everyone's household budget. Although the slaughter of animals increased, per capita calories from meat remained minimal and, furthermore, benefited only those with livestock.

Entitlements and Famine Selectivity

In both Vietnam and Java famine occurred very largely in the countryside and disproportionately killed those with limited endowments or entitlements. These were predominantly the landless. Farmers and anyone who owned land had a good chance of surviving the famine. Large sections of Vietnamese and Javanese society – in Tonkin the poorest 50 to 60 per cent and in Java estate and factory workers – had no land and, reliant on earning enough from an endowment of labour to trade for food, lived on the edge of subsistence. High wartime inflation put even the individuals in these groups who were able to find some form of employment in an increasingly difficult position, since money wages tended to be quite inflexible and lagged far behind price rises. Although in Java the Japanese turned over a number of plantations to workers for the cultivation of food crops, attempts to grow enough for subsistence were often unsuccessful.

High mortality also affected Vietnamese fishermen because in northern Vietnam fish was not a staple but more in the nature of a garnish. Fishermen had to trade their catch for rice and were in a weak position when a rise in its price turned the terms of trade against fish. Furthermore, Vietnamese fishermen mainly harvested small fish, shrimp, crabs and frogs; the famine occurred outside the fishing season; and flooding in coastal provinces due to the typhoons hindered fishing.[41]

[40] NIDS, Japan, Java Military Administration, *Gunseika ni okeru Java – Madura no shokuryō jijō to sono taisaku* [Food conditions in Java and Madura] (October 1943), p. 16.

[41] Furuta, 'Survey', pp. 227–37.

Although famine was not principally an urban phenomenon, cities were greatly affected by it through migration from rural areas. People in the famine-ravaged countryside left for urban areas, hoping to find work there, somehow gain an entitlement to rations or, if neither materialized, to live by begging. Even in Hanoi, however, rice rations were inadequate and their distribution irregular.[42] Nevertheless, Vietnamese walked in 'unending lines together with their whole families' along the 'starvation roads' that led to the provincial towns and cities. Many died along the roads. Others stopped occasionally to close the eyes of the dead or to pick up a piece of rag left on bodies.[43]

In Java in April 1944, the Japanese ordered a population registration aimed at establishing how best to distribute rice after the 1943/44 harvest. By then, however, many Javanese, no longer with plantation or factory employment, had drifted to the cities and, on the margins of society, were probably omitted from the registration and so also any entitlement to rice rations. A careful estimation of demographic data found that the registration may have missed as many as 5.66 million people, either by mistake or perhaps often deliberately on the part of neighbourhood associations in charge of local counts and unwilling to share available food among more people. Those left out of the distribution system in residencies within major cities formed a large destitute group and probably account for many of the famine dead in Java's cities.[44] According to a different estimate, some 9.5 million people, about 20 per cent of Java's population, had somehow to find food because they neither lived in cities of 10,000 or more and shared in a distribution there nor made a living in indigenous agriculture.[45] Writing in 1944, an Indo-European woman in Jakarta reported her *kampong* 'flooded with people from the *oedik* [interior]. They can barely walk. In the *oedik* each family got one *batok* [coconut shell] of rice every two weeks.'[46]

FAD_1 and FAD_2 Famines and Institutional Response

Dramatic drops in food availability need not have led to famine in Vietnam. Nor was famine inevitable in Java. In both instances, it could have been avoided by appropriate institutional policies. However, French, Japanese and

42 VNA, MH 3499, 'Rapports journaliers du Chef des Affairs Annamites de Hanoi sur la situation sociale de la ville de Hanoi du 15 Mars au 29 Mai 1945', p. 46, 94, 97 and 3616 Le Commissaire de Police du 2è arrondissement, 'Etat d'esprit des populations', 29 January 1944.

43 Nguyên, 'La famine', pp. 83–84; see also Bàng, 'They starved', pp. 102–7; Le, *Impact*, p. 253.

44 NC, A. Soebardjo, 'The life conditions of the population with regard to the requisition of paddy by the government', 3/7/2604 (1944), pp. 8–9; van der Eng, 'Bridging a gap', pp. 489–92.

45 Centraal Bureau voor de Statistiek, 'De economische toestand van Nederlandsch-Indie', pp. 123–24.

46 Brugmans, *Nederlandsch-Indië*, p. 451.

American responses not only failed effectively to counter famine but often worsened it.

Falls in food availability in Java are largely explained by the destruction of incentives to plant food crops. That was, in turn, the direct consequence of the Japanese policy of fixing prices at which rice mills were expected to purchase paddy from farmers at levels soon outdistanced by rocketing wartime inflation. High inflation, growing food shortages and rice rations that were either small or altogether lacking led to escalating black market rice prices and a brisk trade in 'illegal' rice, much of it taken to large urban areas and in Jakarta organized in no small part by the city's underworld.[47] However, a substantial share of the incentive that price disparities would have provided to grow and trade in rice was dissipated by Japanese suppression of the black market. Penalties were severe and extended to execution for trafficking in rice.

The pre-war colonial government system was to equalize prices and supplies across the year and regions through buying rice in surplus areas, arranging transport and selling in deficit areas. By contrast, the Japanese requisitioned rice but were not at first involved in its purchase.[48] In April 1943, however, forced deliveries of rice were instituted in Java and beginning in September 1943 the Office of Food Supply (initially the *Shokuryō Kanri Zimusho* but later often renamed) ordered mills to buy rice and sell it to the Food Office. When this proved unsuccessful, Japanese administrators turned to a rigorous system of quotas and controlled prices. Farmers were instructed to deliver paddy only to *kumiai*, Japanese-organized co-operatives. Deliveries were meant to contribute to a quota for paddy assigned, although far from systematically or rationally, to all residencies. They, in turn, were to sell paddy to Java's rice mills at controlled prices. The mills, now under the Food Office's jurisdiction, were prevented from operating in the market. They had, instead, to sell to the Food Office at a controlled price. In practice, rice production fell not merely far short of quotas but, crucially, of actual needs. Towards the end of the Japanese occupation, a number of factors combined to accentuate food shortages in addition to the widening gap between free market and controlled prices. These included the decision in October 1943 to close residency boundaries to trade in rice; a poor 1944/45 cropping year; a near-total absence of any consumer goods for farmers to buy; and acute transport shortages and consequent heavy reliance by black market traders on carts or bicycles.[49]

Because Java's highly integrated rice market and colonial government policy tended to equalize supplies and iron out price rises due to crop failures, the

[47] Anon., 'Rijstpellerijen in midden-Java', p. 94; Cribb, *Gangsters*, p. 42.

[48] The remainder of this paragraph draws on van der Eng, 'Regulation and control', pp. 196–99 and *Food supply*, pp. 8–20.

[49] On transport shortages and small-scale black market trade, including transport by bicycles, see Centraal Bureau voor de Statistiek, 'De economische toestand van Nederlandsch-Indie', pp. 123–24; Twang, *Chinese business élite*, pp. 100–3.

Japanese policy to ban the movement of rice across boundaries and order residencies to become self-sufficient was disastrously misguided. It added to the lack of transport in stifling the intra-Java and intra-island movement of food which had been fundamental to Javanese food security, and discouraged the planting of maize and cassava to make up for falls in rice availability.[50] The occupation policy of self-sufficiency 'tipped the balance of undernourishment into famine'.[51]

If one supposes that somehow in Java, despite World War II and Japanese occupation of the rest of Southeast Asia, the pre-war colonial administrative system for rice (including, crucially, control over prices) had been left in place, the Javanese famine would probably have been largely, perhaps even entirely, avoided. The situation would have been different because, unlike Indonesia's wartime Japanese rulers, the colonial government appreciated both the central role of prices in securing rice production and the need to transport large quantities of rice from surplus to deficit areas. Different Japanese policies, even a willingness, perhaps in early 1943, to change policy, might also have prevented famine. Instead, Japanese officials and policymakers showed little understanding of the Javanese rice economy and the importance in it of market mechanisms and incentives. That may have been because of an inflexible, military government; because the Japanese lacked Javanese experience; or, most likely, because it was thought best to adopt a system like that in Japan. When things began to go wrong, Japanese administrators relentlessly moved away from market solutions and enforced ever more restrictions: 'The more the Japanese tried to control rice marketing, the more it slipped out of control.'[52] By the latter part of 1943 it was probably too late to avoid major famine.

For Vietnam, it is less clear which different actors could have implemented effective measures to avoid, or at least greatly reduce, famine. Cochinchina in the south had abundant surplus rice which could have fed the north. Transport was the main problem to be solved. Normally, coastal shipping carried rice south to north, but it could also be moved along the Transindochinois railway, which linked Saigon and Hanoi. The 1,600 to 1,800 kilometres between rice-producing areas in Cochinchina and Hanoi made shipment by road unrealistic.[53]

The French had some responsibility for the failure to avert the 1944–45 famine for two main reasons. One was that although the French tried to organize a junk fleet to take rice northwards, Chinese junk owners were allowed to profit so little from the sale of the rice that sailing along the coast was not worth the risk of American bombs and mines. The other was that the

50 Anon., 'Rijstpellerijen in midden-Java', p. 94; De Jong, *Collapse*, pp. 231, 258.

51 Lucas, *One soul*, p. 36 and see pp. 36–37.

52 Sato, *War, nationalism*, p. 203.

53 VNA, RS 75782, 'Création des offices provinciaux ou régionaux d'alimentation indigène en Indochine pour la lutte contre les crises alimentaires et la famine' and see especially Inspection Générale du Travail, Saigon to Résident Supérieure au Tonkin, 20 August 1937.

possibility of moving rice to famine areas was stifled by requirements for bureaucratic forms and restrictions on flows of the grain imposed by French administrators. As the war went on and shortages of rice and other goods increased, 'the colonial government's prior penchant for paperwork increased relentlessly . . . By early 1945, the control system was clogged by huge quantities of telegrams, letters, commodity samples, price lists, internal memos and formal complaints requiring investigation'.[54]

A third possible consideration in assessing the degree of French responsibility for famine is that in 1944 the French increased a rice levy on growers to 186,000 tons from 130,000 the previous year. However, it is not clear that the levy was enforced effectively. By 1944, the main Japanese economic advisor found that 'the levy system was no longer giving satisfactory results as it had before'.[55] November 1944 harvest quotas would have become difficult to collect not only due to low prices but also because of the sharp fall in output and worsening famine. Together, these circumstances would have encouraged growers to retain rice if at all possible. Nor would the Japanese have had the same strong motive as earlier in the war to enforce collections, since, desperately short of shipping, they could not carry back to Japan even the rice piled up in Saigon (cf. Table 7.1). Although north Vietnamese peasants without rice for the quota were meant to find it from somewhere, whether they would have had the cash to buy rice at escalating black market prices seems doubtful. Insofar as the French collected levy rice, a substantial part of it was meant for distribution to the cities, and this helps to explain why urbanites were less affected by the famine than their rural counterparts (Chapter 8).

A Japanese requirement to plant land in Tonkin and Annam in fibre and oil seed crops in place of rice, although often cited as an important cause of the famine, had little effect. Shifts in cultivation towards non-rice crops, shown by Table 7.5, were marginal because the acreage involved was relatively small and some of it was in areas of Tonkin and Annam outside the coastal provinces. If between 1942 and 1944 additional land planted in non-rice crops had instead been in rice, in 1944 this would have yielded an additional 1,792 tons of rice in Annam and 18,600 tons in Tonkin.

It is apparent, however, that the Japanese had greater power than the French to avoid the famine and, even before the March 1945 coup, could have been more proactive than they were. After the coup, Japan was in total charge of Indochina. Throughout the war, Japan's military largely controlled transport which, instead of being reserved for military purposes, could have been used in 1944 and 1945 to

[54] Marr, *Vietnam: state, war*, p. 318.

[55] AOM, HCI 2/226, 'Mémoires Yokoyama', p. 88 and see Marr, *Vietnam,1945*, pp. 52, 127–28. Marr points out that the Japanese intended, by whatever means, to collect 35,000 tons of June harvest paddy in Tonkin but actually obtained about 11,500 tons.

Table 7.5 *Tonkin and Annam rice, cotton, jute, ramie and oil seed cultivation 1942–1944 (000 hectares)*

	1942	1943	1944
Tonkin			
Rice	1,487	1,386	1,427
Cotton	1.0	3.2	3.0
Jute	3.0	14.2	13.0
Ramie	0.4	1.0	1.2
Oil seeds	14.5	21.9	26.5
Total non-rice	18.9	40.3	43.7
Annam			
Rice	946	1,045	1,146
Cotton	4.5	7.0	9.7
Jute	0.2	0.4	0.7
Ramie	0.8	0.8	0.9
Oil seeds	27.8	26.7	25.2
Total non-rice	33.3	34.9	36.5

Notes: 1. Oil seeds include peanuts, castor oil and sesame.
2. For 1941, data are available only for the whole of Indochina. Comparison of 1941 and 1942 data suggests significant increases in the cultivation of the non-rice crops of jute and peanuts but the location of this increase in Indochina cannot be identified.
3. In 1944 in Annam, average rice productivity was 0.56 tons per hectare, and between 1942 and 1944 an additional 3,200 hectares were devoted to non-rice fibre and oil seed crops. That implies a possible loss of rice output of 1,792 tons, equivalent to 0.83% of rice output in the coastal provinces of North Annam in 1944. Repeating the same calculation for Tonkin indicates a possible loss in hectares of 24,800. Average rice productivity per hectare in 1944 was 0.75 tons per hectare. That implies a possible loss in rice output of 18,600 tons in Tonkin equivalent to 1.7% of rice output in Tonkin in 1944. Adding North Annam and Tonkin suggests a maximum loss in potential rice output from increased cultivation of fibre and oil seed crops of 20,392 tons of rice. That assumes, however, that land chosen for fibre and oil seed crops had at least the average productivity of rice land as a whole. The possible loss of rice in 1944 of 20,392 tons compares with a total decline in rice output of 212,900 tons between 1942 and 1944 in the coastal provinces of Tonkin and Annam.
Sources: Indochina, *Annuaire statistique, 1941–1942*, pp. 87–89; *1943–1946*, pp. 89–93.

carry rice to the famine-affected north. Even so, transport of rice northwards would have been difficult because of American bombing and mining of coastal waters.

In official Vietnamese accounts, the United States is accorded little or no blame for the famine. Yet it would have been much easier to bring rice to the north without the relentless mining and bombing campaigns, beginning in mid-1943, waged by the US 14th Air Force based in China. By April 1944, bombing had effected a 'brutal reduction' in north–south trade.[56] Figure 7.7, based on Japanese reports intercepted by Allied intelligence, shows for December 1944 destroyed or damaged bridges along the Transindochinois railway, including the highly strategic bridge at Than Hoa on the Tonkin–North Annam border which linked Vietnam's north and south. United States bombing raids by Admiral Halsey's carrier fleet were especially important in creating severe

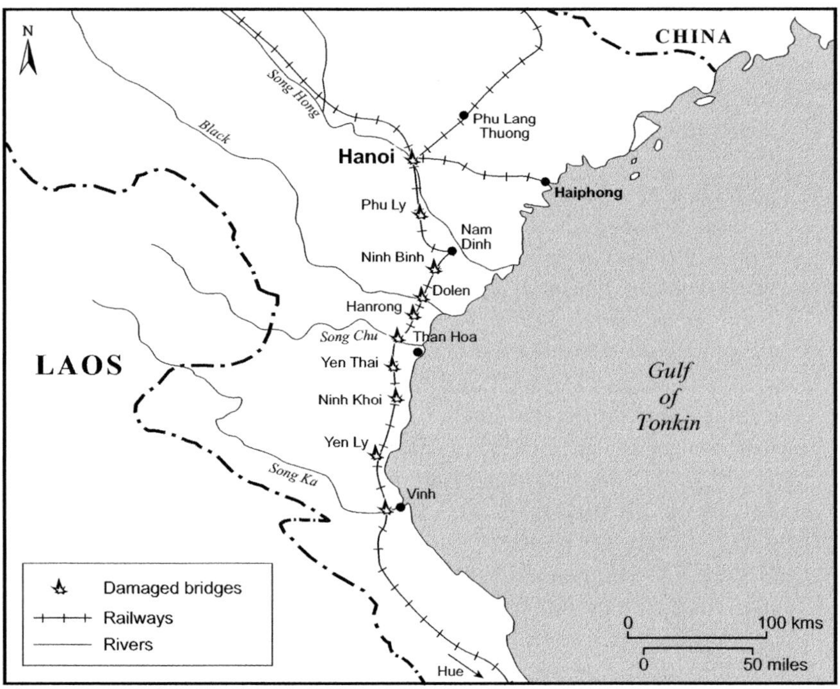

Figure 7.7 Tonkin and North Annam bomb-damaged bridges December 1944
Source: LHC, MAGIC, 'Military: condition of Indo-China coastal railroad bridges', 12 December 1944, p. 2.

[56] VNA, FF 15154, 'Programme de l'utilisation de transports en Indochine 1944', 18 April 1944, p. 20; and on the difficulties of transport to the north see AOM, HCI 2/226, 'Mémoires Yokoyama', p. 95.

transport bottlenecks. By early 1945, these attacks had 'almost eliminated the remaining possibilities of shipping rice and corn to the North'.[57]

It seems probable that US officials were aware of the famine in Vietnam, and by May 1945 it is certain that they were, since Archimedes Patti, in his official capacity as an officer in the Office of Strategic Services, the United States intelligence agency, sent Washington a dossier of photos.[58] Well before that, the Americans, with the benefit of aerial photographic reconnaissance, would have seen how extensively Vietnam's transport network had been damaged. Furthermore, American intelligence in China was in close touch with the Viet Minh in Vietnam and with Washington. Especially after the March 1945 coup, the Viet Minh were instrumental in directing American air strikes and certainly could have passed on information about the devastating famine.[59] The Americans did not doubt the effectiveness of their air campaign: 'the French Indochina rail system, north from Vinh to the China border, was attacked in strength and rendered largely unserviceable'.[60] Probably, the United States, even with knowledge of the famine, remained intent only on the pursuit of war and the continued destruction of Vietnam's communication system. The aims were to deny the Japanese army in the north re-supply from the south and to encourage the population to turn against the Japanese.[61]

The Viet Minh had, of course, its own goals. While the United States may have viewed the famine as an unfortunate by-effect of war, the Viet Minh also saw its positive aspects. As discussed in the Epilogue, the Viet Minh identified famine and an Allied invasion as pre-conditions for a communist revolution.

Food-Deficit Areas: Malaya, Philippines and the Indonesian Outer Islands

Although Malaya, the Philippines and Indonesia's Outer Islands were all food-deficit areas and rice was the staple in each, the contrasts between the three were considerable. They varied in the extent of their food deficits as well as in patterns of scarcity within the areas themselves. Furthermore, transport shortages and fighting impacted food supplies differently both within and across countries.

Malaya

Of the three areas examined in this section, Malaya had by far the greatest pre-war food deficit because its economy had specialized to such a great extent in tin and

57 Tønnesson, *Vietnamese revolution*, p. 294.
58 Patti, *Why Viet Nam?*, pp. 85–86, 347.
59 Spector, 'Allied intelligence', pp. 38–41.
60 USSBS, *Air campaigns*, p. 34 and see p. 23; cf. fig. 5.
61 AOM, HCI 2/226, 'Mémoires Yokoyama', p. 92.

rubber, and because it had little land suited to rice cultivation (Chapter 4). In 1940 in Malaya, imported food, including livestock, provided an average of 1,400 calories a day per person and local production a further 1,162 calories, a total of 2,562.[62] Rice accounted for the largest share of calorie consumption, livestock hardly any. By the 1930s, Malaya produced less than a quarter of the rice it consumed; the rest, about 610,000 metric tons, came as imports, making apparent the supply problem during occupation of obtaining Malaya's customary quantities of rice.

The main rice-producing parts of Malaya were in the north, and included Kedah, Perlis and northern Kelantan near the Thailand border (Figure 4.5). Between 1937/40 and 1943/44, rice output in Kedah, the most important Malayan producer, fell by 25 per cent. In Malaya as a whole, rice output declined by 29 per cent between 1939 and 1945, from 341,000 tons to 241,000 tons. Production dropped mainly because the incentive to farmers to grow and sell rice was undermined by three factors: a lack of consumer goods available in exchange; compulsory delivery schemes at low fixed purchase prices set by Japanese administrators; and the commandeering of rice both by the Japanese and anti-Japanese, mainly ethnic Chinese, guerrillas. Further reasons for decreased rice output were the slaughter of water buffalo for food, a fall in labour hours due to increased malaria and loss of workers to forced labour, bad weather and a breakdown in communal harvesting when, during the latter stages of occupation, women no longer had clothes to wear. In rice-surplus areas, the Japanese used the *mata-mata padi*, or rice police, to collect grain for military use and for distribution elsewhere in Malaya, and to try to deny food to guerrillas. During 1944–45, Japanese pressure to obtain rice intensified as part of a military build-up in north-western Malaya against invasion. Along with falling output, rice distribution from the three northern producers to the rest of Malaya was probably also affected to some extent by Japan's July 1943 decision to cede these states, together with Trengganu, to Thailand (Chapter 2).[63]

Shrinking rice output and a high dependence on external food supplies increased the apparent likelihood that Malaya, including its large cities of Singapore, Penang and Kuala Lumpur, would suffer wartime famine. In October 1945, after the re-occupation of Malaya, the British 'expected that there would be areas in the country where the civilian population would be starving. This was not so. Practically the only cases of frank starvation were found amongst the prisoners of war and displaced people who had been used by the Japanese as labour forces.'[64] By the late stages of the war, however, most Malayans were malnourished. In contrast to Malaya, and despite having been

[62] Nicholls, 'Nutrition', p. 37.

[63] Ibid., p. 37; Harper, *End*, p. 39; Jaafar bin Hamzah, 'Malays in Tasek Gelugur', pp. 58–59; Nonini, *British colonial rule*, p. 105; Lee, 'Study of the rice trade', p. 105.

[64] Bourne, 'Nutrition work', p. 266.

seemingly better placed to avoid food scarcity, by 1944 it was the Philippines and various of Indonesian's Outer Islands that had pockets of famine.

Four main reasons largely explain why Malaya's population did not experience a worse food crisis or even famine. One is a relatively high standard of living in pre-war Malaya which enabled Malayans to consume daily on average 1.1 pounds (450 grams or 1,611 calories) of rice.[65] That and the ability of many Malayans to obtain other constituents of a nutritious diet meant that a substantial share of the population was not in an already weakened state at the start of the occupation.

Second, Malaya's production structure and demography both favoured food cultivation as an alternative to imports. Malaya had a large smallholder sector, and although many of its farmers produced for export, they could turn to subsistence cultivation. Smallholders who grew rubber might already cultivate subsistence crops in conjunction with *hevea* or have done so before entirely specializing in it as a cash crop (Chapter 4). For non-agriculturalists, land on which to grow food was available because of Malaya's low man-to-land ratio. Land availability enabled the Japanese to drive large numbers of people away from the towns and villages to outlying areas, where appreciable tracts of jungle, state land and rubber plantings were felled to allow food cultivation.[66] Other people voluntarily moved to food-growing areas of towns and larger villages.[67] Some Chinese left the towns entirely to settle in more isolated areas of Malaya, where in 1947 many were found squatting.[68]

Third, Malaya benefited from an insular geography and location near mainland Southeast Asia's principal rice-producing countries. Malaya could obtain rice much more easily than the Philippines or even Indonesia's Outer Islands, because of its proximity to Thailand. From Thailand, small vessels carrying rice could sail down either coast of the Malay peninsula. High black market prices gave ethnic Chinese traders in Thailand and Malaya an incentive to facilitate flows of rice and growers a reason to produce it. Although statistics for non-Japanese-organized rice imports to Malaya are not available, after 1943 rice production in Thailand, despite a sharp drop in exports to Japan, did not fall (Table 4.3). Unchanged Thai output suggests that the gap left by the cessation of exports to Japan was at least partly filled by shipments to Malaya and Indonesia.

Finally, after occupation Japanese administrators soon realized the enormity of the problem of feeding Malayans and began to ration rice (Chapter 6). Moreover, throughout the war the Japanese did much to help avoid mass hunger through orchestrated 'grow more food' campaigns aimed at persuading people to plant

65 NA, WO203/2647, 'Summary of economic intelligence (Far East) no. 130', 15 October 1945, p. 3; ANM, 1957/0575131 Intelligence 506/30, 'Appreciation of the economic position of Malaya', 30 June 1944, p. 3.

66 Malayan Union, *Report on agriculture . . . 1946*, pp. 3, 61.

67 Malaya, *Report on the 1947 census*, p. 35.

68 Malayan Union, *Annual report of the labour department 1947*, p. 24.

high-calorie substitutes for previously imported rice and by providing instruction on how to prepare and cook new foods in various ways.[69] The two principal rice substitutes were cassava and sweet potatoes, easily grown, quick-yielding root crops with high calorific values. Both are, however, almost devoid of protein, which must be obtained from other sources such as fish or meat. For the bulk of the population, these foods were available in no more than small amounts, if at all. Other substitutes for rice included maize, groundnuts and ragi. By all accounts, Malayans universally despised tapioca. It could, however, be prepared in a variety of forms, including as flour for a hard and tasteless kind of bread, and contributed substantially to preventing mass starvation.

Despite the advantages of geography, the efforts of Japanese administrators and the resourcefulness of many Malayans, nutritional standards fell sharply for almost everyone in Malaya because there was less food, an unvaried diet and shortages of nutritionally important items like oils, fats and vegetables. Most people relied on coconut oil as a source of fat. Overall, wartime nutrition hovered around 'the minimum nutritional level which could permit the Government of the country to function'.[70] By 1945, almost all people had lost substantial amounts of weight, malnutrition was widespread and semi-starvation 'fairly common'.[71] Among the worst aspects of food shortages was a complete absence of milk, and this may help to explain why both in cities and in rural areas the health of children seems to have suffered disproportionately during the war.[72] In 1946 at welfare centres, two-year-old children weighing 10 pounds and unable to walk were not uncommon.[73]

Malayan death and birth data are incomplete, but overall trends are clear (Table 7.6). Between 1940 and 1944, the number of deaths rose by 58.4 per cent and might well be shown to have continued to increase in 1945 if data were complete. Over the same 1940 to 1944 period, births declined by 17.6 per cent but in 1946 recovered to their pre-war level. Nutritional deficiencies do not, of course, explain all of the increase in deaths. The incidence of malaria rose sharply due to Japanese neglect of preventive measures and a shortage of quinine.[74] Most rubber estates were highly malarious.[75] In Selangor between 1939 and 1942, the death rate from malaria on rubber estates climbed tenfold to 7.2 per thousand.[76]

69 ANM, 1957/0575131 Intelligence 506/30, 'Appreciation of the economic position of Malaya', 30 June 1944, p. 4 and see pp. 3–4; Bourne, 'Nutrition work', p. 267; Turnbull, *History*, p. 201.

70 Bourne, 'Nutrition work', p. 303.

71 MacGregor, 'Medical history', p. 162 and see Bourne, 'Nutrition work', pp. 266–68, 288.

72 Bourne, 'Nutrition work', pp. 272, 281.

73 British Military Administration, *Final report of the nutrition unit*, appx. p. A(ii) p. 6 and Bourne summary, p. 2.

74 Malayan Union, *Report of the medical department 1946*, pp. 19, 51.

75 NARA, RG226, entry 19, box 146, R&A XL10702, *Interrogation on medical conditions in Malaya*, 5 June 1945, p. 2.

76 ANM, 1957/0292074 R. C. Selangor 296/1947, *Report of the Medical Department 1941–1946*, p. 11.

Table 7.6 *Malay states births and deaths 1940–1946*

	Births	Crude birth rate	Deaths	Crude death rate
1940	186,028	37.2	92,491	18.5
1941	142,339*	28.5	63,436*	12.7
1942	151,181*	30.2	99,257	19.9
1943	176,669	35.3	123,282	24.7
1944	153,198	30.6	146,476	29.3
1945	103,747*	20.7	110,112*	22.0
1946	183,960	36.8	105,040	21.0

Notes: 1. An asterisk indicates incomplete records. However, as the report (p. 8) points out, the general trends during the Japanese occupation are clear.
2. For 1942 to 1945, deaths are only those from natural causes.
3. Birth and death rates are per 1,000 population and assume a population of 5 million for the Malayan Union and are approximate. The report (cited below) estimated that the population increased from 4.8 million in 1940 to 5.0 million in 1946. Accordingly, birth and death rates are underestimates for earlier years, especially for the earliest years. The maximum likely error is around 4.3% for births, that is a 1940 figure of 38.8 for a population of 4.8 million, not the 37.2 for a population of 5.0 million. A similar maximum error applies for deaths and is also 4.3%, a 1940 death rate of 19.3 for a population of 4.8 million.
Source: Malayan Union, *Report on the registration of births and deaths, 1941–1946*, pp. 2–3.

Food deprivation and malnourishment varied greatly both among racial groups and spatially. The two were correlated, and a full understanding of this correlation requires some explanation of Malayan economic and settlement patterns (Table 7.7 and Figure 4.5). Excluding Singapore, considered in Chapter 8, the population in Malaya divided into 45.5 per cent Malay, 38.1 per cent Chinese, 14.8 per cent Indian and a tiny proportion of others. Malays were overwhelmingly rural dwellers, and comprised the bulk of settlement in the 'traditional' parts of Malaya. These included Malaya's east coast states, none of which had been more than partially drawn into the tin and rubber export economy, and Kedah and Perlis in the far north-west. Although many Malays were rubber smallholders, the majority followed other, more traditional pursuits which, as well as rice cultivation, included fishing. Chinese settled disproportionately in the towns and in a rubber and tin belt which began in southern Kedah and continued southwards along the entire peninsular west coast to Singapore. While Malays comprised almost three-quarters of the population in Malaya's 'traditional' areas, Chinese accounted for almost half of those living along the west coast, where Malaya's export economy

Table 7.7 *Malay states distribution of population 1940 (000 persons)*

		Malays	Chinese	Indians	Others	Total
Traditional and rice states	Kedah	340.2	108.4	61.8	14.9	525.3
	Perlis	46.9	8.6	1.2	2.1	58.8
	Kelantan	338.9	30.9	11.5	9.0	390.3
	Trengganu	185.7	18.7	2.1	1.4	207.9
	Pahang	128.5	73.9	17.0	2.1	221.8
Total traditional		1,040.3	240.6	93.8	29.4	1,404.1
% traditional		74.1	17.1	6.7	2.1	100.0
West coast tin and rubber	Perak	335.4	450.2	196.1	11.1	992.7
	Selangor	152.7	339.7	193.5	15.6	701.6
	Negri Sembilan	106.0	125.8	59.3	4.9	296.0
	Malacca	110.0	90.2	28.3	3.7	232.2
	Johore	309.5	346.6	76.2	5.2	737.6
	Penang and P. Wellesley	117.5	225.9	60.7	7.8	411.8
Total tin and rubber		1,131.0	1,578.4	614.1	48.4	3,371.8
% tin and rubber		33.5	46.8	18.2	1.4	100.0
Total Malay states population		2,171.3	1,819.0	707.9	77.8	4,776.0
% of Malay states population		45.5	38.1	14.8	1.6	100.0

Source: Malayan Union, *Report of the medical department 1946*, p. 11.

predominated. Many Chinese were rubber smallholders or tin miners. Indians, chiefly Tamils, provided the bulk of the labour force for European-owned rubber estates and so were concentrated along Malaya's west coast and especially in Selangor and Perak.

During the Japanese occupation, people in rural Malaya suffered greater nutritional deprivation than most of those in the large cities. At the beginning of 1946, rural areas such as those in Selangor 'without exception appeared very unhealthy'.[77] One reason for the occupation's more detrimental effect on rural than urban areas was the concentration of rationing and organized relief programmes in the larger cities; during the occupation, people in rural areas received 'very little rice'.[78] Furthermore, many in rural Malaya did not own land,

[77] ANM, 1957/0290683 Sel. CA 232/46 BMA, Nutrition Unit report, January/February 1946, p. 2.

[78] Malayan Union, *Report on the British military administration*, p. 43; see also MacGregor, 'Medical history', p. 162.

and for the landless thrown out of work with the collapse in export agriculture the countryside offered few paid employment opportunities.

Indians were the most nutritionally deprived racial group and Chinese the least.[79] In Selangor, about half of the Chinese population could, at the outset of 1946, be regarded as healthy.[80] To some extent, Chinese were probably less seriously affected nutritionally than Indians or Malays because a high proportion resided in large cities or sizeable urban settlements. The Chinese also tended to live in the wealthier part of Malaya, and included a substantial middle class which, with higher pre-war incomes and more assets than Indians and Malays, was better able to turn to wartime black markets than most of those in the other racial groups. Chinese also seem to have adapted more successfully than either Indians or Malays to food shortages. A significant proportion of Chinese either moved just outside urban areas to become market gardeners or, as indicated above, began subsistence cultivation in remote areas.

Indian estate labourers suffered especially, because they had almost always come to Malaya as contract workers, and when a demand for rubber disappeared so too did their jobs. By the end of the war, the number of people living on rubber estates had fallen from a pre-war 370,000 to 190,000 and actual labourers from 148,000 to 70,000, of whom some 28,000 now grew only food.[81] A death rate for Indians living on estates of around 42 per thousand in 1939 can be regarded as approximately normal, but by 1945 stood at around three or four times that level, an increase far above the rise of 58.4 per cent for Malaya as a whole.[82] Many former estate workers drifted to towns. For those remaining on estates, it often proved difficult, as it had in the 1930s downturns, to turn successfully to self-sufficient agriculture.

A lack of entitlements frequently deepened the predicament of unemployed Indian estate workers. In contrast to the 1930s, when there was an entitlement to return at no cost to India, Indians now had no way to get home.[83] Furthermore, many had come alone to Malaya, and so might be without family or kinship networks which would probably have afforded some entitlement to help. Unlike other ethnic communities, Indians lacked institutional support and this further compromised their position.[84] Imported Javanese estate

[79] Federation of Malaya, *Report on the state of health*, pp. 8–9; Malayan Union, *Medical department report, 1946*, p. 19; WL, Heussler Papers, Gullick, 'My time in Malaya', June 1970, p. 34.

[80] ANM, 1957/0290683 Sel. CA 232/46 BMA, Nutrition Unit report, January/February 1946, p. 4.

[81] NARA, RG226, entry 19, box 317, R&A XL23209, *Malaya–Japanese penetration of the rubber manufacturing industry*, 12 October 1945, p. 18; NA, WO325/57, Document J, Shinozaki Mamoru, 'Information on the enlistment of Malayan coolies'.

[82] ANM, 1957/0292074 R. C. Selangor 296/1947, *Report of the medical department 1941–1946*, pp. 11–15; Malayan Union, *Report of the medical department 1946*, p. 19.

[83] Huff, 'Entitlements', pp. 306–7.

[84] Rai, *Indians*, pp. 261–63, 266–67.

workers were in a similar situation and, once jobless, their mortality rate was very high.[85]

Even when whole Indian families had lived on estates, wives and children often found themselves in desperate circumstances during the war, because husbands had been taken by the Japanese to work on the Thailand–Burma railway, leaving the family without its main breadwinner.[86] By 1945, Indian estate workers were the Malayan population group by far the most frequently reduced to semi-starvation, although labourers and coolies were also poorly off.[87] An eyewitness just after the war later reported some Indian children in a state of emaciation 'comparable to photographs I have seen of Biafra or Belsen'.[88]

Malays were generally at an advantage to Indians, and among Malays the group that did best was *kampong* Malays, who had access to land.[89] Nevertheless, all Malays were quite adversely affected by the war. In Negri Sembilan, Malay villagers were so discouraged by increasing Japanese rice requisitions that they stopped cultivating their fields.[90] The cultivation of paddy was similarly abandoned in Selangor.[91] A British colonial official recalls visiting the Lenggeng Valley in Negri Sembilan just after the war and finding that 'the undergrowth (*belukar*) over the rice fields (*sawah*) was in places five feet high. One could no longer see the line of the main distribution channel (*tali ayer*) from the irrigation dam. The condition of rice fields in the Labu Valley was almost as bad.' Loss of rice cultivation, together with shortages of food and medicines, destroyed local Malay communities: 'Sickness had taken its toll. As one walked through the coconut trees along the side of the Lenggeng Valley one came on groups of houses standing empty – all the householders were dead or had moved away. The people who remained were dispirited and half-starved.'[92]

Among rural Malays, a mild form of scabies was common before the war, but by its late stages had become universal and severe. Yaws, uncommon prior

[85] ANM, 1957/0290683 Sel. CA 232/46 BMA, Nutrition Unit report, January/February 1946, p. 6.

[86] British Military Administration, *Final report of the nutrition unit*, April 1946, appx. D, p. 4; Malayan Union, *Annual report of the labour department 1947*, p. 24. The same desperate circumstances affected Burmese families when cultivators were conscripted for work on the Thailand–Burma railway or for labour camps. IOR, Clague Papers, Mss Eur E252/44, 'Situation in Burma', p. 21.

[87] MacGregor, 'Medical history', p. 162; Bourne, 'Nutritional work', pp. 291–93, 303.

[88] WL, Heussler Papers, Gullick, 'My time in Malaya', June 1970, p. 34.

[89] ANM, 1957/0290683 Sel. CA 232/46 BMA, Nutrition Unit report, January/February 1946, pp. 5–6.

[90] WL, Heussler Papers, Gullick, 'My time in Malaya', June 1970, p. 34.

[91] ANM, 1957/0290166, Selangor, Department of Agriculture, Report I preliminary report, September 1945, pp. 7–8.

[92] WL, Heussler Papers, Gullick, 'My time in Malaya', June 1970, p. 36.

to the war, was rampant in remote districts by 1945.[93] Malays seem often to have ended the war in an even less healthy state than might have been anticipated, because of a tendency for *kampong* Malays to starve themselves of foods like eggs and coconuts and instead sell these goods on the market, where they fetched high prices.[94]

Land was important in explaining why at the end of the 1940s, for two representative survey groups near Malacca in western Malaya, Malays came out better than Indians. After the collapse in demand for rubber, the Indian estate labourer had 'either had to cultivate poor soil to produce food for himself and his family or to follow some other occupation for which he had no training'.[95] By contrast, the Malays, although not self-sufficient in rice, were surrounded by land on which root crops could easily be grown. Within the Malay group, unlike in Tonkin, fishermen were better off than agriculturalists because of a sharp increase in the price of fish relative to rice. Fish prices rose because supply fell due to a Japanese ban on night fishing. Malays benefited from resulting high prices since in that part of western Malaya Chinese fished at night and Malays during the day.[96]

The advantage of being a fisherman was, however, far from universal. In Kelantan on Malaya's east coast, where there were few Chinese, coast-dwelling Malay fishermen were at a disadvantage relative to their inland Malay rice-cultivating counterparts. Kelantan relied partly on imports of rice, and its price rose faster than that of fish, since for these Malays fish merely served as a garnish. The war was a time of 'considerable hardship' for Kelantan fishermen.[97]

A theme running throughout this book, and illustrated by the wartime plight of Kelantan fishermen, is that virtually all of Southeast Asia was at least partly integrated into the global economy, the wartime suspension of which seriously affected living standards in even seemingly remote or 'traditional' regions. Kelantan fishermen, as well as being short of rice, found it expensive, or even impossible, to obtain many goods on which they had come to depend, and which had to be bought with cash. These included clothing, thread, tobacco, cigarettes, coffee, soap, nails, lamp oil, torches, matches and batteries. Cloth was almost totally lacking. Some people wore mainly clothing of gunny sacks; others made clothing of thin rubber sheeting and sold it.[98] Among Malays throughout rural Malaya, family members often shared whatever garments were available and to avoid theft never left clothes hanging outside the house at night.[99]

93 MacGregor, 'Medical history', p. 162.
94 Bourne, 'Nutrition work', p. 304.
95 Federation of Malaya, *Report on the state of health*, p. 9.
96 Ibid.
97 Firth, *Malay fishermen*, p. 298 and see pp. 3–4, 298–300 and 'Coastal people', pp. 197, 201.
98 Firth, *Malay fishermen*, p. 299, *Housekeeping*, p. 136 and 'Economics', p. 69.
99 Abu Talib Ahmad, *Malay Muslims*, pp. 45–46.

Philippines

In 1941, the Philippines appeared in a stronger position than Malaya to avoid a food crisis after occupation, because the Islands' dependence on imported food was far lower. Furthermore, less of the Philippine labour force specialized in export production; and a relatively high proportion of this exported output was food or, in the case of sugar, a quasi-food. An August 1942 US intelligence report, apparently assuming essentially unimpeded movement of food, concluded that 'Japanese control over the Philippines will not introduce any difficult food problems in the Islands ... Filipinos will suffer little food shortages'. Before the war, imports comprised only 5 per cent of total annual food consumption of 5 million tons. Fish, some rice, meat, breadstuffs, fruits and vegetables were all imported and while, the report continued, after occupation imports of dairy products would cease, self-sufficiency in every important foodstuff was high. The average Filipino relied on rice, other grains and root crops for 80 per cent of calorie intake. Although invasion and fighting had caused a 20 to 30 per cent decline in the 1941/42 rice and corn harvest, it was thought that root crops could compensate for temporary shortfalls. Furthermore, new crops could be produced in four or five months, while in the longer term a shift from export agriculture would make up for most previously imported foods.[100]

During the war, however, acute food shortages became the norm over much of the Philippines. Immediately after Japanese occupation, war-devastated areas of Luzon had to contend with scarcity. By 1943 in the Philippines, it was apparent that low, administered prices had caused food output to fall and that the government lacked sufficient control over the country to distribute food effectively and keep large parts of the Islands from experiencing scarcities. In response to the spread of food shortages over much of the Islands, President Laurel declared in 1943 that his duty was 'to save our people from starvation'.[101]

Through the latter half of 1943 and during 1944, government price controls, the difficult geography of the Philippines, the localization of food production, a lack of transport, and widespread guerrilla resistance combined to worsen food shortages and led to instances of famine. In May 1944, editorials in the *Manila Tribune* reported a crop decline of 25 to 30 per cent compared to the previous year.[102] The Philippines divided into 'have' and 'have not' food regions (see Figure 4.8). While the former, the Commissioner for the Visayas observed in June 1944, are 'naturally egotistical, in instinct of self-preservation', the latter are 'beggars, help-clamorers, trying to get what they can from other provinces'.

[100] OSS, R&A 324, *Philippine agriculture under Japanese control*, p. 36 for the quotations and passim.

[101] Kerkvliet, 'Withdrawal', p. 185.

[102] Friend, *Blue-eyed enemy*, pp. 157–58.

The central and northern parts of Luzon were 'rice baskets', but many sugar-specialized regions needed somehow to find food from other parts of the Islands. The major sugar-growing area of Negros had, along with Cebu and Bohol, to depend on Leyte and Panay for food.[103] Those in Leyte's granary areas in the north-west, including the towns of San Isidro and Villaba, found it profitable to sell to other nearby provinces, which left food-deficit areas in the south of the island hungry.[104] The Visayas, as their Commissioner pointed out, had a 'big food problem' which 'we must solve, or we perish'.[105] Ports in Mindanao through which food might have come, the Commissioner lamented, were closed to the Visayas.

Both Japanese demands and guerrilla activity re-directed available rice, and probably also discouraged production, due to a disincentive to contribute rice to one side or another and because of continued instability. According to the Philippines Interior Minister, speaking in October 1944, the people were beset 'with fears and confusion . . . A feeling of insecurity [results in] the paralysis of all activity . . . The farmer does not till the soil . . . causing starvation among the people . . . other people lose their occupations'.[106] Additionally, the Japanese took over substantial amounts of rice land, for example in the province of Laguna, which before the war had itself partly depended on the central Luzon province of Nueva Ecija for rice.[107]

Filipino guerrillas, described as 'a formidable obstacle to Japanese administrative organization', gained strength as the war continued, making wartime disruption in the Philippines second only to Burma.[108] Guerrillas controlled a number of food-growing areas and might, as in Leyte, afford rice-harvesters protection from the Japanese. Merchants in non-Japanese-occupied parts of Leyte had to secure a permit from guerrilla commanders to take food to areas of shortage.[109] For self-preservation and to hedge bets, those with food often supplied both the Japanese army and guerrillas.

A geography of many islands, few railways, an acute lack of shipping, specialization in non-food crops and Japanese and guerrilla demands were not, however, the whole explanation for the wartime food crisis in the Philippines. Corruption was pervasive, and prevented an equitable distribution of rice, as well as probably somewhat reducing its overall availability through unnecessary loss. By the latter part of 1943, the government in

[103] UP, Roxas Papers, box 13, Paulino Gullas, Commissioner for the Visayas to President Laurel, 20 June 1944.
[104] Lear, *Japanese occupation*, p. 133 and see p. 12.
[105] UP, Roxas Papers, box 13, Gullas to President Laurel, 20 June 1944.
[106] Weston, 'Co-Prosperity fails', p. 26 quoting a report in *Domei.*
[107] UP, Roxas Papers, box 44, Jesus Bautista, Governor of Laguna to Chairman, Economic Planning Board, 11 May 1944.
[108] OSS, R&A 2357S, *Guerrilla resistance*, p. 1.
[109] Lear, *Japanese occupation*, pp. 132–33, 138, 140–42; Jose, 'Rice shortage', p. 206.

Manila had, even in Luzon, at best limited control over rice supplies. The National Rice and Corn Corporation (NARIC), the first of a series of government buying agencies, soon became, in the words of President Laurel, a 'rotten apple'; it was 'shot through with corrupt individuals'.[110] NARIC's replacement, Bigasang Bayan (BIBA), established in early January 1944 and put under the personal charge of Manuel Roxas as head of the Economic Planning Board, was no more successful nor probably less corrupt.[111] As official prices increasingly fell behind those on the black market, it became difficult for BIBA to obtain rice or corn. In June 1944, a BIBA representative in the Visayas wired the Food Administrator requesting permission to buy on the black market.[112]

Cabinet minutes record that 'many provincial governors, in connivance with their respective municipal mayors, are engaged in the illicit traffic and sale of rice at exorbitant prices'.[113] Outlaws, whose activities included derailing trains to loot rice, were better armed than the Philippine Constabulary.[114] But that probably made little difference, since many of the Constabulary, distrusted and disliked by the people, 'are engaged in all sorts of graft, racketeering and bribery'.[115] In Leyte, the Constabulary was so corrupt that over a large part of the island little food could be procured.[116]

In July 1944, almost no surplus palay (unmilled rice) existed, and whatever was available was 'in some few strong hands'.[117] Big landlords with rice bribed local officials to avoid selling through official channels. They were, however, only one component of a network of illegal rice trafficking that Colonel N. Utunomiya (Utsunomiya), the Japanese military attaché liaising with the Philippines government, described in July 1944 as comprised of 'non-cooperative governors, constabulary chiefs, town mayors and landlords'.[118] He singled out in particular corruption in the central Luzon rice-growing provinces of Nueva Ecija and Tarlac, but this was far from a comprehensive list. Certain towns in Bulacan, a province just north of Manila, became centres for black marketeers, and acquired a boom-town atmosphere.[119]

110 The quotations are from Friend, *Blue-eyed enemy*, p. 157 and Jose, 'Rice shortage', p. 206.

111 Jose, 'Rice shortage', p. 206; Garcia, *Documents*, p. 252.

112 UP, Roxas Papers, box 13, Memo, Commissioner for the Visayas to the President, 20 June 1944.

113 UP, Japanese Occupation Papers, box 17, Cabinet minutes, 29 November 1943, p. 3.

114 UP, Japanese Occupation Papers, box 17, Cabinet minutes, 8 February 1944, p. 2 and Roxas Papers, box 13, Memo, Rigoberto J. Atienza, Chief, Inspection Division to Food Administrator, Manila, 4 August 1944.

115 UP, Japanese Occupation Papers, box 17, Cabinet minutes, 29 November 1943, p. 3.

116 Ara, 'Food supply problem', pp. 73–75.

117 UP, Roxas Papers, box 4, Memorandum for the General Manager, BIBA, 28 July 1944, p. 1.

118 UP, Roxas Papers, box 44, Colonel N. Utunomiya to Manuel A. Roxas, Chairman, Economic Planning Board, 18 July 1944, p. 3.

119 UP, Japanese Occupation Papers, box 17, Cabinet minutes, 8 February 1944, p. 2.

Throughout the latter part of the war, Manila faced severe food shortages but it was not unique (Chapter 8). As early as August 1943, according to the Governor of Nueva Ecija, people in his province were 'on the verge of starvation'.[120] That, if correct, suggests a major failure in distribution, since Nueva Ecija normally produced about a fifth of all Philippine palay. In the autumn of 1944, a food crisis, partly due to an inflow of migrants from Manila, gripped Baguio and its surrounding area, including many small towns. By December, the Military Governor of the region, the second military district, warned that 'Unless the Government do something immediately to alleviate the present situation, the residents of the city of Baguio will in no time begin to starve'.[121] Reports from other parts of the Philippines spoke of extreme hardship and hundreds dying from lack of food, but not of mass starvation.[122] In August 1944, the Governor of Negros Oriental tried to barter sugar for rice to alleviate food shortages that had caused hunger in large centres and some indigents to die of starvation.[123]

The Japanese, although aware of the seriousness of food scarcities, and mindful of possible resulting civil unrest, especially in Manila, appear to have been largely powerless to act. They themselves got only part of the rice procured by the Philippine buying agencies and as this declined the Japanese food supply was threatened.[124] Colonel Utunomiya complained of endemic corruption: the 'big offenders are among those who enjoy political influence and are connected with big financial groups'. 'Some of the big offenders', Colonel Utunomiya suggested, 'should be executed publicly and their names published in the papers'. But the Japanese army would not, he said, 'overstep its authority'. Executions do not appear to have happened; or, if they did, had no discernible effect on rice supplies.[125]

A partial palliative, and an outcome of the need of both the Japanese and the Philippine government to obtain rice supplies, was the adoption of a plan discussed at the end of July 1944. The plan accorded the market a greater role than already given it in April 1944, when those selling rice to BIBA at the official price were allowed to sell an equal amount of rice on the free market, or if they sold palay to BIBA this would be milled free of charge and the rice equivalent of 40 per cent of the palay delivered to the sellers' warehouse.[126]

[120] Hartendorp, *Japanese occupation*, p. 598.

[121] UP, Roxas Papers, box 30, Lorenzo B. Andrada, Special Representative Ministry of Economic Affairs to Minister for Economic Affairs, Manila, 2 December 1944.

[122] Kerkvliet, 'Withdrawal', pp. 186–87.

[123] UP, Roxas Papers, box 44, Minutes Economic Planning Board, 22 August 1944, p. 2.

[124] Hartendorp, *History of industry*, p. 144.

[125] UP, Roxas Papers, box 44, 'Conference between Colonel Utunomiya and Secretary [of the Interior] Sabido and Mr. Sanvictores', 5 June 1944, p. 1.

[126] UP, Roxas Papers, box 44, 'Regulations concerning the supply of rice, corn, etc.', 20 April 1944 and 'New rice policy', 25 April 1944.

Under the new plan, those who supplied rice received an increased price of 51 pesos for every sack plus 4 pesos worth of so-called prime commodities, meaning basic consumer goods including textiles, matches and soap. The latter could be sold on the black market for much more than 4 pesos and, unlike payment in cash, held their value under the prevailing runaway inflation. The Japanese tabled strong reservations to the plan because they argued (correctly) that it would encourage black market dealings and also undermine the Philippines currency. Agreeing to the plan, Colonel Utunomiya stipulated, probably principally as a face-saving exercise, that the new, more market-realistic measures were only temporary, necessitated by emergency, and that efforts to combat the black market would be re-doubled.[127]

In late November 1944, BIBA was abolished and replaced by the Rice and Corn Association (RIOCA). By then, the Americans had invaded (General MacArthur landed on Leyte on 20 October 1944), and the Japanese desperately needed to secure a supply of rice. Colonel Utunomiya was appointed vice chairman of the board of RIOCA. Moreover, all the agency's new departments of administration, procurement, distribution and transport were headed by Japanese; Filipinos took orders from them. RIOCA enabled the Japanese to gain rice for themselves, though not for the Filipino people.[128]

While severe, the food crisis in the Philippines was not still worse for six main reasons. One, applicable to large urban areas and particularly Manila, was rationing and food relief (Chapter 8). Second, government campaigns which persuaded people to cultivate their own food, or compelled them to do so through compulsory labour schemes, made a contribution, although less so than in Malaya.

A third reason, more important than the first two, was that between half and 55 per cent of all cultivated areas consisted of subsistence crops. Agriculturalists on this land already produced much of their own food. Furthermore, most of the other about 45 per cent of cultivated land was planted with coconuts (27 per cent of all Philippines cultivation), sugar cane (6 per cent) and abaca or tobacco (8.5 per cent).[129] These last two could not, of course, contribute to food intake. However, sugar, a high-calorie source, did so to some extent, since in the pre-war Philippines a fifth of sugar output was consumed locally.[130] Moreover, coconuts were an important foodstuff and before the war, along with fish, a normal part of diets almost everywhere in the Islands. During the war, coconuts could

127 UP, Roxas Papers, box 44, Colonel Utunomiya to Manuel Roxas, 31 July 1944.

128 Hartendorp, *History of industry*, p. 144; Jose, 'Rice shortage', p. 211–12; Garcia, *Documents*, pp. 251–52; Friend, *Blue-eyed enemy*, pp. 158–59.

129 Hainsworth and Moyer, *Agricultural geography*, pp. 14–29. For a map of food-deficit areas, see Spencer, *Land*, p. 124.

130 Sacay, 'Food supply', p. 204.

continue to fulfil this role since, unlike field crops, the trees neither required re-planting nor are easily damaged.[131]

Fourth, as in Malaya, a low man-to-land ratio helped those without land to return to subsistence cultivation. In Leyte, landless farmers mostly evacuated to the interior mountains to cultivate the land of absentee landlords, and grow vegetables for the guerrillas and to sell on the black market.[132] Fifth, friends and relatives constituted a network that seems to have entitled many Filipino evacuees to help. Apparently, among the first questions Filipinos, when talking of the war, asked each other was 'Where did you evacuate to?'[133] Finally, in Manila resistance by Japanese forces ended on 4 March, and this relatively early lifting of occupation almost certainly prevented the food crisis from intensifying over the Islands.

Indonesian Outer Islands

In the Outer Islands food availability and deprivation showed many of the same features as in other deficit regions. Before the war, the Outer Islands, although generally with a food-surplus district or districts on each island, typically depended on feeding themselves by trading non-food crops and the output of cottage industries for food. That, in turn, meant a reliance on a demand for Outer Island output and on Indonesia's intra- and inter-island and Southeast Asia's intra-regional transport network to bring food, including rice, from Java and elsewhere in Southeast Asia. The near-total destruction of intra- and inter-island shipping was, even more than the wartime collapse in demand for non-food exports, a main explanation for the emergence from 1943 of food scarcity throughout almost all of Outer Island Indonesia.

Initially, deficit regions had food to fall back on because the Dutch colonial government had set up rice stores to hedge against a poor harvest and counter shortages until the next harvest. In March 1942 in the Riow (Riau) archipelago, Bangka (Belitung), Billiton, Borneo (Kalimantan), Menado (Mando), the Moluccas and Sumatra's east coast (North Sumatra), this amounted to enough rice for three to five months' consumption. Furthermore, in the pre-war years there had been an expansion, partly through compulsion, of food crop cultivation, especially the planting of root crops such as cassava and sweet potatoes. However, beginning in 1943, food emergencies developed on Sumatra's east coast, Bangka, Billiton, Timor and its adjacent islands, and in the Moluccas. A loss of fishing in the Moluccas due to Allied action put further pressure on food availability there; nearly all the sago crop was consumed, and the coconut crop

131 Hainsworth and Moyer, *Agricultural geography*, p. 31.
132 Ara, 'Food supply problem', pp. 73–75.
133 Kerkvliet, 'Withdrawal', p. 184.

had to be used as a reserve food.[134] In Celebes, 'the food situation [became] very difficult'.[135]

At the same time, in most Outer Island food-surplus districts, rice and corn output fell, despite the neglect or replacement of export crops. These drops further increased pressure on deficit regions. As in other Southeast Asian areas, output decreases were explained by low prices, Japanese confiscation, transport shortages and a lack of inputs. In the pre-war surplus areas of south Celebes, Bali and Lombok, rice surpluses disappeared and 20 to 25 per cent of *sawah* remained unplanted. Rat and pig infestations, along with a lack of imported pesticides, further reduced output.[136] Bali was an Outer Island exception in experiencing no food shortage.[137]

In contrast to Java with a population density of 316 per square kilometre, Outer Island densities were 21, 17 and 5 per square kilometre in Celebes, Sumatra and Borneo respectively.[138] Low man-to-land ratios afforded an important safety valve in the prevention of more severe food crises and avoidance of anything but a few instances of famine. Those with access to land had the opportunity to plant food crops, if perhaps at the cost of abandoning cash crops or felling forest areas, and for them that usually made the nutritional impact of occupation less disastrous than for the pre-war landless.[139] Apart from a scarcity of rice, and even allowing for a weekly food levy enforced by the Japanese military, people living on their own land in north-east Celebes were reported as not suffering any shortage of food.[140] By contrast, in parts of East Sumatra, where population densities were high and military troops most concentrated, 'food deficits quickly assumed acute proportions'.[141]

East Sumatran plantations were among the areas of the Outer Islands most severely affected by a lack of food but here, as typically in Southeast Asia, where land was available this helped to mitigate severity. The plantation belt in East Sumatra stretched from just north of the cities of Deli and Medan, and encompassed them to run southwards along the coast for some distance. Estates, mostly European owned, grew principally tobacco or rubber, but

134 Centraal Bureau voor de Statistiek, 'De economische toestand van Nederlandsch-Indie', pp. 124–25; Fruin, *Het economisch*, pp. 42–43.

135 NIMH, 010A/18, 'Netherlands Forces interrogation report 184, part 3', 18 October 1944, p. 2.

136 Centraal Bureau voor de Statistiek, 'De economische toestand van Nederlandsch-Indie', pp. 124–25; Fruin, *Het economisch*, p. 44.

137 Sutter, *Indonesianisasi*, p. 243.

138 Naval Intelligence Division, *Netherlands East Indies*, vol. 2, pp. 130–35.

139 Fruin, *Het economisch*, p. 44.

140 NIMH, 010B/34, Netherlands Forces Intelligence Service, 'Compilation of NEFIS interrogation reports 1239–1243', 26 March 1945, p. 6.

141 Stoler, *Capitalism*, p. 97.

also tea or oil palm, and depended almost entirely on a large migrant Javanese labour force.[142] In 1942, Sumatra's estate labour force had some 339,000 'full consumers', defined as those plantation residents for whom estate owners were required to find food and counting each male plantation worker as 1.0, a woman as 0.8 and a child as 0.5. Overall, some 450,000 people lived on plantations, equivalent to a quarter of East Sumatra's 1943 population of 1.86 million.[143] That was probably only somewhat more than the number living on Malayan rubber estates, which in 1940 employed 324,000 workers, of whom 214,000 were Indians.[144]

A heavy reliance on imports made food security for East Sumatra's plantation workers precarious. In 1939, the Dutch colonial government tried to put estate food supply on a more secure basis by enacting a compulsory cultivation ordinance to encourage subsistence production. During most of 1942, this requirement, and stocks of rice sufficient for three to six months' supply which planters' associations required member estates to maintain, largely averted food shortage.

Beginning in 1943, however, new measures were needed to counter acute food scarcity. These were formulated under Japanese auspices, and made use of the relative abundance of land on and around estates in East Sumatra. Estate workers were initially conscripted to grow food on estates, but before long this changed to an allocation of estate land in parcels of 0.6 hectares, on two-year leases renewable for a further two years, for cultivating food. Tobacco estates were the most easily converted to subsistence cultivation but on the perennial-crop estates of rubber, oil palm and tea some 52,600 hectares (129,977 acres) of land, amounting to 14.3 per cent of the 1942 planted area, were cleared. According to Pelzer, '[T]housands of landless laborers formerly dependent upon the food rations . . . were suddenly able to grow their own food. Many left the plantation barracks, built simple houses on their newly acquired lots, and began to develop small garden plots by planting fruit trees, bushes and hedgerows.'[145] This analysis may, however, apply principally to single wage labourers. They were generally housed in barracks (*pendopok*) and, without seeds or tools, almost entirely dependent on external food supplies.

The altered status of single wage labourers was not the only wartime change. Possibly it was not even the main one, since many other wage labourers lived on estates with their families. By 1940, these workers were generally housed in company-provided family dwellings arranged as compounds/villages scattered

142 Pelzer, *Pioneer settlement*, p. 228.

143 In 1930 in Sumatra, 435,298 Indonesians lived on the grounds of estates. Netherlands Indies, *Volkstelling 1930*, vol. 4, p. 104.

144 Malaya, *Rubber statistics handbook 1940*, p. 34.

145 Pelzer, *Planter*, p. 125 and see pp. 123–27; Stoler, *Capitalism*, pp. 97–100.

across estate lands. The dwellings came with attached garden plots and the workers had seeds, tools, storage facilities and mutual assistance during the harvest. Given this access to the requirements for more cultivation, it seems likely that when estate production slumped, families cleared additional plots for subsistence farming, a usual reaction throughout Southeast Asia to harsh conditions of rural dwellers with access to land.[146]

Single labourers may therefore have been the main group to leave estates and trek to nearby cities. Possibly families were often the plantation workers referred to by Stoler, who had acquired squatters' rights, having exercised an undefined, quasi-entitlement contingent on continued ties to their former estate. With the impetus which occupation afforded, a 'massive squatter movement emerged'. After the war, it gained strength and squatters encroached further onto estate land.[147]

Despite many East Sumatran plantation workers gaining access to land, malnutrition and malaria took a heavy toll. According to 1946 Dutch intelligence reports, only 15 to 25 per cent of estate workers were physically fit to work.[148] They were, nevertheless, better off than many other estate workers drafted by the Japanese as forced labour. For estate workers, due to inadequate food and medical care, death rates were high and largely explain a reduction by 15 per cent in the number of 'full consumers', from 339,000 in 1942 to 288,000 in 1945.[149]

The population of larger urban areas in the Outer Islands tended to increase substantially during the Japanese occupation because people, now no longer with work in the countryside, drifted to cities in the hope of somehow finding sufficient food. There was a cityward drift in East Sumatra.[150] Although the outcome there of an urban migration strategy is unknown, it would not necessarily have proved successful for migrants, as shown by the experience of many displaced Java estate workers. As in Java, in other Indonesian settings without a hinterland of estates, migration to urban areas shifted rather than solved the problem of hunger. Many people in Macassar, where population increased by 50 per cent, died of starvation after the rice crop in south Celebes failed and the second maize crop completely dried up due to an exceptionally dry west monsoon.[151] By 1944, although in Macassar food was less scarce, the city

146 I owe this analysis to Pierre van der Eng in private communication.
147 Stoler, *Capitalism*, p. 207 and see p. 98.
148 Ibid., p. 99.
149 Pelzer, *Planter*, pp. 126–27.
150 Ibid., p. 125.
151 OSS, assemblage 45, *Manpower in Japan and occupied areas*, vol. 2, p. 286; NIMH, 010A/10, Netherlands Forces Intelligence Service, 'Interrogation of three Boeginese survivors', 24 July 1944, p. 5.

of Menado had serious shortages and all former Chinese shopkeepers now cultivated their own gardens.[152]

Rice-Producing Areas: Cochinchina, Thailand and Burma

Even in specialized rice-producing areas wartime declines in welfare were considerable and, furthermore, worsened substantially by the latter part of the war. Welfare levels fell for two main reasons. One was a loss in income from export markets along with the disappearance of imported consumer goods; the other that rice land was often poorly suited to alternative crops. Both considerations applied particularly to Lower Burma. Living standards there fell much more than in Southeast Asia's other rice bowls of Cochinchina and Thailand's central plain.[153]

Of the two latter, each, of course, suffered the deprivations common to Southeast Asia of a lack of clothing, other basic consumer goods, medicines and some previously imported food, notably milk. However, the ready availability of rice, indeed a superfluity, which left large unused stocks especially in Saigon after 1943, and more diversified economies than Lower Burma's ensured that most people could obtain adequate calories and a reasonably balanced diet. In the south of Indochina, it was reported in May 1946, 'there has been no famine, nor are there at present any signs of serious malnutrition among the public or patients coming to the reopened hospitals'. Almost certainly, vital statistics would reveal a more nuanced picture of the effects of occupation on birth rates and the causes of death. However, as the report observed for Indochina: 'During the Japanese occupation no vital statistics appear to have been kept; and nearly all the records of previous years were destroyed or lost. The hospitals were empty and the equipment was looted.'[154] An increased death rate in Indochina as a whole was attributed mainly to malaria, due to a lack of quinine which before the war had been largely imported.[155]

By Southeast Asian standards, food shortages in Thailand, as in Cochinchina, were modest. The first and most important reason for this was that specialization in rice, rather than a non-food like rubber, helped to ensure the availability of the staple food for the large majority of the population. Rice apart, Thailand was probably less subject to scarcities than Cochinchina, and in many instances, with the notable exceptions of tinned milk and salt, these were felt by only a small minority of people, mainly those living in Bangkok.

[152] NIMH, 010A/18, Netherlands Forces Intelligence Service, 'Netherlands Forces interrogation report 184, part 3', 18 October 1944, p. 2.

[153] Andrus, *Burmese economic life*, pp. 335–36; Christian, *Burma*, p. 124.

[154] ANM, 1957/0619022 MU #442/1946A, 'Special commissioner in South East Asia conference on nutrition May 1946', p. 17.

[155] OSS, R&A 1715, *Indochina's war-time government*, p. 44.

The Kingdom's population of about 15 million split between around 6 million in Central Thailand and 9 million in the rest of the country. Central Thailand encompassed Thailand's great rice-exporting region, but most other areas also had rice surpluses with which to feed themselves. The extension of the railway had stimulated rice production in the north beyond Uttaradit and in the north-east past Khorat and enabled these areas, like the centre, to become rice exporters (Figure 5.1).[156] The Kra Isthmus and the island of Phuket were tin-mining and rubber-growing areas, and although with acreages under rice, also depended on imports from Burma. That trade was interrupted by the war, causing shortages. In peninsular Thailand including Phuket, significant numbers of workers, many of them Chinese, were partly or even chiefly dependent on rubber cultivation or tin mining.[157] Rubber estates were often rather small and commonly relied on hired hands. During the war, although many estates ceased production, estate workers, as noted in Chapter 4, were apparently frequently able to migrate to more highly paid occupations.[158] In Thailand's mountainous northern and western districts and on the Khorat Plateau, upwards of a million people depended on shifting cultivation for food, and during the war this probably continued more or less uninterrupted.[159]

The second principal reason why in comparison to most Southeast Asians Thai were much less affected by the war – nutritionally as well as by shortages of consumer goods – derived from Thailand's economic structure of widespread land ownership and high degree of self-sufficiency. The Thai economy, Ingram observed, had 'an extremely broad subsistence base onto which the money economy has been grafted'.[160] Some 80 per cent of peasants lived mainly in a self-subsistent economy.[161] Salient features of Thailand's rural economy were that agriculture engaged 89 per cent of people in 1937, and a similar proportion raised rice for their own use; 90 per cent or more of cultivated land was under rice; 85 per cent of cultivated land was operated by owners; and a relatively small proportion of farmers were in debt. Furthermore, rural indebtedness was mainly to family or friends, and abundant land still existed for anyone without land.[162] Rice and fish were the main constituents of the Thai diet. Fish could be caught even in canals and

156 Ingram, *Economic change*, pp. 45–47; Kakizaki, *Laying*, pp. 171–81.
157 Ouyyanont, *Regional economic history*, pp. 247–58.
158 NA, WO203/2647, 'Summary of economic intelligence (Far East) no. 130', 15 October 1945, p. 3.
159 Dobby, *Southeast Asia*, pp. 270–71.
160 Ingram, *Economic change*, p. 128 and see Yang, *Multiple exchange rate system*, pp. 4–5; Reeve, *Public administration*, pp. 4–5.
161 de Young, *Village life*, p. 193.
162 Kingdom of Thailand, *Thailand economic farm survey*, pp. 62–63, 250–51; Ingram, *Economic change*, pp. 50, 55, 57, 66–67, 144; de Young, Village life, p. 186; Manarungsan, *Economic development*, p. 70.

waterholes. Thai farmers also generally grew vegetables, although those in the country's centre concentrated on rice. People in the north-east were disadvantaged because they had to depend on dried fish during most of the year and because the region lacked sufficient water for vegetable cultivation.[163] It is unclear, however, to what extent the wartime disruption of transport exacerbated those disadvantages by making it difficult to trade with other parts of Thailand.

Even in Thailand's central plain, farmers' consumption had quite a low import content.[164] Textiles, yarns, kerosene and tinned milk were widely consumed, but otherwise the wartime cessation of imports had relatively little effect on the bulk of the population, since most other imported goods were bought chiefly by the foreign community, by Chinese and by higher income groups, all located principally in Bangkok. Consumer-goods imports, apart from a few items like medicines, kerosene and salt, do not seem to have been necessary to maintain the basic minimum standard of living.[165] Outside Bangkok, living standards in Central Thailand were probably more affected by the war than in many other regions. Because of a high specialization in rice, average incomes in Central Thailand were considerably above those in most of rural Thailand and there was a greater reliance on imported goods, many of which were in short supply during the war. While throughout Thailand serious shortages of textiles developed and this brought out some of the old spinning wheels and looms, even here the Thai were better placed than other Southeast Asians, since, as noted in Chapter 4, Thailand manufactured about a third of domestic textile requirements, a high proportion for Southeast Asia.[166] However, by 1944, salt, because of the difficulties of transport, became hard to obtain in some parts of Thailand; a picul cost 6 baht in Bangkok but 120 to 200 baht in the north.[167]

A third reason for the war's limited effect on Thailand was that the country suffered war damage only relatively late in hostilities and there was no major anti-Japanese guerrilla presence, as in Malaya and the Philippines. Fighting did not seriously affect rice production. Nor was Thailand divided into autarkic zones like most other Southeast Asian countries, with consequent disruption of the flow of goods additional to transport shortages.

Vital statistics for Thailand may be incomplete and skewed because of the disproportionate inclusion of Bangkok, areas contiguous to it and a few other cities (Table 7.8).[168] Nevertheless, available data afford an indication of the war's impact on Thai living standards, pressured by the uncertainties of occupation, alliance with Japan, Allied bombing and shortages of some essential

[163] de Young, *Village life*, pp. 183–84.
[164] Manarungsan, *Economic development*, p. 80.
[165] Ingram, *Economic change*, pp. 130–31; Reeve, *Public administration*, p. 67.
[166] de Young, *Village life*, p. 103.
[167] Numnonda, *Thailand*, p. 89.
[168] Anamwathana, 'Economic policy', p. 84.

Table 7.8 *Thailand crude birth, death and infant mortality rates 1937/38–1950*

	Births	Deaths	Infant mortality (per 1,000 live births)
1937/38	34.9	17.2	104
1938/39	34.2	15.1	91
1939/40	36.5	16.9	101
1940	35.5	17.0	110
1941	35.4	16.6	100
1942	32.6	15.1	95
1943	33.9	17.1	97
1944	30.8	16.9	99
1945	25.7	16.4	106
1946	24.0	15.1	95
1947	23.7	13.4	80
1948	23.9	10.7	68
1949	27.8	10.5	66
1950	28.4	10.0	62

Sources: Kingdom of Thailand, *Statistical yearbook, 1939/40–1944*, p. 96; *1945–1955*, p. 94.

goods. Deaths did not rise above those recorded in the 1930s, which is consistent with a preservation of general nutrition (as argued above). In other ways, the picture was mixed. The birth rate, which had held steady at around 35 per thousand during the 1930s, dropped to 25.7 in 1945 and did not start to recover until 1949. Despite the stability of overall death rates, deaths from malaria, owing to the lack of quinine, rose by 60 per cent, from 213.6 per 100,000 of population in 1940 to a peak of 341.0 in 1943, and then declined slightly.[169] Infant mortality increased significantly in 1945, but during the war did not show the decisive upwards trend which might have been expected because of the upsurge in malaria and possibly also a shortage of tinned milk. Almost as soon as the war ended, infant deaths fell sharply, suggesting that this might have occurred earlier except for the occupation. However, much of the later improvement was probably because government concern about infant deaths led to post-war maternal and child health programmes on a national scale.[170]

169 de Young, *Village life*, p. 177; Kingdom of Thailand, *Statistical yearbook, 1939/40–1944*, p. 98.

170 Kingdom of Thailand, *Public health*, p. 11.

Unlike ethnic Thai, large numbers of Chinese in rural areas and small towns did not escape occupation lightly. Even before occupation and continuing into 1943, the Thai government specified numerous 'prohibited areas' for aliens, the status of many Chinese living in Thailand. Said to be strategically sensitive, these areas included *changwat* (regional divisions) which had army bases, and most of the route of the Thailand–Burma railway. Anti-Chinese discrimination, as part of Prime Minister Phibun's Thai-ification programme beginning in December 1938, was probably also behind the prohibition. Forced evacuation at short notice from prohibited areas created large flows of destitute Chinese refugees, most of whom went south, including to Bangkok. Many of those who ended up there were induced to sign contracts to work on the Thailand–Burma railway.[171]

The maintenance of food security in Burma differed from Thailand in two crucial respects. One was that each of Burma's main regions, although surplus in some essential foodstuffs, was deficit in others, the second that this made transport fundamental to food supplies. Reflective of Burma's status as the world's greatest exporter of rice, a reduction of even 40 per cent in paddy cultivation would still have left the country self-sufficient in rice. It was anticipated that in Burma, 'there should be no shortages or starvation provided distribution is good'.[172] However, it was not: the destruction by 1943 of about half of Burma's transport system (Chapter 5), and the extension of Japanese control over almost all remaining modern transport, made serious food shortages inevitable. In 1944, distribution was further impeded by the division of Burma into four administrative regions as part of General Ogawa's plan for local self-sufficiency because, as elsewhere in potential Southeast Asian war zones, this was militarily desirable.-[173] Shortages affected all of Burma with the possible exception of some sparsely populated areas in the horseshoe of hills surrounding the Irrawaddy Valley where Shans, Kachins and Chins predominated, and where transport was so poor that people had, of necessity, to be largely self-sufficient. However, remote regions of Burma with difficulties of transport between valleys had a history of isolated famines and, as noted below, famine may have happened to some extent at the end of the Japanese occupation, or just after it.[174]

Rice cultivation was concentrated in Lower Burma, the delta area in the south near Rangoon, which encompassed the 13 so-called principal rice-growing districts. Lower Burma (also referred to as the Lower Burma Wet Zone) was 'a great one-crop area': rice was the only crop of any importance. That largely reflected geographical reality and comparative advantage: much of the land, about a third of which was only slightly above the high tide level, was

171 Skinner, *Chinese society*, pp. 264–78.
172 Burma Intelligence Bureau, *Burma*, vol. 1, p. 67 and see pp. 66–67.
173 OSS, R&A 2077, *Economic reorganization of Burma*, pp. 3–4.
174 Burma Intelligence Bureau, *Burma*, vol. 2, pp. 173, 175; Spate, 'Burmese village', pp. 527–28; Richell, *Disease*, pp. 12, 211–14; Andrus, *Burmese economic life*, p. 336.

of little use for alternative crops.[175] Clothing and other foodstuffs except fish and salt had to be brought from the Central Burma Dry Zone (also called the Upper Burma Dry Zone), which included Mandalay, or imported from abroad. Central Burma, deficit in rice, obtained it from Lower Burma, sometimes in great quantity, as well as from a second, but much smaller, rice-growing district north of Burma's dry centre, the Upper Burma Wet Zone. The central region also consumed *ngapi* (pastes made of fish or shrimp) and dried and salt fish originating in the delta and along the sea coast. In return, Central Burma supplied Lower Burma with cooking oil, vegetables, gram (bean flour) and a number of other products widely eaten in the south.[176]

By late 1943, substantial price differences between the regions, which widened over the remainder of the war, indicate the progressive breakdown of transport in Burma and increasing local shortages and surpluses. Japan had no transport available to move rice northwards from Lower Burma nor the means to carry it to the home islands or elsewhere in Asia. Despite large output contractions, big rice surpluses quickly built up in Lower Burma.[177] Figure 7.8 and Table 7.9 show the great disparity in rice prices across Burma by the autumn of 1943 and spring of 1944. In much of the southern delta area, even without adjusting for high inflation, prices fell below a pre-war level of 3.5 Burma rupees (Rs.) a basket (75 lbs). The centre and north experienced shortages which drove up rice prices to large multiples of those in the south.

To analyse the divergence of rice prices across space and time, Table 7.9 and Figure 7.9 divide Burma into five main areas: one is three districts near the 13 principal rice-growing districts, shown with their different administrative district names (Karenni, Salween and Tavoy). The other four are the divisions of Arakan, Magway, Mandalay and Sagaing, each of which comprised a number of districts. Between 1940/41 and 1943/44, the disparity in prices between the 13 rice-growing districts and the rest of Burma widened markedly. For Burma as a whole, the coefficient of variation (the standard deviation divided by the mean and so a measure of dispersion) rose from around 0.17 before the war to 0.51 in 1942/43 and then in 1943/44 more than doubled to 1.10, as transport became ever more difficult. In 1946/47, the coefficient dropped back to 0.14, about its pre-war level, because an at least partial restoration of transport enabled markets again to function efficiently.

Before the war, rice prices in Mandalay were about the same as, or even lower than, in the 13 principal rice-growing districts. By 1943/44, however, Mandalay prices exceeded those in the south by a factor of almost 10, before falling back in 1945/46 to about double southern prices as communications

[175] Burma Intelligence Bureau, *Burma*, vol. 2, p. 173 for the quotation and see Dobby, *Monsoon Asia*, p. 182; Andrus, *Burmese economic life*, p. 63.

[176] Burma Intelligence Bureau, *Burma*, vol. 2, pp. 173, 184.

[177] Ibid., vol. 1, p. 19, vol. 2, p. 180.

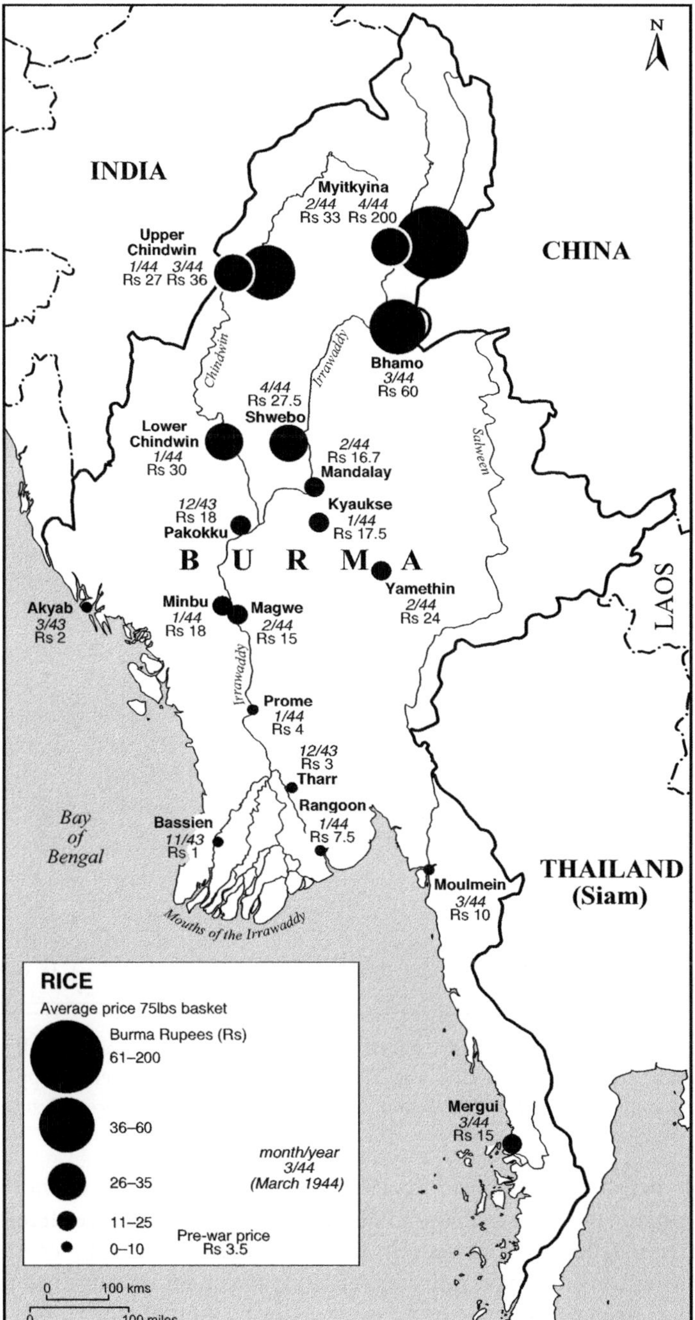

Figure 7.8 Burma rice price disparities 1943 and 1944
Source: Burma Intelligence Bureau, *Burma*, vol. 2, p. 177.

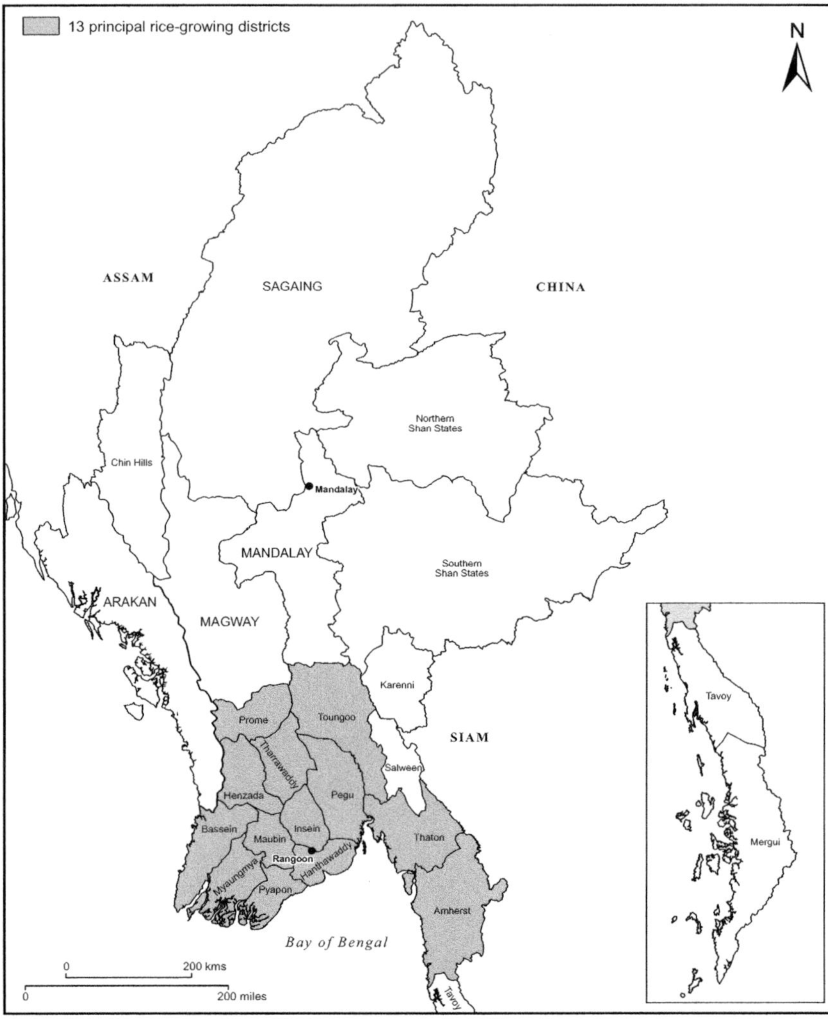

Figure 7.9 Burma 13 principal rice districts and other main geographical divisions
Sources: India, *Census of India, 1931. vol. XI. Burma. part I, Report*, p. between pp. x and 1; India, *Census of India, 1921. vol. X. Burma. part I. Report*, p. 2; Cheng, *Rice industry*, p. xxvi.

channels began to normalize. By 1943/44 in Sagaing in the far north, rice prices, roughly the same as in the 13 districts before the war, were almost seven times higher. The lesser increase in the north compared to the central area around Mandalay may have reflected relatively lower demand due to a smaller, poorer, less urban population and a greater substitution of other foods for rice prompted by high transport costs to so distant a region.

Table 7.9 *Burma harvest-time paddy prices and price differences of other areas of Burma from the 13 principal rice-growing districts 1938/39–1946/47*

	1938/39	1939/40	1940/41	1942/43	1943/44	1945/46	1946/47
a) Burma paddy prices coefficient of variation	0.21	0.16	0.17	0.51	1.10	0.42	0.14
b) Burma paddy prices and price differences							
	1938/39	1939/40	1940/41	1942/43	1943/44	1945/46	1946/47
	Average price in 13 principal rice districts (rupees per 100 baskets)						
	84.9	107.8	123.5	45.8	124.6	159.8	281.7
	Difference from average price in 13 principal rice districts (%)						
Three districts near the 13 districts	84.4	99.7	113.0	83.6	328.9	377.4	355.6
Arkan	107.2	114.2	128.4	70.7	229.6	153.1	296.7
Magwe % of price in 13 districts	82.4	117.8	120.1	94.2	651.2	321.5	292.0
Magway	82.4	117.8	120.1	94.2	651.2	321.5	292.0
Mandalay	77.7	113.0	128.4	117.8	1177.5	302.6	293.2
Sagaing	64.8	104.8	115.4	109.5	710.1	376.8	280.3

Notes: The 13 principal rice-growing districts are: Pegu, Tharrawaddy, Hanthawaddy, Insein, Prome, Bassein, Henzada, Myaumgmya, Maubin, Pyapon, Thaton, Amherst and Toungoo. The 3 districts near the 13 districts are: Salween, Tavoy and Mergui. Arkan consists of Akyab, Northern Arakan, Kyaukse and Sandoway. Magway consists of Thayetmyo, Minbu, Magway and Pakkoku. Mandalay consists of Mandalay, Kyaukse Meiktila, Myingyan and Yamethin. Sagaing consists of Bhamo, Myitkyina, Shwebo, Sagaing, Katha, Upper Chindwin and Lower Chindwin.

Sources: Burma, *Season and crop report*, 1938/39–1946/47; Takahashi, 'Regional differences', p. 166.

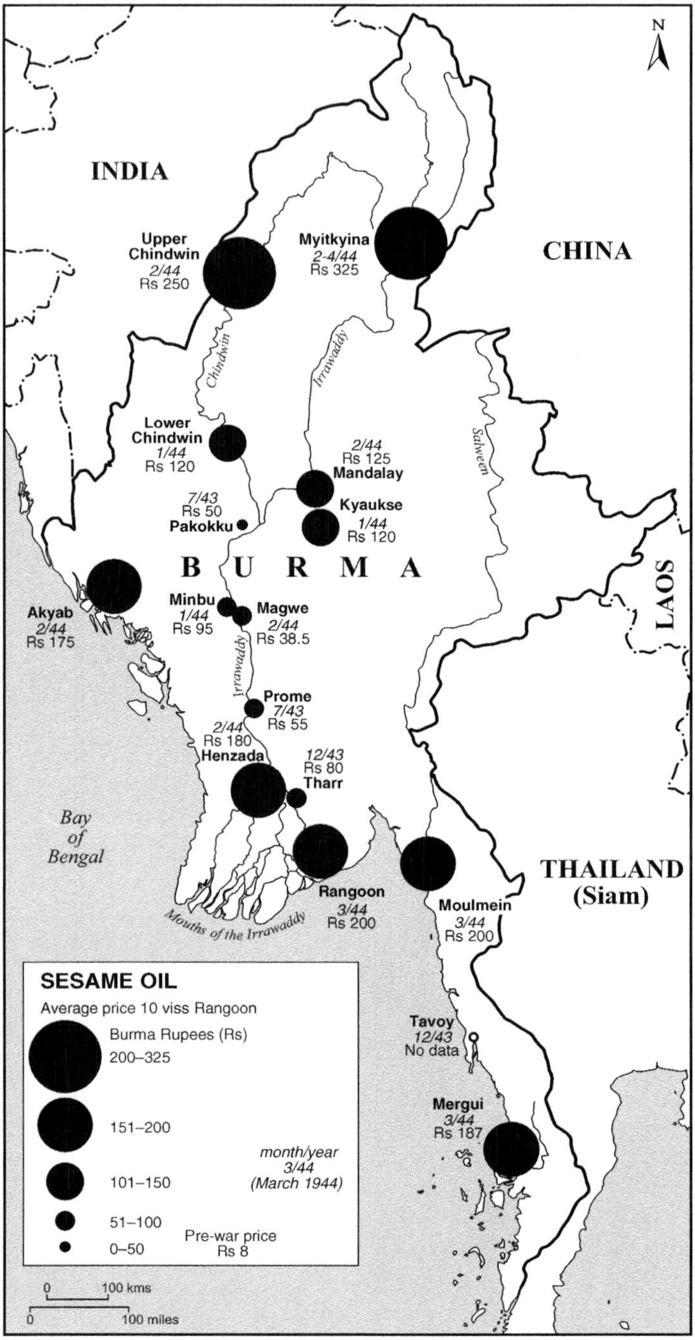

Figure 7.10 Burma sesame oil price disparities 1943 and 1944
Source: Burma Intelligence Bureau, *Burma*, vol. 2, p. 178.

The pattern for sesame oil, basic to Burmese cooking, contrasted markedly with rice (Figures 7.8 and 7.10). Central Burma produced some 95 per cent of Burma's output of oil. Compared to the pre-war level, prices in the centre, including around Mandalay, did not skyrocket, but in late 1943 and early 1944 in Lower Burma were still about twice as high and even higher in the north.

Before the war, Burma relied heavily on imported cotton goods, partly owing to the coarseness of locally grown cotton (Chapter 5). However, some traditional textile production existed everywhere in the country. Domestic output was most concentrated in the north, where the economy was relatively little specialized and cotton was grown. Figure 7.11 depicts the large rise in the price of cotton *longyis*, worn by nearly all Burmese, from a pre-war average of Rs.1.5 to around 30 times that level by the latter stages of the war. While these higher prices must have cut into living standards throughout the country, price rises were somewhat less in northern areas, perhaps reflecting more traditional spinning and weaving. However, only inhabitants of remote hill areas and a few villages in cotton-growing districts spun enough thread to provide for their own clothing.[178]

The lack of transport that prevented rice from reaching Central Burma also impeded a flow of goods from there to Lower Burma. Whether, by the end of the war, its rural population suffered as high an incidence of malnutrition as Rangoon (Chapter 8) is uncertain but likely. Certainly, the south, as well as facing acute shortages of cloth, clothing and thread to repair garments, was short of cooking oil and other usual foods. Diets also deteriorated due to a great diminution in the fish catch, only partly made good by the slaughter of work cattle.[179] As rice prices fell relative to those for indispensable household items, foodstuffs and cloth, Lower Burma cultivators increasingly turned to other, non-agricultural pursuits including trade, war-related jobs and manual labour. Earnings from these subsidiary occupations were, according to the 1943/44 crop report, 'what saves the cultivator from disaster'.[180]

The shortage of transport made famine a danger in Central and Upper Burma by mid-1944. In Mandalay, the rice situation was described as 'serious'.[181] The Burmese government feared that the scarcity of rice might lead to food riots.[182] Upper Burma was also threatened with famine. While the

178 NARA, RG226, entry 154, box 79, file 1310, 'A survey of processing capacity in Burma', 18 October 1944, p.4.

179 Burma Intelligence Bureau, *Burma*, vol. 2, pp. 70–71, 114, 173–92 and vol. 1, pp. 66–67, 77–80; Guyot, 'Uses of Buddhism', pp. 50–51.

180 Burma, *Season and crop report 1944*, p. 13.

181 IOR, Clague Papers, Mss Eur E252/44, U Htin Wa, 'Eyewitness account', p. 6.

182 Burma Intelligence Bureau, *Burma*, vol. 2, p. 180.

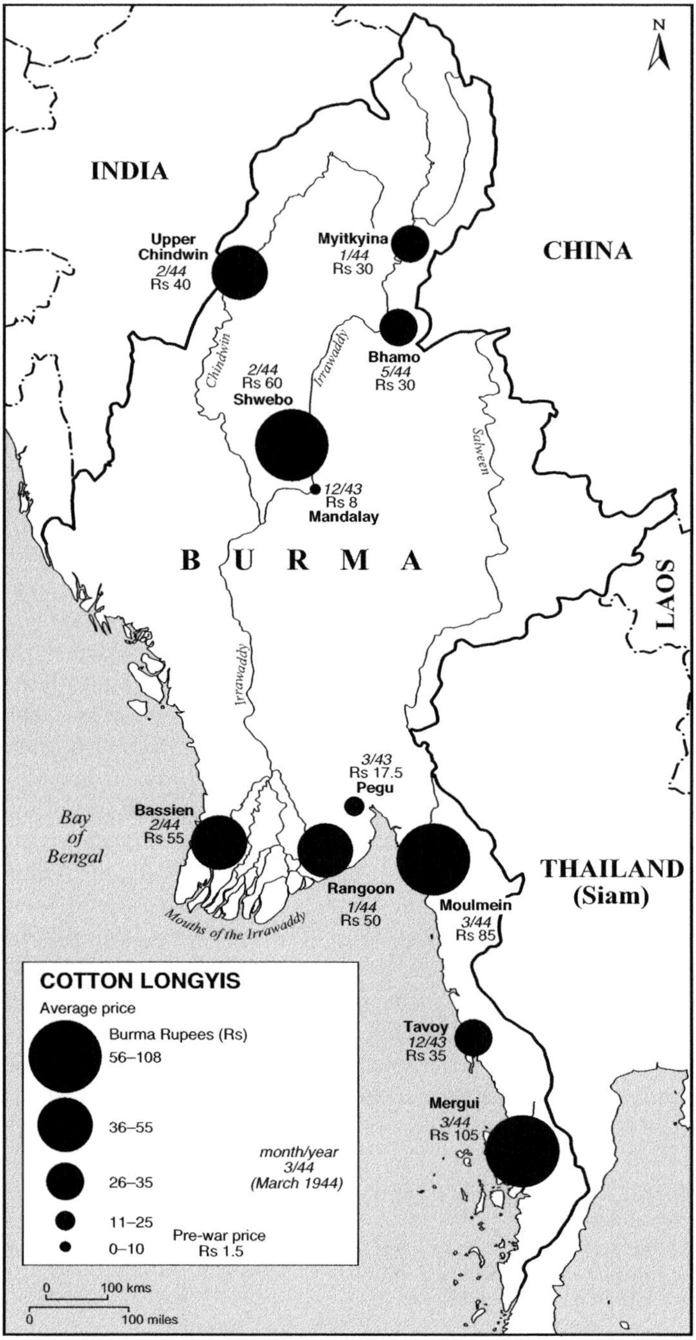

Figure 7.11 Burma cotton *longyis* price disparities 1943 and 1944
Source: Burma Intelligence Bureau, *Burma*, vol. 2, p. 179.

Ba Maw government did not control transport which would have allowed rice shipments to avert possible famine, the Burmese District Political Advisor formulated a strategy of preparing a series of rough cart tracks over which 'convoys of food' could move northwards.[183] The plan may not, however, have materialized as fierce fighting spread over Burma. In 1946, Upper Burma was said to be on the 'verge of famine'.[184]

One scholar states that in Burma's northern areas there is 'little doubt that the famine was a substantial one'.[185] The assertion is not, however, accompanied by evidence, although the disruption of war resulted in many refugees and displaced persons, exacerbated food shortages and badly affected those in more remote hill areas. However, by the time of British re-occupation even Tharrawaddy in Lower Burma and, to a lesser extent, Prome, were thronged with refugees starved out of the Pegu Yomas (the area between the lower Irrawaddy and Sittang rivers). In August 1945, the British military administration reported that: 'Cases of starvation, rare in Burma, have occurred among the hill people in Hsipaw [in the Shan area]. A special relief camp for these destitutes has been opened.'[186] There was also 'news of up to 30,000 starving people in the Loikaw area [in the Karen states] on the Japanese retreat lines from the Kalaw area who will need immediate assistance as soon as they can be reached'.[187]

Conclusion

As in nearly every aspect of Southeast Asian economic life, food supply during the war and Japanese occupation emphasized how globally integrated the region had become over the first four decades of the twentieth century. Due to this integration, when, beginning in 1942, Southeast Asia was almost entirely cut off from international trade and domestic exchange was sharply curtailed, living standards suffered badly and in some areas catastrophically. Even less globalized parts of Southeast Asia, the 'traditional' halves of its dual economies, did not stand apart from high pre-war economic integration and so were caught up in the scarcities of food and nearly all basic consumer goods that affected the region. In occupied Southeast Asia, cuts in consumption described in this chapter were in food and non-durable goods. Because of this, the hardships

183 OSS, R&A 2015, *Japanese administration of Burma*, 10 July 1944, p. 54 and see pp. 54–55, 60.

184 Tinker, *Union of Burma*, p. 287.

185 Scott, 'Approach', p. 280.

186 MNA, 1/5 98 BMA progress report no. 6 to 15 August 1945, p. 2.

187 MNA, 1/5 98 BMA Report, June 1945, p. 3 and Fortnightly progress report no. 6 to 15 August 1945, p. 2.

imposed were greater and more widespread than if cuts had been mainly confined to durable goods. Poor and lower income groups suffered badly and probably disproportionately owing to the pattern of consumption reductions, which fell heavily on the common necessities, not just the luxuries of relatively few.

Areas specialized in food exports, which principally meant rice, weathered the occupation better than their non-food-specialized counterparts. However, a lack of transport was a constraint in all of Southeast Asia, and impacted food-growing regions. In Burma, despite large rice surpluses, transport shortages prevented rice from moving northwards where it was needed, while in the south virtually complete specialization in growing paddy left its cultivators without a number of basic foods normally supplied by the north.

Where population density was high and land at a premium, in northern Vietnam and Java, famine prematurely ended the lives of some 3.4 million people. Although unfavourable weather (Tonkin and North Annam) and Japanese policies and to some extent drought (Java) caused these famines, they could largely have been avoided if different policy decisions had been taken. A willingness to divert some transport from the military and to use it instead to carry food to affected areas could have substantially reduced death rates in Vietnam.

Land was a key consideration in avoiding occupation's most detrimental consequences for food and nutrition. Access to land enabled large numbers of people in Malaya, Indonesia's Outer Islands and the Philippines to grow sufficient of their own food to scrape through the occupation. However, adaptation towards self-sufficiency proved difficult for former estate workers, Indians in Malaya and Javanese in East Sumatra, possibly because they did not have experience in growing food, because they lacked necessary tools and other inputs, and because in getting started they needed advice and help which were in short supply within their own social group.

Southeast Asia's major cities, although seriously short of food, were on the whole less impacted by food shortages than the countryside. Chapter 8 deals with urban food scarcity and efforts to counter it through rationing and the cultivation of any available land in the cities or peripheral areas. An important point made in the chapter is that city and countryside were not separate but part of a single, linked economy. Because of this linkage, several of the main Southeast Asian cities received large inflows of migrants fleeing rural food scarcity.

Illustration 10 Plywood boat construction in Singapore 1944 (HERMES-IR: Pre-World War II Asia, Ref. code: 2713. Hitotsubashi University Library).
Japanese forces lacked sufficient local transport in Southeast Asia and, as pictured here, tried to build boats using locally available materials (Chapter 5).

Illustration 11 Singapore factory producing rubber coverings 1944 (HERMES-IR: Pre-World War II Asia, Ref. code: 2666. Hitotsubashi University Library).
The Japanese attempted to develop industry in Southeast Asia to contribute to the war effort. The photo illustrates one such attempt while the use of what appears to be child labour reflects the labour shortage the Japanese faced by 1944 (Chapter 5).

Illustration 12 Train on the Thailand–Burma railway crossing a bridge over the Mae Klong (Kwai Yai) River c. 1945 (AWM P00761027).
Southeast Asian transport ran predominantly north–south, while Japan's military required east–west transport links. The Thailand–Burma railway was one of the Japanese attempts to construct these links (Chapter 5).

Illustration 13 Penang Japanese-issued peace living certificate (NAS, 19980005536–0018).
In Malaya, a certificate like this one was needed to obtain food rations.

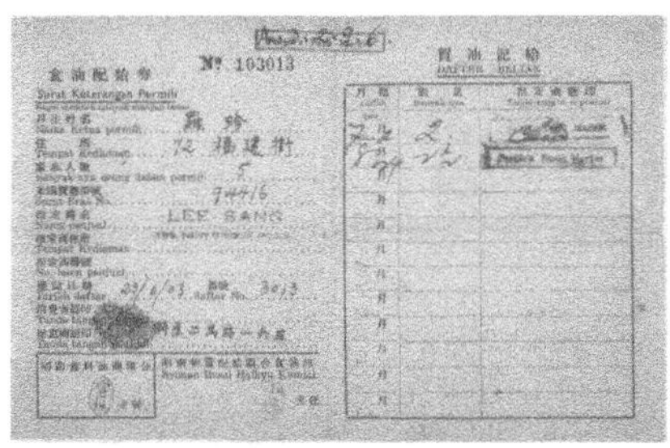

Illustration 14 Singapore Japanese-issued ration card in Malaya (NAS, 19980005130–0047).
Every Southeast Asian country had to institute food rationing and many Southeast Asians relied on rations to help them stay alive under wartime conditions of acute scarcity (Chapters 6, 7 and 8).

Illustration 15 Transport in Southeast Asia (HERMES-IR: Pre-World War II Asia, Ref. code: 2587. Hitotsubashi University Library).
Acute transport shortages soon developed throughout Southeast Asia. Almost all Southeast Asians had to rely on walking or on pre-modern transport, as shown in this Singapore street scene.

Illustration 16 ABCD encirclement (Reddit courtesy Carlos Menica).
Japan, as shown here, promised to break the ABCD (American, British, Chinese and Dutch) ring of chains binding Southeast Asia and liberate its peoples from colonialism and oppression.

Illustration 17 Vietnam famine victims, early 1945 (NARA, RG226, entry 139, box 5, file 60).
3.4 million Southeast Asians died prematurely due to wartime famines in Vietnam and Java. The photo shows some of Vietnam's famine victims (Chapter 7).

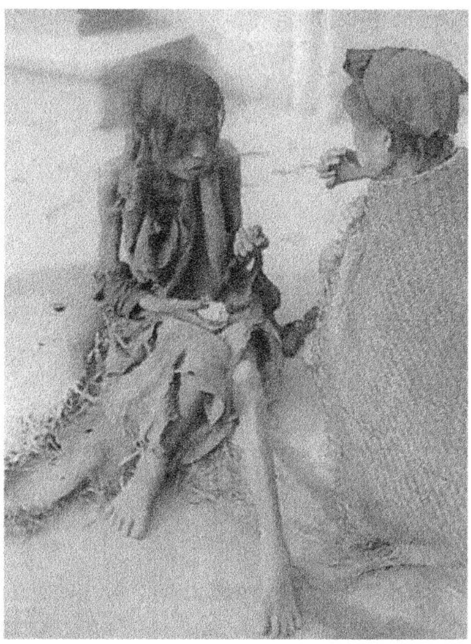

Illustration 18 Vietnam famine, early 1945 (NARA, RG226, entry 139, box 5, file 60). In the Vietnamese famine many had nothing to wear but rags and straw matting. The famine was fundamental to the September 1945 Viet Minh/communist revolution (Chapter 7 and Epilogue).

8

Food and Living Standards in Urban Southeast Asia

Just ten cities comprised all the large pre-war cities in their respective six Southeast Asian countries: Rangoon, Bangkok, Singapore, Penang, Kuala Lumpur, Jakarta, Surabaya, Saigon-Cholon, Hanoi and Manila. This chapter constructs the first set of World War II population data for the ten cities and analyses population movements in them. Both trends and fluctuations could be sizeable and are principally accounted for by two factors. One was the availability of food, the key determinant of living standards for the great majority of Southeast Asians. The other was personal safety. Although this included a desire to avoid the Japanese occupiers, the main motive was to move away from the havoc of warfare. Throughout the war, urban populations responded to the trade-off between food and fear: people weighed the risks of insufficient food against arbitrarily imposed external war-related dangers. The shifting balance between these risks substantially explains two contrasting patterns of wartime urbanization: rapid population growth in some cities but evacuation and population loss in others.

Analysis of wartime demographic trends helps to correct a misperception that World War II brought de-urbanization to Southeast Asia. According to Scott, the war reversed a pre-war demographic pattern of a movement from village to city. There was a general retreat from the urban economy as people fled cities in favour of subsistence agriculture.[1] Similarly, Collingham speaks of the war as 'undoing the process of urbanization and driving the hungry population back into the countryside to undertake subsistence farming'.[2] Contrary to any such substantial wartime return to the countryside, Southeast Asia's main cities typically gained large numbers of new inhabitants.[3] In such cities, the decisive factor was some existing entitlement to food or other means of obtaining it. On the whole, cities best met these needs, and throughout occupied Southeast Asia population shifted accordingly. The Japanese occupation had significance for post-war Southeast Asian urbanization because it confirmed and solidified the region's pre-war urban pattern. In Singapore, Penang, Kuala Lumpur, Jakarta, Surabaya and Manila, the war and the Japanese occupation led to historically unprecedented urban growth.

1 Scott, 'Approach', p. 271.
2 Collingham, *Taste*, p. 235.
3 Clear exceptions were Rangoon and Hanoi.

Urbanization Determinants

Four principal features of pre-war Southeast Asian development, discussed in earlier chapters, had particular relevance in determining wartime urbanization. One key aspect was the region's extreme specialization in a handful of staple commodities. The second, closely associated with the first, was Southeast Asia's division into the non-food specialized countries of Malaya, Indonesia and the Philippines and the rice producers of Burma, Thailand and Indochina. Easy wartime absorption of population back into the surrounding countryside, as limited pre-war urbanization might suggest, did not occur. One reason for this was a third feature of pre-war development: the importance of international immigration from China and India in peopling Southeast Asia. Before the war, when the economy contracted, Chinese and Indian immigrants returned in great numbers to their home countries. After the Japanese occupation, however, this migration 'safety valve' was not available, except for Indians in Burma. Furthermore, by 1941 all Southeast Asia's main cities had a substantial middle class for whom turning to subsistence agriculture was unattractive or even impossible.

A fourth pre-war feature that became a major determinant of wartime demographic shifts was the uneven spread of population across Southeast Asia. Java and Indochina's Tonkin delta and North Annam depended on the option of being able to import food if necessary, a dependence which assumed crisis proportions under occupation conditions of enforced autarky and lack of transport (Chapter 7). When food shortage and famine struck, it caused migration from rural areas to large cities. Just as in Southeast Asia, a similar trend characterized the 1943 Bengal famine and a number of other famines.[4] Although by July 1943 Calcutta was littered with corpses of migrants, there was nevertheless 'little doubt that a destitute who found his way into Calcutta had a much better chance of survival than anywhere else in Bengal'.[5]

Wartime Urbanization

This section analyses how the economic and demographic characteristics of Southeast Asia's urban hinterlands interacted with Japanese military policy largely to determine the urban wartime gain (or loss) of population. Two main patterns of demographic change are evident (Table 8.1 and Figure 8.1).[6] Singapore, Penang, Kuala Lumpur, Jakarta, Surabaya and Manila, lacking hinterlands specialized in producing rice, had restricted wartime access to this staple food. In this group of cities, population grew rapidly and far above historic averages. Between the end of the 1930s or beginning of the 1940s and 1944, growth ranged from 5.6 per cent per annum in Manila to over 6.0 per cent in

4 Ó Gráda, *Black '47*, pp. 11, 93–94, 104, 161–63 and *Famine*, pp. 81–89, 102.

5 Sen, *Poverty*, p. 57.

6 On contrasting urban growth patterns, see also Huff and Huff, 'Urban growth', pp. 527–30.

Singapore and Jakarta. Penang's population came close to doubling between 1941 and 1947. Population gains arose from inwards migration; natural increase was slight, and by the latter part of the war probably negative, in all cities. Wartime Singapore and Jakarta grew to nearly a million; Manila topped that level.

Surabaya and Hanoi resembled Singapore, Penang, Kuala Lumpur, Jakarta and Manila in lacking easy access to rice, but showed interesting variations on the rice-deficit pattern. Throughout the war, Surabaya, a pre-war sugar port, conformed to the classic rice-deficit model. Between 1940 and September 1945, population grew by over half from 403,000 to 618,000. But fear rather than food charted Surabaya's early post-war demography. In November 1945, three months after Japan's surrender, fierce fighting between Indonesian Republicans and British troops emptied the city.[7] Consequently, Surabaya again matched its pre-war population only in 1948. While a dominance of fear of Allied bombing caused Hanoi to lose population until 1944, subsequent famine-induced inwards migration may have

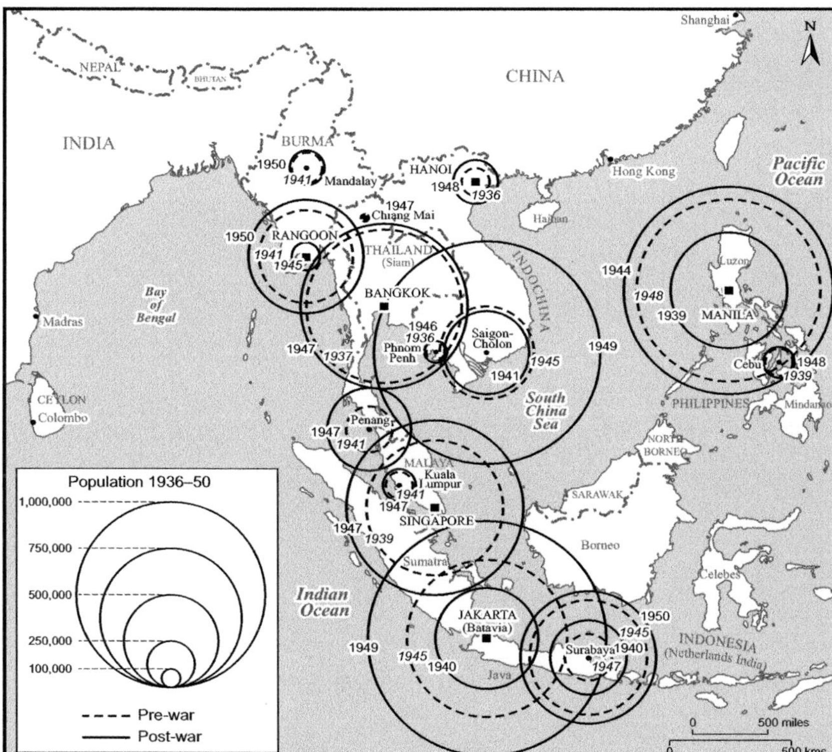

Figure 8.1 Southeast Asia main cities population pre- and post-World War II
Sources: Chapter appendix; Huff and Huff, 'Urban growth', p. 528.

[7] Dick, *Surabaya*, p. xviii.

Table 8.1 *Southeast Asia main city populations 1936–1950 (000 persons)*

	Rangoon	Bangkok	Singapore Island	Penang	Kuala Lumpur	Jakarta	Surabaya	Saigon-Cholon	Hanoi	Manila
1936			603.2					256.0	149.0	
1937		827.3								
1938										
1939			727.6							623.5
1940						544.8	403.0			
Jun. 1941	501.2			247.5	144.4			450.0		
Jan. 1942			1,000.0							
Mar. 1942										300.0
Aug. 1942							464.5			873.0
Sept. 1942	300.0				150.9					
Mar. 1943	400.0					846.6	500.0			940.0
Dec. 1943									119.7	
Feb. 1944										1,093.0
Mar. 1944						863.0				
Jul. 1944	400.0		866.8		200.0		579.8			
Feb. 1945	150.0									174.0
Sept. 1945							618.0			
Dec. 1945							209.0			
1945						847.5		500.0		
1946								492.2		
1947		889.5	940.8	446.3	176.0					
Nov. 1948							400.0			
1948						1,050.0			237.1	983.9
1949							600.0	1,200.0		
1950	687.0						715.0			

Source: Chapter appendix.

Table 8.2 *Southeast Asia pre- and post-World War II urban primacy (ratio of first- to second-largest city)*

		Pre-war	Post-war
Burma	1938, 1950	3.1	3.7
Malaya	1938, 1947	2.9	2.1
Thailand	1947		23.3
Indonesia	1940, 1948	1.4	2.6
Indochina	1936, 1946	1.7	2.1
Philippines	1938, 1947	4.2	5.9

Note: For 1939, Penang data are for 1941.
Source: Chapter appendix.

made up for some of the earlier losses. Between 1943 and 1948, the population of Hanoi, including, in 1948, its suburbs, doubled to 237,146, but by 1948 Hanoi was already subject to new, large population fluctuations due to the shifting balance between food and fear arising from the First Indochina War.[8]

The second pattern, that of cities with rice-specialized hinterlands, is found in Burma, Thailand and Indochina. Wartime growth rates in Rangoon, Bangkok and Saigon did not much exceed, or even fell below, their long-term trends of around 2.5 per cent per annum. Although Rangoon lost population at the outset of the war owing to a mass exodus of Indians, the in-migration of Burmese fleeing an anarchic countryside and Indians searching for work helped to replace departures, and between 1941 and 1950 Rangoon grew substantially.

Pre- and post-war measures of urban primacy (defined as a country's most populous city being twice or more the size of the second-largest city) reflect wartime urbanization and show its disproportionate impact. The war extended the primate city, already a feature of Southeast Asia, to the entire region and strengthened it everywhere except Malaya. Jakarta and Saigon became primate cities for the first time. Manila's primacy ratio widened dramatically (Table 8.2).

Food and Fear

The pull exerted by the availability of food was the dominant demographic determinant in the rapidly growing cities of Singapore, Penang, Kuala Lumpur, Jakarta, Manila and, until 1945, Surabaya. Famine, although not entirely absent from the main cities in food-deficit areas, was overwhelmingly a rural phenomenon. Although famine affected Jakarta and Manila, in neither was it a mass phenomenon, and in both chiefly an externality attributable to population inflows from surrounding areas.

[8] Turley, 'Urbanization', pp. 370–72.

Five principal sources of food availability, already discussed in earlier chapters, account for the ability of main cities in food-deficit areas largely to circumvent famine and to attract hinterland migrants. One was that, as apparent from discussion throughout this book, main cities offered numerous chances for part-time and casual employment and so a variety of possible sources of income to buy food. 'Portfolio diversification' of this sort was far less available in rural areas. The other four sources, elaborated below, were: Japanese rationing systems; cultivation in urban areas and the surrounding fringes; imports both from nearby hinterlands and abroad; and food relief. Apart from the last, which generally meant feeding on the spot, black markets tied together and augmented urban food sources. These markets re-distributed some of the food given as rations or paid as wages (Chapters 2 and 6). Moreover, black market prices drew food to urban Southeast Asia and furnished a price mechanism that stimulated food production. Flourishing black markets increased the attraction of Southeast Asia's cities, since many Southeast Asians bought or sold in these markets.

Rationing

In food-deficit Southeast Asia, rationing in urban, but generally not in rural, areas was basic to attracting substantial net in-migration. Rations, although increasingly inadequate in themselves, reduced the risk in cities of grossly inadequate nutrition by putting a floor under food availability. An exception was Manila, where in late 1944 rationing stopped (Chapter 6). In Malaya, Japanese rationing never operated effectively outside the larger settlements, and during the latter half of 1943 ceased entirely.[9] By contrast, rations in Singapore, although declining substantially as described in Chapter 6, remained available throughout the war. In Java, rationing was heavily skewed towards main urban centres and, as in Malaya, disparities widened over the course of the war. An 'adequate' distribution of *beras* (husked but uncooked rice) was considered by Javanese to be 400 grams (0.88 of a pound) a day per person, although consumption per capita in the 1930s averaged only 230 grams. By January 1945, distribution outside Java's five largest cities, chief among them Jakarta, was irregular and as little as 500 grams of *beras* per family per month. By contrast, as a rule those in Jakarta received regular distributions of *beras*, reported to be 180 grams per person per day.[10]

Food rationing in Surabaya began early in the occupation, and in some areas was backed up by a coupon system for the needy and soup kitchens. General rationing, even initially, provided only just enough to eat from a combination of rice supplemented with maize and soybeans. But for Surabaya, food

[9] Malaya, *Report on the 1947 census*, p. 34; Malayan Union, *Report on the British military administration*, p. 43; Kratoska, *Japanese occupation*, p. 257.

[10] Kurasawa, 'Mobilization', pp. 116, 161; Anderson, 'Problem of rice', pp. 82, 90–91; Anon., 'Rijstpellerijen in midden-Java', p. 84; van der Eng, *Food supply*, p. 34 gives a Jakarta ration near the end of 1944 of 120 grams a day but see Anderson, 'Problem of rice', p. 91.

availability and a smaller chance of recruitment as forced labour 'explain the rapid growth in urban population'.[11]

Initially, the reaction to the Japanese occupation of Manila was mass evacuation caused by a lack of food and fear of the Japanese military. Population quickly fell from its pre-war peak of 623,500 to 300,000 (Table 8.1). The Japanese, however, soon established food rationing in Manila, and food availability together with unsettled conditions in the countryside brought large numbers back to the city.[12] Some evacuees found that they were ill-suited to agriculture and in the Philippines, more than anywhere else in Southeast Asia, widespread guerrilla resistance and danger in rural areas discouraged more than temporary evacuation to the countryside.[13] By March 1943, Manila's population had reached 940,000, over 300,000 more than before the war. In February 1944, population peaked at just under 1.1 million (Table 8.1).

The continued inflow of population to Manila added to pressure on rice rations which were already uncertain and declining. Even so, a programme to provide free transport to move people from Manila, by then with unemployment of some 25 per cent, to Cebu, Iloilo and Sorsogon apparently persuaded just 200 people to leave.[14] Near the end of the war, fear temporarily reversed population inflows to Manila. The Allied offensive to re-take Manila, and Japan's last-ditch defence, produced some of World War II's fiercest fighting and greatest urban destruction. In February 1945, when Manila fell, only some 174,000 people remained there. But encouraged by Allied-supplied food, people flooded back, and Manila's population soon again reached a million (Table 8.1).

Urban Cultivation and Squatter Settlements

Growing food, both in central urban areas and on land adjacent to cities, became a third nutritional source. The cultivation of root crops like cassava and sweet potatoes, encouraged by the Japanese, increased the calorific yield per unit of land. Home gardens helped people to stay in Manila, and urban cultivation further expanded after gardening one day a week in community gardens became compulsory.[15] By 1943 in Kuala Lumpur, every scrap of spare urban land was planted; Health Department staff were, for example, sent to garden at the Golf Club.[16] Singapore municipality, where still in 1947 half the

[11] Dick, *Surabaya*, p. 78; see also Frederick, *Visions*, p. 101.

[12] Hartendorp, *History of industry*, pp. 192–93; Jose, 'Food production', p. 70.

[13] NARA, RG226, entry 16, box 208, 'Economic conditions in the Philippines', 15 October 1942, p. 2; Agoncillo, *Fateful years*, pp. 555–56, 565.

[14] OSS, assemblage 33, *Programs of Japan in the Philippines*, p. 370.

[15] NARA, RG226, entry 16, box 144, 'Conditions in the Philippine Islands', 23 August 1942, pp. 38–39; Hartendorp, *History of industry*, p. 133.

[16] ANM, 1957/0292074, R. C. Selangor 296/1947, Selangor, *Report of the Medical Department 1941–1946*, p. 14. And see Malayan Union, *Report of the medical department 1946*, p. 8 for the same point.

population lived on 11 per cent of Singapore island, was quite densely packed and offered limited scope for cultivation.[17] However, some Singapore residents kept chickens and ducks which they fed on the city's two-inch cockroaches trapped in the sewers at night.[18] Outside central Singapore, grass verges, said once to have been neatly cut, were largely replaced with stringy papaya trees and tapioca plants around which *lalang* (coarse grass) grew unchecked.[19]

Urban cats and dogs, although not always easily caught, afforded an obvious source of high protein. In Singapore, these animals disappeared in sufficiently great numbers to qualify as endangered species.[20] The 1946 Malayan Union Medical Department Report laconically observed that 'food was very scarce and no dogs were to be seen'.[21] Manila residents referred to dog meat as *azucena*, a species of flower, the first two syllables of which sounded like the Tagalog word *aso*, dog.[22]

World War II gave impetus to squatter settlements, and so began to re-configure Southeast Asia's urban geography. In Manila, many squatters occupied bomb-damaged areas in the city's inner core.[23] Food in the form of rations and welfare provision no doubt helped to determine this squatter settlement pattern and so also a broader population shift characterized, as Table 8.1 shows, by considerable net movement into Manila. In both Singapore and Kuala Lumpur, large squatter settlements appeared for the first time on urban fringes and added significantly to population. The area in Singapore under market gardens expanded from 1,500 acres to 7,000 acres, although this expansion fell far short of being able to feed all of the 263,600 additions to Singapore's population between 1938 and 1944.[24] By 1942, almost all vacant land in and around Kuala Lumpur had been utilized for food production. Accompanying this, and encouraged partly by a 'Plant More Food' campaign, unauthorized temporary buildings 'sprang up like mushrooms' in both the city and its outskirts.[25] Between 1941 and 1947, the near doubling of population on Penang island, but slower expansion in Georgetown, suggests the growth of squatter communities. Easy access to central urban districts afforded squatters a ready market for surplus production. Urban marketing opportunities probably help to explain inwards migration from rural

17 Singapore Department of Social Welfare, *Social survey*, p. 24.

18 NAS, Oral History, Lee Tian Soo, p. 29.

19 Gilmour, *With freedom*, p. 116.

20 He, *Syonan interlude*, p. 156.

21 ANM, 1957/0292074, R.C. Selangor 296/1947, Selangor, *Report of the Medical Department 1941–1946*, p. 17; and see ANM, 1957/0292046, R.C. Selangor 269/1947, *Report of the Kuala Lumpur Town Board 1946*, p. 6.

22 Agoncillo, *Fateful years*, p. 585.

23 McGee, *Southeast Asian city*, pp. 144, 157–58.

24 ANM, 1957/0572056, CA (MPU) War Office M.G.D. AGM/22, O. W. Gilmour, 'Assessment of war damage', 15 April 1944, p. 5.

25 ANM, 1957/0290027, Syuseityo Kanbo 108/2603, *Report of the Kuala Lumpur Sanitary Board 2062* (1942), p. 12 and see p. 15 and Malayan Union, *Report of the medical department 1946*, p. 30.

Southeast Asia, and perhaps also, as in Kuala Lumpur, outwards movement from central districts to urban fringes.[26] Just after the war, the spread of squatter settlements was one of Singapore's most prominent features.[27]

Squatter cultivation and urban gardening were, however, a supplement not a replacement for other food sources. For peninsular Malaya, compared to an average pre-war calorie intake of some 2,500, in 1945 the production of root crops, bananas, maize, ragi, groundnuts and sugar provided an average of 520 calories per person per day, far short of adult requirements.[28] Almost certainly, gardening in the main Southeast Asian cities yielded fewer calories than this due to limited land availability.

Food Imports

Geography, transport availability and guerrillas are fundamental in explaining the varying abilities of rice-deficit cities to import food. At the start of the war, Manila, although occupied, was not expected to encounter serious food shortages.[29] Almost immediately, however, scope to import rice or other food to Manila, which normally received rice from central Luzon, was greatly restricted owing to destruction by departing American forces of large numbers of vehicles and most gasoline stocks; by endemic corruption, making it hard for even the government to obtain rice; and by falling output due to a lack of incentive for farmers to grow rice, as described in Chapter 7.[30] Widespread guerrilla activity in rural areas further discouraged cultivation and hindered transport to Manila.[31] In May 1942, one could travel for miles outside Manila without seeing a cultivated field.[32]

Soon after Laurel's Philippines government assumed office in October 1943, it found difficulty in supplying rice to the city. Beginning in late 1943 a series of food policy reforms, which included turning a blind eye to black market supplies, temporarily eased shortages in Manila.[33] By the end of May 1944, however, the government had only 4,177 tons of polished rice stockpiled. Existing distribution of just 2.1 ounces (59.6 grams) of rice per person per day implied supplies for only another 50 days.[34] Although the Japanese

[26] Sandhu, 'Saga of the "squatter"', pp. 145–49. Kuala Lumpur also had a large increase in unsanitary, unauthorized dwellings in the town. ANM, 1957/0292046, R.C. Selangor 269/1947, *Report of the Kuala Lumpur Town Board 1946*, p. 36.

[27] Gilmour, *With freedom*, p. 112.

[28] Kratoska, *Japanese occupation*, p. 266.

[29] OSS, R&A 324, *Philippine agriculture under Japanese control*, pp. 18, 35–36.

[30] NARA, RG226, entry 16, box 208, 'Economic conditions in the Philippines', 15 October 1942, pp. 2, 8–11; Hainsworth and Moyer, *Agricultural geography*, p. 31.

[31] Buencamino, 'Manila under Japanese occupation', pp. 15, 16, 25, 28.

[32] Hartendorp, *Japanese occupation*, p. 205.

[33] Jose, 'Rice shortage', pp. 207–8 and 'Food production and food distribution', p. 79; Hartendorp, *History of industry*, pp. 117–21, 132–33.

[34] LHC, MAGIC, 'Economic: Manila', 30 June 1944, p. 11.

had imported rice for Manila soon after occupying it, this became increasingly difficult because of Manila's distance from Southeast Asia's rice-surplus countries and the Japanese navy's progressive surrender of control of the high seas. During the latter part of the war, the Allies sank many of the ships bringing rice to Manila.[35]

Jakarta was, by contrast, relatively well placed geographically to obtain rice from elsewhere in Java, even in the face of acute transport shortages. The residency of Jakarta, the area around the city, which had a population of about 1.7 million additional non-urban inhabitants, grew and milled rice.[36] Despite the acute shortage of rice in Java, Jakarta's proximity to a rice-growing region gave it an advantage in drawing in supplies, both through sanctioned and, as discussed below, black market channels. Surabaya lacked a similar opportunity, because nearby areas in East Java were heavily rice-deficit.[37]

Singapore's location in so great a rice-deficit country as Malaya might suggest almost inevitable wartime famine. The key geographical factor in keeping famine at bay was the island's centrality in Southeast Asia, facilitating the transport by coastal shipping of rice and other foodstuffs from Thailand, Burma, Indonesia and the Malay Peninsula. Junks with rice sailed regularly from Burma to Singapore (and also Penang) as well as from Thailand to both cities.[38] In October 1944, the sanctioning of 'private importers rice', which legalized imports from Songkhla in southern Thailand, made bringing food to Singapore more straightforward. Sanctioned imports and, with them, added scope for unsanctioned ones enhanced both trade and black market opportunities. Singaporeans responded with a flurry of boat-building. Wartime possession of a junk, a Singapore trader recalled, was 'like owning six ships during peace time'.[39]

Relief Efforts

Relief schemes to provide food for the poor were established in all the main cities but were especially prominent in Manila. After the onset of occupation and prior to rationing, Red Cross relief fed some 100,000 Manila residents.[40] High unemployment and worsening shortages left the Laurel government with

35 Jose, 'Food production', p. 72.
36 Kurasawa, 'Mobilization', pp. 135, 157.
37 De Vries, 'Vital statistics', p. 18.
38 The Thai trade is well known. For Burma, see NARA, RG226, entry 16, box 927, no. 78667, OSS, R&A Branch, Regular Intelligence Reports, 'Junk transport – general and economic conditions, 27 June 1944', pp. 2–3.
39 NAS, Oral History, Jack Kim Boon Ng, p. 42 and on Japanese liberalization of the rice trade see NIDS, Nansei Gunsei –18 Japan, Southern Military Administration Chōsabu, *Syonan tokubetsu shi wo chūshin to seru bukka taisaku* [Counter-measures for prices in Syonan Municipality] (March 1944), passim.
40 Hartendorp, *History of industry*, pp. 192–93.

little option but to establish community kitchens to give cooked rice to the destitute. As early as February 1943, many of the some 25 per cent of those unemployed in Manila depended on charity, while others relied on relief.[41] By October 1943 and up to Allied re-occupation, Manila had 17 welfare stations and 94 community kitchens, and 240,000 people received direct relief.[42]

Black Markets

Faltering Japanese rationing systems and restricted scope for urban cultivation left black markets with a major role in urban food provision. Black market food, essential in feeding much of World War II occupied Europe, may have had an even greater importance in many of the large cities of rice-deficit Southeast Asia.[43] Without black markets, wartime malnutrition in these cities would have been far worse, and in some mass starvation might even have occurred.

Jakarta was the destination for heavy black market trafficking of rice organized through the city's underworld and by networks of smugglers. Underworld leaders could use their contacts and organizations to evade regulations and so were especially well placed to make significant profits from trafficking rice, which in turn strengthened their social positions. Attracted by prices some ten times above village levels, rice smugglers relied on bribes, network organization and a degree of luck to circumvent legal prohibitions and the threat of severe penalties, even death, if apprehended with black market cargoes. Large holders of rice land preferred to channel supplies to Jakarta, and a quarter to a third of milled (as opposed to smallholder pounded) rice was said to go to the black market in cities, chiefly Jakarta, where it was sold mainly by Chinese shopkeepers. The diversion of rice to the urban black market and falling output contributed to rice shortages in the countryside.[44]

A common sight along the route into Manila's Tutuban railway station, where a black market in food centred, was smugglers throwing first sacks of rice and then themselves from moving trains. They were met by clusters of people begging to buy rice.[45] The inability of the Laurel government to control rice supplies from November 1943 left Manila heavily and increasingly dependent on the black market.[46]

Throughout Malaya, black market food was 'crucial' in maintaining the health and welfare of the population.[47] Penang had a thriving black market in

41 OSS, assemblage 45, *Manpower in Japan and occupied areas*, vol. 2, p. 310.

42 Weston, 'Co-prosperity fails', p. 24.

43 League of Nations, *World economic survey 1942/44*, pp. 125, 129.

44 Cribb, *Gangsters*, p. 42; Kurasawa, 'Mobilization', pp. 133–34, 148, 164–65; Sato, *War, nationalism*, pp. 132–135, 143.

45 Agoncillo, *Fateful years*, pp. 545–47.

46 Hartendorp, *History of industry*, p. 83.

47 Kratoska, *Japanese occupation*, p. 175 and see p. 254.

all basic foodstuffs.[48] In Singapore, commercial networks of the city's Chinese firms combined with the port's central location in Southeast Asia to facilitate the clandestine transport of rice and other foodstuffs from nearby areas, while the city's accumulated pre-war stocks of gold and other tangible wealth, as well as essential goods and materials, provided readily accepted means of payment.[49] As an offshoot of Singapore's wartime commerce and black market, Karimun-Bali, previously an obscure fishing island, functioned as the unofficial trade centre of Malaya, Sumatra and Java. Known as 'little Syonan' and just 28 nautical miles from its Singapore namesake, Karimun became home to over 100 firms, the port for a flotilla of small vessels and a hub of smuggling and black marketeering. Although well known to the Japanese military command, it turned a blind eye to Karimun, partly in the interest of food supplies for Singapore.[50]

Black markets were a wartime resource for Southeast Asia's middle class seeking to maintain nutrition by extensive sales of jewellery, gold, furniture and other tangible possessions. George Bogaars describes how his family had to sell their piano and furniture to survive and how he became part of the black market, selling goods to a Chinese acquaintance for onwards sale.[51] In Singapore and Manila, specialized city-centre markets acquired institutional status as centres for the sale of gold, jewellery and other valuables. One set of Singapore dealers, trading in jewellery and property and operating mainly in the High Street or Chulia Street off Raffles Place, bought from a middle-class 'parting with family heirlooms in order to stay alive'.[52] A similar, flourishing jewellery mart grew up in Manila's Azcárraga Street between Rizal Avenue and San Bernardo.

Two vital functions performed by black markets had much wider significance than middle-class survival. Both helped to put food within the reach of a range of urban consumers. One was partially to substitute for the lack of well-functioning markets. Black markets drew food to cities by compensating sufficiently for the effort of growing it, and then the risk and danger of transporting produce illegally from surrounding areas. Although black markets undoubtedly re-allocated food to the better off, the more food that came to cities for black market sale the lower was its price there.

Second, black markets, along with associated smuggling, provided substantial employment in a burgeoning informal economy. This helped to replace pre-war work, much of which had disappeared, and to accommodate the large increase in street vendors and sellers of empty bottles and old clothes characteristic of Southeast Asia's wartime cities. Multiple layers of agents, brokers and dealers appeared, along with their many subordinates and runners.

48 NARA, RG226, entry 16, box 1279, no. 112749, OSS, R&A Branch, Regular Intelligence Reports, 'General conditions in Malaya (Penang island), 11 January 1945', p. 4.

49 Chin, *Malaya upside down*, p. 59.

50 Twang, *Chinese business élite*, pp. 94–96; Kratoska, *Japanese occupation*, p. 254.

51 NAS, Oral History, George Edwin Bogaars, pp. 29, 33–34.

52 Lee, *Singapore story*, p. 66.

Numerous small traders, '*une multitude de petites gens*', formed the base of Indochina's black market and, perhaps partly because of their weight of numbers, seem often to have been left alone by the authorities.[53] New to Jakarta's informal sector were itinerant traders drawn to *cha-tu* or black marketeering. These Jakarta and Surabaya Chinese often relied on supplies from other Chinese, usually Hokchia or Hinhua, engaged in smuggling known as overland *danbang*. Responsive to arbitrage profits averaging 300 per cent, smugglers travelled by train or along Java's back roads, riding or pushing bicycles carrying tens of kilograms of goods.[54]

In the wartime environment of uncertainty and highly imperfect information, black market dealings were, of course, risky. One risk was informers; another that the '"market" was populated with assorted kinds of people: the sharpers, the cheats, the "double-crossers", the embezzlers, the blackmailers, and even the naive'.[55] In Singapore, retail black market distribution of basic goods like food was generally through coffee shops, eating shops and hawkers, since most 'wholesale' distributors assessed contact with the public as too dangerous.[56]

Black market transactions probably effected a substantial re-distribution of wealth. The sale of valuables by middle-class Singaporeans to buy food has been described above. Farmers in the Philippines used their surplus rice to obtain a whole range of goods new to them. Outwards from Manila, 'Along the road to the provinces, one could see "push-carts" loaded with wardrobes, tables, chairs, sofas, pianos, narra beds, and other paraphernalia of the wealthy city residents'.[57] Some Southeast Asians amassed sizeable fortunes, through black market dealings, by supplying the Japanese, or with monopolies granted by them, for example in distributive trades or gambling farms. In Manila, F. C. de la Rama, even allowing for later exaggeration and the hyperbole of his autobiography, became fabulously wealthy, threw lavish parties and was widely celebrated in popular culture. Like other of Manila's so-called 'buy-and-sell' merchants, he played a double game of cultivating links with Japanese army and navy officers and also channelling large sums to several guerrilla organizations, including that of Tomás Confesor, the civilian leader of the resistance in Panay.[58] A few black market kings, already described in Chapter 6 for Rangoon and known in Singapore as mushroom millionaires, became rich, if, at least initially, perhaps mainly in Japanese paper money. But profits also filtered down to local communities, although also frequently to corrupt Japanese officials.[59]

53 VNA, FF 133394, 'Sur le contrôle des prix', 11 August 1944, p. 88.
54 Twang, *Chinese business élite*, pp. 100–4.
55 Agoncillo, *Fateful years*, p. 569.
56 Kratoska, *Japanese occupation*, p. 169.
57 Agoncillo, *Fateful years*, pp. 561–62 and see pp. 563, 575–76; Jose, 'Rice shortage', p. 212.
58 Agoncillo, *Fateful years*, pp. 572–75; Rama, *I made millions*.
59 Chin, *Malaya upside down*, pp. 36–38; IER, Azb: 3 Japan, Malayan Military Administration Chōsabu, *Syonan tōnai shokuryō zōsan saku ni tsuite* [Policy for food

Hanoi: Fear and Famine

As a city that lost population, despite being surrounded by a food-deficit countryside, Hanoi was atypical. The dominance of fear, not food, largely explains the drop in Hanoi's population from 149,000 in 1936 to 119,700 by 1943 (Table 8.1). Unlike the other main cities with adjoining food-deficit hinterlands, Hanoi and its port of Haiphong were principal targets for Allied air attacks.[60] As early as 1942, bombing by aircraft based in China damaged Hanoi and Haiphong.[61] An intensification of air raids left Hanoi, Haiphong and the town of Nam Dinh 'partially deserted'.[62] The exodus of population from Haiphong put yet more pressure on rice supplies in the nearby province of Kien An.[63]

While the seemingly unending stream of famine victims trying to walk to Hanoi, noted in Chapter 7, is consistent with large cityward migration in food-deficit areas, it is unclear how far these famine inflows contributed to population increase because of high death rates among famine victims. Many of the starving newcomers to Hanoi probably died soon after arrival. For Hanoi residents, the famine dead became an accustomed sight; '50 to 70 corpses crouching along the pavement' were picked up daily.[64] Oxcarts made regular runs at 12 noon and 5 p.m. to pick up the dead and dying piling up on pavements and street corners.[65]

Barricades at entrances to Hanoi and other cities, erected by the French colonial administration to prevent the inwards migration of famine victims, were abandoned after the March 1945 Japanese coup and installation of a Vietnamese puppet government.[66] Refugees pouring into Hanoi were described by a contemporary observer as 'more corpses, yet more corpses' dragging themselves towards the city.[67] In Hanoi and other large cities, 'tens of thousands of rural folk [wandered] the streets, begging pitifully, often clad in nothing but straw matting'.[68] Hanoi became the 'capital of beggars'. High famine deaths among Hanoi's inwards migrants were likely, since relief efforts by the French authorities were only partial. The Japanese, after the March coup, made less effort than the French to alleviate famine.[69] In June 1945, when famine deaths were estimated at between 100 and 200

production on Syonan island] (October 1944), p. 12; Kurasawa, 'Mobilization', p. 151; Kratoska, *Japanese occupation*, pp. 169–74.

60 Gunn, 'Great Vietnamese famine', p. 9; Andrus, *Basic problems*, p. 35.

61 LHC, MAGIC, 'Hanoi', 17 August 1942, p. 2.

62 Andrus, *Basic problems*, p. 29.

63 AOM, RSTNF/1393 'Inspection économique Kiên An', 9 May 1944, p. 4.

64 Nguyên, 'Japanese food policies', p. 218; For daily reports of bodies collected on the streets of Hanoi, see VNA, MH 3499, 'Rapports journaliers du Chef des Affairs Annamites', 15 March to 29 May 1945, a file of 142 pages.

65 Bàng, 'They starved', p. 105; Huỳnh, 'Vietnamese August revolution', p. 769.

66 Le, *Impact*, p. 256.

67 The quote is from the poem by Bàng, 'They starved', pp. 101–7.

68 Marr, *Vietnam 1945*, p. 101.

69 Le, *Impact*, p. 254.

a day, corpses were buried by the hundred in shallow pits of about two metres square in Hanoi's Hop Thien cemetery. The pits, covering an area of about two mậu (7,000 square metres), emitted a stench that hung over parts of the city.[70]

Food-Surplus Cities: Rangoon, Bangkok and Saigon

In Rangoon, Bangkok and Saigon, located in rice areas and the constituents of Southeast Asia's other principal urbanization pattern, wartime population movements primarily reflected fear. Plentiful supplies led to falls in the real price of rice. Although other basic foods might be either unobtainable or expensive, they were not generally to be found by going to the countryside.

Rangoon's three main wartime population movements are all explained principally by a search for safety. U Sein Tin describes Indian labourers beginning to leave Rangoon just after bombing started on 23 December 1941, an attack quickly followed by bombing on Christmas Day which killed some 2,000 to 2,500 people. About 70,000 Indians managed to depart by sea, but most aimed to walk the about 250 miles to India over some of the roughest track in existence.[71] Between late December 1941 and mid-1942, 400,000 to 450,000 Indians left Burma.[72] Departures even included school boys in short pants hoping to reach India on their bicycles, and also a number of Europeans.[73] Estimates of Indian deaths on Burma's 'forgotten long march' extend upwards to 100,000, but the likely range is between 10,000 and 50,000.[74] The dead, often unburied, marked the difficult points along the route where, sometimes as couples, mothers with infants, or in family groups, they had lain down by the side of mountain paths to die.[75] Because Indians made up about half of Rangoon's pre-war population and the city's Indian residents accounted for most of those leaving Burma, their exodus largely explains the drop in the city's population from half a million before the war to 300,000 in September 1942 (Table 8.1).

A second, reverse population flow began as Burmese and Indians moved back to Rangoon. By March 1943, population had increased to some 400,000 (Table 8.1). Many Burmese returned because the danger of remaining in the countryside outweighed that of the city, despite regular air raids. U Nu remembered Burmese in rural areas being bullied by the military police; 'those who escaped their clutches came streaming into Rangoon'.[76] However, the city itself was far

[70] AOM, GF/58, Nishimura, Délégation Impériale au Tonkin to Mayor of Hanoi 26 June 1945 and reply from the Mayor 9 July 1945.

[71] Tin, *Wartime*, pp. 12, 20; Christian, *Burma*, p. 114; Collis, *Last and first*, p. 20.

[72] Tinker, 'Forgotten long march', pp. 1–4. Donnison, *British military administration*, p. 280, gives a figure of half a million who left Burma in 1941 and 1942 as does Burma Intelligence Bureau, *Burma*, vol. 2, p. 184.

[73] Tin, *Wartime*, p. 140.

[74] Tinker, 'Forgotten long march', pp. 1–4.

[75] Allen, *Burma*, pp. 80–90.

[76] Nu, *Burma under the Japanese*, p. 35 and see p. 47.

from safe in the lawless early occupation climate of violence, robbery and looting of 'the country folk ... robbing the townspeople and the townspeople ... robbing each other'.[77] Coming to Rangoon 'was like dodging a snake and treading on a scorpion'.[78] In Rangoon soon after Japanese occupation, numerous bazaars appeared selling 'all stolen property'.[79] As well as those seeking Rangoon's comparative safety, Indians migrated to the city. About half of Burma's pre-war Indian population had remained in the country. They were encouraged to come to Rangoon by the Japanese, in need of labour for urban services to function and for the war effort. By the end of 1943 agricultural labourers were flocking to towns and labour camps to find work.[80]

The third of Rangoon's population movements occurred after its re-occupation by the Allies in May 1945. By then, perhaps no more than 100,000 residents remained. Few, if any, urban services, including street lighting, still operated.[81] Nor were surrounding areas safe. However, throughout the delta, once the Japanese forces retreated and danger abated, thousands of people walked into the towns and looted. Evacuation from Rangoon proved temporary. After Allied re-occupation and the restoration of a measure of order in Rangoon, the city again filled up.[82] The departure of Indians at the start of the war was, however, largely permanent. It transformed Rangoon from an Indian into a Burmese city, and was the principal Southeast Asian instance of a lasting war-induced change in urban racial composition.

Bangkok and Saigon were much less affected than Rangoon by the war. In Bangkok, although shortages of medicines, tyres, petrol and fuel oil increasingly developed during the war, rice and most other basic foods remained plentiful. However, wartime inflation, as Reynolds observes, 'severely affected the urban classes'.[83] Bangkok civil servants were hit by forced contributions to patriotic funds and, moreover, suffered a drastic fall in real wages (Chapter 9).[84] The effects of rapid inflation on earnings extended down the social scale: the wages of Bangkok's unskilled labourers nearly halved between 1938 and 1945 (Table 8.3).

The 1941 to 1943 flow to Bangkok of Chinese forced out of northern Thailand by Phibun's discriminatory policies was a special case (Chapter 7). Otherwise, the continued ready availability of rice throughout much of Thailand prevented food from being a reason for inwards migration to Bangkok. Additionally, a preference of many Thai for rural life helps to explain

[77] Tin, *Wartime*, pp. 108–9, 142, 190.
[78] Nu, *Burma under the Japanese*, pp. 35, 47.
[79] Pe, *Narrative*, p. 11.
[80] Burma Intelligence Bureau, *Burma*, vol. 1, pp. 48–49, vol. 2, p. 114.
[81] Ibid., vol. 2, pp. 120–32.
[82] Pe, *Narrative*, p. 95.
[83] Reynolds, *Thailand's secret war*, p. 431.
[84] NARA, RG59, entry 205, box 5834, file 892.00 233, Chapman, 'Conditions in Thailand December 1941 to June 1942', 18 August 1942, p. 36.

Table 8.3 *Thailand unskilled labour daily wages and real wages 1938–1945*

	Bangkok		Rural	
	Baht	Real wages	Baht	Real wages
1938	0.80	100.0	1.125	100.0
1939	0.72		1.6	
1940			2.0	
1941		0.0	2.0	135.7
1942	1.25	88.3	1.75	87.9
1943	1.25	59.0	1.75	58.7
1944				
1945	4.00	55.4	2.5	24.6

Notes and sources: Wages: Ouyyanont, 'Bangkok', p. 82. Both Bangkok and rural wages are for construction workers. For rural wages the figure for 1938 is wages for 1937. Daily rural wages in 1939 were 1.6 baht. *Prices:* Ingram, *Economic change*, p. 164. Ingram derives his data from Bank of Thailand figures and specifies that these are for the cost of living and based on the family budget of white-collar workers and wage earners in Bangkok.

the capital's relatively slow wartime population growth, as does Allied bombing beginning in late 1943, discussed below. For much of the war, Bangkok wages would not have exerted any pull on rural dwellers. Rural money wages remained substantially above those in Bangkok (Table 8.3), while in 1943 real wages in the countryside had declined no more than in Bangkok. By 1945, although both nominal and real rural wages had dropped further than in Bangkok and were less than money wages there, Allied bombing and growing shortages of goods in the city probably made migration to it unattractive.

It seemed at first that, 'as far as our personal safety and welfare are concerned we [people in Bangkok] have been viewing the world's worries from an armchair'.[85] This changed during the war's latter stages and, as in Rangoon, fear motivated large population fluctuations. After severe Allied bombing in late 1943, Chinese associations organized first aid and disaster relief.[86] In February, a Japanese official reported to Tokyo that: 'It is impossible to describe the falling of the bombs, the blazing of the incendiaries, the danger involved in the severe attacks and the damage resulting therefrom.'[87] Bombing intensified, and some

[85] Chaya, *Passing hours*, p. 3 and see pp. 17–18, 60–61, 79, 90; Landon, 'Thailand', pp. 391–92.
[86] Skinner, *Chinese society*, p. 278.
[87] NARA, RG457, entry 9011, box 62, file 51625, Bangkok to Tokyo, 3 February 1944.

12 bombing raids in May 1944 sufficiently unnerved Bangkok residents that an estimated 60 per cent of the population vacated the centre.[88] A sense of crisis and dislocation was heightened after the destruction by Allied bombs of Bangkok's two power stations in April 1945, leaving the city without electricity for the rest of the war. The atmosphere of emergency further intensified when, in July, Bangkok's newspapers began to be printed on straw paper.[89]

Until late 1942, Saigon's economy remained relatively buoyant and may even have benefited disproportionately from French government industrial initiatives and support for commodity prices.[90] Increasingly, however, Saigon, like Hanoi, became a principal Allied target and intensive bombing drove residents from the city. By 1944, many of Saigon's workers had sought safety in the countryside, and the difficulty that the Japanese experienced in finding replacements left them heavily dependent on recruiting from the religious and political sect of the Cao Đài to supply a workforce.[91] In addition, prisoners of war were used as stevedores in Saigon.[92] Although data are lacking, it seems unlikely that new recruits fully made up for Saigon-Cholon residents who left the city.

Urban Health and Nutrition

During the war, almost no one in the main cities in Southeast Asia's rice-deficit areas escaped significant nutritional deprivation and associated impairments to health. Famine had a profound impact on both Hanoi and Jakarta, and, although far less severe, was all too apparent in Manila. By late 1944, people there were dying by the hundreds of starvation, and famine corpses become a common sight.[93]

The fate of rural famine victims crowding into Hanoi has already been described. Much the same happened in Jakarta, where by the late stages of the war a daily round of garbage trucks picked up the dead.[94] Many, and quite possibly most, of Jakarta's famine dead appear to have originated from outside the city. They likely comprised some of the millions of people who, predominantly landless labourers and factory workers no longer in employment, were

88 Reynolds, *Thailand*, pp. 171, 174, 204. See also NARA, RG59, entry 205, box 5835, file 892.00/11-2444, Powell, 'Political conditions in Thailand', 22 September 1944, p. 8 which gives an evacuation figure of 70 per cent.

89 BT, Bank of Thailand, *Bank of Thailand economic and financial report, 1945*, p. 33; Chaya, *Passing hours*, pp. 3, 17–18, 60–61, 79, 90; Skinner, *Chinese society*, p. 278. On the shortage of newsprint dating from May 1943, see Reynolds, '"International orphans"', pp. 383–84.

90 'J. V.', 'La hausse des prix', p. 34; Le, *Impact*, p. 248.

91 Tràn, 'Working', p. 291.

92 LHC, MAGIC, 'Economic value of Indo-China to Japan', 5 July 1944, p. 12.

93 LHC, MAGIC, 'Economic', 11 December 1944; Hartendorp, *History of industry*, p. 145; Jose, 'Rice shortage', p. 213 and 'Food production', p. 90.

94 Friend, *Indonesian destinies*, pp. 34.

left out of the rice distribution system (Chapter 7).[95] The lower town, where the famine dead were a common sight, was said to be 'flooded with people from the country who were so weak they could hardly walk'.[96] An eyewitness account of Jakarta in 1944 recorded a horrible scene of misery:

> Beggars dressed in haversacks or totally naked were lying at the roadside with the most hideous wounds. Their faces full moons and their bellies terribly swollen. Downtown I saw how corpses were loaded onto a lorry, a Jap kicked his booted foot against many other wretches who, if they gave any sign of life, were allowed to stay where they were.[97]

The most detailed health and nutrition data for Southeast Asia are for Singapore and Kuala Lumpur. Although neither city suffered famine, malnutrition increased as occupation continued, and became widespread and severe. In Singapore by the end of the war, 'a very large percentage of the population was suffering from serious under-nourishment'.[98] Between about two-fifths and two-thirds of Singapore school children were malnourished by pre-war standards.[99] Most children showed stunted growth and very poor musculature.[100]

In Kuala Lumpur, Singapore and Jakarta, health services and anti-malarial programmes were, as typically in Japanese-occupied Southeast Asia, progressively abandoned. Death rates surged due to declining health services, serious shortages of quinine, reduced availability of clean water, an end to imports of condensed milk and inadequate diets, this last evidenced, for example, by a much higher incidence of beri-beri (dietary deficiencies associated with an overload of carbohydrates) and infantile convulsions (poorly fed women unable to obtain milk or suckle infants and infants weaned on cereals).[101] Between 1941 and 1944, Singapore's crude death rate more than doubled. For most of the war, birth rates fell less rapidly than death rates rose, but by 1945 Singapore's crude birth rate per thousand of 27.5 was not much above half its 1940/41 average and far below the crude death rate of 39.8. The turning point in Jakarta did not come until mid-1944, after which a large excess of deaths over births similar to Singapore's appeared. In Kuala Lumpur, the birth rate approximately halved during the war, before, as in Singapore, largely

95 van der Eng, *Food supply*, pp. 37–38, 70–71.

96 Abeyasekere, *Jakarta*, p. 141.

97 Brugmans, *Nederlandsch-Indië*, p. 450.

98 Singapore, *Annual report of the medical department 1946*, p. 13 and see Singapore Department of Welfare, *First report*, p. 15; NIDS, Nansei Gunsei –18 Japan, Southern Military Administration Chōsabu, *Syonan tokubetsu shi wo chūshin to seru bukka taisaku* [Counter-measures for prices in Syonan Municipality] (March 1944), pp. 31–32.

99 Bourne, 'Nutrition work', p. 286.

100 ANM, BMA Dept/1/3 pt. II, British Military Administration, 'Final report nutrition unit' (April 1946), Appx. A(i); and see Bourne, 'Nutrition work', pp. 286–87.

101 Singapore, *Annual report of the medical department 1946*, p. 2; ANM, 1957/0290027, Syuseityo Kanbo 108/2063, *Report of the Kuala Lumpur Sanitary Board 2602* (1942), pp. 5, 8; Nicholls, 'Nutrition', p. 38.

Table 8.4 *Singapore, Kuala Lumpur and Jakarta crude birth and death rates 1940–1947 (births and deaths per 1,000 population)*

		Singapore		Kuala Lumpur		Jakarta Municipality	
		Births	Deaths	Births	Deaths	Births	Deaths
1939		45.0	20.0	65.0	22.9	28.0	16.0
1940				59.3		28.0	16.0
1941		44.8	20.8	48.6			
1942		34.6	37.3	22.4			
1943		37.7	26.4	39.2		29.0	18.0
1944		36.9	49.7	35.8	20.7		
1944	(1)					22.0	19.0
1944	(2)					17.0	23.0
1945		27.5	39.8			15.0	28.0
1946		42.3	16.7	41.7	16.3		
1947		45.8	13.3	50.9			

Notes: 1. For 1940, 1942, 1943 and 1944 for Kuala Lumpur, births are estimated using an estimated mid-year 1941 population figure of 144,414 and are indicative of trends only. Figures for 1943 and 1944 are almost certainly overstated due to wartime population inflows.
2. Death rates, in particular, may be understated for Singapore and Kuala Lumpur due to non-reporting.
3. Data for Jakarta Municipality for 1944 labelled (1) and (2) refer to the first and second half of the year respectively.
4. Jakarta Municipality includes a substantial area around the city. Statistics for it are therefore not entirely comparable with Singapore and Kuala Lumpur, but point to likely trends in urban Jakarta.
Sources: Singapore, *Annual report on the registration of births and deaths, 1940–47*, pp. 6, 8, 12; AN, 1957/ 0289720, Sel. Secretariat G. 466/1940, *Report of the Kuala Lumpur Sanitary Board, 1939*, p. 22; AN, 1957/0292046, R.C. Selangor 269/1947, *Report of the Kuala Lumpur Town Board, 1946*, p. 22; AN, 1957/0294190, Selangor Secretariat 554/1948, *Report of the Kuala Lumpur Town Board, 1947*, p. 17; Netherlands, Centraal Bureau voor de Statistiek, 'De economische toestand van Nederlandsch-Indie', p. 127.

recovering in 1946. By 1947, the Kuala Lumpur birth rate had regained its pre-occupation level (Table 8.4).

Infant mortality is a good indicator of health trends and, in particular, a usual measure of access to clean water. In Singapore and, though less so, in Kuala Lumpur, the infant death rate rose markedly during the Japanese occupation (Table 8.5). Between 1940 and 1942, an 86 per cent rise in

Singapore's infant death rate and 48 per cent increase in Kuala Lumpur's compares with a 40 per cent increase in occupied Europe over a similar period and indicates how quickly and how greatly conditions deteriorated.[102] Between 1942 and 1945 in Singapore, infant deaths accounted for a quarter of total deaths but for a much higher share of the increase in deaths. In comparison to 1940, between 1942 and 1945, while average annual deaths excluding infants increased by 56 per cent, infant deaths rose by 256 per cent. Among Singapore's main racial groups, Indians suffered the largest increase in infant deaths, although in 1945 in absolute numbers they remained just behind the Malays. Between 1940 and 1944, infant death rates for Singapore as a whole doubled, while among Indian infants they were 2.7 times higher (Table 8.5, panel b).

Rangoon showed that even being in a rice-surplus area did not necessarily protect against sharp deterioration in diet and health. Although not so badly impacted as Mandalay, where serious rice shortages developed, Rangoon did not escape the 'very great' wartime drop in urban living standards which occurred throughout the country.[103] Burma's high degree of regional specialization, near-complete breakdown in civilian transport and extreme dependence on imported goods, now unavailable, made lower living standards inevitable among Rangoon's middle class. However, much-reduced living standards spread downwards through the social spectrum. In Burma, rice, salt and fish were the three most universal foods. Although Rangoon had large surpluses of rice, scarcities of fish developed because of a lack of imported twine for nets and because the Japanese military requisitioned almost all boats. Residents of Rangoon and elsewhere in Lower Burma suffered from a lack of sesame oil, vegetables, gram and a number of other products normally obtained from Central Burma (Chapter 7). At the same time, Mandalay, in the centre, could not easily obtain rice or dried fish from the south. By the end of the war, Rangoon's and Mandalay's populations were seriously malnourished.[104]

The effect of general malnutrition in Rangoon in weakening resistance to disease was greatly compounded by an abrupt deterioration of urban services. After the bombing of Rangoon at the start of the war, the exodus of the Indian day and night conservancy sweepers made it difficult to keep the city clean. Furthermore, the intermittent municipal water supply became unsafe due to the unavailability of purifying agents. Endemic dysentery took hold, there were outbreaks of cholera and smallpox spread in Rangoon. Venereal disease increased due to a lack of medicines and the great upsurge in prostitution evident in Rangoon, as in all Southeast Asia's large cities.[105] Although Burmese blamed

[102] League of Nations, *World economic survey 1941/42*, p. 18.

[103] Burma Intelligence Bureau, *Burma*, vol. 2, p. 175 and see IOR, Clague Papers, Mss Eur E252/44, U Htin Wa, 'Eyewitness account', pp. 6, 10–11.

[104] Burma Intelligence Bureau, *Burma*, vol. 2, p. 175.

[105] See, for example, Singapore, *Annual report of the medical department 1946*, p. 13.

Table 8.5 *Singapore and Kuala Lumpur infant mortality rates 1940–1947 (deaths per 1,000 children under 1 year old)*

a)	Singapore	Kuala Lumpur
1939	130	111
1940	143	124
1941		136
1942	266	184
1943	194	170
1944	285	155
1945	216	82
1946	90	79
1947	87	

b) Singapore infant mortality by race	Chinese	Indian	Malay
1940	138	111	210
1943	183	268	239
1944	276	296	339
1945	200	286	293
1946	82	95	140
1947	79	76	143

Notes: For Kuala Lumpur, data are for January to October for 1941, May to December for 1942 and September to December for 1945.

Sources: Singapore, *Annual report on the registration of births and deaths, 1940–1947*, p. 9; AN, 1957/0289720, Sel. Secretariat G. 466/1940, *Report of the Kuala Lumpur Sanitary Board, 1939*, p. 22; AN, 1957/0292046, R.C. Selangor 269/1947, *Report of the Kuala Lumpur Town Board, 1946–1948*, p. 23.

Japanese for what was thought to be a new and virulent type of venereal disease, and called it 'Japanese typhoid', the infection may have been a variety of pseudo typhus. A plague epidemic which started in late 1942 remained very bad until June 1943. In response, the Japanese railed off suspect houses, distributed rat traps and undertook extensive anti-plague inoculation. The market response to the Japanese military police beating up householders who did not catch at least one rat a month was to create a flourishing trade in dead rats. Official figures for the first five months of 1943 show almost 5,000 urban deaths from plague, smallpox and cholera, but this was considered a gross under-estimate.[106]

[106] Burma Intelligence Bureau, *Burma*, vol. 2, pp. 41, 51.

Conclusion

A World War II breakpoint that reversed seven decades of continuous urbanization could have been expected if, as has been suggested, a search for food security had dispersed large urban populations to the countryside to take up subsistence cultivation. What actually happened was that, where food was scarce, substantial numbers of people moved to the main cities. They voted with their feet for urban residence because of a greater likelihood of the assurance of at least some food in main cities through the issue of rations, work, relief initiatives and recourse to large black markets. These last both drew food supplies disproportionately to cities and encouraged cultivation in and around them.

Because relatively greater food availability pulled people to main cities, the war was marked, more often than not, by enhanced rates of urbanization. In most of Southeast Asia's main cities, a pattern of swift urban growth continued in the 1950s (Table 8.1). During the Japanese occupation, even cities in food-surplus areas – Rangoon, Bangkok and Saigon-Cholon – where a search for safety was a principal determinant of rural–urban movements, evacuations were temporary. Although a pre-war phenomenon, the primate city became, as a result of the Japanese occupation, even more a feature of Southeast Asia.

In 1953, D. W. Fryer heralded the emergence of the million city in Southeast Asia.[107] In fact by 1943, as this chapter has shown, urban populations were already near to, or above, a million in three of Southeast Asia's main cities. Furthermore, urbanization patterns generally associated with the largest Southeast Asian cities of the 1950s and 1960s appeared in the 1940s. Rapid wartime urbanization and enhanced opportunities for market gardening helped fundamentally to change the geography of settlement. In Singapore and Kuala Lumpur, large squatter communities emerged for the first time. Squatter settlement also expanded in Manila and probably in Penang, and, due to the large inflow of unemployed landless labourers, almost certainly in Jakarta.

Wartime dislocation encouraged a transition towards a new post-war phase of large-scale internal migration rather than international migration from China and India as a driver of Southeast Asian urban growth. Migrant inflows during the war must, in time, have helped to make cities feel less 'alien' to new arrivals from nearby areas. If so, this would have tended to discourage reverse migration and, moreover, is likely to have promoted migration through the 'friends and relatives' attraction exerted on potential migrants. Such migration, along with much-increased post-war urban birth rates, were the motive forces for Southeast Asia's urban explosion after 1950.

[107] Fryer, 'Million city'.

9

Labour and the Japanese

Chapter 3 dealt with the methods that Japan used to finance the war and provided some examples of Japanese plunder. These were not, however, the only ways in which Japan acquired resources: Japan procured Southeast Asian labour. Southeast Asians worked for the Japanese as forced labour, as 'volunteers' under varying degrees of compulsion, and as a matter of choice. Although the Japanese sent only a few Southeast Asians to work in Japan or elsewhere in the Empire outside Southeast Asia, they made considerable use of Southeast Asian labour within the region. Recourse to Southeast Asians, often as forced labour, increased substantially as the war turned against Japan. Large labour surpluses, a feature of the early months of occupation as plantations and mines closed, turned to scarcity beginning by about mid-1943.

This chapter considers five main ways in which Southeast Asians worked for the Japanese and contributed to Japan's war effort. Three of these are notorious and remain the subject of widespread condemnation: the shipment beginning in June 1942 of labour for the Thailand–Burma railway and the use of Indonesians to build three other railways, in Java, Sumatra and south-west Celebes; the recruitment of *romusha* in Indonesia; and the provision of so-called comfort women for Japanese soldiers. A fourth use of Southeast Asian labour, less controversial, was in Japanese factories, where employment rose towards the latter part of the war with increased efforts to manufacture both war and import-substitution goods. Fifth, Japan, badly short of manpower, trained some Southeast Asians as soldiers and, probably, more important in terms of numbers, needed local labour to act as military auxiliaries and construct defence installations. Unlike railway workers, large numbers of *romusha* and almost all comfort women, the majority of labourers in the fourth and fifth groups voluntarily entered Japanese employment, often, and increasingly, as the best way to obtain food.

Including temporary workers, perhaps as many as 15 million Southeast Asians worked at some point for the Japanese. In Indonesia, Malaya and Burma, Japan relied heavily on Southeast Asian labour. Out of Java's population of about 50 million, the Japanese calculated a potential workforce of some 12.5 million. At one time or another a high proportion of these individuals worked for the Japanese, most on a temporary basis but 2.6 million as permanent *romusha*.[1] As labour shortages developed in Southeast Asia, paid labour in Japanese factories or defence installations might be more remunerative than the available alternatives, or in terms of rice even than pre-war work in export industries. That happened in Burma, where the 1942 exodus of Indians created a shortage of workers.[2] Insofar as Southeast Asian workers earned less than they could otherwise have done, the difference was in effect a tax.[3] For Southeast Asia, due to a lack of data such taxation cannot be measured although it clearly existed in the case of forced labour and 'volunteers' meant to work for nothing in their spare time. Implicit labour taxation became more important as the war progressed and as Japan's need for labour increased.

In many instances, however, a concept of implicit taxation lacks relevance for the Japanese occupation. One reason for this is that working for the Japanese might be the only way to obtain food, as for many labourers in Indonesia. Under these circumstances, the line between voluntary and forced labour blurs. Second, high death rates among some groups of forced labourers and the sheer affront to human dignity of the sexual slavery of comfort women make irrelevant a concept of comparative rates of pay, even if these individuals were paid, which generally they were not except for receiving some food and accommodation.

Apart from acquiring resources, the Japanese had two other objectives in their mobilization of Southeast Asians. One, important chiefly in the early stages of the war, was to counter unemployment and underemployment due to wartime economic collapse. The other, most prominently associated with military and para-military training, was to promote nationalism among Southeast Asians and to try to foster a shared (Japanese-inclusive) Asian identity. 'Spiritual' indoctrination was a notable component of this Japanese labour initiative, and also numerous Japanese-sponsored civilian organizations. However, few people in Burma or Indonesia, where such organizations were especially numerous, were persuaded to a strong allegiance to Japan, and fewer still in Malaya and the Philippines. Conversion to *Dai Nippon* and the concept of a common Asian identity would always have been difficult to achieve in Southeast Asia. As the war went on, it became harder still against a backdrop of precipitate falls in GDP, few consumer goods, high inflation, widespread experience of abuse by Japanese, and their arrogant and contemptuous attitude of racial superiority towards Southeast Asians.[4]

1 Sato, *War, nationalism*, pp. 156–58.

2 Pe, *Narrative*, p. 56; Christian, *Burma*, pp. 131–32; Burma Intelligence Bureau, *Burma*, vol. 1, pp. 81–82.

3 Rockoff, *America's economic way*, pp. 25–27 and *Until it's over*, p. 8.

4 Dower, 'Race, language and war', pp. 259, 271, 277.

Manual Labour, Factory Workers and Civil Servants

This section looks at the deployment of Southeast Asian labour, the bulk of which was unskilled, for Japanese construction projects and Japanese-run factories; both were organized mainly by the military. Main topics in the section are: an estimate of the number of workers utilized by the Japanese in various Southeast Asian countries and an indication of their distribution across countries; discussion of food as an incentive to secure labour; the position of civil servants; and some evaluation of labour efficiency.

As well as providing construction and factory labour, many Southeast Asians filled administrative roles. Japan preferred to take over pre-war government structures as far as possible and lacked personnel once Europeans left or were interned (Chapter 2). Here, I refer to administrative workers mainly in regard to their living standards. In Indonesia, Burma, Malaya and, after March 1945, in Vietnam, the wartime promotion of Asians to positions formerly occupied by Europeans within government administrations had a notable impact in giving indigenous administrators more experience of exercising authority.

There were several reasons why Japan, although itself short of labour, sent almost no Southeast Asians to work in the home islands. One was that, unlike Koreans, very few Southeast Asians spoke Japanese, and a second the paucity of skilled Southeast Asian workers. Third, with the exception of the Chinese, the Japanese had a low opinion of Southeast Asian workers. Fourth, when Southeast Asia had large labour surpluses early in the war, Japan was not as badly in need of labour as it was subsequently. During the war's later stages, when labour became acutely scarce in Japan, the Japanese required a large number of workers in Southeast Asia to produce import-substitution goods and construct defence installations. By then, too, the Japanese were desperately short of shipping and probably would not have wanted to divert tonnage to bring Southeast Asian workers to Japan.

Many of the possibly 15 million Southeast Asians who worked, if sometimes briefly, for the Japanese were in war-related construction since, as shown in Chapter 5, the Japanese did not start many new factories and large parts of the plantation and mining sectors shut down during the war. Geographically, worker numbers were skewed heavily towards Indonesia and Burma, and these were also the countries in which workers suffered most, principally due to a predominance of forced labour. The Japanese initiated numerous 'voluntary' labour schemes. Although with a strong compulsory element, these generally involved labour only for short periods such as turning out after work or for one day a week. For example, on Sunday mornings public works staff in Perak, Malaya had to do two hours of 'free labour service', mainly *changkolling* (clearing ground) in connection with food production.[5] Similarly

[5] WL, MSS. Ind. Ocn. s. 172, K. N. Sinnathamby and T. G. Seshan, 'Resume of works done during the period Jan. 1942–Aug. 1945', 3 December 1945, p. 3.

in 1944 in Malaya, Free Labour Corps members of the Peace Preservation Corps were sent to military establishments to do a day's work.[6] Despite the required and usually unpaid character of such work, it is excluded from the category of forced labour on the grounds that this involved the long-term impressment of workers, often under poor conditions. After looking briefly at Japanese-recruited labour in Thailand, Malaya, the Philippines and Indochina, the section more fully discusses Indonesia and Burma.

Thailand

A benefit of Thailand's alliance with Japan was that Thailand had the smallest number of people who worked for the Japanese. Most of these Thai workers were in fact Chinese living in Thailand and included, as discussed later in the chapter, some 18,000 organized by Bangkok's Chinese Chamber of Commerce to labour on the Thailand–Burma railway. Additionally, Japan built a number of roads and various other infrastructure for military purposes, for which a substantial, but unknown, number of Thai as well as Chinese workers were recruited.

Malaya

As in Thailand, the largest group of labourers from Malaya working on a single Japanese project were those, perhaps as many as 91,000, transported to the Thailand–Burma railway. As the war progressed and Allied invasion became more likely, the Japanese increasingly recruited men, and also some women, for military transport and construction projects such as airfields, earth works and lumbering, sometimes resorting to forced labour to obtain these workers. Many older school pupils married to avoid forced labour.[7] Even by April 1943, recruitment for the Thailand–Burma railway had made it hard for Perak's Department of Public Works to obtain staff, and beginning in 1944 the use of labour for war installations and military preparations worsened shortages. The Department found itself partly reliant on hiring women and dependants of those sent to Thailand by the Japanese.[8]

Labour for the Japanese, even if not forced, could be an unhealthy undertaking. Between 1942 and 1943, a labour force of 2,500, housed in temporary huts, was employed at the Port Swettenham aerodrome. Sanitation was primitive and anti-malaria measures absent. In 1943, three or four workers

[6] NARA, RG226, entry 16, box 1472, no. 128585, OSS, R&A Branch, Regular Intelligence Reports, 'Malaya under the Japanese, March 1945', p. 7.

[7] Malayan Union, *Annual report on education ... 1946*, p. 6.

[8] WL, MSS. Ind. Ocn. s. 172, K. N. Sinnathamby and T. G. Seshan, 'Resume of works Jan. 1942–Aug. 1945', 3 December 1945, p. 1.

died every day, mainly from malaria and malnutrition. It became necessary to recruit 500 new labourers monthly to keep up the numbers.[9]

On 20 December 1943, the Japanese responded to growing labour shortages by creating a Labour Service Corps, the *Seicho*, with branches throughout Malaya and organized mainly on racial lines. For every 250 inhabitants, 20 men aged 15 to 45 were required to be *Seicho* members, amounting to a total of roughly 400,000 people and including government employees. Most work undertaken by *Seicho* groups, generally construction or food cultivation, took place in members' 'free' time, but was sometimes for longer periods. By the end of 1944, a further tightening of labour availability led to a stricter, but apparently far from comprehensive, enforcement of employment regulations that required men to move from non-essential occupations to war-related activities. At this time, too, police took workers off estates and beggars from the streets to obtain labour.[10]

In Singapore, about 70,000 people, including 45,000 in Japanese-managed factories, were employed by the Japanese and accounted for more than a fifth of all employment.[11] These Singaporeans were subject to accusations of being sympathizers. However, it is difficult to know how many genuinely sympathised as opposed to working for the Japanese to obtain food or housing.[12]

Philippines

Unemployment in the Philippines did not give way to a serious shortage of unskilled labour until about the beginning of 1944, when Japan's military, under growing Allied threat, began to construct airfields, air-raid shelters and defensive works on a massive scale. The Japanese had to try to obtain labour by working through the government of the independent Philippine Republic. However, like other Japanese attempts to manage the economy, whether themselves or through the intermediary of a quasi-independent Philippine government, that proved frustrating. Nor could the Philippine government itself effectively mobilize labour to increase food output.

Early in 1944, in response to worsening food shortages, the government ordered the recruitment of all able-bodied persons aged between 16 and 60 to participate in emergency food production. In Manila on 14 May 1944, the first day of this compulsory labour service, 300,000 of an expected 420,000 turned out for work. Not all were assigned to food cultivation: some were taken

9 ANM, 1957/0292074, RC Sel. 296/1947 Selangor, *Report of the Medical Department 1941–1946*, p. 12.

10 OSS, assemblage 45, *Manpower in Japan and occupied areas*, vol. 2, pp. 237, 244; NARA, RG226, entry 16, box 1472, no. 128585, OSS, R&A Branch, Regular Intelligence Reports, 'Malaya under the Japanese, March 1945', p. 7; Chin, *Malaya upside down*, p. 49; Kratoska, *Japanese occupation*, pp. 186–94 and 'Labor', p. 243; Harper, *End*, p. 40.

11 Huff and Majima, *World War II Singapore*, pp. 250, 336.

12 NAS, Oral History, Chan Chee Seng, pp. 38–40 and Wong Lau Eng, pp. 5–11.

to do military-related jobs like working on airfields or digging air-raid shelters. Among those meant to grow food, many came without their own tools nor were tools available for them to use. There were no further attempts at mass labour mobilization, although this one Japanese effort did mean that a few hundred thousand Filipinos spent some time, if perhaps briefly, engaged in compulsory labour.[13]

In April 1944, the government response to pressing Japanese demands for labour was to create the Labor Recruitment Agency, which was intended to strike a balance between Japanese labour requirements and the rights of Filipino workers. Japan's army and navy requested the immediate supply of more than 80,000 workers, but the Agency could not meet this, partly because of low real wages, inadequate transport and poor communications, and partly because Filipinos were reluctant to work for the Japanese. As a result, Japanese civilians in the Philippines were mobilized for war work, leading to the scaling down or closure of less important Japanese enterprises like restaurants and shops.

Intense Japanese pressure for President Laurel to provide Filipino labour came after he declared martial law on 21 September 1944, and two days later war against the United States and United Kingdom. Laurel responded to Japanese urgings and their threat to introduce military conscription by issuing an order on 2 November requiring all males aged 18 to 50 to do forced labour. Even before that, the Japanese had started to recruit forced labour through neighbourhood associations in the provinces. Finally, the Japanese, balked by a failure to obtain sufficient labour, annoyed by an insufficiently co-operative government and faced with relentless Allied attack, began to pull people off the streets at bayonet point.[14]

Indochina

In Vietnam, Japan was not in a strong position to obtain forced labour or, as it did in most of Southeast Asia, to set up patriotic associations which might have the dual purpose of attempting to instil pro-Japanese attitudes and obtaining 'voluntary' labour. The Japanese operated mainly through the Cao Đài and the Hòa Hảo (Chapter 2). Both groups worked for the Japanese as part of a more general policy of co-operation. In the case of the Hòa Hảo, most of whose members were farmers, the contribution appears to have been principally through maintaining rice production. In 1944, when Allied bombing caused many workers to leave Saigon in search of safety in the countryside, the Cao Đài voluntarily supplied labourers to fill the gap. The Cao Đài managed work

[13] Jose, 'Labor usage', pp. 279–81; Hartendorp, *Japanese occupation*, pp. 132–34; OSS, assemblage 45, *Manpower in Japan and occupied areas*, vol. 2, pp. 303–04, 307.

[14] Jose, 'Labor usage', pp. 282–83; Friend, *Blue-eyed enemy*, pp. 167–68.

sites with minimal Japanese interference and their management avoided the brutality that characterized Japanese projects elsewhere in Southeast Asia.[15]

After the March 1945 coup, companies of *heiho*, or auxiliary troops, were organized and put under the command of Japanese officers. *Heiho* companies consisted of selected Vietnamese members of the former colonial army, now in Japanese uniforms. Typically unskilled, *heiho* served as coolies, doing jobs like building roads and digging trenches, and as transport drivers. They might also undertake guard duties.[16]

Indonesia

In Indonesia, the Japanese initiated numerous volunteer labour programmes. As one example, in June 1944 it was reported that a million students had started to participate in several labour services. Work included digging bomb shelters, farming, weeding, cleaning machinery and the manufacture of wooden vehicles.[17]

More important, Indonesia, mainly Java, supplied by far Southeast Asia's largest contingent of forced labour because of its many *romusha*. Some Indonesians became *romusha* as a way to get food but large numbers were obtained, often through trickery, by Japanese and Indonesian officials to fill quotas. Systematic recruitment of *romusha* began in November 1943, and their number quickly rose as in Java Japanese labour mobilization entered a new, defence-oriented phase of building airstrips, pillboxes, trenches and tunnels. The some 2.6 million Javanese *romusha* in November 1944 represents the number of regular and rotation workers for whom the Japanese had to supply rice, and is probably a more accurate count of *romusha* than the 4.1 million claimed by the Indonesians in regard to war reparations.[18] Ill treatment of *romusha* was commonplace and a lack of adequate food the rule, but in Java how *romusha* fared also depended significantly on the approach towards these workers of the local *pangreh praja* (an administrative corps of local Indonesian officials).[19]

Most *romusha* in Java worked locally but a large number, some 300,000 in all, were taken outside Java. When a departing *romusha* had been the main breadwinner, families left at home faced desperate circumstances.[20] *Romusha*

[15] Tràn, 'Working', pp. 287–95 and 'Japan and Vietnam's Caodaists', pp. 186–87: OSS, R&A 1249, *Japanese penetration in French Indo-China*, pp. 1–3.

[16] Marr, *Vietnam 1945*, p. 109.

[17] OSS, R&A 3170 and second edition of assemblage 22, *Programs of Japan in Java*, p. 146.

[18] IC, 400 4985, 'Documents on *romusha*', n.d.; Reid and Akira, *Japanese experience*, p. 247; Sato, 'Oppression and romanticism', p. 176.

[19] De Jong, *Collapse*, pp. 241, 242, 250, 251; Totani, *Tokyo War Crimes Trial*, p. 180; Lucas, *One soul*, p. 41.

[20] Sato, 'Oppression and romanticism', p. 177.

returning to Java usually reached their villages with infection, especially skin diseases and malaria.[21]

Data exist for 294,100 *romusha* who were transported from their home areas. Of these, 120,000 were sent to Sumatra, 80,400 to North and South Borneo, 32,400 to the Soenda (Sunda) Islands, Celebes and 31,000 to Malaya. Records show that of the 294,100 *romusha* 77,000 returned home.[22] For example, *romusha* were moved from Java to labour in the South Borneo diamond mines.[23] Probably at least half of all *romusha* taken from their homes died. The summary of a court exhibit for the Tokyo War Crimes Trial submitted by a former *romusha* sent to Tanjung Pinang in Indonesia stated that '[i]n 9 months 400 out of 750 coolies died'. Another Javanese civilian provided the Tribunal with an affidavit that he was made to work at Kampong Barrow in Singapore where 'only 1,000 among 2,000 coolies were physically able to work' and '4 to 6 died everyday'.[24]

The substitution of labour for capital, a prominent feature of Japan's use of Southeast Asian workers, was especially pronounced in Indonesia. Java had Southeast Asia's greatest surplus of labour, and Javanese, as well as being shipped throughout the region, were often used almost to the exclusion of capital equipment in construction projects. Between February 1943 and July 1944 in East Java, the Japanese directed the expenditure of 2 million person days to construct a drainage tunnel 800 metres long and 2 metres in diameter. Possibly as much as 10 per cent of the residency's population worked on the tunnel at one time or another; many died and even more contracted diseases. During the last year of the war, the completed tunnel at best slightly reduced flood damage. Soon after 1945 it began to cave in and fill up with silt.[25] Similarly, an irrigation project in Yogyakarta that was begun in July 1944 and lasted for a year used 2.51 million person days of paid labour and a further 0.21 million person days of unpaid forced labour. When it became doubtful that the project would be completed before the rainy season, school children were mobilized to work on it.[26]

Burma

Just after the Japanese occupation, Burma differed from most Southeast Asian countries in that in contrast to their labour surpluses, labour shortages almost

[21] Anderson, 'Problem of rice', p. 93.
[22] IC, 400 2431, 'Numbers of *romusha* sent from Java from mid-1943 to mid-1945, registered by destination'; De Jong, *Collapse*, pp. 249–51; Friend, *Blue-eyed enemy*, p. 163; Raben, 'Indonesian *rōmusha*', pp. 208–10.
[23] Keppy, *Politics*, pp. 136, 145.
[24] Totani, *Tokyo War Crimes Trial*, p. 180.
[25] Sato, *War, nationalism*, pp. 190–98.
[26] Sato, 'Relocation', pp. 256–57.

immediately developed, especially in Rangoon, due to the early 1942 exodus of Indians. Nearly all essential labour had been Indian, half or more of whom had left. It was thought that by August 1942 the Japanese had secured all remaining Indian labour, and were trying to obtain Burmese labour for work important to the military effort, such as the repair of Rangoon docks, loading and unloading military stores at the docks, and repairs to the roads and railway. In Rangoon, Burmese workers were, however, paid less, and more irregularly, than Indian. Upcountry, the Japanese used forced labour which might or might not be paid.[27]

Although the completion in October 1943 of the Thailand–Burma railway, discussed below, eased the Japanese demand for labour, other projects, mainly construction and the repair of docks, roads and bridges, required all the labourers who could be requisitioned. To some extent, the collapse in rice exports provided this labour supply through causing many Burmese agricultural workers to migrate to the towns or Japanese camps in search of paid work. An increase in daily wages from around 8 annas a day to as much as Rs. 4 by the end of 1943 or early 1944 amounted to an eightfold increase in nominal wages. Despite a more or less similar rise in prices over the same period, this suggests a tight labour market in Burma. That conclusion is further strengthened by smaller rises in nominal wages relative to inflation in some other Southeast Asian countries.[28]

In April 1943, even before Burma's independence in August, Ba Maw announced the formation of four armies: the Blood Army, referred to as the Burma National Army and considered below; the Leadership Army, another name for Ba Maw's sole party, *Dobama Sinyetha Asi Ayon*; the Circle Army; and the Sweat Army. The Circle Army, alias the National Service (*Wunhtan*) Association (NSA), was formed in December 1943 as a 'voluntary' civilian service organization, and described in official pronouncements as 'for those who cannot afford to offer help to the Blood or Sweat Armies'.[29] All government servants except those in the Burma National Army had to join the NSA, but it was open to anyone born in Burma and included a section for boys and girls aged 12 to 18. Recruitment to the Sweat Army appealed to the goal of Burmese independence and labour service on a patriotic basis, emphasizing that Burmese not permitted to shed their blood for Burma's freedom ought to be willing to sweat for it. The first batch of recruits for Burma's 'Sweat Army', and most thereafter, were sent to work on the Thailand–Burma railway. Many youths joined the BurmaNational Army to avoid being in the Sweat Army.[30] After the war, Ba Maw offered an apologia mixed with self-justification for this use of Burmese labour, describing it as a 'shocking tragedy' but labelling the

[27] Burma Intelligence Bureau, *Burma*, vol. 1, pp. 48–49.
[28] Ibid., vol. 2, pp. 114, 204–5.
[29] Ibid., vol. 2, p. 133.
[30] OSS, R&A 2015, *Japanese administration of Burma*, p. 81; Burma Intelligence Bureau, *Burma*, vol. 2, pp. 136, 171.

labourers 'who knew they were doomed to die' as 'among the truest heroes of Burma'.[31]

The NSA was divided under the heads of national service, meant to denote a variety of activities to promote public welfare, such as health and physical training, and Civil Defence to include assisting troops and police and guarding lines of communication. Some of these functions overlapped with those of the *Kayboaing* Associations (Civil Defence Corps), formed about mid-1943, and the East Asian Youths' League. Although described as voluntary labour, the Burmese apparently regarded the NSA as little better than Japanese impressment of labour, and it proved a 'complete failure', mainly due to the apathy of its government-paid officers.[32]

Recruitment for the Sweat Army or *Let Yon Tat* practically amounted to conscription. The Army, which numbered some tens of thousands of workers and included unskilled and skilled labour, was raised by special labour recruitment officers and also by headmen who were ordered to produce a specified number of men from their jurisdiction. Some headmen used this opportunity to exact bribes for excusing men from Sweat Army service, while doctors sold certificates of physical unfitness. The Sweat Army was primarily used to build the Thailand–Burma railway, although also for other tasks. Service in Sweat Army labour camps in Burma was not permanent, and labourers were allowed to return home after work on which they were engaged was finished. The Cart Corps, meant to supply carts on demand for army transport, paralleled the Sweat Army but may have existed mainly on paper due to the scarcity of bullocks.[33]

Food as an Incentive

Chapter 2 considered food as a means of social control; this section explores the somewhat different use of food as an incentive to recruit labour. From early in the war in rice-deficit areas, the promise of food was a major consideration that drew Southeast Asian workers to Japanese-sponsored projects. Unemployment in Indonesia, Malaya and the Philippines was sudden and severe.[34] In Indonesia, various relief works were started in response to high unemployment, which was partly due to the closure of Dutch estates.[35] For many in Java, accepting any work from the Japanese soon became almost the only way to avoid starvation.[36] Unemployment in Manila in February 1943 was

31 Maw, *Breakthrough*, p. 292 and see pp. 293–97.

32 Burma Intelligence Bureau, *Burma*, vol. 2, p. 134.

33 Ibid., vol. 2, pp. 133–38; OSS, assemblage 45, *Manpower in Japan and occupied areas*, vol. 2, pp. 213–14.

34 Rōyama and Takéuchi, *Philippine polity*, p. iii; Kratoska, 'Labor', pp. 237–38; Jose, 'Labor usage', pp. 274, 278.

35 Sato, 'Oppression and romanticism', p. 176.

36 Sato, 'Economic soldiers', p. 148.

roughly 25 per cent of the labour force.[37] A Domei (Japanese news bureau) story in July 1942 reported the success of persuading Filipinos of the 'sheer joy and satisfaction of building things [so that in two months they] were enthusiastically working around the clock, asking no extra pay'. A more realistic assessment is that food shortages and high unemployment not long after Japanese occupation meant that 'the workers in the cities and towns were glad to work for a bowl of rice or a mess of *camotes*' (sweet potatoes).[38]

After mid-1943, when the Japanese started to require large quantities of Southeast Asian labour, food became an increasingly important way to secure workers and probably also a greater incentive for Southeast Asians. For the Japanese, an ability to offer food became more valuable because the pool of available workers shrank due to higher Japanese labour demand; and because, as the likelihood of harsh physical discipline or even serious physical abuse in Japanese employment became common knowledge, fewer Southeast Asians were willing to accept this employment. From the point of view of Southeast Asians, the attraction of being paid in food increased as it became scarcer and money wages lagged behind inflation. A Japanese research report observed food to be the 'surest method of securing a work force'.[39] Chin explained in similar terms: 'By the lure of special rice-allocations to labourers the various branches of the Military, the various factories and foundries of the Kaishas, and the various reconstruction departments of the Railway Administration and the Government, got their labour forces.' Higher wages were not enough; rice was necessary and 'the infallible draw ... people who had vowed never to work under the Japanese had to swallow their pride and give way because of rice ... many women and girls of poor families succumbed to necessity and became Japanese mistresses because of rice'.[40]

The supply of labour available to Japanese mining enterprises in Malaya depended on the rations of rice that each concern could offer. Mining firms outside rice-growing areas considered that their location unduly restricted output by limiting access to rice and so also labour.[41] Labour supply was not, however, solely determined by rice. It was also a function of the availability of land for subsistence cultivation and the fear of being taken by the Japanese as forced labour. In 1944 in Malaya, the offer by Japanese-operated tin mines of a rice ration of 16 lbs a month (242 grams daily for a 30-day month) in addition to money wages attracted relatively few workers. Nor were workers enticed by the inducement to Chinese-operated mines of the cash value of every picul (133.3 lbs) of tin

37 OSS, assemblage 45, *Manpower in Japan and occupied areas*, vol. 2, p. 310.

38 Hartendorp, *History of industry*, p. 81: Agoncillo, *Fateful years*, pp. 564–65.

39 IER, Azb: 5 Japan, Malayan Military Administration Chōsabu, *Shōnan tokubetsu shi rōmu jijō chōsa* [Study of the labour situation in Syonan Municipality] (October 1944), p. 10.

40 Chin, *Malaya upside down*, p. 60.

41 NA, WO203/2647, 'Summary of economic intelligence (Far East) no. 132', 29 October 1945, p. 3.

ore produced plus 16 lbs of rice.[42] The pre-war consumption of the mining workers would probably have been considerably in excess of 242 grams, perhaps even twice as much.

The deplorable living standards and high probability of death that were the lot of the great majority of forced labourers have already been indicated. Many of the Southeast Asians who voluntarily worked for the Japanese also experienced a considerable drop in living standards, if one generally less severe than for those not employed by the Japanese. Inadequate nutrition only partly accounts for this. Workers, as Thompson points out, might also suffer from dislocations, regimentation and a general deterioration of working conditions. An exception was some workers who received a limited amount of training to create a nucleus of skilled labour needed by the Japanese.[43] Additionally, a few individuals made themselves more comfortably off by working for the Japanese security services such as the police and *kempeitai*. In the small Malayan town of Tasek Gelugur in Province Wellesley such officials used the power arising from their association with the Japanese to exact material advantage, which probably included bribes and food.[44]

Civil Servants

Although some government administrators were able to turn employment by the Japanese to considerable personal benefit, many were not. In Malaya, civil service wages were initially cut, then restored at least in Singapore, but before long were badly eroded by inflation. Some civil servants supplemented their incomes by re-selling in the black market goods like medicine, vegetables and cigarettes that they could purchase at preferential rates.[45] However, the British-trained Malay bureaucratic elite did well socially and economically. The Japanese relied heavily on the services and advice of Malay bureaucrats and paid them well.[46] By contrast, in Vietnam, although lower-grade civil servants received ration coupons allowing them to buy rice and some consumer goods at official prices, inflation ate away at real wages and their circumstances were described as bad.[47]

In Bangkok and elsewhere in Thailand, as in much of Southeast Asia, inflation sharply reduced civil servants' real wages. Ordinary government employees had permanent jobs while special government employees were hired on a temporary basis for specific projects. For both groups average annual nominal wages remained almost constant from 1941 to 1944, but real wages dropped by three-quarters or more (Table 9.1). Between 1944 and 1945, a near doubling of inflation further greatly eroded real wages. Falls in real wages of the magnitude

42 Yip, *Tin mining industry*, pp. 295–96.
43 Thompson, *Labor problems*, p. 9.
44 Jaafar bin Hamzah, 'Malays in Tasek Gelugur', p. 59.
45 Kratoska, *Japanese occupation*, pp. 68–69, 204.
46 Cheah, *Red star*, p. 43.
47 Le, *Impact*, p. 250.

Table 9.1 *Thailand annual average government employees' daily wages 1937/38–1944*

1937/38 = 100	Ordinary employees		Special employees		
	Nominal wages	Real wages	Nominal wages	Real wages	Prices
1937/38	100.0	100.0	100.0	100.0	100
1941	130.0	99.2	86.7	66.2	131
1942	125.8	71.1	79.2	44.7	177
1943	126.7	47.8	79.2	29.9	265
1944	125.0	26.6	87.5	18.6	470

Notes and sources: Kingdom of Thailand, *Statistical yearbook, 1937/38–1955*, p. 415. Prices are from Ingram, *Economic change*, p. 164. Ingram derives his data from Bank of Thailand figures and specifies that these are for the cost of living and based on the family budget of white-collar workers and wage earners in Bangkok.

shown in Table 9.1 are inconsistent with sustainable livelihood for nearly all of Thailand's some 82,500 civil servants, especially since money wages were low, even taking into account bonuses. Many middle-ranking civil servants had some capital and could live partly off that as well as by taking second jobs or petty trading, known at the time as *seng lee*. However, the majority, along with lower-grade civil servants, had little choice but to take graft. Continued rapid inflation after the end of the war, coupled with still low civil service wages, worsened the problem of civil service corruption and helped to institutionalize it, since real wages for civil servants never regained pre-war levels.[48]

Upon occupying the Philippines, the Japanese immediately reduced the wages of government employees by about half. Thereafter, salary bonuses which were small relative to inflation, an end to rice rations by mid-1944 and a lack of access to community kitchens left government servants in increasingly desperate circumstances. Although for most civil servants public transport by city bus or *carretela* (horse-drawn carriage) was expensive, it was apparently cheaper than walking, due to the high price of shoes.[49]

Worker Efficiency

As observed for Indonesian *romusha*, it is likely that, for almost all forced labour, poor nutrition reduced the effort and efficiency of workers.[50] Perhaps

48 Reeve, *Public administration*, pp. 67–74; Warr and Nidhiprabha, *Thailand's macroeconomic miracle*, pp. 23–26.

49 UP, Roxas Papers, box 11, unsigned letter to President of the Republic of the Philippines, 4 July 1944.

50 Reid and Akira, *Japanese experience*, p. 249.

more surprisingly, the same was true of Singapore factory workers in receipt of apparently generous priority rations as an inducement to work for the Japanese. In 1944, the daily ration of 400 grams (1,432 calories) of rice for workers in Japanese factories was far above average Singapore rice consumption at the time and not greatly less than average pre-war rice consumption (Table 6.2). Added to the priority rice ration was a small money wage. Nevertheless, priority workers could suffer from a lack of nutrition. One reason for this was that the workers often sold part of their priority rice on the black market, leaving themselves short of the main food staple. A further nutritional impairment was that virtually every other constituent of a balanced diet, including oils, fats and protein, was in short supply, so that black market proceeds from selling rice bought only small quantities of other essential foods or goods like soap or clothing. Poor nutrition and the long periods spent using Singapore's public transport made it difficult to secure adequate work effort and gave rise to chronic absenteeism (Chapter 5).[51]

Japanese Railways

Of the five wartime railways built by the Japanese in Southeast Asia, the Thailand–Burma railway was the only one that became fundamental to Japan's war effort in the region. Once committed to occupying Burma (and later to full-scale war there), it was essential for Japan to transfer soldiers and supplies through Thailand to Burma. Construction of a 150-mile (241-kilometre) link that joined Thailand's and Burma's existing rail networks would avoid a 2,000-mile sea journey between the two countries and reduce the Japanese need to sail in the increasingly dangerous waters of the Indian Ocean and around the Straits of Malacca (Figure 5.2). That, in turn, would save shipping for use on other runs.[52] Not long after initial planning for the railway in early 1942, Japanese shipping was already under serious pressure due to naval setback in May 1942 in the Coral Sea and defeat during the first week in June at Midway. In June, Tokyo ordered the railway to be built.[53]

Construction of a Thailand–Burma railway was a monumental, seemingly near-impossible, undertaking. A railway would have to traverse an extremely inhospitable terrain of mountains, rivers and jungle. A Japanese newspaper report may have erred in favour of hyperbole but it was not so wide of the mark in describing the area as inhabited only by giant ants, leeches as long and thick as an index finger and ready to drop from overhanging branches on anyone

[51] IER, Azb: 5 Japan, Malayan Military Administration Chōsabu, *Shōnan tokubetsu shi rōmu jijō chōsa* [Study of the labour situation in Syonan Municipality] (October 1944), pp. 13, 18–20.

[52] OSS, R&A 1286.1, *Additional strategic objective*, p. 1.

[53] NA, WO203/6325, SEATIC bulletin no. 246, 1946, 'Burma–Siam railway', pp. 3, 7.

underneath, and a species of lizard larger than the average Japanese. The report might also have added that during the rainy season from May to early October the railway's route had some of the world's highest rainfall and, more important, that 70 per cent of it was through thick, malaria-infested jungle.[54]

Remoteness was a major barrier to construction. Materials, including track, wagons and engines, and labour had largely to be transported from elsewhere. Engineering studies for a railway between Thailand and Burma dated from 1905, but the project's intractability and scant economic justification had prevented implementation. Japanese engineers drew on earlier surveys and, eschewing caution, chose the most difficult Three Pagodas Pass route which would take the railway through the pass of the same name, 903 feet above sea level (Figure 5.2). That option was, as the Japanese pointed out, the shortest route. It had, however, been rejected by British engineers as too demanding. A company which had tried to build a railway following the route later chosen by the Japanese abandoned construction due to impossible conditions.[55]

The completed railway was single track with numerous loops and sidings to permit two-way traffic. It had 688 bridges, an average of 28.5 for every 10 kilometres of track. Most bridges were short, but 63 were over 50 metres in length and one measured 200 metres. Almost all bridges were fashioned from local materials; 680 used locally felled wood, a telling indication of the completed railway's high labour content. Ba Maw, who travelled on the railway to escape Burma when the Japanese retreated, described bridges made of wood and bamboo and often held together by wire or rope and even thongs in places.[56] For military usefulness, a road to connect Thailand and Burma might have been superior to a railway, especially because so many bridges offered easy bombing targets. However, acute shortages of motorized transport and petrol told against a road.[57] The one constructed, which eventually paralleled the Thailand–Burma railway, was of variable quality.[58]

Railways built by the Japanese were good examples of Japan's policy of commandeering physical capital in Southeast Asia and, as discussed in the next paragraphs, of substituting labour for capital. The Japanese minimized real resource transfers to Southeast Asia by taking around two-thirds of the equipment for the Thailand–Burma railway from Southeast Asia's rail networks. Japan supplied 45 of 113 locomotives, 400 of 1,800 stock wagons and about half of the steel rails. Much of the rest of the track came from Malaya. As noted in Chapter 5, the Japanese removed a large part (around 300 kilometres,

54 *Japan Times and Advertiser*, 17 June 1942 cited in Reynolds, 'History, memory, compensation', p. 327; NA, WO203/6325, 'Burma–Siam railway', pp. 8–9.

55 NA, WO203/6325, 'Burma–Siam railway', p. 27.

56 Maw, *Breakthrough*, p. 296.

57 NA, WO203/6325, 'Burma–Siam railway', pp. 10, 12.

58 NARA, RG226, entry 154, box 80, file 1387, OSS, R&A/SEAC no. 54K, *The location and installations of the Burma–Thailand Railroad*, 15 January 1945, pp. 26–28.

although the post-war claim was for 182 kilometres) of the Malayan east coast line (Figure 5.2). In Burma, a considerable proportion of the second track of the double-tracked part of the Rangoon–Mandalay line was torn up for use on the new railway. Rails were also brought from Java. Burma and Malaya were principal Southeast Asian sources of locomotives and wagons, although locomotives were also taken from Java, Thailand and Indochina. About 25 locomotives came from Burma. Of the 30 locomotives taken from Malaya to Burma, some were presumably used for the Thailand–Burma railway. Malaya furnished 1,000 wagons for the railway and Burma 400. While just 9 locomotives were taken from Java for the Thailand–Burma railway, the Japanese removed 25 locomotives from the island to meet Malayan needs. Although a comparatively small part of Java's railway, this removal of locomotives constituted a substantial loss of physical capital. The eleven-span bridge over the Mae Klong (Kwai Yai) River at Kanchanaburi was brought from Java. Contributions exacted from Thailand's government included supplying a proportion of the labour and materials for the Thailand–Burma railway and printing baht to finance both it and the Kra Isthmus railway.[59]

To accelerate completion of the Thailand–Burma railway, construction started simultaneously at both its ends, at Ban Pong in Thailand and Thanbyuzayat in Burma (Figure 5.2). Neither area had sufficient labour for Japanese requirements, and local workers soon became hard to attract as news of working conditions spread. Highly labour-intensive techniques during the 16 months of railway construction are indicated by Japanese use during this period of up to 300,000 Allied prisoners of war and Asian workers. Most of the latter were men but there were also female labourers. They apparently suffered a good deal of molestation from Japanese army personnel until, after July 1943, prostitutes, possibly comfort women, were imported for Japanese men engaged in the project. A considerable number of people also went to the site of railway construction in Thailand and Burma as dependants, since with the main breadwinner gone it became hard for families to survive.[60]

Some Asians, especially in the early stages of construction, were attracted by (almost always false) promises of good wages or payments to their families, but the great majority went as forced labour. Many workers were simply rounded up off the streets, from amusement parks, or from their work in plantations or fields.[61] Others were gathered through trickery. Free cinema shows were advertised, and after the theatre was full the doors were locked and adult

[59] Malayan Union, *Railways report 1946*, p. 1; United Nations, *Reconstruction: Burma*, pp. 29–30; Silverstein, 'Transportation', p. 7; De Vries, 'Tracing', p. 36; OSS, R&A 1007, *Japanese use of land transport*, p. 5; Reynolds, 'History, memory, compensation', pp. 327, 332–33.

[60] Totani, *Tokyo War Crimes Trial*, pp. 166–67; Nakahara, 'Labour recruitment', p. 221.

[61] Reynolds, *Thailand*, p. 177; Nakahara, 'Labour recruitment', pp. 222–26; Rai, *Indians*, pp. 251–53.

males seized and sent to the railway.[62] Probably the largest number of Asian workers were secured as part of quotas supplied by headmen – a common way in Burma – or by others with a position of leadership in their country. A headman sometimes took the opportunity to compile a list of candidates which included all his enemies as well as some wealthy individuals who could be squeezed for large bribes not to go to the railway.[63] In early 1943, the Thai government refused to recruit more workers for the railway due to concern about labour conditions, and at the beginning of April local military authorities put pressure on the Chinese Chamber of Commerce to supply 10,000 Chinese coolies for construction work on the railway. The Chamber, as well as recruiting in all about 18,000 people as railway labourers, raised some 2 million baht to fund recruitment.[64]

There is ample reason to refer to the Thailand–Burma railway as the 'Death railway', but quantification of worker numbers and mortality is approximate. The best estimates are that 68,000 Allied prisoners of war and at least 183,000 Southeast Asians were used to build the railway. The latter consisted of about 92,000 from Burma and 91,000 from Malaya, Java, Thailand and Indochina. The number of Thai, as contrasted with ethnic Chinese Thai, is the least certain. Despite Thai government recruitment of workers for the railway, no definite labour enlistment scheme existed. Burmese workers were mainly conscripts in the Burma Sweat Army, although some were from the Labour Service Corps.[65]

Figures for worker mortality rely heavily on Allied reconstruction soon after the war, since most Japanese records were destroyed and post-war Japanese figures are suspect on the grounds of trying to minimize the number of deaths.[66] Official British data for deaths are 12,399 Europeans, amounting to 18.2 per cent of these workers, and a minimum of 74,025 Asians, and so 40.6 per cent of their number (Table 9.2). An estimate of the incidence of death by the historian of Britain's military administration in the Far East gives figures of a third for prisoners of war, over 40 per cent for workers from Burma and half for those from Malaya.[67] Mortality was higher among Asians than Europeans because

62 Nakahara, 'Malayan labor', p. 256.

63 Burma Intelligence Bureau, *Burma*, vol. 2, pp. 132, 136; Maw, *Breakthrough*, pp. 294–95.

64 LHC, MAGIC, 'Summary 402', 2 May 1943, p. 2; Reynolds, 'History, memory, compensation', pp. 332–33 and '"International orphans"', pp. 376–78. Some estimates suggest many more Chinese Thai workers on the railway than the figure cited above. See Subrahmanyan and Sturma, 'Asian Labourers'.

65 NA, WO203/6325, 'Burma–Siam railway', pp. 25–26 and WO325/56, 'Report on coolie camp conditions on the Burma Siam railway during the period November 1943 to August 1945', pp. 11–14.

66 NA, WO325/56, 'Coolie camp conditions', pp. 68–69. For a 1946 statement by Capt. Yamamoto on employment on the railway as of the end of September 1945, see NA, WO325/57, Documents illustrating report on coolie camp conditions on the Burma Siam railway, document D.

67 Donnison, *British military administration*, p. 281.

Table 9.2 *Japanese World War II railways and Yunnan railway comparative construction deaths*

	Construction dates	Length km	Number of workers	Number of deaths	Deaths per km of railway
Yunnan railway (Lao Kay (Hekou)–Kunming)	1898–1910	464.0	60,000 at any one time	24,000	51.7
Thailand–Burma railway (Ban Pong–Thanbyuzayat)	June 1942–Oct. 1943	402.3			
Total			250,503	86,424	214.8
Europeans			68,007	12,399	30.8
Asians			182,496	74,025	184.0
Bayah railway (Bayah–Saketi)	June 1943–March 1944	89.3	200,000	about 35,000	392.0
Central Sumatra railway (Moeara–Pakan Baroe)	c. May 1944–15 Aug. 1945	221.0	Many romusha; 1,937 POWs	82,000	371.0

Notes and sources: Yunnan: Naval Intelligence Division, *Indo-China*, pp. 420–21; Robequain, *Economic development*, pp. 91–92; Rousseau, 'Imperial railway failure', pp. 10, 13. Of the 929 Europeans who worked on the line, 44 lost their lives. *Thailand–Burma: Europeans:* NA, WO203/6325, Burma–Siam railway, pp. 22–24. *Asians:* NA, WO325/56, Coolie camp conditions, p. 75; see also NA, WO203/6325, Burma–Siam railway, pp. 25–26, which gives slightly different figures for Asians. The estimation of Asian deaths is specified as a minimum. *Bayah:* Poeze, 'Road', p. 165; Sato, *War, nationalism*, p. 185. Perhaps an average of roughly 40,000 workers were employed on any given day. *Central Sumatra:* Hovinga, *Sumatra railroad*, pp. 11–12, 16.

the latter, most of whom had been among the some 140,000 prisoners of war after Singapore fell, had generally better treatment than Asians and a military structure in place which included medical officers and a clear chain of command. Military organization enabled them, unlike the Asians, to establish procedures and enforce discipline to try to avoid epidemics, especially cholera, which constantly threatened labour camps along the railway. After completion, the railway required constant maintenance. During this period, Asian worker death rates fell from about 4 per cent of employed workers a month to 1.5 per cent a month.[68]

Desertion was much easier for Asians than Europeans. Thai and Burmese in particular had a chance of blending into the countryside and could secure help in ways that Europeans could not. Substantial numbers of Asians, probably at least a third, deserted. In Thailand, the Salesian Convent at Hua Hin (about 200 km south of Bangkok) was an important station on the 'underground route' followed by deserters.[69] One estimate for Burmese suggests that 87,000 were recruited via the Sweat Army and 166,000 by the Labour Service Corps. Among the latter, 74,000 deserted en route to the railway and a further 13,200 soon after arriving at the line.[70] Many deserting workers probably died before they could reach safety, but the numbers of deserters and survivors can never be known, a further reason for inexact data for deaths and number of Burmese railway workers. Additionally, Japanese officials apparently recorded some deaths at the labour camps as desertions, and this further clouds death statistics.

Table 9.2 compares death rates in the construction of Southeast Asian railways. Data for the Yunnan railway, built between 1897 and 1910 and a notoriously difficult and dangerous Southeast Asian railway project, affords a benchmark of what might be regarded as 'normal' mortality for this type of undertaking in Asia. Thailand–Burma deaths per kilometre of track were over four times higher than in Yunnan, and are indicative of Japanese treatment of workers as an expendable input. The Japanese had, as an Allied intelligence report observed, 'unlimited labour at their disposal and were in a position to effect rapid renewals when necessary'.[71] That also applied to the Japanese railways in Java and Sumatra, discussed below.

Four main factors combined to account for high worker deaths on the Thailand–Burma railway. One is that because of increased shipping losses and an anticipated Allied counter-attack in Burma, it was decided to complete the railway four months in advance of the originally scheduled date of December 1943. The railway became operational on 17 October 1943, somewhat behind the revised August date due to problems in transporting supplies to the railway over impassable roads and to worker sickness and disease. Even

[68] NA, WO325/56, 'Coolie camp conditions', pp. 73, 75.

[69] Ibid., pp. 14–15.

[70] NA, WO203/6325, 'Burma–Siam railway', p. 7.

[71] Ibid., p. 10.

so, the railway was finished some two months ahead of the original schedule. Accelerated completion was achieved by a fanatical Japanese desire to meet the new target, by working the labour force longer and harder, by much cruelty mixed with some sadistic enjoyment, and by a near-total disregard by those in command of the human costs of building the railway.

Asians suffered considerably more than Europeans from all of the other three factors accounting for high mortality – worker management, food and medical attention. Conditions varied along the railway, and while it is difficult to get an overall picture, it is clear that nowhere did workers, European or Asian, escape serious physical abuse and appalling deprivations.[72] An affidavit for the Tokyo War Crimes Trial taken from Thakin Sa, a Burmese and former labour superintendent, stated that railway workers were treated like slaves and that '[w]hips and sticks were freely used on the labourers'.[73] Conditions were worst in the several labour camps along the line and for construction workers and those who had, against time, to repair the bridges and track. Workers in the repair shops and engaged in maintenance, and so doing more skilled jobs, had better conditions.[74]

Worker management, a second reason for high deaths, favoured pain incentives rather than ordinary rewards to a degree extreme even by the standards of slave labour. For skilled work, slaves are most efficiently used through a relatively greater emphasis on the incentive of rewards; unskilled work is more effectively extracted by the fear of punishment.[75] Construction of the Thailand–Burma railway involved largely unskilled work such as moving earth, laying track and felling and hauling timber. Consistent from a Japanese point of view with this skill mix and imperative for quick completion, work on the railway was achieved through the use of constant and extreme physical violence. Workers might have to walk long distances before reaching construction sites. Workdays began at 7.30 a.m. and might last as late as darkness for Europeans and until five o'clock for Asians, with perhaps an hour off for lunch. Long hours and violence might have been the only ways to drive men, often ill and always with inadequate diets, to work beyond what they would do under any other circumstances. Nevertheless, high sickness rates, discussed below, suggest wasteful use of manpower, even if labour was considered unlimited.

Unlike the prisoners of war, Asians did not have commanding officers to try to mediate with the Japanese in charge. They were guarded by *gunzoku* (civilians in military employ), described as 'the illiterate, undisciplined, the

[72] Ibid., p. 15.
[73] Totani, *Tokyo War Crimes Trial*, p. 166.
[74] NA, WO325/56, 'Coolie camp conditions', pp. 19–21.
[75] Fenoaltea, 'Slavery'.

scum of Japan'.[76] Off-duty coolies were 'at the mercy of an illiterate, usually a drunkard and often a sadist, but more often just plain stupid' force of overseers.[77] Physical violence and corporal punishment were the norms in the Japanese army and were liberally transferred to workers. Partly because of this, partly because of a weak command structure and partly due to the assumption that Asians were innately inferior, it was stated in a report on coolie camp conditions that with one exception 'no responsible Japanese authority appeared to show the slightest concern at the suffering of the coolies'.[78]

Third, food given workers was grossly inadequate even for those not engaged in hard labour. Although food is often used as an incentive to promote work effort, for the Thailand–Burma railway evidence of this approach is lacking.[79] Typically, food consisted of little more than small amounts of rice and some dried vegetables three times a day for Europeans doing construction work and for Asians possibly just twice a day. The midday meal for Asians was sometimes rice starch and vegetables. Dried fish is also mentioned, but appears to have been the exception. Europeans had occasional fruit and eggs.[80]

Japanese supervisors might have gained more work if there had been an incentive structure that relied less on pain and somewhat more on food but that did not accord with their inclinations. In any case, the tactic of using food as an incentive was not easily implemented due to the remoteness of the region, monsoon rains rendering roads impassable and wartime shortages of goods. One of the main Japanese concessions in regard to food appears to have been a fried rice ball made with Japanese tinned meat for Europeans at Christmas.[81]

Fourth, high mortality can be explained by a near-total absence of medical facilities as well as Japanese attitudes towards sick workers. Large numbers of men were going down 'with various forms of disease', wrote a British medical officer in his diary of 23 June 1943, 'so the Jap engineers, who do not regard ill health as a reason for not working (at least among the slaves), are working the remainder harder and harder as time gets shorter and they feel less certain of getting their railway finished by the date aimed at'.[82] The Japanese did not

[76] NA, WO325/56, 'Coolie camp conditions', p. 13.

[77] Ibid., p. 26.

[78] Ibid., p. 10.

[79] Cf. Tooze, *Wages*, pp. 538–51.

[80] NA, WO325/56, 'Coolie camp conditions', pp. 21–23, 27.

[81] NA, WO203/6325, 'Burma–Siam railway', p. 27.

[82] Hardie, *Burma–Siam railway*, p. 100. For other, first-hand, vivid accounts of the lack of food and appalling conditions for workers on the Thailand–Burma railway, see NA, HS1/71, 'Report of interrogation of four recovered British P.O.W who were rescued in the South China Sea after the sinking of the "Rakuyo Maru"', 31 January/1 February 1945, pp. 26–32 and 'P.O.W. in Siam', May 1943 revised to 28 August 1943, pp. 1–4.

consider that malaria exempted a man from work. Every morning those least unfit were selected for work. Even so, it was not uncommon for half of the workforce to be in 'hospital'.[83] These were rudimentary at best, and many of those taken to hospital died there.[84]

Endemic sickness, untreated by medical intervention, was usual in Asian camps. A British POW later recalled what he saw at a Tamil camp about 132 kilometres above Kanchanaburi:

> The sight was enough to cause a fit man to throw up. These were men with great ulcers chewing away their arms and legs, others, totally blind being led by others practically unable to support themselves, let alone assist others. Women suffering from ulcers and palagra [sic], mostly in a state of undress, which didn't matter, they had lost all resemblance to women and their bones showed through in the same places as the men.[85]

Similarly, the July 1943 diary of the British medical officer records that: 'People who have been near these [Asian] camps speak with bated breath of the state of affairs – corpses rotting unburied in the jungle, almost complete lack of sanitation, frightful stench, overcrowding, swarms of flies. There is no medical attention in these camps, and the wretched natives are of course unable to organise any communal sanitation.'[86]

Cholera, of which the Japanese were terrified, was probably the largest single cause of death. Asians, lacking the structure of commanding officers and medical personnel that the Europeans had, were particularly affected, and those with cholera were taken to makeshift shelters in the jungle, or to a shelterless cemetery where they were left without food or water. The British medical officer cited above, who spent more than two years on the railway, observed of these cholera victims that: '[I]f they have friends who will look after them, these do what they can. If they have not, so much the worse.'[87] Anxious to dispose of cholera sufferers as quickly as possible, the Japanese, including doctors, might ensure early death by administering tainted food or medicine, including overdoses of morphine or other poisonous injections. Sometimes they compelled other workers to brain Asian cholera cases with a hammer, or to bury them while still alive. A British POW, Arthur Lane, estimated that in 10 days his crew of 15 buried about 2,000 corpses of the cholera dead in 7 large pits.[88]

[83] NA, WO203/6325, 'Burma–Siam railway', p. 16.
[84] Ibid., p. 55.
[85] Lane, *Lesser gods*, p. 163.
[86] Hardie, *Burma–Siam railway*, p. 102.
[87] Ibid., p. 108.
[88] Totani, *Tokyo War Crimes Trial*, p. 167; Hardie, *Burma–Siam railway*, p. 109; Lane, *Lesser gods*, pp. 172–74.

In summary, although the written testimony of Lt. Col. S. W. Harris, a British officer who had been a POW in Changi before his transfer and that of his men to the railway, should be read in full, it is illuminating to reproduce extracts from his first-hand account of conditions even for some Europeans:

> The working day started with reveille and breakfast in darkness at about 0600–0700 hours . . . Breakfast consisted of ¾ pint of plain rice . . . [after parade at first light] Engineers took over. If the numbers were not up to demand there was a scene on parade, sometimes ending with the striking of officers in charge. The daily task of selecting the last few men to go out from a number of convalescents really all unfit to go was heartbreaking . . . [going to work] often entailed a considerable march of 5 to 10 kilos. Many men (in June up to 80%) were without usable boots. Marching was always through deep mud with many snags in the way of rocks and sharp bamboo roots . . . The work itself was mostly very heavy – beyond the strength of an average fully fit man and far beyond the capacity of our starved and debilitated men . . . [building the big bridge at Sonkrai] often entailed working in swift cold water up to the waist, sometimes even to the armpits . . . the Engineer O.Rs. in charge of parties drove the prisoners savagely with blows from fists, boots, sticks and wire whips . . . It is necessary to emphasise that most of this continual beating was not disciplinary but was used to drive men as beasts to efforts beyond their strength [underlining in the original] . . . [often work was continuous for three hours with no break.] A short interval, sometimes only a few minutes was allowed for the midday meal – a pint of rice with a few beans . . . Long after dark . . . the march back began – a nightmare performance in the mud, rain and darkness. Tools had to be checked in and this was frequently made an excuse for further harsh treatment and delay . . . At last the party would arrive back in camp at 2200 hrs or even later tired, worn out and dispirited. Numbers had again to be checked before they were dismissed to eat their evening meal (1 pint of rice and usually ½ pint of some form of vegetable stew) and turn in to their sleeping quarters – 2 ft. by 6 ft. or less per man – to get what sleep they could before the next day's agony started. Those who were sick had to be examined by fire-light.[89]

The railway never provided its planned logistical contribution. Allied bombing was a major, and increasing, hindrance. By the latter part of 1944, it restricted the railway to about 50 per cent of capacity, or four to five trains a day instead of a possible eight.[90] Railway spurs were built to protect trains against Allied air attack, and beginning in early 1944 all movement was at night. Bombing necessitated the rebuilding of many bridges as often as six times. That tested even the Japanese, widely acknowledged as the world's most

89 NA, WO203/6325, 'Burma–Siam railway', pp. 52–53.
90 Ibid., pp. 3, 12; Burma Intelligence Bureau, *Burma*, vol. 2, p. 216.

efficient bridge re-builders. Allied sorties hit several bridges daily, and along one stretch of 200 bridges up to 20 a day. An eight-metre bridge took four days to repair and a 12-metre bridge a week. It required four hours to unload a train for transport by ferry while bridges were being rebuilt.[91]

In January 1946, the Thailand–Burma railway was in a poor state and close to unworkable. The bridges had been built by the Japanese with the expectation of a two-year lifespan. By the end of the war in August 1945, they were capable of lasting until April 1946 with systematic renewal and maintenance.[92] In 1947, Thailand's government bought the railway from the British and the Dutch for £1.25 million, paid in five instalments. The price represented negotiated compensation for track, locomotives, wagons and workshop equipment removed from Malaya and Java and also bridges from Java.[93]

Military logistics had been the only justification for the railway, and before long it fell into disuse. Today its remaining traces consist of some parts of the line, the tourist attraction of the Kwae Yai River bridge, an Allied war cemetery at Kanchanaburi, a cemetery at Thanbyuzayat where 3,700 workers from Burma were buried and the graves of some 8,400 Asian labourers in cemeteries along the railway line.[94] The mass graves of Southeast Asians who died while building and maintaining the wartime railway are covered by jungle and known, if at all, only by rumour.

Railway construction was a principal way that Japan tried to overcome its east–west Southeast Asian transport problem, indicated above and in Chapters 1 and 5, of needing to move troops and supplies across Southeast Asia. The first of Japan's east–west railways was the Kra Isthmus railway, about 92 kilometres long and built by labourers from Malaya. Construction began in June 1942 and was completed at the beginning of December 1943. The line, with a capacity of about 1,000 tons a day, opened for transportation on 10 January 1944. It gave supply ships from Japan a relatively direct route to Burma. Ships coming to Bangkok could unload directly onto railway trucks for transport of materials and men southwards to Chumphon on the Kra Isthmus line and then along it to Khao Huagang. From there it was only a short sea journey to connect to the Burma railway system at Moulmein (Figure 5.2).[95] For shipping to and from Burma, the Kra railway, like the Thailand–Burma railway, increased the importance of the port of Bangkok. With this in mind, even before completion

[91] NA, WO203/6325, 'Burma–Siam railway', pp. 11–14.

[92] ANM, 1957/0620360, MU #5172/1946 British Military Administration 936, Col. J. O. Sanders report for ALFSEA, 12 January 1946.

[93] ANM, 1957/c BMA Misc 51 92/46, Lt. Col. K. A. Warmenhoven, 1 December 1946.

[94] Donnison, *British military administration*, p. 281.

[95] JM 167, *Malay operations record*, p. 2; LHC, MAGIC, 'Summary 619', 5 December 1943, pp. 1–4; NA, WO208/516, 'Railway developments in S. E. Asia', 8 March 1944; Rawson, 'Two new railways', pp. 86–87: Burma Intelligence Bureau, *Burma*, vol. 2, p. 223; Kratoska, *Japanese occupation*, pp. 188–89.

of the Thailand–Burma railway efforts were made to speed up work on dredging the bar at the river entrance to Bangkok harbour.[96]

Little is known about the 20,000 people who worked on the Kra railway. When labour recruiting for the railway opened at the Selangor Club in Kuala Lumpur, thousands of men went, attracted by the offer of $200 cash down.[97] Even less information than for the Kra railway exists for the Tondongkura railway in south-west Celebes, apparently meant to serve a coal mine near Makassar. The rest of this section concentrates on the central (Pekanbara) Sumatra and Java railways. Despite high human costs, the Java railway proved of little use during the war, while the line across Sumatra was completed only on the day that Japan surrendered. Soon after 1945 both railways became derelict and for them, as well as the Kra and Tondongkura railways, at most a few remnants and perhaps a rusting locomotive or two remain.

In Java, the Bayah railway was meant to transport coal from a mine. The railway ran across mountains to Saketi and from there linked to Java's pre-war rail system for onwards shipment (Figure 9.1). However, the railway was not completed until March 1944 and the mine produced only 4,000 tons of coal annually, rather than the target amount of 300,000 tons.[98]

The main purpose of the Sumatra railway (also referred to as the Pekanbaru Death railway) was to carry coal across the island, and so limit the possibility that shipping would encounter Allied navies in the Indian Ocean (Figure 9.2).[99] Before the war, a Sumatran railway to connect to existing lines on either side of the island and provide rail transport across the island's centre had been considered by the Dutch but rejected as impractical because of the swampland that would have to be traversed.[100] Since the railway was still in the planning stage in late 1944, many of the Japanese engineers who had worked on the Thailand–Burma railway could be transferred to the Sumatra project. Most labourers were Indonesians but 500 came from Malaya.[101] Rails, rolling stock and other capital goods were taken mainly from Indonesia's pre-war railways.

The Bayah and Sumatra railways, although more poorly remembered than the Thailand–Burma railway, were even more deadly. Available data show that for both railways, mortality per kilometre of track was not far from around twice as high as the Thailand–Burma railway and approximately eight times

96 LHC, MAGIC, 'Summary 402', 2 May 1943, p. 3.

97 NARA, RG226, entry 16, box 1100, no. 95618, OSS, R&A Branch, Regular Intelligence Reports, 'General information on Malaya, 5 Sept. 1944', p. 3. Near the end of the war, Allied intelligence reported the Tondongkura railway was finished only as far as Maros. NA, FO371/46363, Foreign Office, 'Six-monthly report', 30 June 1944, p. 33.

98 Poeze, 'Road', pp. 171–72; Sato, *War, nationalism*, p. 185.

99 Sato, 'Relocation', p. 259.

100 OSS, R&A 2134.1, *Changes in South Sumatra*, p. 15.

101 ANM, 1957/0290267, Sel. Civil Affairs, 250/1945, Translation of interrogation of Japanese government officials in the Japanese government, 29 October 1945.

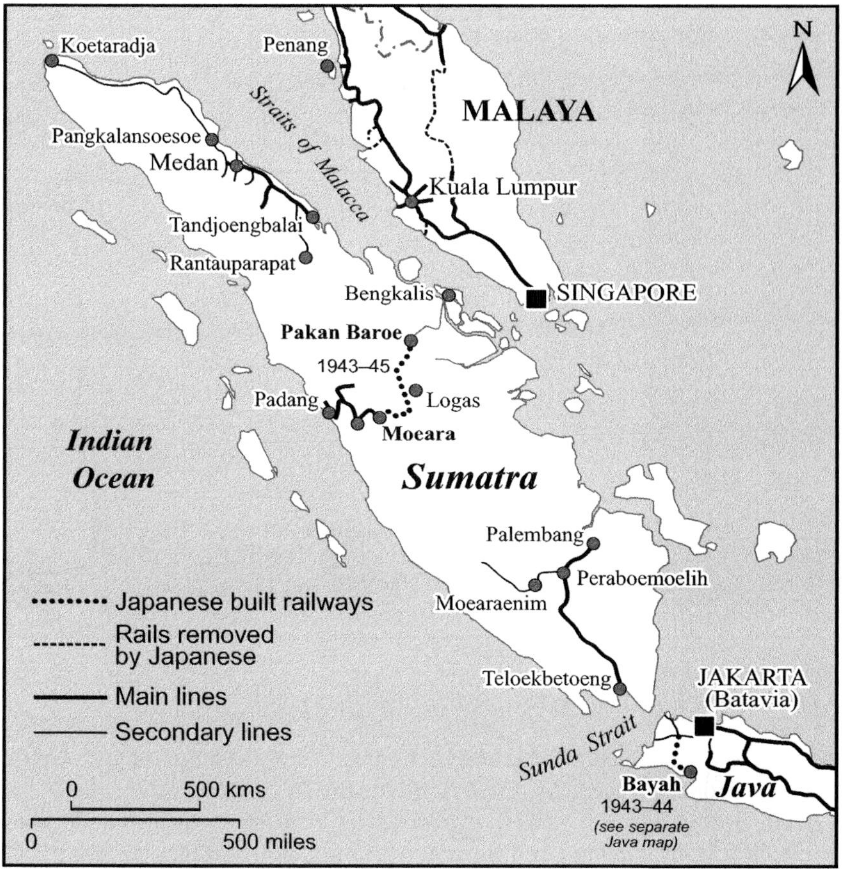

Figure 9.1 Central Sumatra railway
Source: Hovinga, *Sumatra railroad*, p. 8.

that of the Yunnan railway (Table 9.2). However, worker numbers and death rates for the two Japanese railways are impossible to know accurately, because the vast majority of workers were Indonesian *romusha* and because there were not the same careful post-war enquiries as for the Thailand–Burma line. Apparently, a total of some 200,000 labourers were employed to build the Bayah railway, with an average workforce on any one day of perhaps 40,000. The average working life of those who survived was estimated to be 60 days before the onset of physical exhaustion. The worker force was changed continuously.[102] Estimates for deaths during the construction of the Bayah railway vary from 15,000 to 60,000, and the figure of 35,000 in Table 9.2 is used

[102] Sato, *War, nationalism*, p. 185.

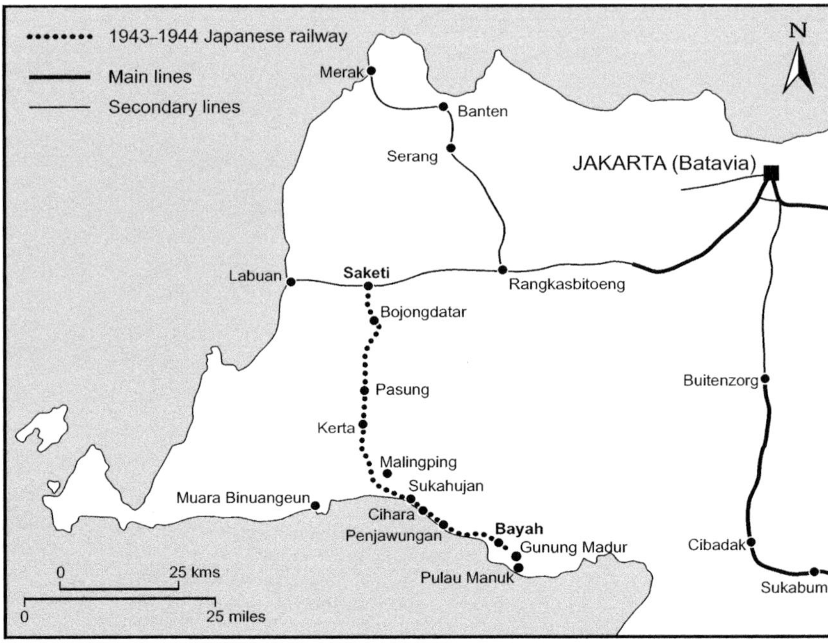

Figure 9.2 Bayah railway
Sources: Poeze, 'Road', p. 153; Sato, *War, nationalism*, p. 182.

here as around the median of a range of figures.[103] For the Sumatra line, 82,000 deaths is probably acceptably close to the truth (Table 9.2).

High death rates are mainly explained by even more inhospitable geographies than in Thailand and Burma, wartime food shortages leaving many new workers already weak, a lack of medical facilities, and poor, if any, measures to enforce sanitation. For both projects working conditions were unspeakably bad and, as for the Thailand–Burma line, the indifference of Japanese in charge was palpable. The historian of the Sumatra line describes 'a green hell full of snakes, bloodsuckers and – even worse – swarms of malaria mosquitos [and] the sadistic violence of Korean and Japanese guards'.[104] The area traversed by the Bayah line was 'a sparsely populated out-of-the way place, covered with jungles, swamps and mountains, infested with predators ... and also rife with various endemic diseases'.[105] A first-hand account of the Bayah railway reported the 'death daily of dozens of *romushas*, who were made to do slave labor, received very bad and insufficient food and almost no medical treatment ... The Japanese did not care

[103] Poeze, 'Road', p. 165.
[104] Hovinga, *Sumatra railroad*, p. 12.
[105] Sato, *War, nationalism*, p. 181.

what happened to them, after all there was a new supply of *romushas* every week.'[106] Another account by an Indonesian, Haji Moh. Mukhandar, recalled some years later how: 'Without human feeling the supervisors beat the workers when they saw them slack off in their work, or when they couldn't proceed because of exhaustion. The workers ate the remains of food for which they fought, while the Japanese entertained themselves by throwing sand or water at them, laughing their heads off as if at a funny play.'[107]

Common features of the Thailand–Burma, Bayah and Sumatra railways were poor working conditions, high death tolls and Japanese disregard of human costs. Subsequent enquiry has made all this abundantly clear. At the time, however, the Japanese focus on a successful war outcome was to the near-total exclusion of other considerations. Almost nothing was done to try to alleviate the suffering of those who worked on the railways. A British officer said that while the Thailand–Burma railway was being built, again and again 'we pressed the question of Japanese obligations under the '06 and '07 agreements and asked how they thought JAPAN would be able to explain things away. The answer was that a victorious JAPAN would not have to explain to anybody.'[108] Perhaps, as much as anything, that encapsulated Japan's attitude towards the suffering and death associated with its construction of railways in Southeast Asia.

Japanese Military Comfort System

During the Pacific War, comfort stations where Japanese army and navy personnel had sexual access to women kept for that purpose were established throughout Southeast Asia. They were government sanctioned and entirely under military control. Government sponsorship, established beyond dispute by Yoshimi Yoshiaki, a professor at Chūō University in Tokyo, is important to bear in mind, because it institutionalized military sexual slavery.[109] One main aim of this section is to estimate the number of comfort women and to indicate their nationalities and the means by which they were obtained. The other principal aim is to describe the workings of the Japanese military comfort system. It stands, along with the use of labour to build Japanese railways and as *romusha* in Indonesia, as a prominent case of forced labour in Southeast Asia on a mass scale. Like the use of labour to construct wartime railways and

106 Poeze, 'Road', p. 162 quoting from a statement by an Indo-Dutchman, R. Sadhinoch, who, under a Japanese chief, handled personnel matters.
107 Ibid., p. 164.
108 NA, WO203/6325, 'Burma–Siam railway', p. 54.
109 Totani, *Tokyo War Crimes Trial*, p. 107.

romusha, the exploitation of comfort women, both sexual and financial, was systematic and so extreme as to constitute atrocities.

The destruction of practically all Japanese records immediately after the war prevents more than an estimate of the total number of comfort women during the Pacific War. There were probably between 80,000 and 100,000 such women at any one time in the Pacific Theatre, but allowing for turnover the likely total was much greater than this.[110] A small number of the women were Japanese. Typically, they had been professional prostitutes, either in Japan or Southeast Asia. Some of these women were promised that if they died their spirits could be enshrined at the Yasukuni Shrine where spirits of the war dead are enshrined and worshipped.[111] Koreans, typically the victims of deceit and false promises, comprised the great majority of comfort women, around 80 per cent of the total. Southeast Asians made up about 20 per cent of all comfort women, but a larger share than this within Southeast Asia. In September 1942, the region had 100 out of a total of 400 Japanese comfort stations in the Pacific Theatre. Almost all the Southeast Asians who were comfort women were Chinese, Burmese, Javanese, Sumatrans or Filipinas, although there is also evidence of Vietnamese women being forced to serve in military brothels.[112] Among Southeast Asian comfort women, there were few Thai, Malays or Indians, because Japanese policy was to avoid antagonizing these racial groups due to their anticipated roles in a post-war Greater East Asia Co-Prosperity Sphere.

The great majority of Southeast Asian comfort women were obtained by force or deception which might include procurement with the help of local leaders acting on requests from military officers backed up by the *kempeitai*.[113] Forcible abduction was especially frequent in the Philippines, and a reason for the strength of guerrilla opposition to the Japanese, although Filipino Chinese business leaders were also asked to supply women and, fearful for their own safety, did so.[114] In Indonesia, initially a number of the comfort women were Dutch (80,000 Dutch were interned during the war). Some women volunteered to go to comfort stations in the hope of better living conditions and food than in the internment camps; others, under pressure when Japanese came to the camps for women, went to save young girls from being taken. In 1943 in Pontianak, when the Japanese navy set up nine or ten new brothels, the navy special police (*tokkeitai*) formally took charge of hunting for local women on the streets, having them medically examined and putting them into

[110] Tanaka, *Japan's comfort women*, pp. 8, 31; Yoshimi, *Comfort women*, pp. 91–94.
[111] Yoshimi, *Comfort women*, pp. 100–1.
[112] Tanaka, *Japan's comfort women*, pp. 27, 31–32; Chung, 'Origin', p. 311; Totani, *Tokyo War Crimes Trial*, pp. 181–82.
[113] Tanaka, *Japan's comfort women*, pp. 22–23, 45, 80–81.
[114] Yoshimi, *Comfort women*, pp. 125–27; Tanaka, *Japan's comfort women*, pp. 47–50.

brothels.[115] Beginning in 1943, large numbers of Javanese began to be rounded up as comfort women.[116] The commonest method was indirect recruitment through local village administrators. Often 'signed consent' was obtained, but most women had no idea of what they were signing.[117] Many of the Javanese women were sent elsewhere in Southeast Asia.[118]

Strategies by women and their families to avoid becoming victims of Japanese soldiers or being forced into brothels included staying out of sight, disguise, blacking the face and skin, and hasty marriage. It was estimated that in Malaya a few thousand young Chinese women of respectable families were kidnapped from their houses and taken as comfort women.[119] In Tasek Gelugur, Province Wellesley, many Chinese girls cut their hair and dressed as boys. Others dressed as Malay girls, since the Japanese were more cautious in their treatment of Malays.[120] The Japanese presence encouraged hasty marriages in Singapore, many of which survived after the war on only shaky foundations. There were also de facto wartime Chinese–Japanese marriages, but these involved girls outside the existing social structure and norms.[121] Marriages between very young couples in Manila increased sharply from the beginning of the occupation because the Japanese were said to be encouraging 'marriage' between young women and soldiers.[122]

Types of comfort stations varied according to their designated users. Those restricted to Japanese officers, frequently called 'officers' clubs', had mainly, or even all, Japanese women and most of the comfort women who were Japanese were in these clubs. Comfort stations for officers might be located in grand settings such as old colonial houses or expensive restaurants or hotels. Almost immediately after Singapore fell, the Raffles Hotel was used by Japanese officers as a comfort station, while in Rangoon an officers' club called the *Suikōen* was a special branch of a famous high-class restaurant in Kurume in Japan of the same name.[123]

Comfort stations for non-commissioned officers and enlisted men were typically assembly-line operations and it was in these, as discussed below, that the women suffered the most degrading and sub-human conditions. Almost any large building might be converted to a comfort station by partitioning off many small rooms. The Singapore Chinese Girls School became

115 Totani, *Tokyo War Crimes Trial*, p. 176.
116 Tanaka, *Japan's comfort women*, pp. 66–67, 79; Hicks, *Comfort women*, pp. 101, 108.
117 Hicks, *Comfort women*, pp. 102–3.
118 Tanaka, *Japan's comfort women*, p. 81.
119 ANM, 1957/0572010, 'Brief review of Chinese affairs', *c.* September 1945, pp. 2–3.
120 Jaafar bin Hamzah, 'Malays in Tasek Gelugur', p. 58.
121 Freedman, *Chinese family*, pp.114, 119, 125, 159, 188.
122 Hartendorp, *Japanese occupation*, p. 224 and *History of industry*, p. 92; Buencamino, *Manila under Japanese occupation*, p. 10.
123 Yoshimi, *Comfort women*, pp. 90, 124.

a comfort station, as did the otherwise nondescript Tan Lock Hotel in Penang.[124] A third type of comfort station, different from those for officers and men, was that established for local men mobilized as auxiliary troops (*heiho*). In Mandalay, one of a total of nine comfort stations was reserved for Burmese auxiliary troops. It, and three more stations, had Burmese women; three stations had Korean women; and one had Chinese women. Uminooya station for officers had Japanese women.[125]

Comfort stations operated from early morning until late at night, and the women kept in them were expected to be available throughout these hours, apart from perhaps two days off a month. Women had often been gang-raped and otherwise intimidated before being sent to comfort stations. Data for the number of men a comfort woman was expected to service vary from a low figure of four to five daily to, apparently not unusually, from seven or eight to ten.[126] A comfort woman in Penang recalled 30 men a day and that, with no time to get dressed between men, she would just lie on the bed naked.[127] Conditions in Burma, which supported a Japanese force of 200,000 men and had influxes of Japanese soldiers preparatory to battles, were especially bad.[128] An average of about 10 men each day increased to 30 or 40 before or after combat operations. Exceptionally in Burma, women were forced to have intercourse with 60 men in a day, after which a woman needed to rest for three days.[129] A Korean woman who came to the front lines in China described a life which was probably not unlike that experienced by comfort women during combat operations in Burma:

> When it is busy, I just lie down on my back, eating rice balls with my legs spread apart, and the soldiers come and mount me and leave, mount me and leave. Finally, I am beyond pain. From the waist down I get numb and lose all feeling. It's a struggle just getting up each day. When the feeling [in my lower body] returns little by little my legs cramp up and my abdomen gets cramped as well. There's a heavy, dull pain that lasts all day. I know that if I rested for two or three days, it would get better. But the customers come one after another so I can't rest. When people talk about a living hell, this is exactly what they mean.[130]

Women who did not comply with the expected regime were forced to through being beaten or restrained.[131] A soldier in charge of women in

[124] Malayan Union, *Report on the British military administration*, p. 102; Nakahara, '"Comfort women"', pp. 583, 587.
[125] Yoshimi, *Comfort women*, p. 90.
[126] Hicks, *Comfort women*, pp. 104–5; Yoshimi, *Comfort women*, pp. 139, 141.
[127] Nakahara, '"Comfort women"', p. 588.
[128] Allen, *Burma*, p. 565.
[129] Yoshimi, *Comfort women*, p. 139; Tanaka, *Japan's comfort women*, p. 52.
[130] Yoshimi, *Comfort women*, pp. 147–48.
[131] Nakahara, '"Comfort women"', p. 584.

Singapore who protested after four or five men recounted how, in the face of threatened riot from lines of soldiers waiting for the women, he 'tied the womens' arms and legs to their beds and forced them to continue'.[132] Closely guarded, comfort women usually found escape impossible. Drugs offered a respite, and suicide, although less frequent than might be imagined, a way out.

Financial exploitation paralleled sexual enslavement and atrocities. There were instances of women returning to Japan or Korea after the end of their contracts with some savings. Most Southeast Asian women, however, appear not to have been paid and, even if they were, had nothing at the end of the war. During their enslavement as comfort women, money was deducted for lodgings and food, and it was not uncommon for unscrupulous brothel keepers to take financial advantage.[133] Soldiers paid in military scrip, and any of this which women had been able to save became, with the exceptions of areas in Burma and Indonesia, worthless after the Japanese surrender. A Japanese army paymaster recorded the sad description of Japanese and Korean comfort women following retreating Japanese troops in Burma but continually falling behind:

> They carried large pieces of luggage on their backs. The heavy burden they carried in knapsacks, in bundles wrapped in cloth, and in trunks hefted on their backs was military currency from the Imperial Army in Burma. They wouldn't let anyone carry these things for them and insisted on carrying them themselves. They practically crawled over the ground, backs bent over under the weight.[134]

Japanese Trained Armies and Military Auxiliaries

There were considerable differences through Southeast Asia in the military training given Southeast Asians by the Japanese and Japan's motives for doing so. Although the Japanese organized military training in every country except Thailand, it assumed real importance only in Burma and Indonesia. Nowhere in the region did Southeast Asian armies have significance as combat forces. This was not a role that the Japanese ever envisaged them performing, nor were these armies fully trusted by those in charge of the Japanese military. Nevertheless, as discussed in the Epilogue, Japanese-trained armies had a fundamental impact on the post-war histories of Burma and Indonesia. This section first briefly comments on the absence of Japanese military training in Thailand and explains why it had no more than minor importance in

132 Yoshimi, *Comfort women*, p. 124.
133 Ibid., pp. 142–44;Tanaka, *Japan's comfort women*, p. 56.
134 Yoshimi, *Comfort women*, pp. 143–44.

Indochina, the Philippines and Malaya. The emergence of Japanese-trained armies and auxiliary forces in Burma and Indonesia is then considered.

Thailand, Indochina, the Philippines and Malaya

There were three possible reasons for the Japanese to train an army in Southeast Asian countries: to create a force for independence from colonialism; to afford propaganda value as an indigenous institution with the credibility of being an organization and having armed might; and to fulfil support roles for Japan's military. None of these considerations was important in Thailand. As an independent country before the war, Thailand already had an army and, moreover, one which, as noted in Chapter 2, in May 1942 embarked on a campaign in Burma's Shan states.[135] Another factor was that, in the face of growing opposition among influential Thai to the Japanese presence, the Thai military was important in preserving the Thai–Japanese wartime alliance, which would have been pivotal in post-war Japanese plans for Thailand to be a puppet state.

Indochina was somewhat similar to Thailand in being nominally ruled by an Allied government and one already with men under arms – the French colonial army. That probably helped to discourage Japanese military training. So too did Japanese contacts and alliances with both the Cao Đài and the Hòa Hảo, two religious-cum-political organizations to whom the Japanese gave paramilitary training.[136] Although Japan began a military training programme after the March 1945 coup against the French, that was too late to have much effect. In some instances, Vietnamese labourers were recruited to work for the Japanese army and promised that they would be given military training in off hours.[137] Furthermore, Japan, by the time it had taken full control of Indochina, was badly discredited by the famine, and nationalism had a dynamic which the Japanese had little chance of turning to advantage. They had powerful and implacable opponents in Ho Chi Minh and the Viet Minh.

The Philippines also offered an unpromising environment for training an army to promote independence or to support Japanese armed forces. Fertile ground did not exist for a Japanese-trained army because a regular Philippines army already existed; because of the strength of guerrilla resistance; because of the pro-American stance of most Filipinos; and because beginning in 1935 the Philippines had already gained a considerable degree of political autonomy and was soon to have full independence. By December 1941, General MacArthur had trained and armed over 100,000 Filipinos, some of whom

135 Murashima, 'Commemorative character', pp. 1055, 1072.
136 Tràn, 'Working', pp. 293–95.
137 Nitz, 'Japanese military policy', p. 349.

faded out of the regular army to come back as guerrillas.[138] The sympathies of many Filipinos, increasingly shaped by the harsh policies and privations of the Japanese occupation, lay with the guerrilla groups. In December 1943, the Japanese created the Patriotic League of Filipinos (*Makapili*) from among radical tenant farmers, but it functioned more as supplementary troops providing labour than a volunteer army.[139]

There was also limited room in Malaya and Singapore for manoeuvre. Chinese comprised the largest share of the population (44.7 per cent in 1947 compared to 38.2 per cent for Malays). Few Chinese actively supported the Japanese, and the allegiance of most was to China in its war against Japan. The British surrender at Singapore included some 50,000 Indian troops, about half of whom quickly joined the Indian National Army, while many others joined later. Organization of the army began in April 1942, and by June 1943 it was firmly under the leadership of Subhas Chandra Bose following his return to Southeast Asia from exile in Germany. A month later, the army had its official debut. The Indian National Army was not, however, trained by the Japanese but seen by them as useful mainly for propaganda purposes and to promote anti-British sentiment. Even during the Burma campaign the Japanese were reluctant to see the Indian National Army evolve into a larger fighting force.[140]

The Japanese decided to establish the Malaya Volunteer Army (the *Giyūgun*) only in December 1943, and officers around whom the army would be formed were not commissioned until February 1944.[141] Members of the volunteer army, consisting mainly of Malays, received regular army pay, uniforms and a certain amount of training.[142] The organization never consisted of more than about 2,000 men, possibly in part owing to a small pool of potential recruits due to the shipment of large numbers of Malays to work on the Thailand–Burma railway.[143]

Burma and Indonesia

Before the war, as well as for part of it, Japanese support for a Burmese army was motivated by the strategic and political value of an independent Burma as a buffer between India and Thailand on the western border of a Japanese-

138 Friend, *Blue-eyed enemy*, pp. 178–79.

139 Lebra, 'Japanese military model', p. 226 and *Japanese-trained armies*, p. 141.

140 Lebra, 'Japanese policy and the Indian National Army', pp. 36, 38, 43, 45, 49; OSS, assemblage 47, R&A 2702, *Indians in Japan and occupied areas*, p. 51.

141 OSS, assemblage 45, *Manpower in Japan and occupied areas*, vol. 2, pp. 244–46.

142 Lebra, *Japanese-trained armies*, pp. 116–20; OSS, R&A 1791, *Implementation study of Malaya, part I morale objectives*, pp. 9–10; Abu Talib Ahmad, *Malay Muslims*, pp. 75, 104, 114.

143 Lebra, *Japanese-trained armies*, pp. 116–20; OSS, R&A 1791, *Implementation study of Malaya, part I morale objectives*, pp. 9–10; Kratoska, *Japanese occupation*, pp. 86–88.

dominated East Asia. A Burmese army might also help militarily to contain any unrest in Thailand and limit its spill-over into Burma by providing greater border security.[144] By contrast, Japan did not plan for Indonesian independence. Military training in Indonesia had its rationale in Japanese war reversals and the need by mid-1943 to recruit a local volunteer force to provide manpower for non-combat roles.

Japanese military training had an immediate and long-term impact in Burma and Indonesia because it concentrated on majority ethnic groups previously by-passed by colonial governments; because it emphasized overtly military training, especially in Burma, and so created a revolutionary potential; and because it established institutions which could, and did, fill vacuums left by the Japanese surrender and discredited colonial regimes. Colonial armies in Burma and Indonesia were drawn from ethnic minorities and had European officers. The British in Burma relied mainly on Karens (pro-British and often Christians) and to a lesser extent on Kachins and Chins. In 1939 in Burma, Burmans comprised three-quarters of the population but just 12.3 per cent of those in the army.[145] Even at that time there was considerable tension between Burman and Karen villages in Lower Burma, because Karens had taken a major role in suppressing various Burman disturbances during the 1920s and the Saya San rebellion in the early 1930s.[146] In sharp contrast to Burma's pre-war military, the Burma Independence Army promoted by the Japanese was dominated by Burmans.

Before World War II in Indonesia, the Dutch traditionally recruited in the Outer Islands and particularly from loyal and Christian groups like those in Ambon in the Moluccas and Minahasa in northern Celebes.[147] Asians in the British and Dutch colonial armies performed chiefly internal police functions. Peta (*Pembela Tanah Air*, variously translated as Fatherland Defence Corps or Defenders of the Homeland) was the most militarily important of a number of Indonesian armies formed by the Japanese and, moreover, unlike the army in colonial Indonesia, consisted largely of Javanese.

The Burma Independence Army originated in the conjunction of the initiative of a Japanese officer, Colonel Suzuki Keiji, and the nationalism and ambitions for political independence of a small, elite group of Burmans. Suzuki, who had been trained in the Japanese Army's Intelligence School (*Nakano Gakkō*), came to Burma in June 1940. His mission was to study Burma and instigate revolution.[148] At first, he operated under cover as a journalist for the Japanese newspaper *Yomiuri Shimbun*, and then, still

[144] Lebra, *Japanese-trained armies*, p. 41.
[145] Furnivall, *Colonial policy*, p. 184; Allen, *Burma*, p. 13; Sadan, 'Ethnic armies', pp. 601–26.
[146] Christie, *Modern history*, p. 61.
[147] Feith, *Decline*, p. 5; Taufik Abdullah, 'Nationalist activities', p. 119.
[148] Than, *Roots*, p. 14.

operating clandestinely, became leader of Japan's *Minami Kikan* (Organization South) intelligence mission. While in pre-war Burma, Suzuki became a passionate supporter of Burma's independence, adopted a name symbolic of revolution and deliverance, Bo Mogyo ('Thunderbolt'), married a local woman and, most important, arranged rigorous military training in Japan for a small group of hand-picked Burmans.

These men became Burma's much mythologized Thirty Comrades from the self-designated Thakins (see Chapter 2 for a definition). In the Leninesque manner of a committed core, they constituted the commanding nucleus of the Burma Independence Army formed in December 1941. Among the 30 were Aung San, instrumental in bringing about Burma's independence in 1948, and Ne Win, elevated to command of Burma's armed forces in 1949 and the general who headed Burma's government after the army took control in 1958 and again in 1962.

In helping to form the Burma Independence Army, Suzuki, who thought of himself as a 'Lawrence of Arabia' figure, was probably aided by Japanese disorganization: in early 1942 in Rangoon alone, eight functionally autonomous army, navy and intelligence operations were vying with each other in an attempt to establish control.[149] There was not, however, official support for the immediate Burmese independence advocated by Suzuki. His superiors disliked Suzuki's swashbuckling manner, eccentric nature, romantic character, and, furthermore, his command of what was in effect a private army. Soon after its formation the Burma Independence Army began to spiral out of Japanese control and contribute to Burma's widespread lawlessness.[150] At its height, the Burma Independence Army had 30,000 members, of whom half were said to be 'bad hats' and unpopular with both the Burmese and Japanese.[151]

Suzuki was a Burman partisan in conflicts between Burmans and Karens or Burmans and Indians. When a Burman officer was killed in a Karen attack on a Burman village, Suzuki immediately ordered two Karen villages, Kanazogon and Tayagon, to be razed to the ground and their inhabitants exterminated.[152] 'Open race war' ensued; Burman refugees flocked into the town of Myaungmya (in south-west Burma). Karens and Indians fled to protected Karen centres.[153]

149 Callahan, *Making enemies*, p. 51.

150 Allen, *Burma*, pp. 17–22; Lebra, *Japanese-trained armies*, p. 8. For discussion of the 'Lawrence of Arabia' description, see Allen, 'Fujiwara and Suzuki', pp. 269–70 and 'Transfer of power', pp. 185–94; Myint-U, *River*, p. 229.

151 NARA, RG226, entry 154, box 80, file 1366, 'The Burma National Army', 2 June 1945, p. 1; Burma Intelligence Bureau, *Burma*, vol. 1, p. 58; Christian, *Burma*, p. 132. Membership numbers for the Burma Independence Army vary from 10,000 to 200,000. A figure of 30,000 is conservative and close to the figure of 23,000 considered safe by Selth, 'Race', p. 490.

152 Allen, *Burma*, pp. 557–59.

153 Maw, *Breakthrough*, pp. 188–90; see p. 189 for the quotation and p. 188 for reference to 'a full-scale communal gang war in the delta'.

In July 1942, the Japanese military administration renamed the Burma Independence Army the Burma Defence Army and reduced its size to 3,000 men. At the same time, Suzuki was transferred back to Japan and *Minami Kikan* abolished. Nevertheless, a military college to train officers for the Burma Independence Army had been established, and an organized, trained Burmese military cadre existed.[154] Crucially, mass nationalist support had been mobilized in Burman areas. In August 1944, Burma's army and revolutionaries outside it joined together.[155]

On 27 March 1945, Burma's Japanese-trained military, since at least 1944 progressively more distrusted by the Japanese, switched sides to support the British.[156] The practical consideration was that, after the disastrous Japanese campaign a year earlier to try to capture the key town of Imphal in Assam, Japan was obviously losing the war. There was also dissatisfaction with the independence given Burma under the 1943 Ba Maw government; in an August 1944 speech, Aung San voiced the widespread view that independence was not real.[157]

In Indonesia, as also in Burma and Malaya, the Japanese army established a system of auxiliary troops to obtain labour. Some 2 million Javanese, about 4.8 per cent of the population, received some military training from the Japanese. Almost all of these were members of para-military groups, of which Japan established at least six. The largest was a Civilian Defence Corps (1.3 million) and the *Seinendan* or youth groups numbering over half a million. Training for para-military groups was perfunctory, and the trainees were armed, if at all, only with bamboo spears. The main roles envisaged by the Japanese for these groups were mutual co-operation and support for the war.[158] The Japanese concentrated on military and para-military training in Java, but also trained a Sumatran volunteer force (*Giyūgun*) of several thousand. The main duty of the trainees was to protect the island's oil refineries.[159]

About 25,000 Javanese served the Japanese as military auxiliaries, or *heiho*. These men were single, aged 16 to 25 and had some education in Japanese. After about two months' training, *heiho*, in reality labourers in uniform, were deployed for guard duty, construction projects like digging trenches and roadbuilding and various supplemental functions. Although of substantial

154 Burma Intelligence Bureau, *Burma*, vol. 2, p. 49; OSS, assemblage 45, *Manpower in Japan and occupied areas*, vol. 2, pp. 216–17; Than, *Roots*, pp. 24, 35–36, 38.

155 Nu, *Burma*, pp. xvi–xxvi, 105.

156 NARA, RG226, entry 154, box 80, file 1366, 'The Burma National Army', 2 June 1945, p. 3.

157 Than, *Roots*, p. 45.

158 Lebra, *Japanese-trained armies*, pp. 97–98; Taufik Abdullah, 'Nationalist activities', pp. 113, 119.

159 Lebra, *Japanese-trained armies*, pp. 123, 127; Taufik Abdullah, 'Nationalist activities', pp. 118, 131.

use to the Japanese military, it is unclear how far these workers could have found alternative, more remunerative employment, and so were in effect taxed. However, thousands of Indonesian *heiho* were sent abroad, some as labourers for the Thailand–Burma railway, where their functions might merge into being *romusha* and forced labour. That represented a tax on workers, and often a death sentence, levied by the Japanese.[160]

The only Indonesians in receipt of genuine military training belonged to Peta. Beginning in late 1943, it grew into a volunteer army of some 35,000, including about 1,500 in Bali. Peta officers, drawn largely from the more privileged strata of Indonesian society, were sent to elite training colleges in Indonesia set up by the Japanese. Training was founded on the Japanese spiritual virtues of sacrifice, self-reliance and endurance of hardship. Javanese trained by the Japanese or who taught in the School for Free Indonesia (*Asrama Merdeka Indonesia*), established in 1944, included most of the men who became generals and the principal politicians in independent Indonesia. Among their number were Sukarno, Mohammad Hatta and Suharto. In the 1970s, Peta officers were the most significant element of Indonesia's political-military elite, and comprised three-quarters of the top ranks of the army.[161] As in Burma, Japanese military training in Indonesia gave rise to a new, and ultimately powerful, elite.[162]

Conclusion

Beginning in 1942, Japan drew heavily on Southeast Asian workers to build railways, and during the last two years of the war to construct defence installations and perform auxiliary functions for the military. As a result, throughout the region large numbers of Southeast Asians came into direct contact with the Japanese, although often as forced labour. Japan's deployment of Southeast Asian labour during the war offers an extreme example of the intensive use of labour to create capital. That strategy occupies a place in the development economics literature most prominently associated with Lewis's 'unlimited' supplies of labour and with Nurkse's idea of setting surplus people to work on capital-creating projects such as roads, railways, drainage and buildings.[163] While Japanese motives differed from those suggested by development economists, the logic of abundant labour at near-zero cost was similar. In Southeast Asia, labour was used intensively because Southeast Asian

160 Maekawa, '*Heiho*', pp. 189, 195; Burma Intelligence Unit, *Burma*, vol. 2, p. 137; Lebra, *Japanese-trained armies*, p. 97; McVey, 'Post-revolutionary transformation, part I', p. 135.

161 Lebra, *Japanese-trained armies*, pp. 176–77.

162 Benda, 'Indonesian Islam', p. 354.

163 Lewis, 'Economic development'; Nurkse, *Problems*, pp. 36–37; Little, *Economic development*, p. 88.

workers often came at no greater outlay than minimal food, which in any case Japan might have had to provide to avoid mass starvation, or which workers themselves might be expected to grow; and because Southeast Asians were regarded as easily expendable. These considerations help to explain why Japanese undertakings like railway construction in Sumatra and East Java and attempts to build infrastructure might exact high human costs but prove near valueless.

The Japanese never had sufficient confidence or trust in the Southeast Asian armies that they trained or in the Indian National Army to envisage them in combat roles. The Burma National Army functioned as garrison and internal security troops and reconnaissance troops on the India–Burma frontier, but was regarded primarily as a vehicle to promote nationalism and independence.[164] In Indonesia, defence and supply requirements, not independence, were Japan's priorities. Japanese attitudes towards Peta and numerous non-military groups created by Japanese policy initiatives were tempered by a fear that organized Javanese leadership might turn against Japan.[165]

Events discussed in this chapter resonated after the end of the war. Extreme ill treatment of railway workers and comfort women generated feelings of bitterness towards Japan that remain in much of Asia. In Burma and Indonesia, armies sponsored by the Japanese created a basis for post-independence ruling military elites. These became of great political importance to Southeast Asia and are considered in the Epilogue.

[164] NARA, RG226, entry 154, box 80, file 1366, 'The Burma National Army', 2 June 1945, p. 3.

[165] Lebra, *Japanese-trained armies*, p. 94.

10

Costs of War and Lessons of Occupation

Japan embarked on a Pacific war driven by strongly military-influenced politics and a fatalistic determination to liberate itself economically. In Southeast Asia, Japan intended to obtain resources and hoped to convert the region's populations to a Japanized culture. This concluding chapter evaluates the overall benefits and costs of the Pacific War for Japan and for Southeast Asia in terms of GDP, loss of life and physical destruction. It also considers why Japan failed so entirely to achieve its objectives in Southeast Asia, decimating the region's economies. What lessons emerge for the economics of occupation and Southeast Asian development?

By early August 1945, 8 million people in Japan were homeless and dispersed; near famine, or famine, appeared likely within a matter of months.[1] Japan's wartime leaders, however, cared little for 'the sufferings of Japanese civilians. A great many military men were willing to fight on when the war was obviously lost – no matter how many civilians would die of hunger, disease, and high explosives'.[2] The Japanese government and military showed even less regard for the lives of the citizens whose countries it had invaded. For Southeast Asians – bystanders caught up in a conflict between great nations – the consequences of war were undeserved and utterly disastrous, the costs even greater than for the Japanese.

The lessons of war and occupation begin with the well-known observation that in conventional warfare over a sustained period, superior economic strength is decisive. Ignoring this reality, Japan initiated a war that was probably unwinnable and certainly so if it lasted more than two years. Furthermore, the decision for war compounded the earlier Japanese misjudgement of the advisability of war in China. Japan engaged in a second war – an air and sea war in the Pacific – partly to try to extricate itself from the China conflict by firmly closing supply routes through Burma and Indochina for Chiang Kai-shek's Nationalist Chinese forces. Although the two wars merged into what became known as the Pacific War, by 1943, Japan found itself effectively fighting separate wars, one in China and one in Southeast Asia,

[1] Feis, *Japan subdued*, p. 107; Johnson, *Japanese food management*, pp. 140, 149.

[2] Gann, 'Reflections', p. 354; see also USSBS, *Oil*, p. 41, which observes of Japan's whole war planning 'the callous disregard for the human welfare' including that of its own citizens.

because a lack of transport largely prevented the movement of troops between the two theatres.[3] Limited home economic capacity ruled out the possibility that Japan could substitute for Southeast Asia's pre-war imports to feed and clothe Southeast Asians. Japanese unwillingness in Southeast Asia to utilize economic incentives made it virtually impossible to mobilize resources and contributed to a downwards spiral in regional output. In Southeast Asia, coercion, terror and torture provided poor substitutes for positive incentives and the provision of human and physical capital as means of mobilizing production, although these negative instruments achieved social compliance. There were no major rebellions and resistance was mainly in the form of various guerrilla movements, notably in the Philippines and Malaya.

Japan: War Costs and Benefits

An influential thesis, associated with the work of Peter Lieberman in regard to industrial societies including Japan's, is that occupation can yield substantial net gains for the occupier: conquest pays.[4] Japan, Lieberman points out, greatly increased its material strength and resources available for war by conquering and then developing the backward, agrarian societies of Taiwan, Korea and Manchuria. It is certainly true that between the Meiji Restoration and 1937 militarism and war served the Japanese economy well.[5]

An occupier's failure to impose compliance may limit the gains of conquest, as Lieberman argues, citing the Belgian and French 1923–24 occupation of the Ruhr-Rhineland. Such a lack of political will to implement compliance was not, however, a Japanese shortcoming in Southeast Asia. Japan was ruthless in its use of massive repression to enforce acquiescence. Nevertheless, as this chapter also shows, for Japan the costs of war, both material and human, far outweighed its benefits. The possibility of wealth and strategic gains from Southeast Asia's resources was soon erased by the Allied military response to Japanese aggression, in Lieberman's terminology the mobilization of a countervailing coalition. For the Japanese, the balance tipped further and further towards debit as shipping losses mounted and Japan committed more resources in an attempt to hold Southeast Asia. Over three and a half years, the costs of conquering Southeast Asia became enormous.

Japan went to war in Southeast Asia for economic reasons. At first, and no doubt with the positive results achieved historically in Taiwan, Korea and Manchuria in mind, a policy of war to increase economic strength in East Asia looked an excellent investment. Japan lost a mere 3,500 men in the conquest of

[3] Hata, 'Continental expansion', p. 302.
[4] Liberman, *Does conquest pay?*
[5] Boulding and Gleason, 'War as an investment', pp. 245–49; Goldsmith, *Financial development of Japan*, pp. 35–36.

Malaya; for Burma the toll was another 2,000. The rest of Southeast Asia fell with few casualties. '[T]o destroy the British Empire in the Far East', Louis Allen remarked, this was 'Not, surely, an inordinate price'.[6]

The eventual costs of World War II to Japan are well known: almost 3 million dead, about half of the area of 66 Japanese cities levelled, two-thirds of Tokyo, Osaka and Nagoya reduced to rubble and burnt ruins, utter devastation throughout the home islands until the 1950s, the destruction of 35 per cent of national wealth, and a decade and a half for national income to regain its 1937 level.[7] Per capita income did not reach its 1938 level until 1953, although by 1956 increase had become rapid (Table 10.1). Added to the economic toll were the costs to the Japanese psyche of having to bear the unbearable of unconditional surrender, disarmament and indictment of Japanese citizens as war criminals; of coping with a devastated economy, widespread poverty, malnutrition, runaway inflation and a rampant black market; of living amid a culture of blame and guilt; and of experiencing the loss of empire, American occupation and an evaporation of moral authority. Japan returned to the status of the small island state which it had been before the Sino-Japanese War of 1894–95.[8] A feeling of antagonism towards Japan remains even today in much of Asia. No doubt, only a proportion of these overall war costs should be assigned to the occupation of Southeast Asia, but assignment is beyond the scope of this book. Instead, in the remainder of this section I assume that the occupation of Southeast Asia was separate from the rest of the war and evaluate its cost to Japan in terms of military expenditure in Southeast Asia and the return on this expenditure.

Japan was rather successful in financing war in Southeast Asia (Chapter 3). Financial dexterity and the policy of living off the land limited the cost of occupation. Nevertheless, between 1941 and 1944, Japan's military spending directly attributable to Southeast Asia averaged 6.2 per cent of GDP, jumping to 16.3 per cent in 1944, when Allied invasion threatened (Table 10.2).

The net transfer of tangible goods from Southeast Asia to Japan was both tiny and a fraction of the outlay on military expenditures (Table 10.2). Between 1942 and 1945, trade surpluses with Southeast Asia were 2.5 per cent of military expenditure on the region. From 1942 to 1944, trade surpluses amounted to just 0.4 per cent of Japanese GDP (Table 10.2, panels a and b). The picture is clear: the flow of tangible goods to Japan during the war could not offset large costs.

Yet it might be that these small imports had huge strategic value. So long as Japan still had merchant shipping, rice was important. Southeast Asia also yielded two raw materials unobtainable elsewhere and fundamental to Japan's

6 Allen, 'Burma', p. 301.

7 Dower, *Embracing*, pp. 98, 45–48, 118, 558–59; USSBS, *Effects of strategic bombing*, pp. 2, 54–55; Cohen, *Japan's economy*, pp. 406–9; Ōuchi, *Keizai tōkei shū*, p. 343; Hara, 'Japan: guns', 262.

8 Hata, 'Continental expansion', p. 314.

Table 10.1 *Southeast Asia and Japan GDP per capita 1870–1980*

	Burma	Malaya	Thailand	Singapore	Indonesia	Indochina	Philippines	Japan
a) 1990 Geary-Khamis $								
1870	504	663	608	682	608	505	624	737
1913	685	939	841	1,367	869	727	988	1,387
1938	**740**	**1,452**	**826**	**2,070**	**1,057**	**831**	**1,440**	**2,449**
1939		1,708	826	2,379	1,038	886	1,508	2,816
1940			841		1,104	803	1,507	2,874
1941			846		1,158	763		2,873
1942			743		925	698		2,818
1943			812		738	659		2,822
1944			759		579	515		2,659
1945			682		512	407		1,346
1946			716		527	473	646	1,444
1947			775		602	498	875	1,541
1948			**838**		694	512	993	1,725
1949			826		758	562	1,025	1,800
1950	396	**1,665**	836	**2,219**	784	658	1,070	1,921
1956	490	1,505	930	2,333	955	764	1,410	**2,948**
1957	510	1,455	910	2,318	977	775	**1,442**	3,136
1959	555	1,467	992	2,186	987	792	1,501	3,554
1960	564	1,530	1,078	2,310	1,015	799	1,476	3,986
1962	606	1,637	1,149	2,520	1,025	**885**	1,537	4,777
1970	642	2,079	1,694	4,439	**1,231**	735	1,764	9,714
1978	**756**	3,271	2,422	7,752	1,740	806	2,262	12,585
1980	828	3,657	2,554	9,058	1,898	757	2,376	13,428

b) 1938 = 100

	Burma	Malaya	Thailand	Singapore	Indonesia	Indochina	Philippines	Japan
1870	68.1	45.7	73.6	33.0	57.5	60.8	43.3	30.1
1913	92.6	64.7	101.7	66.0	82.2	87.5	68.6	56.6
1938	100.0	100.0	100.0	100.0	100.0	100.0	100.0	100.0
1939		117.6	99.9	114.9	98.2	106.7	104.7	115.0
1940			101.8		104.4	96.7	104.6	117.4
1941			102.4		109.5	91.8		117.3
1942			89.9		87.5	84.0		115.1
1943			98.3		69.8	79.3		115.2
1944			91.8		54.8	62.0		108.6
1945			82.5		48.5	49.0		55.0
1946			86.6		49.8	57.0	44.9	59.0
1947			93.8		57.0	59.9	60.8	62.9
1948			101.4		65.7	61.6	68.9	70.4
1949			99.9		71.7	67.6	71.1	73.5
1950	53.5	114.7	101.2	107.2	74.1	79.2	74.3	78.4
1956	66.2	103.7	112.5	112.7	90.4	91.9	97.9	120.4
1957	69.0	100.2	110.1	112.0	92.5	93.3	100.1	128.0
1959	75.0	101.1	120.0	105.6	93.4	95.3	104.2	145.1
1960	76.2	105.4	130.5	111.6	96.0	96.2	102.5	162.8
1962	82.0	112.7	139.1	121.8	96.9	106.5	106.7	195.0
1970	86.7	143.2	205.0	214.5	116.4	88.5	122.5	396.6
1978	102.2	225.2	293.0	374.5	164.7	96.9	157.0	513.8
1980	112.0	251.8	309.1	437.6	179.5	91.1	164.9	548.2

Notes: 1. See notes and sources for Table 4.1.
2. The years in bold indicate when Southeast Asian countries re-gained at least 1938 per capita GDP levels.

Table 10.2 *Japan home islands costs and benefits of Southeast Asia occupation 1940–1945*

	1940	1941	1942	1943	1944	1945
a) Costs						
Military expenditure on SE Asia, million yen		321.0	1,373.0	3,328.0	12,166.0	1,186.0
Military expenditure on SE Asia % Japan GDP		0.7	2.5	5.2	16.3	
b) Benefits						
Trade balance with SE Asia, million yen		370.5	192.5	563.0	44.8	31.8
Trade balance with SE Asia % military expenditure		115.4	14.0	16.9	0.4	2.7
c) Strategic imports Co-Prosperity Sphere (000 tons)						
Bauxite	275	150	305	909	376	16
Coal	7,011	6,459	6,388	5,181	2,635	548
Iron ore	6,073	6,309	4,700	4,298	2,153	341
Iron and steel	621	921	993	977	1,097	170
Lead	100	87	11	25	17	4
Tin	11	6	4	27	24	4
Zinc	24	8	9	10	6	3
Rubber	28	68	31	42	32	18
Phosphorite and phosphate	710	397	342	237	90	23
Dolomite and magnesite	410	506	469	438	287	66
Rice and paddy	1,694	2,233	2,629	1,136	783	151
Soybean cake and soybeans	1,042	910	1,148	895	1,114	770
Other grains and flours	269	267	823	750	507	231
d) Southeast Asia % of Co-Prosperity Sphere imports						
Bauxite		100.0	100.0	100.0	100.0	100.0
Coal		5.4	6.6	2.8	0.0	0.0
Iron ore		33.9	4.6	6.3	4.5	7.9
Iron and steel		0.0	0.0	0.0	0.0	0.0
Lead		10.7	20.7	34.1	1.3	0.0
Tin		100.0	100.0	100.0	100.0	100.0
Zinc		38.0	38.8	30.0	9.8	0.0
Rubber		100.0	94.6	95.2	89.2	92.2
Phosphorite and phosphate		20.2	83.3	76.0	26.2	0.0
Dolomite and magnesite		0.0	0.0	0.0	0.0	0.0
Rice and paddy		64.3	58.1	75.4	9.4	0.1
Soybean cake and soybeans		0.0	0.0	0.0	5.4	0.0
Other grains and flours		80.2	17.9	85.2	70.0	0.0

Table 10.2 (*cont.*)

	1940	1941	1942	1943	1944	1945
e) Crude oil and refined products (000 barrels)						
Production in Southeast Asia		65,100	25,939	49,626	36,928	6,546
Oil received in Japan			10,524	14,500	4,975	0
Oil consumed or lost in Southeast Asia			15,415	35,126	31,953	6,456

Notes: Tons are metric tons.

1. Total military expenditure includes both army and navy expenditure and refers to expenditure made in Japan.
2. Imports of scrap iron are excluded. They were (in 000 tons) 2,124 in 1940 and 181 in 1941, but then became negligible.
3. For 1941, iron ore for Southeast Asia includes imports from countries outside the Co-Prosperity Sphere.
4. GDP data from Ohkawa and Shinohara do not differ greatly from that in USSBS, *Effects of strategic bombing*, p. 84. 6. Oil data are approximate due to destruction by the Japanese of records in Singapore. No division between oil consumed in Southeast Asia and oil lost in the region is possible.

Sources: Military expenditure: USSBS, *Effects of strategic bombing*, p. 85; Japan, Ministry of Finance, Shōwa Finance History Compilation Office, *Shōwa zaisei shi IV: Rinji gunji hi* (Shōwa finance history IV: extraordinary military expense). *Trade and strategic imports:* USSBS, *Effects of strategic bombing*, pp. 189–96; Japan, Ministry of Finance, *Nihon gaikoku bōeki nenpyō* (Return of foreign trade of Japan), 1941–1944–48. *Oil supplies:* Cohen, *Japan's economy*, p. 140. *GDP:* Ohkawa and Shinohara, *Patterns*, p. 269.

war effort (Table 10.2, panels c and d). One was bauxite, used to make aluminum, which was essential for aircraft manufacture. Imports from Southeast Asia enabled Japan to stay in what was, above all, an air and sea war.[9] Japan was less fortunate with the other critical raw material, oil, because Allied depletion of Japan's oil tanker fleet increasingly interdicted oil shipments. By 1944, Japan's two years' pre-war oil stockpile was exhausted, and little oil from Southeast Asia reached the home islands (Table 10.2, panel d). Again, strategic inputs cannot balance an investment decision to make Southeast Asia part of an East Asian Japanese Empire.

9 USSBS, *Japanese aircraft industry* and *Effects of strategic bombing*, pp. 23–25, 49–50.

Japanese Failure in Southeast Asia

The single unambiguous Japanese success in Southeast Asia was the destruction of Western colonialism. Rhetoric for a Co-Prosperity Sphere indicated that as a goal. Towards this end, Japan aimed to engineer changes in Southeast Asia which, had they succeeded, would have ranked among the most fundamental ever effected in an occupied region in any other war or short period.[10] Between 1941 and 1945, Japan entirely altered economic and social life in Southeast Asia, but change was not as intended. Economic weakness is central to explaining Japan's comprehensive failure in Southeast Asia.

Failure is attributable to three economic reasons. First, other than oil, the Japanese economy was too small to use more than a fraction of the main products Southeast Asia produced. Mass unemployment in Southeast Asia soon followed the disappearance of a market for its exports. Second, Japan was unable to provide shipping to move significant amounts of goods within the region. Pre-war Southeast Asia was highly integrated and economically interdependent. The region included the world's three great rice exporters, together accounting for some 80 per cent of world exports and responsible for feeding much of Asia. The result of a lack of shipping was that large rice surpluses built up in rice-specialized areas, especially Lower Burma, while hunger was widespread elsewhere, notably in Upper Burma, Malaya, Indonesia, the Philippines and northern Vietnam.

Third, Japan's home economy had limited productive capacity. Moreover, this did not increase during the war. Pre-war capacity had to be diverted to the production of war goods. There was, as Nakamura emphasizes, no way that Japan could maintain living standards in wartime Southeast Asia, or even supply goods to the region.[11] As with Germany in its plans to reconstruct France as part of the Third Reich, Japanese efforts to provide food were motivated chiefly by an interest in avoiding Southeast Asians dying of starvation or outbreaks of revolution in the region.[12] The decline in living standards was drastic, pushing Southeast Asians to, or below, late nineteenth-century levels.

It was unrealistic to expect that malnourished, poorly clad people deprived of basic necessities would be enlisted in support of Japan or believe the extensive Japanese propaganda of 'Holy War' and pan-Asian nationalism. Nor was pan-Asianism, despite some claims to the contrary, the determining Japanese reason for war.[13] Rather, Japan aimed to replace one kind of imperialism with another and, if the years of occupation are a guide, an even crueller, more exploitative one. Japanese inducements for a Co-Prosperity Sphere could not be taken seriously in

[10] Bloc and Hoselitz, *Economics*, p. 108.
[11] Nakamura, *Lectures*, p. 116.
[12] Milward, *New order*, p. 58.
[13] For the idea that pan-Asianism was 'the driving force' (p. 579) in the establishment of the Greater East Asia Co-Prosperity Sphere, see Matthiessen, 'Re-orienting', pp. 560–81.

Southeast Asian regimes where terror was a basic policy and arrogance and abuse the usual mode of behaviour towards ordinary Southeast Asians.

Southeast Asia: War Costs and Benefits

War and occupation benefits to Southeast Asians are hard to discover and were heavily outweighed by costs. Many Southeast Asians worked for the Japanese or served their needs and a number of traders and merchants, together with some civil servants and possibly a few labourers, gained materially from this. Many ordinary merchants benefited through being able to trade in a sellers' market and supply not least the Japanese. Local Chinese merchants in Thailand were said to have realized big wartime profits.[14] Probably the greatest Southeast Asian beneficiaries of the war were black market traders or fixers such as the 'buy and sell' merchants of Manila, Singapore's mushroom millionaires and Burma's New Order Brokers (Chapters 6 and 8). In Burma, classes which also prospered from Japanese rule were 'certain politicians [and] contractors many of whom had made fortunes from supply'.[15]

As a result of occupation, Thailand, on the basis of Japanese investment, may have moved towards somewhat more industrialization. But with this possible exception, Southeast Asia's economies realized few, if any, advances in technological change or innovation. Manufacturing during the occupation mainly involved the Japanese taking control of plant and equipment that had operated in 1941 and turning it to military use. Unlike, for example, the United Kingdom, war did not yield improvements in health and education in Southeast Asia. Large numbers of schools closed and if they re-opened it was usually to try to teach Japanese and improve pupils spiritually. That consisted largely of compulsory mass physical exercise and rote learning of songs and a few Japanese phrases.

Two gains from the war and occupation are discernable, both of which are considered in the Epilogue. One was that under Japanese rule Southeast Asians acquired greater experience of government, either as part of puppet regimes or through promotion to higher grades in the civil service, as happened in Indonesia, for Malays in Malaya and for Vietnamese and Laotians after the March 1945 coup. For many Javanese, the Japanese occupation meant a rise to a social status that they could not otherwise have hoped to attain.[16] The other gain was to hasten the independence of Southeast Asian countries, if probably at the cost of greater bloodshed than would have occurred as part of a negotiated transition to self-government (Epilogue).

14 IOR, Clague Papers, Mss Eur E252/44, 'Situation in Burma, p. 12; Reynolds, 'International orphans', pp. 379–80 and *Thailand*, p. 178; 'Bewildered', Post Mailbag, *Bangkok Post*, 29 November 1946.

15 IOR, Clague Papers, Mss Eur E252/44, U Htin Wa, 'Eyewitness account', p. 6.

16 Palmier, *Social status*, p. 102; Stuart-Fox, *History*, p. 57.

Earlier chapters detailed a number of economic and social costs to Southeast Asians and these do not need more than brief recall. Chapters 4 and 5 showed that throughout Southeast Asia, Thailand apart, per capita wartime incomes contracted by half or more. There was a near cessation of foreign trade and drastic declines in the availability of transport and public services. As the pre-war stock of imported cloth, manufactures, soap, cigarettes and medicines dwindled, or even disappeared, Southeast Asia's lack of pre-war industrialization and extreme dependence on imported goods became increasingly apparent. Southeast Asians, as described in Chapter 6, had little choice but to try to fashion substitutes from whatever materials were locally available. The drop in welfare due to acute shortages of basic consumer goods was paralleled by falls in the availability of food. Chapters 7 and 8 made the point that, again except in Thailand, most Southeast Asians who survived occupation ended it malnourished to a greater or lesser degree.

GDP and Per Capita Income

Table 10.1 indicates losses of GDP to Southeast Asian countries due to the Japanese occupation. As shown in Chapter 4 and Table 10.1, by the late stages of the war in most of Southeast Asia GDP per capita had fallen to near, or even less than, its 1870 level. Declines in living standards were commensurate with such a sharp drop in incomes. The costs of lost GDP continued after the war. To estimate lost GDP due to the Japanese occupation, 1938 is identified as the pre-war benchmark to avoid taking into account war-related booms in primary commodities, which began in 1939 and in some instances lasted until 1941.

One measure of lost GDP is to ask how much overall GDP fell below its 1938 level in the years 1942 to 1947. Loss can then be defined as the cumulative amount of GDP per capita for 1942 to 1947, assuming that for each of these years incomes had been the same as in 1938 and subtracting from this the total for actual GDP from 1942 to 1947. This difference taken as a percentage of GDP in 1938 measures lost years of GDP. The measure is only indicative because losses after 1945 cannot be wholly attributed to occupation. Although post-1945 national incomes were heavily influenced by war and occupation, internal political choices, ethnic conflict and revolution also played a part. These considerations became increasingly important in the late 1940s, and make it difficult after 1947 to assign GDP losses wholly to Japanese occupation. Under conditions of no war, GDP per capita might have been expected to increase during the 1940s rather than remaining at its 1938 level. However, the increase would probably not have been large. Between 1913 and 1938 income growth was slight, and in Thailand negative, so that if the growth rate for these 25 years were applied to the period for 1938 onwards, it would not greatly augment 1938 GDP per capita.

Of available data, Thailand and Malaya were the only two countries in which GDP per capita before 1950 again matched that of 1938. Both countries

Table 10.3 *Thailand, Indonesia and Indochina years of lost GDP at 1938 levels 1942–1947*

	Actual GDP 1942–47	GDP 1942–47 if same as 1938 GDP	Years of lost GDP (actual as % of GDP if same as in 1938)
Thailand	4,487	4,959	0.57
Indonesia	3,884	6,342	2.33
Indochina	3,250	4,986	2.09

Source: Table 10.1.

profited from sellers' markets arising from post-war shortages, Thailand for rice and Malaya mainly for rubber. In Thailand, GDP during the war never plummeted as elsewhere in Southeast Asia, and for 1942 to 1947 the loss in GDP was just 57 per cent of a year of 1938 GDP. The loss in Indonesia was 2.33 years of 1938 GDP and in Indochina 2.09 years. In Malaya, the Philippines and Burma, losses for 1942 to 1947 were probably at least as large as, or in excess of, those in Indonesia and Indochina but cannot be estimated due to lack of data (Tables 10.1 and 10.3).

While in 1953 Japan's economy first generated a per capita income as great as in 1938, incomes more or less similar to the 1938 benchmark were not seen until significantly later in many parts of Southeast Asia. Malaya, Singapore and Thailand were the only countries in which by 1950 GDP per capita again matched that of 1938. The Philippines first recovered to a 1938 level in 1957 and Vietnam reached this mark in 1962 before sliding backwards with the escalation of the Second Indochina War. Indonesia nearly matched 1938 GDP per capita in 1961 but full recovery to the 1938 level occurred only in 1970, after the end of the Sukarno era. Burma finally regained 1938 income 40 years later, in 1978 (Table 10.1).

In the next three subsections, I draw together information on other principal costs of the Japanese occupation for Southeast Asians. These fall into three main categories. One, already indicated at various points in the book, is mass death. Second, I summarize physical destruction. A third comes under the broad grouping of individual suffering, including torture and displacement. Torture and other suffering has already been described in Chapters 2 and 9, and here I consider only evidence of displaced persons and refugees at the end of the war.

Mass Death and Atrocities

One can easily count over 4 million Southeast Asian dead as a result of major famines in Vietnam and Java, the three main Japanese railway projects, the treatment of Indonesian *romusha*, the Indian exodus from Burma, and deaths in Singapore in 1942 and in the Philippines during 1944 and 1945 (Table 10.4).

Table 10.4 *Premature death of Southeast Asians due to Japanese occupation 1941–1945 (million persons)*

Vietnam famine	1.000
Java famine	2.400
Java *romusha*	0.200
Singapore *sook ching*	0.023
Japanese railways	0.191
Burma Indian exodus	0.030
Philippines	0.500
Others	0.100
Total	4.444

Note: The estimate for the Philippines may include the deaths of some Filipino combatants. All other data refer to civilians. 'Others' is an estimate, and includes numerous smaller atrocities of a few thousand people or less.
Sources: Vietnam famine: Marr, *Vietnam, 1945*, p. 104. *Java famine*: van der Eng, *Food supply*, p. 38. *Java romusha*: De Jong, *Collapse*, p. 249; Friend, *Blue-eyed enemy*, p. 163; Raben, 'Indonesian *romusha*', pp. 208–10. *Singapore sook ching*: Cheah, *Red star*, pp. 20–24; Akashi, 'Japanese policy', pp. 66–68; MacGregor, 'Medical history', p. 159. *Japanese railways:* NA, WO325/56, Coolie camp conditions, p. 75; Poeze, 'Road', p. 165; Hovinga, *Sumatra railroad*, pp. 11–12, 16. *Burma Indian exodus:* Tinker, 'Forgotten long march', pp. 1–4; Donnison, *British military administration*, p. 280.

Alternative, less conservative estimates than in this chapter would produce totals of 5 or even 6 million premature dead. The United Nations Working Committee on Asia and the Far East, for example, estimated for Java 3 million deaths from execution by the Japanese, from hunger and disease and from a lack of medical attention and a further 1 million deaths in the Outer Islands.[17] As well as events involving death on a scale of 20,000 or more, there were numerous smaller instances ranging from the slaughter of a few thousand people to just one or two individuals who incurred Japanese displeasure. In all, such incidents may have added 100,000 to the wartime total of premature Southeast Asian deaths, on average about 17,000 per country but probably more than this in Burma, the Philippines and Indonesia. Using the estimate of 100,000 and the other numbers cited above for mass death on a large scale gives a total of 4.44 million civilians, or 3.1 per cent of Southeast Asia's 1941

[17] Dower, *War*, p. 296.

population of 145 million people. Civilians comprised the vast majority of all Southeast Asian dead.

Under normal circumstances, between 1942 and 1945 many more Southeast Asians would have been born than in fact were. In Malaya, for example, if the 1941/42 average of births in excess of deaths had persisted, over the four years 1942–45 population would have increased by 436,000. In reality, it rose by just under 100,000, a population deficit of roughly 336,000.[18] Remembering that Malaya accounted for only about 3.5 per cent of the population of pre-World War II Southeast Asia, this implies a large population deficit in the region as a whole. However, a lack of demographic data for most of Southeast Asia precludes any reliable estimate of overall wartime population shortfall caused by fewer births. I do not attempt to suggest how many more Southeast Asians might have been born in the absence of Japanese occupation. Nor do I speculate on the impairment to life chances of those who lived through the war. I confine this discussion to known deaths.

Most deaths resulted from economic conditions and forced labour. Lengthy conflict occurred only in Burma and the Philippines. Among Southeast Asians, Filipinos alone were involved in combat on a large scale. In Vietnam, Ho Chi Minh referred to 2 million famine deaths in his 2 September 1945 Independence Day speech. Although that number is still cited in Vietnamese textbooks, 1 million is probably a more accurate estimate.[19] Precise quantification of Java's massive human tragedy is probably impossible, but 2.4 million has been shown to be the likely figure (Chapter 7).

While the Thailand–Burma railway has been popularized as the 'Death railway', Japanese railway projects in Java and central Sumatra were even more lethal. Together the three railways claimed the lives of some 191,000 Southeast Asians and a further 12,000 Europeans. The Kra line added an unknown, but relatively small, number of deaths.

Available data for Indonesian *romusha* transported outside their home areas suggest that some 200,000 died before they could return. Added to this, but not included in Table 10.4 for want of precise information, should be some proportion of the about 2 million *romusha* who worked locally and died due to causes such as overwork, disease and poor food.[20] Most of those in Burma's 'Sweat Army', forced labour like the *romusha*, worked on the Thailand–Burma railway. The figure of 191,000 railway deaths would include these Burmese deaths. There is no good basis to estimate non-railway 'Sweat Army' deaths. The same applies to Thailand. No doubt Thai died when labouring on Japanese construction projects, but ethnic Chinese labourers living and recruited in Thailand for the Thailand–Burma railway may account for Thailand's largest single incidence of

[18] Malaya, *Report on the 1947 census*, pp. 35, 37.
[19] Marr, *Vietnam 1945*, pp. 104, 533.
[20] De Jong, *Collapse*, p. 249; Totani, *Tokyo War Crimes Trial*, p. 180.

death. Some 4,000 conscripted workers perished labouring on Phibun's 1943–44 project to construct a new, more strategically located capital at Phetchabun to counter Japanese influence.[21] Other records for Thailand include Japanese reports in early 1944 of several hundred deaths from Allied bombs and incendiary bombs. Fires due to the latter destroyed 600 buildings including shops, homes and temples in one raid.[22] The highest figure cited for deaths is 1,300 in Bangkok during 1944, although air raids continued in 1945.[23]

Heavy Japanese bombing of Rangoon on 23 and 25 December 1941 killed 2,500 people.[24] The Japanese began to attack Burma in earnest on the first of January, and from then until the fall of Rangoon on 8 March an unknown, but probably substantial, number of people died. Between the initial bombing of Rangoon and mid-1942, around half Burma's pre-war Indian population left the city, mostly on foot. Estimates of deaths on the march back to India range upwards to 100,000, but the probable figure is from 10,000 to 50,000.[25] Table 10.4 adopts a mid-point estimate of 30,000.

In Malaya, some 7,000 Singapore civilians were killed or died of wounds as a result of Japanese attacks between 8 December 1941 and 15 February 1942, when the city fell.[26] Soon afterwards in Singapore, and then in the Malay peninsula, Japan began the systematic mass murder of Chinese as part of a *sook ching*, or 'purification by elimination'. In the Chinese village of E-Lang-Lang in Negri Sembilan, babies were thrown into the air and pierced with bayonets and swords on the way down. *Sook ching* executions in Singapore were said by the Japanese to be about 6,000 and by the Chinese to number as many as 40,000. I use 23,000, as the mid-point between these conflicting assessments.[27]

Intense fighting occurred in the Philippines, and this creates difficulty in separating civilian deaths from those of combatants.[28] Friend gives the number of Filipinos dead from battles, malnutrition and Japanese occupation as 500,000.[29] A Philippines government evaluation that during the war 1 million Filipinos, or 6.3 per cent of the 1938 population, were killed or wounded may be broadly consistent with Friend's figure of half a million dead. Filipino deaths compare with 625,000 Japanese troops sent to the Philippines, of whom 80 per cent never returned home.[30]

21 Reynolds, *Thailand*, p. 171.
22 NARA, RG457, entry 9011, box 60, file 49613–14 and file 49952–55; box 62, file 51264–65.
23 Numnonda, *Thailand*, p. 51; Reynolds, *Thailand*, pp. 172–73.
24 Christian, *Burma*, p. 114.
25 Tinker, 'Forgotten long march', pp. 1–4; Donnison, *British military administration*, p. 280.
26 MacGregor, 'Medical history', p. 157.
27 Cheah, *Red star*, pp. 20–24; Akashi, 'Japanese policy', pp. 66–68; MacGregor, 'Medical history', p. 159; Bayly and Harper, *Forgotten armies*, pp. 214, 489; Blackburn and Hack, *War memory*, p. 40.
28 Friend, *Between two empires*, p. 267.
29 Friend, *Blue-eyed enemy*, pp. 242, 264.
30 Ikehata, 'Japanese occupation period', p. 1.

In battles that began with the 3 February 1945 United States attack on Manila, 100,000 Filipino civilians died; almost 2,000 civilians were slaughtered in the town of Calamba, Laguna.[31] The Japanese systematically destroyed Manila and killed thousands of civilians as part of a planned army operation. A documented United States enquiry, accompanied by many photographs, emphasizes that the Manila massacres were deliberate. They included the practices of burning people alive by first barricading houses and then throwing in grenades; going from house to house to gather men and boys who were then shot in the street; and bayoneting babies and people whose hands had been tied behind their backs.[32]

The number of deaths of relatively small groups of people or of a few individuals, through atrocities of one kind or another, can never be known, but the total of 100,000 suggested at the beginning of this section is probably not an overstatement. War crimes, as Drea observes, are not unusual, but the Japanese in the Pacific War stand out 'because the scope of Japan's atrocities was so excessive'.[33] Atrocities against Allied troops are well known: the Bataan Death March in which about 600 American and 5,000 to 10,000 Filipino troops died, and the Sandakan Death March which 6 of 2,390 prisoners of war survived.[34] The focus here, however, is on Southeast Asian civilians.

Whole villages in Burma were wiped out for harbouring offenders.[35] In rural Sumatra, Captain Inoue put down an *aron* (a group of villagers who harvest collectively) movement by personally decapitating five of its leaders in a public display.[36] Everyone in a leper colony in Malaya was burned to death.[37] An October 1943 Chinese rebellion in British Borneo led to the systematic extinction by the Japanese of an entire tribe, the Suluk, who had assisted the rebels. Men were hunted down, some 4,000 in all, until there were no males left to transmit the cultural heritage. The torture and execution of all Suluk men and boys was judged to be the same or only a little worse than that of the Chinese, of whom some 700 were tortured and executed. Suluk women and children were either killed or deported elsewhere to work as slave labour. In the opinion of the British war crimes investigator, the treatment of the Suluks was standard for any people deemed to be 'anti-Japanese'.[38]

31 Ibid., pp. 17–18. Dower, *War*, pp. 296–97 gives a total figure of 90,000 civilian deaths.
32 Philippines, Office of the Resident Commissioner, *Destruction of Manila*, pp. 1–114; Totani, *Tokyo War Crimes Trial*, pp. 155–58.
33 Drea, *Japan's imperial army*, p. 259.
34 Ibid., p. 224; Coox, 'Pacific War', pp. 345–47; Ooi, *Japanese occupation*, pp. 87–91.
35 OSS, R&A 2015, *Japanese administration of Burma*, p. 39.
36 Reid and Saya, 'Rural unrest', pp. 118–19.
37 NARA, RG226, entry 16, box 1279, no. 112749, OSS, R&A Branch, Regular Intelligence Reports, 'General conditions in Malaya (Penang island), 11 January 1945', p. 5.
38 Totani, *Tokyo War Crimes Trial*, pp. 168–69; Ooi, *Japanese occupation*, pp. 99, 121.

In Pontianak between October 1943 and June 1944, 1,500 Indonesian, Chinese and Indian civilians were arrested on suspicion of participating in an underground resistance movement. The vast majority were tortured and murdered, although some women were not killed but raped by members of the Japanese Naval Police and forced to become comfort women.[39] One individual incident stands for many including the bayoneting of children. A resident of a small village in Malaya recalled how Lee Cheng Fatt, a tailor, was bayoneted in front of his family after refusing to surrender some pieces of cloth demanded by two Japanese soldiers.[40]

Physical Destruction

By the end of the war, the Philippines, Burma and Indonesia had sustained the greatest damage to physical infrastructure and cities but nowhere escaped entirely. In British Borneo, 70 per cent of Jesselton and almost all of Sandakan were destroyed. So, too, was much of the railway, including locomotives, rolling stock and bridges.[41] Destruction in Thailand was mostly due to US bombing, as it also was in Indochina. Thailand's railway was a principal bombing target. Allied bombs had entirely destroyed or made unfit for further service 28 railway bridges (including the three largest), 22 principal stations, half the rolling stock, almost all repair shops, numerous buildings and enormous quantities of equipment.[42] Additional to this was damage to Thai industry and infrastructure other than building and transport equipment, assessed as 1945US$7.8 million. In comparison, damage in Indochina (chiefly Vietnam), including $148 million to industrial plants, was put at a total 1945US$2 billion. It included the demolition of a third of all bridges, the inoperability of a large share of port installations and cuts in the railway so numerous that only short stretches of it could be used. About half of junks over 16 tons, private cars and motorcycles as well as 90 per cent of heavy vehicles were lost.[43]

Much of wartime destruction in Malaya, assessed as 'widespread and serious', resulted from the attempts by retreating Allied troops to deny infrastructure and machinery to the Japanese and by Allied bombing.[44] During the war, Singapore was heavily bombed, especially the naval base and Empire Dock area.[45] There was also destruction caused by the Japanese. That was to

39 Tanaka, *Japan's comfort women*, p. 79; Ooi, *Japanese occupation*, pp. 102–17.
40 Jaafar bin Hamzah, 'Malays in Tasek Gelugur', p. 58; Ooi, *Japanese occupation*, pp. 87–91.
41 United Nations, *Economic reconstruction: British Borneo*, p. 3.
42 Kingdom of Thailand, *Report of the financial adviser 1941–1950*, p. 47.
43 United Nations, *Economic reconstruction: Thailand*, p. 3; United Nations, *Economic reconstruction: Indochina*, pp. 5, 20, 22, 24; Le, *Impact*, p. 272.
44 Federation of Malaya and Singapore, *Report of the War Damage Commission*, p. 4.
45 See, for example, NARA, RG226, entry 16, box 1411, no. 123318, OSS, R&A Branch, Regular Intelligence Reports, 'Damage assessment report no. 45' and RG226, entry 16,

some extent intentional, but more due to neglect or short-term policies on the use of assets. Proposals for a Malayan war damage compensation scheme were made in 1948, and the commission dealing with claims finally reported in 1953. Claims, numbering tens of thousands and amounting to hundreds of millions of Malayan dollars, were received. The aim of compensation was to apply funds to restore the economy to its 1941 productive capacity, for which Malayan$435 million were allocated, an amount which partly reflected the straitened circumstances of the United Kingdom economy. In 1942, Keynes had warned against Britain accepting responsibility for making good war damage in the empire, and by 1945, anxious to protect the UK exchequer, advised that the Treasury should 'stand firm' on Malaya and leave the local government to cope with 'hard cases'.[46] The sum of Malayan$435 million equalled 12.2 per cent of 1948 Malayan GDP, and was far short of claims submitted, although these may have been inflated in the expectation that only a percentage of the sums sought would be paid. Rubber estate and smallholding interests submitted claims for Malayan$376 million, of which a large part was for trees felled to plant food crops, and were paid Malayan$85 million (£9.9 million). Tin mining claims also had an allocation of Malayan$85 million, meant to cover among other items the loss of pre-war stocks and lost and damaged machinery, of which dredges were a major item.[47]

The Philippines emerged from the war with most of its physical capital destroyed, damaged or depleted. War damage was estimated as 1945US $1.6 billion although this included the value of goods the Japanese paid for with the currency that they had printed. If not demolished, nearly all factories and mines were no longer operable. In Manila, the main Philippines manufacturing centre, few factories were left standing, and this was also true in other industrial cities like Cebu and Iloilo. A Committee on Industry and Manufacturing organized by the Philippines Chamber of Commerce summarized: 'what it took almost a half century to build will have to be rebuilt again'.[48] Transportation facilities including railways, Manila's 100 street cars, bridges, the inter-island fleet of 160 ships and wharves had been destroyed, and the power and communications infrastructure severely damaged.[49]

box 1408, no. 123005, OSS, R&A Branch, Regular Intelligence Reports, 'Damage assessment report no. 47, 12 March 1945'.

46 NA, T247/4, 'War risks insurance', 19 February 1942 and T220/52, 'Note for Young', 14 May 1945.

47 Federation of Malaya, *Proposals for Malayan war damage*, pp. 1, 6, 21–23; Federation of Malaya and Singapore, *Report of the War Damage Commission*, pp. iii, 1–4, 83–113. For 1948 GDP, see Benham, *National income*, p. 89.

48 UP, Roxas Papers, box 39, Teodoro, 'Philippine manufacturing industry', 12 July 1945, p. 1.

49 United Nations, *Economic reconstruction: Philippine Republic*, pp. 3, 21–24, 32; United States, Department of State, *Economic survey mission to the Philippines*, p. 6.

At least four-fifths of Greater Manila was razed to the ground, the former 'Pearl of the Orient' gone. Among the world's great cities, the World War II devastation suffered by Manila came second only to Warsaw. The business district was virtually destroyed. In late April 1945, the only electricity supply in Manila was from army generators; there were no buses or street cars. The number of sunken ships in Manila harbour was said to rank behind only Naples. Not much remained of many larger Philippine towns except their names.[50]

The principal form of aid provided by the United States to the Philippines consisted of expenditure under the Philippine Rehabilitation Act. Payments for private war damage claims amounted to US$390 million. This was, as in Malaya, substantially below claims submitted, although the total sum was judged by the Economic Survey Mission to the Philippines (the Bell Commission) sufficient to 'enable reconstruction to begin promptly'. In all, US$141 million was authorized for the reconstruction of public buildings, roads, the port of Manila, health and other public purposes.[51]

Ba Maw later maintained that his relationship with Tōjō was important in saving Burma from total destruction at the end of the war.[52] If so, and recalling end-of-war Manila, that was fortunate. Nevertheless, Allied bombing combined with Japanese disinterest and an inability to effect repairs left Rangoon's entire dock area in ruin.[53] Rangoon itself had fallen into 'a state of indescribable filth [and] the City was in the hands of looters and bad hats'.[54] The Governor of Burma, Sir Hubert Rance, assessed Rangoon as 25 per cent destroyed.[55] Manufactured goods were scarce and a black market flourished.[56] In October 1945, public transport was practically non-existent, water was available only from fire hydrants and there was no possibility of municipal electricity for at least several months.[57] Even after the organization of basic

50 BE, OV149/1, 'Banking business in Philippines reported in chaotic condition', *New York Herald Tribune*, 24 April 1945; Hartendorp, *Japanese occupation*, pp. 153–54, 197; Friend, *Between two empires*, p. 231.

51 United States, Department of State, *Economic survey mission to the Philippines*, pp. 102–3; Golay, *Philippines*, pp. 59–66.

52 Maw, *Breakthrough*, p. 324.

53 United Nations, *Reconstruction: Burma*, p. 32; Tinker, *Union of Burma*, p. 286.

54 MNA, 1/5 98 BMA Report, October 1945, Annexure A, 'Note on the achievements of the BMA in no. 1 area up to the 16 Oct.', p. 33; see also BE, OV79/17, A. K. Potter to C. E. Key, War Office, 29 September 1945.

55 'Burmese seek mastery of own country', *Daily Telegraph*, 1 November 1946.

56 OSS, R&A/SEAC no. 8-R in NARA, RG226, entry 154, box 81, file 1406, *Economic conditions in Rangoon May–June 1945*, 29 June 1945, pp. 1–2.

57 OSS, R&A/SEAC no. 35-R in NARA, RG226, entry 154, box 81, file 1433, *Living conditions in Rangoon*, 18 October 1945, p. 1. In November 1946, 500,000 people in the city were still without piped water ('Burmese seek mastery of own country', *Daily Telegraph*, 1 November 1946).

cleaning and restoration of greater order, Rangoon looked, in Collis's description, 'like a shanty town'.[58] Elsewhere, large parts of Burma were also damaged. Mainly due to British and American air raids, most towns 'were not just badly blitzed, they were completely laid waste, wiped off the map'.[59] The southern portion of Moulmein and its river frontage were completely gutted and the entire town overgrown with jungle.[60] Thaton town was badly smashed in the bazaar area and generally overgrown.[61] Even before the end of the war, British bombing had destroyed the old Legislative Building in Rangoon, perhaps, as was remarked, symbolic of the beginning of the end of an attempt at British Parliamentary democracy in Burma.[62]

Colonial officials in Indonesia assessed direct damage as US$2.2 billion in 1938 values and that this rose to $3.5 billion taking into account losses to food crops, commercial crops and mining output.[63] Damage to Indonesia's capital stock during the occupation and subsequent war of independence remains uncertain but appears to have been considerable. For the purpose of claiming reparations from Japan, the colonial government planned to calculate wartime losses but never completed its calculations. However, van der Eng identified sources with 1947 estimates of the destruction of physical capital in Indonesia. These put total damage at 4.1 billion florins. On the basis of pre-war replacement cost, this is equivalent to a loss of 34 per cent of Indonesian capital stock. While that percentage is considerably higher than losses in wartime Europe, the estimate covers a longer period in providing a comprehensive measure of decade-long destruction. Included in the estimate are the defensive destruction of machinery and equipment by the Dutch colonial government in 1942 and the dismantling and shipment overseas of factories and railway stock by the Japanese military government, as well as damage sustained during the war of independence, particularly during 1946 and 1947. Capital-stock destruction divides about equally between foreign-owned enterprises and infrastructure.[64]

Societal Costs

Wartime scarcities and almost universal poverty bred, along with black markets, corruption and decadence throughout Southeast Asia such that, by 1945, societal infrastructure had been severely damaged. During the war, gambling

[58] Collis, *Last and first*, p. 263; see also Nu, *Saturday's son*, p. 215.
[59] Dorman-Smith, 'Burma', p. 261.
[60] MNA, 1/11 Secret Reports, 'Progress report no. 9', report to 30 September 1945.
[61] MNA, 1/11 141 Monthly reports of SCAO, Thaton and neighbouring SCAO's, September 1945.
[62] Pe, *Narrative*, p. 14.
[63] United Nations, *Economic reconstruction: Netherlands Indies*, p. 3.
[64] van der Eng, 'Capital formation and capital stock', p. 18.

and brothels proliferated.[65] Singapore became 'one big city of gamblers' as everyone tried to supplement incomes.[66] The Singapore amusement parks, Great World and New World, were gambling centres and, in all, about 300 gambling houses were scattered over the city.[67] As well as Singapore, Malaya had two 'Monte Carlos', in Seremban, Negri Sembilan and Kampar, Perak.[68] Gambling proliferated in Penang and 'had become so rife' in Bangkok as to prompt the formation of an Anti-Gambling League.[69] Whole blocks of Manila houses and apartments became brothels.[70] In the Philippines, divorce was legalized for the first time, partly owing to an upsurge in prostitution by married women attempting to feed their families.[71] By the latter part of the war in Rangoon, there was a 'great increase in restaurants, drinking, prostitution and other means of indulgence' and many of the new restaurants advertised for attractive young women to act as waitresses.[72]

In the Philippines, war and occupation resulted in social breakdown, a spiritual erosion that was said to have left people prey to 'cynicism, corruption, and a philosophy of *agaw-buhay*: "snatch-life"'.[73] The effects of this unfolded gradually, manifested in 'the general lawlessness and contempt for government, the violence and criminality, marked by a barbaric disregard of the value of human life [and] the general blunting of the moral sense and abandonment of ethical standards'.[74] In Thailand, wartime corruption was said to be the war's worst legacy.[75] The black market, which had become a way of life in Singapore, continued to flourish after the war.[76] For Malaya, the effect of Japanese occupation was summed up as 'four years of psychological and physical deterioration'.[77]

The social consequences of Japanese conscription of women as 'comfort women' for the troops, the closing of schools, a breakdown in social services and the spectre of starvation lasted well beyond the end of the war. The convergence in Singapore of all these aspects of Japanese occupation 'made

65 NA, CO273/673/1, 'Conditions in enemy-occupied Malaya', *c.* April 1944, p. 1.
66 NAS, Oral History, George Edwin Bogaars, p. 37.
67 ANM, 1957/0572010, 'Brief review of Chinese affairs', p. 3.
68 BE, OV65/3, 'Extract from a Chinese newspaper translated by Peck Pia Jin, Oversea-Chinese Banking Corporation, Chungking', *c.* August 1944.
69 NARA, RG 226, entry 16, box 1279, no. 112749, OSS, R&A Branch, Regular Intelligence Reports, 'General conditions in Malaya (Penang island), 11 Jan. 1945', p. 4 ; Chaya, *Passing hours*, p. 70.
70 Hartendorp, *Japanese occupation*, pp. 444–45.
71 Agoncillo, *Fateful years*, pp. 589–90.
72 Burma Intelligence Bureau, *Burma*, vol. 2, p. 152.
73 Friend, *Between two empires*, p. 266.
74 Hartendorp, *History of industry*, p. 167.
75 Numnonda, *Thailand*, p. 95; and see LHC, MAGIC, 'Economic summary', 23 September 1943, p. 5; 'Reformation at large', *Bangkok Post*, 29 November 1946; United Kingdom, *Burma statement of policy*, Cmd. 6635.
76 Gilmour, *With freedom*, p. 139; Gilmour, *My role*, p. 6.
77 Malayan Union, *Annual report on education … 1946*, p. 93.

easier the revival of the practice of selling female children to brothel keepers and others who trained them for prostitution'. In 1946, Singapore's medical authorities drew attention to the large numbers of girls aged 10 to 14 appearing for the treatment of venereal disease.[78]

Displaced Persons and Refugees

At the end of the war, Southeast Asia had tens of thousands of displaced persons. The region also had many, although only a fraction, of the 6.6 million Japanese outside Japan. By 1950, the Allies had repatriated some 3 million Japanese from far-flung parts of the Co-Prosperity Sphere.[79] Apart from the Japanese in Southeast Asia, numerous others who had emigrated to Southeast Asia or had been brought to Southeast Asia during the war wanted to return home. Numbers of Indians who had been trapped in Burma in 1942 now sought passage to India. Also in need of repatriation were Chinese labourers brought to Thailand from elsewhere during the war and who by the end of August 1945 began to arrive in Bangkok 'destitute, ill or starving in many cases, and penniless'.[80]

Pre-war Southeast Asian residents comprised a large share of displaced persons. About 35,000 of those deported by the Japanese to labour on the Thailand–Burma railway were found when Allied forces entered Thailand. The British military administration in Malaya worked to repatriate them, although in April 1946 several thousand of these workers were still awaiting repatriation.[81] Other survivors of the railway, including those who had successfully deserted during the war or were freed at its end, made their own efforts to get home, if necessary by walking and gradually moving from place to place. Many only arrived home in 1946. A villager from Tasek Gelugur in Malaya finally reached home in mid-1948, and as late as 1950 there were still Malay forced labourers in Thailand appealing for repatriation.[82] Malaya's post-war communal violence increased the number of refugees by thousands.[83]

In early 1947, a large percentage of the Javanese used as labourers by the Japanese had still to be repatriated and were scattered over various of the Indonesian islands and throughout Malaya, Thailand, Burma and Indochina.[84] The returning British found large numbers of Javanese labourers brought to Malaya by the Japanese. Arrangements were made to collect and accommodate

[78] Singapore Department of Social Welfare, *First report*, pp. 37–38.
[79] Milward, *War, economy*, p. 215; Drea, *Japan's imperial army*, p. 261.
[80] Skinner, *Chinese society*, p. 289.
[81] Malayan Union, *Report on the British military administration*, p. 71; United Nations, *Reconstruction: Malayan Union & Singapore*, p. 7; Harper, *End*, p. 41.
[82] Abu Talib Ahmad, *Malay Muslims*, p. 71; Jaafar bin Hamzah, 'Malays in Tasek Gelugur', p. 63; Blackburn and Hack, *War memory*, p. 248.
[83] Harper, *End*, p. 41.
[84] United Nations, *Economic reconstruction: Netherlands Indies*, p. 6.

2,000 of them at Kuala Lumpur. It was also necessary to repatriate to Malaya some 4,000 refugees stranded in India. Altogether in Malaya, 105,000 destitute persons received relief accommodation and about three times as many were helped by the distribution of relief supplies.[85]

Pre-war Asian residents of Malaya were scattered throughout Asia. Notable among them were a group of Chinese carpenters who had been drafted to the Andaman Islands and a large body of people, known as the 'lost legion', who had been taken by the Japanese to Hollandia, Dutch New Guinea as forced labour for the construction of aerodromes. Singapore functioned as a clearing house for the 'wake of human wreckage in South East Asia'.[86] It was described by a contemporary observer as 'a huge transit camp with thousands of troops going both East and West, thousands of displaced persons seeking passages to all points of the compass and thousands of refugees seeking safety'.[87]

Lessons of Occupation and Development

Four main economic lessons emerge from Japanese wartime policy and the collapse in regional economies to which it contributed. The lessons derive from the natural experiment created by the war of an abrupt change from the open economies and essentially laissez-faire approach of pre-war governments to the largely autarkical and administered economies of the Japanese occupation. Analysis of Southeast Asian economies during the war which this book set out to provide is valuable in helping to understand the region's pre-war economic development.

One lesson involves the rationale for Southeast Asian pre-war specialization in a handful of primary commodity staples, and the obstacles to a departure from this pattern. Much of pre-war development was based on comparative advantage associated with quite specific geographical characteristics and dependence on access to a global market. Southeast Asian delta regions were extremely well suited to rice, as were Malaya and Indonesia to rubber, while temperate fibre crops were ill adapted to the tropics of Southeast Asia. For reasons of geography, Southeast Asian cultivators often could not successfully switch to new crops when required to do so by Japanese planners or to meet subsistence needs. In some instances a strategy of survival probably made peasant farmers reluctant to shift from food crops, while in others they may have tried to avoid starting new lines of production because of an expectation that the war would soon end and the Japanese would leave. Technologies for economic re-configuration from agricultural commodities which Japan tried to implement often drew on Japanese historical experience. However,

[85] Malayan Union, *Report on the British military administration*, p. 71.
[86] Singapore Department of Welfare, *First report*, p. 3.
[87] Gilmour, *With freedom*, p. 140.

technologies and approaches that were successful in Northeast Asia often proved inappropriate to Southeast Asian conditions.

Second, economic incentives were fundamental to pre-war development, but were largely ignored by wartime Japanese economic planners and administrators. Those in charge of the region's economies gave little attention to the role of prices and the availability of inducement goods like textiles and simple manufactures as stimuli to production. Japan intended, as it had in 1930s Manchuria, to organize Southeast Asia's economies through planning and to effect plans by relying on large monopoly or semi-monopoly corporations with close links to the government. However, agrarian economies, heavily dependent on numerous small cultivators spread over a large area, are poorly suited to centralized direction and coercion. Production in such economies has typically required positive incentives. These were lacking in wartime Southeast Asia, because there was no longer a market for many of its main products, and because the Japanese tried to secure products they wanted at artificially low prices without offering incentives of food and consumer goods in exchange.

Third, Japanese attempts at manufacturing in Southeast Asia demonstrate the major barriers to industrialization in economies which were not national but in effect miscellaneous collections of factors of production. The region's economies were still in the early stages of development and had weak transformation capacity. An extensive industrial base had yet to be built, education levels were typically low and there were few skilled workers. Any such economy would struggle to move into different types of production of even basic consumer items, especially when, as in wartime Southeast Asia, raw materials and capital goods were no longer available through international trade. The war economy left Japan itself with chronic shortages of skilled labour and engineers. There was little scope to despatch trained Japanese personnel to Southeast Asia. Although Japan sent Southeast Asia some capital equipment, especially textile machinery from closed-down Japanese factories, this was generally no more than partially, if at all, useable for want of raw material inputs and complementary human capital.

Fourth, culture has a role in economic development. Japanese economic planning for Southeast Asia resembled the Soviet-like command economy operational in Japan from the late 1930s.[88] There, social cohesion and the belief of almost all the population in the rightness of the state aided the enforcement of wartime planning and production. In Southeast Asia, a similar Japanese cultural tradition was absent and coercion was a poor substitute. Pre-war Southeast Asian development was heavily reliant on numerous individuals acting in response to market forces. There were also, in Japan, means of enforcement lacking in Southeast Asia. Unlike Southeast Asia, Japan was

[88] Nakamura, 'Japanese war economy', p. 20.

small, homogeneous and highly urbanized, and had at its disposal a large number of economic police.

Before the war, a substantial number of Japanese merchants, traders and shipping companies operated in Southeast Asia. Japan's government, drawing partly on intelligence from individuals living in Southeast Asia and also through its own initiatives, tried to gather information about the economies of the region and its peoples. However, the mistakes made by Japan during the war suggest that little had been learned or understood. The lessons that arise from Japan's three and a half years of occupation reflect in large part this lack of understanding. As this book has shown, the consequences of Japan's weak economy compounded by a failure to appreciate the nature of Southeast Asia, indifference, insistence on the Japanese way and an ever worsening military position, were catastrophic for Southeast Asia.

Conclusion

Even though Japan's decision for a Pacific war was, as Milward has argued, an understandable attempt to add substantially to its economic strength, many of those responsible for the decision knew that it was a gamble.[89] War with the United States, as the comparison of American and Japanese economic power in Chapter 1 showed, was no small matter. A war could easily go wrong. The odds were strongly skewed in that direction if war lasted more than two years. Despite possible failure, few if any Japanese could have envisaged the Pacific War's eventual enormous costs to Japan.

The costs of the war to Southeast Asia, detailed in this chapter and throughout the book, were not in all respects greater than Japan's for the war as a whole. But they were far higher for civilians and greatly outweighed Japanese costs encountered in Southeast Asia alone. Moreover, the loss of life and destruction visited on Southeast Asia was not of its own making. For Southeast Asians, it was, in Collis's description of the plight of the Burmese, like 'innocents strayed into a giant's battle'.[90]

World War II led to far-reaching and fundamental changes in Southeast Asia. That was only to be expected after the routing of the region's colonial powers and the events recorded throughout this book. The Epilogue traces some of the legacies of the war and main post-1945 changes for which war and occupation were responsible.

[89] Milward, *War, economy*, p. 15.
[90] Collis, *Last and first*, p. 82.

Illustration 19 Indian refugees flee Burma, early 1942 (IWM JAR1213).
During early 1942, half a million Indians left Burma, most attempting to walk back to India. Some 50,000 died en route (Chapters 8 and 10).

Illustration 20 Burmese women unloading a freight wagon on the Thailand–Burma railway c. 1943 (AWM P00761027).
Extensive use was made of Southeast Asians to support the Japanese military, as soldiers, comfort women and, in this photo, as labourers (Chapter 9).

Illustration 21 Comfort women liberated on the Andaman Islands (IWM SE5226). The Japanese use of comfort women was notorious. As the photo shows, these women were on the whole quite ordinary individuals caught up in a terrible war (Chapter 9).

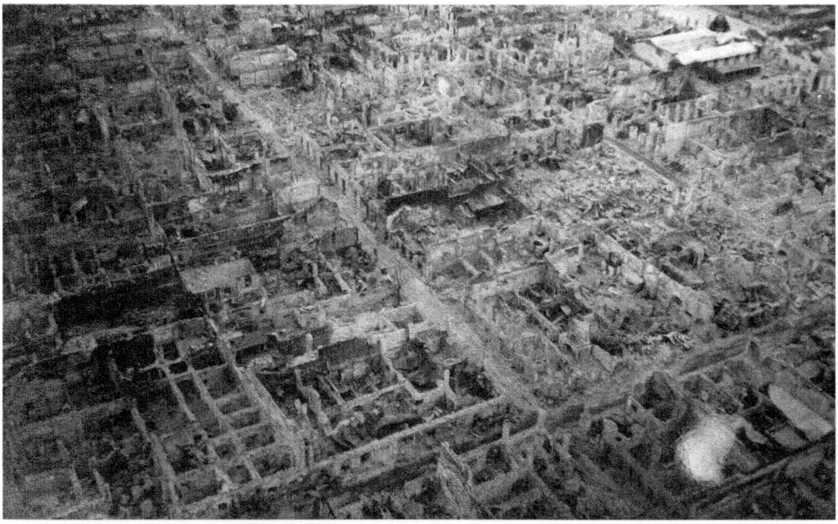

Illustration 22 Destruction in the central Manila inner city core and old Spanish fort district of Intramuros (NARA box 290 211523).
The costs to Southeast Asia of occupation were great. Manila was essentially flattened (Chapter 10).

Illustration 23 Devastation of the Rangoon docks, September 1945 (IWM C5356).
Extensive wartime destruction of infrastructure in some Southeast Asian countries retarded post-war economic recovery (Chapter 10).

Illustration 24 Japanese digging trenches in Singapore under Allied supervision, September 1945 (NARA box 836 392677).
The Singapore Supreme Court provides the backdrop for this example of one kind of Allied retribution after Japan's August 1945 surrender (Epilogue).

Illustration 25 Philippines Independence Day parade, 4 July 1946 (NARA box 434 251860).
The Japanese occupation led quickly to independence for much of Southeast Asia, although, as here with a replica of the US Statue of Liberty, the Philippines alone had warm feeling for the ex-colonial power (Epilogue).

Epilogue and Conclusion

World War II and the Japanese occupation set in motion changes that for two decades did much to shape Southeast Asian history. Chief among the changes were altered Southeast Asian political environments; an end, often swift, to colonial rule; and frequently turbulent transitions to independence. Every country except Thailand experienced civil war or revolution. There was 'no return to the old peaceful, stable, free-and-easy Singapore', as Lee Kuan Yew remarked of an area of Southeast Asia less troubled than much of the region.[1]

This final part of the book first briefly describes the post-war realization of independence for Southeast Asian countries. I then assess how wartime events influenced Southeast Asia's post-World War II political and economic configuration. The balance between continuity and change differed markedly between countries: Burma, Indonesia and Vietnam went through great upheavals while Thailand, Malaya and the Philippines steered steadier, less radical courses. After considering the political repercussions of occupation, I turn to the economic consequences. Both are basic to understanding post-1945 change in Southeast Asia.

Independence, Political Change and Nationalism

The principal longer-term impact of the Second World War on Southeast Asia was the push it gave independence and accompanying political changes. No doubt colonialism would eventually have ended in Southeast Asia. But Japan's military conquest, the Japanese interregnum and its sudden collapse in August 1945 hastened the end of colonial rule. The discontinuities of war and occupation probably made decolonization more violent than it would otherwise have been. If post-war Southeast Asia had quickly stabilized politically, more economies in the region might have recovered to at least near 1938 levels of GDP per capita by the 1950s.[2] However, the geographically varied

[1] Lee, *Singapore story*, p. 85.

[2] Andrus, *Burmese economic life*, pp. 64, 338; Ingram, *Economic change*, pp. 155, 157; United States, Department of State, *Economic survey mission to the Philippines*, p. 6; Golay, *Philippines*, p. 68; Paauw, 'Economic progress', pp. 71–73; International Bank for Reconstruction and Development, *Economic development of Malaya*, p. 13.

consequences of Japanese rule and war affected recovery times. After independence, politics in Southeast Asian countries often pointed, if in varying degrees, to new, more interventionist economic strategies and these impacted economic recovery. In Burma, Indonesia and Vietnam, internal warfare, revolution and experiments with changed political systems lengthened recovery times (Chapter 10).

Thailand and the Philippines were exceptions to the general pattern of accelerated independence, Thailand because it was never a colony and the Philippines because American policy already ensured independence. Despite wartime alliance with Japan, Thailand's post-war leaders and diplomats reached accord with the Allies and succeeded in protecting the country's pre-1940 independence and borders. The United States had begun to prepare for an independent Philippines as early as the 1916 Jones Act. United States legislation in 1934 made the Philippines autonomous in domestic affairs and set out a 12-year timetable for full Philippines independence. In 1935, the Philippine Commonwealth became colonial Southeast Asia's first self-governing country and the first with a president drawn from the local population.[3]

The Japanese interregnum did not deflect the Philippines from the course charted before the war. As American troops advanced through the Philippines, Laurel's government disintegrated.[4] The Japanese announced the arrival in Tokyo of Laurel and Benigno S. Aquino, the wartime Speaker of the National Assembly and director of the Kalibapi, on 4 July 1945. Both were returned to the Philippines after the Japanese surrender.[5] Aquino died in 1947 but the Aquinos continued in the post-war years as one of the most powerful families in the Philippines. Although Laurel was charged with treason, he was never brought to trial due to a general amnesty granted by Manuel Roxas, elected president of the new republic following Philippines independence on 4 July 1946. Like the Aquinos, the Laurels remained a prominent family in Philippines politics.

Elsewhere in Southeast Asia, even in the late 1930s there appeared little prospect that the region's colonial rulers would soon leave. The Governor-General of Netherlands India (Indonesia) surely engaged in hyperbole when, in 1937, he observed that it would require another 300 years of colonial rule to prepare for independence.[6] Nevertheless, similar sentiments, though perhaps envisaging shorter time spans, characterized mainstream thinking in other colonial powers except the United States. Writing in Simla, India during the

[3] Friend, 'Philippine sugar industry', pp. 179–80 and *Blue-eyed enemy*, pp. 33, 270; Bastin and Benda, *History*, p. 171.

[4] Friend, *Between two empires*, p. 244.

[5] OSS, R&A 3208, *Philippines: finale of the puppet government*, pp. 1–2.

[6] Benda, 'Pattern', pp. 590–91 and Feith, *Decline*, p. 5 where the Governor-General is quoted.

war, the pre-war British superintendent of the Intelligence Branch observed that the Burman's desire for freedom was 'the great political factor which operated against us . . . Not only did we fail to grant freedom but we in Burma did little or nothing, despite our promises, to show that we had any intention of granting freedom.'[7]

Before the war, although nationalist movements existed throughout Southeast Asia, none seemed likely to provide an effective force for independence.[8] Nationalism derived almost entirely from the urban intelligentsia, and, unlike religious movements in the region, lacked roots in rural Southeast Asia and therefore a significant power base.[9] And yet within just over a decade after the end of the Second World War virtually all of Southeast Asia had gained independence.

After appointment as Governor of Burma in August 1946, Sir Hubert Rance was instructed to co-operate with Aung San and his Anti-Fascist People's Freedom League in realizing Burma's independence as soon as possible. Burma, until 1937 a province of India, soon followed it in gaining independence and became the independent Union of Burma on 4 January 1948. U Nu had been made Prime Minister after the assassination of Aung San in July 1947, and continued in that role in independent Burma. He remained Prime Minister for almost all of the next 14 years until in July 1962 he was removed by a coup led by General Ne Win. Both U Nu and Ne Win had been members of the We Burmans Association and Ne Win, along with Aung San, one of the Thirty Comrades (Chapter 2).

On 17 August 1945, just after the Japanese surrender, Sukarno and Hatta proclaimed Indonesia independent. The proclamation is said to have 'had an electrifying effect on the mass of Indonesians'.[10] That must, however, have applied principally to Java, as in most parts of Indonesia it took from one to three months for Indonesians to hear of the proclamation and to believe it. Finally in December 1949, after bitter Dutch-Indonesian hostilities and in some areas guerrilla warfare, Indonesia achieved independence with the signing in Amsterdam of a transfer of sovereignty.

In Vietnam, Ho Chi Minh announced independence on 2 September 1945. There soon followed the First Indochina War, fought against the French who were supported by the United States with hardware and advisors. The conflict lasted until 1954, after which, during the Second Indochina War, American military involvement in Vietnam escalated. Under the settlement negotiated in Geneva in July 1954, Vietnam was partitioned into two zones divided at the

7 IOR, Dorman-Smith Papers, Mss Eur E145/6 (6), S. D. Jupp, 'The attitude of Burmese people in the recent campaign in Burma', *c.* December 1942, p. 1.

8 Silverstein, 'Importance of the Japanese occupation', p. 7 and see Trocki, 'Political structures', p. 104; Emerson, Mills and Thompson, *Government*, pp. 15–35, 127.

9 Benda, 'Structure', pp. 131, 135.

10 Anderson, *Some aspects*, p. 98.

17th parallel, the northern zone as the Democratic Republic of Vietnam, the southern as the State of Vietnam. This division of Vietnam was intended to be temporary, with a general election to be held two years later to reunify the country, but the southern zone, backed by the United States, refused to allow the election. Thus, North Vietnam, in effect, retained sovereignty. Both North and South Vietnam needed extensive reconstruction, lacked capital, suffered from corruption and depended on the support of major powers.[11] Vietnam was finally united in 1975 following the defeat, in the Second Indochina War, of the Americans and the South Vietnam government they had backed with massive commitments of troops and money.

For Cambodia and Laos, Indochina's other pre-war constituents, Japanese occupation and the March 1945 coup marked the beginning of the end of French colonialism. Shortly after the coup and under pressure from the Japanese, King Sisavangvong declared Laos independent. A month after proclaiming Cambodian independence on 13 March 1945, King Norodom Sihanouk declared: 'the Empire of the Rising Sun, liberator of the Asian people, gives this gift to Khymer history, the inestimable gift which is Cambodian independence'.[12] Sihanouk, 'a creature of World War II', without which he might never have been a major political figure, pressed for independence after the war.[13] In 1953, the French, buffeted by events in Vietnam, caved in to his demands. A year later Cambodia became fully independent from France as part of the Geneva settlement. From 1955 to 1970, Sihanouk, now Prince Sihanouk, had a monopoly of political power in Cambodia, which did much to set the stage for subsequent political chaos and the Khmer Rouge.[14]

Under the Geneva agreement, Laos also became independent but was de facto a divided country. Three years of negotiation finally overcame the country's division. However, political unity did not last. Like Indochina's other pre-war French administrations, the post-war history of Laos was marked by conflict and near-continuous intervention by external powers.[15]

After the war, Britain planned to form and rule as a single entity a Malayan Union consisting of the Malay states, together with Penang and Malacca, but not Singapore which was to become a separate Crown Colony. The Malayan Union foundered almost immediately because of opposition by Malays who

[11] Shabad, 'Economic developments', pp. 38–41, 45; Thien, 'Economic development', pp. 56–58; C. L. Sulzberger, 'Liberation in reverse – who is rolling back whom?' *New York Times*, 8 December 1954; BE, OV98/2, K. B. Gibson, 'Enclosure to despatch no. 71 (E)', 20 November 1959, p. 18.

[12] NAC, Fonds de la Résidence supérieure du Cambodge 23709, box 2805, Préparation d'un mouvement révolutionnaire, Texte du discours de S. M. Norodom Sihanouk, 15 April 1945.

[13] Chandler, 'Legacies', p. 27.

[14] Chandler, *History*, pp. 227–32.

[15] Stuart-Fox, *History*, pp. 59–89.

considered that insufficient recognition had been given to their political power.[16] Revised proposals for a Federation of Malaya, with the same components as the Union and under British control, were accepted and the Federation came into being in February 1948.

Throughout the Federation's existence, British Commonwealth forces fought the guerrilla (mainly Chinese) units of the Malayan National Liberation Army, the successor to the Malayan People's Anti-Japanese Army and military wing of the Malayan Communist Party. The war, known as the Malayan Emergency by the British and as the Anti-British National Liberation War by their opponents, was bloody. Many of the World War II guerrilla strongholds served likewise for the Liberation Army and became the Emergency's principal battlegrounds.[17] Malayan independence in 1957 was peaceful and ceremonial, even though the Emergency did not formally end until 1960. The Federation was joined in 1963 by Singapore and Sabah and Sarawak in the former British Borneo to create Malaysia, but this union lasted only until 1965, when Singapore was expelled and set its own course as a city state.

War, Occupation and Political Change

Japanese occupation contributed to political change and decolonization in Southeast Asia in three important ways. One was accelerated independence; the second an impetus to Southeast Asian nationalism; and the third, power vacuums after Japan surrendered which gave scope for opportunistic political change. This subsection discusses these political factors in turn, while the next considers economic legacies.

The speed of Japan's military advance in late 1941 and early 1942 and humiliating defeats inflicted by the Japanese on Europeans made it apparent to Southeast Asians that, even if Japan lost the war, European rule would soon end. The fall of Singapore, Churchill later wrote, was 'the worst disaster and largest capitulation in British history'.[18] A nearly 1,000-mile retreat from Burma was 'the longest . . . ever carried out by a British army'.[19] The United Kingdom, an official military historian observed, 'has a long, and in many ways honourable, tradition of unpreparedness for war'.[20] Beginning in late 1941, however, few of those in Southeast Asia, whether Asian or European, perceived

[16] MacMichael, *Report on a mission to Malaya*. On Colonial Office plans for the Malayan Union, see NA, CO273/675/7, 'Future policy in Malaya'. Possible British options for charting Malaya's post-war political configuration are discussed in NA, CO273/677/11, Sir Shenton Thomas, 'Memorandum on post-war Malaya', 29 February 1944.

[17] Harper, *End*, pp. 49–50.

[18] Churchill, *Hinge*, p. 81.

[19] Smyth, 'Long retreat', p. 954.

[20] Donnison, *British military administration*, p. 435.

that tradition favourably. Although Thailand was only in Britain's informal empire, for Thai supporters of Britain 'our collapse in the Far East came as a cruel disillusionment to those . . . who had learnt to regard us as their special friends'.[21] Nor could Britons any longer so easily justify the pre-war approach of some like Financial Advisor, W. A. M. Doll, that: 'The British point of view has always been to humour the Siamese and treat them as the children that they are.'[22] In Indonesia, 'The weak, half-hearted defence put up by most Dutch land forces against the invading Japanese made a tremendous impression on Indonesians'.[23] Pearl Harbor stood out as the United States' greatest ever naval defeat.[24]

Abject defeat at the hands of the Japanese left Europe's colonial powers doubting the rightness of reasserting colonial rule. Drained by war in Europe, they were also economically less able to do so. European uncertainty and military weakness combined with a new, greater determination among Southeast Asians to compress the time frame for decolonization. On returning to Malaya, the British 'found that its people were not prepared to accept their rule for an indefinite period'.[25] The population of Burma was said to have adopted an attitude of 'amazement and resentment mixed with indifference' on seeing 'the British, who had been considered all-powerful, pushed out of the country by the Japanese'.[26] By 1945, the end of British rule in Burma 'was assured'.[27] If any doubt remained over independence for Burma, Britain's decision to make India independent eradicated it.

By the time the Dutch returned to Indonesia, they 'found a new world, one that now belonged to exultant Indonesians. The red and white flag of the republic flew from public buildings, shops and houses.'[28] The Dutch, weakened by war in Europe and facing Republican opposition entrenched in most of Java and parts of Sumatra, were unable to re-assert their rule in these key areas of Indonesia. Eventually in 1949, partly owing to the pressure of the United States' threats to stop military and economic aid through the Marshall Plan, the Netherlands agreed to Indonesian independence.[29]

In Indochina, Japanese support for a French administration helped to prop up colonialism. However, the March 1945 Japanese coup ended this fragile

21 Crosby, *Siam*, p. 149.
22 NARA, RG59, entry 205, box 5834, file 892.00/217, W.A.M. Doll to Frederic Dolbeare, American Foreign Affairs Advisor in Thailand, 19 November 1940.
23 Kahin, *Nationalism*, p. 101.
24 Hudson and Rajchman, *Explanatory atlas*, pp. 132–33; Friend, *Between two empires*, pp. 195, 217.
25 Butcher, *British in Malaya*, p. 227.
26 Christian, *Burma*, p. 110; and see Taylor, 'Burma', pp. 132, 135.
27 Taylor, 'Burma', p. 132.
28 Bayly and Harper, *Forgotten wars*, p. 168.
29 van der Eng, 'Marshall aid', pp. 335, 342–45; see also Friend, *Blue-eyed enemy*, pp. 222–23, 237, 267, 269.

equilibrium and created disruption in Vietnam's major cities.[30] The coup signalled 'the sudden and complete collapse of French prestige'.[31] On 13 September 1945, the British commander General Douglas Gracey arrived in Saigon to secure the city, disarm the Japanese and maintain law and order. Within ten days, Gracey allowed the French to mount a coup in Saigon against the communist-led Viet Minh national front government. The coup was followed, Gracey recorded, by 'unnecessary violence by French soldiers, their police and civilians [which] invited active countermeasures as soon as the Annamites [Vietnamese] could gather themselves together'.[32] Saigon became a scene of Vietnamese rioting and mob violence on both sides until a brief truce which, Gracey wrote, remained only until 10 October and then 'doubtfully in force'.[33] Over the next several months, the British, with 20,000 troops from the 20th Indian Division and the co-operation of the Japanese military, occupied Saigon, suppressed the Viet Minh and then engaged them in open warfare.

During 1946 in the south of Vietnam, the Viet Minh were finally driven underground by the British and French, aided by Japanese soldiers. Early in these operations, according to Gracey: 'the French troops [under General LeClerc] are leaving a pretty good trail of destruction behind them, which will result in such resentment that it will become progressively more difficult for them to implement their new policy and, I am convinced, will result in guerrilla warfare, increased sabotage and arson as soon as we leave the country'.[34]

Japanese occupation also brought a crumbling of French prestige elsewhere in Indochina. In Laos, the March 1945 Japanese coup ended any remaining illusion of French might; a triumphal French return in 1946 could not disguise their defeat by the Japanese.[35] Cambodian independence, 'impractical and almost inconceivable in 1939, had become primarily a matter of time' by the end of 1945.[36]

The second way that the war promoted political change was in the scope and support, if often unintended, that Japan and the Japanese interregnum gave Southeast Asian nationalism. Almost from the start, Japan's own intense

30 AOM, HCI 2/112, 'Rapport sur l'historique des événements en Indochine depuis le 9 mars 1945', 31 May 1945.

31 Smith, 'Japanese period', p. 286 and 'Work of the provisional government', p. 572.

32 LHC, Gracey Papers 4/8, Saigon Control Commission, 'Political report', 13 September 1945 to 9 October 1945.

33 LHC, Gracey Papers 4/12, Reports from the Saigon Control Commission, 'Build-up of 80 Ind Inf Bde at Saigon', 22 October–7 November 1945.

34 LHC, Gracey Papers 4/12, Major General D. D. Gracey to General Sir W. J. Slim, 5 November 1945.

35 Stuart-Fox, *History*, p. 59.

36 Chandler, *History*, p. 201.

nationalism helped to awaken corresponding indigenous nationalisms among Southeast Asians. In Thailand, the Japanese presence was said to be largely responsible for a tide of nationalism among the Thai.[37] Japanese efforts in the Philippines to eradicate pre-war Western cultural influences encouraged Filipinos towards a 'positive cultural nationalism', the use of Tagalog and glorification of Filipino institutions.[38] Even in Malaya, notable for its political quiescence before the war, 'the sudden change of masters and impact of violent Japanese nationalism and pan-Asianism was a most intense school for nationalist feelings and thoughts about political questions'.[39] That also applied, and to a much greater extent, in Burma and Indonesia. In these countries, nationalism gained momentum both through its own internal dynamic and from a mounting Japanese wartime advocacy of nationalistic feeling to try to foster loyalty to the Japanese Empire and create Southeast Asian military capabilities.

By 1943, among the Burmans, who comprised about 75 per cent of the population, the Burma National Army, rural masses and urban intellectuals were already strongly integrated. Nationalist forces further strengthened in August 1944 when Burma's army and revolutionaries in the country came together.[40] Nationalism was such that if the British had tried to arrest Aung San there could have been 'a full scale military rebellion comparable to the fatal and futile Dutch "police actions" in Indonesia'.[41] Britain was in no position in 1947 to find troops and money to deal with an uprising in Burma.[42]

War and occupation in Burma, described as an 'ethnic archipelago', widened and increased a fervent Burman ethno-nationalism from which the country's minority groups have subsequently suffered. During the war, the Japanese allied with the Burmans, while minority groups, the Karens and various hill peoples, were recruited by the Allies. At least a dozen clandestine and para-military organizations operated in Burma, many of which were controlled from London or Washington. At one level, Selth points out, World War II in Burma was fought between the British and Japanese Empires, but at another, intra-country level, it became an ethnic Burma conflict, Burmans on one side, the minorities on the other. Within six months of independence, 'the Union of Burma was wracked by a number of insurgencies'. One was essentially intra-Burman due to communists being denied a place in the new government, but four others were inspired by ethnic antagonisms with Karens, Kachins, Mons and the Muslims in Arakan, all of whom asserted separatist claims against the Burman-dominated government

37 Numnonda, *Thailand*, p. 27.
38 Steinberg, 'Ambiguous legacy', p. 181.
39 Silcock and Aziz, 'Nationalism in Malaya', p. 289.
40 Nu, *Burma*, pp. xvi–xxvi, 105.
41 Trager, 'Review', p. 382. 'Police actions' against Indonesian Republicans occurred from 21 July to 5 August 1947 and again during 19 to 20 December 1948.
42 Collis, *Last and first*, pp. 258, 271, 277.

in Rangoon.[43] Because the war provided the reasons and allowed the means to mobilize separate ethnic identities in post-war Burma, 'ethnic politics [were] raised from the condition of inchoate aspiration to the pivot of political action'.[44] Ethnic conflict between the centre and periphery has remained a principal feature of Burma's history since World War II.

In Indonesia, as in Burma, the Japanese initiated local nationalist-oriented youth groups and gave indigenous officials power which, if often minor, was greater than any they had previously exercised. The Japanese political style presented Indonesian youth with a new, radical mode of political life and action.[45] During occupation in Indonesia, Japanese encouragement of a nationalist content to religious expression worked to integrate rural masses and urban intellectuals and make them a force beyond Japanese control. Although Japan, hoping to mobilize support against Allied invasion, granted Indonesia independence just before the August 1945 surrender, by then it was unclear on whose side many Indonesian youth groups and guerrilla bands would have fought.[46] The Japanese surrender removed 'very quickly the repressive apparatus that had for so long held the Indonesian nationalist movement in check'.[47]

For Cambodians, the period after the Japanese coup was the first time that patriotic ideas could be aired openly and the first encouragement to the formation by Cambodians of politically oriented groups.[48] Lao nationalism, mainly with a cultural orientation, had been supported by Indochina's Governor-General Decoux. The March 1945 Japanese coup opened the way for more sweeping nationalist demands, now with real political content.[49]

The war's third impetus to political change was that Japan's sudden, unanticipated surrender created power vacuums in Malaya, Indonesia and Vietnam. Nationalists, communists and the many guerrilla groups trained and armed by the Allies were now able to operate with few restrictions. In Malaya, the Japanese had favoured the Malays, and deployed largely Malay units in operations against a predominantly Chinese resistance movement. During a 15 August to 3 September 1945 power vacuum prior to re-occupation by the British, inter-racial conflicts between Malays and Chinese descended

43 Selth, *Race*, pp. 484 and 483 for the quotations; passim for the analysis set out in this paragraph. Sadan, 'Ethnic armies' questions for Kachins the link between wartime loyalty to the British and Burma's subsequent ethnic and racial ruptures.

44 Taylor, 'Perceptions', p. 9 and see p. 8; Smith, 'Burma and World War II'.

45 Anderson, *Java*, p. 33.

46 Benda, 'Japanese interregnum', pp. 77–79 and 'Structure', pp. 131–38; Feith, *Decline*, p. 22; Yoichi, 'Outlines of Japanese policy', pp. 184–86.

47 Kahin, 'Indonesian politics', p. 71.

48 Chandler, *History*, p. 209.

49 Stuart-Fox, *History*, pp. 55–59.

into chaos, described as 'near-anarchy'.[50] As the Japanese army retreated to the cities, the wartime armed communist guerrilla Malayan People's Anti-Japanese Army, almost entirely ethnic Chinese, took control of some 70 per cent of smaller towns and villages as well as large parts of the peninsula. Chinese reprisals against Malays accused of collaboration were severe. Malays retaliated savagely. Fighting ceased after the British return, but soon resumed with increased intensity and lasted until March 1946, by which time the Malays had emerged as clear winners.

The assertion by Malays of political power was manifest in their rejection of the 1946 British plan for a Malayan Union, expressed through civil disobedience and refusal to participate in the process of government. British abandonment of the Malayan Union and its replacement by the Federation of Malaya in February 1948 marked 'a crucial turning point in Malaya's nation-building history'.[51] When Malaya became independent in 1957, the tacit bargain was the primacy of Malay political power but Chinese economic dominance.

In Indonesia, the Japanese interregnum unloosed a 'whirlwind of a many-faceted-revolution'.[52] Dutch troops did not reach Java in any numbers until March 1946 and concentrated on trying to safeguard the lives of non-ethnic Indonesians in urban areas. Indonesian Republican forces held sway everywhere in Java except in six large cities and part of a seventh controlled by the Dutch.[53] The Japanese-trained army Peta, the Fatherland Defence Corps (Chapter 9), became a main basis for Indonesian Republican forces. They were armed largely with Japanese weapons and fought against both the British (until their departure beginning in March 1946) and the Dutch military attempting to regain control of Indonesia.[54] In the longer term, 'the drawn out struggle with the Dutch imbued political life generally with a radicalism and potential violence that proved difficult to contain'.[55]

During the 1950s, the Indonesian army, strengthened by its role in the 1945–49 revolution, gained great power and could not be effectively challenged by any other social group. Army leaders had always refused to accept civilian control over military affairs and considered that the army embodied the revolution's spirit and fighting strength.[56] A State of Emergency in

50 Jones, *Japan's new order*, p. 390.
51 Cheah, *Red star*, p. xiii and see pp. xiii–xiv and 'Sino-Malay conflicts', pp. 108–11; Harper, *End*, pp. 49–51.
52 Benda, 'Decolonization', p. 1061.
53 Cribb, 'Political dimensions', pp. 113–36.
54 Kahin, *Nationalism*, pp. 108–109; Anderson, *Some aspects*, pp. 97–98, 118–19, 126; Allen, *End of the war*, p. 95.
55 Bastin and Benda, *History*, p. 183.
56 McVey, 'Post-revolutionary transformation, part I', pp. 131–32.

April 1957 allowed Indonesia's already socially dominant military to expand its activities into economic and political spheres.[57]

At the time of the Japanese coup in March 1945, the Indochina Communist Party, led by Ho Chi Minh, also the organizing force behind the Viet Minh, was still not in a strong position.[58] However, the Viet Minh and Ho correctly identified three opportunities for revolution: the Japanese coup; the climax of the Pacific War; and the 1944–45 famine. After famine struck, 'the Viet Minh came out of hiding and mobilized the population to seize rice that both the French and Japanese had stored in case of food shortages'.[59] Goscha summarizes: 'famine, more than anything else, ushered in change'.[60] Able to call on the rural masses, the Viet Minh filled the power vacuum that existed between Japan's surrender on 15 August 1945 and around mid-September, when Allied troops arrived in some force.

In textbook Leninist fashion, the Viet Minh with at most 900 men took control of Hanoi on the night of 19 August 1945. Tens of thousands of peasants, activated by famine and revolution, immediately supported the revolution by marching on Hanoi, Haiphong and Hue. Ho Chi Minh publicly proclaimed independence on 2 September 1945. He was, like Sihanouk, Sukarno and Ne Win, a World War II creation. At the outset of the First Indochina War, beginning in 1946, the Viet Minh were reinforced by Japanese weapons, instructors and soldiers.[61]

Economic Legacies

In Southeast Asia, political and economic legacies are not easily disentangled. Apart from the interruption to Southeast Asian growth (Chapter 10), three substantially economic legacies require brief consideration. One was pressure to industrialize; a second the Japanese model of comprehensive government economic controls; and the third internationally uncompetitive real exchange rates. Together they helped to determine post-war economic policy and to create a strong bias towards industrialization through import substitution. Although varying between countries, throughout Southeast Asia the difference between the state's pre- and post-independence roles was striking.

The wartime lack of basic consumer goods and demonstration of an extreme reliance on importing manufactured goods comprehensively exposed Southeast Asia's narrow economic specialization. War scarcities reinforced pre-war arguments for greater industrialization already rooted in sharp 1930s

57 McVey, 'Post-revolutionary transformation, part II', p. 147.
58 Marr, *Vietnamese tradition*, p. 415.
59 Brocheux, *Ho Chi Minh*, p. 90.
60 Goscha, *Penguin history*, p. 211.
61 AOM, HCI 2/141, 'Rapport mensuel de la direction de la police et de la sûreté fédérales', October 1946, p. 32; August 1946, p. 19; December 1946, p. 51.

falls in commodity prices and the examples of Japanese and Soviet economic development. Furthermore, a lesson not lost on Southeast Asian leaders was that Japan's industrialization enabled it to challenge the colonial powers and, as Asians, assert authority over other Asians.

While strengthening a desire among Southeast Asians for industrialization, the Japanese occupation did not bequeath a significant industrial inheritance on which to build, with the partial exceptions of Thailand and Vietnam. Post-war Thailand, as described in Chapter 5, was able to make use of some of the machinery brought by Japanese companies as well as a structure of state–private sector partnerships which these enterprises helped to promote. In Vietnam, more relevant than industrial plant left by the Japanese was that the small local Asian industries which emerged during the war became important for the Viet Minh government during the First Indochina War. Although the post-World War II government in the north favoured state-owned enterprises and heavy industry, its survival strategy was based on local self-sufficiency in agriculture and handicrafts.[62]

Elsewhere in Southeast Asia, most notably the Philippines, the Japanese legacy was chiefly the destruction of pre-war industrial equipment. In Burma, contrary to a hoped-for post-war stimulus, wartime Japanese industries do not appear to have had much lasting impact. After the war, many of the spinning factories erected by the Japanese were looted for essential parts.[63] Industries in Indonesia had been established under the pressure of military need, not in the context of commercial success. After the war, the economic justification for wartime Japanese manufacturing was often questionable.[64] While occupation gave some Indonesian administrators experience in supervising industry, it did little to create entrepreneurs.[65]

An inheritance, though not industrial, that proved useful to Singapore in the months after occupation was small wooden ships built by the Japanese, a wartime growth industry. Singapore traditionally relied on the islands of the nearby Rhio-Lingga Archipelago for part of its food and fuel, and the release of the Japanese ships to Chinese traders enabled these supplies again to come to Singapore. At the end of 1945, there were actually more total craft of all sizes entering and leaving the port than before the war, although total tonnage was much smaller.[66]

By 1947 in Singapore, 'many of the mushroom industries of the occupation folded up in the face of competition with imported goods which were both

62 Marr, *Vietnam: state, war*, p. 638, n. 4; Brocheux,'Economy of war', pp. 314, 317, 326.

63 MNA, 1/9 Village industries, Lt. Gen. GOC in-c Twelfth Army to HQ ALFSEA, August 1945.

64 Department of Economic Affairs, Batavia, 'Industries', pp. 21, 24 and 'Economic prospects of the Indonesian islands', p. 6; Fruin, *Het economisch*, p. 45.

65 Sutter, *Indonesianisasi*, pp. 267, 271.

66 Malayan Union, *Report on the British military administration*, p. 109.

better and cheaper'.[67] The Japanese occupation did not leave a legacy of industrialization; Singapore's industrial success dates from the late 1960s, and is not explained by World War II experience.

Wartime administrations created a second legacy, that of economic controls, through abundant Japanese examples of the use of government power over the economy to institute state direction, monopoly and administered pricing. In Thailand, the military government became increasingly involved in the economy during the war, while after it other Southeast Asian governments drew on the Japanese legacy to varying degrees. Some countries combined it, like the Japanese, with military involvement in the economy or, at the least, implemented repressive economic policies reminiscent of wartime Japanese administrations.

Burma, Southeast Asia's most laissez-faire pre-war economy but highly controlled after the war, provides an example of the role of the Japanese occupation in helping to shift economic policy towards an interventionism unacceptable under pre-war colonial rule.[68] Already in 1944, Burma's New Order Plan argued that 'the Burmese Government must have the widest scope and facilities . . . in devising a war-time civilian economic structure to undertake, organize and control, either partly or completely according to requirements, all activities relating to [the Burmese people's basic material] necessities'.[69] Although the returning British administration introduced greater state control and established a rice marketing board, after independence the Burmese government nationalized much of the economy and assumed a central role in it.[70]

The third economic legacy was the path that post-war Southeast Asian industrialization had to take. Import substitution for goods like textiles and basic manufactures was natural due to high pre-war consumption of these goods and simple production technologies. However, for all industrialization, uncompetitive real exchange rates, rather than manufacturing for export, made import substitution the only realistic option. Wartime inflation in Southeast Asia (Chapter 3) far exceeded world inflation. Despite post-war internal price and wage structures at least some five to six times higher than pre-war levels, Southeast Asian governments typically re-established official exchange rates at pre-war parities rather than devaluing to offset wartime inflation and create the competitive real exchange rates required for manufacturing for export.[71]

[67] Malaya, *Report on the 1947 census*, p. 35.
[68] Owen, 'Economic and social change', pp. 143–44.
[69] Burma, *Burma's New Order Plan*, p. 36.
[70] Tinker, *Union of Burma*, p. 255.
[71] Power and Sicat, *Philippines*, pp. 32–33, 51; Golay, *Philippines*, pp. 117–18; United States, Department of State, *Economic survey mission to the Philippines*, pp. 12–14, 18; Manarungsan, *Economic development*, p. 189; Ingram, *Economic change*, pp. 165–67;

Divisions in Post-war Southeast Asia

World War II and the Japanese occupation ended seven decades of continuity in Southeast Asian economic history during which globalization had been the dominant force. A Southeast Asia emerged that was now divided into two groups. One, consisting of Thailand, Malaya (including Singapore) and the Philippines, remained part of what Benda calls the Atlantic system, and continued their pre-war orientation towards world markets.[72] In this group, nationalism was moderate and the economy and industrialization remained substantially dependent on private enterprise. The other group, comprising Burma, Indonesia and Vietnam, turned away from the global economy. Strong nationalisms found expression in socialism, state direction, anti-Westernism and anti-globalization.[73] The split corresponds to Myint's categorization of outwards- and inwards-looking Southeast Asian countries.[74]

Varying colonial and wartime experiences, the ideologies these encouraged and different paths to independence help to explain Southeast Asia's division. Outwards-looking Thailand, Malaya and the Philippines shared two important historical features. One was either relatively benign experiences of colonialism or, for Thailand, only being in Britain's informal empire; the other distinctly muted post-war nationalisms. In Thailand, beginning with the 1932 revolution, a pattern of conservative, military rule was established. Military dominance, although briefly broken in 1944, became the norm beginning in 1947. Britain hoped to retain its earlier influence in post-war Thailand and possibly take control of the Kra Isthmus.[75] However, for post-war Thailand America replaced Britain as a patron. Thailand afforded a staging post for the United States military during the Vietnam War, much as it had for Japanese forces in the Pacific War.

In Malaya, the Japanese encountered a relatively weak nationalism and the war did not augment this to the same extent as in some Southeast Asian countries.[76] The Philippines and less so Malaya were the only two Southeast Asian countries where in 1945 Southeast Asians viewed the return of colonial rulers in anything like a positive light. Filipinos welcomed back Americans as 'liberators'.[77]

Yang, *Multiple exchange rate system*, pp. 26–33, 134; Malayan Union, *Report on the British military administration*, pp. 36–37, 44; Donnison, *British military administration*, p. 238; Department of Economic Affairs, Batavia, 'Economic data . . . 1948', pp. 19–22.

72 Benda, 'Japanese interregnum', pp. 69–74; Bastin and Benda, *History*, p. 156.

73 Elsbree, *Japan's role*, pp. 168–69.

74 Myint, 'Inward and outward looking countries', pp. 1–13. Myint's 1967 list did not include either North or South Vietnam.

75 NARA, RG226, entry 106, box 81, file 483, 'Situation report: Thailand current developments', 11 December 1944, p. 4; Aldrich, *Key to the south*, pp. 24–30.

76 Yoichi, 'Some aspects', pp. 264–66, 256.

77 Friend, *Between two empires*, p. 272.

Pre-war Philippine nationalism had been firmly under the control of a conservative elite: 'leaders of the middle and upper classes seized hold of nationalism early in the century, won the confidence of the masses, and never surrendered the issue or their following'.[78] During the war, the Japanese did not win Filipino allegiance, advance pan-Asian nationalism or create Filipino militancy.[79] Until the 1950s, nationalism in the Philippines was directed 'more against Oriental [Chinese and Japanese] minorities than against Occidental rulers'.[80] A pre- and post-war continuity of elites and conservatism in politics in Malaya and the Philippines ruled out wholesale political change even with the attainment of independence.[81]

In Indonesia, Vietnam and Burma, pre-war antipathy to colonial rule had been considerable, and post-war nationalism was intense. Vietnam and Indonesia were Southeast Asia's two most repressed colonies and in both a dislike of colonialism was widespread.[82] In Burma, nationalist feeling was strongest among the Burman majority. Anti-British and anti-Indian sentiments fused into a nationalism which in many respects hoped to return to an idyllic pre-colonial past.[83]

War and occupation fundamentally shaped post-war Burma, Indonesia and Vietnam through giving rise to a new social group: a military controlled by the population's principal ethnic component. At the same time as creating an ethnic-majority military elite, the Japanese interregnum widened and deepened nationalism, which grew from the preserve of the urban intelligentsia into a potent, countrywide force.[84] In Indonesia, radicalism fused with an Islamic revival which had been encouraged by Japanese policies.[85] Independent Indonesia emerged as resolutely opposed to the West, characterized as 'an independent nation sealed against neocolonialism'.[86] This was also true of Vietnam which aligned with the Soviet Union and after 1949 with China.

The Islamization of Indonesia that Japan promoted during the occupation left a legacy basic in shaping Indonesia's post-war history. Japan did much to empower an Islamic elite which emerged as squarely behind the independence struggle.[87] Revolution in Indonesia, although, Feith points out, not revolution

78 Ibid., p. 34.
79 Steinberg, 'Ambiguous legacy', pp. 179–83.
80 Friend, *Between two empires*, p. 34.
81 Bastin and Benda, *History*, p. 167.
82 Osborne, *Region*, p. 81.
83 Guyot, 'Burma Independence Army', pp. 53–61; Silverstein, *Burma*, pp. 15–17; Taylor, 'Disaster or release', p. 56.
84 See, for example, Benda, *Crescent*, p. 200; Yoon, 'Military expediency', pp. 264–67; Taylor, 'Disaster or release', p. 51.
85 Benda, 'Indonesian Islam', pp. 81–82.
86 Friend, *Blue-eyed enemy*, p. 257 and see Higgins, *Indonesia's economic stabilization*, pp. 96, 105.
87 Benda, *Crescent*, pp. 135, 175, 187.

in the same sense as in the French, Russian and Chinese revolutions, 'certainly involved a deeper shattering of social foundations' than in other post-war independence struggles, except Vietnam's.[88] The revolutionary effects in Java of occupation have been judged as greatest at the lowest social levels: inflation, a lack of clothing, smuggling, forced labour and inwards urban migration turned society upside down.[89]

When the British returned to Burma they found, as a British military administration report observed in August 1945, the Patriotic Burmese Forces (successor to the Burma National Army and dominated by Burmans) 'the sole effective political organization in the country' and strong enough to impose its will on all other political groups.[90] During the 1950s and 1960s, a chief objective of Burman nationalism and the military responsible for its political and economic expression was 'to erase capitalism'.[91] While in outward-looking Southeast Asia the pre-war Western superstructure remained in place, the new governments in Burma, Indonesia and Vietnam liquidated most European economic interests.[92]

The Japanese-trained armies in Burma and Indonesia and the Viet Minh in Indochina could, and did, wrap themselves in post-war strident nationalism. Taking strength from nationalism, armed forces in all three countries assumed major political roles from independence onwards.[93] In all three countries, World War II created groupings and entrenched leaders analogous to the 'Brezhnev generation' in the Soviet Union, where wartime leaders, all ethnic Russians, retained their hold on the levers of power and dominated Soviet political life through the 1960s, 1970s and 1980s.[94] The military in inwards-looking Southeast Asia was 'born and tested in revolution and anticolonial war' and by virtue of this could lay claim to moral authority and legitimacy.[95] Power could be solidified largely due to an absence of other organized, disciplined and trained groups to contest military dominance.[96] Post-war military elites in the three countries became self-perpetuating military oligarchies able to enforce their views on the conduct of the economy and society. In 1985, the generation of Indochinese Communist Party members who 'had survived repression and jail in the 1930s, and who disseminated the Viet Minh message before

88 Feith, *Decline*, p. 1.

89 Anderson, *Some aspects*, p. 44.

90 MNA, 1/5 86 British Military Administration Report, August 1945 (dated 29 September 1945), p. 8.

91 Silverstein, *Burma*, p. 32,

92 Bastin and Benda, *History*, p. 158.

93 For a study of the army's evolution into a political force in Indonesia, see Crouch, *Army and politics*, pp. 24–42.

94 Harrison, 'Soviet Union', pp. 295–96.

95 Bastin and Benda, *History*, p. 194.

96 Ibid., pp. 181–94; Huff, 'Finance and long-term development issues', pp. 58–61; Fenichel and Huff, 'Colonialism', pp. 321–35; Brown, *Burma's economy*, pp. 3–4, 210.

August 1945' still commanded Vietnam's armed forces and governed the country.[97] World War II army leaders and their direct successors remained almost equally as influential in Burma and Indonesia.

While in outward-looking Southeast Asia the Western superstructure created during the colonial era continued to function, for decades after World War II the military-dominated governments in Burma and Vietnam and to some extent in Indonesia pushed politics towards forms of socialism or communism and away from the global economy.[98] The Burman nationalist orientation was not to bend to global capitalism, including the rule of law, force of the market, international trade and the modern state, but to resist and reject it.[99] Only during the second decade of the twenty-first century did this begin to change, although even after Burma's 2015 election, in which Aung San Suu Kyi's National League for Democracy won a landslide victory, the military, among them many of the direct successors of the World War II military, remained central to politics and outside the control of politicians.[100]

Under Sukarno, Indonesia had no real development strategy between 1948 and 1965, but beginning in 1966, after economic collapse into hyperinflation and Sukarno's overthrow, turned outwards towards the global economy under the New Order. Vietnam maintained a war economy between the end of World War II and 1975, and continued until 1986 to implement a system like that in the Soviet Union and to plan the Vietnamese economy centrally. It was only after serious famine and malnutrition in the winter of 1987–88 that Vietnam began decisively to free the market, manufacture for the global market and again become a major world rice exporter.[101]

Final Remarks

This Epilogue and Chapter 10 have indicated some of the longer-term economic, social and political consequences of the Pacific War for Southeast Asia, and to a limited extent also for Japan. Here I ask what might have happened if Japan had not decided for war. One possible scenario may help further to draw out the war's implications for Southeast Asia: that Japan stayed safely on the sidelines during a European-only war in which the United States became involved. How much difference did the Japanese occupation make politically and economically in Southeast Asia?

97 Marr, *Vietnam 1945*, p. 552 and see Marr, *Vietnamese tradition*, pp. 411–12.
98 Bastin and Benda, *History*, p. 180; Indonesia nationalized Dutch enterprises in 1957 and 1958.
99 Taylor, 'Disaster or release', p. 56.
100 Guyot, 'Burma Independence Army', pp. 51, 61.
101 Perkins, *East Asian development*, pp. 121–47.

Japan

I suggest that had Japan remained an observer to war, it might have got much of what it wanted in Southeast Asia relatively cheaply and at a far lower cost than shown in Chapter 10, as well as without the toxic legacies of occupation. War-ravaged Europe would have been weak in the face of a Japanese forward movement into Southeast Asia's economies. The determination of the United States to run Pacific Asia as a pax-Americana region was partly an outcome of Pearl Harbor and crushing World War II victories in Asia. Furthermore, the Philippines would have been granted independence even without a Pacific war and an end to formal United States involvement in Asia would have encouraged isolationist sentiment in America.

After a war fought chiefly in Europe, Japan would have been in a strong position in Southeast Asia. Its best option would have been, not a Co-Prosperity Sphere, but to try to promote as open a trading environment as possible. From World War I onwards, Japan invested in Southeast Asian resource development, and Japanese shipping companies and commercial interests had made considerable inroads into Southeast Asia, especially the Indonesian market, by the 1930s.[102] In 1936, the Singapore *Straits Budget* reported 'widespread feeling in Singapore that immediate action should be taken to prevent Japanese domination of the whole trade and banking of the Colony'.[103] Able to take advantage of an economically weakened Europe, Japan could probably quickly and successfully have built on these relationships. That, not the choice of war, would have been the wise 1941 investment decision (Chapter 1).

During the war, the Japanese preserved most Malayan rubber acreage rather than felling trees to clear land for food and attempted to maintain tin production. That suggests that for a commercially and imperially assertive Japan bolstered by an increasingly strong position in Southeast Asia, a regional development pattern substantially according to economic comparative advantage would have been the beneficial Japanese policy (Chapters 4 and 7). Japanese firms could have sold on the world market Southeast Asian rubber and tin, along with some other regional commodities such as palm oil and spices, to earn foreign currency, the lack of which had pushed Japan towards a Greater East Asia Co-Prosperity Sphere (Chapter 1). Foreign exchange earned in Southeast Asia would have allowed Japan to pay for oil, cotton and other raw materials essential for industrialization but largely lacking in Japan and hard, or impossible, to produce elsewhere in the 1941 Japanese Empire.

Japan would obviously have benefited from maintaining Southeast Asia as a source of rice. Since in pre-war Southeast Asia Western companies controlled relatively little of the trade in rice, Japan could easily have tapped the

[102] For quantification of pre-war Japanese investment in Southeast Asia by country and sector, see Hara, 'Daitōa', p. 12.

[103] 'Japan's trade war in Malaya', *Straits Budget*, 30 July 1936.

region for this source of food. Cheap Southeast Asian rice would have limited wage growth in an urbanizing Japan and so boosted the profits share in national income, allowing the high capital accumulation through business re-investment consistent with internationally competitive industrialization. At the same time, Korea, and possibly Taiwan, now freed to shift labour from food-producing agriculture into industry, could, as Japan wanted of the Korean economy during World War II, have moved towards industrialization complementary to Japan's rather than remaining chiefly agricultural appendages in the Japanese Empire.

Southeast Asia

In the absence of Japanese occupation, decolonization would have probably taken longer in most of Southeast Asia. It seems likely that it would also have been less violent and possibly that stronger, more stable governments would have emerged. Clearly, measured as GDP per capita, much of Southeast Asia would have been better off without the Japanese occupation. Countries in the region would not have started in 1945 from the disrupted economies, low GDP per capita, diminished infrastructure and social breakdown that prevailed everywhere in the region after the Pacific War (Chapters 4 to 10). With the exception of industry in Thailand, Japan's occupation contributed almost nothing to post-war Southeast Asian industrialization or to technical change in agriculture (Chapters 4 and 5).

The Japanese claim that occupation liberated Southeast Asians from colonialism has no validity for either Thailand or the Philippines. Elsewhere, Japan's contribution to the early independence of Southeast Asian countries is strongly tempered by the weak governments and history of war and civil strife that occupation left in its wake. Without a Pacific war, Thailand might have ended up in a Japanese orbit rather than an American one. That placement of Thailand flowed largely from United States hegemony in the Pacific, and was reinforced by the American fear of a communist Southeast Asia, a possibility which occupation went a considerable way towards creating. Occupation propelled the rise of the Viet Minh, the Emergency in Malaya, the Huk insurgency in the Philippines, and intense nationalism and leftwards moves in Indonesia and Burma (Chapters 7 and 10).

In charting Thai history, more important than the occupation was the 1932 revolution. Thailand emerged from World War II with a similar elite and on much the same historical trajectory as in 1941. Just as had been the pre-war state of affairs, in post-war Thailand 'nationalism is the nationalism of an *elite* group which sees the economic interest of the Thai people largely in terms of its own economic interest'.[104] Japanese occupation helped to extend and

[104] Silcock, 'Promotion', p. 258.

solidify, rather than create, patterns of state control of Thai industry and alliances between Thai political leaders and ethnic Chinese business. Wartime industrial ventures, frustrated by a lack of inputs, were largely unsuccessful. However, for Thailand's government to undertake these or participate jointly with the Japanese, Thai politicians needed the economic skills of Thailand's ethnic Chinese. A symbiotic relationship between Thai politicians and Chinese business, already evident in the 1930s, became considerably stronger (Chapter 5). The wartime state–private sector strengthening of a union between the Thai political elite and Chinese economic management, based on government controls, accommodation and mutual benefit, proved to be a prominent feature of post-war Thailand's financial and industrial development.[105] The main impact of Japanese occupation was to strengthen, and provide some of the equipment and technology for, a development trajectory on which Thailand was already embarked by the late 1930s.

The Philippines would almost certainly have become independent in the late 1940s, much as in fact happened anyway in 1946. After independence, it would have had the same dysfunctional economy, overspecialized in sugar, as at the end of American colonialism, although not an occupation-ravaged infrastructure. A Philippine elite was in place before the war, functioned during the war with varying degrees of willingness to assist Japanese rule, and persisted after the war. Occupation did not much change the upper echelons of Filipino social structure. Although bossism and corruption already had strong roots in the pre-war period, the Japanese occupation probably encouraged Filipinos towards more corruption than would otherwise have prevailed.[106] Furthermore, consequences of the occupation were the release of large quantities of arms and the formation of private armies, both of which were major factors in the Philippines' turbulent post-war politics.[107]

Malaya, able quickly to revive its pre-war rubber industry, suffered less economically than most of post-war Southeast Asia. That story could have been different in the absence of the Pacific War. There would probably not have been a Korean War, and so also not the rubber boom from which Malaya benefited at the beginning of the 1950s (Chapter 5). Because Japan's occupation of Malaya favoured the Malays and spawned the Chinese-dominated Malayan People's Anti-Japanese Army, it transformed latent tensions in Malaya's plural society into open and long-lasting conflict.[108] Without the Pacific War, the distribution of political power in Malaya might have been configured differently from the post-war settlement of Malay dominance.

[105] Suehiro, *Capital accumulation*, pp. 133–34, 154; Hewison, *Bankers*, pp. 66–77, 88; Reynolds, '"International orphans"', pp. 387–88.

[106] Fagan, 'Social history', pp. 114–17; Sidel, 'Capital, coercion', pp. 947–66.

[107] Beckett, 'Defiant and compliant', p. 406.

[108] Cheah, *Red star*, p. 17.

Independence for Malaya could possibly have come not too much later than it actually did, even though the British would have wanted to hold Malaya for its US dollar earnings from rubber and tin and, at the least, Singapore as a Crown Colony due to its strategic location and robust British mercantile presence. Without the war, high inflation and resulting post-war overvalued real exchange rate, Singapore and the rest of Malaya would have been in stronger positions to industrialize by supplementing import-substitution policies with export-oriented manufacturing.

Burma, Indonesia and Vietnam were all greatly affected by the Pacific War and occupation. For these countries, the war made a profound difference. Even with no Pacific war, India would likely have become independent not long after it did in 1947. If so, Burma, as historically a colony of India but an entity beginning in 1937 to move towards greater autonomy, may well have gained independence soon after India. The key difference in the post-Pacific-War world was that in Burma, and also Indonesia, substantial Japanese-trained armies more or less ensured that the military would assume power. That, in turn, led to groups of leaders, whatever their revolutionary and military merits, illiterate in economics. Without the push that the Japanese occupation gave towards heightening civil strife and hastening an independent Burma, a less turbulent transition to Burmese independence is plausible. In the absence of World War II, it has in retrospect been observed of Burma that 'one could probably see a very different country emerging'.[109]

For Indonesia, although occupation added to the difficulties of a move to independence through exacerbating religious and social fragmentation, it seems questionable that the colonial power would have failed to contest a handover to an independent government. The Dutch depended more on their colony than any other colonial power in Asia. Dependence was due partly to Indonesia's economic value to the Netherlands and partly to the many Netherlanders living there. Additionally, rule in Indonesia encompassed an element of the Dutch national psyche. The Netherlands ranked as the world's third or fourth colonial power, but without Indonesia the Dutch Empire would collapse, leaving Holland, as one observer unkindly put it, 'a cold little country on the North Sea'.[110] Between 1947 and 1949, the Netherlands battled determinedly to keep hold of Indonesia. That attitude might also have prevailed in the face of rising Indonesian nationalism, although the latter would have needed to find some other source than the Japanese occupation to unite the urban revolutionary intelligentsia with the rural masses. The defeated Japanese became a source of arms and some soldiers for the Indonesian revolution.

109 Taylor, 'Legacies', p. 62.

110 Feith, *Decline*, p. 2. On the economic importance of Indonesia to the Netherlands, see van der Eng, 'Marshall aid', pp. 336, 340, 347.

In the absence of occupation, Vietnam's post-1944 history could hardly have been more tragic and bloody than it was. Nor can the Vietnamese economy reasonably be imagined to have spiralled so far downwards as it did (Chapter 10). Japanese occupation created the environment that permitted mass famine and death, fundamentally affecting Vietnamese history. Without a Pacific war, Japan, as in Indonesia, could probably have secured a strong political and economic position in Vietnam. It could likely also have extended its presence throughout Indochina to Cambodia and Laos, since both were influenced by Vietnam and Thailand.

The French were committed colonialists. In light of this, a Vietnamese war of independence could well have still transpired. However, if the conflict had depended chiefly on the French unsupported by aid from the United States, the struggle, although nasty, would likely have been less protracted than the First Indochina War, and the Second, with its deep American involvement, might never have happened.

In the longer term, Indochina would have been attractive to Western multinationals as a source of cheap labour. That occurred from the 1990s, much later into the second phase of globalization dating from the late 1960s than it might otherwise have done. Unencumbered by the World War II inheritance of an overvalued real exchange rate, Vietnam could have begun some manufacturing for export even before the second phase of globalization.

In directing much of Southeast Asia down a markedly different path than it would otherwise have followed, the Japanese occupation also put the region on a worse path and one beginning from a lower GDP per capita than by any reckoning countries would otherwise have had. The occupation did not conduce to political stability nor lay foundations for post-1945 economic development in manufacturing or agriculture. Formal education largely ceased during the three and a half years of occupation and with this human capital formation suffered (Chapter 2). The Japanese left little useful infrastructure: their wartime construction was directed towards immediate military, not long-term economic, requirements (Chapters 5 and 9). Although described as perhaps 'the most remarkable achievement of the Japanese in South-East Asia', the Thailand–Burma railway, like Japan's other wartime railways, became totally redundant.[111] The post-war elites in Burma, Indonesia and Vietnam and military governments, whose emergence occupation facilitated, adopted policies that led to economic dead ends.

Historical Perspective

The main aim of this book has been to consider World War II in Southeast Asia as an economic event and to understand its impact on and consequences

[111] NARA, RG226, entry 154, box 79, file 1313, 'Note on the Burma–Siam railway', 9 July 1945, p. 1.

for Southeast Asia's economies and societies. Parts of the book have looked backwards to emphasize how specialized and globalized Southeast Asian countries had become before the war in serving the Atlantic economic system of the United States and western Europe. Southeast Asia's pre-war reliance on exports, specialization leading to monoeconomies and lack of industrialization were extreme. These economic characteristics made Southeast Asia highly vulnerable to damage from the economic constraints imposed by Japanese occupation.

It was partly to avoid economic dependence on the Atlantic economy and global forces that Japan, previously a junior partner in the Atlantic system, rejected it in December 1941 in favour of constructing a larger Japanese Empire to strengthen the home economy. Japan's motives, driven by an ascendant military, a rhetoric of national survival and a belief in innate racial superiority, centred on a desire to create and dominate an economically self-sufficient East Asia as a path to greater Japanese industrialization. But Japan's use of war as an instrument of policy was badly misconceived, and its wartime empire lacked cohesion. The Southeast Asian constituent of empire was assembled in a chaotic few months and disintegrated in a little over three years. Nevertheless, efforts by Japan to further Asian nationalism and sudden Japanese military collapse in August 1945 led to sweeping political change in Burma, Indonesia and Vietnam, and revolution in the latter two. Without the Japanese occupation and power vacuums after Japan's surrender, the balance in Southeast Asian decolonization between continuity and change might well have tipped towards the former.[112] Where change was dramatic enough to be thought a transformation – in Burma, Indonesia and Vietnam – it seemed from the perspective of the 1960s permanently to have undermined the historical unity of Southeast Asia so evident during the first, 1870 to 1940, era of globalization. Even as late as 1980, that view was expressed by some leading Southeast Asian scholars in a highly influential collection of essays.[113]

The Japanese interregnum has often been seen as a turning point in Southeast Asian history, and the centrality of the occupation period in shaping post-war politics in Burma, Indonesia and Vietnam would be hard to deny.[114] From a long-term perspective, however, the war does not stand out as a turning point in the economic and social history of Southeast Asia: it did not permanently alter the region's fundamental orientation towards the global economy nor effectively counter the forces of global change on Southeast Asia. To be sure, the war hastened and affected the end of colonialism to create large

112 Cf. Benda, 'Structure', p. 134; Marr, *Vietnam 1945*, pp. 150–51.

113 Cf. Elsbree, *Japan's role*; Benda, 'Beginnings', *Crescent*, 'Structure' and 'Japanese interregnum'; McCoy, *Southeast Asia*. For this point and a re-assessment in favour of historical continuity, see McCoy, 'Circles', p. 977; Harper, 'Long view', pp. 7–8.

114 Benda, 'Structure', pp. 133–34.

differences in post- compared to pre-war Southeast Asia. Attitudes changed towards the importance of industrialization in economic development, the need for indigenous ownership and governments' responsibility in achieving both. But, with the possible exception of Burma, even in those countries where after the war nationalism had its fullest expression, the striking long-term feature of late twentieth- and early twenty-first-century Southeast Asian economic history and development was the reassertion of openness to opportunities in the world economy, a subordination of nationalism to globalization. The main difference between countries within Southeast Asia, it has been suggested, was 'the mode of post-independence re-integration into the world capitalist economy and the global political order'.[115] For almost all of Southeast Asia, re-integration, if by the sharply contrasting paths sketched in this Epilogue and conclusion, has now substantially occurred. That was probably to be expected after the new phase of globalization dating from the late 1960s began to assert itself. In the long term, Southeast Asia will always be driven by global forces and be, as it was particularly during World War II, substantially at their mercy.

The re-assertion of globalization as the dominant historical force affecting Southeast Asia parallels the decades 1870 to 1940 and gives Southeast Asian history a long-term coherence. This continuity makes World War II and the Japanese occupation appear, rather than a turning point, a catalyst for accelerated change. Historical perspective does not, however, diminish the war's devastating impact on Southeast Asian societies and the enormous human and economic costs incurred from the relatively brief Japanese interregnum.

[115] Sidel, 'Fate', p. 116.

APPENDIX TO CHAPTER 3: MONEY SUPPLY, PRICE, GDP AND EXCHANGE RATE DATA SOURCES

Money supply data derive from Japan's Ministry of Finance records and from Thailand's and Indochina's government accounts. These data are reliable until various dates in 1945, when Japanese record-keeping deteriorated or ceased. Subsequently, Allied reconstructions of Japanese policy provide additional information (see NA, T236/108, 'Report on Japanese financial manipulations in French Indo-China' by Lt. Colonel T. H. Sweeny, *c.* November 1945 and WO203/4190, 'Notes on the Southern Regions Development Bank' (Nanpo Ginko), 15 October 1945, p. 24; Longmuir, *Money trail*, pp. 42–43, 100; Swan, 'Thai-Japan relations', pp. 317–20; Kratoska, 'Banana money'; Nitz, 'Japanese military policy', pp. 336–37). Statistics are typically monthly for the four military-administered countries and annual for Thailand and Indochina. Data for the Philippines exist through January 1945, for Indonesia until July 1945, and for Malaya and Burma until 12 and 15 August 1945 respectively. Rapid money supply expansion during the war's last two months, and especially its final two weeks in August when surrender was inevitable, makes Malayan and Burmese data not entirely comparable with those for Indonesia and the Philippines.

Burma

Money supply: MFA, Diplomatic Archives, Navy Ministry, Southeast Asia, Navy-I-1–6, 'Monthly balance of Southern Regions Development Bank notes'; Bank of Japan, Economic Research Department, *Nihon kin'yū-shi shiryō* [Materials on monetary history of Japan], p. 384; Longmuir, *Money trail*, p. 43. *Prices:* Prices are for Rangoon and from Bank of Japan, Economic Research Department, *Nihon kin'yū-shi shiryō* [Materials on monetary history of Japan], p. 385.

Malaya

Money supply: MFA, Diplomatic Archives, Navy Ministry, Southeast Asia, Navy-I-1–6, 'Monthly balance of Southern Regions Development Bank notes'; Bank of Japan, Economic Research Department, *Nihon kin'yū-shi shiryō* [Materials on monetary history of Japan], p. 384. *Prices*: Prices are for Singapore and up to December 1944 from a wholesale price index from Bank of Japan, Economic Research Department, *Nihon kin'yū-shi shiryō* [Materials on monetary history of

Japan], p. 385. December 1944 prices are linked to a cost of living index from NA, CO852/726/3, 'Validity of contracts entered into before and during the Japanese occupation'. The cost of living index was constructed by British authorities after the war using Japanese records of a large variety of retail prices and records from a number of government bodies. Weights are: foodstuffs 0.65; tobacco 0.04; light and water 0.04; transport 0.10; clothing 0.08; and rent 0.09. For May to 12 August 1945, this cost of living index is linked to an index of the value of the British-issued Malayan dollar in terms of occupation currency. Throughout the occupation the cost of living and value of Malayan dollar indexes moved closely together. However, the Bank of Japan wholesale price index records substantially higher inflation than the British reconstruction of a cost of living index.

Thailand

Money supply and yen credits: Kingdom of Thailand, Department of Commerce and Statistics, *Statistical yearbook 1939–40–1944*, p. 435; Kingdom of Thailand, *Report of the financial adviser 1941–1950*, p. 54. Payments to Japan are yen credits plus Thailand's trade surplus. The annual trade surplus and sale of gold by Japan are from Shenoy, 'Currency', p. 291. Towards the end of the war, baht duplicated by the Allies in the event of invasion were air dropped into five provinces, adding slightly to Thailand's published money supply data ('Dropped by plane in error', *Bangkok Post,* 2 December 1945). In the official statistics the inclusion of yen credits as imports gives the misleading impression that Thailand ran a large trade deficit with Japan. See Kingdom of Thailand, *Report of the financial adviser 1941–1950,* pp. 7–14. *Prices*: Ingram, *Economic change*, p. 164, derived from Bank of Thailand figures for the cost of living and based on the family budget of white-collar workers and wage earners in Bangkok. According to Ungphakorn and Suvarnsit ('Fiscal and other measures', p. 70) the inflation figures cited in Ingram are 'lower than most people would consider as representing the actual level of prices'. For an alternative, somewhat different but apparently less reliable, price index, see Kingdom of Thailand, *Report of the financial adviser 1941–1950*, p. 55. *Government revenue and expenditure*: Kingdom of Thailand, *Report of the financial adviser 1941–1950*, pp. 1–3.

Indonesia

Money supply: MFA, Diplomatic Archives, Navy Ministry, Southeast Asia, Navy-I-1-6, 'Monthly balance of Southern Regions Development Bank notes'. The 1941 figure is from Shibata, 'Monetary policy', p. 702, which gives a figure of 316 million guilders for 6 December 1941. Payments to Japan are the annual change in money supply. *Prices:* Bank of Japan, Economic Research Department, *Nihon kin'yū-shi shiryō* [Materials on monetary history of Japan], p. 385. Prices are for Jakarta and in some instances these differ from prices for Medan reported in the same source.

Indochina

Money supply, yen credits and trade surplus: Indochina, *Annuaire statistique 1941–1942*, pp. 176, 245 and *1943–46*, pp. 179–80, 287. Yen credits are expenditure by Japanese armed forces in Indochina and from NA, FO371/53959, 'Second report on Japanese financial manipulations in French Indo-China'. After the 9 March 1945 coup the Japanese took over Indochina. They printed large amounts of currency near the end of the war, but much of it appears not to have been put into circulation. *Prices*: Vietnam, *Annuaire statistique du Viêtnam, 1949–1950*, p. 283. Price data are for the Saigon working class cost of living. For 1945 data are an average of the first two quarters. *Government revenue and expenditure*: Indochina, *Annuaire statistique 1943–46*, pp. 257–60, 304. The budget deficit is quantified as 'VII. Recettes extraordinaires' on p. 260. A similar entry does not appear for 1942. See Indochina, *Annuaire statistique 1941–1942*, p. 245.

Philippines

Money supply: Romualdez, 'Financial problems', pp. 450–52. Money supply data include the 230 million pesos of pre-war treasury certificates. Before 1945 money supply data from Romualdez and MFA, Diplomatic Archives, Navy Ministry, Southeast Asia, Navy-I-1-6, 'Monthly balance of Southern Regions Development Bank notes', are in close agreement but for 1945 the Bank's data shows a smaller increase in money supply. *Prices*: Romualdez, 'Financial problems', pp. 461–62. Price data are unavailable after January 1945.

Note on Pre-war Currency and Money Supply Data

In military-administered Southeast Asia, money supply data during the first year of the Japanese occupation exclude, except for the Philippines, pre-war currency issue. During this period, before the use of colonial currencies was prohibited, data are the subject of some uncertainty since it is unknown at what rate pre-war money disappeared from circulation

GDP

Notes: For Burma, the Philippines and Japan all data are from Maddison. Figures for Malaya, Thailand, Indonesia and Vietnam benchmark GDP per capita in Maddison (1938 benchmark for Thailand and Indonesia; 1913 for Malaya and Indochina) and use GDP per capita data from van der Eng and Bassino, transformed into indexes, to extend Maddison's data. The indexes are multiplied by Maddison's benchmark 1990 GK$. Results of this estimation procedure agree closely with 1950 figures from Maddison. Malaya comprises the Malay peninsula (including Penang and Malacca) and Singapore. Account is taken of higher per capita income for Singapore than the peninsula as follows. For both 1913 and 1950,

Maddison shows Singapore per capita income to be 42 per cent higher than peninsular. Accordingly, peninsular per capita income is multiplied by 1.42 to estimate Singapore's income. Malayan income to include Singapore is weighted, for 1938–40, by Singapore's share of 12.9 per cent of Malayan population recorded by the 1931 census and, for 1949 and 1950, the 16.1 per cent share recorded by the 1947 census. Per capita income in Indochina is assumed to be the same as in Vietnam and estimated to include Cambodia and Laos by multiplying the 1936 share in total Indochina population of those two provinces by Vietnam's GDP and adding the result to Vietnam GDP. In 1936, Vietnam contained 82.4 per cent of the pre-war Indochinese population. While GDP measures are the estimates of highly knowledgeable scholars of Thailand and Indochina respectively, they are nevertheless likely to incorporate a margin of error. Estimates may also understate GDP due to difficulties in taking into account black market transactions.

Sources: Maddison, *World economy: historical statistics*, pp. 180–85; van der Eng, *Historical estimates of GDP in Malaysia/West Malaysia*; van der Eng, *Thailand estimates of GDP based on Sompop's work*; van der Eng, 'Real domestic product of Indonesia', pp. 368–69; Jean-Pascal Bassino, personal communication, Vietnam national income, 6 Feb. 2011.

Exchange Rates

Van der Eng, *Silver standard.*

APPENDIX TO CHAPTER 8: POPULATION DATA SOURCES

Data are drawn from a number of sources. For the pre- and post-war periods, it comes principally from censuses or official population counts and estimates. Wartime data for Thailand and Indochina, where pre-war administrations remained in place, are mainly from official publications. Data for Rangoon, Singapore, Kuala Lumpur, Jakarta, Surabaya and Manila derive chiefly from Japanese sources. Rationing and a desire for social control gave the Japanese strong motives to mount censuses and population counts, which, although unambitious in scope, are reliable.

Burma

Andrus, *Burmese economic life*, p. 25; Murphey, 'New capitals', p. 226; Rangoon, 14 September 1942: NARA, RG262, Foreign Broadcast Intelligence Service, box 114, September 1942, radio report on the Far East no. 3; Rangoon, March 1943: Burma Intelligence Bureau, *Burma*, vol. 2, p. 63; Rangoon, 8 September 1942: OSS, assemblage 45, *Manpower in Japan and occupied areas*, vol. 2, p. 212; Rangoon, July 1944 and February 1945: Collis, *Last and first*, p. 88. The date for the July population figure is approximate, and refers to the size of Rangoon prior to the Indian exodus before Rangoon fell. Rangoon, June 1945: MNA 1/5 98 BMA report for June 1945, p. 3. This report gives a 1941 population for Rangoon of 500,800 excluding suburbs in Insein civil district. The June 1945 figure is for Rangoon town (240,455) and Rangoon suburbs (69,077) but excludes Insein town (24,345). Rangoon, January 1950: Cressey, *Rangoon*, p. 5; Rangoon and Mandalay, 1953: Burma, Census Department, *Towns classified*, p. 2. In Table 8.2 the ratio for Rangoon: Mandalay is the 1953 population for Mandalay and the 1950 population for Rangoon. By 1953, Rangoon was four times the size of Mandalay. For Rangoon for 1956, Murphey ('New capitals', p. 226) estimates a population of 750,000.

Thailand

Murphey, 'New capitals', p. 226.

Malaya and Singapore

Malaya, *Report on the 1947 census*, pp. 39, 44, 589; Huff, *Economic growth*, p. 158; Federation of Malaya, *1957 population census*, pp. 8, 52–53. Population for 1936 for Kuala Lumpur is estimated assuming proportionate population growth between 1931 and 1947. Penang, 1941: NARA, RG226, entry 16, box 21417, Security Intelligence for Planning Section Proforma A strategical: Penang and Province Wellesley. Penang populations for 1941 and 1947 are island populations and so comparable with Singapore populations for 1939 and 1947. For data from a mid-1941 British population estimate, from a 1942 Japanese census, and from a 1946 British population estimate, see ANM, 1957/0292046, RC Sel. 269/1947, Report of the Kuala Lumpur Town Board, 1 April 1946–31 December 1946, pp. 5, 22. For the mid-1941 population, see also ANM, 1957/0290027, Syuseityo Kanbo 108/2603, Kuala Lumpur Sanitary Board, Annual report 2062 (1942), pp. 3, 5, 7. Singapore, 31 January 1942: Allen, *Singapore 1941–1942*, p. 161. This figure must be treated with caution. It is reported as 'close on 1,000,000' and was said to be swollen by troop reinforcements as well as by refugees. Since General Percival had 85,000 men under his command, the population may have been no more than 900,000. One scholar suggests a 15 February 1942 population of 800,000 swollen by the addition of half a million refugees from the peninsula, or a total of 1.3 million, but this seems too high: Thio, 'Syonan years', p. 95; Singapore, 8 January 1943: OSS, assemblage 45, *Manpower in Japan and occupied areas*, vol. 2, p. 235, gives a Singapore municipality population figure of 760,000; Singapore Island, July 1944: Malaya, *Report on the 1947 census*, p. 589: Singapore Island, 1946: Harper, *End*, p. 42; Singapore Island, 1947: Malaya, *Report on the 1947 census*, p. 39. This 1947 island figure is for the Colony of Singapore, and so may slightly overstate island population; Singapore, 1957: Singapore, *Report on the census of population 1957*, p. 43.

Indonesia

Jakarta, January 1941 (but in source end of December 1940): 'Batavia's bevolking' ['Batavia's population'], *De Sumatra Post,* 10 February 1941. Jakarta, April 1943 and April 1944: OSS, assemblage 45, *Manpower in Japan and occupied areas,* vol. 2, p. 257. Surabaya's population in March 1943 is estimated as 500,000: ibid., vol. 2, p. 258. Jakarta, June 1945: 'Hasil pendaftaran tjatjah djiwah di Djakarta' ['Result of census population Jakarta'], *Soeara Asia,* 30 June 1945 (no. 157 Soerabaja). Jakarta and Surabaya, 1940 and 1945, and for Jakarta, 1948: Dick, *Surabaya,* p. 123. The 1945 figure is for a complete census of Jakarta including Batavia and Meester Cornelis, and consisted of 676,261 Indonesians and 137,206 Chinese: Sutter, *Indonesianisasi,* p. 269; Jakarta, October 1948: 'De bevolking van Batavia' ['The population of Batavia'], *De Nieuwsgier,* 4 October 1948. This figure should, however, be treated with some caution; see 'De bevolking van Batavia', *De Nieuwsgier,* 11 October 1948. Jakarta, 1949: 'Djakarta's bevolking' ['Djakarta's population'], *Java-bode: Nieuws, Handels- en Advertentieblad voor Nederlandsch-Indie,* 7 January 1950. Surabaya, 1942 and 1944: Peters, *Surabaya,* pp. 7, 73. Other data in this source for 1940, 1946, 1948 and 1950 agree closely with the figures in Table 8.1. Surabaya, 1947: 'Djoemlah pendoedoek Soerabaja' ['Total number of inhabitants of Surabaya'], *Pelita Rakjat,* 28 January 1948. Surabaya, November 1948: 'Djoemlah pendoedoek Soerabja meningkat' ['The total number of inhabitants of Surabaya has increased'], *Pelita Rakyat,* 23 December 1948. Surabaya, 1951:'Bevolking van Surabaja' ['Population of Surabaya'], *De Vrije Pers: Ochtendbulletin,* 14 December 1951. Jakarta and Surabaya, 1951 and 1956: Murphey, 'New capitals', p. 227. Data for Jakarta's wartime population vary somewhat in sources but are typically of like magnitudes. For example, van der Eng, *Food supply,* p. 37, gives a 1941 Jakarta population of 544,820 and Sato, '"Economic soldiers"', p. 131, reports the growth of Jakarta's population as 594,000 to 844,000 during the occupation.

Indochina

Data for Saigon-Cholon and for Hanoi for 1936 and 1943 are from Indochina, *Annuaire statistique, 1943–46,* pp. 27–28, and *1947–48,* pp. 19–21. For Saigon-Cholon the 1941, 1945 and 1949 populations of 450,000, 500,000 and 1,200,000 are from Brocheux and Hémery, *Indochina,* pp. 131, 373. The figure of 500,000 for Saigon-Cholon from Brocheux and Hémery is confirmed by the *Annuaire statistique, 1943–46,* p. 27, which gives a 1946 population of 492,200. For Saigon-Cholon the 1936 figure may be an under-count. The 1948 figure for Hanoi (but not for Saigon-Cholon) includes the suburban population, and so is not comparable with earlier data for Hanoi. Hanoi, November 1948, 1951, 1953, 1954: Turley, 'Urbanization', pp. 372–73. The figure of 10,000 for November 1948 is an estimate based on the known mass exodus from Hanoi after its near-complete destruction. It may be that the figure of 10,000 refers to the inner city population and, if so, would represent the departure of at least

30,000 and compare with an inner city population of 80,000 in 1951. Cf. Goscha, 'Colonial Hanoi', p. 228. For 1956, data for Saigon-Cholon and Hanoi are for 1960 from Mitchell, *International historical statistics*, pp. 40–42. A rough estimate for Saigon for 1956 is 1.8 million, a figure said to be explained by refugees from Tonkin and civil disorder in the south; Murphey, 'New capitals', p. 216.

Philippines

Manila, 1939: Philippines, *Census of the Philippines 1939*, vol. 2, p. 59; Manila, March 1942: Kerkvliet, 'Withdrawal', p. 184; Manila, October 1942: Philippines, *In commemoration*, p. 2. It is not clear to what extent, if any, the boundaries of Manila as defined by the Japanese in this publication (*In commemoration*) may have differed from the boundaries of the 1939 census. Manila, March 1943: NARA, RG56, entry 72A245, box 31, 'Labor conditions in Manila'. This March 1943 Japanese estimate puts Manila's population at 940,000 and the population of Greater Manila, including suburban towns, at over a million. During 1943 and 1944 population data vary but make clear the great increase in Manila's population. There is a November 1943 estimate of 1,300,000, while early in 1944 a Tokyo broadcast reported the population of Manila as some 1,500,000. I prefer the figure of February 1944 of 1,093,000 because it is based on a survey by the mayor's office and reports of neighbourhood associations. The various estimates are reported in OSS, assemblage 45, *Manpower in Japan and occupied areas*, vol. 2, p. 292, which can also be found in NARA, RG407, Foreign Occupied Areas box 2229, file 5; Manila, February 1945: NARA, RG407, entry 427, Philippines Civil Affairs Unit no. 20, 'History of Philippines Civil Affairs Unit no. 20 November 1944–June 1945'. This Civil Affairs Unit was in Manila from 6 February and took a census which found the population to be around 174,000. The Unit estimated that 60 per cent of the population needed relief and described a city in flames. For post-war statistics, see: Philippines, Bureau of the Census and Statistics, *Yearbook of Philippine statistics 1946*, p. 10; Philippines, *Handbook [of] Philippine statistics*, p. 8; Murphey, 'New capitals', p. 227. Urban population for 1948 and 1958 may be somewhat overstated for cities other than Manila because of the conventions of official Philippine statistics which record population in political areas rather than the usual definition of a city as an unbroken urban area.

BIBLIOGRAPHY

Japanese, Chinese and Vietnamese names appear as surname followed by first or given name and not separated by a comma.

Archives

Burma (Myanmar)

National Archives of Myanmar, Yangon (MNA)

Cambodia

National Archives of Cambodia, Phnom Penh (NAC)
  Fonds de la Résidence supérieure du Cambodge

France

Centre des Archives d'Outre-Mer, Aix-en-Provence (AOM)
  Affaires économiques (AFFECO)
  Affaires politiques (AP)
  Fonds du gouvernement de fait (GF)
  Gouvernement général de l'Indochine (GGI)
  Haut commissariat pour l'Indochine (HCI) formerly CP: Fonds conseiller politique
  Indochine nouveau fonds (INF)
  Journal officiel (JO)
  Papiers d'agents (FP)
  Résidence supérieure du Tonkin nouveau fonds (RSTNF)

Japan

Hitotsubashi University, Institute of Economic Research Library (IER)
Kishi Kōichi Collection, Institute of Developing Economies, Japan External Trade Organization (IDE-JETRO) (KKC)
Ministry of Foreign Affairs, Diplomatic Archives, Navy Ministry Southeast Asia (MFA)

National Institute for Defense Studies, Military History Research Centre (NIDS)
Nishijima Collection, Waseda University, Tokyo (NC)

Malaysia

Arkib Negara Malaysia (National Archives of Malaysia) (ANM)

Netherlands

Indische Collectie, Instituut voor Oorlogs-, Holocaust- en Genocidestudies, (Collection Netherlands East Indies, Institute for War, Holocaust and Genocide Studies), Amsterdam (IC)
Koninklijk Instituut voor Taal-, Land- en Volkenkunde (Royal Netherlands Institute of Southeast Asian and Caribbean Studies), Leiden (KITLV)
Nationaal Archief (National Archives), The Hague (NAH)
Nederlands Instituut voor Militaire Historie (Netherlands Institute for Military History), The Hague (NIMH)

Philippines

Philippine National Library (PNL)
University of the Philippines, Diliman Main Library (UP)
  Filipiniana Section
  Japanese Occupation Papers
  Manuel A. Roxas Papers

Singapore

National Archives of Singapore (NAS)

Thailand

Bank of Thailand Archives (BT)

United Kingdom

Bank of England Records, London (BE)
  OV25 (Thailand)
  OV65 (Malaya, Singapore and Borneo)
  OV66 (Far East General)
  OV79 (Burma)
  OV85 (Dutch East Indies/Indonesia)
  OV85 (Indochina)
  OV149 (Philippines)

India Office Records, British Library, London (IOR)
Clague Papers Mss Eur E252
Dorman-Smith Papers Mss Eur E215

Liddell Hart Centre for Military Archives, King's College, London (LHC)
Gracey Papers
MAGIC

National Archives, Kew (NA)
CO273 Straits Settlements original correspondence
CO852 Colonial Office economic general department
FO371 Foreign Office general files
HS1 Special operations executive (SOE): Far East files, 1941–1946
T236 Treasury: overseas finance division
T247 Lord Keynes' personal files Far East (Malaya, etc.)
WO106 Directorate of military operations and military intelligence: correspondence and papers
WO203 War of 1939–45; military headquarters papers, Far East
WO208 War Office: directorate of military operations and intelligence
WO325 War crimes South-East Asia: trials

Weston Library, University of Oxford (WL)
Heussler Papers

United States

National Archives and Records Administration (NARA)
RG56 General records of the Department of the Treasury
RG59 General records of the Department of State
RG226 Records of the Office of Strategic Services (OSS)
RG262 Records of the Foreign Broadcast Intelligence Service
RG319 Records of the Army Staff
RG407 Records of the Adjutant General's Office (Foreign Occupied Areas)
RG457 Records of the National Security Agency/Central Security Service
111-SCA Records of the Office of the Chief Signal Officer

US Army Center of Military History
Japanese Monographs (JM) (Prepared by the Military History Section of the Headquarters, Army Forces East, distributed by the Office of the Chief of Military History, Department of the Army)
No. 24 *History of the Southern Army 1941–1945*
No. 103 *Outline of administration in occupied areas, 1941–1945*
No. 150 *Political strategy prior to the outbreak of war, part iv, January–December 1941*
No. 167 *Malay operations record January 1944–August 1945*

Vietnam

National Archives Center I, Hanoi (VNA)
 Fonds de la direction des finances de l'Indochine (FF)
 Fonds de la résidence supérieure au Tonkin (RS)
 Fonds de la mairie de Hanoi (MH)
 Fonds du contrôle financier de l'Indochine (FC)

Official Publications

Burma

Burma, *Report on the progress of cotton work in Burma 1939–40* (Rangoon: Superintendent, Government Printing and Stationery, 1940).
Burma, *Season and crop report of Burma* (annual series) 1939/40 to 1946/47 (Rangoon: Superintendent, Government Printing and Stationery).
Burma, *Burma's new order plan* (Rangoon: Bureau of the State Printing Presses, 1944).
Burma, *Report of the Committee on Currency* (Rangoon: Bureau of the State Printing Presses, 1944).
Burma, *Report on mining and mineral production in Burma 1946* (Rangoon: Superintendent, Government Printing and Stationery, 1948).
Burma, *Report on the land records administration of Burma 1946* (Rangoon: Superintendent, Government Printing and Stationery, 1948).
Burma, *Two-year plan of economic development for Burma* (Rangoon: Superintendent, Government Printing and Stationery, 1948).
Burma, *Report on the state of public health in Burma during 1947* (Rangoon: Superintendent, Government Printing and Stationery, 1949).
Burma, *The national income of Burma* (Rangoon: Ministry of National Planning, 1951).
Burma, Census Department, *Towns classified by population with decennial variations from 1881 to 1953* (Rangoon: Superintendent of Government Printing and Stationery, 1954).
Burma Currency Board, *Report of the Burma Currency Board, 1 April 1947 to 30 September 1948* (London: Solicitors' Law Stationery Society, 1949).
Burma Intelligence Bureau, *Burma during the Japanese occupation*, vol. 1 (Simla: Government of India Press, 1943).
Burma Intelligence Bureau, *Burma during the Japanese occupation*, vol. 2 (Simla: Government of India Press, 1944).
India, *Census of India, 1921. vol. X. Burma. part I. Report* by S. G. Grantham (Rangoon: Superintendent, Government Printing and Stationery, 1923).
India, *Census of India, 1931. vol. XI. Burma. part I. Report* by J. J. Bennison (Rangoon: Superintendent, Government Printing and Stationery, 1932).

Indochina and Vietnam

Indochina, *Annuaire statistique de l'Indochine*, irregular series covering the years 1913–46 and published 1927–48 (Hanoi).

Indochina, *Atlas de l'Indochine* (Paris: Service Géographique de l'Indochine, 1928).

Vietnam, *Thống kê niên giám Việt-Nam* (Annuaire statistique du Viêtnam), *1949–1950* (Hanoi: Institut de la Statistique et des Études Économique du Viêtnam, 1951).

Vietnam, *Annuaire statistique du Viêtnam*, irregular series covering the years 1949–50 to 1954–55 and published 1951–57 (Saigon).

Indonesia

Indonesia, Department of Economic Affairs, Central Bureau of Statistics, *Statistical pocket book of Indonesia 1941* (Batavia: Central Bureau of Statistics, 1947).

Netherlands Indies, *Volkstelling* [Population census] *1930*, 8 vols. (Batavia: Departement van Landbouw, Nijverheid en Handel, 1933–34).

Japan

Bank of Japan, Economic Research Department, *Nihon kin'yū-shi shiryō: Shōwa XXVII: Senji kin'yū kankei shiryō* [Materials on the monetary history of Japan: Shōwa XXVII: Materials on wartime monetary relations], ed. Takao Tsuchiya (Tokyo: Finance Ministry Printing Bureau, 1970).

Bank of Japan, Statistics Department, *Meiji ikō honpō shuyō Keizai tōkei* [Hundred-year statistics of the Japanese economy] (Tokyo: Statistics Department, Bank of Japan, 1966).

Japan, Cabinet Planning Board, *Gendai shi shiryō (43) Kokka sōdōin (1) Keizai* [Materials on recent history, vol. 43, National total mobilization, part 1, Economy] (Tokyo: Misuzu Shobo, 1970).

Japan, Ministry of Finance, *Nihon gaikoku bōeki nenpyō* [Annual return of the foreign trade of Japan], annual series, 1937–1944–48 (Tokyo: variously published by Ministry of Finance, Cabinet Printing Office, Finance Association of the Ministry of Finance, and Ministry of Printing, 1941–51).

Japan, Ministry of Finance, Shōwa Finance History Compilation Office, *Shōwa zaisei shi IV: Rinji gunji hi* [Shōwa finance history IV: Extraordinary military expense] (Tokyo: Toyo Keizai Shinpō Sha, 1955).

Japan, Philippines Military Administration, *Gunsei kōhō* [Official journal of the military administration] (Nichi-nichi Shimbun Sha), 3rd edn., vol. 1 (Manila: Manila Nichi-Nichi Shimbun Sha, 1943).

Malaya and Singapore

British Military Administration, Malaya, *Gazette of the Malay peninsula* (Kuala Lumpur, 1945).

British Military Administration, *Final report of the nutrition unit* (April 1946).

Federated Malay States, *Report of the rice cultivation committee*, 2 vols. (Kuala Lumpur: Government Press, 1931).

Federated Malay States Railways, *Fifty years of railways in Malaya 1885–1935* (Kuala Lumpur: Federated Malay States Railways, 1935).

Federation of Malaya, *Memorandum on proposals for a Malayan war damage compensation scheme* (Kuala Lumpur: Government Press, 1948).

Federation of Malaya, *A report on the state of health, the diet and the economic conditions of groups of people in the lower income levels in Malaya* by R. C. Burgess and Laidin Alang Musa (Federation of Malaya: Division of Nutrition, Institute for Medical Research, 1950).

Federation of Malaya, *1957 population census of the Federation of Malaya, report no. 14, final report* by H. Fell (Kuala Lumpur: Department of Statistics, Federation of Malaya, 1960).

Federation of Malaya and Singapore, *Report of the war damage commission, Federation of Malaya and Singapore* by Richard Graham (Kuala Lumpur: Government Press, 1953).

Malaya, *British Malaya, a report on the 1931 census* by C. A. Vlieland (Singapore: Government Printing Office, 1932).

Malaya, *Report upon the mining industry of Malaya* by Lewis Leigh Fermor (Kuala Lumpur: Government Press, 1939).

Malaya, *Rubber statistics handbook 1940* (Singapore: Government Printing Office, 1940).

Malaya, *Malaya, A report on the 1947 census of population*, by M. V. Del Tufo (London: Crown Agents, 1949).

Malayan Union, *Report on the British military administration of Malaya* by H. R. Hone (Kuala Lumpur: Malayan Union Government Press, 1946).

Malayan Union, *Annual report of the electricity department 1946* by F. P. Egerton (Kuala Lumpur: Malayan Union Government Press, 1947).

Malayan Union, *Annual report on education in the Malayan Union 1946* by H. R. Cheeseman (Kuala Lumpur: Malayan Union Government Press, 1947).

Malayan Union, *Annual report on the mines department and the mining industry of the Malayan Union 1946* by A. Bean (Kuala Lumpur: Malayan Union Government Press, 1947).

Malayan Union, *Railways report 1946* by J. O. Sanders (Kuala Lumpur: Malayan Union Government Press, 1947).

Malayan Union, *Report of the medical department 1946* by R. B. MacGregor (Kuala Lumpur: Malayan Union Government Press, 1947).

Malayan Union, *Report on agriculture in Malaya 1946* by F. Burnett (Kuala Lumpur: Malayan Union Government Press, 1947).

Malayan Union, *Report on the registration of births and deaths for the years 1941 to 1946* by R. B. MacGregor (Kuala Lumpur: Malayan Union Government Press, 1948).

Malayan Union, *Annual report of the labour department 1947* by R. G. D. Houghton (Kuala Lumpur: Government Press, 1948).

Malayan Union and Singapore, *Interim report on wages by the Joint Wages Commission* (Kuala Lumpur: Malayan Union Government Press, 1947).

Singapore, *Annual report of the medical department 1946* by W. J. Vickers (Singapore: Government Printing Office, 1947).

Singapore, *Report on the census of population 1957* by S. C. Chua (Singapore: Government Printer, 1964).

Singapore and Federation of Malaya, *Malayan statistics: monthly digest of economic and social statistics*, monthly series, 1952–56 (Singapore: Government Printing Office).

Singapore Department of Social Welfare, *A social survey of Singapore* (Singapore: Department of Social Welfare, 1947).

Singapore Department of Social Welfare, *First report of the Singapore Department of Social Welfare, June to December 1946* (Singapore: G. H. Kiatt, 1947).

Singapore, *Annual report on the registration of births and deaths for the years 1940–47* by E. J. Phillips (Singapore: Government Printing Office, 1948).

Straits Settlements, *Report of the commission to enquire into and report on the trade of the colony*, 5 vols. (Singapore: Government Printing Office, 1934).

Netherlands

Centraal Bureau voor de Statistiek, 'De economische toestand van Nederlandsch-Indie tijdens de Japanse bezetting, 1942–45' [The economic situation of the Dutch Indies during the Japanese occupation 1942–45], *Statistische en econometrische onderzoekingen*, 2, 4 (1947), pp. 118–27.

Philippines

Philippines, *Annual report of the Bank Commissioner of the Philippine Islands to the Honorable Secretary of Finance for the fiscal year ended December 31, 1930* (Manila: Bureau of Printing, 1931).

Philippines, *Yearbook of Philippine statistics 1940* (Manila: Bureau of Printing, 1940).

Philippines, *Census of the Philippines 1939*, 4 vols. (Manila: Bureau of Printing, 1942).

Philippines, *In commemoration of the twelve new administrative districts of Manila: Manila, Philippines October 31, 1942* (Manila: Bureau of Printing, 1942).

Philippines, 'Central Bank statistical bulletin', 2, 4 (1950).

Philippines, *Handbook [of] Philippine statistics 1903–1959* (Manila: Bureau of Printing, 1960).

Philippines, *NEDA statistical yearbook 1974* (Manila: National Economic and Development Authority, 1974).

Philippines, Bureau of Commerce, *Statistical bulletin of the Philippine Islands*, annual series, 1918–46 (Manila: Bureau of Printing).

Philippines, Bureau of the Census and Statistics, *Yearbook of Philippine statistics 1946* (Manila: Bureau of Printing, 1947).

Philippines, Commission of the Census, *Special bulletin no. 1, census of the Philippines 1939* (Manila: Bureau of Printing, 1939).

Philippines, Japanese Military Administration, *Ideals of the new Philippines* (edited and published by the Propaganda Corps, Imperial Japanese forces, 1942).

Philippines, Japanese Military Administration, *The voice of the new Philippines: a collection of lectures on current topics* (Manila: Department of Information, 1942).

Philippines, Japanese Military Administration, *Ano ang Kalibapi?* [What is the Kalibapi?] (Department of Information, Imperial Japanese Army, 1942–43).

Philippines, Japanese Military Administration, *Our independence is at hand!* (Manila: Bureau of Information and Security, Department of the Interior, 1943).

Philippines, Japanese Military Administration, *The voice of the new Philippines: volume II: reconstruction* (Manila: Department of Information, 1943).

Philippines, Office of the Resident Commissioner of the Philippines to the United States, *Report on the destruction of Manila and Japanese atrocities* (Washington, DC, 1945).

Thailand

Bank of Thailand, *Bank of Thailand economic and financial report*, annual series, 1942–50 (Bangkok).

Kingdom of Siam [or Thailand], *Statistical yearbook of the Kingdom of Siam [or Thailand]*, annual series, 1920–1955 (Bangkok).

Kingdom of Siam [or Thailand], Department of Commerce and Statistics, *Statistical year book of Thailand* (irregular annual series, 1920–1939–40–1944; 1952, 1945–55).

Kingdom of Thailand, *Report of the financial adviser in connection with the budgets of the Kingdom of Thailand 1939–1941* (Bangkok, 1941).

Kingdom of Thailand, *Annual statements of the foreign trade and navigation of the Kingdom of Thailand 1942–1945* (Bangkok: Department of His Majesty's Customs, c. 1947).

Kingdom of Thailand, *Report of the financial adviser covering the years 1941 to 1950* (Bangkok, 1951).

Kingdom of Thailand, Ministry of Public Health, *Public health in Thailand* (Bangkok: Ministry of Public Health, 1957).

Kingdom of Thailand, Thailand, Division of Agricultural Economics, *Thailand economic farm survey*, 1953 by John C. Kassebaum (Bangkok: Ministry of Agriculture, 1955).

United Kingdom

Burma statement of policy by His Majesty's Government, Cmd. 6635 (London: HMSO, 1945).

MacMichael, Sir Harold, *Report on a mission to Malaya (October, 1945–January, 1946)* (London: HMSO, 1946).

Thailand no. 1 (1940) treaty of non-aggression between the United Kingdom and Thailand, Bangkok, June12, 1940, Cmd. 6211 (London: HMSO, 1940).

United States

United States, *Reports of General MacArthur*, 2 vols. (Washington, DC: US Department of the Army, 1966).

United States, Department of State, *Peace and war: United States foreign policy 1931–1941* (issued by US Department of State reprinted by HMSO) (London: HMSO, 1943).

United States, Department of State, *Report to the President of the United States by the economic survey mission to the Philippines* (the Bell mission) (Washington, DC: Department of State, 1950).

JISPB (Joint Intelligence Study Publishing Board Studies, University Microfilms, Ann Arbor, MI)

JISPB, *Joint Army-Navy intelligence study of Indochina*, chapter 7, 'Transportation and communications' (Washington, DC: United States Strategic Bombing Survey, October 1945).

JISPB, *Joint Army-Navy intelligence study of Indochina*, chapter 8, 'Cities and towns in French Indochina' (Washington, DC: United States Strategic Bombing Survey, October 1945).

JISPB, *Joint Army-Navy intelligence study of Indochina*, chapter 10, 'People and government' (Washington, DC: United States Strategic Bombing Survey, October 1945).

JISPB, *Joint Army-Navy intelligence study of Indochina*, chapter 11, 'Health and sanitation' (Washington, DC: United States Strategic Bombing Survey, October 1945).

These studies can also be accessed at NARA, entry 319 (NM3) 82A Records of the Army Staff. Office of the Assistant Chief of Staff, G-2, Intelligence. Collections and Dissemination Division. Document Library Branch. Reports and Messages, 1950–1951. Chapters 7 and 8 box 395/Chapters 10 and 11 box 396.

United States Office of Strategic Services (OSS), Research and Analysis Branch (R&A): Assemblages, Reports and South East Asia Command (SEAC) (published in Washington DC or Honolulu or in NARA)

Assemblages (University Microfilms, K Ann Arbor, MI)

33 *The programs of Japan in the Philippines*, 1 September 1944.

43 (R&A 2280) *Handbook of Japanese industry in Japan and occupied areas*, 10 June 1944.

43 (R&A 2280.1) *Handbook of Japanese industry in Japan and occupied areas*, 15 December 1944.

44 (R&A 2629) *Financial programs of Japan in Japan and occupied areas*, vol. 2, part 3: *Southeast Asia*, 20 September 1944.

45 *Manpower in Japan and occupied areas*, 2 vols., 25 August 1944.

47 (R&A 2702) *Indians in Japan and occupied areas: their support of Indian independence; biographies*, 20 October 1944.

55 (R&A 3170 and second edition of assemblage 22) *Programs of Japan in Java and Bali with biographies*, 18 June 1945.

59 (R&A 3373) *Programs of Japan in Sumatra*, 10 September 1945.

Reports (University Microfilms, K Ann Arbor, MI)

R&A 34 *Singapore*, 12 December 1941.

R&A 44 *Resources of Burma*, 18 January 1942.

R&A 92 *The factor of increased Japanese influence in Thailand*, August 1941.

R&A 272 *Social conditions, attitudes and propaganda in Burma with suggestions for American orientation toward the Burmese*, 6 April 1944.

R&A 274 *Social conditions, attitudes and propaganda in British Malaya with suggestions for American orientation toward the Malayans*, 1 April 1942.

R&A 301 *Social conditions, attitudes and propaganda in Thailand with suggestions for American orientation toward the Thai*, 19 June 1945.

R&A 324 *Philippine agriculture under Japanese control*, 7 August 1942.

R&A 551 *Results of Japanese conquest of Burma*, 5 May 1942.

R&A 552 *Development of Thai cooperation with Japan*, 9 June 1944.

R&A 597 *Studies based on census of the Philippines 1939*, 19 March 1942.

R&A 719 *Strategic survey of Indo-China*, 14 March 1942.

R&A 1007 *Japanese use of land transport in Southeast Asia*, 15 May 1944.

R&A 1249 *Some methods of Japanese penetration in French Indo-China previous to the war*, 31 August 1943.

R&A 1253 *The problem of law and order in occupied Burma*, 14 March 1944.

R&A 1278 *Personnel of 'independent' Burma government*, 27 August 1943.

R&A 1286 *Selection of S. O. objectives in the Southeast Asia theatre*, 11 November 1943.

R&A 1286.1 *An additional strategic objective (Appendix to selection of S. O. objectives in the Southeast Asia theatre R&A 1286)*, 8 December 1943.

R&A 1433 *Political and economic changes effected by the Japanese in Malaya*, 1 December 1943.

R&A 1526 *The psychological warfare problem in Burma*, 12 November 1943.

R&A 1712 *The structure of the government in Thailand*, 20 March 1944.

R&A 1713 *The structure of the government of Burma*, 29 September 1944.

R&A 1715 *Indochina's war-time government and main aspects of French rule*, 10 July 1945.

R&A 1752 *The government of the new Philippines (a study of the present puppet government in the Philippines)*, 15 May 1944.

R&A 1752.2 *Status of the Philippine puppet government as of 14 October 1944*, 14 October 1944.

R&A 1791 *Implementation study of Malaya, part 1 morale objectives*, 15 March 1944.

R&A 1931 *Problems confronting the Free Thai movement*, 25 February 1944.

R&A 1992 *Burma (New Delhi area report no. 1)*, 15 May 1944.

R&A 1992A *Burma (situation report no. 1)*, 25 February 1944.
R&A 2015 *Japanese administration of Burma*, 10 July 1944.
R&A 2072 *Japanese administration in Malaya*, 8 June 1944.
R&A 2077 *Economic reorganization of Burma*, 1944.
R&A 2114 *Political aspects of Allied occupation of Thailand*, 14 July 1944.
R&A 2134.1 *Changes in south Sumatra under Japanese administration*, 14 October 1944.
R&A 2137 *Industrial facilities in Malaya*, 15 May 1944.
R&A 2368 *Japanese domination of Thailand*, 18 September 1944.
R&A 2380 *Education in the Philippines*, 19 December 1944.
R&A 2357S *Guerrilla resistance in the Philippines*, 21 July 1944.
R&A 2423 *Singapore under Japanese domination*, 8 September 1944.
R&A 2451 *Control of inflation in Japan*, 1 October 1945.
R&A 2589 *The rubber industry of Southeast Asia: an estimate of present conditions and anticipated capabilities*, 16 December 1944.
R&A 2594 *Selected industrial installations in Indo-China*, 1 January 1945.
R&A 2595 *Selected industrial installations in Thailand*, 15 June 1945.
R&A 2644 *Rough summary of information on inflation in Southeast Asia*, 15 October 1944.
R&A 2695 *The status of the Chinese in Thailand*, 13 March 1945.
R&A 2731 *Price inflation in Burma*, 15 December 1944.
R&A 2753 *Japanese use of Burmese industry*, 1 November 1945.
R&A 2771 *Proposed British policies for post-war Burma and probable Burmese reactions*, April 1945.
R&A 3186S *The kempei in Japanese-occupied territory*, 15 July 1945.
R&A 3208 *The Philippines: finale of the puppet government*, 9 July 1945.
R&A 4409 *Financial relations between Siam and Japan, 1940–45*, 1 July 1947.

XL R&A Reports (in NARA)
R&A XL2332 *H.M.S. Statesman patrol report*, 23 September 1944.
R&A XL10702 *Interrogation on medical conditions in Malaya*, 5 June 1945.
R&A XL10747 *Interrogation on Malaya*, 1 June 1945.
R&A XL21411 *Tactical – Perak*, 12 June 1945
R&A XL20728 *Notes on group attitudes in southern Malaya*, 2 October 1945.
R&A XL23209 *Malaya–Japanese penetration of the rubber manufacturing industry*, 12 October 1945.

South East Asia Command Reports (in NARA)
R&A/SEAC no. 8-R *Economic conditions in the Rangoon area May–June 1945*, 29 June 1945.
R&A/SEAC no. 23-R *Burma economic review July–August*, 21 August 1945.
R&A/SEAC no. 35-R *Living conditions in Rangoon*, 18 October 1945.
R&A/SEAC no. 54K *The location and installations of the Burma–Thailand Railroad*, 15 January 1945.

United States Strategic Bombing Surveys and Reports (USSBS)

United States Strategic Bombing Survey, *Air campaigns of the Pacific War* (Washington, DC: Military Analysis Division, United States Strategic Bombing Survey, 1946).

United States Strategic Bombing Survey, *Chemicals in Japan's war* (Washington, DC: Oil and Chemicals Division, United States Strategic Bombing Survey, 1946).

United States Strategic Bombing Survey, *Japan's struggle to end the war* (Washington, DC: Office of the Chairman, United States Strategic Bombing Survey, 1946).

United States Strategic Bombing Survey, *Oil in Japan's war* (Washington, DC: Oil and Chemicals Division, United States Strategic Bombing Survey, 1946).

United States Strategic Bombing Survey, *Summary report (Pacific war)* (Washington, DC: Office of the Chairman, United States Strategic Bombing Survey, 1946).

United States Strategic Bombing Survey, *The effects of strategic bombing on Japan's war economy* (Washington, DC: Overall Economic Effects Division, United States Strategic Bombing Survey, 1946).

United States Strategic Bombing Survey, *The Japanese aircraft industry* (Washington, DC: US Government Printing Office, 1946).

United States Strategic Bombing Survey, *The war against Japanese transportation 1941–1945* (Washington, DC: Transportation Division, United States Strategic Bombing Survey, 1947).

International Organizations

International Bank for Reconstruction and Development, *The economic development of Malaya* (Washington, DC, 1955).

International Tin Research and Development Council, *Statistical year book 1938* (The Hague: International Tin Research and Development Council, 1938).

League of Nations, *Report of the committee for the study of the problem of raw materials*, number A.27. 1937. II. B. (Geneva: League of Nations, 1937).

League of Nations, *World economic survey 1941/42* (Geneva: League of Nations, 1942).

League of Nations, *Food rationing and supply 1943/44* (Geneva: League of Nations, 1944).

League of Nations, *World economic survey 1942/44* (Geneva: League of Nations, 1945).

United Nations, Department of Economic Affairs, *Salient features of the world economic situation 1945–47* (New York: United Nations, 1948).

United Nations, Economic and Social Council, 2nd year, 4th session. *Report of the working group for Asia and the Far East.* Supplement no. 10 (1947).

United Nations, Economic and Social Council, E/CN.1/Sub.1/C.2/W.8. *Economic reconstruction of devastated areas working group for Asia and the Far East, part II country studies. H. Philippine Republic* (New York: United Nations, January 1947).

United Nations, Economic and Social Council, E/CN.1/Sub.1/C.2/W.11. *Economic reconstruction of devastated areas working group for Asia and the Far East, part II country studies. K. Netherlands Indies* (New York: United Nations, January 1947).

United Nations, Economic and Social Council, E/CN.1/Sub.1/C.2/W.2. *Economic reconstruction of devastated areas working group for Asia and the Far East, part II country studies. B. Indo-Chinese Federation* (New York: United Nations, January 1947).

United Nations, Economic and Social Council, E/CN.1/Sub.1/C.2/W.10. *Reconstruction of devastated areas working group for Asia and the Far East, part II country studies. J. Burma* (New York: United Nations, January 1947).

United Nations, Economic and Social Council, E/CN.1/Sub.1/C.2/W.5. *Economic reconstruction of devastated areas working group for Asia and the Far East, part II country studies. E. Siam* (New York: United Nations, January 1947).

United Nations, Economic and Social Council, E/CN.1/Sub.1/C.2/W.3. *Reconstruction of devastated areas working group for Asia and the Far East, part II country studies. C.&D. Malayan Union: Singapore* (New York: United Nations, January 1947).

United Nations, Economic and Social Council, E/CN.1/Sub.1/C.2/W.9. *Economic reconstruction of devastated areas working group for Asia and the Far East, part II country studies. I. British Borneo* (New York: United Nations, January 1947).

Unpublished Manuscripts

Osmeña, Sergio, Jr. 'Dear dad', n.d. (but c. 1947).

Newspapers

Bangkok Post
Daily Telegraph
New York Herald Tribune
New York Times
Shanghai Evening Post
The Economist
The Times

Theses

Anamwathana, Panarat, 'Economic policy and development in Thailand during and after World War II', M.Phil. diss., Oxford University, 2016.

Kurasawa Aiko Inomata, 'Mobilization and control: a study of social change in rural Java, 1942–1945', Ph.D. diss., Cornell University, 1988.
Nazrin, Raja, 'Essays on economic growth in Malaysia in the twentieth century', Ph.D. diss., Harvard University, 2000.
Prasertkul, Seksan, 'The transformation of the Thai state and economic change, 1855–1945', Ph.D. diss., Cornell University, 1989.
Sugimoto Ichiro, 'Economic growth of Singapore in the twentieth century', Ph.D. diss., University of Malaya, Kuala Lumpur, 2008.
Twang Peck Yang, 'Indonesian Chinese business communities in transition', Ph.D. diss., Australian National University, Canberra, 1987.
Vu Ngu Chieu, 'Political and social change in Viet-Nam between 1940 and 1946', Ph.D. diss., University of Wisconsin, Madison, 1984.
Yoon Won Zoon, 'Japan's occupation of Burma, 1941–1945', Ph.D diss., New York University, 1971.

Books and Articles

A Correspondent lately in Burma [Reginald Dorman-Smith], 'Burma: the struggle for power', *Round Table*, 37, 146 (1947), pp. 146–52.
Abeyasekere, Susan, *Jakarta: a history* (Singapore: Oxford University Press, 1989).
Abu Talib Ahmad, 'Japanese policy towards Islam in Malaya during the occupation: a reassessment', *Journal of Southeast Asian Studies*, 33, 1 (2002), pp. 107–22.
Abu Talib Ahmad, *The Malay Muslims, Islam and the rising sun: 1941–1945* (Kuala Lumpur: Malaysian Branch of the Royal Asiatic Society, 2003).
Adas, Michael, *The Burma delta: economic development and social change on an Asian rice frontier, 1852–1941* (Madison, WI: University of Wisconsin Press, 1974).
Agoncillo, Teodoro A., *The fateful years: Japan's adventure in the Philippines, 1941–45*, 2 vols. (Quezon City: R. P. Garcia Publishing Company, 1965).
Aisha Akbar, *Aishabee at war: a very frank memoir* (Singapore: Landmark Books, 1990).
Akashi Yoji, 'Japanese policy towards the Malayan Chinese 1941–1945', *Journal of Southeast Asian Studies*, 1, 2 (1970), pp. 61–89.
Akashi Yoji, 'The Japanese occupation of Malaya: interruption or transformation', in Alfred W. McCoy, ed., *Southeast Asia under Japanese occupation* (New Haven, CT: Yale University Southeast Asia Studies, 1980), pp. 54–74.
Akashi Yoji, 'Bureaucracy and the Japanese military administration with specific reference to Malaya', in William H. Newell, ed., *Japan in Asia, 1942–1945* (Singapore: Singapore University Press, 1981), pp. 46–82.
Akashi Yoji and Yoshimura Mako, eds., *New perspectives on the Japanese occupation in Malaya and Singapore, 1941–1945* (Singapore: NUS Press, 2008).

Aldrich, Richard J., 'A question of expediency: Britain, the United States and Thailand, 1941–42', *Journal of Southeast Asian Studies*, 19, 2 (1988), pp. 209–44.

Aldrich, Richard J., *The key to the south: Britain, the United States and Thailand during the approach of the Pacific War, 1929–1942* (Kuala Lumpur: Oxford University Press, 1993).

Allen, Louis, 'Japanese military rule in Burma', *Modern Asian Studies*, 3, 2 (1969), pp. 177–81.

Allen, Louis, 'Studies in the Japanese occupation of South-East Asia, 1942–1945 (I)', *Durham University Journal*, 63, 1 (1970), pp. 1–15.

Allen, Louis, *The end of the war in Asia* (London: Hart-Davis, MacGibbon, 1976).

Allen, Louis, *Singapore 1941–1942* (London: Davis-Poynter, 1977).

Allen, Louis, *Burma: the longest war 1941–45* (London: J. M. Dent & Sons, 1984).

Allen, Louis, 'The Japanese coup of 9 March 1945 in Indo-China', *1945 in South-East Asia, Part one*, London School of Economics International Studies 1985/116, pp. 1–29.

Allen, Louis, 'The transfer of power in Burma', *Journal of Imperial and Commonwealth History*, 13, 2 (1985), pp. 185–94.

Allen, Louis, 'Burma: the longest war, 1941–45', in Ian Nish and Mark Allen, eds., *War, conflict and security in Japan and Asia-Pacific, 1941–1952: the writings of Louis Allen* (Folkestone: Global Oriental, 2011), pp. 297–305.

Allen, Louis, 'Fujiwara and Suzuki: the Lawrence of Arabia syndrome', in Ian Nish and Mark Allen, eds., *War, conflict and security in Japan and Asia-Pacific, 1941–1952: the writings of Louis Allen* (Folkestone: Global Oriental, 2011), pp. 267–76.

Anderson, Benedict, *Some aspects of Indonesian politics under the Japanese occupation: 1944–1945* (Ithaca, NY: Southeast Asia Program, Department of Far Eastern Studies, Cornell University, 1961).

Anderson, Benedict, 'The languages of Indonesian politics', *Indonesia*, 1 (1966), pp. 89–116.

Anderson, Benedict, 'The problem of rice [Stenographic notes on the fourth session of the Sanyo Kaigi, January 8, 1945]', translated with an introduction by Anderson, *Indonesia*, 2 (1966), pp. 77–123.

Anderson, Benedict, *Java in a time of revolution: occupation and resistance, 1944–1946* (Ithaca, NY: Cornell University Press, 1972).

Anderson, Benedict, 'Review of South-East Asia from colonialism to independence by Jan Pluvier', *Journal of Asian Studies*, 35, 1 (1975), pp. 171–73.

Anderson, Benedict, 'Old state, new society: Indonesia's new order in comparative historical perspective', *Journal of Asian Studies*, 42, 3 (1983), pp. 477–96.

Anderson, Benedict, *Imagined communities: reflections on the origin and spread of nationalism* (London: Verso, 1991).

Anderson, Benedict, *The spectre of comparisons: nationalism, Southeast Asia and the world* (London: Verso, 1998).

Andō Yoshio, ed., *Kindai Nihon keizaishi yōran* [Handbook of modern Japanese economic history], 2nd edn. (Tokyo: University of Tokyo Press, 1979).

Andrus, J. Russell, *Basic problems of relief, rehabilitation and reconstruction in South-East Asia* (New Delhi: Indian Council of World Affairs, 1946).

Andrus, J. Russell, *Burmese economic life* (Stanford, CA: Stanford University Press, 1948).

Anon., 'Monetary situation in the south', *Oriental Economist* (December 1942), pp. 561–62.

Anon., '"Co-prosperity" takes shape', *The Economist* (18 December 1943), pp. 812–13.

Anon., 'Japan's war economy', *The Economist* (6 November 1943), p. 615.

Anon., 'De rijstpositie van Nederlandsch-Indie' [The rice situation in the Dutch Indies], *Economisch Weekblad voor Nederlandsch-Indië*, 12, 11 (25 May 1946), pp. 81–82.

Anon., 'Rijstpellerijen in midden-Java gedurende de Japansche bezetting' [Rice mills in central Java during the Japanese occupation], *Economisch Weekblad voor Nederlandsch-Indië*, 12, 21 (3 August 1946), pp. 93–94.

Anon., 'L'agriculture indochinoise pendant la guerre', *Bulletin de Renseignements Économiques*, 9 (15 April 1947), pp. 17–20; 10 (15 May 1947), pp. 13–16.

Anon., 'Burma: what next?', *Round Table*, 37, 148 (1947), pp. 352–55.

Anon., 'History of railways in Indonesia' (2004), http://keretapi.tripod.com/history.html

Ara Satoshi, 'Food supply problem in Leyte, Philippines, during the Japanese occupation (1942–1944)', *Journal of Southeast Asian Studies*, 39, 1 (2008), pp. 59–82.

Aragon, Lorraine V., '"Japanese time" and the mica mine: occupation experiences in the central Sulawesi highlands', *Journal of Southeast Asian Studies*, 27, 1 (1996), pp. 49–63.

Arita Hachiro, 'The Greater East Asian Sphere of common prosperity', *Contemporary Japan*, 10, 1 (1941), pp. 9–15.

Asakura Kōkichi and Nishiyama Chiaki, eds., *Nihon keizai no kaheiteki bunseki* [A monetary analysis of the Japanese economy] (Tokyo: Sōbunsha, 1974).

Aso, Michitake, *Rubber and the making of Vietnam: an ecological history, 1897–1975* (Chapel Hill, NC: University of North Carolina Press, 2018).

Baker, A. C., 'A general survey of labour problems in Burma', *Burma Labour Gazette*, 2, 4 (April 1949), pp. 2–5.

Bàng Bá Lân, 'They starved, they starved', *Vietnam Forum*, 5 (1985), pp. 101–07.

Banyai, Richard A., *Money and banking in China and Southeast Asia during the Japanese military occupation 1937–1945* (Taipei: Tai Wan Enterprises, 1974).

Barendregt, Jaap, *The Dutch money purge: the monetary consequences of German occupation and their redress after liberation, 1940–1952* (Amsterdam: Thesis Publishers, 1993).

Barkai, Avraham, *Nazi economics: ideology, theory, and policy* (Oxford: Berg, 1990).

Barker, Randolph and Robert W. Herdt, *The rice economy of Asia* (Washington, DC: Resources for the Future, 1985).

Barro, Robert J. and José F. Ursúa, 'Macroeconomic crises since 1870', *Brookings Papers on Economic Activity*, 39, 1 (Spring 2008), pp. 255–335.

Bartholomew-Feis, Dixee R., *The OSS and Ho Chi Minh: unexpected allies in the war against Japan* (Lawrence, KS: University Press of Kansas, 2006).

Bassino, Jean-Pascal, 'Preliminary estimates of Vietnam GDP: north–south economic divide in historical perspective, 1800–1970', in K. Odaka, Y. Kiyokawa and M. Kuboniwa, eds., *Constructing a historical macroeconomic database for the trans-Asian regions* (Tokyo: Hitotsubashi University, 2000), pp. 9–41.

Bassino, Jean-Pascal, *Asian historical statistics: Vietnam* (Tokyo: Toyo Keizai, forthcoming).

Bassino, Jean-Pascal and Séverine Blaise, 'Linking pre-1945 and post-1945 series for estimating North Vietnam and South Vietnam long-term economic performances', in Jean-Pascal Bassino, Jean-Dominique Giacometti, Konosuke Odaka and Suzanne Ruth Clark, eds., *Quantitative economic history of Vietnam 1900–1990* (Tokyo: Hitotsubashi University Institute of Economic Research, 2000), pp. 409–28.

Bassino, Jean-Pascal and Pierre van der Eng, 'Asia's "little divergence" in the twentieth century: evidence from PPP-based direct estimates of GDP per capita, 1913–69', *Economic History Review*, 73, 1 (2020), pp. 185–208.

Bastin, John and Harry J. Benda, *A history of modern Southeast Asia* (Englewood Cliffs, NJ: Prentice Hall, 1968).

Batson, Benjamin A., 'The fall of the Phibun government, 1944', *Journal of the Siam Society* 62, 2 (1974), pp. 89–120.

Batson, Benjamin A., 'Siam and Japan: the perils of independence', in Alfred W. McCoy, ed., *Southeast Asia under Japanese occupation* (New Haven, CT: Yale University Southeast Asia Studies, 1980), pp. 221–50.

Batson, Benjamin A. and Shimizu Hajime, *The tragedy of Wanit: a Japanese account of wartime Thai politics* (Singapore: Southeast Asian Studies Special Publications, 1990).

Bauchar, R., *Raffles sur l'Indochine* (Paris: L. Fournier, 1946).

Bauer, P. T., 'Some aspects of the Malayan rubber slump 1929–1933', *Economica*, 11 (1944), pp. 190–98.

Bauer, P. T., *The rubber industry: a study in competition and monopoly* (Cambridge, MA: Harvard University Press, 1948).

Bayly, Christopher and Tim Harper, *Forgotten armies: the fall of the British in Asia, 1941–1945* (London: Allen Lane, 2004).

Bayly, Christopher and Tim Harper, *Forgotten wars: freedom and revolution in Southeast Asia* (Cambridge, MA: Harvard University Press, 2007).

Beasley, W. G., *Japanese imperialism 1894–1945* (Oxford: Clarendon Press, 1987).

Beckett, Jeremy, 'The defiant and the compliant: the *datus* of Magindanao under colonial rule', in Alfred W. McCoy and Ed. C. de Jesus, eds., *Philippine social history: global trade and local transformations* (Honolulu: University of Hawaii Press, 1982), pp. 391–414.

Benda, Harry J., 'Indonesian Islam under Japanese occupation', *Pacific Affairs*, 28, 4 (1955), pp. 350–62.

Benda, Harry J., *The crescent and the rising sun: Indonesian Islam under Japanese occupation 1942–1945* (The Hague: W. van Hoeve, 1958).

Benda, Harry J., 'The structure of Southeast Asian history: some preliminary observations', *Journal of Southeast Asian History*, 3, 1 (1962), pp. 106–38.

Benda, Harry J., 'Decolonization in Indonesia: the problem of continuity and change', *American Historical Review*, 70, 4 (1965), pp. 1,058–73.

Benda, Harry J., 'The pattern of administrative reforms in the closing years of Dutch rule in Indonesia', *Journal of Asian Studies*, 25, 4 (1966), pp. 589–605.

Benda, Harry J., 'The Japanese interregnum in Southeast Asia', in Grant K. Goodman, ed., *Imperial Japan: a reassessment* (New York: East Asian Institute, Columbia University, 1967), pp. 65–79.

Benda, Harry J., 'The beginnings of the Japanese occupation in Java', in Harry J. Benda, *Continuity and change in Southeast Asia* (New Haven, CT: Yale University Southeast Asian Studies, 1972), pp. 63–82.

Benda, Harry J., James K. Irikura and Kishi Koichi, eds., *Japanese military administration in Indonesia: selected documents* (New Haven, CT: Yale University Southeast Asia Studies, 1965).

Benham, Frederic, *The national income of Malaya, 1947–49 (with a note on 1950)* (Singapore: Government Printing Office, 1951).

Bernardini, Jean-J., *Sous la botte Nippone* (Paris: Editions de la Pensée Universelle, 1971).

Bernholz, Peter, 'Currency substitution during hyperinflation in the Soviet Union 1922–1924', *Journal of European Economic History*, 25, 2 (1996), pp. 297–323.

Berreman, Joel V., 'The Japanization of far eastern occupied areas', *Pacific Affairs*, 17, 2 (1944), pp. 168–80.

Biggs, David, *Quagmire: nation-building and nature in the Mekong delta* (Seattle, WA: University of Washington Press, 2010).

Bisson, T. A., *Japan's war economy* (New York: Institute of Pacific Relations, 1945).

Bix, Herbert P., 'Japanese imperialism and the Manchurian economy, 1900–31', *China Quarterly*, 51 (1972), pp. 425–43.

Blackburn, Kevin and Karl Hack, *War memory and the making of modern Malaysia and Singapore* (Singapore: NUS Press, 2012).

Blanchard, Olivier, Alessia Amighini and Francesco Giavazzi, *Macroeconomics: a European perspective* (Harlow: Prentice Hall, 2010).

Bloc, Henry Simon and Bert F. Hoselitz, *Economics of military occupation: selected problems*, revised edn. (Chicago, IL: University of Chicago Press, 1944).

Boissarie, Delphine, 'Indochina during World War II: an economy under Japanese control', in Marcel Boldorf and Tetsuji Okazaki, eds., *Economies under occupation: the hegemony of Nazi Germany and Imperial Japan in World War II* (London: Routledge, 2015), pp. 232–44.

Boldorf, Marcel and Tetsuji Okazaki, eds., *Economies under occupation: the hegemony of Nazi Germany and Imperial Japan in World War II* (London: Routledge, 2015).

Booth, Anne, *The Indonesian economy in the nineteenth and twentieth centuries* (London: Macmillan, 1998).

Booth, Anne, *Economic change in modern Indonesia: colonial and post-colonial comparisons* (Cambridge: Cambridge University Press, 2016).

Bose, Sugata, 'Starvation amidst plenty: the making of famine in Bengal, Honan and Tonkin, 1942–45', *Modern Asian Studies*, 24, 4 (1990), pp. 699–727.

Boulding, Kenneth E. and Alan H. Gleason, 'War as an investment: the strange case of Japan', in Kenneth E. Boulding and Tapan Mukerjee, eds., *Economic imperialism: a book of readings* (Ann Arbor, MI: University of Michigan Press, 1972), pp. 240–61.

Bourne, Geoffrey H., 'Nutrition work in Malaya under the British Military Administration', *International Review of Vitamin Research*, 21 (1949), pp. 265–307.

Boyce, Robert and Esmonde M. Robertson, eds., *Paths to war: new essays on the origins of the Second World War* (London: Macmillan, 1989).

Brennan, Lance, Les Heathcote and Anton Lucas, 'War and famine around the Indian Ocean during the Second World War', *Research in Ethical Issues in Organizations*, 18 (2017), pp. 5–70.

Broadberry, Stephen and Mark Harrison, eds., *The economics of World War I* (Cambridge: Cambridge University Press, 2005).

Brocheux, Pierre, *The Mekong delta: ecology, economy and revolution, 1860–1960* (Madison, WI: Center for Southeast Asian Studies, University of Wisconsin, 1995).

Brocheux, Pierre, 'The economy of war as a prelude to a "socialist economy": the case of Vietnamese resistance against the French', in Pierre Brocheux and Gisele Bousquet, eds., *Viêt Nam exposé: French scholarship on twentieth-century Vietnamese society* (Ann Arbor, MI: University of Michigan Press, 2002), pp. 313–30.

Brocheux, Pierre, *Ho Chi Minh: a biography* (Cambridge: Cambridge University Press, 2007).

Brocheux, Pierre, *Une histoire économique du Viet Nam 1850–2007: la palanche et le camion* (Paris: les Indes savants, 2009).

Brocheux, Pierre and Daniel Hémery, *Indochina: an ambiguous colonization 1858–1954* (Berkeley, CA: University of California Press, 2009).

Brodrick, Alan Houghton, *Beyond the Burma road* (London: Hutchinson & Co., 1944).

Broek, Jan O. M., 'Diversity and unity in Southeast Asia', *Geographical Review*, 34, 2 (1944), pp. 175–95.

Brown, Ian, 'British firms and the end of empire in Burma', *Asian Affairs*, 40, 1 (2009), pp. 16–33.

Brown, Ian, 'The economics of decolonization in Burma', in Toyin Falola and Emily Brownell, eds., *Africa, empire and globalization: essays in honor of A. G. Hopkins* (Durham, NC: Carolina Academic Press, 2011), pp. 433–44.

Brown, Ian, *Burma's economy in the twentieth century* (New York: Cambridge University Press, 2013).

Brugmans, I. J., *Nederlandsch-Indië onder Japanse bezetting: gegevens en documenten over de Jaren 1942–1945* [The Dutch East Indies under Japanese occupation: data and documents for the years 1942–1945] (Franeker, 1960).

Buencamino, Victor, *Memoirs of Victor Buencamino* (Mandaluyong, Metro Manila: Jorge B. Vargas Filipiniana Foundation, 1977).

Buencamino, Victor, 'Manila under Japanese occupation (January 1–April 30, 1942), *Bulletin of the American Historical Collection*, 7, 3–4 (1979), pp. 7–29.

Bui Minh Dung, 'Japan's role in the Vietnamese starvation of 1944–45', *Modern Asian Studies*, 29, 3 (1995), pp. 573–618.

Butcher, John G., *The British in Malaya 1880–1941* (Kuala Lumpur: Oxford University Press, 1979).

Butow, Robert J. C., *Tojo and the coming of the war* (Princeton, NJ: Princeton University Press, 1961).

Cagan, Philip, 'The monetary dynamics of hyperinflation', in Milton Friedman, ed., *Studies in the quantity theory of money* (Chicago, IL: University of Chicago Press, 1956), pp. 25–117.

Callahan, Mary P., *Making enemies: war and state building in Burma* (Ithaca, NY: Cornell University Press, 2003).

Callis, Helmut G., *Foreign capital in Southeast Asia* (New York: Institute of Pacific Relations, 1942).

Campbell, Bruce M. S., 'Nature as historical protagonist: environment and society in pre-industrial England', *Economic History Review*, 63, 2 (2010), pp. 281–314.

Carter, Susan B., Scott Sigmund Gartner, Michael Haines, Alan Olmstead, Richard Sutch and Gavin Wright, eds., *Historical statistics of the United States: earliest times to the present*, 5 vols. (Cambridge: Cambridge University Press, 2006).

Catling, David, *Rice in deep water* (London: Palgrave Macmillan/International Rice Research Institute, 1992).

Catton, Philip E., *Diem's final failure: prelude to America's war in Vietnam* (Lawrence, KS: University Press of Kansas, 2002).

Chandler, David, 'Legacies of World War II in Indochina', in David Koh Wee Hock, ed., *Legacies of World War II in South and East Asia* (Singapore: Institute of Southeast Asian Studies, 2007), pp. 23–35.

Chandler, David P., *A history of Cambodia*, 4th edn. (Boulder, CO: Westview Press, 2008).

Chandler, David P., Robert Cribb and Li Narangoa, eds., *End of empire: 100 days in 1945 that changed Asia and the world* (Copenhagen: Nordic Institute of Asian Studies, 2016).

Chao Kang, *The economic development of Manchuria: the rise of a frontier economy* (Ann Arbor, MI: Center for Chinese Studies, University of Michigan, 1982).

Chapman, F. Spencer, 'Travels in Japanese-occupied Malaya', *Geographical Journal*, 110, 1–3 (1947), pp. 17–36.

Chapman, F. Spencer, *The jungle is neutral* (London: Chatto and Windus, 1949).

Charney, Michael W. and Atsuko Naono, 'The Burmese economy under the Japanese occupation', in Marcel Boldorf and Tetsuji Okazaki, eds., *Economies under occupation: the hegemony of Nazi Germany and Imperial Japan in World War II* (London: Routledge, 2015), pp. 218–31.

Chaya, Prem and Alethea, *The passing hours: a record of five amazing years* (Bangkok: Chatra Books, 1945).

Cheah Boon Kheng, 'Sino-Malay conflicts in Malaya: communist vendetta and Islamic resistance', *Journal of Southeast Asian Studies*, 12, 1 (1981), pp. 108–17.

Cheah Boon Kheng, *Red star over Malaya: resistance and conflict during and after the Japanese occupation, 1941–1946*, 3rd edn. (Singapore: Singapore University Press, 2003).

Chen, King C., *Vietnam and China 1938–54* (Princeton, NJ: Princeton University Press, 1969).

Cheng Siok-Hwa, *The rice industry of Burma 1852–1940* (Kuala Lumpur: University of Malaya Press, 1968).

Chesneaux, Jean, *The Vietnamese nation: contribution to a history* (Sydney: Current Book Distributors, 1966).

Chaiyasoot, Naris, 'Commercial banking', in Peter G. Warr, ed., *The Thai economy in transition* (Cambridge: Cambridge University Press, 1993).

Chickering, Roger, Stig Förster and Bernd Greiner, *A world at total war: global conflict, and the politics of destruction, 1937–1945* (Cambridge: Cambridge University Press, 2005).

Chin Kee Onn, *Malaya upside down* (Singapore: Jitts & Co., 1946).

Chinese commercial directory of Singapore, Penang, Malacca, Kuala Lumpur, Batu Pahat, Maur (Singapore: Nanyang Advertising, 1932).

Chou Shun-Hsin, *The Chinese inflation 1937–1949* (New York: Columbia University Press, 1963).

Christian, John L., *Burma* (London: Collins, 1945).

Christian, John L., *Burma and the Japanese invader* (Bombay: Thacker and Company, 1945).

Christie, Clive J., *A modern history of Southeast Asia: decolonization, nationalism and separatism* (London: L. B. Tauris, 1996).

Chung Chin-Sung, 'The origin and development of military sexual slavery in imperial Japan', in Paul H. Kratoska, ed., *Asian labor in the wartime Japanese Empire* (Armonk, NY: M. E. Sharpe, 2005), pp. 303–25.

Churchill, W. S., *The hinge of fate* (London: Cassell, 1951).

Clark, Grover, *The balance sheets of imperialism: facts and figures on colonies* (New York: Columbia University Press, 1936).

Clutterbuck, Richard, *Riot and revolution in Singapore and Malaya 1945–1963* (London: Faber and Faber, 1973).
Cohen, Jerome B., *Japan's economy in war and reconstruction* (Minneapolis, MN: University of Minnesota Press, 1949).
Cole, D. H., *Imperial military geography: general characteristics of the Empire in relation to defence*, 7th edn. (London: Sifton Praed & Co., 1933).
Collingham, Lizzie, *The taste of war: World War II and the battle for food* (London: Allen Lane, 2011).
Collis, Maurice, *Last and first in Burma (1941–1948)* (London: Faber and Faber, 1956).
Commodity Research Bureau, *Commodity year book 1939* (New York: Commodity Research Bureau, 1939).
Coox, Alvin D., 'The Pacific War', in Peter Duus, ed., *The Cambridge history of Japan*, vol. 6: *The twentieth century* (Cambridge: Cambridge University Press, 1989), pp. 315–82.
Costello, John, *The Pacific War* (London: Pan Books, 1985).
Cramb, R. A., 'Agriculture and food supplies during the Japanese occupation', in Paul H. Kratoska, ed., *Food supplies and the Japanese occupation of Southeast Asia* (Houndmills: Macmillan, 1998), pp. 135–66.
Cressey, Paul F., *Rangoon: a brief social survey* (Rangoon: Rangoon Gazette, 1950).
Cressey, Paul F., 'The ecological organization of Rangoon, Burma', *Sociology and Social Research*, 40, 3 (1956), pp. 166–69.
Cribb, Robert, 'Political dimensions of the currency question 1945–1947', *Indonesia*, 31 (1981), pp. 113–36.
Cribb, Robert, *Gangsters and revolutionaries: the Jakarta people's militia and the Indonesian revolution 1945–1949* (Honolulu: University of Hawaii Press, 1991).
Cribb, Robert, 'Institutions', in Peter Post et al., eds., *The encyclopedia of Indonesia in the Pacific War* (Leiden: Brill, 2009), pp. 102–13.
Crosby, Josiah, 'Observations on a post-war settlement in South-East Asia', *International Affairs*, 20, 3 (1944), pp. 357–68.
Crosby, Josiah, *Siam: the crossroads* (London: Hollis & Carter, 1945).
Crouch, Harold, *The army and politics in Indonesia* (Ithaca, NY: Cornell University Press, 1978).
Crowley, James B., *Japan's quest for autonomy: national security and foreign policy, 1930–1938* (Princeton, NJ: Princeton University Press, 1966).
Crowley, James B., 'A new Asian order: some notes on prewar Japanese nationalism', in Bernard Silberman and Harry Harootunian, eds., *Japan in crisis: essays on Taishō democracy* (Princeton, NJ: Princeton University Press, 1974), pp. 270–98.
Crozier, Brian, *The rebels: a study of post-war insurrections* (London: Chatto and Windus, 1960).
Cruz, Eugenio E., 'The Philippine fiber industry', in Philippines, Bureau of Agriculture, *A half-century of Philippine agriculture* (Manila: Bureau of Agriculture, 1952), pp. 115–46.

'D. S. E.', 'Mise au point sur la situation actuelle de l'économie indochinoise', *Bulletin Économique de l'Indochine*, part 1 (February 1943), pp. 1–13.

Daniels, Gordon, ed., *A guide to the reports of the United States Strategic Bombing Survey, I: Europe, II: The Pacific* (London: Offices of the Royal Historical Society, 1981).

De Boer, M. G. and J. C. Westerman, *Een halve eeuw paketvaart 1891–1941* [Half a century of package shipping 1891–1941] (Amsterdam, 1941).

De Jong, Louis, *The collapse of a colonial society: the Dutch in Indonesia during the Second World War* (Leiden: KITLV Press, 2002).

De Vries, E., 'Vital statistics under Japanese rule', *Economic Review of Indonesia*, 1, 1 (1947), pp. 18–19.

De Vries, W. A. D., 'Tracing removed property', *Economic Review of Indonesia*, 1, 2 (1947), pp. 35–36.

De Young, John E., *Village life in modern Thailand* (Berkeley, CA: University of California Press, 1955).

Decoux, Admiral, *A la barre de l'Indochine: histoire de mon gouvernement général (1940–1945)* (Paris: Plon, 1949).

Department of Economic Affairs, Batavia, 'Economic prospects of the Indonesian islands beyond Java and Sumatra', *Economic Review of Indonesia*, 1, 1 (1947), pp. 1–8.

Department of Economic Affairs, Batavia, 'Produce shipped by the Japanese from the Netherlands Indies', *Economic Review of Indonesia*, 1, 3 (1947), pp. 54–56.

Department of Economic Affairs, Batavia, 'The economic condition of Indonesia in mid-1947', *Economic Review of Indonesia*, 1, 8 (1947), pp. 117–30.

Department of Economic Affairs, Batavia, 'The export of pre-war agrarian produce during the Japanese occupation', *Economic Review of Indonesia*, 1, 10 (1947), pp. 163–69.

Department of Economic Affairs, Batavia, 'The industries of the Indies since the Japanese capitulation', *Economic Review of Indonesia*, 1, 2 (1947), pp. 21–24.

Department of Economic Affairs, Batavia, 'The native agriculture and its recovery', *Economic Review of Indonesia*, 1, 11 (1947), pp. 165–69.

Department of Economic Affairs, Batavia, 'The rice production in Indonesia', *Economic Review of Indonesia*, 1, 1 (1947), pp. 9–12.

Department of Economic Affairs, Batavia, 'Industrial recovery in Indonesia', *Economic Review of Indonesia*, 2, 10 (1948), pp. 161–70.

Department of Economic Affairs, Batavia, 'The recovery of the Java sugar industry', *Economic Review of Indonesia*, 2, 2 (1948), pp. 17–23.

Department of Economic Affairs, Batavia, 'Economic data on Indonesia to the end of 1948', *Economic Review of Indonesia*, 3, 1 (1949), pp. 5–22.

Devillers, Philippe, *Histoire du Viêt-Nam de 1940 à 1952* (Paris: Éditions du Seuil, 1952).

Dick, Howard, 'Japan's economic expansion in the Netherlands Indies between the first and second world wars', *Journal of Southeast Asian Studies*, 20, 2 (1989), pp. 244–72.

Dick, Howard, *Surabaya, city of work: a socioeconomic history, 1900–2000* (Athens, OH: Ohio University Press, 2002).

Dick, Howard, Vincent J. H. Houben, J. Thomas Lindblad and Thee Kian Wee, *The emergence of a national economy: an economic history of Indonesia, 1800–2000* (Leiden: KITLV Press, 2002).

Do Phong Chau, 'La famine de 1944–1945 au Tonkin', *Magazine Good Morning* (February 2011), http://aejjrsite.free.fr/goodmorning/gm118/gm118_LafamineDe1944-45.pdf

Dobby, E. H. G., *Monsoon Asia* (London: University of London Press, 1961).

Dobby, E. H. G., *Southeast Asia*, 9th edn. (London: University of London Press, 1966).

Doeppers, Daniel F., *Manila 1940–1941: social change in a late colonial metropolis* (Manila: Manila University Press, 1984).

Donnison, F. S. V., *British military administration in the Far East 1943–1946* (London: Her Majesty's Stationery Office, 1956).

Dorman-Smith, Reginald, 'Civil government under invasion conditions', *Journal of the United Services Institute of India*, 73 (1943), pp. 240–52.

Dorman-Smith, Reginald, 'Burma', *United Empire* (November–December 1946), pp. 259–65.

Dower, John, *War without mercy: race and power in the Pacific War* (New York: Pantheon Books, 1986).

Dower, John, 'Race, language, and war in two cultures', in John Dower, *Japan in war and peace: essays on history, culture and peace* (London: Harper Collins, 1995), pp. 257–85.

Dower, John, *Embracing defeat: Japan in the aftermath of World War II* (London: Penguin, 1999).

Drabble, John H., *Malayan rubber: the interwar years* (Houndmills: Macmillan, 1991).

Drake, P. J., 'Natural resources versus foreign borrowing in economic development', *Economic Journal*, 82 (1972), pp. 951–62.

Drea, Edward J., *Japan's imperial army: its rise and fall, 1853–1945* (Lawrence, KS: University Press of Kansas, 2009).

Duiker, William J., *The communist road to power in Vietnam*, 2nd edn. (Boulder, CO: Westview Press, 1996).

Duiker, William J., *Ho Chi Minh: a life* (New York: Hyperion, 2000).

Dunlop, E. E., *The war diaries of Weary Dunlop: Java and the Burma–Thailand railway, 1942–1945* (London: Viking, 1989).

Duus, Peter, 'Imperialism without colonies: the vision of a Greater East Asia Co-Prosperity Sphere', *Diplomacy & Statecraft*, 7, 1 (1996), pp. 54–72.

Duus, Peter and Daniel I. Okimoto, 'Comment: Fascism and the history of pre-war Japan: the failure of a concept', *Journal of Asian Studies*, 39, 1 (1979), pp. 65–76.

Earhart, David C., *Certain victory: images of World War II in the Japanese media* (Armonk, NY: M. E. Sharpe, 2008).

Eckert, Carter J., *Offspring of empire: the Koch'ang Kims and the colonial origins of Korean capitalism, 1876–1945* (Seattle, WA: University of Washington Press, 1991).

Edelstein, Michael, 'War and the American economy in the twentieth century', in Stanley L. Engerman and Robert E. Gallman, eds., *The Cambridge economic history of the United States*, vol. 3 (Cambridge: Cambridge University Press, 2000), pp. 329–405.

Ellis, John, *The World War II databook: the essential facts and figures for all the combatants* (London: Aurum, 1993).

Ellman, Michael, 'The 1947 Soviet famine and the entitlement approach to famines', *Cambridge Journal of Economics*, 24, 5 (2000), pp. 603–30.

Elsbree, Willard H., *Japan's role in Southeast Asian nationalist movements 1940–1945* (New York: Institute of Pacific Relations, 1953).

Emerson, Rupert, Lennox A. Mills and Virginia Thompson, *Government and nationalism in Southeast Asia* (New York: Institute of Pacific Relations, 1942).

Emery, Robert F., *The financial institutions of Southeast Asia* (New York: Praeger, 1970).

Emmerson, Donald K., '"Southeast Asia": what's in a name', *Journal of Southeast Asian Studies*, 15, 1 (1984), pp. 1–21.

Fagan, Brian, 'The social history of a central Luzon barrio', in Alfred W. McCoy and Ed. C. de Jesus, eds., *Philippine social history: global trade and local transformations* (Honolulu: University of Hawaii Press, 1982), pp. 91–129.

Fall, Bernard B., 'Indochina since Geneva', *Pacific Affairs*, 28, 1 (1955), pp. 3–25.

Farrell, Brian P., *The defence and fall of Singapore 1940–1942* (Stroud: Tempus, 2005).

Fear, Sean A., 'The ambiguous legacy of Ngô Đình Diệm in South Vietnam's Second Republic (1967–1975)', *Journal of Vietnamese Studies*, 11, 1 (2016), pp. 1–75.

Feeny, David, *The political economy of productivity: Thai agricultural development 1880–1975* (Vancouver: University of British Columbia Press, 1982).

Feis, Herbert, *The road to Pearl Harbor: the coming of the war between the United States and Japan* (Princeton, NJ: Princeton University Press, 1950).

Feis, Herbert, *Japan subdued: the atomic bomb and the end of the war in the Pacific* (Princeton, NJ: Princeton University Press, 1961).

Feith, Herbert, *The decline of constitutional democracy in Indonesia* (Ithaca, NY: Cornell University Press, 1962).

Femor, Sir Lewis Leigh, 'Burma's mineral resources and the war', *Asiatic Review*, 37 (1941), pp. 154–66.

Fenichel, A. H. and Gregg Huff, *The impact of colonialism on Burmese economic development* (Montreal: McGill Centre for Developing Area Studies, 1971).

Fenichel, A. H. and Gregg Huff, 'Colonialism and the political economy of an independent Burma', *Modern Asian Studies*, 9 (1975), pp. 321–35.

Fenoaltea, Stefano, 'Slavery and supervision in comparative perspective: a model', *Journal of Economic History*, 44, 3 (1984), pp. 635–68.

Ferguson, Bernard, 'Upper Burma, 1943–44', *Geographical Journal*, 57, 1–2 (1946), pp. 1–10.

Ferrara, Frederico, *The political development of modern Thailand* (Cambridge: Cambridge University Press, 2015).

Fine, Herbert A., 'The liquidation of World War II in Thailand', *Pacific Historical Review*, 34, 1 (1965), pp. 65–82.

Firth, Raymond, 'Economics of a Malayan fishing industry', *Man*, 41 (1941), pp. 69–73.

Firth, Raymond, 'The coastal people of Kelantan and Trengganu, Malaya', *Geographical Journal*, 101, 5/6 (1943), pp. 193–210.

Firth, Raymond, *Malay fishermen: their peasant economy*, 2nd edn. (London: Routledge & Kegan Paul, 1966).

Firth, Rosemary, *Housekeeping among Malay peasants*, 2nd edn. (London: Athlone Press, 1966).

Fischer, Stanley, 'Seigniorage and the case for a national money', *Journal of Political Economy*, 90, 2 (1982), pp. 295–313.

Fisher, Charles A., 'The Thailand–Burma railway', *Economic Geography*, 23, 2 (1947), pp. 85–97.

Fisher, Charles A., 'The railway geography of British Malaya', *Scottish Geographical Magazine*, 64, 3 (1948), pp. 123–36.

Fisher, Charles A., *South-east Asia: a social, economic and political geography* (London: Methuen, 1964).

Fisher, Charles A., 'Economic myth and geographical reality in Indonesia', *Modern Asian Studies*, 1 (1967), pp. 155–89.

Frederick, William H., *Visions and heat: the making of the Indonesian revolution* (Athens, OH: Ohio University Press, 1989).

Freedman, Maurice, *Chinese family and marriage in Singapore* (London: HMSO, 1957).

French, Paul, *China Rhyming*, www.chinarhyming.com/2011/05/08/the-wartime-burma-road-map/

Friedman, Milton, 'Price, income, and monetary changes in three wartime periods', *American Economic Review*, 42, 2 (1952), pp. 612–25.

Friend, Theodore, 'The Philippine sugar industry and the politics of independence, 1929–1935', *Journal of Asian Studies*, 22, 2 (1963), pp. 179–92.

Friend, Theodore, *Between two empires: the ordeal of the Philippines 1929–1946* (New Haven, CT: Yale University Press, 1965).

Friend, Theodore, *The blue-eyed enemy: Japan against the West in Java and Luzon, 1942–1945* (Princeton, NJ: Princeton University Press, 1988).

Friend, Theodore, *Indonesian destinies* (Cambridge, MA: Harvard University Press, 2003).

Fruin, Thomas A., *Het Economisch Aspect van het Indonesisch Vraagstuk* [The economic aspect of the Indonesian issue] (Amsterdam: Vrij Nederland, 1947).

Fryer, D. W., 'The "million city" in Southeast Asia', *Geographical Review*, 43, 4 (1953), pp. 474–94.

Fujiwara Akira, *Uejini shita eiyūtachi* [The spirit of heroes starved to death] (Tokyo: Aoki Shoten, 2001).

Furnivall, J. S., 'The political economy of the tropical Far East', *Journal of the Royal Central Asiatic Society*, 29, 3–4 (1942), pp. 195–210.

Furnivall, J. S., *Colonial policy and practice: a comparative study of Burma and Netherlands India* (Cambridge: Cambridge University Press, 1948).

Furnivall, J. S., 'Twilight in Burma: independence and after', *Pacific Affairs*, 22, 2 (1949), pp. 155–72.

Furnivall, J. S., *An introduction to the political economy of Burma*, 3rd edn. (Rangoon: Peoples' Literature Committee & House, 1957).

Furuta Motoo, 'A survey of village conditions during the 1945 famine in Vietnam', in Paul H. Kratoska, ed., *Food supplies and the Japanese occupation of Southeast Asia* (Houndmills: Macmillan, 1998), pp. 227–37.

Gallman, Robert E., 'Gross national product in the United States, 1834–1909', in Dorothy S. Brady, ed., *Output, employment, and productivity in the United States after 1800, Studies in Income and Wealth*, vol. 30 (New York: National Bureau of Economic Research, 1966).

Gann, L. H., 'Reflections on the Japanese and German empires of World War II', in Peter Duus, Ramon H. Myers and Mark R. Peattie, eds., *The Japanese wartime empire, 1931–1945* (Princeton, NJ: Princeton University Press, 1996), pp. 335–62.

Garcia, Mauro, *Documents on the Japanese occupation of the Philippines* (Manila: Philippine Historical Association, 1965).

Garcia, Mauro, 'More documents on the Japanese occupation of the Philippines', *Historical Bulletin*, 11, 1 (1967), pp. 73–97, and 11, 2 (1967), pp. 198–226.

Garnaut, Anthony, 'A quantitative description of the Henan famine of 1942', *Modern Asian Studies*, 47, 6 (2013), pp. 2007–45.

Gatrell, Peter and Mark Harrison, 'The Russian and Soviet economies in two world wars: a comparative view', *Economic History Review*, 46, 3 (1993), pp. 425–52.

Gaudel, André, *L'Indochine Française en face du Japon* (Paris: J. Susse, 1947).

Geertz, Clifford, *The religion of Java* (New York: Free Press of Glencoe, 1960).

Geertz, Clifford, *Agricultural involution: the process of ecological change in Indonesia* (Berkeley, CA: University of California Press, 1963).

Geertz, Clifford, *The social history of an Indonesian town* (Cambridge, MA: MIT Press, 1965).

Geertz, Clifford, 'After the revolution: the fate of nationalism in new states', in Clifford Geertz, ed., *The interpretation of cultures: selected essays* (New York: Basic Books, 1973), pp. 234–54.

Geertz, Clifford, 'The integrative revolution: primordial sentiments and civil politics in the new states', in Clifford Geertz, ed., *The interpretation of cultures: selected essays* (New York: Basic Books, 1973), pp. 255–310.

Gellner, Ernest, *Nationalism* (London: Phoenix, 1998).

Gilmour, Andrew, *My role in the rehabilitation of Singapore, 1946–1953* (Singapore: Institute of Southeast Asian Studies, 1973).

Gilmour, O. W., *With freedom to Singapore* (London: Ernest Benn, 1950).

Golay, Frank H., *The Philippines: public policy and economic development* (Ithaca, NY: Cornell University Press, 1961).

Goldsmith, Raymond W., 'The power of victory: munitions output in World War II', *Military Affairs*, 10, 1 (1946), pp. 69–80.

Goldsmith, Raymond W., *The financial development of Japan, 1868–1977* (New Haven, CT: Yale University Press, 1983).

Goodman, Grant K., 'The Japanese occupation of the Philippines: Commonwealth sustained', *Philippine Studies*, 36 (1988), pp. 98–104.

Goodstein, M. E., *The pace and pattern of Philippine economic growth: 1938, 1948 and 1956* (Ithaca, NY: Cornell Southeast Asia Program, data paper no. 48, 1963).

Gorce, Paul-Marie de la, *L'empire écartelé 1936–1946* (Paris: Denoël, 1988).

Goscha, Christopher E., 'Colonial Hanoi and Saigon at war: social dynamics of the Viet Minh's "underground city", 1945–1954', *War in History*, 20, 2 (2013), pp. 222–50.

Goscha, Christopher E., *The Penguin history of modern Vietnam* (London: Allen Lane, 2016).

Goto Ken'ichi, 'Cooperation, submission, and resistance of indigenous elites of Southeast Asia in the wartime empire', in Peter Duus, Raymond H. Myers and Mark Peattie, eds., *The Japanese wartime empire, 1931–1945* (Princeton, NJ: Princeton University Press, 1996), pp. 243–73.

Goto Ken'ichi, *Tensions of empire: Japan and Southeast Asia in the colonial and postcolonial world* (Athens, OH: Ohio University Press, 2003).

Gourou, Pierre, *Les paysans du delta tonkinois, étude de géographie humaine* (Paris: Les Éditions d'Art et d'Histoire, 1936).

Gourou, Pierre, *L'utilisation du sol en Indochine française* (Paris: P. Hartmann, 1940).

Gourou, Pierre, *The standard of living in the delta of the Tonkin (French Indo-China)* (New York: Institute of Pacific Relations, 1945).

Gourou, Pierre, *L'Asie* (Paris: Hachette, 1953).

Gourou, Pierre, *Tropical world* (London: Longmans Green, 1953).

Grajdabzev, A. J., 'Japan's co-prosperity sphere', *Pacific Affairs*, 16, 3 (1943), pp. 311–28.

Grew, Joseph C., *Ten years in Japan: a contemporary record drawn from the diaries and private and official papers of Joseph C. Grew, United States ambassador to Japan 1932–1942* (London: Hammond, Hammond & Company, 1944).

Grist, D. H., *An outline of Malayan agriculture* (Kuala Lumpur: Department of Agriculture, Straits Settlements and Federated Malay States, 1935).

Guglielmo, Mark, 'The contribution of economics to military intelligence during World War II', *Journal of Economic History*, 68, 1 (2008), pp. 109–50.

Gullick, J. M., 'Prelude to merdeka: public administration in Malaya, 1945–1957', *South East Asia Research*, 5, 2 (1997), pp. 155–73.

Gunn, Geoffrey C., 'The great Vietnamese famine of 1944–45 revisited', *Asia-Pacific Journal* 9, 5/4 (2011), www.japanfocus.org/-Geoffrey-Gunn/3483

Gunn, Geoffrey C., *Rice wars in colonial Vietnam: the great famine and the Viet Minh road to power* (Lanham: Rowman and Littlefield, 2014).

Guyot, Dorothy, 'The Burma Independence Army: a political movement in military garb', in Josef Silverstein, ed., *Southeast Asia in World War II: four essays* (New Haven, CT: Yale University Southeast Asia Studies, 1966), pp. 51–65.

Guyot, Dorothy, 'The uses of Buddhism in wartime Burma', *Asian Studies*, 7, 1 (1969), pp. 50–80.

Hack, Karl and Tobias Rettig, *Colonial armies in Southeast Asia* (London: Routledge, 2006).

Haggard, Stephen and Marcus Noland, 'Famine in North Korea redux?', *Journal of Asian Economics*, 20 (2009), pp. 384–95.

Hainsworth, Reginald G. and Raymond T. Moyer, *Agricultural geography of the Philippine Islands* (Washington, DC: United States Department of Agriculture, Office of Foreign Agricultural Relations, 1945).

Hara Akira, 'L'économie Japonaise pendant la deuxième guerre mondiale', *Revue d'histoire de la Deuxième Guerre Mondiale*, 23e Année, no. 89, *La guerre en Asie* (January 1973), pp. 33–56.

Hara Akira, '"Daitōa kyōei ken" no keizai-teki jittai' [The economic reality of the 'Greater East Asia Co-Prosperity Sphere'], *Tochi-seido shigaku*, 71, 3 (1976), pp. 1–28.

Hara Akira, 'Japan: guns before rice', in Mark Harrison, ed., *The economics of World War II* (Cambridge: Cambridge University Press, 1998), pp. 224–67.

Hara Fujio, 'Japan and Malaysian economy: an analysis of the relations started with reparations after the end of World War II', in Hara Fujio, ed., *Formation and restructuring of business groups in Malaysia* (Tokyo: Institute of Developing Economies, 1993), pp. 119–40.

Hardie, Robert, *The Burma-Siam railway: the secret diary of Dr Robert Hardie 1942–45* (London: Imperial War Museum, 1983).

Hardy, Andrew, 'The economics of French rule in Indochina: a biography of Paul Bernard (1892–1960)', *Modern Asian Studies*, 32, 4 (1998), pp. 807–48.

Harper, T. N., *The end of empire and the making of Malaya* (Cambridge: Cambridge University Press, 1999).

Harper, T. N., 'A long view on the great Asian war', in David Koh Wee Hock, ed., *Legacies of World War II in South and East Asia* (Singapore: Institute of Southeast Asian Studies, 2007), pp. 7–20.

Harrison, Mark, *Accounting for war: Soviet production, employment and the defence burden, 1940–1945* (Cambridge: Cambridge University Press, 1996).

Harrison, Mark, ed., *The economics of World War II: six great powers in international comparison* (Cambridge: Cambridge University Press, 1998).

Harrison, Mark, 'The economics of World War II: an overview', in Mark Harrison, ed., *The economics of World War II* (Cambridge: Cambridge University Press, 1998), pp. 1–42.

Harrison, Mark, 'The Soviet Union: the defeated victor', in Mark Harrison, ed., *The economics of World War II* (Cambridge: Cambridge University Press, 1998), pp. 268–301.

Hart, Donn V., 'Guerrilla warfare and the Filipino resistance on Negros island in the Bisayas, 1942–1945', *Journal of Southeast Asian History*, 5, 1 (1964), pp. 101–25.

Hart, G. H. C., 'Recent development in the Netherlands-Indies', *Geographical Journal*, 99, 2 (1942), pp. 81–102.

Hartendorp, A. V. H., *History of industry and trade of the Philippines* (Manila: American Chamber of Commerce of the Philippines, 1958).

Hartendorp, A. V. H., *The Japanese occupation of the Philippines*, 2 vols. (Manila: Bookmark, 1967).

Hata Ikuhiko, 'Continental expansion, 1905–1941', in Peter Duus, ed., *The Cambridge history of Japan*, vol. 6: *The twentieth century* (Cambridge: Cambridge University Press, 1989), pp. 271–314.

Hayami Yujiro, 'Rice policy in Japan's economic development', *American Journal of Agricultural Economics*, 54, 1 (1972), pp. 19–31.

Hayashi Saburo with Alvin D. Coox, *Kogun: the Japanese army in the Pacific War* (Quantico, VA: Marine Corps Association, 1959).

Hayashi Yoko and Hikita Yasuyuki, 'Japanese business in wartime Indonesia', in Peter Post et al., *The encyclopedia of Indonesia in the Pacific War* (Leiden: Brill, 2009), pp. 234–45.

He Wen-Lit, *Syonan interlude* (Singapore: Mandarin Paperbacks, 1991).

Hefner, Robert W., *The political economy of mountain Java: an interpretive history* (Berkeley, CA: University of California Press, 1990).

Henderson, H. D., *Colonies and raw materials* (Oxford: Clarendon Press, 1939).

Hewison, Kevin, *Bankers and bureaucrats: capital and the role of the state in Thailand* (New Haven, CT: Yale University Southeast Asian Studies, 1989).

Hicks, George, *The comfort women* (St Leonards: Allen & Unwin, 1995).

Hicks, George, 'The "comfort women"', in Peter Duus, Ramon H. Myers and Mark R. Peattie, eds., *The Japanese wartime empire, 1931–1945* (Princeton, NJ: Princeton University Press, 1996), pp. 305–23.

Higgins, Benjamin, *Indonesia's economic stabilization and development* (New York: Institute of Pacific Relations, 1957).

Higuchi Hiroshi, *Nihon no tai-Shi tōshi ken'kyū* [Study of Japanese investment in China] (Tokyo: Seikatsu Sha, 1939).

Hikita Yasuyuki, *Nanpō kyōei ken: Senji Nihon no Tōnan Ajia keizai shihai* [Southern Co-prosperity Sphere: Japanese economic control in Southeast Asia during the war] (Tokyo: Taga Shuppan, 1995).

Hikita Yasuyuki, 'Japanese companies' inroads into Indonesia under Japanese military domination', *Bijdragen tot de Taal-, Land- en Volkenkunde*, 152, 4 (1996), pp. 656–98.

Hill, David T., *Journalism and politics in Indonesia: a critical biography of journalist Mochtar Lubis (1922–2004) an editor and author* (London: Routledge, 2010).

Hionidou, Violetta, 'The demography of a Greek famine: Mykonos, 1941–1942', *Continuity and Change*, 10, 2 (1995), pp. 279–99.

Hionidou, Violetta, *Famine and death in occupied Greece, 1941–1944* (Cambridge: Cambridge University Press, 2006).

Hlaing, U Aye, *A study of the economic development of Burma, 1870 –1940* (Rangoon: Department of Economics, University of Rangoon, 1964).

Hlaing, U Aye, 'Trends of economic growth and income distribution in Burma, 1870–1940', *Journal of the Burma Research Society*, 47 (1964), pp. 89–148.

Ho, Samuel P.-S., 'Agricultural transformation under colonialism: the case of Taiwan', *Journal of Economic History*, 28, 3 (1968), pp. 313–40.

Ho, Samuel P.-S., *Economic development of Taiwan* (New Haven, CT: Yale University Press, 1978).

Hoàng Văn Đức, *Comment la révolution a triomphé de la famine (La campagne des cultures sèches en novembre 1945–avril 1946 au Viêt-Nam)* (Hanoi: République Démocratique du Viêt-Nam, Service d'information, 1946).

Hofileña, Josefina D., 'Life in an occupied zone: one Negros planter's experience of war', *Journal of Southeast Asian Studies*, 27, 1 (1996), pp. 82–94.

Honrado, Primo A., 'Philippine sugar: the long view', in Philippines, Bureau of Agriculture, *A half-century of Philippine agriculture* (Manila: Bureau of Agriculture, 1952), pp. 190–98.

Hooley, Richard, 'Long-term growth of the Philippine economy', *Philippine Economic Journal*, 7, 1 (1968), pp. 1–24.

Hooley, Richard, 'A century of Philippine foreign trade: a quantitative analysis', in E. DeDios and R. Fabella, eds., *Choice, growth and development* (Manila: University of the Philippines Press, 1996), pp. 255–303.

Hooley, Richard, 'American economic policy in the Philippines, 1902–1940: exploring a dark age in colonial statistics', *Journal of Asian Economics*, 16 (2005), pp. 464–88.

Horowitz, Donald L., *Ethnic groups in conflict*, 2nd edn. (Berkeley, CA: University of California Press, 2000).

Hovinga, Henk, *The Sumatra railroad: final destination Pakan Baroe 1943–1945* (Leiden: KITLV Press, 2010).

Hoyle, R. W., 'Famine as agricultural catastrophe: the crisis of 1622–4 in east Lancashire', *Economic History Review*, 63, 4 (2010), pp. 974–1002.

Hoyt, Edwin P., *Japan's war: the great Pacific conflict* (New York: McGraw-Hill, 1986).

Hudson, G. F. and Marthe Rajchman, *An explanatory atlas of the Far East* (London: Faber and Faber, 1942).

Huff, Gregg, *The economic growth of Singapore: trade and development in the twentieth century* (Cambridge: Cambridge University Press, 1994).

Huff, Gregg, 'Entitlements, destitution and emigration in the 1930s Singapore great depression', *Economic History Review*, 54, 2 (2001), pp. 290–323.

Huff, Gregg, 'Monetization and financial development in Southeast Asia before the Second World War', *Economic History Review*, 56, 2 (2003), pp. 300–45.

Huff, Gregg, 'Financial transition in Pre-World War II Japan and Southeast Asia', *Financial History Review*, 14, 2 (2007), pp. 149–75.

Huff, Gregg, 'Globalization, natural resources and foreign investment: a view from the resource rich tropics', *Oxford Economic Papers*, 59, 5 (2007), pp. 127–55.

Huff, Gregg, 'Finance and long-term development issues in Southeast Asia', *Asian-Pacific Economic Literature*, 25, 1 (2011), pp. 56–78.

Huff, Gregg, 'Export-led growth, gateway cities and urban systems development in pre-World War II Southeast Asia', *Journal of Development Studies*, 48, 10 (2012), pp. 1431–52.

Huff, Gregg, 'Finance for war in Asia and its aftermath', in Michael Geyer and Adam Tooze, eds., *The Cambridge history of the Second World War*, vol. 3 (Cambridge: Cambridge University Press, 2015), pp. 56–93.

Huff, Gregg, 'Causes and consequences of the Great Vietnam Famine, 1944–1945', *Economic History Review*, 72, 1 (2019), pp. 286–316.

Huff, Gregg, 'The great World War II Vietnam and Java Famines', *Modern Asian Studies*, 72, 1 (2019), pp. 286–316.

Huff, Gregg and Luis Angles, 'Globalization, industrialization and urbanization in pre-World War II Southeast Asia', *Explorations in Economic History*, 48, 1 (2011), pp. 20–36.

Huff, Gregg and Gillian Huff, 'Urban growth and change in 1940s Southeast Asia', *Economic History Review*, 68, 2 (2015), pp. 522–47.

Huff, Gregg and Gillian Huff, 'Substitution in a war-affected economy: Southeast Asia, 1941–1945', *Journal of Asian Cultures*, 18 (2016), pp. 511–24.

Huff, Gregg and Gillian Huff, 'The Second World War Japanese occupation of Singapore', *Journal of Southeast Asian Studies*, 51, 1 and 2 (2020), pp. 243–70.

Huff, Gregg and Shinobu Majima, 'The Japanese occupation of World War II Southeast Asia', *South East Asia Research*, 19, 2 (2011), pp. 848–69.

Huff, Gregg and Shinobu Majima, 'Financing Japan's World War II occupation of Southeast Asia', *Journal of Economic History*, 73, 4 (2013), pp. 938–78.

Huff, Gregg and Shinobu Majima, 'The challenge of finance in World War II Southeast Asia', *War in History*, 22, 2 (2015), pp. 191–210.

Huff, Gregg and Shinobu Majima, trans. and ed., *World War II Singapore: the Chōsabu reports on Syonan* (Singapore: NUS Press, 2018).

Hughes, T. L., *What happened in Burma* (London: Britain Publishing Co., 1945).

Hurstfield, J., *The control of raw materials* (History of the Second World War United Kingdom civil series) (London: HMSO, 1953).

Huỳnh Khánh Kim, 'The Vietnamese August revolution reinterpreted', *Journal of Asian Studies*, 30, 4 (1971), pp. 761–82.

'I. G. M. I.', 'L'effort d'industrialisation de l'Indochine', *Bulletin Économique de l'Indochine*, part 1 (February 1943), pp. 161–93.

Ike, Nobutaka, ed. and trans., *Japan's decision for war: records of the 1941 policy conferences* (Stanford, CA: Stanford University Press, 1967).

Ikehata Setsuho, 'The Japanese occupation period in Philippine history', in Setsuho Ikehata and Ricardo Trota Jose, eds., *The Philippines under Japan: occupation policy and reaction* (Manila: Manila University Press, 1999), pp. 1–20.

Ikehata Setsuho, 'Mining industry development and local anti-Japanese resistance', in Setsuho Ikehata and Ricardo Trota Jose, eds., *The Philippines under Japan: occupation policy and reaction* (Manila: Manila University Press, 1999), pp. 197–61.

Ikehata Setsuhuo and Ricardo Trota Jose, eds., *The Philippines under Japan: occupation policy and reaction* (Manila: Manila University Press, 1999).

Ingram, James C., 'Thailand's rice trade and the allocation of resources', in C. D. Cowan, ed., *The economic development of South-East Asia* (London: George Allen and Unwin, 1964), pp. 102–26.

Ingram, James C., *Economic change in Thailand 1850–1970* (Stanford, CA: Stanford University Press, 1971).

Inouyé Jihei, 'The necessity of foreign trade adjustment', *Contemporary Japan*, 5, 2 (1936), pp. 236–44.

Institute of Social Sciences, *The Nishijima collection: materials on the Japanese military administration in Indonesia* (Tokyo: Waseda University, 1973).

Iriye Akira, 'The failure of military expansionism', in James Morley, ed., *Dilemmas of growth in prewar Japan* (Princeton, NJ: Princeton University Press, 1971), pp. 107–38.

Iriye Akira, *Power and culture: the Japanese-American war 1941–1945* (Cambridge, MA: Harvard University Press, 1981).

Iriye Akira, 'Japan's drive to great power status', in Marius P. Jansen, ed., *The Cambridge history of Japan*, vol. 5: *The nineteenth century* (Cambridge: Cambridge University Press, 1989), pp. 721–82.

Ishii Kanji, Hara Akira and Takeda Haruhito, eds., *Nihon Keizaishi Senji, Sengo-ki* [Japanese economic history, vol. 4, WWII and postwar periods] (Tokyo: Tokyo University Press, 2007).

Isoart, P., ed., *L'Indochine française, 1940–1945* (Paris: Presses Universitaires de France, 1982).

Iwatake Teruhiko, *Nanpō gunseika no keizai shisaku: Malaya, Sumatra, Java no kiroku* [The economic policies in the Southern Regions under the military administration: record of Malaya, Sumatra and Java], 2 vols. (Tokyo: Kyūko Shoin, 1981).

Iwatake Teruhiko, *Nanpō gunsei ronshū* [Essays on southern military administration] (Tokyo: Gan'nandō Shoten, 1989).

'J. V.', 'La hausse des prix en Indochine', *Bulletin Economique de l'ndochine*, I (1942), pp. 28–55.

Jaafar bin Hamzah, 'The Malays in Tasek Gelugur during the Japanese occupation', *Malaysia in History*, 21, 2 (1978), pp. 56–64.

Japan Statistical Association, *Historical statistics of Japan*, 5 vols. (Tokyo, 1987).

Java Rikuyu Sōkyoku Shi Kankōkai, *Java Rikuyu Sōkyoku shi* [History of Java General Bureau of Land Transport] (Tokyo: Java Rikuyu Sōkyokushi Kankōkai, 1976).

Jayanama, Direk, *Siam and World War II* (Bangkok: Social Science Association of Thailand Press, 1978).

Jeffrey, Robin, ed., *Asia – the winning of independence* (Houndmills: Macmillan, 1981).

Jennings, Eric T., *Vichy in the tropics: Pétain's national revolution in Madagascar, Guadeloupe and Indochina, 1940–1944* (Stanford, CA: Stanford University Press, 2001).

Johnson, B. F., *Japanese food management in World War II* (Stanford, CA: Stanford University Press, 1953).

Johnston, David B., 'Rice cultivation in Thailand: the development of an export economy by indigenous capital and labor', *Modern Asian Studies,* 15, 1 (1981), pp. 107–26.

Jones, Clarence F., 'Industrial capacity and supplies of raw materials', in Samuel van Valkenburg, ed., *America and war: a geographical analysis* (New York: Prentice-Hall, 1943), pp. 150–99.

Jones, F. C., *Japan's new order in East Asia: its rise and fall 1937–45* (London: Oxford University Press, 1954).

Jose, Ricardo T., 'Food production and food distribution programmes in the Philippines during the Japanese occupation', in Paul H. Kratoska, ed., *Food supplies and the Japanese occupation of Southeast Asia* (Houndmills: Macmillan, 1998), pp. 67–100.

Jose, Ricardo T., 'The rice shortage and countermeasures during the Japanese occupation', in Ikehata Setsuho and Ricardo Trota Jose, eds., *The Philippines under Japanese occupation* (Manila: Manila University Press, 1999), pp. 197–214.

Jose, Ricardo T., 'Labor usage and mobilization during the Japanese occupation of the Philippines, 1942–45', in Paul H. Kratoska, ed., *Asian labor in the wartime Japanese empire* (Armonk, NY: M. E. Sharpe, 2005), pp. 267–84.

Kahin, George McTurnan, *Nationalism and revolution in Indonesia* (Ithaca, NY: Cornell University Press, 1952).

Kahin, George McTurnan, 'Indonesian politics and nationalism', in William L. Holland, ed., *Asian nationalism and the West* (New York: Macmillan, 1953), pp. 67–196.

Kakizaki Ichiro, *Laying the tracks: the Thai economy and its railways 1885–1935* (Kyoto: Kyoto University Press, 2005).

Kalaw, Maximo M., 'Filipino opposition to the Japanese', *Pacific Affairs,* 18, 4 (1945), pp. 340–45.

Kathigasu, Sybil, *No dram of mercy* (London: Neville Spearman, 1954).

Kawashima Midori, 'The records of the former Japanese army concerning the Japanese occupation of the Philippines', *Journal of Southeast Asian Studies,* 27, 1 (1996), pp. 124–31.

Keppy, Peter, *The politics of redress: war damage compensation and restitution in Indonesia and the Philippines, 1940–1957* (Leiden: KITLV Press, 2020).

Kendrick, John W., *Productivity trends in the United States* (Princeton, NJ: Princeton University Press, 1961).

Kerkvliet, Benedict J. Tria, *The Huk rebellion: a study of peasant revolt in the Philippines* (Berkeley, CA: University of California Press, 1977).

Kerkvliet, Benedict J. Tria, 'Withdrawal and resistance: the political significance of food, agriculture and how people lived during the Japanese occupation in the Philippines', in Laurie J. Sears, ed., *Autonomous histories, particular truths* (Madison, WI: University of Wisconsin Center for Southeast Asian History, 1993), pp. 175–93.

Keukens, Leo, 'With nothing but our lives', http://leokeukens.com/wp-content/uploads/2013/04/java_new_map_medium_colordots.jpg

Keyes, Charles F., 'Buddhist politics and their revolutionary origins in Thailand', *International Political Science Review*, 10, 2 (1989), pp. 121–42.

Keynes, J. M., *A tract on monetary reform*, in *The collected writings of John Maynard Keynes*, vol. 4 (London: Macmillan for the Royal Economic Society, 1971).

Keynes, J. M., 'How to pay for the war', in *The collected writings of John Maynard Keynes*, vol. 9: *Essays in persuasion* (London: Macmillan, 1972).

Keynes, J. M., *The general theory of employment, interest and money*, in *The collected writings of John Maynard Keynes*, vol. 7 (London: Macmillan for the Royal Economic Society, 1973).

Khérian, G., 'Le problème démographique en Indochine', *La Revue Indochinoise: Juridique & Économique*, nos. 1–2, pt. 1 (1937), pp. 3–38.

Khérian, G., 'Les méfaits de la surpopulation deltaïque', *La Revue Indochinoise: Juridique & Économique*, nos. 7–8, pt. 2 (1938), pp. 476–505.

Khin Myo Chit, Daw, *Three years under the Japs* (Sanchaung: Khin Myo Chit, 1945).

Kiernan, Ben, *Việt Nam: a history from the earliest times to the present* (New York: Oxford University Press, 2017).

King, Frank H. H., *Money in British East Asia* (London: HMSO, 1957).

Kirby, William C., 'The Chinese war economy', in James C. Hsiung and Steven I. Levine, eds., *China's bitter victory: the war with Japan 1937–1945* (Armonk, NY: M. E. Sharpe, 1992), pp. 185–212.

Knorr, K. E., *World rubber and its regulation* (Stanford, CA: Stanford University Press, 1945).

Kobayashi Hideo, '"Daitōa kyōei ken" to Nihon kigyō' [Greater East Asian Co-prosperity Sphere and Japanese firms], in Wada Haruki et al., eds., *Higashi Ajia kingendaishi* [East Asian modern history] (Tokyo: Iwanami Shoten, 2011), vol. 6, pp. 102–21.

Koh, David Wee Hock, ed., *Legacies of World War II in South and East Asia* (Singapore: Institute of Southeast Asian Studies, 2007).

Koh, Denis Soo Jin and Tanaka Kyoko, 'Japanese competition in the trade of Malaya in the 1930s', *Journal of Southeast Asian Studies*, 21, 4 (1984), pp. 374–99.

Kornai, János, *The socialist system: the political economy of communism* (Oxford: Clarendon Press, 1992).

Kratoska, Paul H., 'Banana money: consequences of the demonetization of wartime Japanese currency in British Malaya', *Journal of Southeast Asian Studies*, 23, 1 (1992), pp. 322–45.

Kratoska, Paul H., ed., *Food supplies and the Japanese occupation of Southeast Asia* (Houndmills: Macmillan, 1998).

Kratoska, Paul H., ed., *Southeast Asian minorities in the wartime Japanese empire* (London: Routledge, 2002).

Kratoska, Paul H., ed., *Asian labor in the wartime Japanese empire* (Armonk, NY: M. E. Sharpe, 2005).

Kratoska, Paul H., 'Labor in the Malay peninsula and Singapore under Japanese occupation', in Paul H. Kratoska, ed., *Asian labor in the wartime Japanese empire* (Armonk, NY: M. E. Sharpe, 2005), pp. 237–48.

Kratoska, Paul H., *The Japanese occupation of Malaya and Singapore: a social and economic history* (Singapore: NUS Press, 2018).

Kratoska, Paul H. and Ken'ichi Goto, 'Japanese occupation of Southeast Asia', in R. J. B. Bosworth and Joseph Maiolo, eds., *The Cambridge history of the Second World War*, vol. 2: *Politics and ideology* (Cambridge: Cambridge University Press, 2015), pp. 533–57.

Kublin, Hyman, 'The evolution of Japanese colonialism', *Comparative Studies in Society and History*, 2, 1 (1959), pp. 67–84.

Kubo Ryō, 'Higashi Ajia no sō-dōin tōsei' [Total war system in East Asia], in Wada Haruki et al., eds., *Higashi Ajia kingendaishi* [East Asian modern history] (Tokyo: Iwanami Shoten, 2011), vol. 6, pp. 48–72.

Kurasawa Aiko, 'Forced delivery of paddy and peasant uprisings in Indramayu, Indonesia: Japanese occupation and social change', *Developing Economies*, 21, 1 (1983), pp. 52–72.

Kurasawa Aiko, 'Propaganda media on Java under the Japanese 1942–1945', *Indonesia*, 44 (1987), pp. 59–116.

Kurasawa Aiko, 'Rice shortage and transportation', *Bijdragen tot de Taal-, Land- en Volkenkunde*, 152, 4 (1996), pp. 633–55.

Kurasawa Aiko, 'Transportation and rice distribution in Southeast Asia during the Second World War', in Paul H. Kratoska, ed., *Food supplies and the Japanese occupation* (Houndmills: Macmillan, 1998), pp. 32–66.

Kurihara, Kenneth K., *Labor in the Philippine economy* (Stanford, CA: Stanford University Press, 1945).

Kyi, U Khin Maung, 'Western enterprise and economic development in Burma', *Journal of the Burma Research Society*, 53 (1970), pp. 25–49.

Kyi, U Khin Maung, 'Problems of agricultural policy in some trade dependent small countries: a comparative study of Burma and Thailand', *Kajian Economy Malaysia*, 16, 1–2 (1980), pp. 344–62.

'L. A.', 'L'Indochine depuis la guerre', *Bulletin Économique de l'Indochine*, part 1 (February 1942), pp. 1–27.

La Feber, Walter, 'Roosevelt, Churchill, and Indochina: 1942–1945', *American Historical Review*, 80, 5 (1975), pp. 1277–95.

Landon, Margaret, 'Thailand under the Japanese', *Asia and the Americas*, 44, 9 (1944), pp. 389–93.

Lane, Arthur, *Lesser gods, greater devils* (Stockport: Lane Publishers, 1993).

Larkin, John A., 'Philippine history reconsidered: a socioeconomic perspective', *American Historical Review*, 87, 3 (1982), pp. 595–628.

Larkin, John A., *Sugar and the origins of modern Philippine society* (Berkeley, CA: University of California Press, 1993).

Le Manh Hung, *The impact of World War II on the economy of Vietnam 1939–45* (Singapore: Eastern Universities Press, 2004).

Lear, Elmer Norton, *The Japanese occupation of the Philippines, Leyte, 1941–1945* (Ithaca, NY: Southeast Asia Program, Cornell University, 1961).

Lebra, Joyce C., 'Japanese policy and the Indian national army', *Asian Studies*, 7, 2 (1969), pp. 31–49.

Lebra, Joyce C., ed., *Japan's Greater East Asia Co-Prosperity Sphere in World War II* (Kuala Lumpur: Oxford University Press, 1975).

Lebra, Joyce C., 'The significance of the Japanese military model for Southeast Asia', *Pacific Affairs*, 48, 2 (1975), pp. 215–29.

Lebra, Joyce C., *Japanese-trained armies in Southeast Asia* (Singapore: Institute of Southeast Asian Studies, 2010).

Lee Kam Hing, 'Malaya: new state and old elites', in Robin Jeffrey, ed., *Asia: the winning of independence* (Basingstoke: Macmillan, 1981), pp. 213–57.

Lee Kuan Yew, *The Singapore story* (Singapore: Times Editions, 1998).

Lee Say Lee, 'A study of the rice trade in Kedah before and during the Japanese occupation', *Malaysia in History*, 24 (1981), pp. 109–16.

Lee Ting Hui, 'Singapore under the Japanese, 1942–1945', *Journal of the South Seas Society*, 17, 1 (1961), pp. 31–69.

Lent, John A., 'Guerrilla press of the Philippines, 1941–45', *Asian Studies*, 8, 2 (1970), pp. 260–74.

Lester, Richard A., *International aspects of wartime monetary experience*, Princeton Essays in International Finance, no. 3 (Princeton, NJ: International Finance Section, Department of Economics, 1944).

Lester, Richard A., 'Review of Bloc and Hoselitz, *Economics of military occupation*', *American Economic Review*, 34, 2, part 1 (1944), pp. 394–97.

Lewis, W. Arthur, 'Economic development with unlimited supplies of labour', *Manchester School of Economic and Social Studies*, 22, 2 (1954), pp. 139–91.

Li, Lincoln, *The Japanese army in north China, 1937–1941: problems of political and economic control* (Tokyo: Oxford University Press, 1975).

Liberman, Peter, *Does conquest pay?: the exploitation of occupied industrial societies* (Princeton, NJ: Princeton University Press, 1996).

Lim Chong-Yah, *Economic development of modern Malaya* (Kuala Lumpur: Oxford University Press, 1967).

Lim Pui Huen, P., 'Memoirs of the war in Malaya', in Paul H. Kratoska, ed., *Malaya and Singapore during the Japanese occupation* (Singapore: Journal of Southeast Asian Studies, 1995), pp. 121–47.

Lindblad, Thomas J., 'The eclipse of the Indonesian economy under Japanese occupation', in Marcel Boldorf and Tetsuji Okazaki, eds., *Economies under occupation: the hegemony of Nazi Germany and Imperial Japan in World War II* (London: Routledge, 2015), pp. 205–17.

Little, Ian M. D., *Economic development: theory, policy and international relations* (New York: Basic Books, 1982).

Lockard, Craig A., 'John Smail and the Wisconsin search for world history', in Laurie J. Sears, ed., *Autonomous histories, particular truths* (Madison, WI: University of Wisconsin Center for Southeast Asian History, 1993), pp. 261–80.

Lockwood, William W., *The economic development of Japan: growth and structural change* (Princeton, NJ: Princeton University Press, 1968).

Loh, Grace, Goh Chor Boon and Tan Teng Lang, *Building bridges, carving niches* (Singapore: Oxford University Press, 2000).

Longmuir, Marilyn, *The money trail: Burmese currencies in crisis, 1937–1947* (DeKalb: Northern Illinois University Center for Southeast Asian Studies, 2002).

Lotzer, L., 'Notes pour servir à l'histoire du paysan indochinois', *Bulletin Économique de l'Indochine*, part 1 (February 1943), pp. 14–45.

Low, N. I., *When Singapore was Syonan-to* (Singapore: Eastern Universities Press, 1973).

Low, N. I. and H. M. Cheng, *This Singapore (our city of dreadful night)* (Singapore: Ngai Seong Press, 1946).

Lucas, Anton, 'Social revolution in Pemalang, central Java, 1945', *Indonesia*, 24 (1977), pp. 87–122.

Lucas, Anton, *One soul, one struggle: region and revolution in Indonesia* (Sydney: Asian Studies Association of Australia in association with Allen and Unwin, 1991).

MacGregor, R. B., 'Medical history of the war in Malaya', *Medical Journal of Malaya*, 3, 3 (1949), pp. 146–72.

MacIntyre, Kate, 'Famine and the female mortality advantage', in Tim Dyson and Cormac Ó Gráda, *Famine demography: perspectives from the past and present* (Oxford: Oxford University Press, 2002), pp. 240–59.

MacLean, Ken, 'History reformatted: Vietnam's great famine (1944–1945) in archival form', *Southeast Asian Studies*, 5, 2 (2016), pp. 187–218.

Maddison Project Database, version 2013. J. Bolt and J. L. van Zanden, 'The Maddison Project: collaborative research on historical national accounts', *Economic History Review*, 67, 3, pp. 627–51.

Maddison, Angus, *Monitoring the world economy 1820–1992* (Paris: OECD, 1995).

Maddison, Angus, *The world economy: a millennial perspective* (Paris: OECD, 2001).

Maddison, Angus, *The world economy: historical statistics* (Paris: OECD, 2003).

Maddison, Angus, *Historical statistics of the world economy: 1–2008 A.D.*, www.ggdc.net/maddison/Maddison.htm

Maekawa Kaori, 'The *heiho* during the Japanese occupation of Indonesia', in Paul H. Kratoska, ed., *Asian labor in the wartime Japanese Empire* (Armonk, NY: M. E. Sharpe, 2005), pp. 152–78.

Majima Shinobu, 'The Chōsabu: its members and socio-economic research activities, 1942–1943', unpublished ms, July 2017.

Majima Shinobu, 'The Chōsabu members and the Chōsabu reports', in Gregg Huff and Shinobu Majima, trans. and ed., *World War II Singapore: the Chōsabu reports on Syonan* (Singapore: NUS Press, 2018), pp. 47–125.

Makinen, Gail E., 'The Greek hyperinflation and stabilization of 1943–1946', *Journal of Economic History*, 46, 3 (1986), pp. 795–805.

Manarungsan, Sompop, *Economic development of Thailand, 1850–1950: response to the challenge of the world economy* (Groningen: University of Groningen, 1989).

Marr, David G., 'World War II and the Vietnamese revolution', in Alfred W. McCoy, ed., *Southeast Asia under Japanese occupation* (New Haven, CT: Yale University Southeast Asia Studies, 1980), pp. 104–31.

Marr, David G., 'Vietnam: harnessing the whirlwind', in Robin Jeffrey, ed., *Asia: the winning of independence* (Basingstoke: Macmillan, 1981), pp. 163–207.

Marr, David G., *Vietnamese tradition on trial 1920–1945* (Berkeley, CA: University of California Press, 1981).

Marr, David G., 'Vietnam 1945: some questions', *Vietnam Forum*, 6 (1985), pp. 155–93.

Marr, David G., *Vietnam 1945: the quest for power* (Berkeley, CA: University of California Press, 1995).

Marr, David G., *Vietnam: state, war and revolution (1945–1946)* (Berkeley, CA: University of California Press, 2013).

Marshall, Jonathan, *To have and have not: Southeast Asian raw materials and the origins of the Pacific War* (Berkeley, CA: University of California Press, 1995).

Marston, Daniel, ed., *The Pacific War companion: from Pearl Harbor to Hiroshima* (Oxford: Osprey, 2005).

Martin, Bernd and Alan S. Milward, eds., *Agriculture and food supply in the Second World War* (Ostfildern: Scripta Mercaturae, 1985).

Marzouk, G. A., *Economic development and politics: case study of Thailand* (Rotterdam: Rotterdam University Press, 1972).

Matsuoka Yosuké, 'The new order in East Asia', *Contemporary Japan*, 8, 1 (1939), pp. 1–9.

Matsusaka Yoshihisa Tak, 'Managing occupied Manchuria', in Peter Duus, Ramon H. Myers and Mark R. Peattie, eds., *The Japanese wartime empire, 1931–1945* (Princeton, NJ: Princeton University Press, 1996), pp. 97–135.

Matsusaka Yoshihisa Tak, *The making of Japanese Manchuria, 1904–1932* (Cambridge, MA: Harvard University Asia Center, 2001).

Matthiessen, Sven, 'Re-orienting the Philippines: the KALIBAPI party and the application of pan-Asianism, 1942–45', *Modern Asian Studies*, 53, 2 (2019), pp. 560–81.
Maung, E., 'Enemy legislation and judgments in Burma', *Journal of Comparative Legislation and International Law*, 30, 3/4 (1948), pp. 11–17.
Maw, Ba, *Breakthrough in Burma: memories of a revolution, 1939–1946* (New Haven, CT: Yale University Press, 1968).
Mazower, Mark, *Inside Hitler's Greece: the experience of occupation, 1941–44* (New Haven, CT: Yale University Press, 1993).
McCoy, Alfred W., '"Politics by other means": World War II in the Western Visayas, Philippines', in Alfred W. McCoy, ed., *Southeast Asia under Japanese occupation* (New Haven, CT: Yale University Southeast Asia Studies, 1980), pp. 158–203.
McCoy, Alfred W., *Southeast Asia under Japanese occupation* (New Haven, CT: Yale University Southeast Asia Studies, 1980).
McCoy, Alfred W., 'The Philippines: independence without decolonisation', in Robin Jeffrey, ed., *Asia: the winning of independence* (Basingstoke: Macmillan, 1981), pp. 23–65.
McCoy, Alfred W., 'Circles of steel, castles of vanity: the geopolitics of military bases on the South China Sea', *Journal of Asian Studies*, 75, 4 (2016), pp. 975–1017.
McCoy, Alfred W. and Ed. C. de Jesus, eds., *Philippine social history: global trade and local transformations* (Honolulu: University of Hawaii Press, 1982).
McGee, T. G., *The Southeast Asian city: a social geography of the primate cities of Southeast Asia* (London: G. Bell and Sons, 1967).
McIntyre, W. David, 'The strategic significance of Singapore 1917–1942: the naval base and the Commonwealth', *Journal of Southeast Asian History*, 10, 1 (1969), pp. 69–94.
McVey, Ruth, 'The post-revolutionary transformation of the Indonesian army, part I', *Indonesia*, 11 (1971), pp. 131–76.
McVey, Ruth, 'The post-revolutionary transformation of the Indonesian army, part II', *Indonesia*, 13 (1972), pp. 147–81.
Medlicott, W. N., *The economic blockade*, vol. 2 (London: HMSO, 1952).
Merino, Gonzalo, 'Introduction', in Philippines, Bureau of Agriculture, *A half-century of Philippine agriculture* (Manila: Bureau of Agriculture, 1952), pp. ix–xix.
Mickelsen, Martin L., 'A mission of vengeance: Vichy France in Indochina in World War II', *Air Power History*, 55, 3 (2008), pp. 30–45.
Midlarsky, Manus I., *The killing trap: genocide in the twentieth century* (Cambridge: Cambridge University Press, 2005).
Miller, Edward S., *Bankrupting the enemy: the US financial siege of Japan before Pearl Harbor* (Annapolis, MD: Naval Institute Press, 2007).
Mills, Geoffrey and Hugh Rockoff, 'Compliance with price controls in the United States and United Kingdom during World War II', *Journal of Economic History*, 47, 1 (1987), pp. 191–213.
Milward, Alan S., *The German economy at war* (London: Athlone Press, 1965).

Milward, Alan S., *The new order and the French economy* (Oxford: Clarendon Press, 1970).

Milward, Alan S., *The fascist economy in Norway* (Oxford: Clarendon Press, 1972).

Milward, Alan S., *War, economy and society, 1939–1945* (London: Allen Lane, 1977).

Mimura, Janis, *Planning for empire: reform bureaucrats and the Japanese wartime state* (Ithaca, NY: Cornell University Press, 2011).

Mitchell, B. R., *International historical statistics: Africa, Asia and Oceania 1750–2000*, 4th edn. (Houndmills: Palgrave Macmillan, 2003).

Mitchell, Kate L., *Industrialization in the western Pacific* (New York: Institute of Pacific Relations, 1942).

Mitter, Rana, *China's war with Japan, 1937–1945: the struggle for survival* (London: Allen Lane, 2013).

Modder, Ralph, *The Singapore Chinese massacre: 18 February to 4 March 1942* (Singapore: Horizon Books, 2004).

Morley, James William, ed., *The fateful choice: Japan's advance into Southeast Asia, 1939–1941* (New York: Columbia University Press, 1980).

Murashima Eiji, 'Commemorative character of Thai historiography: the 1942–43 Thai military campaign in the Shan states depicted as a story of national salvation and the restoration of Thai independence', *Modern Asian Studies*, 40, 4 (2006), pp. 1053–97.

Murashima Eiji, 'The Thai-Japanese wartime alliance and the Chinese of Thailand, in Paul H. Kratoska, ed., *Southeast Asian minorities in the wartime Japanese empire* (London: Routledge, 2002), pp. 192–222.

Murfett, Malcolm H., John N. Miksic, Brian P. Farrell and Chiang Ming Shun, *Between two oceans: a military history of Singapore from the first settlement to final British withdrawal* (Oxford: Oxford University Press, 1999).

Murphey, Rhoads, 'New capitals of Asia', *Economic Development and Cultural Change*, 5, 3 (1957), pp. 216–43.

Muscat, Robert J., *The fifth tiger: a study of Thai development policy* (Armonk, NY: M. E. Sharp, 1994).

Myers, Ramon H., 'Creating a modern enclave economy: the economic integration of Japan, Manchuria and North China, 1932–1945', in Peter Duus, Ramon H. Myers and Mark R. Peattie, eds., *The Japanese wartime empire, 1931–1945* (Princeton, NJ: Princeton University Press, 1996), pp. 136–70.

Myers, Ramon H. and Adrienne Ching, 'Agriculture development in Taiwan under Japanese colonial rule', *Journal of Asian Studies*, 23, 4 (1964), pp. 555–70.

Myint, Hla, 'The gains from international trade and the backward countries', *Review of Economic Studies*, 22 (1954–5), pp.129–42.

Myint, Hla, 'The "classical" theory of international trade and the underdeveloped countries', *Economic Journal*, 68 (1958), pp. 317–37.

Myint, Hla, 'The inward and outward looking countries of Southeast Asia', *Malayan Economic Review*, 12, 1 (1965), pp. 1–13.

Myint-U, Thant, *The river of lost footsteps: a personal history of Burma* (London: Faber and Faber, 2007).

Nagano Toshio, 'America's Pacific policy', *Contemporary Japan*, 9, 9 (1940), pp. 1131–39.

Nagano Yoshiko, 'Cotton production under Japanese rule, 1942–1945', in Setsuho Ikehata and Ricardo Trota Jose, eds., *The Philippines under Japanese occupation* (Manila: Manila University Press, 1999), pp. 171–96.

Nakahara Michiko, 'Labour recruitment in Malaya under the Japanese occupation: the case of the Burma-Siam railway', in K. S. Jomo, ed., *Rethinking Malaysia* (Kuala Lumpur: Malaysian Social Science Association, 1999), pp. 215–45.

Nakahara Michiko, '"Comfort women" in Malaysia', *Critical Asian Studies*, 33, 4 (2001), pp. 581–89.

Nakahara Michiko, 'Malayan labor on the Thailand–Burma railway', in Paul H. Kratoska, ed., *Asian labor in the wartime Japanese Empire* (Armonk, NY: M. E. Sharpe, 2005), pp. 249–64.

Nakamura Takafusa, *Lectures on modern Japanese economic history 1926–1994* (Tokyo: International Library Foundation, 1994).

Nakamura Takafusa, *The postwar Japanese economy: its development and structure, 1937–1994*, 2nd edn. (Tokyo: University of Tokyo Press, 1995).

Nakamura Takafusa, 'The yen bloc, 1931–1941', in Peter Duus, Raymond H. Myers and Mark Peattie, eds., *The Japanese wartime empire, 1931–1945* (Princeton, NJ: Princeton University Press, 1996), pp. 171–86.

Nakamura Takafusa, 'The Japanese war economy as a "planned economy"', in Erich Pauer, ed., *Japan's war economy* (London: Routledge, 1999), pp. 9–22.

Nakano Satoshi, 'In the language of the occupier: recent work on the Japanese period in the Philippines', *Social Science Japan Journal*, 2, 2 (1999), pp. 267–72.

National Archives of Singapore, *Reflections and memories of war*, vol. 2: *Syonan years 1942–1945: living beneath the rising sun* (Singapore: National Archives of Singapore, 2009).

Naval Intelligence Division, *Indo-China* (London: Naval Intelligence Division of the Admiralty, 1943).

Naval Intelligence Division, *Netherlands East Indies*, 2 vols. (London: Naval Intelligence Division of the Admiralty, 1944).

Nazrin, Sultan Shan, *Charting the economy: early 20th century Malaya and contemporary Malaysian contrasts* (Oxford: Oxford University Press, 2017).

Nelson, John, 'Social memory as ritual practice: spirits of the military dead at Yasukuni Shinto Shrine', *Journal of Asian Studies*, 62, 7 (2003), pp. 443–67.

Nemoto Kei, *Reconsidering the Japanese military occupation in Burma (1942–45)* (Tokyo: Research Institute for Languages and Cultures of Asia and Africa (ILCAA), Tokyo University of Foreign Studies, 2007).

Nenryō Konwa Kai [Fuel Study Group], ed., *Nihon kaigun nenryō shi* [History of Japanese naval fuels], 2 vols. (Tokyo: Hara Shobō, 1972).

Newell, William H., ed., *Japan in Asia* (Singapore: Singapore University Press, 1981).

Ngô Thiéu Hiêu, Vũ Thi Minh Huong, Philippe Papin and Vũ Văn Theyên, *Guide des fonds d'archives d'époque coloniale: conservés au centre n 1 des Archives Nationales à Hanoi* (Hanoi, 2001).

Ngô Viñh Long, *Before the revolution: the Vietnamese peasants under the French* (New York: Columbia University Press, 1991).

Nguyên Thê Anh, 'La famine de 1945 au Nord-Viêt-Nam', *Vietnam Forum*, 5 (1985), pp. 81–100.

Nguyên Thê Anh, 'La campagne nord-vietnamienne de la dépression économique de 1930 à la famine de 1945', *Vietnam Forum*, 9 (1987), pp. 120–37.

Nguyên Thê Anh, 'Japanese food policies and the 1945 great famine in Indochina', in Paul H. Kratoska, ed., *Food supplies and the Japanese occupation* (Houndmills: Macmillan, 1998), pp. 208–26.

Nguyen Van Huyen, *Le problème de la paysannerie Annamite au Tonkin* (Hanoi: Tendances, 1939).

Nicholls, Lucius, 'Nutrition in Singapore during Japanese occupation', *British Medical Journal*, I, 4548 (1948), pp. 37–39.

Nish, Ian, 'Greater East Asian Co-Prosperity Sphere', in I. C. B. Dear, ed., *The Oxford companion to the Second World War* (Oxford: Oxford University Press, 1995), pp. 500–03.

Nish, Ian and Mark Allen, eds., *War, conflict and security in Japan and Asia-Pacific, 1941–1952: the writings of Louis Allen* (Folkestone: Global Oriental, 2011).

Nishijima Shigetada and Kishi Koichi, *Japanese military administration in Indonesia* (Washington, DC: United States Department of Commerce Technical Services, 1963).

Nitz, Kurusu Kiyoko, 'Japanese military policy towards French Indochina during the Second World War: the road to the *meigo sakusen* (9 March 1945)', *Journal of Southeast Asian Studies*, 14, 2 (1983), pp. 328–50.

Nitz, Kurusu Kiyoko, 'Independence without nationalists? The Japanese and Vietnamese nationalism during the Japanese period, 1940–45', *Journal of Southeast Asian Studies*, 15, 1 (1984), pp. 108–33.

Noda Katsuhisa, ed., *Nanpō chi'iki genchi jikatsu kyōhon* [Textbook for survival and self-support in the local areas of the southern region] (Tokyo: Fuji Shuppan, 1999).

Noda Katsuhisa, ed., *Nanpō hōmen kaigun shiryō* [Materials on the southern region navy] (Tokyo: Fuji Shuppan, 2001).

Nonini, Donald M., *British colonial rule and the resistance of the Malay peasantry, 1900–1957* (New Haven, CT: Yale University Southeast Asia Studies, 1992).

Norman, E. Herbert, 'The Genyosha: a study in the origins of Japanese imperialism', *Pacific Affairs*, 17, 3 (1944), pp. 261–84.

Nu, Thakin [U Nu], *Burma under the Japanese: pictures and portraits*, ed. and with introduction by J. S. Furnivall (London: Macmillan, 1954).

Nu, U, *Saturday's son* (New Haven, CT: Yale University Press, 1975).

Numnonda, Thamsook, *Thailand and the Japanese presence, 1941–1945* (Singapore: Institute of Southeast Asian Studies, 1977).

Numnonda, Thamsook, 'Pibulsongkram's Thai nation-building programme during the Japanese military presence, 1941–1945', *Journal of Southeast Asian Studies*, 9, 2 (1978), pp. 234–47.

Nurkse, Ragnar, *Problems of capital formation in underdeveloped countries and patterns of trade and development* (New York: Oxford University Press, 1967).

Ó Gráda, Cormac, *Black '47 and beyond: the great Irish famine in history, economy and memory* (Princeton, NJ: Princeton University Press, 1999).

Ó Gráda, Cormac, 'Making famine history', *Journal of Economic Literature*, 43, 1 (2007), pp. 5–38.

Ó Gráda, Cormac, 'The ripple that drowns? Twentieth-century famines in China and India as economic history', *Economic History Review*, 61, S1 (2008), pp. 5–37.

Ó Gráda, Cormac, *Famine: a short history* (Princeton, NJ: Princeton University Press, 2009).

Occhino, Filippo, Kim Oosterlinck and Eugene N. White, 'How occupied France financed its own exploitation during World War II', *American Economic Review*, 97, 2 (2007), pp. 295–99.

Occhino, Filippo, Kim Oosterlinck and Eugene N. White, 'How much can a victor force the vanquished to pay? France under the Nazi boot', *Journal of Economic History*, 68, 1 (2008), pp. 1–45.

Offer, Avner, 'War economy', in John Eatwell et al., eds., *The new Palgrave*, 4 vols. (London: Macmillan, 1987), vol. 4, pp. 875–77.

Offer, Avner, *The First World War: an agrarian interpretation* (Oxford: Oxford University Press, 1989).

Offer, Avner, 'Going to war in 1914: a matter of honor?', *Politics and Society*, 23, 2 (1995), pp. 213–41.

Offer, Avner, 'The blockade of Germany and the strategy of starvation, 1914–1918', in Roger Chickering and Stig Förster, eds., *Great war, total war: combat and mobilization on the Western Front 1914–1918* (Cambridge: Cambridge University Press, 2000), pp. 169–88.

Office of Population Research, 'French Indo-China: demographic imbalance and colonial policy', *Population Index*, 11, 2 (1945), pp. 68–81.

Ohkawa Kazushi and Henry Rosovsky, *Japanese economic growth* (Stanford, CA: Stanford University Press, 1973).

Ohkawa Kazushi and Shinohara Miyohei, eds., *Patterns of Japanese economic development: a quantitative appraisal* (New Haven, CT: Yale University Press, 1979).

Ohta Tsunezo, 'Japanese military occupation of Burma – the dichotomy', *Intisari*, 2, 3 (1967), pp. 25–39.

Oka Yoshitake, *Konoe Fumimaro 'Unmei' no Seijika* [Konoe Fumimaro: a politician of 'destiny'] (Tokyo: Iwanami Shoten, 1983).

Okazaki Tetsuji, 'Strategies and organizations for managing the "Greater East Asia Co-Prosperity Sphere"', in Marcel Boldorf and Tetsuji Okazaki, eds., *Economies under occupation: the hegemony of Nazi Germany and Imperial Japan in World War II* (London: Routledge, 2015), pp. 24–36.

Okazaki Tetsuji and Okuno-Fujiwara Masahiro, eds., *The Japanese economic system and its historical origins* (Oxford: Oxford University Press, 1999).

Ooi Keat Gin, 'For want of rice: Sarawak's attempts at rice self-sufficiency during the period of Brooke rule, 1841–1941', *Journal of Southeast Asian Studies*, 29, 1 (1998), pp. 8–23.

Ooi Keat Gin, ed., *Japanese empire in the tropics: selected documents and reports of the Japanese period in Sarawak, Northwest Borneo 1941–1945*, 2 vols. (Athens, OH: Ohio University Center for International Studies, 1998).

Ooi Keat Gin, *Rising sun over Borneo: the Japanese occupation of Sarawak 1941–1945* (London: Macmillan, 1999).

Ooi Keat Gin, *The Japanese occupation of Borneo, 1941–1945* (London: Routledge, 2011).

Oosterlinck, Kim, 'French stock exchanges and regulation during World War II', *Financial History Review*, 17, 2 (2010), pp. 211–37.

Oosterlinck, Kim, 'Sovereign debts and war finance in Belgium, France and the Netherlands', in Christoph Buchheim and Marcel Boldorf, eds., *Europäische volkswirtschaften unter deutscher hegemonie 1938–1945* (Munich: Schriften des Historischen Kollegs, 2012), pp. 93–106.

Osborne, Milton, *Region of revolt: focus on Southeast Asia* (Harmondsworth: Penguin Books, 1971).

Ōuchi Hyōbei, *Nihon keizai tōkei shū – Meiji, Taishō, Shōwa* [Collected statistics of the Japanese economy: Meiji, Taisho, Showa] (Tokyo: Nihon Hyōron Shinsha, 1958).

Ouyyanont, Porphant, 'Bangkok as a magnet for rural labour: changing conditions, 1900–1970', *Southeast Asian Studies*, 36, 1 (1998), pp. 78–108.

Ouyyanont, Porphant, *A regional economic history of Thailand* (Singapore: ISEAS, 2017).

Overy, R. J., *War and economy in the Third Reich* (Oxford: Clarendon Press, 1994).

Owen, Norman G., *Prosperity without progress: Manila hemp and material life in the colonial Philippines* (Manila: Ateneo de Manila, 1984).

Owen, Norman G., 'Economic and social change', in Nicholas Tarling, ed., *The Cambridge history of Southeast Asia*, vol. 2, part 2: *From World War II to the present* (Cambridge: Cambridge University Press, 1999), pp. 139–99.

Owen, Norman G., ed., *The emergence of modern Southeast Asia* (Honolulu: University of Hawaii Press, 2005).

Paauw, Douglas S., 'Economic progress in Southeast Asia', *Journal of Asian Studies*, 23, 1 (1963), pp. 69–92.

Paine, S.C.M., *The Japanese Empire: grand strategy from the Meiji restoration to the Pacific War* (Cambridge: Cambridge University Press, 2017).

Palairet, Michael, *The four ends of the Greek hyperinflation of 1941–1946* (Copenhagen: Museum Tusculanum Press, 2000).

Palmier, L. H., *Social status and power in Java* (London: Athlone Press, 1969).

Parillo, Mark P., *The Japanese merchant marine in World War II* (Annapolis, MD: Naval Institute Press, 1993).

Patti, Archimedes L. A., *Why Viet Nam?: prelude to America's albatross* (Berkeley, CA: University of California Press, 1980).

Pauer, Erich, ed., *Japan's war economy* (London: Routledge, 1999).

Pe, U Hla, *Narrative of the Japanese occupation of Burma* (Ithaca, NY: Southeast Asia Program, Cornell University, 1961).

Peattie, Mark R., *Ishiwara Kanji and Japan's confrontation with the West* (Princeton, NJ: Princeton University Press, 1975).

Peattie, Mark R., 'The Japanese colonial empire, 1895–1945', in Peter Duus, ed., *The Cambridge history of Japan,* vol. 6: *The twentieth century* (Cambridge: Cambridge University Press, 1989), pp. 217–70.

Peattie, Mark R., 'Forecasting a Pacific war, 1912–1933: the idea of a conditional Japanese victory', in James W. White, Michio Umegaki and Thomas R. H. Havens, eds., *The ambivalence of nationalism: modern Japan between east and west* (Lanham, MD: University Press of America, 1990), pp. 115–31.

Peattie, Mark R., '*Nanshin*: the "southward advance," 1931–1941, as a prelude to the Japanese occupation of Southeast Asia', in Peter Duus, Raymond H. Myers and Mark Peattie, eds., *The Japanese wartime empire, 1931–1945* (Princeton, NJ: Princeton University Press, 1996), pp. 189–242.

Peattie, Mark R., Edward Drea and Hans van de Ven, eds., *The battle for China: essays on the military history of the Sino-Japanese War of 1937–1945* (Stanford, CA: Stanford University Press, 2011).

Pelzer, Karl J., *Pioneer settlement in the Asiatic tropics: studies in land utilization and agricultural colonization in Southeastern Asia* (New York: Institute of Pacific Relations, 1945).

Pelzer, Karl J., *Planter and peasant: colonial policy and agrarian struggle in East Sumatra, 1863–1947* (The Hague: Martinus Nijhoff, 1978).

Perkins, Dwight H., *East Asian development: foundations and strategies* (Cambridge, MA: Harvard University Press, 2013).

Peters, Robbie, *Surabaya, 1945–2010: neighbourhood, state and economy in Indonesia's city of struggle* (Singapore: NUS Press, 2013).

Peterson, Alec, 'Britain and Siam: the latest phase', *Pacific Affairs*, 19, 4 (1946), pp. 364–72.

Pham, David Lan, *Two hamlets in Nam Bo: memoirs of life in Vietnam through Japanese occupation, the French and American wars, and communist rule, 1940–1986* (Jefferson, NC: McFarland & Company, 2000).

Pluvier, Jan M., *A handbook and chart of South-East Asian history* (Kuala Lumpur: Oxford University Press, 1967).

Pluvier, Jan M., *South-East Asia from colonialism to independence* (Kuala Lumpur: Oxford University Press, 1974).

Poeze, Harry A., 'The road to hell: the construction of a railway line in West Java during the Japanese occupation', in Paul H. Kratoska, ed., *Asian labor in the wartime Japanese empire* (Armonk, NY: M. E. Sharpe, 2005), pp. 152–78.

Porter, Catherine, 'The future of Philippine-American relations', *Pacific Affairs*, 16, 3 (1943), pp. 261–76.

Post, Peter, 'Policing society', in Peter Post et al., eds., *The encyclopedia of Indonesia in the Pacific War* (Leiden: Brill, 2009), pp. 148–60.

Post, Peter, William H. Frederick, Iris Heidebrink et al., eds., *The encyclopedia of Indonesia in the Pacific War* (Leiden: Brill, 2009).

Power, John H. and Gerardo P. Sicat, *The Philippines industrialization and trade policies* (London: Oxford University Press, 1971).

Pratt, Sir John, *Japan and the modern world* (Oxford: Oxford University Press, 1942).

Prest, A. R., *War economics of primary producing countries* (Cambridge: Cambridge University Press, 1948).

Prillwitz, P. M., 'The estate agriculture during the Japanese occupation', *Economic Review of Indonesia*, 1, 1 (1947), pp. 13–17.

Purcell, Victor, *Malaya: communist or free?* (London: Victor Gollancz, 1954).

Raben, Remco, 'The Indonesian *rōmusha* and coolies under naval administration: the eastern archipelago, 1942–45', in Paul H. Kratoska, ed., *Asian labor in the wartime Japanese empire* (Armonk, NY: M. E. Sharpe, 2005), pp. 197–212.

Rai, Rajesh, *Indians in Singapore 1819–1945: diaspora in the colonial port city* (New Delhi: Oxford University Press, 2014).

Rama, F. C. de la, *I made millions and lost them* (Manila: Nation-Ad Philippines, 1957).

Ránki, György, *The economics of the Second World War* (Wein: Bohlau Verlag, 1993).

Rawson, Rees, 'Two new railways in South-East Asia', *Geographical Journal*, 103, 1/3 (1946), pp. 85–88.

Reeve, W. D., *Public administration in Siam* (London: Royal Institute of International Affairs, 1951).

Reid, Anthony, *The Indonesian national revolution, 1945–1950* (Hawthorne: Longman Australia, 1974).

Reid, Anthony, 'Indonesia: from briefcase to Samurai sword', in Alfred W. McCoy, ed., *Southeast Asia under Japanese occupation* (New Haven, CT: Yale University Southeast Asia Studies, 1980), pp. 13–26.

Reid, Anthony, 'Indonesia: revolution without socialism', in Robin Jeffrey, ed., *Asia: the winning of independence* (Basingstoke: Macmillan, 1981), pp. 113–57.

Reid, Anthony, *The blood of the people: revolution and the end of traditional rule in northern Sumatra*, 2nd edn. (Singapore: NUS Press, 2014).

Reid, Anthony and Oki Akira, eds., *The Japanese experience in Indonesia: selected memoirs of 1942–1945* (Athens, OH: Ohio University Center for International Studies, 1986).

Reid, Anthony and Shiraishi Saya, 'Rural unrest in Sumatra, 1942: a Japanese report', *Indonesia*, 21 (1976), pp. 115–33.

Reinhart, Carmen M. and Kenneth S. Rogoff, *This time is different: eight centuries of financial folly* (Princeton, NJ: Princeton University Press, 2009).

Reitsma, S. A., *Gedenkboek der staatsspoor- en tramwegen in Nederlandsch-Indië 1875–1925* [Commemorative book of the state railways and tramways in the Dutch East Indies 1875–1925] (Weltevreden: Topografische Inrichting, 1925).

Reynolds, E. Bruce, 'Aftermath of alliance: the wartime legacy in Thai-Japanese relations', *Journal of Southeast Asian Studies*, 21, 1 (1990), pp. 66–87.

Reynolds, E. Bruce, *Thailand and Japan's southern advance 1940–1945* (London: Macmillan, 1994).

Reynolds, E. Bruce, 'Anomaly or model? Independent Thailand's role in Japan's Asian strategy, 1941–1943', in Peter Duus, Raymond H. Myers and Mark Peattie, eds., *The Japanese wartime empire, 1931–1945* (Princeton, NJ: Princeton University Press, 1996), pp. 243–73.

Reynolds, E. Bruce, '"International orphans": the Chinese in Thailand during World War II', *Journal of Southeast Asian Studies*, 28, 2 (1997), pp. 365–88.

Reynolds, E. Bruce, 'History, memory, compensation and reconciliation: the abuse of labor along the Thai–Burma railway', in Paul H. Kratoska, ed., *Asian labor in the wartime Japanese empire* (Armonk, NY: M. E. Sharpe, 2005), pp. 326–47.

Reynolds, E. Bruce, *Thailand's secret war: the free Thai, OSS, and SOE during World War II* (Cambridge: Cambridge University Press, 2005).

Rice, Richard, 'Economic mobilization in wartime Japan: business, bureaucracy, and military in conflict', *Journal of Asian Studies*, 38, 4 (1979), pp. 689–706.

Richell, Judith L., *Disease and demography in colonial Burma* (Singapore: NUS Press, 2006).

Riggs, Fred W., *Thailand: the modernization of a bureaucratic polity* (Honolulu: East-West Center Press, 1966).

Rimmer, Douglas, 'Have-not nations: the prototype', *Economic Development and Cultural Change*, 27, 2 (1979), pp. 307–25.

Robequain, Charles, *The economic development of French Indo-China* (London: Oxford University Press, 1944).

Robequain, Charles, *Malaya, Indonesia, Borneo and the Philippines: a geographical, political and economic description of Malaya, the East Indies and the Philippines* (London: Longmans, 1959).

Robertson, C. J., 'The rice export from Burma, Siam and French Indo-China', *Pacific Affairs*, 9, 2 (1936), pp. 243–53.

Rockoff, Hugh, 'Indirect price increases and real wages during World War II', *Explorations in Economic History*, 15 (1978), pp. 407–20.

Rockoff, Hugh, *Until it's over, over there: the US economy in World War I*, National Bureau of Economic Research working paper 10580 (2004).

Rockoff, Hugh, *America's economic way of war: war and the US economy from the Spanish-American war to the Persian Gulf war* (Cambridge: Cambridge University Press, 2012).

Rodenburg, G., 'Java's sugar supply', *Economic Review of Indonesia*, 1, 1 (1947), pp. 25–29.

Rodrigo, P. A., 'The coconut industry since liberation', in Philippines, Bureau of Agriculture, *A half-century of Philippine agriculture* (Manila: Bureau of Agriculture, 1952), pp. 199–201.

Romualdez, Eduardo Z., 'Financial problems created by the war', *Journal of the Philippine National Historical Society*, 10, 4 (1962), pp. 448–518.

Rousseau, Jean-François, 'An imperial railway failure: the Indochina-Yunnan railway, 1898–1941', *Journal of Transport History*, 35, 1 (2014), pp. 1–17.

Roxas, Manuel, 'Brief summary of the activities of Manuel Roxas during the Japanese occupation, with notes by Mauro Garcia', in Mauro Garcia, *Documents on the Japanese occupation of the Philippines* (Manila: Philippine Historical Association, 1965), pp. 238–58.

Royal Institute of International Affairs, *Raw materials and colonies*, Information Department paper no. 18 (London: Royal Institute of International Affairs, 1936).

Rōyama Masamichi and Takéuchi Tatsuji, *The Philippine polity: a Japanese view*, ed. Theodore Friend (New Haven, CT: Southeast Asian Studies, Yale University, 1967).

Sacay, Francisco M., 'The food supply and population of the Philippines', *Philippine Agriculturalist*, 33 (1950), pp. 203–17.

Sadan, Mandy, 'Ethnic armies and ethnic conflict in Burma: reconsidering the history of colonial militarization in the Kachin region of Burma during the Second World War', *South East Asia Research*, 21, 4 (2013), pp. 601–26.

Saito, T. and Lee Kin Kiong, *Statistics on the Burmese economy* (Singapore, 1999).

Sandhu, Kernial Singh, 'The saga of the "squatter" in Malaya', *Journal of Southeast Asian History*, 5, 1 (1964), pp. 143–77.

Sansom, Robert L., *The economics of insurgency in the Mekong delta of Vietnam* (Cambridge, MA: MIT, 1970).

Sargent, Thomas J., 'The ends of four big inflations', in Robert E. Hall, ed., *Inflation: causes and effects* (Chicago, IL: University of Chicago Press, 1982), pp. 41–97.

Sargent, Thomas J. and François R. Velde, 'Macroeconomic features of the French revolution', *Journal of Political Economy*, 103, 3 (1995), pp. 474–518.

Sato Shigeru, *War, nationalism and peasants: Java under the Japanese occupation 1942–1945* (Armonk, NY: M. E. Sharpe, 1994).

Sato Shigeru, 'The pangreh praja in Java under Japanese military rule', *Bijdragen tot de Taal-, Land- en Volkenkunde*, 152 (1996), pp. 64–86.

Sato Shigeru, 'Oppression and romanticism: the food supply of Java during the Japanese occupation', in Paul H. Kratoska, ed., *Food supplies and the Japanese occupation* (Houndmills: Macmillan, 1998), pp. 167–86.

Sato Shigeru, '"Economic soldiers" in Java: Indonesian laborers mobilized for agricultural projects', in Paul H. Kratoska, ed., *Asian labor in the wartime Japanese Empire* (Armonk, NY: M. E. Sharpe, 2005), pp. 129–51.

Sato Shigeru, 'Administrative changes in Java', in Peter Post et al., eds., *The encyclopedia of Indonesia in the Pacific War* (Leiden: Brill, 2009), pp. 92–102.

Sato Shigeru, 'Relocation of labor and the rōmusha issue', in Peter Post et al., eds., *The encyclopedia of Indonesia in the Pacific War* (Leiden: Brill, 2009), pp. 245–61.

Satyawati Suleiman, 'The last days of Batavia', *Indonesia*, 28 (1979), pp. 55–64.

Scherer, Anke, 'Drawbacks to controls on food distribution', in Erich Pauer, ed., *Japan's war economy* (London: Routledge, 1999), pp. 106–23.

Scott, James C., *The moral economy of the peasant: rebellion and subsistence in Southeast Asia* (New Haven, CT: Yale University Press, 1976).

Scott, James C., 'An approach to the problems of food supply in Southeast Asia during World War Two', in Bernd Martin and Alan S. Milward, eds., *Food supply in the Second World War* (Ostfildern: Scripta Mercaturae, 1985), pp. 269–82.

Selth, Andrew, 'Race and resistance in Burma, 1942–1945', *Modern Asian Studies*, 20, 3 (1986), pp. 483–507.

Sen, Amartya, 'Ingredients of famine analysis: availability and entitlements', *Quarterly Journal of Economics*, 96 (1981), pp. 433–64.

Sen, Amartya, *Poverty and famines: an essay on entitlement and deprivation* (Oxford: Clarendon Press, 1981).

Sen, Amartya, *War and famines: on divisions and incentives* (London: London School of Economics, Suntory-Toyota Centre, 1991).

Serrano, Felicisimo B., 'The rice industry and scientific research', in Philippines, Bureau of Agriculture, *A half-century of Philippine agriculture* (Manila: Bureau of Agriculture, 1952), pp. 170–78.

Shabad, Theodore, 'Economic developments in North Vietnam', *Pacific Affairs*, 31, 1 (1958), pp. 36–53.

Shapiro, Carl and Joseph E. Stiglitz, 'Equilibrium unemployment as a worker discipline device', *American Economic Review*, 74, 3 (1984), pp. 433–44.

Shenoy, B.R., 'The currency, banking, and exchange system of Thailand', *IMF Staff Papers*, 1, 2 (1950), pp. 289–314.

Shepherd, Jack, *Industry in Southeast Asia* (New York: Institute of Pacific Relations, 1941).

Shibata Yoshimasa, 'The monetary policy in the Netherlands East Indies under the Japanese administration', *Bijdragen Tot de Taal-, Land- en Volkenkunde*, 152, 4 (1996), pp. 699–724.

Shibata Yoshimasa, *Senryōchi tsūka kin'yū seisaku no tenkai* [The development of monetary and currency policy in the occupied territories] (Tokyo: Nihon Keizai Shinbun Sha, 1999).

Shimazaki Kyūya, *En no shinryaku shi: En kawase hon'i seido no keisei katei* [Invasion of the yen: the making of the yen exchange standard system] (Tokyo: Nihon Keizai Shimbun Sha, 1989).

Shinozaki Mamoru, *Syonan – my story: the Japanese occupation of Singapore* (Singapore: Times Books International, 1975).

Shipway, Martin, *Decolonization and its impact: a comparative approach to the end of empires* (Oxford: Blackwell, 2008).

Shiraishi Masaya, 'Vietnam under the Japanese presence and the August Revolution', *1945 in South-East Asia, Part Two*, London School of Economics International Studies 1985/123, pp. 1–31.

Shiraishi Masaya, 'The background to the formation of the Tran Trong Kim cabinet in April 1945: Japanese plans for governing Vietnam', in Shiraishi Takashi and Furuta Motoo, eds., *Indochina in the 1940s and 1950s* (Ithaca, NY: Cornell Southeast Asia Program, 1992), pp. 113–41.

Shiraishi Takashi and Furuta Motoo, 'Two features of Japan's Indochina policy during the Pacific War', in Shiraishi Takashi and Furuta Motoo, eds., *Indochina in the 1940s and 1950s* (Ithaca, NY: Cornell Southeast Asia Program, 1992), pp. 55–85.

Shu Sang-Chul, *Growth and structural changes in the Korean economy, 1910–1940* (Cambridge, MA: Council on East Asian Studies, Harvard University, 1978).

Siamwalla, Ammar, 'A history of rice policies in Thailand', *Food Research Institute Studies*, 14, 3 (1975), pp. 233–49.

Sicat, Gerardo P., 'The Philippine economy', in Gerardo P. Sicat, ed., *The Philippine economy in the 1960s* (Quezon City: Institute of Economic Development and Research, University of the Philippines, 1964).

Sicat, Gerardo P., 'On the measurement of long-term output', *Philippine Economic Journal*, 7, 1 (1968), pp. 25–41.

Sicat, Gerardo P., 'A historical and current perspective of Philippine economic problems', *Philippine Economic Journal*, 24, 1 (1985), pp. 24–63.

Sicat, Gerardo P., *The Philippine economy during the Japanese occupation, 1941–1945*, School of Economics, University of the Philippines discussion paper 0307 (November 2003).

Sicat, Gerardo P., 'The Philippine economy during the Japanese occupation, 1941–1945', in Marcel Boldorf and Tetsuji Okazaki, eds., *Economies under occupation: the hegemony of Nazi Germany and Imperial Japan in World War II* (London: Routledge, 2015), pp. 191–204.

Sidel, John T., 'Philippine politics in town, district, and province: bossism in Cavite and Cebu', *Journal of Asian Studies*, 56, 4 (1997), pp. 947–66.

Sidel, John T., *Capital, coercion and crime: bossism in the Philippines* (Stanford, CA: Stanford University Press, 1999).

Sidel, John T., 'Social origins of dictatorship and democracy revisited: colonial state origins and Chinese immigrant in the making of modern Southeast Asia', *Comparative Politics*, 40, 2 (2008), pp. 127–47.

Sidel, John T., 'The fate of nationalism in new states: Southeast Asia in comparative historical perspective', *Comparative Studies in Society and History*, 54, 1 (2012), pp. 114–44.

Silcock, Thomas H., 'Promotion of industry and the planning process', in Thomas H. Silcock, ed., *Thailand: social and economic studies in development* (Canberra: Australian National University Press, 1967), pp. 258–88.

Silcock, Thomas H., *The economic development of Thai agriculture* (Canberra: Australian National University Press, 1970).

Silcock, Thomas H., *A history of economics teaching and graduates in Singapore* (Singapore: Department of Economics and Statistics, National University of Singapore, 1985).

Silcock, Thomas H. and Ungku Abdul Aziz, 'Nationalism in Malaya', in William L. Holland, ed., *Asian nationalism and the west* (New York: Macmillan, 1953), pp. 269–345.

Silverstein, Josef, 'Transportation in Burma during the Japanese occupation', *Journal of the Burma Research Society*, 39 (1956), pp. 1–17.

Silverstein, Josef, 'The importance of the Japanese occupation of Southeast Asia to the political scientist', in Josef Silverstein, ed., *Southeast Asia in World War II: four essays* (New Haven, CT: Yale University Southeast Asia Studies, 1966), pp. 1–11.

Silverstein, Josef, *Burma: military rule and the politics of stagnation* (Ithaca, NY: Cornell University Press, 1977).

Sivaram, M., *Road to Delhi* (Rutland: Charles E. Tuttle Co., 1967).

Skinner, G. William, *Chinese society in Thailand* (Ithaca, NY: Cornell University Press, 1957).

Skinner, G. William, *Leadership and power in the Chinese community of Thailand* (Ithaca, NY: Cornell University Press, 1958).

Sluimers, László, *The rice situation in Java and Madura during the Japanese era, 1942–1945* (Amsterdam: Amsterdam: Universiteit van Amsterdam, Antropologisch-Sociologisch Centrum, Vakgroep Zuid- en Zuidoost-Azie, 1983).

Sluimers, László, 'The Japanese military and Indonesian independence', *Journal of Southeast Asian Studies*, 27, 1 (1996), pp. 19–36.

Smethurst, Richard J., *From foot soldier to finance minister: Takahashi Korekiyo, Japan's Keynes* (Cambridge, MA: Harvard University Asia Center, 2007).

Smitabhindu, Thanatphong, 'Domestic developments in Thailand and Japan, 1932–1942', in *1945 in Southeast Asia part one* (London: London School of Economics International Studies, 1985/1), pp. 39–58.

Smith, Martin, 'Burma and World War II', *Cultural Survival Quarterly*, 13, 4 (1989), pp. 1–4.

Smith, Ralph B., 'The Japanese period in Indochina and the coup of 9 March 1945', *Journal of Southeast Asian Studies*, 9, 2 (1978), pp. 268–301.

Smith, Ralph B., 'The work of the provisional government of Vietnam, August–December 1945', *Modern Asian Studies*, 12, 4 (1978), pp. 571–609.

Smurthwaite, David, *War atlas of Asia and the Pacific 1941–1945* (Shrewsbury: Airlife, 2000).

Smyth, Brigadier Sir John, 'The long retreat, the first Burma campaign', in Sir Basil Liddell Hart and Barrie Pitt, eds., *History of the Second World War*, vol. 3, no. 3 (London: Purnell, 1967), pp. 953–63.

Spate, O. H. K., 'Beginnings of industrialization in Burma', *Economic Geography*, 17, 1 (1941), pp. 75–92.

Spate, O. H. K., 'The Burmese village', *Geographical Review*, 35, 4 (1945), pp. 523–43.

Spector, Ronald H., 'Allied intelligence and Indochina, 1943–1945', *Pacific Historical Review*, 51, 1 (1982), pp. 23–50.

Spector, Ronald H., *Eagle against the sun: the American war with Japan* (London: Cassell & Co., 2000).

Spencer, J. E., *Land and people in the Philippines* (Berkeley, CA: University of California Press, 1954).

Stamp, L. Dudley, 'Siam before the war', *Geographical Journal*, 99, 5–6 (1942), pp. 209–24.

Stamp, L. Dudley, *Asia: a regional and economic geography*, 9th edn. (London: Methuen, 1957).

Steinberg, David Joel, *Philippine collaboration in World War II* (Manila: Solidaridad Publishing House, 1967).

Steinberg, David Joel, 'An ambiguous legacy: years at war in the Philippines', *Pacific Affairs*, 45, 2 (1972), pp. 165–90.

Stoler, Ann Laura, *Capitalism and confrontation in Sumatra's plantation belt, 1870–1979*, 2nd edn. (Ann Arbor, MI: University of Michigan Press, 1995).

Stowe, Judith A., 'Japan's relations with Thailand in 1945', in *South-East Asia, part one*, London School of Economics International Studies 1985/1, pp. 30–38.

Stuart-Fox, Martin, *A history of Laos* (Cambridge: Cambridge University Press, 1997).

Subrahmanyan, Arjun and Michael Sturma, 'Asian Labourers, the Thai Government and the Thai-Burma Railway' *Journal of Contemporary History* (2020) https://journals.sagepub.com/doi/abs/10.1177/0022009420922586#.

Suehiro Akira, *Capital accumulation in Thailand 1855–1985* (Tokyo: Centre for East Asian Cultural Studies, 1989).

Sukarno, *Sukarno: an autobiography as told to Cindy Adams* (Indianapolis, IN: Bobbs-Merrill, 1966).

Sutter, John O., *Indonesianisasi: politics in a changing economy, 1940–1955*, vol. 1: *The Indonesian economy at the close of the Dutch period and under the Japanese* (Ithaca, NY: Southeast Asia Program Cornell University data paper 36-I, 1959).

Suzuki Tohmin, 'Is a Pacific War possible?', *Contemporary Japan*, 10, 8 (1941), pp. 977–86.

Swan, William L., 'Thai-Japan relations at the start of the Pacific War: new insight into a controversial period', *Journal of Southeast Asian Studies*, 18, 2 (1979), pp. 270–93.

Swan, William L., 'Thai-Japan monetary relations at the start of the Pacific War', *Modern Asian Studies*, 23, 2 (1989), pp. 313–47.

Swan, William L., 'Japan's intentions for its Greater East Asia Co-Prosperity Sphere as indicated in its policy plans for Thailand', *Journal of Southeast Asian Studies*, 27, 1 (1996), pp. 139–49.

Swan, William L., *Japan's economic relations with Thailand: the rise to 'top trader' 1875–1942* (Bangkok: White Lotus Press, 2009).

Swift, Michael G., 'The accumulation of capital in a peasant economy', *Economic Development and Cultural Change*, 5, 4 (1957), pp. 325–37.

Tabuchi Yukichika, 'Indochina's role in Japan's Greater East Asian Co-Prosperity Sphere: a food procurement strategy', in Shiraishi Takashi and Furuta Motoo, eds., *Indochina in the 1940s and 1950s* (Ithaca, NY: Cornell Southeast Asia Program, 1992), pp. 87–112.

Tai Hue-Tam Ho, *Millenarianism and peasant politics in Vietnam* (Cambridge, MA: Harvard University Press, 1983).

Takahashi Akio, 'Regional differences in agriculture in Burma during the Japanese occupation period', in Nemoto Kei, *Reconsidering the Japanese military occupation in Burma (1942–45)* (Tokyo: Research Institute for Languages and Cultures of Asia and Africa (ILCAA), Tokyo University of Foreign Studies, 2007), pp. 157–77.

Takeuchi Tatsuji, 'Manila diary', in Theodore Friend, ed., *The Philippine polity: a Japanese view* (New Haven, CT: Yale University Southeast Asian Studies monograph no. 12, 1967), pp. 209–81.

Takir Alisjahbana, 'The Indonesian language – by-product of nationalism', *Pacific Affairs*, 22, 4 (1949), pp. 388–92.

Tan Yeok Seong, *The extortion by the Japanese military administration of $50,000,000 from the Chinese in Malaya* (Singapore: Nanyang Book Co., 1947).

Tanaka Yuki, *Japan's comfort women: sexual slavery and prostitution during World War II and the US occupation* (London: Routledge, 2002).

Tanzi, Vito, 'Inflation, lags in collections, and the real value of tax revenue', *IMF Staff Papers*, 24, 1 (1977), pp. 154–67.

Tarling, Nicholas, 'Rice and reconciliation: the Anglo-Thai peace negotiations of 1945', *Journal of the Siam Society*, 66, 2 (1978), pp. 59–111.

Tarling, Nicholas, '"A new and better cunning": British wartime planning for post-war Burma, 1942–43', *Journal of Southeast Asian Studies*, 13, 1 (1982), pp. 33–59.

Tarling, Nicholas, '"An empire gem": British wartime planning for post-war Burma, 1943–44', *Journal of Southeast Asian Studies*, 13, 2 (1982), pp. 310–48.

Tarling, Nicholas, '"An attempt to fly in the face of the ordinary laws of supply and demand": the British and Siamese rice 1945–7', *Journal of the Siam Society*, 75 (1987), pp. 140–86.

Tarling, Nicholas, *A sudden rampage: the Japanese occupation of Southeast Asia 1941–1945* (London: Hurst, 2001).

Taufik Abdullah, 'Nationalist activities during the Japanese period', in Peter Post et al., eds., *The encyclopedia of Indonesia in the Pacific War* (Leiden: Brill, 2009), pp. 113–27.

Taylor, R. H., 'The legacies of World War II for Myanmar', in David Koh Wee Hock, ed., *Legacies of World War II in South and East Asia* (Singapore: Institute of Southeast Asian Studies, 2007), pp. 60–73.

Taylor, Robert H., 'Burma in the anti-fascist war', in Alfred W. McCoy, ed., *Southeast Asia under Japanese occupation* (New Haven, CT: Yale University Southeast Asia Studies, 1980), pp. 132–57.

Taylor, Robert H., 'Perceptions of ethnicity in the politics of Burma', *Southeast Asian Journal of Social Science*, 10, 1 (1982), pp. 7–22.

Taylor, Robert H., *Marxism and resistance in Burma, 1942–1945: Thein Pe Myint's 'Wartime traveler'* (Athens, OH: Ohio University Press, 1984).

Taylor, Robert H., 'Disaster or release: J. S. Furnivall and the bankruptcy of Burma', *Modern Asian Studies*, 29, 1 (1995), pp. 45–63.

Than, U Ba, *For Burma my first five year plan* (Rangoon: Thudammewaddy Press, 1945).

Than, U Ba, *The roots of the revolution: a brief history of the defence services of the Union of Burma and the ideals for which they stand* (Rangoon: Director of Information, 1962).

Thien Ton That, 'Economic development in South Vietnam 1954–60', *Malayan Economic Review*, 6, 1 (1961), pp. 55–80.

Thio, Eunice, 'The Syonan years, 1942–1945', in Ernest C. T. Chew and Edwin Lee, eds., *A history of Singapore* (Singapore: Oxford University Press, 1991), pp. 95–114.

Thomas, Martin, 'Economic conditions and the limits to mobilization in the French Empire, 1936–1939', *Historical Journal*, 48, 2 (2005), pp. 471–98.

Thomas, Martin, 'France and the colonial civil wars, 1940–1945', in R. J. B. Bosworth and Joseph Maiolo, eds., *The Cambridge history of the Second World War*, vol. 2: *Politics and ideology* (Cambridge: Cambridge University Press, 2015), pp. 581–603.

Thomas, R. Murray, 'Educational remnants of military occupation: the Japanese in Indonesia', *Asian Survey*, 6, 11 (1966), pp. 630–42.

Thompson, Virginia, *Labor problems in Southeast Asia* (New Haven, CT: Yale University Press, 1947).

Tin, U Sein, *Wartime in Burma: a diary, January to June1942* (Athens, OH: Ohio University Research in International Studies, 2009).

Tinker, Hugh, *The Union of Burma*, 4th edn. (London: Oxford University Press, 1967).

Tinker, Hugh, 'A forgotten long march: the Indian exodus from Burma, 1942', *Journal of Southeast Asian Studies*, 6, 1 (1975), pp. 1–15.

Tinker, Hugh, 'Burma: the politics of memory', *Pacific Affairs*, 49, 1 (1976), pp. 108–11.

Tinker, Hugh, 'The contraction of empire in Asia, 1945–48: the military dimension', *Journal of Imperial and Commonwealth History*, 16, 2 (1988), pp. 218–33.

Tohmatsu Haruo, 'The strategic correlation between the Sino-Japanese and Pacific Wars', in Mark R. Peattie, Edward Drea and Hans van de Ven, eds., *The battle for China: essays on the military history of the Sino-Japanese War of 1937–1945* (Stanford, CA: Stanford University Press, 2011), pp. 423–45.

Tønnesson, Stein, *The Vietnamese revolution of 1945: Roosevelt, Ho Chi Minh and de Gaulle in a world at war* (London: Sage, 1991).

Tooze, Adam, *The wages of destruction: the making and breaking of the Nazi economy* (London: Allen Lane, 2006).

Totani Yuma, *The Tokyo War Crimes Trial; the pursuit of justice in the wake of World War II* (Cambridge, MA: Harvard University Asia Center, 2008).

Trager, Frank N., 'Review of *Last and first in Burma (1941–1948)*', *Pacific Affairs*, 29, 4 (1956), pp. 381–84.

Trager, Frank N., ed., *Burma: Japanese military administration, selected documents, 1941–1945* (Philadelphia, PA: University of Pennsylvania Press, 1971).

Trâm Huong, 'Famine in northern Viêt Nam', *Vietnamese Studies*, 183 (2012), pp. 79–85.

Tràn Mỹ-Vân, 'Japan and Vietnam's Caodaists: a wartime relationship (1939–45)', *Journal of Southeast Asian Studies*, 27, 1 (1996), pp. 179–93.

Tràn Mỹ-Vân, 'Working for the Japanese: working for Vietnamese independence, 1941–45', in Paul H. Kratoska, ed., *Asian labor in the wartime Japanese empire* (Armonk, NY: M. E. Sharpe, 2005), pp. 287–99.

Tregonning, K. G., *Straits tin: a brief account of the first seventy-five years of the Straits Trading Company, Limited, 1887–1962* (Singapore: Straits Times Press, 1962).

Tregonning, K. G., *Home port Singapore: a history of the Straits Steamship Company Limited, 1890–1965* (Singapore: Oxford University Press, 1967).

Trescott, Paul B., *Thailand's monetary experience: the economics of stability* (New York: Praeger, 1971).

Trocki, Carl A., 'Political structures in the nineteenth and early twentieth centuries', in Nicholas Tarling, ed., *The Cambridge economic history of Southeast Asia*, vol. 3: *1800–1930s*, pp. 75–126.

Tsuji Masanobu, *Singapore 1941–1942: the Japanese version of the Malayan campaign of World War II* (Singapore: Oxford University Press, 1988 [1961]).

Tsutsui Chihiro, 'Our southern reconstruction policy', *Contemporary Japan*, 11, 12 (1942), pp. 1,746–56.

Tun, U Wai, *Burma's currency and credit* (Bombay: Orient Longmans, 1962).

Turley, William S., 'Urbanization in war: Hanoi, 1946–1973', *Pacific Affairs*, 48, 3 (1975), pp. 370–97.

Turnbull, C. M., 'British planning for post-war Malaya', *Journal of Southeast Asian Studies*, 5, 2 (1974), pp. 239–54.

Turnbull, C. M., *A history of Singapore 1819–1988*, 2nd edn. (Singapore: Oxford University Press, 1989).

Twang Peck Yang, *The Chinese business élite in Indonesia and the transition to independence* (Kuala Lumpur: Oxford University Press, 1998).

Ungphakorn, Puey and Renoo Suvarnsit, 'Fiscal and other measures for combating inflation in Thailand', in United Nations, Economic Commission for Asia and the Far East, *Mobilization of domestic capital: report and documents of the first working party of experts* (Bangkok: Department of Economic Affairs, ECAFE, 1952), pp. 70–74.

United States Treasury, War and Navy Departments, 'Occupational currency in the Pacific', *Federal Reserve Bulletin* (March 1944), p. 233.

University Publications of America, *The MAGIC documents: summaries and transcripts of the top-secret diplomatic communications of Japan, 1938–1945* (Frederick, MD: University Publications of America, 1982).

Uyématsu, T., 'The naval conference and after', *Contemporary Japan*, 5, 2 (1936), pp. 159–65.

Valaoras, V. G., 'Some effects of famine on the population of Greece', *Milbank Memorial Fund Quarterly*, 24, 3 (1946), pp. 215–34.

van der Eng, Pierre, 'Marshall aid as a catalyst in the decolonization of Indonesia, 1947–1949', *Journal of Southeast Asian Studies*, 19, 2 (1988), pp. 335–52.

van der Eng, Pierre, *Growth and productivity change in Indonesian agriculture, 1880–1985*, Institute of Economic Research memorandum no. 348 (Groningen: University of Groningen, 1990).

van der Eng, Pierre, 'Indonesian national income' (unpublished paper, 1991).

van der Eng, Pierre, 'Estimates of GDP per capita in Malaya, 1910–1965 (excluding Singapore)' (unpublished paper, 1992).

van der Eng, Pierre, 'The real domestic product of Indonesia, 1880–1989', *Explorations in Economic History*, 29, 3 (1992), pp. 343–73.

van der Eng, Pierre, *The 'colonial drain' from Indonesia, 1823–1990*, Australian National University, Research School of Pacific Studies, Economics Division, working paper no. 93/2 (1993).

van der Eng, Pierre, *The silver standard and Asia's integration into the world economy*, Australian National University, Department of Economic History, working paper no. 175 (1993).

van der Eng, Pierre, 'Assessing economic growth and standards of living in Asia, 1870–1990', in A. J. H. Latham and H. Kawakatsu, eds., *The evolving structure of the East Asian economic system since 1700: a comparative analysis* (Milan: Universita Bocconi, 1994).

van der Eng, Pierre, *Food supply in Java during the war and decolonization, 1940–1950*, University of Hull Centre for Southeast Asian Studies, occasional paper no. 25 (1994); 2nd edn. Munich Personal RePEc Archive (2008).

van der Eng, Pierre, 'Historical estimates of GDP in Malaysia/West Malaysia, 1910–1960' (unpublished paper, 1994).

van der Eng, Pierre, 'Thailand estimates of GDP based on Sompop's work' (unpublished paper, 1994).

van der Eng, Pierre, *Agricultural growth in Indonesia: productivity change and policy impact since 1800* (Houndmills: Macmillan, 1996).

van der Eng, Pierre, 'Regulation and control: explaining the decline of food production in Java, 1940–6', in Paul H. Kratoska, ed., *Food supplies and the Japanese occupation* (Houndmills: Macmillan, 1998), pp. 187–207.

van der Eng, Pierre, 'Food for growth: trends in Indonesia's food supply, 1880–1995', *Journal of Interdisciplinary History*, 30, 4 (2000), pp. 591–616.

van der Eng, Pierre, 'Bridging a gap: a reconstruction of population patterns in Indonesia, 1930–61', *Asian Studies Review*, 26, 4 (2002), pp. 487–509.

van der Eng, Pierre, 'Productivity and comparative advantage in rice agriculture in Southeast Asia since 1870', *Asian Economic Journal*, 18, 4 (2004), pp. 345–70.

van der Eng, Pierre, 'Capital formation and capital stock in Indonesia, 1950–2007', Australian National University, Arndt-Corden Department of Economics working paper 2008–24 (2008).

van der Eng, Pierre, 'Market responses to climate stress: rice in Java in the 1930s', *Australian Economic History Review*, 50, 1 (2010), pp. 62–79.

van der Eng, Pierre, 'All lies? Famines in Sukarno's Indonesia, 1950s–1960s' (unpublished paper, 2012), https://crawford.anu.edu.au/news-events/events/1218/all-lies-famines-sukarnos-indonesia-1950s-1960s.

van der Eng, Pierre, 'Long-term growth in Malaysia, 1910–2010' (unpublished paper, undated but *c.* 2012).

van der Eng, Pierre, 'Government promotion of labour-intensive industrialization in Indonesia, 1930–1975', in Gareth Austin and Kaoru Sugihara, eds., *Labour-intensive industrialization in global history* (London: Routledge, 2013), pp. 176–200.

van der Eng, Pierre, 'Why didn't colonial Indonesia have a competitive cotton textile industry?', *Modern Asian Studies*, 47, 3 (2013), pp. 1019–54.

van der Wee, Herman and Monique Verbreyt, *A small nation in the turmoil of the Second World War: money, finance and occupation (Belgium, its enemies, its friends, 1939–1945)* (Leuven: Leuven University Press, 2009).

van Klaveren, J. J., *The Dutch colonial system in the East Indies* (Rotterdam: Drukkerij Benedictus, 1953).

van Neil, Robert, 'The course of Indonesian history', in Ruth T. McVey, ed., *Indonesia* (New Haven, CT: Southeast Asia Studies, Yale University, 1963), pp. 272–308.

Van Tao and Furuta Motoo, eds., *Nan doi Nam 1945 o Viet Nam: nhung chung tich lich su* [The 1945 famine in Vietnam: historical evidence] (Hanoi: Nhã Nam, 2011).

Yasuba Yasukichi, 'Did Japan ever suffer from a shortage of natural resources before World War II?', *Journal of Economic History*, 56, 3 (1996), pp. 543–60.

Yip Yat Hoong, *The development of the tin mining industry of Malaya* (Kuala Lumpur: University of Malaya Press, 1969).

Yoichi Itagaki, 'Outlines of Japanese policy in Indonesia and Malaya during the war', *Annals of the Hitotsubashi Academy*, 2, 2 (1952), pp. 183–92.

Yoichi Itagaki, 'Some aspects of the Japanese policy for Malaya under the occupation, with special reference to nationalism', in K. G. Tregonning, ed., *Papers on Malayan history* (Singapore: Journal of South-East Asian History, 1962), pp. 256–67.

Yomiuri Shimbun, *Who was responsible?: from Marco Polo Bridge to Pearl Harbor* (Tokyo: Yomiuri, 2006).

Yoon Won Z., 'Military expediency: a determining factor in the Japanese policy regarding Burmese independence', *Journal of Southeast Asian Studies*, 9, 2 (1978), pp. 248–67.

Yoshimi Yoshiaki, *Comfort women: sexual slavery in the Japanese military during World War II*, trans. Suzanne G. O'Brien (New York: Columbia University Press, 1995).

Yoshimura Mako, 'Japan's economic policy for occupied Malaya', in Akashi Yoji and Yoshimura Mako, eds., *New perspectives on the Japanese occupation in Malaya and Singapore, 1941–1945* (Singapore: NUS Press, 2008), pp. 113–38.

Young, Arthur N., *China's wartime finance and inflation, 1937–1945* (Cambridge, MA: Harvard University Press, 1965).

Young, Louise, *Japan's total empire: Manchuria and the culture of wartime imperialism* (Berkeley, CA: University of California Press, 1998).

Yuen Choy Leng, 'Japanese rubber and iron investments in Malaya, 1900–1941', *Journal of Southeast Asian Studies*, 5, 1 (1974), pp. 18–36.

Yu-Jose, Lydia N., *Japan views the Philippines* (Manila: Manila University Press, 1992).

Zagoria, Donald S., 'Peasants and revolution', *Comparative Politics*, 8, 3 (1976), pp. 321–6.

Zainal Abidin b. Abdul Wahid, Datuk, 'The Japanese occupation and nationalisms', in Zainal Abidin b. Abdul Wahid Datuk, ed., *Glimpses of Malaysian history* (Kuala Lumpur: Dewan Bahasa dan Pustaka, 1970), pp. 93–8.

INDEX

Italic page references indicate an illustration or a figure; **bold** page references indicate a table.